Forty Years
of
Screen Credits
1929-1969

Volume 2: K-Z

Compiled by
John T. Weaver

The Scarecrow Press, Inc.
Metuchen, N.J.   1970

K

Ish Kabibble (1908-
1939: That's Right, You're
Wrong
40: You'll Find Out
41: Playmates
42: My Favorite Spy
43: Around the World

Armand Kaliz (1892-1941)
1929: Noah's Ark
Twin Beds
Gold Diggers of Broadway
Marriage Playground
30: The Mysterious Mr. Parkes
Little Caesar
32: Three Wise Girls
33: Secret Sinners
Flying Down to Rio
34: Caravan
35: Diamond Jim
36: Desire
37: Cafe Metropole
38: Josette
Gold Diggers in Paris
A Trip to Paris
Algiers
Vacation from Love
39: Off the Record
40: Down Argentine Way
41: Skylark

Dick Kallman
1957: Hell Canyon Outlaws
58: Born to be Loved
59: Verboten!
61: Back Street
It's All Happening
67: Doctor, You've Got to be
Kidding!

Helen Kane (1904-1966)
1929: Nothing but the Truth
Sweetie
Pointed Heels
30: Paramount on Parade
Dangerous Nan McGrew
Heads Up
32: The Dentist (short)
33: The Pharmacist (short)
34: Counsel on the Fence

PT Marvin Kaplan
1950: The Reformer and the Redhead
51: Angels in the Outfield
Criminal Lawyer
Behave Yourself
52: The Fabulous Señorita
60: Wake Me When It's Over
63: The Nutty Professor
A New Kind of Love
It's a Mad Mad Mad Mad
World
65: The Great Race
68: Dark in the Belleau Wood

Anna Karina (1941-
1961: Cleo from Five to Seven
62: Vivre sa Vie
Le Petit Soldat
63: My Life to Live
64: A Woman Is a Woman
Bande a Part
She'll Have to Go
65: Alphaville
Circle of Love
Pierrot le Fou (or, Crazy
Pete)
66: Made in the U.S.A.
Bands of Outsiders
67: The Stranger

Ronald Reagan with Viveca Lindfors
in "Night Unto Night"

68: The Oldest Profession
    The Magus
    Dragees au Poivre
    Before Winter Comes
69: Laughter in the Dark
    Justine
    The Reckoning
    Michael Kohlhaas

Boris Karloff (1887-1969)
1928: Vultures of the Sea
      (ser.)   S
      The Love Mart   S
      Burning the Wind   S
29:   The Fatal Warning (ser.)S
      King of the Congo (ser.)
      Little Wild Girl   S
      The Devil's Chaplain   S
      Phantoms of the North   S
      Two Sisters   S
      The Unholy Night
      Behind that Curtain
30:   The Bad One
      The Sea Bat
      The Utah Kid
      Mothers Cry
31:   King of the Wild (ser.)
      The Criminal Code
      Cracked Nuts
      Young Donovan's Kid
      Smart Money
      The Public Defender
      I Like Your Nerve
      Five-Star Final
      The Mad Genius
      The Guilty Generation
      The Yellow Ticket
      Graft
      Frankenstein
      Tonight or Never
32:   Business and Pleasure
      Alias the Doctor
      Scarface
      The Cohens and Kellys
       in Hollywood
      The Miracle Man
      Behind the Mask
      The Mummy
      The Old Dark House
      Night World

      Mask of Fu Manchu
33:   Bimi
      The Ghoul
      The Man Who Dared
34:   House of Rothschild
      The Lost Patrol
      The Black Cat
      Gift of Gab
35:   The Bride of Frankenstein
      The Raven
      The Black Room Mystery
36:   The Invisible Ray
      The Walking Dead
      Charlie Chan at the Opera
      The Man Who Changed His
       Mind (or, The Man Who
       Lived Again)
      Juggernaut
37:   Night Key
      West of Shanghai
38:   The Invisible Menace
      Mr. Wong--Detective
39:   Son of Frankenstein
      Mr. Wong in Chinatown
      The Man They Could not
       Hang
      Tower of London
40:   The Fatal Hour
      British Intelligence
      Black Friday
      The Man with Nine Lives
      Devil's Island
      Doomed to Die
      Before I Hang
      The Ape
      You'll Find Out
41:   The Devil Commands
42:   The Bogey Man Will Get
       You
43:   The Climax
45:   House of Frankenstein
      The Body Snatcher
      Isle of the Dead
46:   Bedlam
47:   Lured
      The Secret Life of Walter
       Mitty
      Dick Tracy Meets Gruesome
      Unconquered
48:   Tap Roots

757

49: Abbott & Costello Meet
    the Killer, Boris Karloff
51: The Strange Door
52: The Black Castle
53: The Hindu
    Abbott & Costello Meet
    Dr. Jekyll and Mr. Hyde
    The Monster of the Island
55: Sabaka
57: Voodoo Island
58: Grip of the Strangler (or,
    The Haunted Strangler)
    Frankenstein--1970
61: Days of Thrills and
    Laughter
63: Corridors of Blood
    The Raven
    The Terror
64: Comedy of Terrors
    Black Sabbath
    Scarlet Friday
65: Die, Monster, Die!
66: Monster of Terror
    The House at the End of
    the World
    The Day Dreamer
    Mondo Balordo (narr.)
    Ghost in the Invisible
    Bikini
67: Mad Monster Party
    The Venetian Affair
    Targets
    The Sorcerers
    The Crimson Altar
68: Dreams in a Witch House
69: The Dark

Oscar Karlweiss
1951: St. Benny, the Dip
  52: Anything can Happen
      Five Fingers
  53: Tonight We Sing
      The Juggler
  56: Meet Me in Las Vegas

Roscoe Karns (1893-1970)
1928: Beau Sabreur   S
      Warming Up   S
      Moran of the Marines S
      Something Always
      Happens   S

Jazz Mad   S
Headlines
Flying Ensign
Beggars of Life   PT
29: This Thing Called Love
    Object Alimony
30: Safety in Numbers
    Troopers Three
    The Front Page
    Man Trouble
    Little Accident
    New York Nights
    The Costello Case
31: The Gorilla
    Dirigible
    Left Over Ladies
    Many a Slip
32: The Stowaway
    Roadhouse Murder
    Working Wives
    Two Against the World
    Pleasure
    The Crooked Circle
    Night after Night
    Week End Marriage
    If I Had a Million
    Rockabye
    I Am a Fugitive from a
    Chain Gang
    Under Cover Man
33: 20,000 Years in Sing Sing
    Gambling Ship
    Alice in Wonderland
    One Sunday Afternoon
    Today We Live
    A Lady's Profession
34: Twentieth Century
    Women in His Life
    Shoot the Works
    Come on, Marines!
    Search for Beauty
    Elmer and Elsie
    It Happened One Night
    I Sell Anything
35: Red Hot Tires
    Stolen Harmony
    Four Hours to Kill
    Wings in the Dark
    Two Fisted
    Front Page Woman
    Alibi Ike

36: Woman Trap
Border Flight
Three Cheers for Love
Three Married Men
Cain and Mabel
37: Murder Goes to College
A Night of Mystery
On Such a Night
Clarence
Partners in Crime
38: Scandal Sheet
Dangerous to Know
Tip-Off Girls
You and Me
Thanks for the Memory
39: Everything's on Ice
That's Right, You're
Wrong
Dancing Coed
King of Chinatown
40: His Girl Friday
Saturday's Children
They Drive by Night
Ladies Must Live
Meet the Missus
Double Alibi
41: Petticoat Politics
Footsteps in the Dark
The Gay Vagabond
42: Road to Happiness
A Tragedy at Midnight
Yokel Boy
Woman of the Year
You Can't Escape Forever
43: My Son, the Hero
His Butler's Sister
Old Acquaintance
44: The Navy Way
Hi Good Lookin'!
The Minstrel Man
46: I Ring Doorbells
Avalanche
One Way to Love
It's a Wonderful Life
Down Missouri Way
47: That's My Man
Vigilantes of Boomtown
48: The Devil's Cargo
Inside Story
Speed to Spare

Texas, Brooklyn, and
Heaven
58: Onionhead
64: Man's Favorite Sport?

Anna Kashfi
1956: The Mountain
Battle Hymn
58: Cowboy
59: Night of the Quarter Moon

Kurt Kasznar (1913-
1951: The Light Touch
52: Anything can Happen
Talk about a Stranger
Lovely to Look at
Glory Alley
Happy Time
53: Give a Girl a Break
Lili
Sombrero
Ride, Vaquero!
All the Brothers Were
Valiant
Kiss Me Kate
54: The Last Time I Saw Paris
Valley of the Kings
55: Jump into Hell
My Sister Eileen
Flame of the Islands
56: Fanny
Anything Goes
57: Legend of the Lost
A Farewell to Arms
59: The Journey
For the First Time
62: Arms and the Man
63: 55 Days at Peking
The Thrill of it All
67: The King's Pirate
Code Name: Heraclitus
The Ambushers
The Perils of Pauline
Casino Royale
68: The Smugglers (TV)

Kurt Katch (1896-1959)
1941: Man at Large
42: The Wife Takes a Flyer
Berlin Correspondent

42: Counter Espionage
They Came to Blow Up
America
Edge of Darkness
Quiet Please--Murder
43: Background to Danger
Mission to Moscow
Watch on the Rhine
Ali Baba and the Forty
Thieves
44: The Purple Heart
Mask of Dimitrios
The Conspirators
The Seventh Cross
Make Your Own Bad
45: Salome, Where She Danced
The Mummy's Curse
46: Angel on My Shoulder
Rendezvous 24
Strange Journey
47: Song of Love
54: Secret of the Incas
Adventures of Hajji Baba
55: Abbott & Costello Meet
the Mummy
56: Hot Cars
57: The Pharaoh's Curse
Girl in the Kremlin
58: The Beast of Budapest

Christine Kaufmann (1945-
1959: Embezzled Heaven
60: Last Days of Pompeii
Little Rosie
Silent Angel
Maedchen in Uniform
Winter Vacation
62: Constantine and the Cross
Town Without Pity
Taras Bulba
Escape from East Berlin
Swordsman of Siena
64: Wild and Wonderful
Red Lips

Danny Kaye (1913-
1944: Up in Arms
45: Wonder Man (dual roles)
46: The Kid from Brooklyn
47: The Secret Life of Walter
Mitty

48: A Song Is Born
49: Inspector General
51: On the Riviera
52: Hans Christian Andersen
54: Knock on Wood
White Christmas
(SPECIAL AWARD)
56: The Court Jester
58: Merry Andrew
Me and the Colonel
59: The Five Pennies
61: On the Double
63: The Ambassador at Large
The Man from the Diner's
Club
64: The Sound of Laughter
(doc.)
That's Life
67: The Biggest Bundle of
Them All
69: The Madwoman of Chaillot

Stubby Kaye (1918-
1955: Guys and Dolls
56: You Can't Run Away from
It
It Happened One Night
The Cool Mikado
59: Li'l Abner
62: Forty Pounds of Trouble
64: Sex and the Single Girl
65: Cat Ballou
67: The Way West
69: Sweet Charity
Can Hieronymus Merkin
Ever Forget Mercy
Humppe and Find True
Happiness?
A Woman for Charley (TV)

Edward Keane
1939: Frontier Pony Express
Heroes in Blue
The Roaring Twenties
40: Charlie Chan in Panama
Midnight Limited
Devil's Island
City for Conquest
Money and the Woman
Son of Monte Cristo
41: Riders of the Timberline

760

42: The Man with Two Lives
    Wildcat
    The Traitor Within
43: Truck Busters
    I Escaped from the
    Gestapo
    Mission to Moscow
44: South of Dixie
    Bermuda Mystery
    When Strangers Marry
45: Fashion Model
    Rogues Gallery
46: Angel on My Shoulder
    Night Editor
    Out California Way
    Roll on Texas Moon
47: Trail to San Antonio
    The Hat Box Mystery
    The Invisible Wall
    Roses Are Red
48: Chicken Every Sunday
49: It Happens Every Spring
50: A Modern Marriage
    Twilight in the Sierras
    The Baron of Arizona

Robert Emmett Keane (1883-
1938: Boys Town
  39: Cafe Society
      Confessions of a Nazi Spy
      Pack Up Your Troubles
      The Spellbinder
      One Hour to Live
      Hawaiian Nights
  40: Double Alibi
      Lillian Russell
      The Saint Takes Over
      The Lone Wolf Meets a
      Lady
      Slightly Tempted
      Border Legion
      Tin Pan Alley
      Michael Shayne, Private
      Detective
  41: The Devil and Miss Jones
      Men of Boys Town
      The Cowboy and the
      Blonde
      Wild Geese Calling
      Hello Sucker

    Midnight Angel
42: Remember Pearl Harbor
    The Man Who Wouldn't
    Die
    A-Haunting We Will Go
    Sabotage Squad
43: He Hired the Boss
    Crazy House
    Jitterbugs
44: Hi, Good Lookin'!
    The Impatient Years
    Kansas City Kitty
    Sweet and Low Down
    The Whistler
45: Her Lucky Night
    Scared Stiff
    Why Girls Leave Home
46: Fool's Gold
    Live Wires
    Night Editor
    Rainbow over Texas
    Red Dragon
    The Shadow Returns
    The Strange Mr. Gregory
47: The Beginning or the End?
    Fear in the Night
    Millie's Daughter
    I Wonder Who's Kissing
    Her Now
    News Hounds
48: Return of the Whistler
    Angels' Alley
    The Gentleman from
    Nowhere
    When My Baby Smiles at
    Me
    Incident
    Out of the Storm
    I Surrender, Dear
    The Timber Trail
49: You're My Everything
    Trouble Investigator
    Susanna Pass
    Henry the Rainmaker
    Jolson Sings Again
    The Sickle or the Cross
    There's a Girl in My
    Heart
    Everybody Does It
    Mary Ryan, Detective

49: Navajo Trail Raiders
50: Hills of Oklahoma
     Blondie's Hero
     Father Makes Good
54: The Atomic Kid
56: When Gangland Strikes

Joseph Kearns (1907-1962)
1955: Daddy Long Legs
56: Our Miss Brooks
58: The Gift of Love
59: Anatomy of a Murder

Fred Keating (1902-1961)
1934: The Captain Hates the Sea
  35: The Nitwits
     Shanghai
     I Live My Life
     To Beat the Band
  36: Thirteen Hours by Air
     The Devil on Horseback
  37: When's Your Birthday?
     Melody for Two
  38: Dr. Rhythm
     Prison Train
  39: Society Smugglers
  40: Tin Pan Alley

Larry Keating (1899-1963)
1945: Song of the Sarong
  49: Whirlpool
  50: Mister 880
     Right Cross
     I Was a Shoplifter
     Three Secrets
     My Blue Heaven
  51: The Mating Season
     Come Fill the Cup
     When Worlds Collide
     Francis Goes to the Races
     Follow the Sun
     Bright Victory
     Bannerline
     Too Young to Kiss
     The Light Touch
  52: About Face
     Carson City
     Above and Beyond
     Monkey Business
     Something for the Birds

53: Give a Girl a Break
     A Lion Is in the Streets
     Inferno
54: Gypsy Colt
55: Daddy Long Legs
56: The Eddie Duchin Story
     The Best Things in Life
     Are Free
57: The Buster Keaton Story
     The Wayward Bus
     Stopover Tokyo
60: Who Was that Lady?
62: Boys' Night Out
64: The Incredible Mr. Limpet

Buster Keaton (1896-1966)
1929: Hollywood Revue of 1929
  30: Spite Marriage
     Free and Easy
     The Big Shot
     Doughboys
  31: Speak Easily
     Sidewalks of New York
  32: Parlor, Bedroom, and Bath
     The Passionate Plumber
  33: What, No Beer?
  34: The Champ of the Champs-
     Elysees
  35: An Old Spanish Custom
     Allez Oop
     The Gold Ghost
     Palooka from Paducah
     Tars and Stripes
     Hayseed Romance
     E-Flat Man
     One Run Elmer
  36: The Timid Man
     The Chemist
     Three on a Limb
     Grand Slam Opera
     Blue Blazes
     Mixed Magic
  37: Ditto
     Jail Bait
     Love Nest on Wheels
  38: Life in Sometown, U.S.A.
     Hollywood Handicap
     Streamlined Swing
  39: Hollywood Cavalcade
     The Jones Family in
     Hollywood

39: The Jones Family in
    Quick Millions
    Mooching Through Georgia
    Pest from the West
    Nothing but Pleasure
40: The Villain Still Pursued
    Her
    Li'l Abner
    Pardon My Berth Marks
    The Spook Speaks
    Taming of the Snood
41: So You Won't Squawk
    His Ex Marks the Spot
    General Nuisance
    She's Oil Mine
43: Forever and a Day
44: San Diego, I Love You
    Bathing Beauty
45: That's the Spirit
    That Night with You
46: El Moderno Barba Azul
    (Mex.)
    God's Country
48: Un Duel a Mort (Fr.)
49: You're My Everything
    In the Good Old Summer-
    time
    The Lovable Cheat
    Neptune's Daughter
    A Southern Yankee
50: Sunset Boulevard
52: Limelight
53: The Awakening
    Paradise for Buster
    (never released)
56: Around the World in 80
    Days
57: The Buster Keaton Story
    (supervised Don O'Connor)
59: (SPECIAL AWARD)
60: The Adventures of Huckle-
    berry Finn
    When Comedy Was King
    (doc.)
62: Ten Girls Ago
63: It's a Mad Mad Mad Mad
    World
    The Great Chase
    The Triumph of Lester
    Snapwell

    Thirty Years of Fun (doc.)
64: Big Parade of Comedy
    (doc.)
    Pajama Party
65: Keaton Rides Again
    Beach Blanket Bingo
    The Railroader
    Film (1 pt. of Evergreen
    Theatre trilogy)
    Sergeant Deadhead, The
    Astronaut!
    The Sound of Laughter
    (doc.)
66: How to Stuff a Wild Bikini
    Marines e un General
    (Ital.)
    A Funny Thing Happened
    on the Way to the Forum
    The Scribe
    War--Italian Style

Lila Kedrova (1918-
1955: No Way Back
58: The Lovemaker
59: A Woman Like Satan
60: Human Cargo
64: Zorba the Greek (OSCAR)
65: High Wind in Jamaica
66: Torn Curtain
67: Penelope
68: The Runaround
    Tenderly (Ital.)
69: The Kremlin Letter

Howard Keel (1919-
1948: The Small Voice
    London 1948
49: Hideout
50: Annie Get Your Gun
    Pagan Love Song
51: Three Guys Named Mike
    Show Boat
    Texas Carnival
    Callaway Went Thataway
52: Lovely to Look At
    Desperate Search
53: Ride, Vaquero!
    Fast Company
    Kiss Me Kate
    Calamity Jane

54: Rose Marie
    Seven Brides for Seven
      Brothers
    Deep in My Heart
55: Jupiter's Darling
    Kismet
59: Floods of Fear
    The Big Fisherman
61: The Armored Command
63: The Day of the Triffids
65: The Man from Button
      Willow
66: Waco
67: The War Wagon
    Red Tomahawk
68: Arizona Bushwackers

Ruby Keeler (1909-
1933: 42nd Street
    Gold Diggers of 1933
    Footlight Parade
34: Dames
    Flirtation Walk
35: Go Into Your Dance
    Shipmates Forever
36: Colleen
37: Ready, Willing, and
      Able
38: Mother Carey's Chickens
41: Sweetheart of the Campus
59: The Phynx

Tom Keene (George Duryea)
(1898-1963)
1928: Marked Money   NT
   29: Thunder   NT
       Night Work
       Pardon My Gun
       The Godless Girl   PT
       Honky Tonk
       Tide of Empire   NT
   30: In Old California
       Rodeo Kissin'
       Tol'able David
       Sunset Trail
       Beau Bandit
       Dude Wrangler
       Montana Rider
   31: Freighters of Destiny
       Partners

32: Saddle Buster
    Beyond the Rockies
    Strictly Business
    Ghost Valley
33: Renegades of the West
    Come on, Danger!
    The Cheyenne Kid
    Scarlet River
    Crossfire
    Son of the Border
    Sunset Pass
34: Our Daily Bread
35: Hong Kong Nights
36: Timothy's Quest
    Drift Fence
    Desert Gold
    The Glory Trail
    Rebellion
37: Battle of Greed
    Old Louisiana
    Drums of Destiny
    Where Trails Divide
38: The Painted Trail
41: Wanderers of the West
    Riding the Sunset Trail
    Dynamite Canyon
    The Driftin' Kid
42: Arizona Roundup
    Where Trails End
45: The Enchanted Cottage
    Girls of the Big House
46: San Quentin
50: Trail of Robin Hood
52: Red Planet Mars
58: Once Upon a Horse
59: Plan 9 for Outer Space

Betty Lou Keim (1938-
1956: These Wilder Years
    Teenage Rebel
57: The Wayward Bus
58: Some Came Running

Brian Keith (1921-
1953: Arrowhead
54: Jivaro
    Alaska Seas
    Bamboo Prison
55: Rough Comedy (or, The
      Violent Men)

55: Tight Spot
    Five Against the House
56: Storm Center
    Nightfall
57: Run of the Arrow
    Dino
    Hell Canyon Outlaws (or,
    The Tall Trouble)
    Chicago Confidential
58: Sierra Baron
    Villa!
    The Violent Road
    Desert Hell
    Fort Dobbs
    Appointment with a
    Shadow
59: The Young Philadelphians
60: Ten Who Dared
61: The Parent Trap
    The Deadly Companions
62: Moon Pilot
63: Savage Sam
    The Raiders
64: The Pleasure Seekers
    A Tiger Walks
    Johnny Shiloh (TV)
    Those Calloways
65: The Hallelujah Trail
66: Rare Breed
    Nevada Smith
    The Russians Are Coming,
    The Russians Are
    Coming!
67: Krakatoa--East of Java
    The Tenderfoot
    Reflections in a Golden
    Eye
    Way, Way Out
68: With Six You Get Eggroll
69: Gaily, Gaily
    Suppose They Gave a War
    and Nobody Came
    Dodo Birds Can't Fly
    The MacKenzie Break

Donald Keith (1905-
1929: Just Off Broadway   S
      The Lone Wolf's
      Daughter   PT
      Phantoms of the North S

Should a Girl Marry?
31: First Aid
    Branded Men
32: Midnight Lady
    Speed Madness
    Arms of the Law
33: Outlaw Justice
    The Big Bluff
34: Guilty Parents

Ian Keith (1899-1960)
1929: Light Fingers   PT
      Divine Lady   SSE
      Prisoners   PT
30: Prince of Diamonds
    Abraham Lincoln
    The Great Divide
    Sin Ship
    The Big Trail
    Boudoir Diplomat
31: The Deceiver
    A Tailor-Made Man
    The Phantom of Paris
32: Sign of the Cross
33: Queen Christina
34: Dangerous Corner
    Cleopatra
35: The Crusades
    Three Musketeers
36: Preview Murder Mystery
    Don't Gamble with Love
    Mary of Scotland
    The White Legion
38: The Buccaneer
    Comet over Broadway
40: All this and Heaven too
    The Sea Hawk
42: Remember Pearl Harbor
    Pay-Off
43: Five Graves to Cairo
    The Sundown Kid
    I Escaped from the
    Gestapo
    Wild Horse Stampede
    That Nazty Nuisance
    Here Comes Kelly
    Bordertown Gun Fighters
44: Casanova in Burlesque
    The Chinese Cat
    Arizona Whirlwind

44: Bowery Champs
    The Cowboy from Lone-
      some River
45: Fog Island
    Identity Unknown
    Northwest Trail
    Phantom of the Plains
    She Gets Her Man
    Song of Old Wyoming
    The Spanish Main
    Under Western Skies
46: Dick Tracy vs Cueball
    Mr. Hex
    Singing on the Trail
    Valley of the Zombies
    The Strange Woman
47: Dick Tracy's Dilemma
    Border Feud
    Nightmare Alley
48: The Three Musketeers
54: Black Shield of Falworth
55: Prince of Players
    New York Confidential
    It Came from Beneath
      the Sea
    Duel on the Mississippi
56: The Ten Commandments

Robert Keith (1898-1966)
1939: Spirit of Culver
    Destry Rides Again
49: My Foolish Heart
    Boomerang
50: Branded
    Woman on the Run
    The Reformer and the
      Redhead
    Edge of Doom
51: Fourteen Hours
    Here Comes the Groom
    I Want You!
52: Just Across the Street
    Somebody Loves Me
53: Small Town Girl
    Battle Circus
    Devil's Canyon
54: The Wild One
    Drum Beat
    Young at Heart
55: Underwater!

Guys and Dolls
Love Me or Leave Me
56: Ransom!
    Written on the Wind
    Between Heaven and Hell
57: Men in War
    My Man Godfrey
58: The Lineup
59: They Came to Cordura
    Tempest
    Orazi et Curiazzi
60: Cimarron
61: The Posse from Hell

Cecil Kellaway (1893-
1937: It Isn't Done
38: Everybody's Doing It
    Double Danger
    Law of the Underworld
    Wise Girl
    Night Spot
    Maid's Night Out
    This Marriage Business
    Blonde Cheat
    Tarnished Angel
39: Wuthering Heights
    Intermezzo
    The Sun Never Sets
    Mexican Spitfire
    Lady with Red Hair
    We Are not Alone
40: The Invisible Man Returns
    House of Seven Gables
    The Mummy's Hand
    Diamond Frontier
    Brother Orchid
    Phantom Raiders
    The Mexican Spitfire Out
      West
    The Letter
    South of Suez
41: The Night of January 16th
    A Very Young Lady
    West Point Widow
    Burma Convoy
    Small Town Deb
    Appointment for Love
    Bahama Passage
42: My Heart Belongs to Daddy
    I Married a Witch

42:	The Lady Has Plans	58:	The Proud Rebel
	Take a Letter, Darling	59:	The Shaggy Dog
	Night in New Orleans	60:	The Private Lives of
	Are Husbands Necessary?		Adam and Eve
43:	Crystal Ball	61:	Francis of Assisi
	Forever and a Day		Tammy Tell Me True
	Star-Spangled Rhythm		The Cage of Evil
	The Good Fellows		The Walking Target
	It Ain't Hay	62:	Zotz!
44:	And Now Tomorrow	63:	The Cardinal
	Frenchman's Creek	65:	Hush, Hush, Sweet
	Practically Yours		Charlotte!
	Mrs. Parkington	66:	The Confession
45:	Bring on the Girls		Spin-Out
	Love Letters	67:	The Adventures of Bull
	Kitty		Whip Griffin
46:	The Cockeyed Miracle		Guess Who's Coming to
	Easy to Wed		Dinner?
	Monsieur Beaucaire	68:	Fitzwilly
	The Postman Rings Twice	69:	Getting Straight
47:	Unconquered		

42: The Lady Has Plans
Take a Letter, Darling
Night in New Orleans
Are Husbands Necessary?
43: Crystal Ball
Forever and a Day
Star-Spangled Rhythm
The Good Fellows
It Ain't Hay
44: And Now Tomorrow
Frenchman's Creek
Practically Yours
Mrs. Parkington
45: Bring on the Girls
Love Letters
Kitty
46: The Cockeyed Miracle
Easy to Wed
Monsieur Beaucaire
The Postman Rings Twice
47: Unconquered
Variety Girl
Always Together
48: Portrait of Jennie
Joan of Arc
Decision of Christopher
Blake
Luck of the Irish
49: Down to the Sea in Ships
50: The Reformer and the
Redhead
Harvey
Kim
51: The Highwayman
Half Angel
Katie Did it
Francis Goes to the Races
52: My Wife's Best Friend
Just Across the Street
53: Thunder in the East
The Beast from 20,000
Fathoms
Young Bess
Paris Model
Cruisin' Down the River
55: The Prodigal
Interrupted Melody
Female on the Beach
56: Toy Tiger
57: Johnny Trouble

58: The Proud Rebel
59: The Shaggy Dog
60: The Private Lives of
Adam and Eve
61: Francis of Assisi
Tammy Tell Me True
The Cage of Evil
The Walking Target
62: Zotz!
63: The Cardinal
65: Hush, Hush, Sweet
Charlotte!
66: The Confession
Spin-Out
67: The Adventures of Bull
Whip Griffin
Guess Who's Coming to
Dinner?
68: Fitzwilly
69: Getting Straight

De Forest Kelley (1920-
1947: Fear in the Night
50: Duke of Chicago
55: House of Bamboo
The View from Pompey's
Head
Illegal
56: Tension at Table Rock
57: Gunfight at the O.K.Corral
Raintree County
58: The Law and Jake Wade
59: Warlock
63: Gunfight at Comanche
Creek
64: Where Love Has Gone
65: Black Spurs
Marriage on the Rocks
Town Tamer
66: Apache Uprising
Waco
Johnny Reno

Mike Kellin (1922-
1949: So Young, so Bad
50: At War with the Army
52: Hurricane Smith
58: Lonely Hearts
60: The Mountain Road
The Great Impostor

60: The Wackiest Ship in the
    Army
62: Hell Is for Heroes
64: Invitation to a Gunfighter
67: Banning
    The Incident
68: The Boston Strangler
    The Riot
69: The Phynx
    Run, Shadow, Run
    The Maltese Bippy

Brian Kelly
1963: Thunder Island
  64: Flipper's New Adventure
  66: Around the World Under
      the Sea
  67: Not Buried, but Dead

Gene Kelly (1912-
1942: For Me and My Gal
  43: Pilot No. 5
      Du Barry Was a Lady
      Thousands Cheer
      The Cross of Lorraine
  44: Christmas Holiday
      Cover Girl
  45: Anchors Aweigh
  46: Ziegfeld Follies
  47: Living in a Big Way
  48: The Pirate
      The Three Musketeers
      On an Island with You
      Words and Music
  49: On the Town
      Take Me Out to the Ball
      Game
  50: Summer Stock
      Black Hand
  51: An American in Paris
      (SPECIAL AWARD)
      It's a Big Country
  52: Singing in the Rain
      The Devil Makes Three
  54: Brigadoon
      Crest of the Wave
      Deep in My Heart
  55: It's Always Fair Weather
  56: Invitation to the Dance
  57: The Happy Land

Les Girls
58: Tunnel of Love (dir.)
60: Let's Make Love (cameo)
    Inherit the Wind
62: Gigot (dir.)
64: What a Way to Go!
67: Young Girls of Rochefort
69: Hello, Dolly! (dir.)
    The Cheyenne Social
    Club (dir.)

Grace Kelly (1929-
1951: Fourteen Hours
  52: High Noon
  53: Mocambo
  54: Crest of the Wave
      Dial M for Murder
      Rear Window
      Green Fire
      Country Girl (OSCAR)
      The Bridges at Toko-Ri
  55: To Catch a Thief
  56: The Swan
      High Society

Jack Kelly (1927-
1950: Where Danger Lives
  51: Submarine Command
      The Wild Blue Yonder
  52: The Redhead from Wyoming
      No Room for the Groom
      Red Ball Express
      Sally and St. Anne
  53: The Stand at Apache
      River
      Gunsmoke
      Law and Order
      Column South
  54: Drive a Crooked Mile
      They Rode West
      The Country Girl
  55: The Night Holds Terror
      Double Jeopardy
      To Hell and Back
      Cult of the Cobra
  56: Julie
  57: She-Devil
      Taming Sutton's Girl
  58: The Hong Kong Affair
  61: A Fever in the Blood

64: FBI Code 98
65: Love and Kisses
68: Young Billy Young

Nancy Kelly (1921-
1929: Girl on the Barge   PT
35: Convention Girl
38: Submarine Patrol
    Jesse James
39: Stanley and Livingstone
    Tail Spin
    Frontier Marshal
40: He Married His Wife
    One Night in the Tropics
    Private Affairs
41: A Very Young Lady
    Scotland Yard
    Parachute Battalion
42: To the Shores of Tripoli
    Fly by Night
    Friendly Enemies
43: Tornado
    Women in Bondage
    Tarzan's Desert Mystery
44: Gambler's Choice
    Show Business
    Double Exposure
45: Song of the Sarong
    The Woman Who Came
      Back
    Betrayal from the East
    Follow that Woman
46: Murder in the Music Hall
48: Disaster
56: Crowded Paradise
    The Bad Seed

Patsy Kelly (1910-
1933: Going Hollywood
33-35: various shorts with
      Thelma Todd
34: Countess of Monte Cristo
    The Girl from Missouri
    The Party's Over
35: Go into Your Dance
    Page Miss Glory
    Every Night at Eight
    Thanks a Million
36: Private Number

Sing, Baby, Sing
Pigskin Parade
Kelly the Second
a short
37: Nobody's Baby
    Pick a Star
    Wake Up and Live
    Ever Since Eve
38: Merrily We Live
    There Goes My Heart
    The Cowboy and the Lady
39: The Gorilla
40: The Hit Parade of 1941
41: Road Show
    Topper Returns
    Broadway Limited
    Playmates
42: Sing Your Worries Away
    In Old California
43: My Son, the Hero
    Danger! Women at Work
    Ladies' Day
60: Please Don't Eat the
      Daisies
    The Crowded Sky
64: The Naked Kiss
66: The Ghost in the Invisible
      Bikini
67: Come on, Let's Live a
      Little
68: Rosemary's Baby

Paul Kelly (1899-1956)
1932: Girl from Calgary
33: Broadway Through a Key-
      hole
34: Love Captive
    The President Vanishes
    Blind Date
    School for Girls
    Death on the Diamond
35: When a Man's a Man
    Side Streets
    Star of Midnight
    Public Hero No. 1
    Silk Hat Kid
    My Marriage
36: Here Comes Trouble
    The Song and Dance Man

36: The Country Beyond
    Murder with Pictures
    The Accusing Finger
    It's a Great Life
    Women Are Trouble
37: Join the Marines
    Parole Racket
    Fit for a King
    Navy Blue and Gold
    It Happened Out West
    The Frame Up
38: Island in the Sky
    Nurse from Brooklyn
    The Devil's Party
    The Missing Guest
    Torchy Blane in Panama
    Juvenile Court
39: Adventure in Sahara
    Forged Passport
    The Flying Irishman
    6000 Enemies
    Within the Law
    The Roaring Twenties
40: Invisible Stripes
    Queen of the Mob
    The Howards of Virginia
    Girls Under Twenty-One
    Wyoming
    Flight Command
41: a short
    Ziegfeld Girl
    Parachute Battalion
    I'll Wait for You
    Mystery Ship
    Mr. and Mrs. North
42: Call Out the Marines
    Tarzan's New York
     Adventure
    Tough as They Come
    Not a Ladies' Man
    Flying Tigers
    The Secret Code (ser.)
43: The Man from Music
     Mountain
44: Dead Man's Eyes
    Faces in the Fog
    The Story of Dr. Wassell
    That's My Baby
45: Grissley's Millions
    China's Little Devils

San Antonio
Allotment Wives, Inc.
46: Strange Journey
    The Cat Creeps
    Deadline for Murder
    The Glass Alibi
    Strange Impersonation
47: Crossfire
    Fear in the Night
    Adventure Island
    Spoilers of the North
49: Thelma Jordan
    Side Street
    Guilty of Treason
50: Secret Futy
    Frenchie
51: The Painted Hills
52: Springfield Rifle
53: Gunsmoke
    Split Second
54: Duffy of San Quentin
    Johnny Dark
    The High and the Mighty
    The Steel Cage
55: Square Jungle
    Narcotic Squad
56: Storm Center
57: Bailout at 43,000

Tommy Kelly (1925-
1938: Adventures of Tom Sawyer
     Peck's Bad Boy with the
      Circus
39: They Shall Have Music
40: Curtain Call
    Military Academy
    Gallant Sons
41: Nice Girl?
    Double Date
43: Mugtown

Fred Kelsey (1884-1961)
1928: On Trial   S
     The Wright Idea   S
     Tenderloin   PT
29: The Donovan Affair
    The Faker   S
    The Fall of Eve
    Naughty Baby
    Smiling Irish Eyes

29: The Last Warning
30: Road to Paradise
    Murder on the Roof
    Going Wild
    She Got What She Wanted
    Men Without Law
    The Laurel & Hardy
     Murder Case
    Only Saps Work
31: The Big Jewel Case
    The Subway Express
    Young Donovan's Kid
    The Falling Star
32: Discarded Lovers
    Love in High Gear
    Guilty as Hell
33: a short
    Girl Missing
    Young and Beautiful
    School for Girls
34: Shadows of Sing Sing
    Beloved
    The Crime Doctor
35: Lightning Strikes Twice
    Carnival
    Death Flies East
    One Frightened Night
    Diamond Jim
    Danger Ahead
    Public Menace
    Hot Off the Press
    Sagebrush Troubadour
37: Time Out for Romance
    That I May Live
    Super Sleuth
    All Over Town
39: Rough Riders' Round-Up
    a short
    Too Busy to Work
40: The Lone Wolf Strikes
    The Lone Wolf Meets a
     Lady
    A Little Bit of Heaven
41: The Lone Wolf Takes a
     Chance
    The Invisible Ghost
    The Lone Wolf Keeps a
     Date
42: Murder in the Big House
    Gentleman Jim

X Marks the Spot
43: Counter Espionage
    One Dangerous Night
    Murder on the Waterfront
    True to Life
44: Adventures of Mark Twain
    Crime by Night
    The Great Mystic
45: Come Out Fighting
    How Do You Do?
46: Bringing Up Father
    The Strange Mr. Gregory
48: Jiggs and Maggie in Court
52: O. Henry's Full House
    (The Gift of the Magi
     seq.)
    Hans Christian Andersen
53: Murder Without Tears

Pert Kelton (1907-1968)
1930: Sally
33: Bed of Roses
    The Bowery
    Wine, Women, and Song
34: The Meanest Gal in Town
    Sing and Like it
    Bachelor Bait
    Pursued
35: Lightnin' Strikes Twice
    Hooray for Love
    Annie Oakley
    Mary Burns--Fugitive
36: Kelly the Second
    Sitting on the Moon
    Cain and Mabel
37: Women of Glamour
    Laughing at Trouble
    The Hit Parade
    Meet the Boy Friend
38: Rhythm of the Saddle
    Slander House
39: Whispering Enemies
62: The Music Man
65: Love and Kisses
69: Billy Bright

Ed Kemmer
1956: Behind the High Wall
57: The Sierra Stranger
    Calypso Joe

771

57: Panama Sal
58: The Spider
    Too Much, Too Soon
    Hong Kong Confidential
    The Hot Angel
59: Giant from the Unknown
60: The Crowded Sky
65: Mara of the Wilderness

Jeremy Kemp (1935-
1963: Cleopatra
65: Dr. Terror's House of
    Horrors
    The Great Spy Mission
66: Cast a Giant Shadow
    Operation Crossbow
    The Blue Max
69: A Twist of Sand
    The Strange Affair
    Games

Charles Kemper
1950: Wagonmaster
    Stars in My Crown
    Ticket to Tomahawk
    The Nevadan
    Where Danger Lives
    Mr. Music
    California Passage
51: On Dangerous Ground

Cyrus W. Kendall
1937: Meet the Boy Friend
39: Pacific Liner
    Stand Up and Fight
    Twelve Crowded Hours
    Calling All Marines
    Fugitive at Large
    Angels Wash Their Faces
40: The House Across the Bay
    Men Without Souls
    The Saint Takes Over
    Prairie Law
    Andy Hardy Meets a
    Debutante
    Youth Will be Served
41: Ride, Kelly, Ride
    Robin Hood of the Pecos
    Billy the Kid
    Mystery Ship

Midnight Angel
Johnny Eager
42: Fly by Night
    Tarzan's New York
    Adventure
43: A Lady Takes a Chance
44: The Chinese Cat
    Crime by Night
    Dancing in Manhattan
    Girl Rush
    Lady in the Death House
    The Last Ride
    Laura
    Outlaw Trail
    Roger Touhy--Gangster
    A Wave, a Wac, and a
    Marine
    Whispering Footsteps
    The Whistler
    Wilson
45: The Cisco Kid Returns
    Docks of New York
    Power of the Whistler
    Scarlet Street
    Shadow of Terror
    She Gets Her Man
    Tahiti Nights
    The Tiger Woman
46: Blonde for a Day
    The Glass Alibi
    The Invisible Informer
47: The Farmer's Daughter
    Sinbad the Sailor
    In Self-Defense
48: Fighting Mad
    Sword of the Avenger
    In This Corner
65: Mara of the Wilderness

Kay Kendall (1926-1959)
1945: Caesar and Cleopatra
46: London Town
53: The Shadow Man
    Curtain Up
    My Heart Goes Crazy
54: Genevieve
    A Doctor in the House
55: Constant Husband
56: Adventures of Quentin
    Durward
    Simon and Laura

772

56: Abdullah's Harem
57: Les Girls
58: The Reluctant Debutante
60: Once More with Feeling

Susy Kendall
1966: Up Jumped a Swagman
The Liquidator
Circus of Fear (or, Psycho
Circus)
The Sandwich Man
67: The Penthouse
Up the Junction
To Sir, with Love
68: Thirty Is a Dangerous
Age, Cynthia
Fraulein Doktor
69: The Gamblers
Bird with the Crystal
Plumage
The Betrayal

Arthur Kennedy (1914-
1940: City for Conquest
41: High Sierra
Strange Alibi
Knockout
Bad Men of Missouri
Highway West
They Died with Their
Boots on
42: Desperate Journey
43: Air Force
46: Devotion
47: Boomerang
Cheyenne
49: The Window
Chicago Deadline
Champion
Too Late for Tears
The Walking Hills
50: The Glass Menagerie
51: Red Mountain
Bright Victory
52: Rodeo
Bend of the River
Rancho Notorious
The Girl in White
The Lusty Men
55: The Man from Laramie

Trial
The Naked Dawn
Desperate Hours
Crashout
56: The Rawhide Years
57: Peyton Place
58: Some Came Running
Claudelle Inglish
Twilight for the Gods
59: A Summer Place
60: Elmer Gantry
61: Home Is the Hero
62: Hemingway's Adventures
of a Young Man
Barabbas
Murder She Said
Lawrence of Arabia
63: Il Bravo Gente
64: Cheyenne Autumn
65: Joy in the Morning
Murietta (or, Vendetta)
Italiano Brava Gente
66: Nevada Smith
Attack and Retreat (Ital.)
Fantastic Voyage
67: The Prodigal Gun
68: Day of the Evil Gun
A Minute to Pray, a
Second to Die
69: Anzio
Shark
Hail, Hero!

Douglas Kennedy (1915-
1940: Those Were the Days
Opened by Mistake
Women Without Names
At Good Old Siwash
The Way of All Flesh
Northwest Mounted Police
41: The Roundup
The Great Mr. Nobody
47: Last Train from Hong Kong
Nora Prentiss
Dark Passage
Possessed
The Unfaithful
Deep Valley
Always Together
That Hagen Girl

773

48: To the Victor
Decision of Christopher
  Blake
Whirlpool
Embraceable You
Johnny Belinda
Adventures of Don Juan
49: South of Rio
Look for the Silver Lining
Revenge Agent
Flaxy Martin
One Last Fling
South of St. Louis
The Fighting Man of the
  Plains
Ranger of Cherokee Strip
East Side, West Side
50: Chain Gang
Caribou Trail
Montana
Convicted
51: Oh, Susanna!
I Was an American Spy
Lion Hunters
Callaway Went Thataway
China Corsair
The Texas Rangers
52: Fort Osage
Indian Uprising
For Men Only
The Next Voice You Hear
Last Train from Bombay
Ride the Man Down
53: Torpedo Alley
War Paint
Gun Belt
Sea of Lost Ships
Safari Drums
San Antone
Jack McCall--Desperado
54: Lone Gun
Massacre Canyon
The Big Chase
Ketchikan
Sitting Bull
Cry Vengeance
55: Wyoming Renegades
The Eternal Sea
Strange Lady in Town
56: The Wiretrappers

The Last Wagon
The Strange Intruder
57: Last of the Badmen
Hell's Crossroads
The Land Unknown
Chicago Confidential
Rockabilly Baby
58: The Lone Ranger and the
  Lost City of Gold
59: The Lone Texan
The Alligator People
60: The Amazing Transparent
  Man
61: Flight of the Lost Balloon
67: The Fastest Guitar Alive

Edgar Kennedy (1890-1948)
1929: They Had to See Paris
Unaccustomed as We Are
Trent's Last Case
The Chinese Parrot
Hurdy Gurdy
Dad's Day
30: Night Owls
31: Bad Company
32: Carnival Boat
various short comedies
Hold 'em, Jail!
The Penguin Pool Murder
Little Orphan Annie
33: Duck Soup
Crossfire
Professional Sweetheart
Son of the Border
Tillie and Gus
Scarlet River
34: All of Me
Heat Lightning
Murder on the Blackboard
The Silver Streak
We're Rich Again
Mr. Average Man comedies
  a short
Kid Millions
Twentieth Century
Money Means Nothing
Gridiron Flash
The Marines Are Coming
King Kelly of U.S.A.
Flirting with Danger

35: Living on Velvet
The Cowboy Millionaire
Woman Wanted
The Little Big Shot
In Person
A $1000 a Minute
The Bride Goes Home
Rendezvous at Midnight
36: The Return of Jimmy
Valentine
a short
Small Town Girl
San Francisco
Mad Holiday
Fatal Lady
Yours for the Asking
Robin Hood of El Dorado
Three Men on a Horse
37: a short
When's Your Birthday?
Super Sleuth
A Star Is Born
Double Wedding
True Confession
Hollywood Hotel
38: The Black Doll
Scandal Street
Hey! Hey! U.S.A.
Peck's Bad Boy with the
Circus
a short
39: It's a Wonderful World
Everything's on Ice
Little Accident
Charlie McCarthy,
Detective
Laugh it Off
40: Sandy Is a Lady
Dr. Christian Meets the
Women
The Quarterback
Margie
Who Killed Aunt Maggie?
Remedy for Riches
41: The Bride Wore Crutches
Public Enemies
Blonde in Society
42: Snuffy Smith, Yard Bird
Pardon My Stripes
In Old California

Hillbilly Blitzkrieg
43: The Falcon Strikes Back
Air Raid Wardens
The Girl from Monterey
Hitler's Madman
Crazy House
The Great Alaskan Mystery
44: It Happened Tomorrow
45: Anchors Aweigh
Captain Tugboat Annie
47: Mad Wednesday
Heaven Only Knows
48: Unfaithfully Yours
Variety Time
49: My Dream Is Yours
64: The Sound of Laughter
(doc.)
65: Laurel & Hardy's Laughing
'20s (doc.)

George Kennedy (1925-
1961: Little Shepherd of Kingdom
Come
62: Lonely Are the Brave
63: The Man from the Diner's
Club
Charade
64: Strait-Jacket
McHale's Navy
Island of the Blue Dolphins
65: Hush, Hush, Sweet
Charlotte!
In Harm's Way
Shenandoah
Mirage
66: The Sons of Katie Elder
The Flight of the Phoenix
67: Hurry Sundown
Cool Hand Luke (OSCAR)
The Dirty Dozen
68: The Legend of Lylah Claire
The Ballad of Josie
The Pink Jungle
Bandolero
The Boston Strangler
69: The Guns of the Magnificent
Seven
Gaily, Gaily
Rebellion
The Good Guys and the
Bad Guys

69: Man Against Himself
Airport
Tick...Tick...Tick...
False Witness

Madge Kennedy (1892-
1952: The Marrying Kind
55: The Rains of Ranchipur
56: Three Bad Sisters
The Catered Affair
Lust for Life
58: A Nice Little Bank that
Should be Robbed
59: Plunderers of Painted
Flats
60: Let's Make Love
69: They Shoot Horses, Don't
They?

Merna Kennedy (1908-1944)
1928: The Circus   S
29: Broadway
Barnum Was Right
Skinner Steps Out
30: Embarrassing Moments
King of Jazz
The Rampant Age
Worldly Goods
Midnight Special
31: Stepping Out
32: Lady with a Past
The Gay Buckaroo
Ghost Valley
The All-American
Reputation
Red-Haired Alibi
Laughter in Hell
33: Come on, Tarzan!
Emergency Call
Arizona to Broadway
Don't Bet on Love
Big Chance
Police Call
Easy Millions
Son of a Sailor

Tom Kennedy (1885-1965)
1929: Glad Rag Doll
Post Mortems
Goodbys Broadway (or,
The Shannons of Broad-
way)

Big News
Love over Night
The Cohens and the Kellys
in Atlantic City
30: See America Thirst
Big House
Fall Guy
31: It Pays to Advertise
Gang Busters
Caught
Monkey Business
32: Pack Up Your Troubles
The Devil Is Driving
33: She Done Him Wrong
Blondie Johnson
Man of the Forest
a short
34: Hollywood Party
Down to Their Last Yacht
Strictly Dynamite
a short
35: a short
Bright Lights
36: a short
Hollywood Boulevard
Smart Blonde
37: a short
Fly-Away Baby
Marry the Girl
The Adventurous Blonde
Behind the Headlines
The Big Shot
Forty Naughty Girls
Living on Love
Married Before Breakfast
Armored Car
Swing it Sailor
She Had to Eat
The Case of the Stuttering
Bishop
38: Wise Girl
Go Chase Yourself
Crime Ring
The Long Shot
Pardon Our Nerve
Torchy Blane in Panama
Making the Headlines
Crashing Hollywood
House of Mystery
Blondes at Work
Torchy Gets Her Man
39: Torchy Blane in Chinatown

39: Torchy Runs for Mayor
a short
The Day the Bookies Wept
Covered Trailer
Society Lawyer
Torchy Plays with
Dynamite
40: Remember the Night
Millionaire Playboy
Curtain Call
An Angel from Texas
Pop Always Pays
Sporting Blood
Flowing Gold
The Mexican Spitfire Out
West
41: The Great Swindle
Angels with Broken Wings
Sailors on Leave
The Officer and the Lady
42: Pardon My Stripes
Wildcat
43: The Hit Parade of 1943
Ladies' Day
Dixie
Here Comes Elmer
My Darling Clementine
Petticoat Larceny
44: Rosie the Riveter
The Princess and the
Pirate
Moonlight and Cactus
45: The Man Who Walked
Alone
46: Voice of the Whistler
47: The Pretender
The Burning Cross
The Case of the Baby-
Sitter
48: The Devil's Cargo
Jinx Money
The Paleface
49: The Mutineers
Thunder in the Pines
Maggie and Jiggs in Jack-
pot Jitters
Square Dance Jubilee
50: Border Rangers
51: Havana Rose
Let's Go, Navy!

52: Invasion U.S.A.
Gold Fever

Barbara Kent (1908-
1928: Modern Mothers   S
Retribution   S
Lonesome   PT
29: The Shakedown   PT
Welcome Danger
Night Ride
30: What Men Want
Dumbbells in Ermine
Feet First
31: Indiscreet
Grief Street
Chinatown after Dark
Freighters of Destiny
32: Emma
Vanity Fair
No Living Witness
Exposed
Beauty Parlor
Pride of the Legion
33: Self Defense
Oliver Twist
Her Forgotten Past
Marriage on Approval
35: Swell Head
Old Man Rhythm
Guard that Girl!
41: Under Age

Crauford Kent (1881-1953)
1928: Blindfold   SSE
Man, Woman, and
Wife   SSE
Show People   SSE
29: Seven Keys to Baldpate
Wolf of Wall Street
The Charlatan
Come Across
30: In the Next Room
Sweethearts and Wives
The Second Floor Mystery
The Devil to Pay
Three Faces East
Ladies Love Brutes
31: Body and Soul
Transatlantic
Delicious

777

31: The Feathered Serpent
    Women Men Marry
    His Last Performance
    Goldberg
    Grief Street
32: Sally of the Subway
    Sinister Hands
    The 13th Guest
    File 113
    The Menace
    Murder at Dawn
    The Fighting Gentleman
    Western Limited
33: Humanity
    Eagle and the Hawk
    Only Yesterday
    Sailor be Good
34: The House of Rothschild
    Lost Jungle
35: Vanessa--Her Love Story
36: Magnificent Obsession
    O'Malley of the Mounted
    It Couldn't Have Happened
    Daniel Boone
    Hitchhike to Heaven
    Down the Stretch
37: Navy Spy
38: Love, Honor, and Behave
39: I Was a Convict
    We Are not Alone
40: Foreign Correspondent
    South of Suez
41: Shining Victory
    International Squadron
43: Mysterious Doctor
    The Constant Nymph
44: Black Parachute
45: The Fatal Witness
46: Kitty
50: Tea for Two

Larry Kent
1929: Spirit of Youth   S
     The Devil's Appletree   S
     Midstream   PT
36: Man Hunt
55: A Man Called Peter
    Daddy Long Legs

Robert Kent
1936: The Country Beyond
     The Crime of Dr. Forbes
     King of the Royal Mounted
     Dimples
     Reunion
37: Nancy Steele Is Missing
    Step Lively, Jeeves
    Angel's Holiday
    Born Reckless
    Charlie Chan at Monte
     Carlo
38: The Gladiator
    Mr. Moto Takes a Chance
    Wanted by the Police
    Little Orphan Annie
    Gang Bullets
39: East Side of Heaven
    For Love or Money
    Andy Hardy Gets Spring
     Fever
    Calling all Marines
    The Secret of Dr.Kildare
41: Sunset in Wyoming
    Twilight on the Trail
42: Stagecoach Express
43: Yanks Ahoy
    Find the Blackmailer
    What a Man!
44: Hot Rhythm
45: What Next, Corporal Har-
     grove?
46: Joe Palooka, Champ
50: Federal Agent at Large
    Radar Secret Service
    For Heaven's Sake
53: Rebel City
54: The Country Girl

Doris Kenyon (1897-
1930: Beau Bandit
31: Upper Underworld
    Alexander Hamilton
    Road to Singapore
    The Bargain
    The Ruling Voice
32: Young America
    The Man Called Back

33: Voltaire
No Marriage Ties
Counsellor-At-Law
34: Whom the Gods Destroy
The Human Side
36: Along Came Love
38: Girls' School

Deborah Kerr (1921-
1939: Contraband
41: Major Barbara
Love on the Dole
The Courageous Mr. Penn
(or, Penn of Pennsylvania)
43: The Avengers (or, The
Day Will Dawn)
45: Colonel Blimp
I See a Dark Stranger
Vacation from Marriage
(or, Perfect Strangers)
47: Black Narcissus
The Hucksters
If Winter Comes
The Adventuress
48: Hatter's Castle
49: Edward My Son
50: Please Believe Me
King Solomon's Mines
51: Quo Vadis?
52: The Prisoner of Zenda
53: Dream Wife
Julius Caesar
Thunder in the East
Young Bess
From Here to Eternity
55: The End of the Affair
56: The King and I
The Proud and Profane
Tea and Sympathy
57: Heaven Knows, Mr. Allison
An Affair to Remember
58: Bonjour Tristesse
Separate Tables
59: Count Your Blessings
The Journey
Beloved Infidel
60: The Sundowners
The Grass Is Greener
61: The Innocents
The Naked Edge

64: The Chalk Garden
Night of the Iguana
65: Marriage on the Rocks
Community Property
67: Eye of the Devil
Casino Royale
68: Prudence and the Pill
69: The Gypsy Moths
The Arrangement
The Lonely Passion of
Judith Hearne

John Kerr (1931-
1955: The Cobweb
56: Gaby
Tea and Sympathy
57: The Vintage
58: South Pacific
60: Girl of the Night
The Crowded Sky
61: The Pit and the Pendulum
Seven Women from Hell

Joseph M. Kerrigan (1887-1964)
1929: Lucky in Love
30: Song o' My Heart
New Movietone Follies
Lightnin'
Under Suspicion
31: Don't Bet on Women
Black Camel
Merely Mary Ann
32: Rainbow Trail
Careless Lady
33: Air Hostess
Lone Cowboy
A Study in Scarlet
Paddy, the Next Best Thing
34: The Lost Patrol
A Modern Hero
The Key
Gentlemen Are Born
Treasure Island
The Fountain
Happiness Ahead
35: Mystery of Edwin Drood
Werewolf of London
The Informer
Hot Tip
Barbary Coast

779

35: A Feather in Her Hat
36: Timothy's Quest
Spendthrift
The General Died at Dawn
Colleen
The Prisoner of Shark
Island
Lloyds of London
Laughing Irish Eyes
Hearts in Bondage
Special Investigator
37: The Plough and the Stars
Let's Make a Million
The Barrier
London by Night
38: Vacation from Love
Ride a Crooked Mile
Little Orphan Annie
39: The Great Man Votes
Boy Slaves
The Flying Irishman
Sorority House
Two Thoroughbreds
The Kid from Texas
6000 Enemies
Two Bright Eyes
The Zero Hour
Sabotage
Union Pacific
The Witness Vanishes
Gone With the Wind
40: Congo Maisie
Three Cheers for the
Irish
Young Tom Edison
Curtain Call
Untamed
The Sea Hawk
One Crowded Night
No Time for Comedy
The Long Voyage Home
41: Adventure in Washington
42: Captains of the Clouds
43: An American Romance
None but the Lonely Heart
Mr. Lucky
Action in the North
Atlantic
44: The Fighting Seabees
Wilson

45: Tarzan and the Amazons
The Big Bonanza
The Great John L.
The Spanish Main
She Went to the Races
The Crime Doctor's
Warning
46: Black Beauty
Abie's Irish Rose
48: Call Northside 777
49: Mrs. Mike
The Fighting O'Flynn
51: Sealed Cargo
Two of a Kind
52: The Wild North
Park Row
My Cousin Rachel
53: The Silver Whip
54: 20,000 Leagues Under the
Sea
55: It's a Dog's Life
56: The Fastest Gun Alive

Norman Kerry (1890-1956)
1929: Man, Woman, and
Wife   SSE
Trial Marriage   S
The Bondman   S
30: Ex-Flame
31: Bachelor Apartment
Air Eagles
41: Tanks a Million

Evelyn Keyes (1919-
1938: The Buccaneer
Sons of the Legion
39: Sudden Money
Union Pacific
Gone With the Wind
40: Slightly Honorable
Lady in Question
Before I Hang
41: The Face Behind the Mask
Here Comes Mr. Jordan
Ladies in Retirement
Beyond the Sacramento
42: The Adventures of Martin
Eden
Flight Lieutenant
43: The Desperadoes

44: Nine Girls
Dangerous Blondes
Strange Affair
45: A Thousand and One Nights
46: The Jolson Story
Thrill of Brazil
Renegades
47: Johnny O'Clock
48: Mating of Millie
Enchantment
49: Mr. Soft Touch
Mrs. Mike
50: The Killer that Stalked
New York
51: The Prowler
Smuggler's Island
The Iron Man
52: One Big Affair
53: Shoot First
99 River Street
54: Hell's Half Acre
55: Top of the World
The Seven Year Itch
56: Around the World in 80
Days

Guy Kibbee (1882-1956)
1931: Stolen Heaven
Laughing Sinners
Man of the World
City Streets
Happy Landing
Larceny Lane
New Adventures of Get-
Rich-Quick Wallingford
Blonde Crazy
Side Show
Flying High
32: Play Girl
So Big
Mouthpiece
The Crowd Roars
Gentleman for a Day
High Pressure
Fireman, Save My Child!
Winner Take All
Man Wanted
Taxi!
The Crooner
Strange Love of Molly
Louvain

The Dark Horse
New York Town
Weekend Marriage
Two Seconds
Rain
The Conquerors
Central Park
Big City Blues
33: 42nd Street
Lilly Turner
Silk Express
The Life of Jimmy Dolan
Girl Missing
Scarlet Dawn
Gold Diggers of 1933
Footlight Parade
Lady for a Day
The World Changes
Havana Widows
Convention City
34: Easy to Love
Dames
Big-Hearted Herbert
Harold Teen
Merry Wives of Reno
Wonder Bar
Babbitt
They Had to Get Married
The Merry Frinks
35: While the Patient Slept
Mary Jane's Pa
Crashing Society
Don't Bet on Blondes
Going Highbrow
I Live for Love
Captain Blood
36: Little Lord Fauntleroy
Captain January
I Married a Doctor
The Big Noise
Earthworm Tractors
Three Men on a Horse
M'Liss
37: The Captain's Kid
Mama Steps Out
Don't Tell the Wife
Riding on Air
The Big Shot
Jim Hanvey, Detective
Mountain Justice
38: Bad Man of Brimstone

38: Of Human Hearts
    Three Comrades
    Rich Man, Poor Girl
    Three Loves Has Nancy
    Joy of Living
39: Let Freedom Ring
    It's a Wonderful World
    Babes in Arms
    Bad Little Angel
    Mr. Smith Goes to
    Washington
40: Our Town
    Street of Memories
    Chad Hanna
    Henry Goes Arizona
41: Scattergood Baines
    It Started with Eve
    Design for Scandal
    Scattergood Meets Broad-
    way
    Scattergood Pulls the
    Strings
42: This Time for Keeps
    Sunday Punch
    Miss Annie Rooney
    Whistling in Dixie
    Scattergood Rides High
    Scattergood Survives a
    Murder
43: Cinderella Swings it
    Power of the Press
    White Savage
    Girl Crazy
44: Dixie Jamboree
45: The Horn Blows at
    Midnight
    White Pongo
46: Gentleman Joe Palooka
47: Romance of Rosy Ridge
48: Fort Apache
    Three Godfathers

Michael Kidd (1919-
1952: Where's Charley (choreog.)
53: Band Wagon (choreog.)
54: Seven Brides for Seven
    Brothers (choreog.)
    It's Always Fair Weather
55: Guys and Dolls
58: Merry Andrew (act., dir.)

Richard Kiel
1962: The Magic Sword
63: House of the Damned
65: The Human Duplicators
67: A Man Called Dagger

Jan Kiepura (1904-1966)
1930: The Singing City
32: City of Song
    Ein Lied für Dich
33: Be Mine Tonight
    Das Lied Eine Nach
    Mein Herz Ruft nach Dir
34: Ich Liebe Alles Frauen
35: My Heart Is Calling You
36: Give Us This Night
    Zauber der Boheme
49: La Vie de Boheme

Percy Kilbride (1888-1964)
1933: White Woman
36: Soak the Rich
42: Keeper of the Flame
    George Washington Slept
    Here
43: Crazy House
    Woman of the Town
44: The Adventures of Mark
    Twain
    Guest in the House
    Knickerbocker Holiday
    She's a Soldier too
45: State Fair
    Fallen Angel
    She Wouldn't Say Yes
46: The Well-Groomed Bride
47: Welcome Stranger
    The Egg and I
    Riffraff
48: Black Bart
    You Gotta Stay Happy
    You Were Meant for Me
    Feudin', Fussin', an' A-
    Fightin'
49: The Sun Comes Up
    Free for All
    Mr. Soft Touch
    Ma and Pa Kettle
50: Ma and Pa Kettle Go to
    Town

51: Ma and Pa Kettle Back to
    the Farm
52: Ma and Pa Kettle at the
    Fair
53: Ma and Pa Kettle on
    Vacation
54: Ma and Pa Kettle at
    Home
55: Ma and Pa Kettle at
    Waikiki

Terry Kilburn (1928-
1934: No Greater Glory
38: Lord Jeff
    A Christmas Carol
    Sweethearts
39: Goodbye Mr. Chips
    Andy Hardy Gets Spring
     Fever
    They Shall Have Music
    Adventures of Sherlock
     Holmes
40: Swiss Family Robinson
41: Mercy Island
42: A Yank at Eton
44: National Velvet
45: Keys of the Kingdom
46: Black Beauty
47: Song of Scheherazade
    Bulldog Drummond Strikes
     Back
    Bulldog Drummond at Bay
48: The Challenge
    Thirteen Lead Soldiers
49: The Fan
50: The Fortunes of Captain
    Blood
    Tyrant of the Sea
51: Only the Valiant
53: Slaves of Babylon
58: The Fiend Without a Face

Richard Kiley (1922-
1951: The Mob
52: The Sniper
    Eight Iron Men
53: Pickup on South Street
55: The Blackboard Jungle
    The Phenix City Story
58: The Spanish Affair

67: Pendulum

Victor Kilian (1891-
1929: Valley Forge
    Gentlemen of the Press
32: The Wiser Sex
33: After the Dance
    Bad Boy
    Air Hawks
    Public Menace
    The Girl Friend
36: Riffraff
    I Loved a Soldier
    The Music Goes 'Round
    Shakedown
    Adventure in Manhattan
    Lady from Nowhere
    Road to Glory
    Ramona
    Banjo on My Knee
37: Fair Warning
    Seventh Heaven
    League of Frightened Men
    It's All Yours
    Tovarich
38: Adventures of Tom Sawyer
    Orphans of the Street
    Gold Diggers in Paris
    a short
    Prison Break
    Boys' Town
39: Fighting Thoroughbreds
    Paris Honeymoon
    St. Louis Blues
    The Adventures of Huckle-
     berry Finn
    Return of the Cisco Kid
    Only Angels Have Wings
    Dust be My Destiny
40: Virginia City
    Dr. Cyclops
    Little Old New York
    Young Tom Edison
    Till We Meet Again
    King of the Lumberjacks
    Torrid Zone
    All this and Heaven too
    The Return of Frank James
    Out West with the Peppers
    They Knew What They
     Wanted

40: Tugboat Annie Sails Again
Barnyard Follies
Chad Hanna
41: Western Union
Blood and Sand
I Was a Prisoner on
Devil's Island
Mob Town
A Date with the Falcon
42: Reap the Wild Wind
Atlantic Convoy
43: The Ox-Bow Incident
Bomber's Moon
Hitler's Hangman
Johnny Come Lately
Belle of the Yukon
44: Uncertain Glory
Adventures of Mark Twain
Barbary Coast Gent
45: Dangerous Passage
The Spanish Main
Behind City Lights
Spellbound
The Fighting Guardsman
46: Little Giant
Smoky
47: A Gentleman's Agreement
48: Northwest Stampede
Yellow Sky
49: I Shot Jesse James
Rimfire
Colorado Territory
Wyoming Bandit
50: The Flame and the Arrow
Old Frontier
Return of Jesse James
The Showdown
The Bandit Queen
One Too Many
51: The Tall Target

Aron Kincaid (1943-
1963: Palm Springs Weekend
65: The Girls on the Beach
Ski Party
Beach Ball
66: The Ghost in the Invisible
Bikini
67: The Happiest Millionaire
69: Proud, Damned, and Dead

Alan King
1955: Hit the Deck
56: Miracle in the Rain
The Girl He Left Behind
57: The Helen Morgan Story
65: Operation Snafu
69: Bye Bye, Braverman

Andrea King (1916-
1944: The Very Thought of You
Hollywood Canteen
45: Roughly Speaking
God Is My Co-Pilot
Hotel Berlin
46: Shadow of a Woman
The Man I Love
The Beast with Five Fingers
47: Ride the Pink Horse
My Wild Irish Rose
48: Mr. Peabody and the
Mermaid
49: Song of Surrender
50: Buccaneer's Girl
I Was a Shoplifter
Dial 1119
Southside 1-1000
51: The Lemon Drop Kid
Mark of the Renegade
52: Red Planet Mars
The World in His Arms
56: Silent Fear
57: A Band of Angels
Outlaw Queen
58: Darby's Rangers
69: Daddy's Gone A-Hunting

Charles King (1894-1944)
1929: Broadway Melody
The Girl in the Show
Hollywood Revue of 1929
Slim Fingers
Road Show
30: Chasing Rainbows
Oh Sailor, Behave!
Oklahoma Cyclone
Remote Control
Beyond the Law
Dawn Trail
Fighting Through
32: Gay Buckaroo

32: A Man's Land
The Fighting Champ
Ghost City
Honor of the Mounted
33: The Fighting Parson
Crashing Broadway
Son of the Border
The Lone Avenger
Strawberry Roan
Young Blood
Outlaw Justice
35: Northern Frontier
Outlawed Guns
The Smiling Vagabond
The Ivory-Handled Gun
Just My Luck
Mississippi
Red Blood of Courage
Tumbling Tumbleweeds
His Fighting Blood
36: The Lawless Nineties
Guns and Guitars
O'Malley of the Mounted
Headin' for Rio Grande
Sunset of Power
Desert Phantom
Sundown Sanders
Men of the Plains
Last of the Warrens
Idaho
37: Trouble in Texas
Sing, Cowboy, Sing
Tex Rides with the Boy
  Scouts
Rootin' Tootin' Rhythm
Hittin' the Trail
Headline Crasher
The Trusted Outlaw
A Lawman Is Born
Island Captives
Black Aces
Riders of the Rockies
Mystery of the Hooded
  Horseman
The Red Rope
Ridin' the Lone Trail
38: Starlight over Texas
Where the Buffalo Roam
Gun Packer
Frontier Town

Thunder in the Desert
Song and Bullets
Phantom Ranger
Man's Country
39: Wild Horse Canyon
Song of the Buckaroo
Rollin' Westward
Down the Wyoming Trail
Mutiny in the Big House
Oklahoma Frontier
40: Son of the Navy
West of Carson City
Wild Horse Range
41: Billy the Kid's Fighting
  Pals
Outlaws of the Rio Grande
Roar of the Press
The Lone Ranger in Ghost
  Town
Texas Marshal
Gunman from Bodie
Borrowed Hero
Billy the Kid Wanted
Billy the Kid's Roundup
The Lone Ranger Fights
  Back
42: Ghost Town Law
Riders of the West
Law and Order
Pirates of the Prairie
43: Two-Fisted Justice
The Rangers Take Over
The Ghost Rider
The Stranger from Pecos
Border Buckaroos
Riders of the Rio Grande

Charles King, Jr.
1938: Where the Buffalo Roam
42: Eagle Squadron
45: Law of the Valley
The Navajo Kid
Border Badmen
Devil Riders
Gangsters' Den
His Brother's Ghost
Both Barrels Blazing
Enemy of the Law
Navajo Trails
Oath of Vengeance
Outlaw Roundup
Shadows of Death

785

45: Rustler's Hideout
Three in the Saddle
Arizona Whirlwind
46: Ambush Trail
The Cimarron Trail
Lawless Breed
Thunder Town
Queen of Burlesque
Prairie Badmen
47: Law of the Lash
Three on a Ticket
Ghost of Hidden Valley
48: Killer at Large
Ridin' Down the Trail
Outlaw af the Plains
Oklahoma Blues

Claude King (1879-1941)
1929: Strange Cargo
Madame X
Behind that Curtain
Blue Skies
Black Watch
Mysterious Dr. Fu Manchu
Son of the Gods
In Gay Madrid
Prince of Diamonds
2nd Floor Mystery
Follow Through
Love Among the Million-
aires
31: Rango
The Reckless Hour
Men Love Once
Transatlantic
Devotion
Once a Lady
Heartbreak
Arrowsmith
32: Behind the Mask
He Learned about Women
Sherlock Holmes
33: White Woman
The Big Brain
Charlie Chan's Greatest
Case
34: Long Lost Father
Murder in Trinidad

The Moonstone
Stolen Sweets
The World Moves on
Two Heads on a Pillow
35: Circumstantial Evidence
Smart Girl
$1000 a Minute
The Great Impersonation
36: The Leathernecks Have
Landed
Three on the Trail
It Couldn't Have Happened
Beloved Enemy
Shanghai Gesture
Happy Go Lucky
39: Within the Law
40: New Moon

Dennis King (1897-
1930: Vagabond Kind
Paramount on Parade
31: Fra Diavolo
37: Between Two Worlds
69: The One with the Fuzz

John "Dusty" King (1911-
1939: The Three Musketeers
The Hardys Ride High
Mr. Moto Takes a Vacation
The Gentleman from
Arizona
40: Midnight Limited
Half a Sinner
The Range Busters
Trailing Double Trouble
West of Pinto Basin
41: Trail of the Silver Spurs
The Kid's Last Ride
Tumbledown Ranch in
Arizona
Wranglers' Roost
Fugitive Valley
42: Rock River Renegades
Texas to Bataan
Law of the Jungle
Trail Riders
Boot Hill Bandits
Texas Trouble Shooters
43: Two-Fisted Justice

Joseph King
1935: Front Page Woman
  36: Satan Met a Lady
  39: My Son Is a Criminal
      Off the Record
      You Can't Get Away with
        Murder
      Code of the Secret
        Service
      Smashing the Money Ring
      Destry Rides Again
  40: Three Cheers for the Irish
      Black Friday
      It's a Date
      You're not so Tough
      Charlie Chan at the Wax
        Museum
      Always a Bride
  41: Blondie Goes Latin
      Bullets for O'Hara
  42: The Big Shot
      The Glass Key
  43: She Has What it Takes

Walter Woolf King (1899-
1930: Golden Dawn
  33: Girl Without a Room
      Experience Unnecessary
      Ladies All
      Lottery Lover
      One More Spring
      Spring Tonic
      Ginger
  55: A Night at the Opera
      a short
  37: Call it a Day
  38: Walking Down Broadway
      Swiss Miss
  39: Society Smugglers
      Big Town Czar
      House of Fear
      Balalaika
  40: Go West
  41: Melody for Three
  42: Today I Hang
      Smart Alecks
      A Yank in Libya
  43: Yanks Ahoy
  56: Bottom of the Bottle
  57: The Helen Morgan Story

  58: Kathy O'
      Hong Kong Confidential
  67: Rosie

Walter Kingsford (1884-1956)
1934: Pursuit to Happiness
      The President Vanishes
  35: Frankie and Johnnie
      Mystery of Edwin Drood
      The White Cockatoo
      Naughty Marietta
      Shanghai
      I Found Stella Parish
      The Melody Lingers on
      Professional Soldier
      The Story of Louis Pasteur
  36: Hearts Divided
      Stolen Holiday
      The Invisible Ray
      Little Lord Fauntleroy
      Trouble for Two
      Mad Holiday
      Meet Nero Wolfe
  37: Maytime
      Captains Courageous
      My Dear Miss Aldrich
      Bulldog Drummond Escapes
      Double or Nothing
      The Life of Emile Zola
      League of Frightened Men
      The Devil Is Driving
      I'll Take Romance
      It Could Happen to You
  38: Paradise for Three
      A Yank at Oxford
      The Toy Wife
      The Lone Wolf in Paris
      Lord Jeff
      There's Always a Woman
      Algiers
      The Young in Heart
      Carefree
      If I Were King
      Say it in French
      Young Dr. Kildare
      Juarez
  39: The Man in the Iron Mask
      Miracles for Sale
      Dancing Coed
      The Secret of Dr. Kildare

787

39: The Witness Vanishes
Smashing the Spy Ring
Calling Dr. Kildare
40: Adventure in Diamonds
Dr. Kildare's Strange Case
Star Dust
Lucky Partners
A Dispatch from Reuters
Dr. Kildare Goes Home
Dr. Kildare's Crisis
Kitty Foyle
41: The Devil and Miss Jones
The Lone Wolf Takes a
Chance
The People vs Dr. Kildare
Hit the Road
Ellery Queen and the
Perfect Crime
Dr. Kildare's Wedding Day
Unholy Partners
Dr. Kildare's Victory
The Corsican Brothers
42: My Favorite Blonde
Fly by Night
Fingers at the Window
Calling Dr. Gillespie
The Loves of Edgar Allan
Poe
Dr. Gillespie's New
Assistant
43: Flight for Freedom
Forever and a Day
Bomber's Moon
Dr. Gillespie's Criminal
Case
Hi Diddle Diddle
44: Three Men in White
The Hitler Gang
Mr. Skeffington
Ghost Catshers
Secrets of Scotland Yard
45: Between Three Women
48: Black Arrow
The Velvet Touch
49: Slattery's Hurricane
50: Experiment Alcatraz
51: My Forbidden Past
Tarzan's Peril
The Desert Fox
Two Dollar Bettor

52: Confidence Girl
The Brigand
The Pathfinder
53: Loose in London
Walking My Baby Back
Home
56: Around the World in 80
Days
The Search for Bridey
Murphy
58: Merry Andrew

Natalie Kingston
1929: River of Romance
30: Swellhead
Her Wedding Night
31: Under Texas Skies
33: Forgotten
His Private Secretary

Leonid Kinsky (1903-
1932: Trouble in Paradise
33: Duck Soup
Girl Without a Room
Three-Cornered Moon
34: Fugitive Road
35: Les Miserables
Peter Ibbetson
36: Road to Glory
Garden of Allah
Rhythm on the Range
The General Died at Dawn
37: We're on the Jury
Make a Wish
Espionage
My Dear Miss Aldrich
Cafe Metropole
The Sheik Steps Out
Meet the Boy Friend
38: Outside of Paradise
The Great Waltz
A Trip to Paris
Three Blind Mice
Flirting with Fate
Big Broadcast of 1938
Professor Beware
39: The Story of Vernon and
Irene Castle
The Spellbinder
Exile Express

39: On Your Toes
Everything Happens at
Night
Daytime Wife
40: He Stayed for Breakfast
Down Argentine Way
41: That Night in Rio
So Ends Our Night
Broadway Limited
Week-End in Havana
Ball of Fire
Lady for a Night
42: Brooklyn Orchid
I Married an Angel
Talk of the Town
Casablanca
43: Cinderella Swings It
Gildersleeve on Broadway
Presenting Lily Mars
Let's Have Fun
44: The Fighting Seabees
That's My Baby!
Can't Help Singing
46: Monsieur Beaucaire
49: Alimony
51: Honeychile
52: Gobs and Gals
55: The Man with a Golden
Arm
56: Glory

Lee Kinsolving
1960: All the Young Men
The Dark at the Top of
the Stairs
61: The Explosive Generation

Phyllis Kirk (1929-
1950: A Life of Her Own
Two Weeks with Love
Mrs. O'Malley and Mr.
Malone
Our Very Own
51: Three Guys Named Mike
52: About Face
The Iron Mistress
53: Thunder over the Plains
Adventure
House of Wax (3-D)
54: Crime Wave

River Beat
55: Canyon Crossroads
56: Johnny Concho
Back from Eternity
57: The Sad Sack
58: The Woman Opposite
59: Cry after Midnight

Tommy Kirk (1941-
1957: Old Yeller
59: The Shaggy Dog
60: The Swiss Family Robinson
The Snow Queen
61: The Absent-Minded
Professor
Babes in Toyland
62: Bon Voyage
Moon Pilot
63: Son of Flubber
Savage Sam
64: The Misadventures of
Merlin Jones
Pajama Party
65: The Monkey's Uncle
Village of the Giants
66: The Ghost in the Invisible
Bikini
67: It's a Bikini World
68: How to Stuff a Wild Bikini
The Catalina Caper

Muriel Kirkland (1903-
1933: Fast Workers
Hold Your Man
Cocktail Hour
To the Last Man
Secret of the Blue Room
34: Nana
Little Man, What Now?
The White Parade

Alexander Kirkland (1908-
1931: Tarnished Lady
Surrender
32: Passport to Hell
Devil's Lottery
Almost Married
Strange Interlude
33: Humanity
Black Beauty

James Kirkwood (1883-1963)
1929: Black Waters
The Time, the Place, and
the Girl
Hearts in Exile
30: Devil's Holiday
Worldly Goods
The Spoilers
31: Young Sinners
Over the Hill
A Holy Terror
32: Cheaters at Play
Charlie Chan's Chance
The Rainbow Trail
Lena Rivers
Careless Lady
My Pal, the King
She Wanted a Millionaire
34: Hired Wife
41: The Lady from Cheyenne
No Hands on the Clock
47: Driftwood
48: The Untamed Breed
49: The Doolins of Oklahoma
Red Stallion in the
Rockies
50: The Nevadan
Fancy Pants
Stage to Tucson
51: Man in the Saddle
52: I Dream of Jeanie
53: The Last Posse
54: Passion
56: The Search for Bridey
Murphy

Joe Kirkwood
1946: Joe Palooka-Champ
Gentleman Joe Palooka
47: Joe Palooka in The Knock-
out
48: Fighting Mad
Winner Take All
49: Joe Palooka in The Big
Fight
Joe Palooka in The
Counter-punch
50: Joe Palooka Meets
Humphrey
Joe Palooka in Humphrey
Takes a Chance

61: Marriage-Go-Round

Eartha Kitt (1930-
1954: New Faces
57: St. Louis Blues
58: Anna Lucasta
Mark of the Hawk
61: The Saint of Devil's
Island
65: Synanon

Alf Kjellin (1920-
1952: The Iron Mistress
My Six Convicts
53: The Juggler
54: Illicit Interlude
65: Ship of Fools
66: Assult on a Queen
68: Ice Station Zebra
69: The McMasters (dir.)

Helen Kleeb (1907-
1952: Kansas City Confidential
53: Half a Hero
54: Witness to Murder
Magnificent Obsession
56: Friendly Persuasion
There's Always Tomorrow
A Day of Fury
59: Curse of the Undead
The Gazebo
60: Cage of Evil
61: The Young Savages
62: The Manchurian Candidate
64: Seven Days in May
Sex and the Single Girl
65: Hush, Hush, Sweet
Charlotte!
The Hallelujah Trail
66: The Fortune Cookie
67: Fitzwilly
68: The Party
69: Blue
A Hall of Mirrors

Werner Klemperer
1956: Flight to Hong Kong
Death of a Scoundrel
57: Istanbul
Five Steps to Danger
Kiss Them for Me

790

58: The Goddess
Houseboat
61: Operation Eichmann
Judgment at Nuremberg
62: Escape from East Berlin
64: Youngblood Hawke
65: Ship of Fools
The Intruder (or, Dark
Intruder)
69: The Wicked Dreams of
Paula Schultz

Jack Klugman (1922-
1956: Time Table
57: Twelve Angry Men
58: Cry Terror
62: The Days of Wine and
Roses
63: I Could Go on Singing
The Yellow Canary
Act One
67: Hail Mafia!
68: The Detective
The Split
69: Goodbye, Columbus

Evalyn Knapp (1908-
1930: Sinners' Holiday
Mothers Cry
31: River's End
Gentlemen of the Evening
The Bargain
Tight Squeeze
Hard-Boiled Hampton
Big Time Charlie
Smart Money
The Millionaire
Fifty Million Frenchmen
Side Show
You and I
32: High Pressure
Fireman, Save My Child!
Big City Blues
Madame Racketeer
Bachelor Mothers
Fame
The Strange Love of
Molly Louvain
New York Town
Vanishing Frontier

Sporting Widow
A Successful Calamity
Night Mayor
This Sporting Age
Tess of the Storm Country
Slightly Married
33: State Trooper
Air Hostess
Corruption
His Private Secretary
Police Car 17
Dance, Girl, Dance
Love, Honor, and Oh Baby!
Smooth Guy
Black Market Babies
Haunted
Wednesday at the Ritz
Chills and Fever
Keeping Company
34: Perils of Pauline (ser.)
Speed Wings
A Man's Game
In Old Santa Fe
35: One Frightened Night
Ladies Crave Excitement
Confidential
The Firetrap
36: Laughing Irish Eyes
Three of a Kind
Bulldog Edition
38: Hawaiian Buckaroo
Rawhide
Wanted by the Police
41: The Lone Wolf Takes a
Chance
The Roar of the Press
43: Two Weeks to Live

Robert Knapp
1952: Strange Fascination
56: Jubal
Scandal, Inc.
57: Tomahawk Trail
Revolt at Fort Laramie
The Outlaw's Son
58: Hot Car Girl
The Rawhide Trail
59: Gunmen from Laredo

Felix Knight (1913-
1934: Babes in Toyland
  36: The Bohemian Girl

Fuzzy Knight (1901-
1933: Hell's Highway
      She Done Him Wrong
      Speed Demon
      Her Bodyguard
      Sunset Pass
      Under the Tonto Rim
      This Day and Age
      To the Last Man
      Moulin Rouge
  34: The Last Roundup
      I Hate Women
      Operator No. 13
      Night Alarm
  35: Behold My Wife
      Home on the Range
      George White's Scandals
        of 1935
      The Murder Man
      Mary Burns, Detective
      Wanderer of the Waste-
        land
      Danger Ahead
      The Old Homestead
      Hott Off the Press
      Trails of the Wild
  36: Trail of the Lonesome
        Pine
      And Sudden Death
      The Plainsman
      Song of the Gringo
      The Sea Spoilers
      Song of the Trail
      Rio Grande Romance
      Wildcat Trooper
      Kelly of the Secret
        Service
      Put on the Spot
      With Love and Kisses
  37: The Gold Racket
      Mountain Justice
      County Fair
      Mountain Music
      Courage of the West
  38: Quick Money
      Spawn of the North

      The Cowboy and the Lady
      Silks and Saddles
      Flying Fists
      Border Wolves
      The Last Stand
  39: Oklahoma Frontier
      Union Pacific
      Desperate Trails
      The Oregon Trail (ser.)
  40: Chip of the Flying "U"
      My Little Chickadee
      Johnny Apollo
      West of Catson City
      Riders of Peco Basin
      Bad Man of Red Butte
      Son of Roaring Dan
      Bridham Young
      Law and Order
      Ragtime Cowboy Joe
      Pony Post
  41: Horror Island
      The Cowboy and the Blonde
      Shepherd of the Hills
      Law of the Range
      New York Town
      Badlands of Dakota
      The Masked Rider
      The Man from Montana
  42: Arizona Cyclone
      Butch Minds the Baby
      Juke Girl
      Fighting Bill Fargo
      Apache Trail
      Stagecoach Buckaroo
      The Silver Bullet
      The Boss of Hangtown
        Mesa
      Keep in the Heart of
        Texas
      Little Joe, the Wrangler
  43: He's My Guy
      The Old Chisholm Trail
      Tenting on the Old Camp
        Ground
      Cheyenne Roundup
      Lone Star Trail
      Corvette K-225
      Slick Chick
  44: Hi Good Lookin'!
      The Great Alaska Mystery

44: Arizona Trail
The Cowboy and the
Senorita
Allergic to Love
Take it Big
The Singing Sheriff
Oklahoma Raiders
The Marshal of Gunsmoke
Boss of Boomtown
Trail to Gunsight
Trigger Trail
Riders of the Santa Fe
The Old Texas Trail
45: Frisco Sal
Frontier Gal
The Senorita from the
West
Spng of the Sarong
Swing Out Sister
46: Bad Men of the Border
Code of the Lawless
Girl on the Spot
Gunman's Code
Gun Town
The Lawless Breed
Renegades of the Rio
Grande
Her Adventurous Night
Trail to Vengeance
47: The Egg and I
Rustler's Round-Up
48: Adventures of Gallant
Bess
49: Down to the Sea in Ships
Rinfire
Apache Chief
Feudin' Rhythm
50: Hostile Country
Hills of Oklahoma
West of the Brazos
Marshal of Heldorado
Colorado Ranger
Crooked River
Fast on the Draw
51: Canyon Raiders
Nevada Badmen
Gold Raiders
Honeychile
Rodeo
Lawless Cowboys

Stage from Blue River
52: Oklahoma Annie
Kansas Territory
Fargo
The Gunman
Night Raiders
Feudin' Fools
53: Topeka
54: Vigilante Terror
56: The Naked Hills
58: The Notorious Mr. Monks
59: These Thousand Hills
65: The Bounty Killer
66: Waco
67: Hostile Guns

June Knight (1913-
1933: Take a Chance
Ladies Must Love
34: Cross Country Cruise
Gift of Gab
Wake Up and Dream
35: Broadway Melody of 1935
38: Vacation from Love
40: The House Across the
Bay

Shirley Knight (1937-
1959: Five Gates to Hell
60: Ice Palace
The Dark at the Top of
the Stairs
62: House of Women
Sweet Bird of Youth
63: The Couch
The Terror
64: Flight from Ashiya
66: The Group
67: The Dutchman
The Outsider (TV)
68: Shadow over Elveron (TV)
The Counterfeit Killer
69: The Rain People
Petulia

Don Knotts (1924-
1958: No Time for Sergeants
60: Wake Me When It's Over
61: The Last Time I Saw
Archie

63: It's a Mad Mad Mad Mad
World
Move Over Darling
64: The Incredible Mr. Limpet
66: The Ghost and Mr. Chicken
67: The Reluctant Astronaut
68: The Shakiest Gun in the
West
69: The Love God
Me and My Shadow

Patric Knowles (1911-
1934: Irish Hearts
Abdul the Damned
Royal Jubilee
35: Student's Romance
Honours Easy
Mister Hobo
The Guv'nor
36: Charge of the Light
Brigade
Two's Company
Give Me Your Heart
37: It's Love I'm After
Expensive Husbands
38: Adventures of Robin Hood
The Patient in Room 18
Four's a Crowd
The Sisters
Heart of the North
Storm over Bengal
39: Beauty for the Asking
Five Came Back
The Spellbinder
Torchy Blane in China-
town
Another Thin Man
The Honeymoon's Over
40: Married and in Love
A Bill of Divorcement
Anne of Windy Poplars
Women in War
41: How Green Was My Valley
The Wolf Man
42: No Man's Woman
Mystery of Marie Roget
The Strange Case of Dr.
RX
Lady in a Jam
Sin Town

Eyes of the Underworld
Who Done It?
43: Frankenstein Meets the
Wolf Man
Forever and a Day
Crazy House
All by Myself
Hit the Ice
Always a Bridesmaid
44: Pardon My Rhythm
Chip Off the Old Block
This Is the Life
45: Kitty
Masquerade in Mexico
46: Of Human Bondage
The Bride Wore Boots
Monsieur Beaucaire
O.S.S.
47: Ivy
Variety Girl
48: Dream Girl
Isn't it Romantic?
49: The Big Steal
A Connecticut Yankee in
King Arthur's Court
50: Three Came Home
51: Quebec
52: Mutiny
Tarzan's Savage Fury
53: Jamaica Run
Flame of Calcutta
54: The World Ransom
Khyber Patrol
55: No Man's Woman
57: A Band of Angels
58: Auntie Mame
From the Earth to the
Moon
67: The Way West
68: The Devil's Brigade
In Enemy Country

Alexander Knox (1907-
1938: The Gaunt Stranger
39: Phantom Strikes
Four Feathers
41: The Sea Wolf
42: This Above All
The Commandos Strike at
Dawn

44:	None Shall Escape	68:	Shalako

44: None Shall Escape
Wilson
45: Over Twenty-One
46: Sister Kenny
47: Indian Summer
48: Sign of the Ram
49: The Judge Steps Out
Tokyo Joe
51: Saturday's Hero
I'd Climb the Highest
Mountain
Two of a Kind
The Son of Dr. Jekyll
Man in the Saddle
52: Paula
54: The Greatest Love
The Sleeping Tiger
55: The Divided Heart
Alias John Preston
The Night My Number
Came Up
57: Hidden Fear
Reach for the Sky
High Tide at Noon
Davy
58: The Accident
Chase a Crooked Shadow
Intent to Kill
The Vikings
59: The Passionate Summer
The Two-Headed Spy
The Wreck of the Mary
Deare
60: Crack in the Mirror
Oscar Wilde
Operation Amsterdam
62: The Longest Day
63: In the Cool of the Day
64: Man in the Middle
Woman of Straw
65: Crack in the World
These Are the Damned
Mr. Moses
66: Khartoum
The Psychopath
Modesty Blaise
67: Bikini Paradise
The Accident
The 25th Hour
You Only Live Twice

68: Shalako
Villa Rides!
Fraulein Doktor
How I Won the War
69: The Betrayal
Skullduggery

Elyse Knox (1917-
1940: Free, Blonde, and 21
Youth Will be Served
Lillian Russell
Girl in 313
The Girl on Avenue A
41: Footlight Fever
The Sheriff of Tombstone
Tanks a Million
Miss Polly
42: The Mummy's Tomb
Hay Foot
The Night Monster
Top Sergeant
43: Mr. Big
Don Winslow of the Coast
Guard (ser.)
Keep 'em Slugging
Hit the Ice
Hi Ya, Sailor!
So's Your Uncle
44: A Wave, a Wac, and a
Marine
Moonlight and Cactus
Army Wives
46: Joe Palooka--Champ
Gentleman Joe Palooka
Sweetheart of Sigma Chi
47: Linda be Good
Black Gold
Joe Palooka in The Knock-
out
48: I Wouldn't be Seen in Your
Shoes
Fighting Mad
Winnter Take All
49: Joe Palooka in The Counter-
Punch
Forgotten Women
There's a Girl in My Heart

Peggy Knudsen (1923-
1946: The Big Sleep

46: Never Say Goodbye
    Shadow of a Woman
    A Stolen Life
    Humoresque
47: Stallion Road
    The Unfaithful
    In Self Defense
    Roses Are Red
48: Half Past Midnight
    Perilous Waters
49: Trouble Preferred
50: Copper Canyon
55: Unchained
    Good Morning, Miss Dove
    Betrayed Women
56: Bottom of the Bottle
    Hilda Crane
57: Istanbul

Fred Kohler (1889-1938)
1928: The Spider
    Broadway Daddies   S
29: The Dummy
    The Case of Lena Smith S
    Tide of Empire   S
    The Leatherneck   PT
    Sal of Singapore   PT
    The Quitter   S
    Stairs of Sand   S
    River of Romance
    Say it With Songs
    Thunderbolt
30: Roadhouse Nights
    Hell's Heroes
    Under a Texas Moon
    Light of the Western Stars
    Steel Highway
31: The Lash
    Fighting Caravans
    Right of Way
    Woman Hungry
    Other Men's Women
    Soldiers Plaything
    Corsair
    X Marks the Spot
32: Carnival Boat
    Call Her Savage
    Wild Horse Mesa
    The Fourth Horseman
    Rider of Death Valley

    The Texas Bad Man
33: Under the Tonto Rim
    Constant Woman
    Ship of Wanted Men
    The Deluge
    Fiddlin' Buckaroo
34: The Last Round Up
    Little Man, What Now?
    The Man from Hell
    West of the Pecos
35: Wilderness Mail
    Times Square Lady
    Mississippi
    Goin' to Town
    The Pecos Kid
    Border Brigand
    Hard Rock Harrigan
    Men of Action
    The Trail's End
    Stormy
    Toll of the Desert
    The Frisco Kid
36: Dangerous Intrigue
    I Loved a Soldier
    For the Service
    Heart of the West
    The Accusing Finger
37: Arizona Mahoney
    Slaughter of Shanghai
38: The Buccaneer
    Forbidden Valley
    Blockade
    Gangs of New York
    Billy the Kid Returns
    Painted Desert

Fred Kohler, Jr.
1935: Grand Old Girl
    The Hoosier Schoolmaster
    No More Ladies
    Toll of the Desert
36: Sins of Man
    Pigskin Parade
37: The Holy Terror
    Roaring Timber
    Life Begins in College
38: Prison Nurse
    Hold that Coed
39: Young Mr. Lincoln
41: Two-Gun Sheriff

41: Nevada City
Bahama Passage
42: Raiders of the Range
The Lone Star Ranger
The Boss of Hangtown
Mesa
43: Calling Wild Bill Elliott
44: Up in Mabel's Room
45: The Big Bonanza
Why Girls Leave Home
46: Feudin', Fussin', and A-
Fightin'
Loaded Pistols
47: The Gay Amigo
Tough Assignment
50: The Baron of Arizona
Twilight in the Sierras
51: Spoilers of the Plains
Two Lost Worlds
56: Daniel Boone, Trail
Blazer
58: Terror in a Texas Town
60: Thirteen Fighting Men
68: Custer of the West

Susan Kohner (1936-
1955: To Hell and Back
56: The Last Wagon
57: Dino
Trooper Hook
59: Imitation of Life
The Big Fisherman
The Gene Krupa Story
60: All the Fine Young
Cannibals
61: By Love Possessed
62: Freud (or, The Secret
Passion)
69: Devil's Dolls

Clarence Kolb (1874-1964)
1937: The Toast of the Town
Portia on Trial
Wells Fargo
38: Gold Is Where You Find it
Carefree
Merrily We Live
Give Me a Sailor
The Law West of Tomb-
stone

39: Honolulu
Society Lawyer
Five Little Peppers
I Was a Convict
Good Girls Go to Paris
Beware Spooks!
It Could Happen to You
The Amazing Mr. Williams
Our Leading Citizen
40: His Girl Friday
The Man Who Talked too
Much
No Time for Comedy
Tugboat Annie Sails Again
Michael Shayne, Private
Detective
The Five Little Peppers
at Home
41: Caught in the Draft
Nothing but the Truth
The Night of January 16th
Bedtime Story
Hellzapoppin'!
42: True to the Army
43: True to Life
The Falcon in Danger
44: Standing Room Only
Irish Eyes Are Smiling
Something for the Boys
Three Is a Family
45: Road to Alcatraz
What a Blonde!
46: The Kid from Brooklyn
White Tie and Tails
47: Fun on a Weekend
The Lost Honeymoon
The Pilgrim Lady
Shadowed
The Fabulous Joe
Christmas Eve
48: Blondie in the Dough
49: Impact
Adam's Rib
52: The Rose Bowl Story
57: Man of a Thousand Faces

Henry Kolker (1874-1947)
1929: Pleasure Crazed
Coquette
Good Intentions

797

29: Love, Live, and Laugh
The Valiant
30: The Bad One
Way of All Men
DuBarry--Woman of
Passion
East Is West
31: Don't Bet on Women
The Spy
Indiscreet
I Like Your Nerve
32: Washington Masquerade
The Devil and the Deep
First Year
The Crash
Faithless
Jewel Robbery
33: Baby Face
The Keyhole
The Narrow Corner
Bureau of Missing Persons
A Bedtime Story
Golden Harvest
The Power and the Glory
Blood Money
I Loved a Woman
Meet the Baron
Notorious but Nice
Love, Honor, and Oh Baby!
Gigolettes of Paris
34: Massacre
Wonder Bar
Sisters Under the Skin
The Hell Cat
Whom the Gods Destroy
Journal of Crime
Success at Any Price
The Girl from Missouri
Name the Woman
Madame DuBarry
Now and Forever
Blind Date
Imitation of Life
Exciting Adventure
The Band Plays on
A Lost Lady
Love Time
Million Dollar Ransom
Lady by Choice
Sing Sing Nights

35: Times Square Lady
Red Hot Tires
The Case of the Curious
Bride
Shipmates Forever
Charlie Chan in Paris
Diamond Jim
Three Kids and a Queen
Society Doctor
Mad Love
Here Comes the Band
Red Salute
The Mystery Man
Honeymoon Limited
My Marriage
The Ghost Walks
The Florentine Dagger
The Last Days of Pompeii
One New York Night
Frisco Waterfront
Only Eight Hours
The Black Room Mystery
Ladies Love Danger
36: Collegiate
Bullets or Ballots
Romeo and Juliet
Sitting on the Moon
In His Steps
Great Guy
The Man Who Lived Twice
Theodora Goes Wild
37: They Wanted to Marry
Under Cover of Night
Conquest
Thoroughbreds Don't Cry
Green Lights
Once a Doctor
Without Warning
Maid of Salem
Let Them Live!
The Devil Is Driving
38: Adventures of Marco Polo
The Cowboy and the Lady
The Invisible Menace
Holiday
Safety in Numbers
Too Hot to Handle
39: Let Us Live
Hidden Power
Parents on Trial

59: Hercules
60: Hercules Unchained
Michael Strogoff
Four Queens for an Ace
61: Uncle Was a Vampire
Swordsman of Siena
62: Jessica
The Man in the Iron Mask
63: Three Fables of Love
64: Love on the Riviera
Let's Talk about Women
Love--The Italian Way
65: Juliet of the Spirits
The Little Nuns
Love in Four Dimensions
66: Agent 8 3/4
The Railroad Man
That Man in Istanbul
Love and Marriage
Judex
67: Deadlier than the Male
Made in Italy
68: Three Bites of the Apple
A Lovely Way to Die
The Private War of Harry
Frigg
Charge of the Light
Brigade
69: The Protagonists
Battle on the River
Neretva
Fight for Rome (Pt. 1)
The Hornets' Nest
Baraka X-77
He and She

Martin Kosleck (1907-
1938: Napoleon auf St. Helena S
39: Confessions of a Nazi Spy
Nurse Edith Cavell
Nick Carter, Master
Detective
Espionage Agent
40: Calling Philo Vance
Foreign Correspondent
41: A Date with Destiny
The Mad Doctor
International Lady
Underground
The Devil Pays Off

42: All Through the Night
Fly by Night
Nazi Agent
Berlin Correspondent
Manila Calling
43: Chetniks
Bomber's Moon
The North Star
44: The Hitler Gang
Secrets of Scotland Yard
The Mummy's Curse
45: The Frozen Ghost
Gangs of the Waterfront
Pursuit to Algiers
The Spider
46: Crime of the Century
House of Horrors
Just Before Dawn
Strange Holiday
The Wife of Monte Cristo
She-Wolf of London
47: The Beginning or the End?
48: Assigned to Danger
Half Past Midnight
Smuggler's Cove
61: Hitler
The Flesh Eaters
Something Wild
65: Thirty-Six Hours
The Saboteur, Code Name
Morituri
66: The Agent from H.A.R.M.

Yaphet Kotto
1968: Five Card Stud
Nothing but a Man
69: The Thomas Crown Affair
The Liberation of Lord
Byron Jones

Nancy Kovack (1935-
1960: Strangers When We Meet
61: Cry for Happy
62: The Wild Westerners
63: Jason and the Argonauts
Diary of a Madman
65: Sylvia
The Outlaws Is Coming!
66: The Silencers
Tarzan and the Valley of
Gold

66: The Great Sioux Massacre
     Frankie and Johnny
67: Enter Laughing
69: Marooned

Ernie Kovacs (1920-1962)
1957: Operation Mad Ball
 58: Bell, Book, and Candle
 59: It Happened to Jane
 60: Our Man in Havana
     Strangers When We Meet
     North to Alaska
     Pepe
     Wake Me When It's Over
 61: Sail a Crooked Ship
     Five Golden Hours

Mitchell Kowell
1953: Violated
 55: The Big Bluff
 59: John Paul Jones
 63: 55 Days at Peking
 67: Guests Are Coming
 69: Francesco Bertazzoli,
     Investigator

Werner Kraus (1885-1962)
1928: Jealousy   S
     Unwelcome Children   S
     The Man Who Cheated
     Life   S
 29: Looping the Loop   SSE
     Fighting the Slave
     Traffic   PT
     Three Wax Men   S
     The Jolly Peasant   S
     Nana   S
     Royal Scandal   S
     The Treasure   S

Kurt Kreuger (1917-
1943: The Purple V
     The Moon Is Down
     Sahara
     The Strange Death of
     Adolf Hitler
 44: None Shall Escape
     Mademoiselle Fifi
 45: Escape in the Desert
     Hotel Berlin

Paris Underground (or,
     Madame Pimpernel)
     The Spider
46: The Dark Corner
     Sentimental Journey
48: Unfaithfully Yours
50: Spy Hunt
57: The Enemy Below
58: Legion of the Doomed
66: What Did You Do in the
     War, Daddy?
67: The St. Valentine's Day
     Massacre

Berry Kroeger (1912-
1948: The Iron Curtain
     The Dark Past
     Act of Violence
     Cry of the City
 49: Black Magic
     Chicago Deadline
     Fighting Man of the Plains
     Gun Crazy
     Deadly as the Female
     Down to the Sea in Ships
     Guilty of Treason
 51: The Sword of Monte Cristo
 55: Yellowneck
     Blood Alley
 56: Man in the Vault
 60: Seven Thieves
     The Walking Target
 61: Atlantis (or, The Lost
     Continent)
 62: Hitler
     Woman Hunt
 64: Youngblood Hawke
 66: Chamber of Horros
 69: Nightmare in Wax

Alma Kruger (1868-1960)
1936: These Three
     Craig's Wife
     Love Letters of a Star
 37: Breezing Home
     The Mighty Treve
     Man in Blue
     One Hundred Men and a
     Girl
     Vogues of 1938

38: Toy Wife
Marie Antoinette
The Great Waltz
Mother Carey's Chickens
Tarnished Angel
39: Made for Each Other
The Secret of Dr. Kildare
Balalaika
40: His Girl Friday
Dr. Kildare's Strange Case
Dr. Kildare's Goes Home
Dr. Kildare's Crisis
Anne of Windy Poplars
You'll Find Out
41: Blonde Inspiration
The People vs Dr. Kildare
Puddin'head
Dr. Kildare's Wedding Day
Dr. Kildare's Victory
42: Saboteur
Calling Dr. Gillespie
Dr. Gillespie's New
Assistant
That Other Woman
43: Dr. Gillespie's Criminal
Case
44: Three Men in White
Between Two Women
Our Hearts Were Young
and Gay
Babes on Swing Street
45: Crime Doctor's Warning
46: Do You Love Me?
A Scandal in Paris
47: Forever Amber
Dark Delusion
Fun on a Weekend

Hardy Kruger (1928-
1956: As Long As You're Near
Me
57: The One that Got Away
58: Bachelor of Arts
59: Blind Date
60: The Last Summer
Chance Meeting
The Rest Is Silence
61: Taxi for Tobruk
62: Sunday and Cybele
Hatari!

Confess, Dr. Corda!
65: The Flight of the Phoenix
66: The Defector
67: The Uninhibited
To be a Crook
Sauterelle (or, Grass-
hopper)
68: Femmina
69: The Secret of Santa
Vittoria
Le Francis Cain de
Bourges
The Red Tent
Battle on the River Neretva
The Lady of Monza

Otto Kruger (1885-
1933: Mr. Intruder
a short
Turn Back the Clock
Beauty for Sale
The Prizefighter and the
Lady
Ever in My Heart
Gallant Lady
The Women in His Life
34: Treasure Island
Chained
Paris Interlude
Men in White
The Crime Doctor
Springtime for Henry
35: Vanessa--Her Love Story
Two Sinners
36: Living Dangerously
Dracula's Daughter
Lady of Secrets
37: Glamorous Nights
They Won't Forget
Counsel for Crime
The Barrier
38: Housemaster
Thanks for the Memory
I Am the Law
Exposed
39: Disbarred
The Gang's all Here
Zero Hour
A Woman Is the Judge
Another Thin Man

40: The Story of Dr. Ehrlich's
    Magic Bullet
    A Dispatch from Reuter's
    Scandal Sheet
    Seventeen
    The Hidden Menace
    The Man I Married
41: The Big Boss
    The Men in Her Life
    Mercy Island
42: Saboteur
    Friendly Enemies
    Secrets of a Coed
43: Corregidor
    Night Plane for Chungking
    Hitler's Children
    Stage Door Canteen
    Tarzan's Desert Mystery
    America's Children
44: Knickerbocker Holiday
    Cover Girl
    Storm over Lisbon
    Murder My Sweet
    They Live in Fear
45: The Woman Who Came
    Back
    On Stage Everybody!
    Jungle Captive
    The Chicago Kid
    The Wonder Man
    The Great John L.
    Allotment Wives, Inc.
    Escape in the Fog
    Earl Carroll's Vanities
46: The Fabulous Suzanne
    Duel in the Sun
47: Love and Learn
48: Smart Woman
    Lulu Belle
    Dungeon
50: Valentino
    711 Ocean Drive
51: Payment on Demand
52: High Noon
54: Magnificent Obsession
    Black Widow
55: The Last Command
58: The Colossus of New York
59: The Young Philadelphians
    Cash McCall

The Wonderful World of
    the Brothers Grimm
63: Della
64: Sex and the Single Girl

Jack Kruschen (1922-
1949: Red Hot and Blue
50: Woman from Headquarters
51: Cuban Fireball
52: Tropical Heat
    Confidence Girl
53: War of the Worlds
    Abbott & Costello Go to
    Mars
    Ma and Pa Kettle on
    Vacation
    Blueprint for Murder
    Money from Home
54: Untamed Heiress
    Tennessee Champ
55: Dial Red O
    Carolina Cannonball
    Soldier of Fortune
    The Night Holds Terror
56: Outside the Law
    Julie
57: Badlands of Montana
    Reform School Girl
58: Cry Terror
    Fraulein
    The Decks Ran Red
    The Buccaneer
60: The Last Voyage
    The Apartment
    Studs Lonigan
    The Angry Red Planet
    Seven Ways from Sundown
61: The Ladies' Man
    Lover Come Back
    Where the Boys Are
62: Cape Fear
    Convicts Four
63: McLintock!
64: The Unsinkable Molly Brown
65: Dear Brigitte
    Harlow (Magna.)
67: The Happening
    Caprice

Henry Kulky (1912-1965)
1947: A Likely Story
  49: Tarzan's Magic Fountain
       Bandits of El Dorado
  50: Wabash Avenue
       South Sea Sinner
       Bodyhold
  51: The Guy Who Came Back
       The Love Nest
       The Kid from Amarillo
       Fixed Bayonets
  52: The World in His Arms
       Gobs and Gals
       No Holds Barred
       Target Hong Kong
  53: The Five Thousand
       Fingers of Dr. T
       The Charge at Feather
       River
       Down Among the Shelter-
       ing Palms
       The Glory Brigade
  54: Yukon Vengeance
       Hell and High Water
       Fireman, Save My Child!
       Tobor the Great
       The Steel Cage
  55: Prince of Players
       New York Confidential
       Abbott & Costello Meet
       the Keystone Kops
       Illegal
  57: Sierra Stranger
  59: Up Periscope!
       The Gunfight at Dodge City
  60: Guns of the Timberland

Nancy Kulp
1952: Steel Town
  53: Shane
  54: You're Never too Young
       Count Three and Pray
  56: Forever Darling
  57: God Is My Partner
       Three Faces of Eve
  59: Five Gates to Hell
  61: The Parent Trap
       The Two Little Bears
  63: Who's Minding the Store?
  64: The Patsy

Strange Bedfellows
  66: The Night of the Grizzly

Kay Kuter
1955: Guys and Dolls
  56: Steel Jungle
  57: Under Fire
  60: The Big Night
  68: A Time for Killing

Nancy Kwan (1938-
1960: The World of Suzie Wong
  61: The Flower Drum Song
  63: The Main Attraction
  64: Honeymoon Hotel
       Fate Is the Hunter
       Tamahine
  65: The Wild Affair
  66: Arrivederci, Baby!
       Lt. Robin Crusoe, U.S.N.
  67: The Corrupt Ones
  68: The House of Seven Joys
       Hawaii 5-0 (TV pilot)
       The Wrecking Crew
       The Girl Who Knew Too Much
       Nobody's Perfect
  69: The McMasters
       The Girl from Peking

Kay Kyser (1905-
1939: That's Right, You're Wrong
  40: You'll Find Out
  41: Playmates
  42: My Favorite Spy
  43: Thousands Cheer
       Swing Fever
       Around the World
       Right about Face
  44: Carolina Blues
       To Be or Not to Be

L

Frank Lackteen (1894-
1928: Prowlers of the Sea   S
       Court Martial   S
  29: Hawk of the Hills   S
  31: Hell's Valley   S
       Law of the Tong
  32: Land of Wanted Men

32: Texas Pioneer
33: Nagana
Rustlers' Roundup
Tarzan the Fearless (ser.)
Perils of Pauline (ser.)
35: Escape from Devil's Land
36: Under Two Flags
Mummy's Boys
Isle of Fury
37: I Cover the War
Mysterious Pilot (ser.)
39: The Kansas Terrors
Juarez
40: Stagecoach War
Girl from Havana
Moon over Burma
41: The Sea Wolf
South of Tahiti
42: Bombs over Burma
43: Chetniks
Frontier Badmen
44: Moonlight and Cactus
45: Frontier Gal
47: Oregon Trail Scouts
Singin' in the Corn
48: Man-Eater of Kumoan
49: Daughter of the Jungle
Son of the Badman
The Mysterious Desperado
51: Flaming Feather
53: Northern Patrol
55: Devil Goddess
60: Three Came to Kill

Alan Ladd (1913-1964)
1937: Souls at Sea
38: Goldwyn Follies
Born to the West
Freshman Year
39: Rulers of the Sea
Beasts of Berlin
40: The Light of Western
Stars
In Old Missouri
Meet the Missus
Captain Caution
Her First Romance
Those Were the Days
41: Reluctant Dragon
Petticoat Politics

The Black Cat
Paper Bullets
Gangs, Inc.
42: This Gun for Hire
Joan of Paris
The Glass Key
Lucky Jordan
Star-Spangled Rhythm
43: China
Hollywood in Uniform
(short)
44: Skirmish on the Home
Front (short)
And now Tomorrow
45: Salty O'Rourke
Duffy's Tavern
Hollywood Victory Caravan
46: Two Years before the Mast
Blue Dahlia
O.S.S.
47: Wild Harvest
Calcutta
Variety Girl
The Long Grey Line
48: Beyond Glory
Saigon
Whispering Smith
49: The Great Gatsby
Chicago Deadline
Eyes of Hollywood (short)
50: Branded
Captain Carey, U.S.A.
51: Appointment with Danger
Red Mountain
52: Adventure
The Iron Mistress
53: Desert Legion
Shane
Thunder in the East
Botany Bay
54: Paratrooper
Hell below Zero
Saskatchewan
Black Knight
Drum Beat
55: The McConnell Story
Hell on Frisco Bay
56: Santiago
57: The Big Land (or,
Stampede)

57: Boy on a Dolphin
58: The Deep Six
   The Proud Rebel
   The Badlanders
59: Man in the Net
60: Guns of the Timberland
   All the Young Men
   One Foot in Hell
61: Duel of Champions
   Orazio
62: 13 West Street
64: The Carpetbaggers

Alana Ladd (1943-
1960: Guns of the Timberland
62: Young Guns of Texas

David Ladd (1947
1957: The Big Land
58: The Proud Rebel
59: The Sad Horse
60: A Dog of Flanders
   Raymie
61: Misty

Bert Lahr (1895-1967)
1931: a short
   Faint Heart
   Flying High
33: Mr. Broadway
34: Hizzoner (a short)
36: a short
37: Merry-Go-Round of 1938
   Love and Hisses
38: Josette
   Just Around the Corner
39: Zaza
   The Wizard of Oz
40: DuBarry Was a Lady
42: Sing Your Worries Away
   Ship Ahoy
44: Meet the People
49: Always Leave Them
   Laughing
51: Mr. Universe
54: Rose Marie
55: The Second Greatest Sex
62: Ten Girls Ago
64: Big Parade of Comedy
   (doc.)

   The Sound of Laughter
   (doc.)
65: The Fantasticks
69: The Night They Raided
   Minskey's

Ethan Laidlow (1900-1963)
1929: Outlawed   S
   The Big Diamond
   Mystery   S
   The Little Savage   S
   Laughing at Death   S
   Bride of the Desert
30: Pardon My Gun
31: Dugan of the Bad Lands
33: Speed Demon
35: Powdersmoke Range
36: Yellow Dust
   Two in Revolt
   Silly Billies
   Special Investigator
   The Sea Spoilers
38: I'm from the City
   Rhythm of the Saddle
39: Home on the Prairie
   Night Riders
   Three Texas Steers
   Western Caravans
   Cowboys from Texas
40: The Marines Fly High
   Son of Roaring Dan
   Stage to Chino
   The Tulsa Kid
   Law and Order
   Wagon Train
41: Law of the Range
   The Lone Star Vigilantes
42: Stagecoach Express
43: Riding Through Nevada
   The Desperadoes
   Border Buckaroos
   Fugitive from Sonora
44: Marshal of Gunsmoke
   Oklahoma Raiders
45: Blazing the Western Trail
   Lawless Empire
47: Rustlers' Roundup
   Singin' in the Corn
48: Buckaroo from Powder
   River

```
48:  Six-Gun Law                    38:  Everybody's Doing it
50:  Traveling Saleswoman                Double Danger
     The Great Missouri Raid             Blondie
51:  Flaming Feather                     There Goes My Heart
52:  Montana Territory              39:  Blondie Meets the Boss
53:  Powder River                        Blondie Takes a Vacation
                                         Blondie Brings Up Baby
Frankie Laine (1913-              40:  Blondie on a Budget
1950:  When You're Smiling                Blondie Has Servant
51:  On the Sunny Side of the              Trouble
     Street                              Blondie Plays Cupid
52:  Rainbow 'Round My             41:  Blondie Goes Latin
     Shoulder                            Blondie in Society
55:  Bring Your Smile Along        42:  Blondie Goes to College
56:  Meet Me in Las Vegas                Blondie's Blessed Event
     He Laughed Last                     Blondie for Victory
                                         The Wedding Guest Sat on
Alice Lake (1896-1967)                   a Stone
1929:  Twin Beds                    43:  Footlight Glamour
     Untamed Justice          S    44:  Sailor's Holiday
     Circumstantial Evidence  S         Three Is a Family
     Frozen Justice                      The Ghost that Walks
30:  Young Desire                         Alone
31:  Wicked                        45:  The Big Show-Off
33:  Skyway                              Life with Blondie
34:  Wharf Angel                         Leave it to Blondie
     Glamour                       46:  Blondie's Lucky Day
                                         Blondie Knows Best
Arthur Lake (1905-               47:  Blondie's Holiday
1927:  Cradle Snatchers         S         Blondie's Big Moment
28:  Harold Teen             SSE         Blondie's Anniversary
     Lilac Time              PT    48:  Blondie in the Dough
     Air Circus              S          Blondie's Reward
29:  On with the Show                    Sixteen Fathoms Deep
     Dance Hall                    49:  Blondie's Big Deal
     Tanned Legs                         Blondie Hits the Jackpot
30:  Cheer up and Smile                  Blondie's Secret
     She's My Weakness          50:  Beware of Blondie
31:  Indiscreet                          Blondie's Hero
33:  Midshipman Jack
34:  Girl o' My Dreams             Veronica Lake (1919-
     Silver Streak              1941:  I Wanted Wings
35:  Orchids for You                     Sullivan's Travels
     Women Must Dress          42:  This Gun for Hire
36:  a short                             The Glass Key
     I Cover Chinatown                   I Married a Witch
37:  23 1/2 Hours Leave                  Girls' Town
     Annapolis Salute                    Star-Spangled Rhythm
     Topper                        43:  So Proudly We Hail!
     Exiled to Shanghai            44:  Hour before Dawn
```

45: Bring on the Girls
Hold that Blonde
Duffy's Tavern
Out of this World
Leave it to Blondie
46: Miss Susie Slagle's
The Blue Dahlia
47: Ramrod
Variety Girl
48: Saigon
The Sainted Sisters
Isn't it Romantic?
49: Slattery's Hurricane
52: Stronghold
66: Footsteps in the Snow

Hedy Lamarr (1915-
1929: Ein Sturm im Wasserglas
(Storm in a Water Glass)
32: Man Braucht Kein Geld
(One Doesn't Need Money)
34: Die Koffer des Herr O.F.
(Trunks of Mr.O.F. Herne)
37: Ecstasy
38: Algiers
39: I Take this Woman
Lady of the Tropics
40: Boomtown
Comrade X
41: Come Live with Me
Ziegfeld Girl
H.M. Pulham, Esq.
42: Tortilla Flat
Cross Roads
White Cargo
43: The Heavenly Body
44: The Conspirators
Experiment Perilous
45: Her Highness and the
Bellboy
46: Strange Woman
House of Dracula
47: Dishonored Woman
48: Let's Live a Little
49: Samson and Delilah
50: Copper Canyon
A Lady Without a Pass-
port
51: My Favorite Spy

The Face that Launched
a Thousand Ships (Ital.
never rel. in U.S.A.)
Femina (never rel.)
57: The Story of Mankind
58: The Female Animal

Fernando Lamas (1915-
1945: Lady Windemere's Fan
48: Historia de una Mala
Mujer
50: The Avengers
Rich, Young, and Pretty
51: Law and the Lady
52: The Merry Widow
53: The Girl Who Had Everything
Dangerous When Wet
Diamond Queen
Sangaree
54: Jiavro
Rose Marie
55: Girl Rush
60: The Lost World
61: Magic Fountain
62: Duel of Fire
63: The Revenge of the
Musketeers
67: The Violent Ones
Kill a Dragon
68: A Hundred Rifles
Valley of Mystery
69: The Savarona Syndrome
Backtrack

Gil Lamb (1906-
1942: The Fleet's In
Star-Spangled Rhythm
43: Riding High
44: Rainbow Island
45: Practically Yours
47: Hit Parade of 1947
49: Make Mine Laughs
50: Joe Palooka in Humphrey
Takes a Chance
56: The Boss
58: Terror in a Texas Town
67: The Gnome-Mobile
68: Blackbeard's Ghost

69: The Love Bug
    Norwood

Jack Lambert
1943: The Cross of Lorraine
  46: Abilene Town
      The Harvey Girls
      The Plainsman and the
        Lady
  47: The Vigilantes Return
  48: River Lady
      Belle Starr's Daughter
  49: Big Jack
      Brimstone
      Montana Belle
  50: Dakota Lil
      Stars in My Crown
      West of the Great Divide
      North of the Great Divide
  51: The Enforcer
      Secret of the Convict Lake
  52: Bend of the River
      Blackbeard the Pirate
  53: Scared Stiff
      99 River Street
  54: Vera Cruz
  55: Three Cases of Murder
      Run for Cover
      Kiss Me Deadly
      The Warriors
      Cross Channel
      At Gunpoint
  56: Canyon River
      Track the Man Down
  57: The Little Hut
      Chicago Confidential
  58: Hot Car Girl
  59: Day of the Outlaw
      Alias Jesse James
  60: Freckles
  61: Francis of Assisi
      Grey Friar's Bobby
      The George Raft Story
  62: How the West Was Won
  63: Four f or Texas
  66: Dracula--Prince of Dark-
        ness

Dorothy Lamour (1914-
1936: Jungle Princess

37: Swing High, Swing Low
    College Holiday
    The Last Train from
      Madrid
    High, Wide, and Handsome
    Thrill of a Lifetime
    The Hurricane
38: Big Broadcast of 1938
    The Jungle Love
    Tropic Holiday
    Spawn of the North
39: St. Louis Blues
    Man about Town
    Disputed Passage
40: Johnny Apollo
    Typhoon
    The Road to Singapore
    Moon over Burma
    Chad Hanna
41: The Road to Zanzibar
    Caught in the Draft
    Aloma of the South Seas
42: The Fleet's In!
    Beyond the Blue Horizon
    The Road to Morocco
    Star-Spangled Rhythm
43: They Got Me Covered
    Riding High
    Dixie
44: And the Angels Sing
    Rainbow Island
    Practically Yours
45: A Medal for Benny
    Duffy's Tavern
    Masquerade in Mexico
46: The Road to Utopia
47: My Favorite Brunette
    The Road to Rio
    Wild Harvest
    Variety Girl
48: A Miracle can Happen (or,
      On Our Merry Way)
    Lulu Belle
    Girl from Manhattan
49: Lucky Stiff
    Slightly French
    Manhandled
52: The Greatest Show on Earth
    The Road to Bali
62: The Road to Hong Kong

63: Donovan's Reef
64: Pajama Party
69: The Phynx

Zohra Lampert (1936-
1959: Odds Against Tomorrow
60: Pay or Die
61: Posse from Hell
Splendor in the Grass
Hey, Let's Twist!
66: A Fine Madness
68: Bye Bye, Braverman

Burt Lancaster (1913-
1946: The Killers
47: Desert Fury
I Walk Alone
Brute Force
Variety Girl
48: Sorry, Wrong Number
All My Sons
49: Criss Cross
Rope of Sand
50: Mr. 880
Flame and the Arrow
51: Vengeance Valley
Ten Tall Men
Jim Thorpe--All American
52: The Crimson Pirate
Come Back, Little Sheba
53: South Sea Woman
From Here to Eternity
His Majesty's O'Keefe
54: Apache
Vera Cruz
55: The Kentuckian (act.,dir.)
The Rose Tattoo
56: Trapeze
The Rainmaker
57: Gunfight at the O.K. Corral
Sweet Smell of Success
58: Separate Tables
Run Silent, Run Deep
59: The Devil's Disciple
60: Elmer Gantry (OSCAR)
The Unforgiven
61: The Young Savages
Judgment at Nuremberg
62: Bird Man of Alcatraz
63: The Leopard

A Child Is Waiting
The List of Adrian
Messenger (cameo)
64: Seven Days in May
65: The Train
The Hallelujah Trail
66: The Professionals
67: The Swimmer
68: The Scalphunters
Castle Keep
69: The Gypsy Moths
Airport
Valdez Is Coming

Elsa Lanchester (1902-
1929: The Constant Nymph
31: Potiphar's Wife
32: Blue Bottles
33: The Private Life of Henry
VIII
34: The Private Life of Don
Juan
35: David Copperfield
Naughty Marietta
Bride of Frankenstein
36: The Ghost Goes West
Rembrandt
37: Vessel of Wrath
38: The Beachcomber
41: Ladies in Retirement
42: Son of Fury
Tales of Manhattan
43: Forever and a Day
Thumbs Up
Lassie Come Home
44: Passport to Destiny
Follow the Boys
45: Son of Lassie
46: The Spiral Staircase
The Razor's Edge
47: Northwest Outpost
48: The Bishop's Wife
The Big Clock
49: Come to the Stable
The Secret Garden
Inspector General
50: The Petty Girl
The Buccaneer's Girl
Mystery Street
Frenchie

52: Androcles and the Lion
Dreamboat
Les Miserables
53: The Girls of Pleasure
Island
54: Hell's Half Acre
Three-Ring Circus
55: The Glass Slipper
57: Witness for the Prosecution
58: Bell, Book, and Candle
64: Mary Poppins
Honeymoon Hotel
Pajama Party
65: That Darn Cat
67: Easy Come, Easy Go
68: Blackbeard's Ghost
Me, Natalie
69: Rascal

Martin Landau (c1925-
1959: Pork Chop Hill
The Gazebo
North by Northwest
62: Stagecoach to Dancers'
Rock
63: Cleopatra
65: The Greatest Story Ever
Told
The Hallelujah Trail
66: Nevada Smith

Elissa Landi (1905-1948)
1928: Bolivar   S
29: Underground   S
The Betrayal   S
31: London
Knowing Men
The Price of Things
The Inseparables
Sin
The Parisian
Body and Soul
Always Goodbye
Wicked
Yellow Ticket
Children of Chance
Burnt Offering
32: The Devil's Lottery
The Woman in Room 13

A Passport to Hell
Sign of the Cross
33: The Masquerader
I Loved You Wednesday
34: By Candlelight
Man of Two Worlds
The Count of Monte Cristo
Sisters under the Skin
The Great Flirtation
35: Enter Madame
Without Regret
36: Amateur Gentleman
Mad Holiday
After the Thin Man
37: The 13th Chair
43: Corregidor

Carole Landis (1919-1948)
1937: Varsity Show
A Day at the Races
The Emperor's Candlesticks
Hollywood Hotel
Broadway Melody of 1938
38: Blondes at Work
Adventurous Blonde
Gold Diggers in Paris
Four's a Crowd
Men Are Such Fools
The Noose (or, The Silk
Noose)
39: Daredevils of Red Circle
(ser.)
Three Texas Steers
Cowboys from Texas
40: One Million B. C.
Turnabout
Mystery Sea Raider
41: Road Show
Topper Returns
Moon over Miami
Dance Hall
I Wake Up Screaming (or,
Hot Spot)
Cadet Girl
42: A Gentleman at Heart
My Gal Sal
It Happened in Flatbush
Orchestra Wives
Manila Calling
The Powers Girl

811

43: Wintertime
44: Secret Command
    Four Jills in a Jeep
45: Having a Wonderful Crime
46: Behind Green Lights
    It Shouldn't Happen to a
    Dog
    Scandal in Paris
47: Out of the Blue
48: The Brass Monkey
    The Noose

Jessie Royce Landis (1904-
1930: Derelict
49: Mr. Belvedere Goes to
    College
    It Happens Every Spring
    My Foolish Heart
50: Mother Didn't Tell Me
53: Tonight at Eight-Thirty
54: She Couldn't Say No
55: To Catch a Thief
56: The Swan
    The Girl He Left Behind
57: My Man Godfrey
58: A Private Affair
    I Married a Woman
59: North by Northwest
61: Goodbye Again
62: Bon Voyage!
    Boys' Night Out
63: Critic's Choice
    Gidget Goes to Rome
69: Airport

Michael Landon (1935-
1957: I Was a Teenage Werewolf
58: God's Little Acre
    Maracaibo
59: Legend of Tom Dooley
62: The Errand Boy (cameo)

Abbe Lane (1932-
1953: Wings of the Hawk
54: Ride Clear of Diablo
55: TheAmericano
    Chicago Syndicate
58: Maracaibo

Allan "Rocky" Lane (c1901-
1929: Not Quite Decent   PT
    Forward Pass
30: Love in the Rough
    Madam Satan
31: Honor of the Family
32: The Tenderfoot
    Night Nurse
    Winner Take All
    Miss Pinkerton
36: Stowaway
37: Fifty Roads to Town
    Big Business
    Laughing at Trouble
    The Duke Comes Back
    Charlie Chan at the
    Olympics
    Sing and be Happy
38: Night Spot
    Maid's Night out
    This Marriage Business
    Having a Wonderful Time
    Crime Ring
    Fugitives for a Night
    Law West of Tombstone
39: Pacific Liner
    Twelve Crowded Hours
    They Made Her a Spy
    Panama Lady
    The Spellbinder
    Conspiracy
40: Grand Ole Opry
    King of the Royal Mounted
    (ser.)
41: All American Coed
42: Yukon Patrol
43: Daredevils of the West (ser.)
    The Dancing Masters
44: Tiger Woman (ser.)
    Night Riders of Montana
    Rustlers on Horseback
    Call of the South Seas
    Stagecoach to Monterey
    Sheriff of Sundown
    The Silver City Kid
45: Bells of Rosarita
    Corpus Christi Bandits
    Trail of Kit Carson

45:	The Topeka Terror	58:	The Saga of Hemp Brown
46:	Gay Blades	60:	Hell Bent for Leather
	A Guy Could Change	61:	Posse from Hell
	Night Train to Memphis		

Homesteaders of Paradise
  Valley
Out California Way
Santa Fe Uprising
Stangecoach to Denver

47: Vigilantes of Boomtown
Oregon Trail Scouts
Marshal of Cripple Creek
Rustlers of Devil's Canyon
The Wild Frontier
Bandits of Dark Canyon

48: Bold Frontiersman
Oklahoma Badlands
Carson City Raiders
Desperadoes of Dodge City
Marshal of Amarillo
The Denver Kid
Sundown at Santa Fe
Renegades of Sonora

49: Sheriff of Wichita
Death Valley Gunfighter
Frontier Investigator
Wyoming Bandit
Bandit King of Texas
Navajo Trail Raiders
Powder River Rustlers

50: Code of the Silver Sage
Gunmen of Abilene
Covered Wagon Raiders
The Vigilante Hideout
Frisco Tornado
Rustlers on Horseback

51: Wells Fargo Gunmaster
Night Riders of Montana
Fort Dodge Stampede
Rough Riders of Durango
Desert of Lost Men

52: Leadville Gunslinger
Black Hills Ambush
Thundering Caravans
Desperadoes Outpost
Captive of Billy the Kid

53: Marshal of Cedar Creek
Bandits of the West
Savage Frontier
El Paso Stampede

Charles Lane_ (1899-

1928: Sadie Thompson   S
29: Saturday's Children   PT
The Canary Murder Case
35: Here Comes the Band
Two for Tonight
36: The Milky Way
Mr. Deeds Goes to Town
Neighborhood House
The Crime of Dr. Forbes
Thirty-Six Hours to Kill
Ticket to Paradise
37: We're on the Jury
Interns Can't Take Money
River of Missing Men
Trapped by G-Men
Danger, Love at Work!
Ali Baba Goes to Town
City Girl
38: In Old Chicago
Always in Trouble
Inside Story
Thanks for Everything
Kentucky
Cocoanut Grove
Professor Beware!
You Can't Take it with You
39: Boy Slaves
The Flying Irishman
Rose of Washington Square
Second Fiddle
Lucky Night
News Is Made at Night
They all Come out
Mr. Smith Goes to
  Washington
Cat and the Canary
40: Blondie Plays Cupid
Buck Benny Rides Again
Johnny Apollo
The Crooked Road
On Their Own
We Who Are Young
Queen of the Mob
The Great Profile
Rhythm on the River

40: The Leather Pushers
    Ellery Queen, Master
      Detective
41: Repent at Leisure
    Ellery Queen and the
      Perfect Crime
    Hot Spot
    Never Give a Sucker an
      Even Break
42: The Lady Is Willing
    A Gentleman at Heart
    Tarzan's New York
      Adventure
    Dudes Are Pretty People
    Home in Wyoming
    Through Different Eyes
    Friendly Enemies
44: Arsenic and Old Lace
46: A Close Call for Boston
      Blackie
    The Invisible Informer
    Just Before Dawn
    The Mysterious Intruder
    Swell Guy
47: The Farmer's Daughter
    Louisiana
    Intrigue
    Roses Are Red
48: State of the Union
    Call Northside 777
    Gentleman from Nowhere
    Apartment for Peggy
    Out of the Storm
49: You're My Everything
    Mother Is a Freshman
    Miss Grant Takes Rich-
      mond
50: Riding High
    Borderline
    For Heaven's Sake
53: Remains to be Seen
    The Juggler
    The Affairs of Dobie
      Gillis
56: The Birds and the Bees
57: Top Secret Affair
    God Is My Partner ·
58: Teacher's Pet
59: The Mating Game
    The Thirty Foot Bride
      of Candy Rock

62: The Music Man
63: Papa's Delicate Condition
    It's a Mad Mad Mad Mad
      World
64: Good Neighbor Sam
    The Carpetbaggers
    John Goldfarb, Please
      Come Home
65: Billie
    Looking for Love
    The New Interns
66: The Ugly Dachshund
    The Ghost and Mr. Chicken
67: The Gnome-Mobile
69: The Artocrats (cartoon
      voice)
    What's so Bad about
      Feeling Good?

Jocelyn Lane
1965: The Sword of Ali Baba
    Tickle Me
66: Incident at Phantom Hill
    The Poppy Is Also a
      Flower (TV)
69: Hell's Belles

Lola Lane (1909-
1929: Speakeasy
    Fox Movietone Follies of
      1929
    Girl from Havana
    The Case of Lena Smith S
30: Let's Go Places
    The Costello Murder Case
    Big Fight
    Good News
31: Hell Bound
    Ex-Bad Boy
32: After Tomorrow
34: Public Stenographer
    Burn 'em Up Barnes (ser.)
    Woman Condemned
    Women Who Dared
    Ticket to a Crime
35: Murder on a Honeymoon
    Alias Mary Dow
    His Night Out
    Death from a Distance
    Port of Lost Dreams
36: In Paris A.W.O.L.

37: Marked Woman
    Hollywood Hotel
    The Sheik Steps Out
38: When Were You Born?
    Torchy Blane in Panama
    Mr. Chump
    Four Daughters
39: Daughters Courageous
    Four Wives
40: Convicted Woman
    Girls of the Road
    Zanzibar
    Gangs of Chicago
41: Four Mothers
    Mystery Ship
42: Miss V from Moscow
43: Lost Canyon
    Buckskin Frontier
45: Identity Unknown
    Why Girls Leave Home
    Steppin' in Society
46: They Made Me a Killer
    Deadline at Dawn

Lupino Lane (1892-1957)
1928: The Love Parade
    Show of Shows
30: Bride of the Regiment`
    Golden Dawn
    Yellow Mask
39: Me and My Gal

Nora Lane
1928: The Cohens and the
    Kellys in Paris
    Sunset Pass   S
    Lawless Legion   S
    Masked Emotions   SSE
    One Hysterical Night
    Sally
29: Marquis Preferred
30: The Man Hunter
    Lucky Larkin
    Rain or Shine
    Night Work
31: Young Sinners
    The Cisco Kid
32: Dance Team
    After Tomorrow
    Disorderly Conduct

    Careless Lady
    The Trial of Vivienne Ware
    This Sporting Age
33: The Western Code
34: Jimmy the Gent
35: Western Justice
    Outlaw Deputy
37: Borderland
38: Hopalong Cassidy Rides
    Again
    Cassidy of Bar-20
39: The Gentleman from
    Arizona
40: City of Chance
41: Puddin'head
    Small Town Deb
42: Undercover Man

Priscilla Lane (1917-
1937: Varsity Show
38: Love, Honor, and Behave
    Men Are Such Fools
    The Cowboy from Brooklyn
    Four Daughters
    Brother Rat
39: Yes, My Darling Daughter
    Dust be My Destiny
    The Roaring Twenties
    Four Wives
    Daughters Courageous
40: Brother Rat and a Baby
    Three Cheers for the Irish
    Ladies Must Live
41: Four Mothers
    Million Dollar Baby
    Blues in the Night
42: The Saboteur
    Silver Queen
43: The Meanest Man in the
    World
44: Arsenic and Old Lace
47: Fun on a Weekend
48: Bodyguard

Richard Lane (1900-
1937: Outcasts of Poker Flat
    You Can't Buy Luck
    There Goes My Girl
    New Faces of 1937
    Super Sleuth

37: Life of the Party
Flight from Glory
Saturday's Heroes
Danger Patrol
Wise Girl
38: a short
Everybody's Doing it
Radio City Revels
This Marriage Business
Go Chase Yourself
Blind Alibi
I'm from the City
Mr. Doddle Kicks Off
Charlie Chan in Honolulu
Exposed
Last Warning
His Exciting Night
Crashing Hollywood
39: Union Pacific
For Love or Money
Unexpected Father
Mutiny on the Blackhawk
It Could Happen to You
News Is Made at Night
The Escape
Stronger than Desire
Mr. Moto in Danger Island
Hero for a Day
Main Street Lawyer
The Day the Bookies Wept
40: City of Chance
Sued for Libel
The Biscuit Eater
Free, Blonde, and Twenty
    One
Youth Will be Served
Yesterday's Heroes
Two Girls on Broadway
Boom Town
Sandy Is a Lady
Hired Wife
Brother Orchid
41: Ride, Kelly, Ride
Margie
Meet the Chump
A Girl, a Guy, and a Gob
Meet Boston Blackie
The Penalty
I Wanted Wings
The Cowboy and the Blonde

For Beauty's Sake
San Antonio Rose
The Bride Wore Crutches
Sunny
Time Out for Rhythm
Navy Blues
Tight Shoes
Riders of the Purple Sage
Man at Large
Confessions of Boston
    Blackie
42: To the Shores of Tripoli
Butch Minds the Baby
Doctor Broadway
A-Haunting We Will Go
Drums of the Congo
Time to Kill
43: It Ain't Hay
Corvette K-225
Air Force
Swing Your Partner
Crazy House
Gung Ho!
Fired Wife
Thank Your Lucky Stars
44: Bermuda Mystery
Bowery to Broadway
Brazil
Louisiana Hayride
Mr. Winkle Goes to War
One Mysterious Night
Slightly Terrific
Take it Big
A Wave, a Wac, and a
    Marine
45: What a Blonde
Two O'Clock Courage
Here Come the Coeds
Boston Blackie Rendezvous
Wonder Man
The Bull Fighter
Boston Blackie Booked on
    Suspicion
46: Blackie and the Law
The Phantom Thief
A Close Call for Boston
    Blackie
Girl on the Spot
Gentleman Joe Palooka
Sioux City Sue

816

47: Song of Scheherezade
Out of the Blue
Hit Parade of 1947
Devil Ship
48: Return of the Whistler
Tenth Avenue Angel
The Babe Ruth Story
Trapped by Boston Blackie
The Creeper
49: Take Me Out to the Ball
Game
The Big Wheel
Boston Blackie's Chinese
Venture
Miss Mink of 1949
There's a Girl in My
Heart
50: Quicksand
The Admiral Was a Lady
I Shot Billy the Kid
51: I Can Get it for You
Wholesale
The Jackie Robinson Story

Rosemary Lane (1916-
1937: Hollywood Hotel
Varsity Show
38: Four Daughters
Gold Diggers in Paris
39: The Oklahoma Kid
Blackwell's Island
The Return of Dr. X
Four Wives
Daughters Courageous
40: An Angel from Texas
The Boys from Syracuse
Always a Bride
41: Four Mothers
Time Out for Rhythm
43: Chatterbox
All by Myself
Harvest Melody
44: Trocadero
45: Sing Me a Song of Texas

Charles Lang
1940: One Crowded Night
Wildcat Bus
41: The Invisible Woman
Ellery Queen's Penthouse
Mystery

Dancing on a Dime
Where Did You Get that
Girl?
Six Lessons from Madame
La Zonga
Hit the Road
Keep 'em Flying
42: Bombay Clipper
Secret Enemies
43: Strictly in the Groove
Truck Busters
Guadalcanal Diary
The Ghost Ship
44: Tampico
Roger Touhy--Gangster
Wing and a Prayer
Crime by Night
The Last Ride

June Lang (1915-
1934: Young Sinners
Chandu the Magician
I Loved You Wednesday
The Man Who Dared
Music in the Air
35: Bonnie Scotland
36: Every Saturday Night
Captain January
The Country Doctor
The Road to Glory
White Hunter
37: Nancy Steel Is Missing
Wee Willie Winkie
Ali Baba Goes to Town
38: International Settlement
One Wild Night
Meet the Girls
39: Zenobia
Forged Passport
Captain Fury
For Love or Money
Inside Information
40: Isle of Destiny
Convicted Woman
41: Red Head
The Deadly Game
42: Too Many Women
Footlight Serenade
City of Silent Men
43: Flesh and Fantasy
44: Three of a Kind

817

48: Lighthouse

<u>Glenn Langan</u> (1917-
1939: The Return of Dr. X
A Kiss for Cinderella
43: Riding High
44: Four Jills in a Jeep
Something for the Boys
A Wing and a Prayer
In the Meantime Darling
45: A Bell for Adano
Hangover Square
46: Margie
Sentimental Journey
Dragonwyck
47: Homestretch
Forever Amber
48: Fury at Furnace Creek
The Snake Pit
49: Treasure of Monte Cristo
50: Rapture
Iroquois Trail
52: Hangman's Knot
53: One Girl's Confession
99 River Street
54: The Big Chase
Outlaw Treasure
57: The Amazing Colossal
Man
Junggle Heat
65: Mutiny in Outer Space

<u>Harry Langdon</u> (1884-1946)
1929: Sky Boy
Hotter than Hot
30: The Fighting Parson
The Big Kick
The Head Guy
The Shrimp
The King
See America Thirst
31: Soldier's Plaything
32: The Big Flash
33: Hallelujah, I'm a Bum
My Weakness
Tired Feet
The Hitch-Hiker
Tied for Life
Hooks and Jabs
Marriage Humor
The Stage Hand

Leave it to Dad
On Ice
Pop's Pal
A Roaming Romeo
34: Trimmed in Furs
Goodness! a Ghost
Circus Hoodoo
No Sleep on the Deep
Petting Preferred
Counsel on Defence
Shivers
35: His Bridal Sweet
Atlantic Adventure
The Leather Necker
His Marriage Mixup
I Don't Remember
37: Wise Guys (dir.)
38: A Doggone Mixup
Sue My Lawyer
He Loved an Actress (or,
Mad About Money)
Block Heads
There Goes My Heart (or,
Guest Appearance)
39: Zenobia
Elephants Never Forget
40: A Chump at Oxford
Saps at Sea
Misbehaving Husbands
Cold Turkey
41: Road Show
All-American Coed
Double Trouble
42: House of Errors
What Makes Lizzy Dizzy?
Tire Man, Spare My Tires
Carry Harry
Piano Mooner
43: Spotlight Scandals
A Blitz on the Fritz
Here Comes Mr. Zerk
44: Hot Rhythm
To Heir Is Human
Defective Detectives
Block Busters
Money Dope
45: Swingin' on a Rainbow
Snooper Service
Pistol Packin' Nitwits
64: The Sound of Laughter
(doc.)

Sue Ann Langdon
1964: Roustabout
65: The Rounders
When the Boys Meet the Girls
66: Hold on!
Frankie and Johnny
A Fine Madness
67: A Guide for the Married Man
A Man Called Dagger

Hope Lange (1933-
1956: Bus Stop
57: The True Story of Jesse James
Peyton Place
58: The Young Lions
In Love and War
59: The Best of Everything
61: A Pocketful of Miracles
Wild in the Country
62: How the West Was Won
63: Love Is a Ball
68: Jigsaw

Frances Langford (1913-
1935: Every Night at Eight
Broadway Melody of 1936
36: Collegiate
Palm Springs
Born to Dance
37: The Hit Parade
Hollywood Hotel
40: Dreaming Out Loud
Too Many Girls
The Hit Parade of 1940
Romance and Rhythm
41: All-American Coed
Swing it, Soldier
42: The Mississippi Gambler
Yankee Doodle Dandy
43: This Is the Army
Career Girl
Follow the Band
Cowboy in Manhattan
Never a Dull Moment
44: The Girl Rush
Dixie Jamboree
45: Radio Stars on Parade

46: People Are Funny
The Bamboo Blonde
47: Beat the Band
48: Melody Time
49: Deputy Marshal
Make Mine Laughs
51: The Purple Heart Diary
54: The Glenn Miller Story

Paul Langton (1913-
1943: Destination Tokyo
44: Thirty Seconds over Tokyo
The Thin Man
Gentle Annie
45: They Were Expandable
The Hidden Eye
What Next, Corporal Hargrove?
46: Till the Clouds Roll By
47: My Brother Talks to Horses
Romance of Rosy Ridge
For You I Die
48: A Song Is Born
Fighting Back
49: Trouble Preferred
53: The Big Leaguer
Jack Slade
54: Return from the Sea
The Snow Creature
55: Murder Is My Beat
To Hell and Back
The Big Knife
57: The Incredible Shrinking Man
Utah Blaine
Calypso Heat Wave
Chicago Confidential
Juke Box Jamboree
58: Girl in the Woods
It! the Terror from Beyond Space
59: The Cosmic Man
The Invisible Invaders
60: The Big Night
Three Came to Kill
63: Dime with a Halo
Four for Texas
64: Man's Favorite Sport?
Shock Treatment

819

Angela Lansbury (1925-
1944: Gaslight
National Velvet
45: The Picture of Dorian
Dray
Strangler of the Swamp
46: The Harvey Girls
The Hoodlum Saint
Till the Clouds Roll By
47: If Winter Comes
Private Affairs of Bel
Ami
48: Tenth Avenue Angel
State of the Union
The Three Musketeers
49: The Red Danube
Samson and Delilah
51: Kind Lady
52: Mutiny
53: Remains to be Seen
55: The Purple Mask
A Lawless Street
A Life at Stake
56: The Court Jester
Please Murder Me
58: The Reluctant Debutante
The Long Hot Summer
60: A Breath of Scandal
The Dark at the Top of the
Stairs
61: Blue Hawaii
Season of Passion
62: The Manchurian Candidate
All Fall Down
63: In the Cool of the Day
The Out-Of-Towners
64: Dear Heart
The World of Henry Orient
65: The Greatest Story Ever
Told
The Amorous Adventures
of Moll Flanders
Harlow (Para.)
66: Mr. Buddwing
69: The Rook

Joi Lansing
1948: The Counterfeiters
56: Hot Cars
Fountain of Youth (short)

The Brave One
Hot Shots
59: A Hole in the Head
The Atomic Submarine
60: Who Was that Lady?
65: Marriage on the Rocks
69: Bigfoot

Robert Lansing (1929-
1959: 4-D Man
60: The Pusher
63: A Gathering of Eagles
Under the Yum-Yum Tree
66: An Eye for an Eye
Namu, the Killer Whale
Danger Has Two Faces
It Takes all Kinds
69: God Bless You, Uncle Sam

Mario Lanza (1921-1959)
1949: That Midnight Kiss
50: Toast of New Orleans
51: The Great Caruso
52: Because You're Mine
54: The Student Prince (voice)
56: Serenade
58: Seven Hills of Rome
59: For the First Time

Rosemary LaPlanche (1923-
1943: Manhattan Serenade
Prairie Chickens
Two Weeks to Live
45: Strangler of the Swamp
Swing Your Partner
46: The Devil Bat's Daughter
47: Betty Coed
48: Angel's Alley
An Old-Fashioned Girl
49: Golden Hands of Kurigal

Laura LaPlante (1904-
1929: Last Warning
Scandal
Show Boat
Love Trap
Hold Your Man
30: Captain of the Guard
King of Jazz
31: God's Gift to Women

820

31: Lonely Wives
    Arizona
    Meet the Wife
    Men Are Like that
    The Sea Ghost
46: Little Mister Jim
    Spring Reunion

John Larch
1954: Bitter Creek
55: The Phenix City Story
56: The Killer Is Loose
    Behind the High Walls
    Seven Men from Now
    The Man from Del Rio
    Written on the Wind
57: Gun for a Coward
    The Careless Years
    Man in the Shadow
    Quantez
58: From Hell to Texas
    The Saga of Hemp Brown
60: Hell to Eternity
63: Miracle of the White
    Stallions
68: House of Seven Joys
    The Wrecking Crew
69: Hail Hero!
    The Great Bank Robbery
    Cannon for Cordoba

John Larkin (1902-
1932: Wet Parade
    The Tenderfoot
    Stranger in Town
33: Black Beauty
    Day of Reckoning
34: The Witching Hour
35: The Notorious Gentleman
    Mississippi
    Frankie and Johnnie
36: Hearts Divided

John Larkin (1912-1965)
1949: Saints and Sinners
    Twelve O'Clock High
54: The Detective
64: Seven Days in May
    Those Calloways
65: The Satan Bug

Rod La Rocque (1896-1969)
1928: Captain Swagger
29: Man and the Moment
    The Delightful Rogue
    The One Woman Idea
    Our Modern Maidens
    The Locked Door
    Our Dancing Daughter
30: One Romantic Night
    Beau Bandit
    Let Us be Gay
31: The Yellow Ticket
    Resurrection
33: S. O. S. Iceberg
35: Mystery Woman
    Hold 'em, Yale!
    Frisco Waterfront
3?: The Love Pirate
36: Preview Murder Mystery
    Hi, Gaucho!
    The Dragnet
    Till We Meet Again
37: The Shadow Strikes
38: International Crime
39: The Hunchback of Notre
    Dame
40: Dr. Christian Meets the
    Women
    Beyond Tomorrow
    Dark Streets of Cairo
41: Meet John Doe

Rita La Roy (1907-
1929: Dynamite
    Children of the Ritz   SSE
    Love Trap   PT
    Fashions in Love
    Delightful Rogue
30: Lilies of the Field
    Conspiracy
    Sin Takes a Holiday
    Check and Double Check
    Leathernecking
31: Traveling Husbands
    Gay Diplomat
    Chisellers of Hollywood
    The Holy Terror
    Secret Witness
    The Scoop
31: Playthings of Hollywood

821

31: Woman Pursued
    Terror by Night
    Leftover Ladies
32: While Paris Sleeps
    Amateur Daddy
    Bachelor's Affairs
    Hollywood Speaks
    So Big
    Blonde Venus
    Hot Saturday
    Sinners in the Sun
33: From Hell to Heaven
34: Whirlpool
    One Is Guilty
    Name the Woman
    Fugitive Lady
35: Hollywood Boulevard
    Lady from Nowhere
37: Find the Witness
    The Mandarin Mystery
    Mountain Music
    Flight from Glory
38: Condemned Women
39: Fixer Dugan
40: A Fugitive from Justice
    Hold that Woman

Keith Larsen
1949: Son of Belle Starr
  52: Green Glove
      Flat Top
      The Rose Bowl Story
      Hiawatha
  53: War Paint
      Fort Vengeance
      Frontier Rangers
  54: Arrow in the Dust
      Security Risk
  55: Chief Crazy Horse
      Desert Sands
      Dial Red O
      Wichita
      Night Freight
  57: Badlands of Montana
      Last of the Badmen
      Apache Warrior
  66: Women of the Prehistoric
      Planet
  68: Mission: Batangas

Christine Larson
1950: Trial Without Jury
  51: The Well
      Valley of Fire
  52: Brave Warrior
      Last Train from Bombay
  53: Valley of the Headhunters

Al "Lash" La Rue (1921-
1945: Song of Old Wyoming
  46: The Caravan Trail
      Wild West
  47: Law of the Lash
      Border Feud
      Ghost Town Renegades
      Heartaches
      Pioneer Justice
  48: Return of the Lash
      Fighting Vigilantes
      Stage to Mesa City
      Cheyenne Takes Over
      Mark of the Lash
      The Enchanted Valley
      Prairie Outlaws
  49: Outlaw Country
      Son of the Badman
      Son of Billy the Kid
      Dead Men's Gold
      Frontier Revenge

Frank LaRue
1937: Bar-Z Bad Men
      Gun Lords of Stirrup
      Basin
      A Lawman Is Born
      It Happened Out West
      Boothill Brigade
      Public Cowboy No. 1
      The Colorado Kid
  38: Outlaws of Sonora
      Song and Bullets
      Lightning Carson Rides
      Again
      Overland Stage Raiders
      I Demand Payment
  39: Trigger Pals
      Song of the Buckaroo
      In Old Montana
      Down the Wyoming Trail

39: Port of Hate
    Roll Wagons Roll
40: Westbound Stage
    Riders of Pasco Basin
    Frontier Crusader
    Land of Six-Guns
    Return of Wild Bill
    Fugitive from a Prison
     Camp
    The Durango Kid
    The Range Busters
    Arizona Frontier
41: Beyond the Sacramento
    Robbers of the Range
    Hands Across the Rockies
    Gunman from Bodie
    Prairie Stranger
    A Missouri Outlaw
42: Lawless Plainsmen
    The Cyclone Kid
43: Robin Hood of the Range
    Saddles and Sagebrush
44: Ghost Guns
    The Last Horseman
    Saddle Leather Law
    West of the Rio Grande
45: Blazing the Western Trail
    Devil Riders
    Frontier Feud
    The Lost Trail
46: Border Bandits
    The Fighting Frontiersman
    Frontier Gun Law
    The Gentleman from Texas
    Gunning for Vengeance
    The Haunted Mine
    Silver Range
    Under Arizona Skies
47: Prairie Raiders
    South of Chisholm Trail
    Gun Talk
48: Song of the Drifter
    Frontier Agent
49: Sheriff of Medicine Bow

Jack LaRue (1900-
1932: When Paris Sleeps
    The Mouthpiece
    Blessed Event
    Radio Patrol

    Three on a Match
    Virtue
    Man Against Woman
    Farewell to Arms
    The All-American
33: The Story of Temple Drake
    Woman Accused
    Terror Abroad
    Girl in 419
    Gambling Ship
    To the Last Man
    Headline Shooter
    The Kennel Murder Case
    Christopher Strong
34: Miss Fane's Baby Is
    Stolen
    Good Dame
    Take the Stand
35: No Ransom
    Times Square Lady
    Calling all Cars
    The Daring Young Man
    Under the Pampas Moon
    Men of the Hour
    Headline Woman
    Waterfront Lady
    Little Big Shot
    Special Agent
    Remember Last Night?
    His Night Out
    Secret of the Chateau
    After the Dance
    Hot Off the Press
36: Strike Me Pink
    Dancing Pirate
    It Couldn't Have Happened
    Yellow Cargo
    Go West Young Man
    Mind Your Own Business
    Born to Fight
    Bridge of Sighs
37: That I May Live
    Her Husband Lies
    Captains Courageous
    Dangerous Holiday
    River of Missing Men
    Trapped by G-Men
38: Arson Gang Busters
    Under the Big Top
    Valley of the Giants

38: I Demand Payment
39: Murder in Soho
    The Gang's all Here
    Big Town Czar
    In Old Caliente
40: Charlie Chan in Panama
    Forgotten Girls
    Enemy Agent
    Fugitive from a Prison
      Camp
    East of the River
41: Paper Bullets
    The Hard Guy
    Ringside Maisie
    The Gentleman from Dixie
    Footsteps in the Dark
42: Swamp Woman
    Highways by Night
    X Marks the Spot
    American Empire
    The Pay-Off
43: You Can't Beat the Law
    The Girl from Monterey
    The Desert Song
    Pistol Packin' Mama
    The Sultan's Daughter
    Never a Dull Moment
44: Leave it to the Irish
    Moonlight Fiesta
    The Last Ride
    Machine Gun Mama
    Smart Guy
    Follow the Leader
45: Steppin' in Society
    Dangerous Passage
    The Spanish Main
    Dakota
46: Road to Utopia
    Murder in the Music Hall
    Cornered
    In Old Sacramento
47: Bush Pilot
    Santa Fe Uprising
    Robin Hood of Monterey
    My Favorite Brunette
48: No Orchids for Miss
    Blandish
50: For Heaven's Sake
52: Ride the Man Down
64: Robin and the Seven Hoods

Those Who Think Young

Lassie (1940-
1943: Lassie Come Home
    Courage of Lassie
45: Son of Lassie
48: The Master of Lassie
49: Challenge to Lassie

Frank Latimore (1925-
1944: In the Meantime, Darling
45: The Dolly Sisters
46: The Razor's Edge
    Three Little Girls in Blue
47: 13 Rue Madeleine
49: Black Magic
53: Three Forbidden Stories
58: The Devil's Cavaliers
59: John Paul Jones
    Blazing Sun
63: Zorro the Avenger
66: Cast a Giant Shadow
69: The Sergeant

Charles Laughton (1899-1962)
1929: Piccadilly   SSE
    Wolves (or, Wanted Men)
32: Island of Lost Souls
    The Old Dark House
    The Devil and the Deep
    Payment Deferred
    If I Had a Million
    Sign of the Cross
33: White Woman
    Private Life of Henry VIII
    (OSCAR)
34: The Barretts of Wimpole
    Street
35: Les Miserables
    Frankie and Johnny (short)
    Ruggles of Red Gap
    Mutiny on the Bounty
36: Rembrandt
37: Vessel of Wrath
38: St. Martin's Lane
    The Beachbomber
39: Jamaica Inn
    The Hunchback of Notre
    Dame
    Sidewalks of London

39: A Miracle can Happen
40: They Knew What They
     Wanted
41: It Started with Eve
42: The Tuttles of Tahiti
     Tales of Manhattan
     Stand by for Action
43: Forever and a Day
     This Land Is Mine
     The Man from Down Under
44: The Canterville Ghost
     The Suspect
     The Queen's Necklace
45: Captain Kidd
46: Because of Him
47: The Paradine Case
     Arch of Triumph
48: The Girl from Manhattan
     The Big Clock
49: The Bribe
     The Man on the Eiffel
     Tower
51: The Strange Door
     The Blue Veil
52: O. Henry's Full House
     (The Cop and the Anthem
     seq.)
     Abbott & Costello Meet
     Captain Kidd
53: Young Bess
     Salome
54: Hobson's Choice
55: Night of the Hunter (dir.)
57: Witness for the Prosecu-
     tion
60: Spartacus
     Under Ten Flags
62: Advise and Consent

Stan Laurel (1891-1965) & Oliver
Hardy (1892-1957)
1929: Unaccustomed as We Are
     Double Whoopee   S
     Big Business   S
     Men o' War   S-T
     The Perfect Day   S-T
     Angora Love   S
     Bacon Grabbers   S
     They Go Boom!
     The Hoosegow

Hollywood Revue of 1929
Berth Marks   S-T
Wrong Again
That's My Wife
30: Night Owls
     Blotto
     Be Big
     Brats
     Below Zero
     The Laurel and Hardy
       Murder Case
     Another Fine Mess
     Hog Wild (or, Aerial
       Antics)
     The Rogue Song
31: Chickens Come Home
     Our Wife
     Laughing Gravy
     Come Clean
     One Good Turn
     Helpmates
     Beau Hunks (or, Beau
       Chumps)
     Pardon Us
32: Any Old Port
     The Music Box
     The Chimp
     County Hospital
     Scram
     Their First Mistakes
     Pack Up Your Troubles
33: Busy Bodies
     Towed in a Hole
     Me and My Pal
     Twice Two
     The Midnight Patrol
     Dirty Work
     Fra Diavolo (The Devil's
       Brother)
34: Going Bye-Bye
     Oliver the VIII
     Them Thar Hills
     The Live Ghost
     Sons of the Desert
     Babes in Toyland
     Hollywood Party of 1934
35: Tit for Tat
     The Fixer-Uppers
     Thicker than Water
     Bonnie Scotland

825

36: The Bohemian Girl
      Our Relations
37: Way Out West
      Pick a Star
38: Swiss Miss
      Blockheads
39: The Flying Deuces
40: A Chump at Oxford
      Saps at Sea
41: Great Guns
42: A-Haunting We Will Go
43: Air Raid Wardens
      Jitterbugs
      The Dancing Masters
44: The Big Noise
      Nothing but Trouble
45: The Bullfighters
50: Riding High
52: Atoll-K
55: Utopia
57: The Golden Age of Comedy
      (doc.)
60: When Comedy Was King
      (doc.)
      (SPECIAL AWARD)
64: Big Parade of Comedy
      (doc.)
67: The Crazy World of Laurel
      & Hardy (doc.)
      Further Perils of Laurel
      & Hardy (doc.)
See also: Oliver Hardy

Piper Laurie (1932-
1950: Louisa
      The Milkman
51: Francis Goes to the Races
      The Prince Who Was a
      Thief
52: Son of Ali Baba
      Has Anybody Seen My Gal?
      No Room for the Groom
53: Mississippi Gambler
      The Golden Blade
54: Dangerous Mission
      Johnny Dark
      Dawn at Socorro
55: Smoke Signal
      Ain't Misbehavin'
57: Until They Sail

57: Kelly and Me
61: The Hustler

Rod Lauren
1964: Law of the Lawless
65: The Crawling Hand
67: Once Before I Die
69: Childish Things

Harry Lauter
1950: Experiment Alcatraz
51: Silver City Bonanza
      Thunder in God's Country
      Whirlwind
      According to Mrs. Hoyle
      Hills of Utah
      The Kid from Amarillo
      Valley of Fire
52: Night Stage to Galveston
      Apache Country
      Sea Tiger
      The Steel Fist
      Yukon Gold
53: The Marshal's Daughter
      Prince of Pirates
      Topeka
      Fighter Attack
      Pack Train
54: Dragonfly Squadron
      Yankee Pasha
      Target: Sea of China
      Return to Treasure Island
      The Forty-Niners
55: It Came from Beneath the
      Sea
      The Creature with the Atom
      Brain
      The Crooked Web
      At Gunpoint
56: Earth vs the Flying Saucer
      The Werewolf
      Miami Exposé
      Dig that Uranium
      The Women of Pitcairn
      Island
57: Hellcats of the Navy
      The Badge of Marshal
      Brennan
      Death in Small Doses
      Raiders of Old California

58: Return to Warbow
The Toughest Gun in
Tombstone
The Cry Baby Killer
Missing Monsters
Tarzan's Fight for Life
Good Day for a Hanging
59: The Gunfight at Dodge
City
61: Posse from Hell
62: The Wild Westerners
65: Fort Courageous
Convict Stage
66: Ambush Bay
67: Fort Utah

Lucille LaVerne (1869-1945)
1930: Abraham Lincoln
Sinner's Holiday
31: The Great Meadow
Twenty-Four Hours
An American Tragedy
32: She Wanted a Millionaire
Alias the Doctor
While Paris Sleeps
Hearts of Humanity
Breach of Promise
33: Wild Horse Mesa
Strange Adventure
Pilgrimage
The Last Trail
34: Beloved
School for Girls
Kentucky Kernels
35: A Tale of Two Cities

Daliah Lavi (1940-
1962: Two Weeks in Another
Town
Candida
63: Blazing Sand
Il Demonio
64: What?
65: Lord Jim
And so to Bed
66: The Silencers
Ten Little Indians
67: Casino Royale
Blast-Off
Shatterhand

The Spy with a Cold Nose
Those Fantastic Flying
Fools
68: Some Girls Do
Nobody Runs Forever
69: High Commissioner

John Phillip Law (1937-
1964: What?
65: High Infidelity (The Scandal
seq.)
66: The Russians Are Coming,
The Russians Are Coming!
67: Hurry Sundown
68: Barbarella
Danger: Diabolik!
69: The Sergeant
Skidoo!
The Hawaiians
Death Rides a Horse

Peter Lawford (1923-
1930: Old Bill
38: Lord Jeff
42: Mrs. Miniver
Eagle Squadron
Thunder Birds
A Yank at Eton
43: Sherlock Holmes Faces
Death
Flesh and Fantasy
The West Side Kid
The Purple V
Someone to Remember
The Man from Down Under
Paris after Dark
44: The White Cliffs of Dover
Mrs. Parkington
The Canterville Ghost
45: The Picture of Dorian Gray
Son of Lassie
46: Cluny Brown
My Brother Talks to Horses
Two Sisters from Boston
47: It Happened in Brooklyn
Good News
48: On an Island with You
Easter Parade
Julia Misbehaves
49: Little Women

827

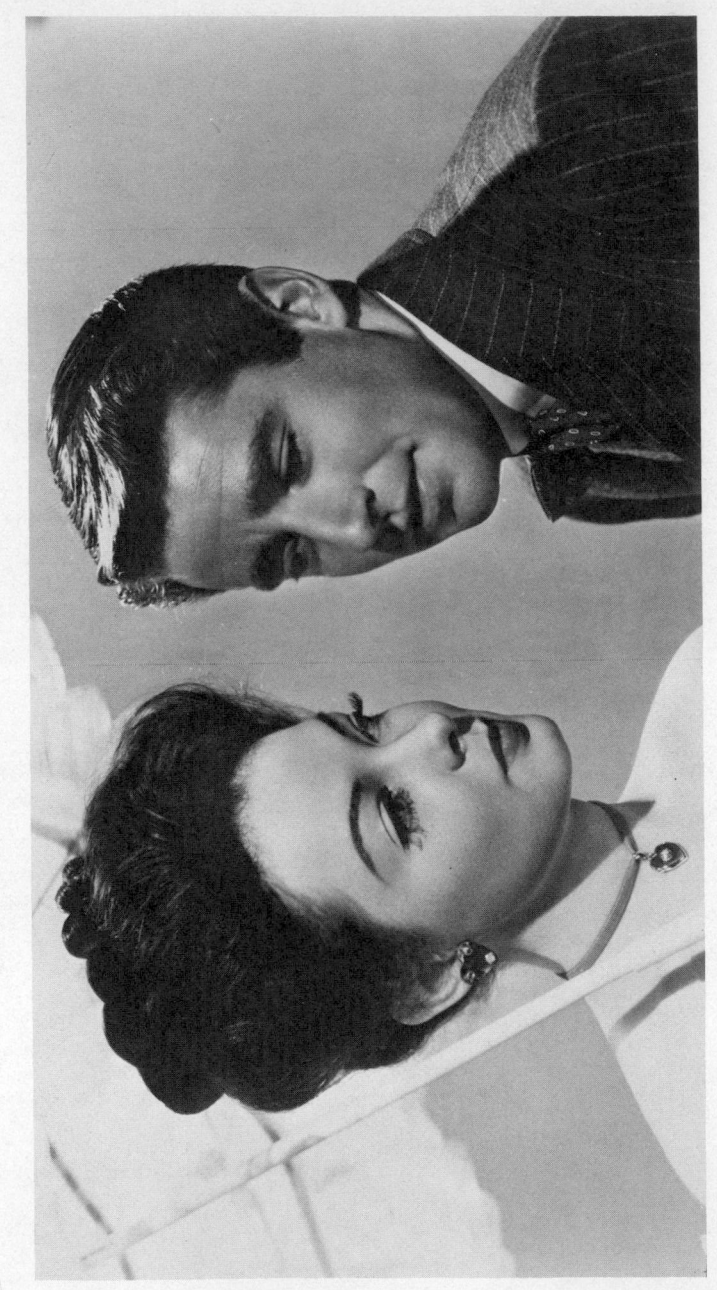

Peter Lawford and Kathryn Grayson in "Meet Me in St. Louis"

49: The Red Danube
50: Please Believe Me
51: Royal Wedding
52: Kangaroo
    Just this Once
    The Hour of Thirteen
    You for Me
    Rogue's March
54: It Should Happen to You
59: Never so Few
60: Pepe
    Exodus
    Ocean's Eleven
62: Advise and Consent
    Sergeants Three
    The Longest Day
63: Johnny Cool
64: Dead Ringer
65: Sylvia
    Billie
    Harlow (Para.)
66: The Oscar
    A Man Called Adam
67: How I Spent My Summer
    Vacation (TV)
68: Salt and Pepper
    Skidoo!
69: Hook, Line, and Sinker
    (cameo)
    The Silent Treatment
    The April Fools
    Buona Sera, Mrs. Camp-
    bell
    Dead Run
    Togetherness
    The Big Blast
    One More Time

Jody Lawrance (1920-
1951: Mask of the Avenger
    The Son of Dr. Jekyll
    The Family Secret
    Ten Tall Men
52: The Brigand
53: All Ashore
    John Smith and Pocahontas
56: The Scarlet Hour
    The Leather Saint
58: Hot Spell
60: The Purple Gang

62: Stagecoach to Dancer's
    Rock

Barbara Lawrence (1928-
1946: Margie
47: Captain from Castile
48: Give My Regards to
    Broadway
    You Were Meant for Me
    Street with no Name
    Unfaithfully Yours
    A Letter to Three Wives
49: Mother Is a Freshman
    Thieves' Highway
51: Two Tickets to Broadway
52: Here Come the Nelsons
53: The Star
    Paris Model
    Arena
54: Jesse James vs the Daltons
    Her Twelve Men
55: Oklahoma!
    Man with the Gun
57: Joe Dakota
    Man in the Shadow
    Kronos

Carol Lawrence (1935-
1954: New Faces
61: West Side Story
62: A View from the Bridge

Gertrude Lawrence (1898-1952)
1929: Battle of Paris
33: No Funny Business
36: Rembrandt
37: Men Are not Gods
50: The Glass Menagerie

Marc Lawrence (1910-
1933: White Woman
35: Men of the Hour
    Little Big Shot
    Dr. Socrates
36: Road Gang
    Desire
    Trapped by Television
    Counterfeit
    The Final Hour
    Night Waitress

829

37: I Promise to Pay
What Price Vengeance?
Racketeers in Exile
Motor Madness
San Quentin
Criminals of the Air
Counsel for Crime
Charlie Chan on Broadway
Murder in Greenwich
Village
The Shadow
38: Penitentiary
Who Killed Gail Preston?
Convicted
I Am the Law
Squadron of Honor
39: Sergeant Madden
Homicide Bureau
Romance of the Redwoods
Ex-Champ
S.O.S. Tidal Wave
Blind Alibi
The Housekeeper's
Daughter
Dust be My Destiny
Beware Spooks!
40: Invisible Stripes
Johnny Apollo
The Man Who Talked too
Much
Charlie Chan at the Wax
Museum
The Great Profile
Brigham Young--Frontiers-
man
The Golden Fleecing
Love, Honor, and Oh Baby!
41: Tall, Dark, and Handsome
A Dangerous Game
The Monster and the Girl
The Man Who Lost Himself
Blossoms in the Dust
Shepherd of the Hills
Hold that Ghost!
Lady Scarface
Sundown
Public Enemies
42: Nazi Agent
This Gun for Hire
Yokel Boy

Call of the Canyon
'Neath Brooklyn Bridge
43: Submarine Agent
The Ox-Bow Incident
Eyes of the Underworld
Calaboose
Hit the Ice
44: The Princess and the
Pirate
Rainbow Island
Tampico
45: Club Havana
Dillinger
Don't Fence Me in
Flame of the Barbary
Coast
Life with Blondie
46: Cloak and Dagger
The Virginian
47: Yankee Fakir
The Captain from Castile
I Walk Alone
Joe Palooka in The Knock-
out
Unconquered
48: Key Largo
Out of the Storm
49: Calamity Jane and Sam
Bass
Jigsaw
Tough Assignment
50: Black Hand
The Asphalt Jungle
The Desert Hawk
51: Gun Moll
Hurricane Island
My Favorite Spy
54: Girls Marked Danger
58: Kill Her Gently
63: Johnny Cool
65: Nightmare in the Sun (act.,
dir.)
66: Johnny Tiger
67: Krakatoa--East of Java
68: Custer of the West

Frank Lawton (1904-1969)
1930: Young Woodley
Birds of Prey
The Outsider

30:	The Skin Game
32:	Michael and Mary
33:	Cavalcade
	Friday the Thirteenth
34:	Voice in the Night
35:	Bar-20 Rides Again
	David Copperfield
36:	The Invisible Ray
	The Devil-Doll
	The Mill on the Floss
39:	The Four Just Men
42:	Went the Day Well?
48:	The Winslow Boy
53:	Rough Shoot
58:	Rising of the Moon
	A Night to Remember

Evelyn Laye (1900-
1930:	Queen of Scandal
	One Heavenly Night
33:	Waltz Time
34:	Evensong
35:	The Night Is Young
	Princess Charming
59:	Make Mine a Million

Cloris Leachman (1927-
1955:	Kiss Me Deadly
56:	The Rack
62:	The Chapman Report
69:	Butch Cassidy and the
	Sundance Kid
	Blood Fiend
	A Hall of Mirrors

Rex Lease (1901-1966)
1928:	Law of the Range	S
29:	The Younger Generation	PT
	Stolen Love
	Two Sisters
	When Dreams Come True
	Girls Who Dare
30:	Troopers Three
	Sunny Skies
	Hot Curves
	So This Is Mexico?
	Why Marry?
	Borrowed Wives
	The Utah Kid
	Wings of Adventure

31:	Chinatown after Dark
	The Monster Walks
	Is There Justice?
	In Old Cheyenne
32:	Cannonball Express
	The Lone Trail
	Midnight Morals
34:	Inside Information
35:	The Ghost Rider
	Custer's Last Stand (ser.)
	The Man from Gun Town
36:	Aces and Eights
	The Clutching Hand
	Gentleman Jim McGee
	Fast Bullets
	Lightnin' Bill Carson
	Roarin' Guns
	Cavalcade of the West
37:	The Silver Trail
	Heroes of the Alamo
	The Freedom
	Swing it, Sailor!
	The Mysterious Pilot (ser.)
38:	Fury Below
	Code of the Rangers
	Desert Patrol
39:	South of the Border
40:	Rancho Grande
	One Man's Law
	Under Texas Skies
	The Trail Blazers
	Lone Star Raiders
41:	Outlaws of the Rio Grande
	The Phantom Cowboy
	Death Valley Outlaws
	Pals of the Range
	Sierra Sue
	Outlaws of the Cherokee
	Trail
42:	Arizona Terrors
	The Silver Bullet
	The Cyclone Kid
	Tomorrow We Live
	The Boss of Hangtown Mesa
43:	Haunted Ranch
	Tenting on the Old Camp
	Ground
	Dead Man's Gulch
44:	Firebrands of Arizona
	Bordertown Trail

44: The Cowboy and the
 Señorita
45: Flame of the Barbary
 Coast
 Frontier Gal
 Texas Ranger
 Santa Fe Saddlemates
46: Days of Buffalo Bill
 Sun Valley Cyclone
 The Time of Their Lives
47: Helldorado
 Slave Girl
 The Wistful Widow of
 Wagon Gap
48: Out of the Storm
49: Ma and Pa Kettle
50: Singing Guns
 Bells of Coronado
 Code of the Silver Sage
 Curtain Call at Cactus
 Creek
 Covered Wagon Raiders
 Hills of Oklahoma
 The Frisco Tornado
52: Ma and Pa Kettle at the
 Fair
53: Ride, Vaquero!

Ivan Lebedeff (1895-1953)
1929: Sin Town   S
 The Veiled Woman   S
 One Woman Idea   SSE
 They Had to see Paris
 Street Girl
30: The Cuckoos
 Midnight Mystery
 The Conspiracy
31: The Gay Diplomat
 The Bachelor Apartment
 The Lady Refuses
 Deceit
 Woman Pursued
32: Unholy Love
33: Made on Broadway
 Bombshell
 Laughing at Life
 Moulin Rouge
34: Kansas City Princess
 The Merry Frinks
 Merry Widow

35: Sweepstakes Annie
 Goin' to Town
 China Seas
36: Golden Arrow
 Pepper
 Love on the Run
37: Fair Warning
 Mama Steps Out
 Conquest
 History Is Made at Night
 Atlantic Flight
 Angel
38: Wise Girl
 Straight Place and Show
39: You Can't Cheat an Honest
 Man
 Trapped in the Sky
 The Mystery of Mr. Wong
 Elsa Maxwell's Hotel for
 Women
40: Passport to Alcatraz
 Elsa Maxwell's Public
 Deb No. 1
41: Blue, White, and Perfect
 Shanghai Gesture
42: Foreign Agent
 Lure of the Islands
43: Mission to Moscow
 Around the World
44: Oh, What a Night!
 Are These Our Parents?
45: Rhapsody in Blue
52: California Conquest
 The Snows of Kilimanjaro

Friedrich Ledebur
1949: The Great Sinner
56: Alexander the Great
 Moby Dick
57: The Man Who Turned to
 Stone
 The Twenty-Seventh Day
 Voodoo Island
58: Roots of Heaven
 Enchanted Island
 The Buccaneer
60: A Breath of Scandal
65: Juliet of the Spirits
66: The Blue Max
67: Oedipus the King

832

Francis Lederer (1906-
1929: Die Wunderbar Lüge der
Nina Petrovna (The
Wonderful Lies of Nina
Petrovna)
Zuflucht (Refuge)
Die der Pandora (Pandora's
Box)
Ihre Majestät die Liebe
(Her Majesty of Love)
30: Atlantis
Haitang
Maman Ceribri
32: The Bracelet
34: Man of Two Worlds
Pursuit of Happiness
Romance in Manhattan
35: The Gay Deception
36: One Rainy Afternoon
My American Wife
37: Cape of Good Hope
38: It's all Yours
The Lone Wolf in Paris
39: Confessions of a Nazi
Spy
Midnight
40: The Man I Married
41: Puddin'head
44: The Bridge of San Luis
Rey
Voice in the Wind
46: The Madonna's Secret
Diary of a Chambermaid
48: Million Dollar Weekend
50: Captain Carey U.S.A.
A Woman of Distinction
Surrender
53: Stolen Identity
56: The Ambassador's
Daughter
Lisbon
58: Maracaibo
The Curse of Dracula
Nights Are Made for Love
Return of Dracula
The Fantastic Disappearing
Man
59: Terror Is a Man
60: A Breath of Scandal

Anna Lee (1914-
1935: First a Girl

The Camels Are Coming
36: The Man Who Changed
His Mind
37: You're in the Army Now
King Solomon's Mines
Non-Stop New York
39: Four Just Men
Youn Man's Fancy
40: Seven Sinners
41: My Life with Caroline
How Green Was My Valley
42: Flying Tigers
The Commandos Strike at
Dawn
43: Forever and a Day
Flesh and Fantasy
Hangmen also Die
44: Summer Storm
Abroad with Two Yanks
46: Bedlam
G.I. War Brides
47: High Conquest
The Ghost and Mrs. Muir
48: The Best Man Wins
Fort Apache
49: Prison Warden
50: Wyoming Mail
51: Triple Cross
G.I. Jane
52: Boots Malone
56: Daniel Boone, Trail Blazer
58: The Last Hurrah
59: This Earth Is Mine
The Horse Soldiers
The Crimson Kimono
Gideon of Scotland Yard
60: The Big Night
Jet over the Atlantic
61: Two Rode Together
62: Whatever Happened to
Baby Jane?
Jack the Giant Killer
64: For Those Who Think
Young
65: The Sound of Music
Seven Women
66: Picture Mommy Dead
67: In Like Flint

Belinda Lee (1935-1961)

50: Eye Witness
54: Blackout
The Runaway Bus
55: Footsteps in the Fog
Man of the Moment
The Bells of St. Trinian's
57: The Gentle Touch
58: The Secret Place
Dangerous Exile
59: Elephant Gun
60: The Nights of Lucretia
Borgia
The Goddess of Love
61: Aphrodite
62: Constantine and the Cross
Joseph and His Brethern
Messalina
63: Long Night at 43
The Devil's Choice
64: Love--The Italian Way

Christopher Lee (1922-
1948: Corridors of Mirrors
Hamlet
49: Scott of the Antarctic
50: Prelude to Fame
The Devil's Agent
51: Valley of the Eagles
52: Moulin Rouge
Sherlock Holmes and the
Deadly Necklace
The Crimson Pirate
55: That Lady
Storm over the Nile
Alias John Preston
Innocents in Paris
56: Moby Dick
Pursuit of the Graf Spee
(or, The Battle of the
River Plate; or, Graf
Spee)
The Cockleshell Heroes
Port Afrique
57: The Curse of Frankenstein
Dracula
A Tale of Two Cities
Beyond Mombasa
58: The Truth about Women
Horror of Dracula
Bitter Victory

She Played with Fire (or,
Fortune Is a Woman)
59: The Traitor (or, The
Accursed)
The Hound of the Baskers-
villes
The Man Who Could Cheat
Death
The Mummy
Treasure of San Teresa
Too Hot to Handle (U.S.
rel. '62: Playgirl After
Dark)
Beat Girl
60: City of the Dead
Two Faces of Dr. Jekyll
The Hands of Orlac
Missile from Hell (or,
Unseen Heroes; or, Battle
of the V-1)
Taste of Fear
The Devil's Daffodil
Red Orchid
61: The Valley of Fear
Katharsis
The Terror of the Tongs
House of Fright (or, The
Two Faces of Dr.Jekyll)
Scream of Fear
62: Faust '63
63: Hot Money Girl
Terror in the Crypt
The Pirates of Blood River
Wild for Kicks
Uncle Was a Vampire
Castle of the Living Dead
The Way and the Body
Carmilla
The Devilship Pirates
Hercules in the Haunted
World
Corridors of Blood
Virgin of Nuremberg
64: The Gorgon
The Sign of Satan
The House of Blood
The Dunwich Horror
Dr. Terror's House of
Horrors
What!

834

65: She
The Skull
The Mask of Fu Manchu
Horror Castle of the
Living Dead
The Bride of Fu Manchu
66: Dracula--The Prince of
Darkness
Rasputin, the Mad Monk
The Face of Dr. Fu
Manchu
Circus of Fear
Golden Dragons
Brides of Fu Manchu
67: Psycho-Circus
68: The Vengeance of Fu
Manchu
Eve
The Devil Rides Out
Kiss and Kill
The Witch House
The Crimson Altar
69: Dracula Has Risen from
the Grave
Three in the Attic
Blood Fiend
The Oblong Box
The Devil's Bride
Assignment: Istanbul
The Magic Christian
(cameo)
Julius Caesar
The Private Life of
Sherlock Holmes

Dixie Lee (1911-1952)
1929: Fox Movietone Follies of
1929
Why Leave Home?
30: Happy Days
Harmony at Home
Let's Go Places
Big Party
Cheer Up and Smile
31: No Limit
Night Life in Reno
34: Manhattan Love Song
35: Love in Bloom
Redheads on Parade

Gwen Lee
1931: Paid
Inspiration
Lawless Woman
Traveling Husbands
Pagan Lady
32: West of Broadway
From Broadway to Cheyenne

Gypsy Rose Lee (1914-
1937: You Can't Have Everything
Ali Baba Goes to Town
38: My Lucky Star
The Battle of Broadway
Sally, Irene, and Mary
43: Stage Door Canteen
44: Belle of the Yukon
45: Doll Face
52: Babes in Bagdad
58: The Screaming Mimi
Wind Across the Everglades
63: The Stripper
66: The Trouble with Angels

Lila Lee (1905-
1929: Little Wildcat   PT
The Man in Hobble's   S
Queen of the Night Clubs
Black Pearl
Honky Tonk
The Argyle Case
Drag
Flight
Dark Streets
The Sacred Flame
Love, Live, and Laugh
30: Second Wife
Double Cross Roads
Murder Will Out
The Unholy Three
Those Who Dance
31: Misbehaving Ladies
The Gorilla
Woman Hungry
32: War Correspondent
Radio Patrol
Exposure
Unholy Love
The Night of June Thirteenth

835

32: False Faces
33: Officer 13
Face in the Sky
Iron Master
The Intruder
34: The Whirlpool
Lone Cowboy
In Love with Life
I Can't Escape
35: Marriage Bargain
The People's Enemy
Champagne for Breakfast
36: The Ex-Mrs. Bradford
Country Gentleman
37: Two Wise Maids
A Nation Aflame

62: Sergeants Three
63: Gun Hawk
Hootenanny Hoot
64: Bullet for a Badman

Andrea Leeds (1914-
1936: Come and Get it
37: Stage Door
It Could Happen to You
38: The Goldwyn Follies
.   Letter of Introduction
Youth Takes a Fling
39: They Shall Have Music
The Real Glory
Swanee River
40: Earthbound

Michele Lee (1944-
1967: How to Succeed in Business
Without Really Trying
68: The Love Bug
69: Billy Bright

Peter Leeds
1949: The Lady Gambles
50: Saddle Tramp
51: Katie Did it
53: 99 River Street
54: The Last Time I Saw Paris
The Atomic Kid
55: Interrupted Melody
Tight Spot
Love Me or Leave Me
I'll Cry Tomorrow
Bobby Ware Is Missing
59: The Thirty Foot Bride of
Candy Rock
Girls Town
The Rookie
60: The Facts of Life
65: Harlow (Para.)
67: Eight on the Lam
68: With Six You Get Eggroll

Palmer Lee (1942-
1951: The Cimarron Kid
52: Red Ball Express
Battle of Apache Pass
Sally and St. Anne
Francis Goes to West
Point
Son of Ali Baba
Back at the Front
The Raiders
The Redhead from Wyoming
53: It Happens Every Thursday
Column South
Veils of Bagdad

Peggy Lee (1920-
1950: Mr. Music
53: The Jazz Singer
55: Pete Kelly's Blues

Fritz Leiber (1882-1949)
1935: A Tale of Two Cities
The Story of Louis Pasteur
36: Sins of Man
Hearts in Bondage
Under Two Flags
Anthony Adverse
Down to theSea
Camille
37: Champagne Waltz
The Prince and the Pauper
The Great Garrick

Ruta Lee (1935-
1955: Twinkle in God's Eye
56: Gaby
57: Funny Face
Witness for the Prosecution
58: Marjorie Morningstar
61: Operation Eichmann

38: The Jury's Secret
Flight into Nowhere
Gateway
39: Nurse Edith Cavell
They Made Her a Spy
The Hunchback of Notre
Dame
Pack Up Your Troubles
40: The Way of all Flesh
All this and Heaven too
The Sea Hawk
Lady with Red Hair
41: Aloma of the South Seas
42: Cross Roads
43: The Desert Song
The Phantom of the Opera
First Comes Courage
44: Are These Our Parents?
Bride of the Vampire
The Impostor
Cry of the Werewolf
45: The Cisco Kid Returns
This Love of Ours
The Spanish Main
46: Humoresque
A Scandal in Paris
Strange Journey
47: High Conquest
Bells of San Angelo
The Web
Dangerous Venture
Monsieur Verdoux
48: Another Part of the Forest
Adventures of Casanova
To the Ends of the Earth
Inner Sanctum
49: Bride of Vengeance
Song of India
Samson and Delilah
Bagdad

Janet Leigh (1927-
1947: Romance of Rosy Ridge
If Winter Comes
48: Hills of Rome
Words and Music
Act of Violence
49: Little Women
The Doctor and the Girl
The Red Danube

That Forsyte Woman
Holiday Affair
51: Two Tickets to Broadway
It's a Big Country
Strictly Dishonorable
Angels in the Outfield
52: Just this Once
Scaramouche
Fearless Fagan
53: The Naked Spur
Confidentially Yours
Houdini
Walking My Baby Back
Home
54: Prince Valiant
Living it Up
The Black Shield of Fal-
worth
Rogue Cop
55: My Sister Eileen
Pete Kelly's Blues
56: Safari
57: Jet Pilot
58: The Vikings
Touch of Evil
Perfect Furlough
60: Psycho
Pepe
Who Was that Lady?
62: The Manchurian Candidate
63: Bye Bye, Birdie
Wives and Lovers
66: Harper
Three on a Couch
Kid Rodelo
The American Dream
67: The Moving Target
68: Where Were You When the
Lights Went Out?
Grand Slam
69: The Girl from Paradise
Hello Down There
The Monk (TV)
The House on Green Apple
Road (TV)
Honeymoon with a Stranger

Nelson Leigh (1914-1967)
1944: Follow the Boys
Texas Masquerade

44: Louisiana Hayride
    U-Boat Prisoner
45: Identity Unknown
48: Angels' Alley
49: The Lost Tribe
    Barbary Pirate
50: Captive Girl
51: Home Town Story
    Hurricane Island
    Yukon Manhunt
52: Thief of Damascus
53: Savage Mutiny
    The Valley of the Head-
    Hunters
54: Jesse James vs the
    Daltons
    The Saracen Blade
    The Outlaw's Daughter
55: The Creature with the
    Atom Brain
56: World Without End
    The First Texan
    Hold Back the Night
57: Gunfight at the O.K.Corral
    God Is My Partner
    Bombers B-52
58: In Love and War
59: These Thousand Hills
60: The Gallant Hours
    Ma Barker's Killer Brood
62: Incident in an Alley
63: A Gathering of Eagles

Vivien Leigh (1913-1967)
1934: Things Are Looking Up
      The Village Squire
35: Look Up and Laugh
    Gentleman's Agreement
36: First and Last
37: Fire over England
    The Dark Journey
    Storm in a Teacup
38: A Yank at Oxford
39: Gone With the Wind
    (OSCAR)
40: Sidewalks of London (or,
    St. Martin's Lane)
    Waterloo Bridge
    Twenty One Days Together
41: That Hamilton Woman

46: Caesar and Cleopatra
48: Anna Karenina
    Hamlet
51: Streetcar Named Desire
    (OSCAR)
55: The Deep Blue Sea
61: The Roman Spring of Mrs.
    Stone
65: Ship of Fools

Margaret Leighton (1922-
1948: The Winslow Boy
      Bonnie Prince Charlie
49: Under Capricorn
50: The Astonished Heart
    The Elusive Pimpernel
51: Calling Bulldog Drummond
    Home at Seven
53: Murder on Monday
54: The Holly and the Ivy
55: Court Martial
    The Good Die Young
    The Teckman Mystery
    Carrington V.C.
    The Constant Husband
59: The Sound and the Fury
    A Novel Affair
62: The Passionate Stranger
    The Waltz of the Toreadors
64: The Best Man
    The Third Secret
65: The Loved One
66: Seven Women
69: The Madwoman of Chaillot

Harvey Lembeck (1923-
1951: You're in the Navy Now
      (or, U.S.S. Teakettle)
      The Frogmen
      Fourteen Hours
      The Program
      Finders Keepers
52: Just Across the Street
    Back at the Front
53: Girls in the Night
    Stalag 17
    Mission over Korea
54: The Command
56: Between Heaven and Hell
61: The Last Time I Saw Archi

61: Sail a Crooked Ship
62: A View from the Bridge
63: Beach Party
    Love with a Proper
    Stranger
64: The Unsinkable Molly
    Brown
    Bikini Beach
    Pajama Party
65: How to Stuff a Wild Bikini
    Beach Blanket Bingo
    Sgt. Deadhead, the Astro-
    naut
66: Fireball 500
    The Ghost in the Invisible
    Bikini
67: The Spirit Is Willing
69: Hello, Down There

Jack Lemmon (1925-
1954: It Should Happen to You
    Phffft!
55: Three for the Show
    My Sister Eileen
    Mr. Roberts (OSCAR)
56: You Can't Run Away from
    it
57: Fire Down Below
    Operation Mad Ball
58: Bell, Book, and Candle
    Cowboy
59: It Happened to Jane
    Some Like it Hot
60: The Apartment
    Pepe
61: The Wackiest Ship in the
    Army
62: The Days of Wine and
    Roses
    Stowaway in the Sky (narr.)
    The Notorious Landlady
63: Irma la Douce
    Under the Yum-Yum Tree
64: Good Neighbor Sam
65: The Great Race
    How to Murder Your Wife
66: The Fortune Cookie
67: Luv (or, Rage)
68: The Odd Couple
69: The April Fools

The Out-Of-Towners
Kotch (dir.)

John Lennon (1940-
1968: How I Won the War
See also: The Beatles

Lotte Lenya (1900-
1930: Three Penny Opera
60: The Roman Spring of Mrs.
    Stone
64: From Russia with Love
69: The Appointment

Queenie Leonard
1941: Ladies in Retirement
    Confirm or Deny
42: This Above All
43: Forever and a Day
    Thumbs Up
44: The Lodger
45: Molly and Me
    And Then There Were None
    My Name Is Julia Ross
46: Cluny Brown
47: Life with Father
    The Lone Wolf in London
51: Thunder on the Hill
52: The Narrow Margin
55: The King's Thief
56: Twenty-Three Paces to
    Baker Street
    D-Day, the Sixth of June
61: A Hundred and One
    Dalmatians (voice)

Sheldon Leonard (1907-
1939: Another Thin Man
41: Tall, Dark, and Handsome
    Weekend in Havana
    Buy Me that Town
    Private Nurse
    Married Bachelor
    Rise and Shine
42: Tortilla Flat
    Lucky Jordan
    Pierre of the Plains
    Street of Chance
43: Taxi, Mister!
    Hit the Ice

44: The Falcon in Hollywood
Uncertain Glory
Gambler's Choice
Timber Queen
To Have and Have Not
Trocadero
45: Why Girls Leave Home
Zombies on Broadway
Shadow of Terror
River Gang
Frontier Gal
Captain Kidd
Radio Stars on Parade
46: Crime, Inc.
The Last Crooked Mile
The Gentleman Misbehaves
Somewhere in the Night
Her Kind of Man
It's a Wonderful Life
Bowery Bombshell
Decoy
Rainbow over Texas
47: The Gangster
Sinbad the Sailor
Violence
The Fabulous Joe
48: If You Knew Susie
Open Secret
Alias a Gentleman
Jinx Money
Madonna of the Desert
Winner Take All
Shep Comes Home
49: My Dream Is Yours
Take One False Step
Daughter of the Jungle
50: Iroquois Trail
51: Abbott & Costello Meet
the Invisible Man
Behave Yourself
Come Fill the Cup
52: Breakdown
Here Come the Nelsons
Young Man with Ideas
Stop, You're Killing Me!
53: Diamond Queen
55: Money from Home
Guys and Dolls
61: A Pocketful of Miracles

Eugenie Leontovich (1894-
1940: Four Sons
41: The Men in Her Life
52: Anything can Happen
The World in His Arms
55: The Rains of Ranchipur
61: Homicidal

Baby Leroy (1932-
1933: A Bedtime Story
Torch Singer
Tillie and Gus
Alice in Wonderland
34: Miss Fane's Baby Is
Stolen
The Old-Fashioned Way
The Lemon Drop Kid
It'a a Gift
36: It's a Great Life

Bethel Leslie (1929-
1959: The Rabbit Trap
63: Captain Newman, MD
65: A Rage to Live
68: The Molly Maguires

Joan Leslie (1925-
1937: Camille
39: Two Thoroughbreds
Winter Carnival
40: Military Academy
Foreign Correspondent
Laddie
Alice in Wonderland
(short)
41: The Great Mr. Nobody
High Sierra
The Wagons Roll at Night
Thieves Fall Out
Sergeant York
42: The Male Animal
Yankee Doodle Dandy
The Hard Way
43: The Sky's the Limit
This Is the Army
Thank Your Lucky Stars
44: Hollywood Canteen
Manhattan Fury
45: Rhapsody in Blue

45: Where Do We Go from
Here?
46: Too Young to Know
Cinderella Jones
Two Guys from Milwaukee
Janie Gets Married
47: Repeat Performance
Royal Flush
48: Northwest Stampede
Bed of Roses
50: Born to be Bad
The Skipper Surprised
His Wife
51: Man in the Saddle (or,
The Outcast)
52: Toughest Man in Arizona
Hellgate
53: The Woman They Almost
Lynched
Flight Nurse
54: Jubilee Trail
55: Hell's Outpost
56: Revolt of Mamie Stover

Nan Leslie (1926-
1946: Sunset Pass
47: The Devil Thumbs a Ride
Woman on the Beach
Under the Tonto Rim
Wild Horse Mesa
48: The Arizona Ranger
Guns of Hate
Western Heritage
Indian Agent
49: Rim of the Canyon
50: Pioneer Marshal
53: Problem Girls
Iron Mountain Trail
59: Miracle of the Hills
60: The Crowded Sky
68: The Bamboo Saucer

Ben Lessy
1943: Thousands Cheer
45: Her Highness and the
Bellboy
47: Dark Delusion
48: The Pirate
50: The Jackie Robinson Story
51: The Purple Heart Diary

52: Just for You
62: It's a Mad Mad Mad Mad
World
63: Gypsy
64: Pajama Party
65: That Funny Feeling
66: The Last of the Secret
Agents?
67: The Fastest Guitar Alive

Buddy Lester
1960: Ocean's Eleven
61: The Ladies' Man
62: Sergeants Three
64: The Nutty Professor

Mark Lester (1958-
1965: Spaceflight IC-I
67: Our Mother's House
68: Oliver!
69: Philip

Vicki Lester
1940: The Great Plane Robbery
41: Tall, Dark, and Handsome
Tom, Dick, and Harry
You're Out of Luck
42: The Miracle Kid

Oscar Levant (1906-
1929: Dance of Life
35: In Person
40: Rhythm on the Range
41: Kiss the Boys Goodbye
(lyrics, music)
45: Rhapsody in Blue
46: Humoresque
47: Romance on the High Seas
48: You Were Meant for Me
The Barkleys of Broadway
51: An American in Paris
52: O. Henry's Full House
(Ransom of Red Chief seq.)
53: The Band Wagon
The I Don't Care Girl
55: The Cobweb

Sam Levene (1905-
1936: After the Thin Man
Three Men on a Horse

38: Yellow Jack
    The Shopworn Angel
39: Golden Boy
40: The Mad Miss Manton
41: Married Bachelor
    Shadow of the Thin Man
42: The Big Street
    Grand Central Murder
    The Sunday Punch
    Destination Unknown
43: Gung Ho!
    Action in the North
     Atlantic
    I Dood it
    Whistling in Brooklyn
44: The Purple Heart
46: The Killers
47: Brute Force
    Boomerang
    A Likely Story
    Killer McCoy
    Crossfire
48: The Babe Ruth Story
50: Guilty Bystander
    Dial 1119
53: Three Sailors and a Girl
56: The Opposite Sex
57: Designing Woman
    Sweet Smell of Success
    Slaughter on Tenth Avenue
    A Farewell to Arms
58: Wink of an Eye
    Kathy O'
63: Act One
69: A Dream of Kings

Cathy Lewis (1918-1968)
1941: Double Trouble
  42: The Kid Glove Killer
  49: My Friend Irma
  50: My Friend Irma Goes
       West
  58: Party Crashers
  61: The Devil at 4 O'Clock

Diana Lewis (1915-
1934: It's a Gift
  35: Enter Madame
      One Hour Late
  38: He Couldn't Say No

Gold Diggers in Paris
40: Forty Little Mothers
    Andy Hardy Meets a
     Debutante
    Bitter Sweet
    Go West
41: The People vs Dr. Kildare
    Johnny Eager
42: Seven Sweethearts
    Whistling in Dixie
43: Cry Havoc
64: Big Parade of Comedy
    (doc.)

Elliott Lewis (1917-
1950: Ma and Pa Kettle Go to
       Town
  51: Saturday's Hero

George J. Lewis (1904-
1929: King of the Campus
      College Love
      Tonight at Twelve
  32: A Parisian Romance
      The Heart Punch
  33: Her Resale Value
  34: Lazy River
      Two Heads on a Pillow
  35: Red Morning
      Headline Woman
      Storm over the Andes
  36: Captain Calamity
  39: Back Door to Heaven
      Beware Spooks!
  40: Outside the Three-Mile
       Limit
  41: Outlaws of the Desert
  42: Phantom Killer
      A Yank in Libya
      The Falcon's Brother
  43: The Black Hills Express
  44: Charlie Chan in the Secret
       Service
      The Falcon in Mexico
      The Laramie Trail
      Shadow of Suspicion
  45: Song of Mexico
      South of the Rio Grande
      Wagon Wheels Westward
  46: Gilda

46: The Missing Lady
Passkey to Danger
Rainbow over Texas
South of Monterey
Tarzan and the Leopard
Woman
Under Nevada Skies
47: Beauty and the Bandit
Twilight on the Rio Grande
Blackmail
Slave Girl
48: Half Past Midnight
Lulu Belle
When My Baby Smiles
at Me
49: Renegades of Sonora
Sheriff of Medicine Bow
The Feathered Serpent
The Big Sombrero
The Dalton Gang
The Lost Tribe
50: Captain Carey, U.S.A.
One Way Street
Hostile Country
Colorado Ranger
Marshal of Heldorado
Crooked River
Fast on the Draw
Short Grass
51: Al Jennings of Oklahoma
Appointment with Danger
Saddle Legion
The Kid from Amarillo
52: Wagon Team
The Raiders
Hold that Line!
53: Desert Legion
Bandits of Corsica
Cow Country
Devil's Canyon
54: Saskatchewan
Border River
Drum Beat
55: Hell on Frisco Bay
56: Santiago
A Cry in the Night
57: The Big Land
The Tall Stranger
59: The Ghost of Zorro
60: The Sign of Zorro

61: The Comancheros

Harry Lewis
1942: Always in My Heart
Busses Roar
44: The Last Ride
Winged Victory
46: Her Kind of Man
47: The Unsuspected
48: Key Largo
49: Deadly as the Female
Joe Palooka in The
Counterpunch
Bomba on Panther Island
50: Blonde Dynamite
68: Pendulum

Jarma Lewis
1954: River of No Return
55: The Prodigal
The Marauders
The Cobweb
The Tender Trap
It's a Dog's Life
57: Raintree County

Jerry Lewis (1926-
(With Dean Martin through '56)
1949: My Friend Irma
50: My Friend Irma Goes West
At War with the Army
51: That's My Boy
52: The Stooge
Jumping Jacks
53: Sailor, Beware!
The Caddy
Scared Stiff
Money from Home
54: Living it Up
Three-Ring Circus
55: You're Never too Young
Artists and Models
56: Pardners
Hollywood or Bust
57: The Delicate Delinquent
The Sad Sack
58: Rockabye Baby
The Geisha Boy
59: Don't Give Up the Ship
60: Visit to a Small Planet

60: Cinderfella
The Bellboy
61: Ladies' Man
62: The Errand Boy
It's Only Money
63: The Nutty Professor
Who's Minding the Store?
64: The Disorderly Orderly
The Patsy
65: The Family Jewels
66: Boeing! Boeing!
Three on a Couch
67: The Big Mouth
Way Way Out
68: Don't Raise the Bridge,
Lower the Water
69: Which Way to the Front?

Mitchell Lewis (1880-1956)
1929: Madame X
The Leatherneck
Linda
The Black Watch
One Stolen Night
The Bridge of San Luis
Rey
30: Girl of the Port
Mammy
a short
The Death Ship
The Cuckoos
Beau Bandit
Sea America Thirst
The Bad One
31: Never the Twain Shall
Meet
The Squaw Man
Son of India
32: World and the Flesh
New Morals for Old
McKenna of the Mounted
Kongo
33: Secret of Madame Blanche
Ann Vickers
34: Count of Monte Cristo
35: Red Morning
A Tale of Two Cities
The Best Man Wins
36: Sutter's Gold
The Bohemian Girl

The Dancing Pirate
Mummy's Boys
37: Waikiki Wedding
Espionage
38: Mysterious Mr. Moto (or,
...of Devil's Island)
41: Meet John Doe
I'll Wait for You
Billy the Kid
42: Cairo
46: Courage of Lassie
51: Man with a Cloak
53: The Sun Shines Bright
All the Brothers Were
Valiant

Monica Lewis (1925-
1951: Inside Straight
Excuse My Dust
52: Everything I Have Is Yours
53: Affair with a Stranger
57: The D.I.

Ralph Lewis (d. 1937)
1928: The Girl in the Glass
Cage   PT
30: The Bad One
Fourth Alarm
The Glass Case
32: American Madness
33: Sucker Money
Somewhere in Sonora
Riot Squad
34: Mystery Liner
Badge of Honor
Fighting Hero
Ready for Love
Terrors of the Plains
35: The Lost City
Behind Green Lights
Sunset Range
36: Swifty
44: The Utah Kid
Shadow of Suspicion
Army Wives
Marked Trails
Trigger Law
45: China's Little Devils
Dillinger
G.I. Honeymoon

45: The Jade Mask
46: Danny Boy
    The Flying Serpent
    Ziegfeld Follies

Robert Q. Lewis (1921-
1964: Good Neighbor Sam
  65: Sky Party
  66: Ride Beyond Vengeance
  67: How to Succeed in
      Business Without Really
      Trying

Sheldon Lewis (1869-1958)
1929: Little Wild Girl
      Untamed Justice
      Seven Footprints to Satan
      River Woman
      Black Magic
  30: Danger Man
      Firebrand Jordan
  32: The Monster Walks
      Tex Takes a Holiday
  33: Tombstone Canyon
  34: Gun Justice
  36: The Cattle Thief

Ted Lewis (1891-
1928: Is Everybody Happy?
  29: Show of Shows
  37: Manhattan Merry-Go-
      Round
  43: Follow the Boys

Vera Lewis (d. 1958)
1929: The Iron Mask
      The Home Towners
  30: Wide Open
  31: Command Performance
      Night Nurse
  33: Hold Your Man
  35: The Man on the Flying
      Trapeze
      Way Down East
      Paddy O'Day
      Never Too Late
  36: Missing Girls
  38: Comet over Broadway
      Four Daughters
      Nancy Drew, Detective

39: Naughty but Nice
    Women in the Wind
    On Trial
    Hell's Kitchen
    The Roaring Twenties
    Four Wives
    Return of Dr. X
    Private Detective
    Nancy Drew and the Hidden
      Staircase
    Sweepstakes Winner
40: They Drive by Night
    Courageous Dr. Christian
    Granny Get Your Gun
    A Night at Earl Carroll's
    Father Is a Prince
41: Four Mothers
    She Couldn't Say No
    Here Come Happiness
    Nine Lives Are not Enough
42: Lady Gangster
    The Busses Roar
43: Moontide
45: Rhythm Roundup
    Hollywood & Vine
46: The Cat Creeps
    Spook Busters
47: It's a Joke, Son

John Leyton
1963: The Great Escape
  64: Guns at Batasi
  65: Von Ryan's Express
      Seaside Swingers
  66: The Idol
PT 68: Krakotoa- East of Java
S
V. Liberace (1919-
1950: South Sea Sinner
  51: Footlight Varieties
  55: Sincerely Yours
  65: When the Boys Meet the
      Girls
      The Loved One

Winnie Lightner (1901-
1928: A Song a Minute
  29: Show of Shows
      Gold Diggers of Broadway
  30: She Couldn't Say No

30: Hold Everything
Life of the Party
31: Sit Tight
Why Change Your Husband?
Side Show
Gold Dust Gertie
32: Play Girl
Eight to Five
Manhattan Parade
33: She Had to Say Yes
Dancing Lady
34: I'll Fix It

Beatrice Lillie (1898-
1927: Exit Smiling   S
29: Show of Shows
30: Are You There?
38: Dr. Rhythm
43: On Approval
56: Around the World in 80
Days
67: Thoroughly Modern Millie

Yvonne Lime
1957: Untamed Youth
I Was a Teenage Werewolf
58: Dragstrip Riot
59: Speed Crazy

Kay Linaker
1939: Charlie Chan in Reno
Drums Along the Mohawk
The Girl from Rio
40: Heaven with a Barbed
Wire Fence
Buck Benny Rides Again
Free, Blonde, and
Twenty-One
Mystery Sea Raider
Kitty Foyle
41: They Dare not Love
Private Nurse
Charlie Chan in Rio
42: The Night Before the
Divorce
Men of Texas
War Dogs
43: Two Weeks to Live
Cinderella Swings it
Let's Face it

44: Men on Her Mind
Lady in the Dark

Eric Linden (1909-
1931: Are These our Children?
Veneer
32: The Crowd Roars
Young Bride
Age of Consent
Big City Blues
Roundhouse Murder
The Phantom of Crestwood
Life Begins
33: The Past of Mary Holmes
Sweepings
The Silver Cord
Flying Devils
35: Let 'em Have it
Ladies Crave Excitement
Born to Gamble
Ah, Wilderness
36: The Voice of Bugle Ann
Old Hutch
In His Steps
Career Woman
Robin Hood of El Dorado
Accent on Love
37: Sweetheart of the Navy
A Family Affair
Good Old Soak
Girl Loves Boy
Here's Flash Casey
38: Midnight Intruder
Romance of the Limberlost
39: Everything's on Ice
Gone With the Wind
41: Criminals Within

Viveca Lindfors (1920-
1940: In Paradise
41: The Crazy Family
If I Could Marry the
Minister
44: Appassionata
45: Interlude
48: Adventures of Don Juan
To the Victor
49: Night unto Night
Anna Lans
The Saga of Sincoalla

50: Dark City
The Flying Missile
No Sad Songs for Me
Backfire
This Side of the Law
51: Gypsy Fury
Journey into Light
Four in a Jeep
Somewhere in the City
52: The Raiders
No Time for Flowers
55: Run for Cover
Moonfleet
Captain Dreyfuss
57: Halliday Brand
58: I Accuse!
Weddings and Babies
59: Tempest
60: The Story of Ruth
61: King of Kings
The Riding Kid
62: No Exit
63: Fanfare for a Death
Scene
64: An Affair of the Skin
65: Sylvia
Brainstorm (or, The
Woman Who Wouldn't Die)
These Are the Damned

Margaret Lindsay (1910-
1932: The All-American
Okay, America
33: Paddy the Next Best Thing
Captured
The Fourth Horseman
Cavalcade
The House on 56th Street
Voltaire
Lady Killer
Private Detective 62
West of Singapore
The World Changes
34: From Headquarters
Merry Wives of Reno
Fog over Frisco
The Dragon Murder Case
Gentlemen Are Born
35: Bordertown
Devil Dogs of the Air

The Florentine Dagger
The Frisco Kid
Dangerous
Personal Maid's Secret
The Case of the Curious
Bride
The G Men
36: The Lady Consents
The Law in Her Hands
Public Enemy's Wife
Isle of Fury
Sinner Take All
37: Green Lights
Slim
Back in Circulation
Song of the City
38: Gold Is Where You Find it
When Were You Born?
Broadway Musketeers
There's that Woman Again
Jezebel
Garden of the Moon
Three Girls on Broadway
39: On Trial
Hell's Kitchen
The Under-Pup
Twenty Thousand Men a
Year
40: British Intelligence
Honeymoon Deferred
House of the Seven Gables
Double Alibi
Meet the Wildcat
Ellery Queen, Master
Detective
41: Ellery Queen's Penthouse
Mystery
Ellery Queen and the
Perfect Crime
Ellery Queen and the
Murder Ring
Hard Boiled Canary
42: A Close Call for Ellery
Queen
The Spoilers
A Desperate Chance for
Ellery Queen
A Tragedy at Midnight
Enemy Agents Meet Ellery
Queen

43: No Place for a Lady
Let's Have Fun
Crime Doctor
44: Alaska
45: Adventures of Rusty
Scarlet Street
46: Club Havana
Her Sister's Secret
47: The Vigilantes Return
Louisiana
Seven Keys to Baldpate
48: Cass Timberlane
B.F.'s Daughter
56: Emergency Hospital
The Bottom of the Bottle
58: The Restless Years
60: Please Don't Eat the
Daisies
Jet over the Atlantic
63: Tammy and the Doctor

Ivan Linow
1929: The River   PT
In Old Arizona
Black Magic   SSE
Speakeasy
The Far Call
The Cockeyed World
30: Temple Tower
Ship from Shanghai
Song of the Flame
The Unholy Three
Numbered Men
Just Imagine
The Silver Horde
Madonna of the Streets
31: Goldie
32: It's Tough to be Famous
Jewel Robbery
Rachety Rax
Scarlet Dawn
34: Wharf Angel

Virna Lisi (1937-
1963: The Doll that Took the
Town
Duel of the Titans
64: The Black Tulip
The Spy I Love
Love, Hate, and Dishonor

65: Eva
Bambole! (The Telephone
Call seq.)
How to Murder Your Wife
Casanova '70
Signore I Signori
Paranoia (Kiss the Other
Sheik seq.)
66: Assault on a Queen
Not with My Wife You
Don't!
The Twenty-Fifth Hour
The Gardens of Finzi
The Girl and the General
Made in Italy
67: Across the River and into
the Trees
The Birds, the Bees, and
the Italians
68: Arabella
A Maiden for a Prince
Better a Widow
Any One can Play
The Tenderness
69: The Runaround
If It's Tuesday, This Must
be Belgium
The Secret of Santa Vittoria
The Christmas Tree
Speak no Evil, See no Evil,
Hear no Evil

John Litel (1892-1964)
1929: The Sleeping Porch
30: Don't Believe it
32: Wayward
37: Fugitive in the Sky
Black Legion
Marked Woman
Midnight Court
Slim
The Life of Emile Zola
The Missing Witnesses
Back in Circulation
38: Alcatraz Island
Gold Is Where You Find it
A Slight Case of Murder
My Bill
Broadway Musketeers
Love, Honor, and Behave

848

38: Jezebel
Over the Wall
Little Miss Thoroughbred
The Amazing Dr. Clitter-
house
Nancy Drew, Detective
Valley of the Giants
Comet over Broadway
39: Wings of the Navy
You Can't Get Away with
Murder
Secret Service of the Air
On Trial
Dodge City
Dust be My Destiny
Dead End Kids on Dress
Parade
The Return of Dr. X
A Child Is Born
One Hour to Live
Nancy Drew, Trouble
Shooter
Nancy Drew and the
Hidden Staircase
40: The Fighting Sixty-Ninth
Castle on the Hudson
Virginia City
It All Came True
Flight Nurse
An Angel from Texas
The Man Who Talked too
Much
They Drive by Night
Murder in the Air
Money and the Woman
Knute Rockne--All-
American
Lady with Red Hair
Santa Fe Trail
Men Without Souls
Flight Angels
Gambling on the High Seas
Father Is a Prince
41: The Trial of Mary Dugan
Father's Son
Thieves Fall Out
The Big Boss
Henry Aldrich for
President
The Great Mr. Nobody

42: Don Winslow of the Navy
(ser.)
41: Sealed Lips
They Died with Their
Boots on
42: The Kid Glove Killer
Henry and Dizzy
The Mystery of Marie
Roget
Mississippi Gambler
Men of Texas
Invisible Agent
A Desperate Chance for
Ellery Queen
Henry Aldrich, Editor
Boss of Big Town
Madame Spy
43: Henry Aldrich Gets Glamour
Submarine Bass
Dangerous Age
Crime Doctor
Murder in Times Square
Henry Aldrich Swings it
Where Are Your Children?
Henry Aldrich Haunts a
House
44: Murder in the Blue Room
Henry Aldrich Plays Cupid
Henry Aldrich's Little
Secret
Henry Aldrich, Boy Scout
Faces in the Fog
My Buddy
Lake Placid Serenade
45: Brewster's Millions
The Enchanted Forest
Salome, Where She Danced
San Antonio
The Crimson Canary
The Daltons Ride Again
Northwest Trail
46: The Crime Doctor's
Warning
The Madonna's Secret
Notorious Gentleman
A Night in Paradise
The Return of Rusty
She Wrote the Book
Sister Kenny
Smooth as Silk

46: Swell Guy   66: Nevada Smith
    Lighthouse
47: Cass Timberlane   Lucien Littlefield (1895-1960)
    The Beginning or the End? 1928: Do Your Duty   S
    Easy Come, Easy Go   Mother Knows Best   PT
    The Guilty   29: Seven Keys to Baldpate
    Heaven Only Knows   Drag
    Christmas Eve   Girl in the Glass Cage   PT
48: Smart Woman   Saturday's Children   PT
    Rusty Leads the Way   Making the Grade   PT
    My Dog Rusty   This Is Heaven   PT
    Pitfall   Clear the Decks   PT
    Valiant Hombre   Wall Street
    Triple Threat   The Man in Hobble's   S
    I, Jane Doe   30: Captain of the Guard
49: The Gal Who Took the   The Great Divide
    West   No, No, Nanette
    Outpost in Morocco   High Society Blues
    Shamrock Hill   Queen of Main Street
    Rusty Saves a Life   His Big Ambition
    Rusty's Birthday   Out for Game
    Woman in Hiding   Getting a Raise
50: Mary Ryan, Detective   The Potters at Home
    The Fuller Brush Girl   The Potters Done in Oil
    Kiss Tomorrow Goodbye   Pa Gets a Vacation
    The Sundowners   Big Money
51: The Cuban Fireball   Misbehaving Ladies
    The Groom Wore Spurs   Tom Sawyer
    Texas Rangers   Clancy in Wall Street
    Little Egypt   She's My Weakness
    $2 Bettor   31: It Pays to Advertise
    Flight to Mars   Reducing
52: Jet Job   Scandal Sheet
    Montana Belle   Young as You Feel
    Scaramouche   32: High Pressure
53: Jack Slade   Broken Lullaby
54: Sitting Bull   Strangers in Love
55: Texas Lady   Shopworn
    Double Jeopardy   Strangers of the Evening
    The Kentuckian   Miss Pinkerton
56: Comanche   Downstairs
    The Wild Dakotas   Speed Madness
57: The Hired Gun   Pride of the Legion
    Decision at Sundown   That's My Boy
58: Houseboat   If I Had a Million
61: Voyage to the Bottom of   Evenings for Sale
    the Sea   33: The Big Brain
    A Pocketful of Miracles   Professional Sweetheart
63: The Gun Hawk   Chance at Heaven
65: The Sons of Katie Elder   Alice in Wonderland

33: East of Fifth Avenue
The Bitter Tea of General
  Yen
Dirty Work
Sailor's Luck
Sweepings
Skyway
Rainbow over Broadway
34: Sons of the Desert
30-Day Princess
Kiss and Make Up
Mandalay
Gridiron Flash
Marrying Widows
Love Time
When Strangers Meet
35: Sweepstakes Annie
Ruggles of Red Gap
Man on the Flying Trapeze
One Frightened Night
The Murder Man
She Gets Her Man
The Return of Peter
  Grimm
I Dream too Much
Cappy Ricks Returns
Magnificent Obsession
36: Rose Marie
Early to Bed
The Moon's Our Home
Let's Sing Again
37: High, Wide, and Handsome
Souls at Sea
Hotel Haywire
Wild Money
Partners in Crime
Bulldog Drummond's
  Revenge
38: Wide Open Faces
Scandal Sheet
Hollywood Stadium Mystery
Born to the West
The Night Hawk
The Gladiator
39: A short
Mystery Plane
Sky Pirate
Tumbleweeds
Unmarried
What a Life!

Sabotage
Jeepers Creepers
40: Money to Burn
Those Were the Days
41: Murder Among Friends
The Great American
  Broadcast
Henry Aldrich for President
Man at Large
The Little Foxes
Mr. and Mrs. North
42: The Great Man's Lady
Castle in the Desert
Hillbilly Blitzkrieg
Bells of Capistrano
Whistling in Dixie
43: Johnny Come Lately
Henry Aldrich Haunts a
  House
44: Casanova in Burlesque
Goodnight Sweetheart
The Cowboy and the
  Senorita
One Body too Many
Lady, Let's Dance
When the Lights Go on
  Again
Lights of Old Santa Fe
45: Scared Stiff
The Caribbean Mystery
Detour
46: Rendezvous with Annie
That Brennan Girl
47: The Hal Roach Comedy
The Fabulous Joe
Sweet Genevieve
48: Lightnin' in the Forest
Jinx Money
Badmen of Tombstone
49: Susanna Pass
52: At Sword's Point
53: Roar of the Crowd
54: Casanova's Big Night
55: Sudden Danger
57: Bop Girl
58: Wink of an Eye

Roger Livesey (1906-
1935: Lorna Doone
36: Rembrandt

38: The Drum
Keep Smiling
39: Spies of the Air
40: Girls in the News
45: Colonel Blimp
47: I Know Where I'm Going
A Matter of Life and
Death
Vice Versa
That Dangerous Age
Green Grow the Bushes
50: If This be Sin
53: The Master of Ballantrae
Intimate Stranger
56: The Finger of Guilt
60: The Entertainer
League of Gentlemen
It Happened in Broad
Daylight
64: Of Human Bondage
65: The Amorous Adventures
of Moll Flanders
67: Oedipus the King
69: Hamlet

Bob Livingston (1908-
1933: Enlighten Thy Daughter
Public Enemy No. 2
34: The Band Plays On
Death on the Diamond
35: West Point of the Air
The Winning Target
Baby Face Harrington
Murder in the Fleet
36: a short
Three Godfathers
Absolute Quiet
The Three Musketeers
The Bold Caballero
37: Larceny on the Air
Come on, Cowboys!
Range Defenders
Wild Horse Rodeo
The Girl Said No (collab.)
Riders of the Whistling
Skull
Renfrew of the Royal
Mounted
Circus Girl
Ghost Town Gold

Roarin' Lead
38: The Purple Vigilantes
Call the Mesquiteers
Arson Gang Busters
Outlaws of Sonora
Ladies in Distress
Riders of the Black Hills
Heroes of the Hills
The Night Hawk
Orphans of the Street
39: Federal Man-Hunt
Kansas Terrors
Cowboys from Texas
Heart of the Rockies
40: Heroes of the Saddle
Pioneers of the West
Covered Wagon Days
Rocky Mountain Rangers
Oklahoma Renegades
Under Texas Skies
The Trail Blazers
Lone Star Rangers
41: Prairie Pioneers
Pals of the Pecos
Saddlemates
Gangs of Sonora
43: Pistol Packin' Mama
Wild Horse Rustlers
Lone Rider in Overland
Stagecoach
44: Beneath Western Skies
Wolves of the Range
Law of the Saddle
Storm over Lisbon
Goodnight Sweetheart
The Laramie Trail
Pride of the Plains
Brazil
45: Lake Placid Serenade
The Big Bonanza
Bells of Rosarita
Steppin' in Society
Dakota
The Cheaters
Tell it to a Star
Don't Fence Me in
46: The Undercover Woman
Valley of the Zombies
48: Daredevils of the Clouds
Grand Canyon Trail

49: The Feathered Serpent
    The Mysterious Desperado
    Riders in the Sky
50: Mule Train
    Law of the Badlands
52: Night Stage to Galveston
53: Winning of the West
58: Once Upon a Horse

Margaret Livingston (1902-
1929: Last Warning   PT
      The Bellamy Trial   PT
      Office Scandal   PT
      The Charlatan   PT
      Innocents of Paris
      Tonight at Twelve
      Acquitted
30:   Seven Keys to Baldpate
      Murder on the Roof
      Big Money
      What a Widow
      For the Love o' Lil
31:   Kiki
      The Lady Refuses
      Broad-Minded
      Smart Money
32:   Call Her Savage
34:   Social Register

Doris Lloyd (1900-1968)
1929: The Careless Age
      The Drake Murder Case
30:   Sarah and Son
      Disraeli
      Off to Reno
      Old English
      Way for a Sailor
      Charley's Aunt
31:   Waterloo Bridge
      Bought
      Transgression
      Bachelor Father
      Once a Lady
      Devotion
32:   Back Street
      Tarzan the Ape Man
33:   Robbers' Roost
      Always a Lady
      Looking Forward
      Peg o' My Heart

A Study in Scarlet
Voltaire
Oliver Twist
Tarzan and His Mate
34: Dangerous Corner
    Kiss and Make Up
    Glamour
    Sisters Under the Skin
    She Was a Lady
    One Exciting Adventure
35: Clive of India
    Straight from the Heart
    Kind Lady
    The Perfect Gentleman
    The Woman in Red
    Motive for Revenge
    Chasing Yesterday
    Becky Sharp
    A Shot in the Dark
    Peter Ibbetson
    A Feather in Her Hat
36: Brilliant Marriage
    Don't Get Personal
    Too Many Parents
    Mary of Scotland
37: The Plough and the Stars
    Tovarich
38: Alcatraz Island
    The Black Doll
39: I'm from Missouri
    The Under-Pup
    Barricade
    First Love
    The Private Lives of
      Elizabeth and Essex
40: Vigil in the Night
    The Great Plane Robbery
    Till We Meet Again
    The Letter
41: The Great Lie
42: Night Monster
    Journey for Margaret
    The Ghost of Frankenstein
43: Mission to Moscow
    The Constant Nymph
    Forever and a Day
44: The Lodger
    The Invisible Man's Revenge
    The Conspirators
    Frenchman's Creek

853

44: Phantom Lady
    Follow the Boys
45: Allotment Wives
    Molly and Me
    My Name Is Julia Ross
    Scotland Yard Investigator
46: Devotion
    G.I. War Brides
    Holiday in Mexico
    Of Human Bondage
    Tarzan and the Leopard
        Woman
    Three Strangers
    To Each His Own
47: Secret Life of Walter
        Mitty
48: Sign of the Ram
50: Tyrant of the Sea
51: King Lady
    The Son of Dr. Jekyll
55: A Man Called Peter
56: The Swan
60: The Time Machine
    Midnight Lace
62: The Notorious Landlady
65: The Sound of Music
67: Rosie

Harold Lloyd (1893-
1929: Welcome Danger
  30: Feet First
  32: Movie Crazy
  34: The Cat's Paw
  36: The Milky Way
  38: Professor Beware!
  41: A Girl, a Guy, and a
        Gob (prod.)
  42: My Favorite Spy (prod.)
    Mad Wednesday (The Sin
        of Harold Diddlebok)
  52: (SPECIAL AWARD)
  57: The Golden Age of Comedy
        (doc.)
  62: Harold Lloyd's World of
        Comedy (film excerpts)
    The Funny Side of Life

Harold Lloyd, Jr.
1959: Girls Town
  60: Platinum High School

65: Mutiny in Outer Space

Sondra Locke (1946-
1968: The Heart Is a Lonely
        Hunter
  69: Lovemakers
    Run, Shadow, Run

Gene Lockhart (1891-1957)
1934: By Your Leave
  35: Ah, Wilderness
    I've Been Around
    Captain Hurricane
    Star of Midnight
    Thunder in the Night
    Storm over the Andes
    Crime and Punishment
  36: Brides Are Like that
    Times Square Playboy
    Earthworm Tractors
    The First Baby
    Career Woman
    The Garden Murder Case
    The Gorgeous Hussy
    The Devil Is a Sissy
    Wedding Present
    Mind Your Own Business
    Come Closer, Folks!
  37: Mama Steps Out
    Too Many Wives
    The Sheik Steps Out
    Something to Sing About
  38: Human Hearts
    Listen, Darling
    A Christmas Carol
    Sweethearts
    Penrod's Double Trouble
    Men Are Such Fools
    Blondie
    Algiers
    Sinners in Paradise
    Meet the Girl
  39: I'm from Missouri
    Hotel Imperial
    Our Leading Citizen
    Geronimo
    Tell no Tales
    Bridal Suite
    Blackmail
    The Story of Alexander
        Graham Bell

854

40: Edison the Man
Dr. Kildare Goes Home
We Who Are Young
South of Pago Pago
A Dispatch from Reuter's
His Girl Friday
Abe Lincoln in Illinois
41: Billy the Kid
Keeping Company
Meet John Doe
The Sea Wolf
All that Money can Buy
One Foot in Heaven
Here Is a Man
Steel Against the Sky
International Lady
They Died with Their
Boots on
42: Juke Girl
The Gay Sisters
You Can't Escape Forever
43: Forever and a Day
Hangmen also Die
Mission to Moscow
Find the Blackmailer
The Desert Song
Madame Curie
Northern Pursuit
44: The White Cliffs of Dover
Going My Way
Action in Arabia
The Man from Brooklyn
45: The House on 92nd Street
Leave Her to Heaven
That's the Spirit
46: Meet Me on Broadway
A Scandal in Paris
She-Wolf of London
The Strange Woman
47: The Shocking Miss Pilgrim
Miracle on 34th Street
The Foxes of Harrow
Cynthia
Honeymoon
Her Husband's Affairs
48: Joan of Arc
Inside Story
That Wonderful Urge
Apartment for Peggy
I, Jane Doe

49: Down to the Sea in Ships
Madame Bovary
The Inspector General
The Sickle and the Cross
50: The Big Hangover
51: I'd Climb the Highest
Mountain
Rhubarb
The Lady from Texas
52: Hoodlum Empire
A Girl in Every Port
Face to Face
Bonzo Goes to College
Androcles and the Lion
Apache War Smoke
53: Francis Covers the Big
Town
Down Among the Sheltering
Palms
Confidentially Connie
The Lady Wants Mink
54: The World for Ransom
55: The Vanishing American
56: Carousel
The Man in the Gray
Flannel Suit
57: Jeanne Eagels

June Lockhart (1925-
1938: A Christmas Carol
40: All This and Heaven Too
41: Sergeant York
Adam Had Four Sons
42: Miss Annie Rooney
43: Forever and a Day
44: Meet Me in St. Louis
45: Son of Lassie
Keep Your Powder Dry
46: Easy to Wed
She-Wolf of London
The White Cliffs of Dover
The Yearling
47: Bury Me Dead
T-Men
It's a Joke, Son!
49: Red Light
57: Time Limit
63: Lassie's Great Adventure

Kathleen Lockhart
1936: The Devil Is a Sissy
      Broadway Playboy
      Brides Are Like that
      Times Square Playboy
      Mr. Cinderella
      Career Woman
37: Something to Sing About
38: Men Are Such Fools
      Penrod's Double Trouble
      Blondie
      A Christmas Carol
      Sweethearts
39: Man of Conquest
      Our Leading Citizen
      What a Lie!
40: All This and Heaven Too
41: Adam Had Four Sons
      Sergeant York
      Love Crazy
42: Are Husbands Necessary?
43: Mission to Moscow
      Lost Angel
      The Good Fellows
44: The Seventh Cross
      Wilson
45: Roughly Speaking
      Bewitched
46: Two Years Before the
      Mast
      Lady in the Lake
47: A Gentleman's Agreement
48: The Snake Pit
49: The Sickle or the Cross
51: I'd Climb the Highest
      Mountain
53: Confidentially Connie
      Walking My Baby Back
      Home
54: The Glenn Miller Story
58: A Certain Smile
60: The Purple Gang

Gary Lockwood (1937-
1961: Wild in the Country
      Splendor in the Grass
62: The Magic Sword
63: It Happened at the World's
      Fair
68: Firecreek

2001: a Space Odyssey
The Model Shop
69: They Came to Rob Las
      Vegas (Ital.)

Margaret Lockwood (1916-
1934: The Case of Gabriel Perry
      Rulers of the Sea
      Susannah of the Mounties
35: Lorna Doone
      Midshipman Easy
36: Beloved Vagabond
37: Dr. Syn
38: Bank Holiday
      The Lady Vanishes
39: The Stars Look Down
      A Girl Must Live
      Gestapo
40: Night Train to Munich
41: Quiet Wedding
      The Girl in the News
43: Alibi
      Give Us the Moon
      Dear Octopus
      The Man in Grey
44: Love Story
      A Place of One's Own
45: I'll be Your Sweetheart
      Wicked Lady
46: Bedelia
47: Hungry Hill
      Jassy
      The Bad Sister
      Madness of the Heart
      White Unicorn
48: The Cardboard Cavalier
50: Highly Dangerous
52: Trent's Last Case
54: Laughing Anne
      Trouble in the Glen
57: Cast a Dark Shadow

John Loder (1898-
1928: The Great Unknown   S
      The Doctor's Secret
29: Sunset Pass   S
      Half an Hour
      Black Waters
      Unholy Night
      Wedding Rehearsal

29: Money Means Nothing
The First Born
Her Private Affair
30: The Racketeer
Rich People
Lilies of the Field
Sweethearts and Wives
One Night at Susie's
The Man Hunter
31: Second Floor Mystery
The Seas Beneath
Men of the Sky
Hot Dogs
32: Money for Speed
33: You Made Me Love You
Paris Plane
Sound City
The Private Life of Henry
VIII
34: Love, Live, and Laughter
Lorna Doone
Rolling in Money
Warn London
The Battle
35: Java Head
Eighteen Minutes
It Happened in Paris
Silent Passenger
36: Ourselves Alone
Guilty Melody
The Man Who Lived Again
The Man Who Changed
His Mind
37: King Solomon's Mines
A Woman Alone
Non-Stop New York
Mademoiselle Docteur
Odd Bob
Peace on the Rhine
39: Menaces
40: Diamond Frontier
Mozart
Tin Pan Alley
Katia
Meet Maxwell Archer
Murder Will Out
Diamonds Are Dangerous
Adventures in Diamonds
41: Scotland Yard
How Green Was My Valley

Confirm or Deny
One Night in Lisbon
42: Maxwell Archer, Detective
Continental Express
Now Voyager
Gentleman Jim
The Eagle Squadron
The Gorilla Man
The Male Animal
43: The Mysterious Doctor
Murder on the Waterfront
Adventure in Iraq
Old Acquaintance
44: Passage to Marseilles
The Hairy Ape
Abroad with Two Yanks
45: Jealousy
The Brighton Strangler
The Woman Who Came
Back
The Fighting Guardsman
46: The Wife of Monte Cristo
One More Tomorrow
A Game of Death
47: Dishonored Lady
57: Woman and the Hunter
The Story of Esther
Costello
59: Gideon of Scotland Yard

John Lodge (1903-
1932: Woman Accused
33: Murders in the Zoo
Under the Tonto Rim
Little Women
34: Scarlet Empress
The Menace
35: The Little Colonel
Konigsmark
36: Ourselves Alone
Sensation
37: Bulldog Drummond at Bay
Bank Holiday (or, Three
on a Weekend)
The Tenth Man
L'Esclave Blanche
Stascera Alle Undice
38: Just Like a Woman
Batticuore
Lightning Conductor

39: White Cargo
40: Mayerling to Sarajevo
Sensation (U.S.)
66: Out of Sight

Jeanette Loff (1906-
1928: Hold 'em, Yale!   S
Black Ace   S
Man-Made Woman   S
Annapolis   SSE
Love over Night   S
29: .45 Calibre War
The Sophomore
The Racketeer
30: Party Girl
King of Jazz
Boudoir Diplomat
Fighting Through
35: Million Dollar Baby
St. Louis Woman

Celia Loftus (1876-1943)
1931: East Lynne
Doctors' Wives
Young Sinners
35: Once in a Blue Moon
39: The Old Maid
On Dress Parade
40: It's a Date
The Blue Bird
Lucky Partners
41: The Black Cat

Ella Logan (1913-1969)
1936: Flying Hostess
37: 52nd Street
Top of the Town
Woman Chases Man
38: Goldwyn Follies

Jacqueline Logan (1900-
1928: Leopard Lady   S
Broadway Daddies   S
Stocks and Blondes   S
River Woman   SSE
Nothing to Wear   S
Midnight Madness   S
The Cop   S
Power   S
Charge of the Gauchos   S

Look-Out Girl   S
29: Ships of the Night   S
The Faker   S
Stark Mad
Bachelor Girl   PT
General Crack

Robert Loggia (1930-
1956: Somebody Up There Likes
Me
57: The Garment Jungle
58: Cop Hater
The Lost Missile
63: Cattle King
69: Che!

Gina Lollobrigida (1928-
1947: Pagliacci
50: Love of a Clown
The City Defends Itself
51: The White Line
Fanfare the Tulip
Time Gone By
52: Belles de Nuit
Tale of Five Women
53: The Young Caruso
The World's Most Beautiful
Woman
54: Beat the Devil
Four Ways Out
Crossed Swords
The Great Game
Beauties of the Night
Bread, Love, and Dreams
55: Wayward Wife
56: Trapeze
Woman of Rome
57: The Hunchback of Notre
Dame
58: Flesh and the Woman
Beautiful but Dangerous
59: Solomon and Sheba
Never so Few
60: Fast and Sexy
Where the Hot Wind Blows!
The Unfaithfuls
61: Go Naked in the World
Come September
Imperial Venus
64: Strange Bedfellows

64: Woman of Straw
65: The Dolls (or, Bambole)
    (M. Cupid seq.)
66: Hotel Paradiso
67: Cervantes
68: The Private Navy of Sgt.
    O'Farrell
69: Assassination Bureau
    A Very Beautiful November
    Me Me Me and the Others
    The Stuntman
    Buona Sera, Mrs. Campbell

Herbert Lom (1917-

1939: Mein Kampf
  42: Tomorrow We Live
      Secret Mission
      Young Mr. Pitt
  43: Dark Tower
  44: Hotel Reserve
  45: The Veil
  46: Night Boat to Dublin
      Appointment with Crime
  47: Dual Alibi
  48: Good Time Girl
      Snowbound
      The Mark of Cain
      The Brass Monkey
  49: The Golden Salamander
  50: State Street
      The Black Rose
  52: The Ringer
      Whispering Smith vs
        Scotland Yard
      Two on the Tiles
      Hell Is Sold Out
      The Gaunt Stranger
  53: Mr. Denny Drives North
      The Paris Express
      Project M-7
      Shoot First
      Rough School
      The Net
      The Love Lottery
      Star of India
      Beautiful Stranger
  54: Twist of Fate
  56: The Ladykillers
      War and Peace
  57: Action of the Tiger

Fire Down Below
58: I Accuse!
    Hell Drivers
    Chase a Crooked Shadow
    Passport to Shame
    No Trees in the Street
    Roots of Heaven
    Intent to Kill
59: Northwest Frontier
    The Big Fisherman
    Third Man on the Mountain
60: Flame over India
    I Aim at the Stars
    Spartacus
61: Mysterious Island
    Mr. Topaza
    El Cid
62: The Frightened City
    I Like Money
    Phantom of the Opera
    The Horse Without a Head
63: Tiara Tahiti
64: A Shot in the Dark
    Uncle Tom's Cabin
65: Return from the Ashes
    Treasure of Silver Lake
66: Gambit
    Bang! Bang! You're Dead!
68: The Assignment
    Ninety-Nine Women
    Eve
    Villa Rides!
69: Doppleganger
    The Happy Ending

Carole Lombard (1909-1942)

1928:	Perfect Crime	PT
	Me, Gangster	SSE
	Show Folks	PT
	Ned McCobb's Daughter	SSE
	Power	S
29:	Dynamite	
	Big News	
	High Voltage	
	Parachute	
30:	Racketeer	
	Fast and Loose	
	The Arizona Kid	
	Safety in Numbers	
31:	It Pays to Advertise	

31: Man of the World
    Ladies' Man
    Up Pops the Devil
    I Take This Woman
32: Virtue
    No One Man
    Sinners in the Sun
    No More Orchids
    No Man of Her Own
    The Match King
33: From Hell to Heaven
    Supernatural
    The Eagle and the Hawk
    White Woman
    Brief Moment
34: Bolero
    We're not Dressing
    Now and Forever
    Twentieth Century
    The Gay Bride
35: Rumba
    Hands Across the Table
36: Love Before Breakfast
    My Man Godfrey
    The Princess Comes
      Across
37: Swing High, Swing Low
    True Confession
    Nothing Sacred
38: Fools for Scandal
39: Made for Each Other
    In Name Only
40: Vigil in the Night
    They Knew What They
      Wanted
41: Mr. and Mrs. North
42: To be or not to be
64: Big Parade of Comedy
    (doc.)

Julie London (1926-
1944: Jungle Woman
  45: Nabonga
    On Stage Everybody!
  46: A Night in Paradise
  47: The Red House
  48: Tap Roots
  49: Task Force
  50: Return of the Frontiers-
      man

51: The Fat Man
55: The Fighting Chance
56: Crime Against Joe
    The Great Man
    A Girl Can t Help it
57: Drango
58: Saddle the Wind
    Voice in the Mirror
    Man of the West
59: The Wonderful Country
    Night of the Quarter Moon
    A Question of Adultery
60: The Third Voice
61: The George Raft Story
    Sanctuary

Tom London (1882-1963)
1929: Border Wildcat   S
      Untamed Justice   S
      Harvest of Hate   S
      Hell's Heroes
      Spell of the Circus
      Lawless Region   S
      The Devil's Twin
      3 serials
  30: Storm
      Firebrand Jordan
      The Woman Racket
      Troopers Three
      Romance of the West
      The Third Alarm
  31: The Secret Six
      Hell Divers
      River's End
      The Men in Her Life
      Dishonored
      Under Texas Skies
      Westbound
      Air Police
      Trails of the Golden West
      Two Gun Man
      Range Law
      Lightnin' Smith Returns
      The Arizona Terror
  32: Freaks
      Without Honor
      Dr. Jekyll and Mr. Hyde
      Night Rider
      Beyond the Rockies
      Gold

32: The Boiling Point
Trailing the Killer
33: Sunset Pass
One Year Later
Iron Master
Outlaw Justice
The Fugitive
34: Mystery Ranch
Outlaw's Highway
Fighting Hero
Burn 'em Up O'Connor
(feature; also as ser.)
35: Toll of the Desert
Tumbling Tumbleweeds
Just My Luck
Sagebrush Troubadour
The Last of the Clintons
Hong Kong Nights
Gun Play
Skull and Crown
36: The Lawless Nineties
Guns and Guitars
O'Malley of the Mounted
The Border Patrolman
Heroes of the Range
37: Bar-Z Bad Men
Law of the Range
Roaring Timber
Springtime in the Rockies
Western Gold
38: Phantom Ranger
Outlaws of Sonora
Prairie Moon
Pioneer Trail
Riders of the Black Hills
Six-Shootin' Sheriff
Santa Fe Stampede
Sunset Trail
39: Song of the Buckaroo
Rollin' Westward
The Renegade Ranger
The Night Riders
Southward Ho!
Mountain Rhythm
Roll, Wagons, Roll!
40: Westbound Stage
Shooting High
Ghost Valley Raiders
Hi-Yo, Silver!
Covered Wagon Days
Wild Horse Range

Stage to Chino
The Kid from Santa Fe
Trailing Double Trouble
Lone Star Raiders
41: Romance of the Rio Grande
Pals of the Pecos
Robbers of the Range
Dude Cowboy
Twilight on the Trail
Stick to Your Guns
Fugitive Valley
Land of the Open Range
42: Arizona Terrors
West of Tombstone
Ghost Town Law
Stardust on the Sage
Down Texas Way
Sons of the Pioneers
American Empire
43: Tenting Tonight on the Old
Camp Ground
Shadows on the Sage
Fighting Frontier
Wild Horse Stampede
Wagon Tracks West
Hail to the Rangers
The Renegade
44: Faces in the Fog
Three Little Sisters
Thoroughbreds
Beneath Western Skies
Yellow Rose of Texas
The San Antonio Kid
Hidden Valley Outlaws
Sheriff of Sundown
Vigilantes of Dodge City
Stagecoach to Monterey
Firebrands of Arizona
Code of the Prairie
The Cheyenne Wildcat
45: Grissly's Millions
Earl Carroll Vanities
Behind City Lights
Three's a Crowd
Sunset in Eldorado
Don't Fence Me in
Corpus Christi Bandits
Marshal of Laredo
The Cherokee Flash
Colorado Pioneers
Wagon Wheels Westward

45: Trail of Kit Carson
The Topeka Terror
Sheriff of Cimarron
Rough Riders of Cheyenne
Oregon Trail
46: Murder in the Music Hall
Sun Valley Cyclone
Passkey to Danger
Sheriff of Redwood Valley
Days of Buffalo Bill
Crime of the Century
California Gold Rush
Alias Billy the Kid
The Undercover Woman
Roll on Texas Moon
The Invisible Informer
Man from Rainbow Valley
Rio Grande Raiders
Red River Renegades
47: Last Frontier Uprising
Homesteaders of Paradise
Valley
Out California Way
Santa Fe Uprising
Saddle Pals
Wyoming
Marshal of Cripple Creek
Rustlers of Devil's Canyon
Along the Oregon Trail
The Wild Frontier
Shootin's Irons
Under Colorado Skies
Code of the Plains
Thunder Gap Outlaws
48: Mark of the Lash
Marshal of Amarillo
49: Red Desert
Sand
Frontier Investigator
South of Rio
San Antone Ambush
Riders of the Sky
Brand of Fear
50: The Old Frontier
The Blazing Sun
51: Rough Riders of Durango
The Secret of Convict Lake
Hills of Utah
52: The Old West
High Noon

Trail Guide
Apache Trail
Blue Canadian Rockies
53: The Marshal's Daughter
Pack Train

Audrey Long (1924-
1944: A Night of Adventure
45: Pan-Americana
47: Song of My Heart
50: David Hardy--Counterspy
Trial Without Jury
The Petty Girl
51: Insurance Investigator
Cavalry Scout
Blue Blood
On the Sunny Side of the
Street
52: Indian Uprising

Richard Long (1927-
1946: Tomorrow Is Forever
The Stranger
The Dark Mirror
47: The Egg and I
48: Tap Roots
49: Crisscross
The Life of Riley
50: Ma and Pa Kettle Go to
Town
Kansas Raiders
51: Ma and Pa Kettle Back
on the Farm
52: Back at the Front
53: All I Desire
All-American
54: Saskatchewan
Return to Treasure Island
Playgirl
55: Cult of the Cobra
56: Fury at Gunsight Pass
He Laughed Last
58: House on Haunted Hill
59: Tokyo after Dark
63: Follow the Boys
64: The Tenderfoot
67: Make Like a Thief

Walter Long (1884-1952)
1928: Grass

862

29: Black Watch
Black Cargoes of the
South Seas   S
30: Beau Bandit
Steel Highway
Conspiracy
31: Sea Devils
The Maltese Falcon
Other Men's Women
Pardon Us
Souls of the Slums
32: Dragnet Patrol
Escapade
Any Old Port
33: Women Won't Tell
34: Six of a Kind
The Live Ghost
Going Bye Bye
35: Drift Fence
The Glory Trail
36: The Bold Caballero
37: Pick a Star
North of the Rio Grande
38: Bar-20 Justice
The Painted Trail
Six-Shootin' Sheriff
Man's Country
39: Wild Horse Canyon
41: Silver Stallion
City of Missing Girls

Richard Loo (c1903-
1933: Secrets of Wu Sin
Bitter Tea of General Yen
37: West of Shanghai
War Lord
The Good Earth
38: Shadows over Shanghai
39: Mr. Wong in Chinatown
Island of Lost Men
Daughter of the Tong
41: Secrets of the Wasteland
42: Little Tokyo, U.S.A.
Bombs over Burma
Across the Pacific
43: The Falcon Strikes Back
Flight for Freedom
China
Yanks Ahoy!
Jack London

44: The Purple Heart
Keys of the Kingdom
The Story of Dr. Wassell
45: God Is My Co-Pilot
Betrayal from the East
China Sky
Back to Bataan
First Yank into Tokyo
Tokyo Rose
Prison Ship
47: Seven Were Saved
The Web of Danger
48: The Cobra Strikes
Half Past Midnight
Rogues' Regiment
49: The Clay Pigeon
State Department File 649
Malaya
51: The Steel Helmet
I Was an American Spy
52: Five Fingers
53: China Adventure
54: Hell and High Water
The Shanghai Story
Living it Up
The Bamboo Prison
55: Soldier of Fortune
Love Is a Many-Splendored
Thing
56: Around the World in 80
Days
Battle Hymn
58: The Quiet American
Hong Kong Affair
61: Seven Women from Hell
62: Confessions of an Opium
Eater
A Girl Named Tamiko
66: The Sand Pebbles
69: Marcus Welby, M.D. (TV
pilot)

Perry Lopez (1931-
1956: The Steel Jungle
57: Omar Khayyam
58: The Deep Six
The Violent Road
59: Cry Tough
61: Man-Trap
62: Taras Bulba

63: McLintock!
66: The Rare Breed
68: Sol Madrid
    The Daring Game
69: Che!
    The Warriors

Trini Lopez (1937-
1966: The Poppy Is Also a
      Flower (TV)
67: The Dirty Dozen

Jack Lord (1930-
1950: Cry Murder
55: The Court-Martial of Billy
    Mitchell
56: The Vagabond King
    The Williamsburg Story
57: Tip of a Dead Jockey
58: The True Story of Lynn
    Stuart
    God's Little Acre
    Man of the West
59: The Hangman
60: Walk Like a Dragon
63: Dr. No
67: The Ride to Hangman's
    Tree
68: The Counterfeit Killer
    The Name of the Game
    Is...Kill
    Hawaii 5-0 (TV pilot)

Marjorie Lord (c1921-
1937: Border Cafe
    Hideaway
    On Again, Off Again
    Forty Naughty Girls
    High Flyers
42: Escape from Hong Kong
    Moonlight in Havana
43: Hi Buddy!
    Shantytown
    Johnny Come Lately
    Flesh and Fantasy
    Sherlock Holmes in
    Washington
47: New Orleans
48: The Argyle Secrets
    The Strange Mrs. Crane

49: Air Hostess
    Masked Raiders
50: Riding High
    The Lost Volcano
    Chain Gang
51: Stop that Cab!
53: Down Laredo Way
    Rebel City
54: Port of Hell
66: Boy, Did I Get a Wrong
    Number!

Pauline Lord (1890-1950)
1934: Mrs. Wiggs of the Cabbage
      Patch

Phillip Lord (Seth Parker)
1932: Way Back Home (or,
      Other People's Business)

Sophia Loren (1934-
1951: Peccato chi Sia una Canaglia
      La Fortuna di Essere Donna
      A Husband for Cynthia
52: Africa Beneath the Seas
    Village of the Bells
    Good People's Sunday
    Neapolitan Carousel (Post-
    cards from Naples Cameo
    seq.; rel. in '61)
    A Day in Court
53: The Sign of Venus
54: Aida
    Girls Marked Danger
    Two Nights with Cleopatra
    (rel. in U.S. in '63)
    Our Times
55: Too Bad She's Bad
57: The Pride and the Passion
    Gold of Naples (Pizza on
    Credit seq.)
    Legend of the Lost
    Boy on a Dolphin
    Scandal in Sorrento
    The Miller's Beautiful Wife
    Woman of the River
    Lucky to be a Woman
58: Attila, Scourge of God
    Desire under the Elms
    Houseboat

864

58: The Key
59: Black Orchid
    That Kind of Woman
    The Anatomy of Love
    (The Camera seq.)
60: A Breath of Scandal
    Heller in Pink Tights
    It Started in Naples
61: Two Women (OSCAR)
    The Millionairess
    El Cid
62: Boccaccio 70 (The
    Raffle seq.)
    The Knife in the Wound
63: Madame (or, Sans Gene)
    Five Miles to Midnight
    The Condemned of Altona
64: Fall of the Roman Empire
    Yesterday, Today, and
    Tomorrow (all 3 seq.)
    Marriage--Italian Style
65: Operation Crossbow (or,
    The Great Spy Mission)
    A Day in Court
66: Judith
    Arabesque
    Lady L
67: The Countess from Hong
    Kong
    More than a Miracle
    Once Upon a Time
68: The Best House in Naples
69: Giovanni
    Ghosts--Italian Style
    This Ecstasy Business
    TheSunflowers
    White, Red, Green

Jon Lormer
1958: Rally 'Round the Flag,
    Boys!
    I Want to Live!
    The Hell Bent Kid
    Take Five from Five
    The Matchmaker
59: Career
    The Gazebo
60: Polyanna
    Where the Boys Are
61: Ada

Commancheros
The Second Time Around
62: Brush Fire!
    The Wonderful World of
    the Brothers Grimm
64: Youngblood Hawke
    The Tiger Walks
    Dead Ringer
    Kisses for My President
    Mountain of Fire
65: One Man's Way (or, The
    Norman Vincent Peale
    Story)
    Two on a Guillotine
    Zebra in the Kitchen
66: The Singing Nun
    A Fine Madness
    Dimension Five
    Three for a Marriage
    The Sand Pebbles

Marion Lorne (1888-1968)
1955: The Girl Rush
67: The Graduate

Peter Lorre (1905-1964)
1931: M
    Thirteen Trunks of Mr.
    O. F.
    White Demon
    De Haute à Bas
    The Man Who Knew too
    Much
33: F. P. No. 1
35: Mad Love
    Crime and Punishment
36: Hidden Power
    Secret Agent
    Crack-Up
37: Nancy Steele Is Missing
    Think Fast, Mr. Moto
    Lancer Spy
    Thank You, Mr. Moto
38: Mr. Moto Takes a Chance
    Mr. Moto's Gamble
    Mysterious Mr. Moto of
    Devil's Island
    I'll Give a Million
    Mr. Moto Takes a Vacation
39: Mr. Moto on Danger Island

865

39: Mr. Moto's Last Warning
40: Strange Cargo
I Was an Adventuress
Island of Doomed Men
The Stranger on the Third
Floor
You'll Find Out
41: The Face Behind the Mask
Mr. District Attorney
They Met in Bombay
The Maltese Falcon
42: All Through the Night
The Invisible Agent
The Boogie Man Will Get
You
Casablanca
In This Our Life (seq. of
The Maltese Falcon)
43: The Constant Nymph
The Cross of Lorraine
Background to Danger
44: Passage to Marseilles
Mask of Dimitrios
The Conspirators
Arsenic and Old Lace
Hollywood Canteen
45: Hotel Berlin
Confidential Agent
46: Three Strangers
The Beast with Five
Fingers
The Verdict
The Black Angel
The Chase
47: My Favorite Brunette
48: Casbah
The Lone One
49: Rope of Sand
50: Quicksand
51: Double Confession
54: Beat the Devil
20,000 Leagues Under the
Sea
56: Around the World in 80
Days
Congo Crossing
57: The Story of Mankind
Silk Stockings
The Buster Keaton Story
The Sad Sack

Hellship Mutiny
59: The Big Circus
60: Scent of Mystery
61: Voyage to the Bottom of
the Sea
62: Five Weeks in a Balloon
Tales of Terror
63: The Raven
Comedy of Terrors
64: The Patsy
Muscle Beach Party

Joan Lorring (1931-
1944: A Song of Russia
The Bridge of San Luis Rey
45: The Corn Is Green
46: The Verdict
Three Strangers
47: The Other Love
The Gangster
The Lost Moment
48: Good Sam
51: The Big Night
53: Stranger on the Prowl

Tilly Losch (1902-
1936: The Garden of Allah
37: The Good Earth
46: Duel in the Sun

Jackie Loughery (1930-
1955: The Naked Street
56: Pardners
57: The D.I.
Eighteen and Anxious
58: The Hot Angel

Anita Louise (1915-
1929: Wonder of Women
Square Shoulders   PT
30: Just Like Heaven
What a Man!
Floradora Girl
The Third Alarm
31: The Great Meadow
Marriage Playground
Millie
Madame Julie
Marriage Interlude
Fraternity House

866

31: Are These Our Children?
32: Pack Up Your Troubles
Phantom of Crestwood
Heaven on Earth
Everything's Rosie
Woman Between
Duck Soup
33: Our Betters
34: The Most Precious Thing
in Life
Are We Civilized?
Madame DuBarry
The Firebrand
Cross Streets
Bachelor of Arts
I Give My Love
Judge Priest
35: A Midsummer Night's
Dream
Personal Maid's Secret
Lady Tubbs
Here's to Romance
The Story of Louis Pasteur
36: Brides Are Like that
Anthony Adverse
37: Green Light
Call It a Day
The Go-Getter
That Certain Woman
First Lady
Tovarich
38: Marie Antoinette
My Bill
Going Places
The Sisters
39: The Little Princess
The Gorilla
These Glamour Girls
Main Street Lawyer
Reno
Hero for a Day
The Personality Kid
40: Wagons Westward
The Villain Still Pursued
Her
Glamour for Sale
41: Two in a Taxi
Harmon of Michigan
The Phantom Submarine
43: Dangerous Blondes

44: Nine Girls
Casanova Brown
45: The Fighting Guardsman
Love Letters
46: Bandit of Sherwood Forest
The Devil's Mask
Shadows
The Swan Song
47: Bulldog Drummond at Bay
Blondie's Big Moment
Shadowed
Blondie's Holiday
52: Retreat, Hell!

Tina Louise (1935-
1955: Kismet
58: God's Little Acre
59: Day of the Outlaw
The Trap
The Hangman
60: The Warrior's Empress
61: Armored Command
Garibaldi
62: Siege of Syracuse
64: For Those Who Think
Young
68: The Wrecking Crew
69: House of Seven Joys
How to Commit Marriage
The Good Guys and the
Bad Guys
The Happy Ending

Bessie Love (1891-
1929: Broadway Melody
Hollywood Revue of 1929
The Idle Rich
Road Show
30: Girl in the Snow
Good News
Chasing Rainbows
Conspiracy
They Learned about Women
See America Thirst
The Swell Head
31: Morals for Women
35: The Old Curiosity Shop
41: Live Again
Atlantic Fury
42: Journey Together

47:	Idol of Paris		Dream Mother
51:	No Highway in the Sky		The Engineer's Daughter
52:	The Magic Box		Love Bound
54:	The Barefoot Contessa		Out of Singapore
55:	Too Young to Love		Midnight Lady
56:	Touch and Go		The Broadway Tornado
57:	The Story of Esther	33:	His Double Life
	Costello	34:	The Menace
58:	No Where to Go		Limehouse Blues
60:	Next to no Time	35:	Clive of India
61:	Loss of Innocence		The Crusades
	The Roman Spring of		The Man Who Broke the
	Mrs. Stone		Bank at Monte Carlo°
64:	Children of the Damned	36:	Country Doctor
66:	Promise Her Anything		Sing, Baby, Sing
67:	The Battle Beneath the		Reunion
	Earth		Lloyds of London
68:	Hot Millions		One in a Million
69:	Loves of Isadora		Sutter's Gold

Montague Love (1877-1943)

				White Angel
1928:	The Haunted House	SSE		Hi Gaucho!
29:	Divine Lady	SSE		Champagne Charlie
	Her Private Life		37:	The Prince and the Pauper
	A Most Immoral Lady			The Life of Emile Zola
	Synthetic Sin	S		Tovarich
	Mysterious Island	PT		Parnell
	Charming Sinners			London by Night
	Midstream	PT		The Prisoner of Zenda
	Bulldog Drummond			A Damsel in Distress
	The Last Warning	PT	38:	The Adventure's End
	Silks and Saddles			The Buccaneer
	The Voice Within			Adventures of Robin Hood
30:	Love Comes Along			Professor Beware!
	The Cat Creeps			Kidnapped
	Kismet			If I Were King
	Back Pay		39:	Gunga Din!
	A Notorious Affair			Juarez
	Double Cross Roads			Man in the Iron Mask
	The Furies			Rulers of the Sea
	Reno			We Are not Alone
	Inside the Lines		40:	Northwest Passage
	Outward Bound			Son of Monte Cristo
	a short			The Story of Dr. Ehrlich's
31:	Lion and the Lamb			Magic Bullet
	Alexander Hamilton			All This and Heaven Too
32:	Stowaway			The Sea Hawk
	The Fighting Tornado			A Dispatch from Reuter's
	Vanity Fair			The Lone Wolf Strikes
	The Silver Lining			Private Affairs
				Northwest Mounted Police
				Mark of Zorro

40: Hudson's Bay
41: The Devil and Miss Jones
Shining Victory
Lady for a Night
The Remarkable Andrew
42: Sherlock Holmes and the
Voice of Terror
Tennessee Johnson
Devotion
43: Forever and a Day
The Constant Nymph
Holy Matrimony

Phyllis Love (1925-
1956: Friendly Persuasion
61: The Young Doctors

Frank Lovejoy (1914-1962)
1948: Black Bart
49: Home of the Brave
50: South Sea Sinner
In a Lonely Place
Three Secrets
Breakthrough
Try and Get Me (or, The
Sound of Fury)
51: Force of Arms
I Was a Communist for
the FBI
Goodbye My Fancy
Starlift
I'll See You in My Dreams
52: Retreat, Hell!
The Winning Team
53: The Hitchhiker
House of Wax
The System
She's Back on Broadway
Charge at Feather River
54: Beachhead
Men of the Fighting Lady
55: The Americano
Top of the World
Mad at the World
Finger Man
The Crooked Web
Shack Out on 101
Strategic Air Command
56: Julie
Country Husband

57: Three Brave Men
58: Cole Younger--Gunfighter

Celia Lovsky
1947: The Foxes of Harrow
48: Sealed Verdict
49: Flaming Fury
50: The Killer that Stalked
New York
Captain Carey, U.S.A.
51: Night into Morning
The Scarf
52: Because You're Mine
54: Rhapsody
The Last Time I Saw Paris
55: New York Confidential
Foxfire
Duel on the Mississippi
56: Death of a Scoundrel
Rumble on the Docks
57: The Garment Jungle
Trooper Hook
The Man of a Thousand
Faces
58: Crash Landing
Twilight for the Gods
Me and the Colonel
I, Mobster
59: The Gene Krupa Story
62: Hitler
64: Thirty-Six Hours
65: Harlow (MTC)
67: The St. Valentine's Day
Massacre
68: The Power

Edmund Lowe (1892-
1929: In Old Arizona
The Cockeyed World
This Thing Called Love
Through Different Eyes
Making the Grade   PT
30: The Painted Angel
Bad One
Born Reckless
Good Intentions
Happy Days
Men on Call
More than a Kiss
Scotland Yard

869

30: Part Time Wife
The Spreading Dawn
31: Women of All Nations
The Spider
The Cisco Kid
Don't Bet on Women
Transatlantic
32: Attorney for the Defense
Guilty as Hell
Chandu the Magician
Misleading Lady
American Madness
The Devil Is Driving
33: Hot Pepper
I Love that Man
Her Bodyguard
Dinner at Eight
34: Let's Fall in Love
No More Women
The Bombay Mail
Gift of Gab
35: Under Pressure
The Great Hotel Murder
Black Sheep
Mr. Dynamite
The Best Man Wins
Thunder in the Night
King Solomon of Broad-
way
The Great Impersonation
36: The Grand Exit
The Wrecker
The Garden Murder Case
Mad Holiday
Doomed Cargo
Girl on the Front Page
37: Under Cover of Night
Espionage
The Squealer
Every Day's a Holiday
Murder on Diamond Row
38: Secrets of a Nurse
39: The Witness Vanishes
Our Neighbors--The Carters
Newsboys' Home
40: The Crooked Road
Honeymoon Deferred
I Love You Again
Men Against the Sky
41: Double Date

Flying Cadets
42: Call Out the Marines
Klondike Fury
43: Dangerous Blonde
Oh, What a Night!
Murder in Times Square
44: Girl in the Case
45: Dillinger
Enchanted Forest
The Great Mystic
46: The Strange Mr. Gregory
48: Good Sam
56: Around the World in 80
Days
57: Wings of the Eagles
58: The Last Hurrah
59: Plunderers of Painted
Flats
60: Heller in Pink Tights

Robert Lowery (1916-
1937: Wake Up and Live
Life Begins in College
38: Passport Husband
Submarine Patrol
39: Young Mr. Lincoln
Charlie Chan in Reno
Hollywood Cavalcade
Drums Along the Mohawk
Mr. Moto in Danger Island
40: City of Chance
Free, Blonde, and Twenty-
One
Shooting High
Star Dust
Charlie Chan's Murder
Cruise
Four Sons
Maryland
Mark of Zorro
Murder over New York
41: Ride on, Vaquero!
Private Nurse
Cadet Girl
42: Who Is Hope Schuyler?
She's in the Army
Criminal Investigator
Lure of the Islands
Rhythm Parade
Dawn on the Great Divide

43: The Immortal Sergeant
Tarzan's Desert Mystery
So's Your Uncle
The North Star
Campus Rhythm
Revenge of the Zombies
44: The Navy Way
Hot Rhythm
Dark Mountain
Dangerous Passage
The Mummy's Ghost
Mystery of the River
Boat (ser.)
45: Thunderbolt
Homesick Angel
Road to Alcatraz
Fashion Model
Highpowered
Prison Ship
The Monster and the Ape
46: Sensation Hunters
They Made Me a Killer
House of Horrors
God's Country
Lady Chaser
The Gas House Kids
47: Big Town
Danger Street
I Cover Big Town
Killer at Large
Queen of the Amazons
Death Valley
Jungle Flight
48: Mary Lou
Heart of Virginia
Highway 13
49: Shep Comes Home
Arson, Inc.
The Dalton Gang
Batman and Robin (ser.)
New Adventures of Batman
(ser.)
50: Gunfire
Border Rangers
Western Pacific Agent
Train to Tombstone
Everybody's Dancing
51: Crosswinds
53: Jalopy
Cow Country

The Homesteaders
55: Lay the Rifle Down
57: The Parson and the Outlaw
60: Rise and Fall of Legs
Diamond
62: When the Girls Take Over
The Deadly Duo
Young Guns of Texas
63: McLintock!
64: Stage to Thunder Rock
65: A Zebra in the Kitchen
66: Johnny Reno
Pride of Virginia
67: The Adventures of Batman
and Robin
The Undertaker and His
Pals
69: The Ballad of Josie

Myrna Loy (1905-
1929: Evidence
Show of Shows
Fancy Baggage   PT
Noah's Ark   PT
Desert Song
The Black Watch
Hard-Boiled Rose   PT
The Squall
King of the Khyber Rifles
30: The Great Divide
Bride of the Regiment
Rogue of the Rio Grande
A Night in Cairo
Crooks in Clover
Isle of Escape
Last of the Duanes
31: The Naughty Flirt
Cameo Kirby
Cock o' the Walk
Under a Texas Moon
Outward Bound
The Truth about Youth
Renegades
Rebound
Body and Soul
Transatlantic
Hush Money
Skyline
Consolation Marriage
A Connecticut Yankee

32: Emma
The Devil to Pay
Wet Parade
Woman in Room 13
Arrowsmith
Vanity Fair
Love Me Tonight
Thirteen Women
The Mask of Fu Manchu
The Animal Kingdom
33: The Barbarian
The Prizefighter and the
Lady
Penthouse
Topaze
When Ladies Meet
Night Flight
34: Men in White
Stamboul Quest
Broadway Bill
The Thin Man
Evelyn Prentice
Manhattan Melodrama
35: Wings in the Dark
Whipsaw
36: Wife versus Secretary
After the Thin Man
To Mary with Love
Petticoat Fever
The Great Ziegfeld
Libeled Lady
37: Parnell
Double Wedding
38: Man-Proof
Test Pilot
Too Hot to Handle
39: Lucky Night
The Rains Came
Another Thin Man
40: Third Finger, Left Hand
I Love You Again
41: Shadow of the Thin Man
Love Crazy
44: The Thin Man Goes Home
45: A Genius in the Family
46: The Best Years of Our
Lives
So Goes My Love
47: The Bachelor and the
Bobby-Soxer

Song of the Thin Man
48: Mr. Blanding Builds His
Dream House
49: The Red Pony
50: Cheaper by the Dozen
If this be Sin
52: Belles on Their Toes
56: The Ambassador's Daughter
58: Lonelyhearts
60: From the Terrace
Midnight Lace
64: Big Parade of Comedy
(doc.)
69: The April Fools

Wilfrid Lucas (d. 1940)
1930: Hello, Sister
Cock o' the Walk
The Arizona Kid
Those Who Dance
Just Imagine
Madam Satan
31: Dishonored
Young Donovan's Kid
Pardon Us
Convicted
32: Cross Examination
Midnight Patrol
The Tenderfoot
The Unwritten Law
33: Racetrack
Sister to Judas
Lucky Larrigan
The Intruder
Fra Diavolo (or, The Devil's
Brother)
Phantom Thunderbolt
I Cover the Waterfront
The Big Game
Breed of the Border
Strange People
The Sphinx
Notorious but Nice
Day of Reckoning
34: The Moth
Count of Monte Cristo
36: Chatterbox
Modern Times
Mary of Scotland
37: Criminal Lawyer

37:	Mile a Minute Love			50 Million Frenchmen
38:	The Baroness and the Butler			Broadminded
				Black Camel
	Crime Afloat		32:	Chandu the Magician
40:	A Chump at Oxford			Murders in the Rue Morgue
	Brother Orchid			White Zombie
	Ragtime Cowboy Joe			The Phantom Creeps (ser.)
	Triple Justice			The Yellow Phantom (ser.)
			33:	Island of Lost Souls

Jack Luden (1902-

1928:	Partners in Crime	S		International House
	Woman from Moscow	S		Night of Terror
	Sins of the Father	S		Whispering Shadow (ser.)
	Fools for Luck	S	34:	The Death Kiss
	Forgotten Faces	S	34:	The Black Cat
	Under the Tonto Rim	S		The Gift of Gab
				Return of Chandu (ser.)
29:	Wild Party		35:	The Best Man Wins
	Wolf of Wall Street			The Raven
	Innocents of Paris			Mark of the Vampire (ser.)
	Dangerous Curves			Mysterious Mr. Wong
	Why Bring that Up?			Murder by Television
30:	Young Eagles			Mystery of the Marie
36:	King of the Royal Mounted			Celeste
38:	Pioneer Trail			Mandrake the Magician (ser.)
	Phantom Gold			(ser.)
39:	Susannah of the Mounties			Chandu on the Magic Isle
	Rolling Caravan			(ser.)
43:	Guadalcanal Diary		36:	The Invisible Ray
44:	Bordertown Trail			S.O.S. Coast Guard
				Postal Inspector

Laurette Luez

1950:	Kim			Shadow of Chinatown (ser.)
	Killer Shark		37:	Blake of Scotland Yard (ser.)
51:	Prehistoric Woman			Phantom Ship
52:	African Treasure		38:	Killer Rats
53:	Siren of Bagdad		39:	Son of Frankenstein
54:	Adventures of Hajji Baba			The Gorilla
	Jungle Gents			Ninotchka
			40:	Fantasia (voice)

Bela Lugosi (1882-1956)

1928:	Viennese Nights			The Saint's Double Trouble
29:	The Thirteenth Chair			You'll Find Out
	Prisoners	PT	41:	Black Friday
	The Veiled Woman		41:	The East Side Meet Bela
30:	Renegades			Lugosi
	Such Women Are Dangerous			Devil Bat
	Oh, What a Man!			Wolf Man
	Wild Company			The Human Monster
31:	Women of All Nations			The Invisible Ghost
	Dracula			Spooks Run Wild
			42:	Black Dragons

42: The Corpse Vanishes
Night Monster
The Ghost of Frankenstein
Bowery at Midnight
The Phantom Killer
43: Ghosts on the Loose
The Ape Man
Frankenstein Meets the
Wolf Man
Eyes of the Underworld
Return of the Vampire
44: One Body too Many
The Black Parachute
Voodoo Man
Return of the Ape Man
45: Zombies on Broadway
The Body Snatcher
46: Genius at Work
My Son, the Vampire
47: Scared to Death
48: Abbott & Costello Meet
Frankenstein
49: Master Minds
52: Old Mother Riley Meets
the Vampire
Bela Lugosi Meets the
Brooklyn Gorilla
Bela Lugosi Meets the
Boys from Brooklyn
53: King Robot (unrel.)
Glen or Glenda
56: Bride of the Monster
Black Sheep
He Lived to Kill
The Shadow Creeps
59: Plan 9 from Outer Space
63: My Son the Vampire
65: The World of Abbott &
Costello

Paul Lukas (1894-
1928: Loves of an Actress
Three Sinners
Woman from Moscow
Hot News
Manhattan Cocktail
Two Lovers
The Night Watch
29: Illusion
Wolf of Wall Street
Half Way to Heaven

Shopworn Angel
30: Behind the Make-Up
The Benson Murder Case
The Devil's Holiday
Slightly Scarlet
Young Eagles
Grumpy
Anybody's Woman
The Right to Love
31: Beloved Bachelor
Women Love Once
Unfaithful
City Streets
Working Girls
Strictly Dishonorable
Vice Squad
32: No One Man
Tomorrow and Tomorrow
Downstairs
Burnt Offering
Rockabye
A Passport to Hell
Thunder Below
33: Grand Slam
Kiss Before the Mirror
Captured!
Sing, Sinner, Sing
Secret of the Blue Room
Little Women
34: By Candlelight
Nagana
Countess of Monte Cristo
Glamour
Affairs of a Gentleman
I Give My Love
Gift of Gab
35: Father Brown, Detective
The Casino Murder Case
The Three Musketeers
I Found Stella Parrish
Age of Indiscretion
36: Dodsworth
Ladies in Love
37: Espionage
Dinner at the Ritz
Mutiny of the Elsinore
38: Dangerous Secrets
Rebellious Daughters
The Lady Vanishes
39: Confessions of a
Nazi Spy

39: Captain Fury
40: Strange Cargo
The Ghost Breakers
Window in London
41: The Monster and the Girl
The Chinese Den
42: They Dare not Love
Lady in Distress
43: Watch on the Rhine
(OSCAR)
Hostages
44: Uncertain Glory
Address Unknown
One Man's Secret
Experiment Perilous
46: Deadline at Dawn
Temptation
48: Berlin Express
50: Kim
54: 20,000 Leagues Under the
Sea
56: The Chinese Bungalow
57: Under Fire
58: Roots of Heaven
60: Scent of Mystery
62: The Four Horsemen of
the Apocalypse
63: 55 Days at Peking
Fun in Acapulco
65: Lord Jim
68: Sol Madrid

Key Luke (1911-
1931: Charlie Chan Carries on
32: Charlie Chan's Chance
33: Charlie Chan's Greatest
Case
34: Charlie Chan's Courage
Charlie Chan in London
35: Charlie Chan in Shanghai
The Painted Veil
Oil for the Lamps of
China
Charlie Chan in Paris
Charlie Chan in Egypt
Shanghai
Mad Love
36: Charlie Chan at the Race-
track
Charlie Chan at the Circus

Charlie Chan's Secret
Charlie Chan at the Opera
37: The Good Earth
Charlie Chan in Monte
Carlo
Charlie Chan on Broadway
Charlie Chan at the
Olympics
38: International Settlement
Mr. Moto's Gamble
Charlie Chan in Honolulu
39: Charlie Chan in Reno
Charlie Chan on Treasure
Island
Charlie Chan in the City
of Darkness
Disputed Passage
Barricade
North of Shanghai
40: Sued for Libel
Charlie Chan in Panama
Charlie Chan's Murder
Cruise
Charlie Chan at the Wax
Museum
41: The Gang's all Here
Let's Go Collegiate
Bowery Blitzkrieg
Burma Convoy
No Hands on the Clock
Mr. and Mrs. North
Charlie Chan in Rio
42: Across the Pacific
A Yank on the Burma Road
A Tragedy at Midnight
North to the Klondike
Spy Ship
The Falcon's Brother
Destination Unknown
Dr. Gillespie's New Assist-
ant
43: Dr. Gillespie's Criminal
Case
Salute to the Marines
44: Charlie Chan in the Secret
Service
Dragon Seed
Three Men in White
Andy Hardy's Blonde
Trouble

875

44: Between Two Women
45: First Yank in Tokyo
     Tokyo Rose
     How Do You Do?
47: Dark Illusion
48: Waterfront at Midnight
     Sleep My Love
49: The Feathered Serpent
     Sky Dragons
53: Fair Winds to Java
54: Hell's Half Acre
     The World for Ransom
     Bamboo Prison
55: Love Is a Many-Splendor-
     ed Thing
56: Around the World in 80
     Days
     Their Greatest Glory
57: Battle Hell
     The Yangste Incident
68: Nobody's Perfect
69: Project X
     The Chairman

Dayton Lummis
1954: Loophole
     Dragon's Gold
     Return to Treasure Island
     The Yellow Mountain
55: Prince of Players
     The Prodigal
     High Society
     View from Pompey's
     Head
     The Court-Martial of
     Billy Mitchell
     Sudden Danger
     The Spoilers
56: Over-Exposed
     A Day of Fury
     The First Texan
     Showdown at Abilene
57: The Wrong Man
     Monkey on My Back
60: The Music Box Kid
     Spartacus
61: The Flight that Dis-
     appeared
62: Deadly Duo
     Jack the Giant Killer

Beauty and the Beast

Barbara Luna
1959: Cry Tough
61: Devil at Four O'Clock
62: Five Weeks in a Balloon
63: Dime with a Halo
64: Mail Order Bride
65: Synanon
     Ship of Fools
67: Winchester 73 (TV)
68: Firecreek
69: Che!
     King Gun

John Lund (1913-
1946: To Each His Own
47: The Perils of Pauline
     Variety Girl
48: The Night Has a Thousand
     Eyes
     A Foreign Affair
     Miss Tatlock's Millions
49: Bride of Vengeance
     My Friend Irma
50: My Friend Irma Goes
     West
     The Duchess of Idaho
     No Man of Her Own
51: The Mating Season
     Darling, How Could You?
52: Steel Town
     Bronco Buster
     Battle of Apache Pass
     Just Across the Street
53: The Woman They Almost
     Lynched
     Latin Lovers
55: Chief Crazy Horse
     White Feather
     Five Guns West
     Hell's Outpost
56: Battle Stations
     High Society
     The Dakota Incident
57: Affair in Reno
60: The Wackiest Ship in the
     Army
62: If a Man Answers

876

William Lundigan (1914-
1937: Armored Car
The Lady Fights Back
38: Black Doll
State Police
Reckless Living
Wives Under Suspicion
Danger on the Air
Missing Guest
Freshman Year
That's My Story!
39: Three Smart Girls Grow
Up
Forgotten Woman
They Asked for it
Legion of Lost Flyers
Dodge City
The Old Maid
40: The Fighting 69th
Three Cheers for the Irish
The Man Who Talked too
Much
The Sea Hawk
East of the River
Santa Fe Trail
a short
41: The Case of the Black
Parrot
A Shot in the Dark
The Great Mr. Nobody
The Bugle Sounds
Highway West
International Squadron
Sailors on Leave
42: The Courtship of Andy
Hardy
The Sunday Punch
Apache Trail
Northwest Rangers
Andy Hardy's Double Life
43: Dr. Gillespie's Criminal
Case
Salute to the Marines
Headin' for God's Country
45: What Next, Corporal
Hargrove?
47: The Fabulous Dorseys
Dishonored Lady
48: Inside Story
Mystery in Mexico

49: State Department File 649
Follow Me Quickly
Pinky
50: I'll Get By
Mother Didn't Tell Me
51: I'd Climb the Highest
Mountain
The House on Telegraph
Hill
Love Nest
Elopement
53: Down Among the Sheltering
Palms
Serpent of the Nile
Inferno
54: Riders to the Stars
Terror Ship
White Orchid
62: The Underwater City
67: The Way West
68: Where Angels Go, Trouble
Follows

Ida Lupino (1916-
1932: Her First Affair
Money for Speed
High Finance
Prince of Arcadia
I Lived with You
The Ghost Camera
34: Search for Beauty
Come on, Marines!
Ready for Love
35: Peter Ibbetson
Paris in Spring
Smart Girl
36: The Gay Desperado
Yours for the Asking
One Rainy Afternoon
Anything Goes
Coast Patrol
Tops Is the Limit
Weather or No
37: Sea Devils
Let's Get Married
Artists and Models
Fight for Your Lady
39: The Lady and the Mob
The Light that Failed
The Lone Wolf Spy Hunt

39: The Adventures of
    Sherlock Holmes
40: They Drive by Night
41: High Sierra
    Out of the Fog
    Ladies in Retirement
42: Moontide
    The Hard Way
    Life Begins at 8:30
43: Forever and a Day
    Thank Your Lucky Stars
44: In Our Time
    Hollywood Canteen
    The Very Thought of You
45: Pillow to Post
46: Devotion
    Escape Me Never
47: The Man I Love
    Deep Valley
48: Road House
    The Queen's Necklace
49: For Those Who Dare
    Woman in Hiding
    Lust for Gold
    Not Wanted
50: Never Fear
    Outrage
51: Hard, Fast, and Beautiful
    On Dangerous Ground
52: Beware, My Lovely
53: Jennifer
    The Bigamist
54: Private Hell No. 36
55: Women's Prison
    The Big Knife
56: While the City Sleeps
    Strange Intruder
66: Trouble with Angels (dir.)
69: I Love a Mystery (TV
    pilot)
    Backtrack

John Lupton
1951: Shadow in the Sky
52: Rogue's March
53: Scandal at Scourie
    All the Brothers Were
    Valiant
    Escape from Fort Bravo
54: Dragonfly Squadron

    Prisoner of War
55: Battle Cry
    Diane
    Man with the Gun
56: Glory
    The Great Locomotive
    Chase
57: Drango
    Taming Sutton's Gal
58: Gun Fever
59: The Man in the Net
    The Rebel Set
    Blood and Steel
60: Three Came to Kill
62: The Clown and the Kid
65: The Greatest Story Ever
    Told
66: Jesse James Meets
    Frankenstein's Daughter

Peter Lupus (1937-
1964: Muscle Beach Party
    Hercules and the Tyrants
    of Babylon
    Goliath at the Conquest
    of Damascus
    The Gladiator Who
    Challenged an Empire

Freeman Lusk
1951: Little Egypt
52: Phone Call from a
    Stranger
53: The Caddy

Jimmy Lydon (1923-
1939: Back Door to Heaven
    Two Thoroughbreds
40: Tom Brown's School Days
    Little Men
41: Bowery Boy
    Naval Academy
    Henry Aldrich for President
42: Henry and Dizzy
    Cadets on Parade
    Henry Aldrich, Editor
43: Henry Aldrich Haunts a
    House
    Henry Aldrich Swings it
    Henry Aldrich Gets Glamour

878

44: Henry Aldrich, Boy Scout
My Best Gal
Henry Aldrich Plays Cupid
Henry Aldrich's Little
    Secret
When the Lights Go on
    Again
The Town Went Wild
45: Strange Illusion
Twice Blessed
46: Affairs of Geraldine
47: Cynthia
Life with Father
Sweet Genevieve
48: Blazing Across the Pecos
The Time of Your Life
Out of the Storm
Joan of Arc
An Old-Fashioned Girl
49: Bad Boy
Miss Mink of 1949
Tucson
50: When Willie Comes
    Marching Home
Destination Big House
Hot Rod
The Magnificent Yankee
September Affair
51: Oh, Susanna!
Gasoline Alley
52: Corky of Gasoline Alley
53: Island in the Sky
54: Desperado
56: Battle Stations
57: Chain of Evidence
60: The Hypnotic Eye
I Passed for White
61: The Last Time I Saw
    Archie
65: Brainstorm
69: Death of a Gunfighter

Ken Lynch
1958: Run Silent, Run Deep
Voice in the Mirror
Young and Wild
Man or Gun
I Married a Monster from
    Outer Space
Unwed Mother

59: Pork Chop Hill
The Legend of Tom Dooley
Anatomy of a Murder
North by Northwest
60: Seven Days from Sundown
The Dark at the Top of
    the Stairs
61: Portrait of a Mobster
The Honeymoon Machine
62: Walk on the Wild Side
The Days of Wine and
    Roses
64: Dead Ringer
FBI Code 48
Apache Rifles
Dear Heart
65: Dr. Terror's House of
    Horrors
66: Mr. Buddwing

Paul Lynde (1926-
1954: New Faces (dir.)
63: Son of Flubber
Bye Bye, Birdie
Under the Yum-Yum Tree
64: For Those Who Think Young
Send Me no Flowers
65: Beach Blanket Bingo
66: The Glass Bottom Boat
67: The Silent Treatment
68: How Sweet it Is

Carol Lynley (1942-
1958: Light in the Forest
59: Holiday for Lovers
Blue Denim
Hound-Dog Man
61: Return to Peyton Place
The Last Sunset
63: The Stripper
Under the Yum-Yum Tree
The Cardinal
64: Shock Treatment
The Pleasure Seekers
65: Bunny Lake Is Missing
Harlow (Magna)
67: The Shuttered Room
68: Danger Route
Shadow on the Land
Sudden Death

68: The Smugglers (TV)
    You Can't Win 'em All
69: The Immortal (TV)
    The Maltese Bippy
    Norwood

Betty Lynn
1948: June Bride
51: Payment on Demand
56: Meet Me in Las Vegas
    Behind the High Wall
57: Gun for a Coward

Diana Lynn (1926-
1940: There's Magic in Music
41: The Hard Boiled Canary
42: The Major and the Minor
    Star-Spangled Rhythm
43: Henry Aldrich Gets
    Glamour
44: The Miracle of Morgan's
    Creek
    Henry Aldrich Plays Cupid
    Four Angels
    And the Angels Sing
    Our Hearts Were Young
    and Gay
45: Out of this World
    Duffy's Tavern
46: Our Hearts Were Growing
    Up
    The Bride Wore Boots
47: Variety Girl
    Easy Come, Easy Go
48: Ruthless
    Texas, Brooklyn, and
    Heaven
    Every Girl Should be
    Married
49: My Friend Irma
50: Paid in Full
    Rogues of Sherwood Forest
    My Friend Irma Goes West
    Peggy
51: Bedtime for Bonzo
    Take Care of My Little
    Girl
    The People Against O'Hara
52: Meet Me at the Fair
53: Plunder of the Sun
54: Track of the Cat

55: An Annapolis Story
    You're Never too Young
    The Kentuckian

Emmett Lynn
1942: Stagecoach Express
    Westward Ho!
    In Old California
    Baby Face Morgan
    Tomorrow We Live
    City of Silent Men
    Queen of Broadway
43: The Sundown Kid
    Girls in Chains
    Dead Man's Gulch
    Carson City Cyclone
    The Law Rides Again
44: Good Night, Sweetheart
    Outlaws of Santa Fe
    Frontier Outlaws
    Return of the Rangers
    Cowboy Canteen
    When the Light Go on
    Again
    The Laramie Trail
    Bluebeard
    The Town Went Wild
    Swing Hostess
45: Song of Old Wyoming
    Shadow of Terror
46: The Caravan Trail
    Romance of the West
    Throw a Saddle on a Star
    Man from Rainbow Valley
    The Fighting Frontiersmen
    Stagecoach to Denver
    Santa Fe Uprising
    Landrush
    Conquest of Cheyenne
47: Code of the West
    Oregon Trail Scouts
    Rustlers of Devil's Canyon
48: Relentless
    West of Sonora
    Grand Canyon Trail
49: Ride, Ryder, Ride!
    Roll, Thunder, Roll!
    The Fighting Redhead
50: Cowboy and the Prizefighter
51: Badman's Gold
    Best of the Bad Men

52: Oklahoma Annie
Skirts Ahoy!
Lone Star
Apache War Smoke
Sky Full of Moon
Monkey Business
Desert Pursuit
53: The Homesteaders
Northern Patrol
The Robe
54: Bait
Ring of Fear
55: A Man Called Peter

George Lynn (1906-
1937: The Duke Comes Back
Charlie Chan at Monte
Carlo
City Girl
39: Mystery Plane
Let Us Live
Wolf Call
Mr. Wong in Chinatown
Quick Millions
40: The Lone Wolf Strikes
Buried Alive
Kit Carson
The Great Dictator
Drums of the Desert
41: Saddlemates
42: To be or not to be
Grand Central Murder
A-Haunting We Will Go
Bombay Clipper
43: Tonight We Raid Calais
44: House of Frankenstein
45: Shady Lady
46: Under Nevada Skies
Tangier
47: Killer at Large
48: The Best Man Wins
Homicide for Three
52: Atomic City
The Bushwackers
54: Magnificent Obsession
56: The Werewolf
The Boss
57: The Man Who Turned to
Stone
I Was a Teenage Frank-
enstein

58: Girl in the Woods

Jeffrey Lynn (1909-
1938: various shorts
Romance and Rhythm
Cowboy from Brooklyn
Four Daughters
When Were You Born?
Out Where the Stars Begin
39: Yes, My Darling Daughter
Daughters Courageous
Espionage Agent
The Roaring Twenties
Four Wives
40: A Child Is Born
The Fighting 69th
It All Came True
All this and Heaven too
My Love Came Back
Money and the Woman
41: Flight from Destiny
Four Mothers
Million Dollar Baby
Law of the Tropics
The Body Disappears
Underground
48: For the Love of Mary
Whiplash
Black Bart
Washington Girl
49: A Letter to Three Wives
Strange Bargain
50: Captain China
51: Home Town Story
Up Front
58: Lost Lagoon
60: Butterfield 8
67: Tony Rome

Sharon Lynn (1910-1963)
1929: Trail of the Horse Thieves
Speakeasy
Red Wine
Fox Movietone Follies of
1929
One Woman Idea
Sunnyside Up
30: Happy Days
Let's Go Places
Crazy that Way
Wild Company

881

30: Man Trouble
    Lightnin'
    Up the River
31: Men on Call
    Too Many Crooks
32: Discarded Lovers
    Big Broadcast
33: Big Executive
34: Enter Madame
35: Go Into Your Dance
36: Way Out West
41: West Point Widow

Ben Lyon (1901-
1928: The Air Legion   S
29: The Flying Marine   PT
    The Quitter   S
    Dancing Vienna
30: The Lummox
    Alias French Gertie
    What Men Want
    Hell's Angels (synch.)
    Queen of Main Street
    Lawful Larceny
31: Compromised
    Her Majesty Love
    Bought
    Hot Heiress
    Misbehaving Ladies
    Indiscreet
    Reputation
    We Three
    Soldiers Plaything
    Aloha
    My Past
    Night Nurse
32: Lady with a Past
    The Big Timer
    Hat Check Girl
    The Crooked Circle
    By Whose Hands?
    Week-Ends Only
    Rackety Rax
    So Big
    Wages of Virtue
    No Greater Love
33: Girl Missing
    I Cover the Waterfront
    I Spy
34: The Morning After

    The Woman in His Life
    Crimson Romance
35: Lightning Strikes Twice
    Call to Arms
    Frisco Waterfront
    Navy Wife
    Beauty's Daughter
36: Dancing Feet
    Down to the Sea
38: He Loved an Actress
39: I Killed the Count
    Treachery on the High
        Seas
41: Hi Gang!
42: This Was Paris
48: Life with the Lyons
56: The Lyons in Paris

Sue Lyon (1946-
1962: Lolita
64: Night of the Iguana
65: Seven Women
67: The Flim Flam Man
    Tony Rome
69: Four Rode Out
    Don't Push--I'll Charge
    When I'm Ready (TV)

Bert Lytell (1888-1954)
1930: Blood Brothers
31: Single Sin
43: Stage Door Canteen

M

James MacArthur (1937-
1957: The Young Stranger
58: The Light in the Forest
59: Third Man on the Mountain
60: Kidnapped
    The Swiss Family Robinson
62: The Interns
63: Cry of Battle
    Spencer's Mountain
65: The Battle of the Bulge
    The Truth about Spring
    The Bedford Incident
66: Ride Beyond Vengeance
67: The Love-Ins
68: The Angry Breed

882

J. Farrell MacDonald (1875-1951)

1929: Masquerade
Masked Emotions   SSE
In Old Arizona
None but the Brave
The Four Devils   PT
South Sea Rose
Strong Boy
30: Painted Angel
Steel Highway
Broken Kishes
Truth about Youth
Song o' My Heart
Born Reckless
31: The Painted Desert
River's End
The Easiest Way
The Millionaire
Woman Hungry
The Maltese Falcon
Other Men's Women
The Squaw Man
Too Young to Marry
The Brat
Sporting Blood
Spirit of Notre Dame
Touchdown
32: Under Eighteen
Discarded Lovers
Hotel Continental
Probation
Phantom Express
Week-End Marriage
The 13th Guest
70,000 Witnesses
The Vanishing Frontier
Hearts of Humanity
This Sporting Age
The Pride of the Legion
No Man of Her Own
Me and My Gal
Steady Company
The Racing Strain
33: The Working Man
Peg o' My Heart
Laughing at Life
Power and the Glory
Myrt and Marge

I Loved a Woman
Murder on the Campus
The Iron Master
Heritage of the Desert
Under Secret Orders
34: Man of Two Worlds
Crime Doctor
Romance in Manhattan
Once to Every Woman
The Crosby Case
Beggar's Holiday
35: The Square Shooter
The Whole Town's Talking
Northern Frontier
Star of Midnight
The Best Man Wins
The Healer
Swell Head
Maybe it's Love
Let 'em Have it!
Out Little Girl
The Irish in Us
Front Page Woman
Danger Ahead
Stormy
Fighting Youth
Waterfront Lady
36: Riffraff
Hitchhike Lady
Florida Special
Exclusive Story
Showboat
37: Shadows of the Orient
Maid of Salem
Mysterious Crossing
The Silent Barriers
Roaring Timber
The Hit Parade
Slave Ship
County Fair
Slim
Topper
My Dear Miss Aldrich
The Game that Kills
Courage of the West
38: My Old Kentucky Home
Numbered Woman
Gang Bullets
State Police
Flying Fists

38: There Goes My Heart
Extortion
Little Orphan Annie
White Banners
Come on, Rangers!
The Crowd Roars
Submarine Patrol
39: Susannah of the Mounties
Mickey the Kid
Conspiracy
The Gentleman from
Arizona
Zenobia
40: Knights of the Range
The Dark Command
Light of the Western
Stars
Prairie Law
I Take this Oath
The Last Alarm
Untamed
Stagecoach War
Friendly Neighborn
41: In Old Cheyenne
Meet John Doe
The Great Lie
Riders of the Timberline
42: Snuffy Smith--Yardbird
Little Tokyo
One Thrilling Night
Phantom Killer
The Living Ghost
Bowery at Midnight
43: The Ape Man
Clancy Street Boys
True to Life
Tiger Fangs
44: The Miracle of Morgan's
Creek
Texas Masquerade
The Great Moment
Follow the Boys
Shadow of Suspicion
45: A Tree Grows in Brooklyn
Nob Hill
Johnny Angel
Pillow of Death
The Woman Who Came
Back
46: Joe Palooka--Champ

Smoky
My Darling Clementine
47: Web of Danger
Keeper of the Bees
Thunder in the Valley
48: Fury at Furnace Creek
Walls of Jericho
Whispering Smith
Belle Starr's Daughter
Panhandle
49: Streets of San Francisco
She Comes Home
Fighting Man of the
Plains
Law of the Barbary Coast
The Beautiful Blonde from
Bashful Bend
The Dalton Gang
50: Woman on the Run
The Dakota Kid
Hostile Country
51: Elopement
Mr. Belvedere Rings the
Bell

Jeanette MacDonald (1906-1965)
1929: The Love Parade
30: The Vagabond King
Let's Go Native°
Monte Carlo
The Lottery Bride
Oh, What a Man!
31: Annabelle's Affairs
Don 't Bet on Women
32: One Hour with You
Love Me Tonight
34: Cat and the Fiddle
Merry Widow
35: Naughty Marietta
36: Rose Marie
San Francisco
37: Maytime
The Firefly
38: Girl of the Golden West
Sweethearts
39: Broadway Serenade
40: The New Moon
Bitter Sweet
41: Smilin' Through
42: I Married an Angel

42: Cairo
44: Follow the Boys
48: Three Daring Daughters
49: The Sun Comes Up
51: Miquette

Kenneth MacDonald
1939: Spoilers of the Range
Outpost of the Mounties
40: Bullets for Rustlers
Two-Fisted Rangers
Texas Stagecoach
Island of Doomed Men
The Durango Kid
Before I Hang
Frontier Vengeance
41: The Devil Commands
Prairie Schooners
The Wildcat of Tucson
Mystery Ship
Hands Across the Rockies
The Son of Davy Crockett
The Confessions of Boston
Blackie
42: The Man Who Returned to
Life
Cadets on Parade
Riders of the Northland
43: Robin Hood of the Range
44: U-Boat Prisoner
West of the Rio Grande
Pride of the Plains
Cowboy from Lonesome
River
45: Shadow of Terror

Wallace MacDonald (1896-
1929: Fancy Baggage
Sweetie
Darkened Rooms
30: Hit the Deck
Dark Skies
The Rogue Song
Madam Satan
Fighting Through
31: Drums of Jeopardy
Fifty Fathoms Deep
Range Feud
Pagan Lady
Branded

32: High Speed
Two-Fisted Law
Daring Danger
The Riding Tornado
The Vanishing Frontier
Hello Trouble
Tex Takes a Holiday
33: Between Fighting Men
King of the Wild Horses

Moyna MacGill
1945: The Picture of Dorian Gray
The Strange Case of Uncle
Harry
46: Black Beauty
47: Green Dolphin Street
48: Three Daring Daughters
Texas, Brooklyn, and
Heaven
51: Kind Lady

Niall MacGinnis (1913-
1935: Turn of the Tide
38: Edge of the World
42: The 49th Parallel (or,
The Invaders)
43: We Dive at Dawn
44: Henry V
48: Hamlet
51: No Highway
53: Martin Luther
54: Betrayed
Hell Below Zero
55: The Battle of the River
Plate
Special Delivery
Helen of Troy
56: Alexander the Great
Lust for Life
57: Night of the Demon
59: The Nun's Story
Shake Hands with the Devil
Tarzan's Greatest Adventure
60: Kidnapped
The Night Fighters
61: Sword of Sherwood Forest
Foxhole in Cairo
62: Billy Budd
63: Jason and the Argonauts
A Face in the Rain

885

64: Becket
65: Johnny Nobody
The War Lord
The Truth about Spring
The Spy Who Came in
from the Cold
66: A Man Could Get Killed
67: Island of Terror
68: The Viking Queen
The Shoes of the Fisher-
man
Krakatoa--East of Java

Jack MacGowran (1916-
1952: The Quiet Man
53: The Titfield Thunderbolt
57: The Rising of the Moon
59: Darby O'Gill and the
Little People
60: Blind Date
65: Lord Jim
66: Cul-De-Sac
67: The Vampire Killers
68: How I Won the War
Age of Consent
69: King Lear

Helen Mack (1913-
1930: Zaza
Pied Piper Malone
Under the Red Robe
Grit
Little Red School House
31: The Struggle
32: Silent Witness
While Paris Sleeps
33: Fargo Express
Sweepings
California Trail
Melody Cruise
Son of Kong
Blind Adventure
Her Sweetheart, Christopher
Bean
34: All of Me
Kiss and Make Up
The Lemon Drop Kid
35: Captain Hurricane
She
The Return of Peter
Grimm

Four Hours to Kill
36: The Milky Way
37: I Promise to Pay
You Can't Buy Luck
Fit for a King
Last Train from Madrid
The Wrong Road
38: King of the Newsboys
I Stand Accused
Secrets of a Nurse
Gambling Ship
39: Calling All Marines
Mystery of the White Room
40: His Girl Friday
Girls of the Road
41: Power Dive
44: And Now Tomorrow
45: Divorce
46: Strange Holiday

Wilbur Mack (1873-1964)
1929: Beauty and Bullets   S
Slim Fingers   S
The Argyle Case
Honky Tonk
30: Scarlet Pages
Remote Control
Sweethearts on Parade
The Girl Said No
Annabella
Up the River
35: Million Dollar Baby
Redheads on Parade
36: The Crime Patrol
37: Larceny on the Air
38: Law of the Texan
39: Tough Kid
40: Half a Sinner
That Gang of Mine
43: Dixie
44: Atlantic City
48: Stage Struck
51: According to Mrs. Hoyle
57: Up in Smoke

Dorothy Mackaill (1903-
1928: Ladies' Night in a Turkish
Bath
Man Crazy   S
Lady be Good   S
The Barker   PT

886

28: Waterfront S The Racket
    The Whip S 52: Deadline, U.S.A.
29: Two Weeks Off PT O. Henry's Full House
    His Captive Woman PT (The Clarion Call seq.)
    Children of the Ritz SSE 53: Tarzan and the She-Devil
    Hard to Get
30: Bright Lights Shirley MacLaine (1934-
    The Great Divide 1955: The Trouble with Harry
    The Love Racket Artists and Models
    The Flirting Widow 56: Around the World in 80
    Strictly Modern Days
    Office Wife 58: Hot Spell
    Man Trouble The Sheepman
31: Safe in Hell The Matchmaker
    Their Mad Moment Some Came Running
    Once a Sinner 59: Ask Any Girl
    Kept Husbands Career
    Party Husband 60: Can-Can
    Reckless Hour The Apartment
32: Love Affair Ocean's Eleven (Cameo)
    Lost Lady 61: All in a Night's Work
    No Man of Her Own Two Loves
33: Neighbors' Wives 62: My Geisha
    The Chief The Children's Hour
34: Curtain at Eight Two for the Seesaw
    Cheaters 63: Irma la Douce
    Picture Brides 64: What a Way to Go!
37: Bulldog Drummond at Bay John Goldfarb, Please
                              Come Home
Kenneth MacKenna (1899-1962) 65: The Yellow Rolls-Royce
1929: Pleasure Crazed 66: Gambit
      South Sea Rose 67: Woman Times Seven
      Love, Live, and Laugh 68: Sweet Charity
30: Crazy that Way 69: The Bliss of Mrs. Blossom
    Men Without Women Two Mules for Sister Sara
    Temple Tower
    Man Trouble Barton MacLane (1902-1969)
    Virtuous Sin 1933: Man of the Forest
    Sin Takes a Holiday Big Executive
60: High Time The Torch Singer
61: Judgment at Nuremberg To the Last Man
62: 13 West Street Tillie and Gus
                    Hell and High Water
Joyce MacKenzie 34: Lone Cowboy
1950: Mother Didn't Tell Me The Thundering Herd
      Destination Murder The Last Round-Up
      Broken Arrow 35: Black Fury
      Stella Go into Your Dance
      Ticket to Tomahawk The Case of the Curious
51: People Will Talk Bride

35: Stranded
Page Miss Glory
Dr. Socrates
I Found Stella Parrish
Ceiling Zero
The G-Men
The Case of the Lucky
Legs
Man of Iron
36: The Frisco Kid
The Walking Dead
Times Square Playboy
Jail Break
Bullets or Ballots
Bengal Tiger
Smart Blonde
God's Country and the
Woman
37: Draegerman Courage
You Only Live Once
Wine, Women, and Horses
San Quentin
The Prince and the Pauper
Born Reckless
Ever Since Eve
Fly Away Baby
The Adventurous Blonde
38: The Kid Comes Back
Blondes at Work
Torchy Gets Her Man
The Storm
Gold Is Where You Find
It
You and Me
Prison Break
39: Stand Up and Fight
Big Town Czar
Torchy Blane in China-
town
I Was a Convict
Mutiny in the Big House
40: Men Without Souls
Torchy Runs for Mayor
Secret Seven
Gangs of Chicago
Melody Ranch
41: Come Live with Me
High Sierra
Western Union
Barnacle Bill

Dr. Jekyll and Mr. Hyde
The Maltese Falcon
Wild Geese Calling
Hit the Road
42: Highways by Night
All Through the Night
The Big Street
In this Our Life (seq. of
The Maltese Falcon)
43: Man of Courage
Bombardier
Song of Texas
The Underdog
The Crime Doctor's
Strangest Case
44: Cry of the Werewolf
The Mummy's Ghost
Marine Raiders
Secret Command
Gentle Annie
Nabonga
45: The Spanish Main
Scared Stiff
Tarzan and the Amazons
Treasure of Fear
46: The Mysterious Intruder
47: Jungle Flight
Cheyenne
Santa Fe Uprising
Tarzan and the Hunters
48: Treasure of the Sierra
Madre
Relentless
Unknown Island
The Dude Goes West
Silver River
The Walls of Jericho
Angel in Exile
49: Red Light
50: Kiss Tomorrow Goodbye
Rookie Fireman
The Bandit Queen
Let's Dance
51: Best of the Badmen
Drums in the Deep South
52: Bugles in the Afternoon
The Half-Breed
Thunderbirds
53: Sea of Lost Ships
Jack Slade

53: Races into Laramie
    Captain Scarface
    Kansas Pacific
    Cow Country
54: Rails into Laramie
    The Glenn Miller Story
    Jubilee Trail
55: Hell's Outpost
    The Treasure of Ruby
     Hills
    The Silver Star
    Foxfire
    The Last of the
     Desperadoes
    Jail Busters
56: Jaguar
    Backlast
    Wetbacks
    The Man Is Armed
    Three Violent People
    The Naked Gun
57: Sierra Stranger
    Naked in the Sun
    The Storm Rider
    Hell's Crossroads
58: Girl in the Woods
    Geisha Boy
    Frontier Gun
60: Gunfighter of Abilene
    Noose for a Gunman
61: A Pocketful of Miracles
64: Law of the Lawless
65: The Rounders
    Town Tamer
68: Arizona Bushwackers
    Buckskin

Ian MacLaren (1886-
1931: The Conquering Horde
    Body and Soul
32: Prestige
    Afraid to Talk
34: Cleopatra
35: Les Miserables
    Let 'em Have it!
37: The Prince and the
     Pauper
    The Prisoner of Zenda
38: The Invisible Enemy
    Little Orphan Annie

39: The Hound of the Basker-
    villes

Mary MacLaren (1896-
1936: King of the Pecos
37: A Lawman Is Born
38: Duke of West Point
40: Misbehaving Husbands
41: Prairie Schooners
44: Lady in the Dark
45: Frontier Feud
    Navajo Trails

Douglas MacLean (1894-1967)
1929: The Carnation Kid
    Divorce Made Easy

Aline MacMahon (1899-
1931: Five-Star Final
32: Heart of New York
    The Mouthpiece
    Weekend Marriage
    One Way Passage
    Life Begins
    Silver Dollar
    Once in a Lifetime
33: Gold Diggers of 1933
    The Life of Jimmy Dolan
    Heroes for Sale
    The World Changes
34: Heat Lightning
    Side Streets
    Big-Hearted Herbert
    Babbitt
    The Merry Frinks
35: While the Patient Slept
    Mary Jane's Pa
    I Live My Life
    Kind Lady
    Ah, Wilderness!
36: A Woman in Her Thirties
37: When You're in Love
39: Back Door to Heaven
41: Out of the Fog
42: The Lady Is Willing
    Tish
43: Stage Door Canteen
    Seeds of Freedom
44: Dragon Seed
    Reward Unlimited

44: Guest in the House
46: The Mighty McGuirk
48: The Search
49: Roseanna McCoy
50: The Flame and the Arrow
53: The Eddie Cantor Story
55: Man from Laramie
60: Cimarron
61: The Young Doctors
62: Diamond Head
63: I Could Go on Singing
     The Lonely Stage
     All the Way Home

Fred MacMurray (1908-
1935: Car No. 99
       Grand Old Girl
       The Gilded Lily
       Hands Across the Table
       The Bride Comes Home
       Alice Adams
       Glad Rag Doll
       Men Without Names
36: Trail of the Lonesome
     Pine
     Thirteen Hours by Air
     The Princess Comes
      Across
     The Texas Rangers
37: Maid of Salem
     Exclusive
     True Confession
     Champagne Waltz
     Swing High, Swing Low
38: Men with Wings
     Cocoanut Grove
     Sing, You Sinners!
39: Cafe Society
     Invitation to Happiness
     Honeymoon in Bali
40: Too Many Husbands
     Rangers of Fortune
     Remember the Night
     Little Old New York
41: Virginia
     One Night in Lisbon
     New York Town
     Dive Bomber
42: The Lady Is Willing
     Take a Letter, Darling

The Forest Rangers
Star-Spangled Rhythm
Girls' Town
43: Flight for Freedom
     Above Suspicion
     No Time for Love
44: And the Angels Sing
     Double Indemnity
     Practically Yours
     Standing Room Only
45: A Tree Grows in Brooklyn
     Murder He Says!
     Where Do We Go from
      Here?
     Captain Eddie
46: Pardon My Past
     Smoky
47: Suddenly it's Spring
     The Egg and I
     Singapore
48: A Miracle can Happen
      (or, On Our Marry Way)
     Miracle of the Bells
     Don't Trust Your Husband
      (or, An Innocent Affair)
     Family Honeymoon
49: Father Was a Fullback
50: Never a Dull Moment
     Borderline
51: Callaway Went Thataway
     Millionaire for Christy
53: Fair Wind to Java
     The Moonlighter
54: The Caine Mutiny
     The Pushover
     Woman's World
55: The Far Horizons
     At Gunpoint
     Rains of Ranchipur
56: There's Always Tomorrow
57: Gun for a Coward
     Quantez
58: Good Day for a Hanging
     Day of the Bad Man
59: The Shaggy Dog
     Face of a Fugitive
     The Oregon Trail
60: The Apartment
61: The Absent-Minded
     Professor

62:	Bon Voyage!		The Man Who Dared
63:	Son of Flubber		The Return of Monte Cristo
64:	Kisses for My President	47:	The Swordsman
66:	Follow Me, Boys!		Down to Earth
67:	The Happiest Millionaire	48:	The Big Clock

Gordon MacRae (1921-

1948:	The Big Punch		The Black Arrow
49:	Look for the Silver Lining		Coroner Creek
50:	Backfire		Beyond Glory
	Return of the Frontiers-		The Gallant Blade
	man	49:	Alias Nick Beal
	Fine and Dandy		Knock on Any Door
	Daughter of Rosie O'Grady		Johnny Allegro
	Tea for Two		The Doolins of Oklahoma
	The West Point Story	50:	The Nevadan
51:	On Moonlight Bay		A Lady Without a Passport
	Starlift		The Desert Hawk
52:	About Face		Fortunes of Captain Blood
53:	By the Light of the		Rogues of Sherwood Forest
	Silvery Moon	51:	Tarzan's Peril
	The Desert Song		The Golden Horde
	Three Sailors and a Girl		Detective Story
55:	Oklahoma!		The Desert Fox
56:	Carousel	52:	Green Glove
	The Best Things in Life	53:	Treasure of the Golden
	Are Free		Condo

George Macready (1909-

1942:	The Commandos Strike		Julius Caesar
	at Dawn		The Stranger Wore a Gun
44:	The Seventh Cross		The Golden Blade
	Wilson	54:	Duffy of San Quentin
	The Story of Dr. Wassell		Vera Cruz
	The Conspirators	56:	Kiss Before Dying
	Follow the Boys		Thunder over Arizona
	The Missing Juror	57:	The Abductors
	Soul of a Monster		Gunfire at Indian Gap
45:	Counter-Attack		Paths of Glory
	Don Juan Quilligan	59:	The Alligator People
	The Fighting Guardsman		Plunderers of Painted
	I Love a Mystery		Flats
	The Monster and the Ape	60:	Jet over the Atlantic
	(ser.)	62:	Two Weeks in Another
	A Song to Remember		Town
	My Name Is Julia Ross		Taras Bulba
46:	Gilda	64:	Seven Days in May
	The Walls Came Tumbling		Dead Ringer
	Down		Where Love Has Gone
	Bandit of Sherwood Forest	65:	The Great Race
		66:	The Human Duplicators
		67:	Fame Is the Name of the
			Game (TV)
		69:	Tora! Tora! Tora!

Guy Madison (1922-
1944: Since You Went Away
46: Till the End of Time
47: Honeymoon
48: Texas, Brooklyn, and
Heaven
49: Massacre River
51: Drums in the Deep South
52: Red Snow
53: The Charge at Feather
River
54: The Command
55: Five Against the House
The Last Frontier
Savage Wilderness
56: The Beast of Hollow
Mountain
On the Threshold of
Space
Hilda Crane
Reprisal!
57: The Hard Man
58: Bullwhip
60: Jet over the Atlantic
Women of Devil's Island
61: The Slave of Rome
62: Sword of the Conqueror
63: Captain Sinbad
Gentleman of the Night
64: Adventures of Tortuga
Dual at Rio Bravo
65: Gunmen of the Rio Grande
66: Apaches Last Battle
Mystery of Thug Island
67: The Bang Bang Kid
Payment in Blood
Shatterhand

Noel Madison (c1905-
1930: Sinners' Holiday
31: Star Witness
32: The Hatchet Man
Play Girl
Symphony of Six Million
The Trial of Vivienne
Ware
The Last Mile
Hat Check Girl
Me and My Gal

Laughter in Hell
33: Humanity
West of Singapore
Destination Unknown
Important Witness
34: House of Rothschild
Journal of a Crime
I Like it that Way
Manhattan Melodrama
35: Four Hours to Kill
The G-Men
What Price Crime?
Woman Wanted
The Girl Who Came Back
Three Kids and a Queen
My Marriage
36: Muss 'em Up!
Murder at Glen Athol
Champagne Charlie
Straight from the Shoulder
Our Relations
Easy Money
Missing Girls
37: Nation Aflame
39: Missing Evidence
Charlie Chan in the City
of Darkness
40: The Great Plane Robbery
41: Ellery Queen's Penthouse
Mystery
Footsteps in the Dark
A Shot in the Dark
Highway West
42: Secret Agent of Japan
Joe Smith, American
Bombs over Burma
43: Miss V from Moscow
Shantytown
Jitterburgs
The Black Raven
49: The Gentleman from No-
where

Anna Magnani (1908-
1934: Blind Woman of Sorrento
Calvary
Down with Misery
46: The Open City
The Bandit
Unknown Men of San
Marino

892

46: Dreams in the Streets
Woman Trouble
47: Before Him All Rome
Trembled
Revenge
48: Angelina
49: Peddlin' in Society
50: The Miracle
53: Volcano
Anita Garibaldi
54: The Golden Coach
Bellissima
We Women
55: The Rose Tattoo (OSCAR)
The Wayward Wife
57: Wild Is the Wind
58: The Awakening
Of Life and Love
60: The Fugitive Kind
The Passionate Thief
61: Wild Women
62: Mama Roma
65: La Lupe
67: Made in Italy
69: The Secret of Santa
Vittoria
Fellini Satyricon
Year of the Lord

George Maharis (1938-
1960: Exodus
64: Quick Before it Melts
65: The Satan Bug
Sylvia
67: A Covenant with Death
The Happening
68: The Desperadoes
69: Destination: Mindanao (or,
Escape to Mindanao)
Last Day of the War
Day of the Landgrabber
You Can't Judge a Book...
The Monk

Jock Mahoney (1919-
1945: Rough Rider of Durango
46: The Fighting Frontiersman
47: South of the Chisholm
Trail

The Stranger from Ponca
City
48: Blazing Across the Pecos
49: The Doolins of Oklahoma
Blazing Trail
Horsemen of the Sierras
Rim of the Canyon
Bandits of El Dorado
Renegades of the Sage
Frontier Marshal
50: The Nevadan
David Harding, Counterspy?
Cow Town
The Texas Dynamo
Hoedown
Lightning Guns
Cody of the Pony Express
(ser.)
51: Santa Fe
The Texas Rangers
Pecos River
Roar of the Iron Horse
(ser.)
52: Smoky Canyon
The Hawk of Wild Canyon
Junction City
The Rough Tough West
The Kid from Broken Gun
Laramie Mountains
54: Overland Pacific
Gunfighters of the North-
west (ser.)
56: Away all Boats
Day of Fury
Showdown at Abilene
Battle Hymn
57: The Land Unknown
Slim Carter
I've Lived Before
Joe Dakota
58: A Time to Love, and a
Time to Die
Last of the Fast Guns
Money, Women, and Guns
60: Tarzan, the Magnificent
Three Blondes in His Life
62: Tarzan Goes to India
63: Tarzan's Three Challenges
California
64: Moro Witch Doctor

64: The Walls of Hell
67: The Glory Stompers
68: Portrait of Violence

Charles Hill Mailes (1870-1937)
1929: Phantom City   S
       The Faker   S
       The Bellamy Trial   PT
       The Carnation Kid   PT
       One Stolen Night   PT
30: Mother's Cry
32: No More Orchids
33: Women Won't Tell

Marjorie Main (1890-
1932: A House Divided
33: Take a Chance
34: Music in the Air
    New Deal Rhythm
    Crime Without Passion
35: Naughty Marietta
37: Love in a Bungalow
    The Man Who Cried Wolf
    Stella Dallas
    Dead End
    The Wrong Road
    The Shadow
    Boy of the Streets
38: Penitentiary
    Girls' School
    Romance of the Limber-
      lost
    Under the Big Top
    King of the Newsboys
    Test Pilot
    Too Hot to Handle
    Prison Farm
    Little Tough Guy
    There Goes My Heart
    Three Comrades
39: They Shall Have Music
    Angels Wash Their Faces
    The Women
    Another Thin Man
    Two Thoroughbreds
    Lucky Night
40: I Take this Woman
    Women Without Names
    The Dark Command
    Turnabout

Wyoming
Susan and God
The Captain Is a Lady
Bad Man from Wyoming
41: The Trial of Mary Dugan
    A Woman's Face
    Wild Man of Boreno
    Barnacle Bill
    Honky Tonk
    Shepherd of the Hills
42: The Bugle Sounds
    We Were Dancing
    The Jackass Mail
    Once Upon a Thursday (or,
      The Affairs of Martha)
    Tish
    Tennessee Johnson
    Woman of the Town
    Melody of Youth
43: Johnny Come Lately
    Heaven can Wait
44: Rationing
    Gentle Annie
    Meet Me in St. Louis
45: Murder He Says
46: The Heavenly Body
    Undercurrent
    Bad Bascomb
    The Show-Off
47: The Egg and I
    The Wistful Widow of Wagon
      Gap
48: Feudin', Fussin', an' A-
      Fightin'
49: Ma and Pa Kettle
    Big Jack
50: Ma and Pa Kettle Go to
      Town
    Summer Stock
    Mrs. O'Malley and Mr.
      Malone
51: Ma and Pa Kettle Back on
      the Farm
    The Law and the Lady
    Mr. Imperium
    It's a Big Country
52: The Belle of New York
    Ma and Pa Kettle at the
      Fair
53: Ma and Pa Kettle on
      Vacation

53: Fast Company
54: The Long, Long Trailer
Rose Marie
Ma and Pa Kettle at Home
Ricochet Romance
55: Ma and Pa Kettle at
Waikiki
56: The Kettles in the
Ozarks
Friendly Persuasion
57: The Kettles on Old Mac-
Donald's Farm
65: The World of Abbott &
Costello

Mako
1966: The Sand Pebbles
The Ugly Dachshund
68: The Private Navy of Sgt.
O'Farrell
69: The Great Bank Robbery
Tora! Tora! Tora!
The Hawaiians

Karl Malden (1914-
1940: They Knew What They
Wanted
44: Winged Victory
47: Boomerang
The Kiss of Death
50: The Gunfighter
Where the Sidewalk Ends
The Halls of Montezuma
51: A Street Named Desire
(OSCAR)
The Sellout
52: Diplomatic Courier
Operation Secret
Ruby Gentry
53: I Confess
Take the High Ground
54: Phantom of the Rue
Morgue
On the Waterfront
55: Desperate Hours
56: Baby Doll
57: Bombers B-52
Fear Strikes Out
The Egghead
Time Limit (dir.)

59: The Hanging Tree
60: Pollyanna
The Great Impostor
61: One-Eyed Jacks
Parrish
62: How the West Was Won
All Fall Down
Birdman of Alcatraz
Gypsy
63: Come Fly with Me
64: Cheyenne Autumn
Dead Ringer
65: The Cincinnati Kid
66: Nevada Smith
Murderers' Row
67: The Adventures of Bullwhip
Griffin
Hotel
Billion Dollar Brain
68: Blue
Hot Millions
69: Patton

Miles Malleson (1888-1969)
1937: Knight Without Armour
38: Six Glorious Years
40: The Thief of Bagdad
45: Dead of Night
51: The Magic Box
52: The Importance of Being
Earnest
53: Trent's Last Case
56: The Man Who Never Was
57: The Admirable Crichton
(or, Paradise Lagoon)
58: Dracula
59: The Hound of the Baskervilles
I'm All Right, Jack
60: Kidnapped
The Day They Robbed the
Bank of England
Man in a Cocked Hat
The Captain's Table
The Brides of Dracula
61: Double Break
62: Phantom of the Opera
Peeping Tom
63: Heavens Above
64: The Magnificent Showman

895

64: Murder Ahoy!
Circus World
First Men in the Moon
A Jolly Bad Fellow
65: The Brain
You Must be Joking!

Rory Mallinson
1945: Pride of the Marines
46: The Big Sleep
Janie Gets Married
Night and Day
47: Nora Prentiss
Possessed
Cry Wolf
Dark Passage
For You I Die
King of the Bandits
Road to the Big House
48: Panhandle
Open Secret
Docks of New Orleans
I Wouldn't be in Your
Shows
The Checkered Coat
Badmen of Tombstone
The Denver Kid
Last of the Wild Horses
49: Prince of the Plains
South of Rio
Angels in Disguise
El Dorado Pass
Task Force
50: Salt Lake Raiders
County Fair
Short Grass
51: Three Desperate Men
Fingerprints Don't Lie
According to Mrs. Hoyle
Rodeo King and the
Senorita
Purple Heart Diary
52: A Yank in Indo-China
Brave Warrior
The Laramie Mountains
Waco
Montana Belle
53: Cow Country
Killer Ape
54: Jesse James vs the
Daltons

Killer Leopard
55: A Bullet for Joey
Seminole Uprising
Shotgun
59: King of the Wild Stallions

Boots Mallory (d-1958)
1932: Walking Down Broadway
Handle with Care
33: Humanity
Hello Sister
Carnival Lady
34: The Big Race
Sing Sing Nights
35: Powdersmoke Range
37: Here's Flash Casey!

Dorothy Malone (1925-
1944: One Mysterious Night
Show Business
Hollywood Canteen
45: Too Young to Know
46: The Big Sleep
Janie Gets Married
Night and Day
48: Two Guys from Texas
To the Victor
One Sunday Afternoon
49: Colorado Territory
Flaxy Martin
South of St. Louis
50: Mrs. O'Malley and Mr.
Malone
The Killer that Stalked
New York
The Nevadan (or, The Man
from Nevada)
Convicted
51: Saddle Legion
52: The Bushwackers (or, The
Rebel)
53: Law and Order
Scared Stiff
Jack Slade
Torpedo Alley
54: The Lone Gun
Loophole
The Pushover
Security Risk
Private Hell No. 36
Young at Heart

896

54: Fast and Furious
55: Battle Cry
At Gunpoint
Five Guns West
Tall Man Riding
Sincerely Yours
Artists and Models
56: Pillars of the Sky (or,
The Tomahawk and the
Cross)
Written on the Wind
(OSCAR)
Tension at Table Rock
57: Man of a Thousand Faces
Tip Off on a Dead Jockey
Quantez
Tarnished Angels
58: Too Much, Too Soon
59: Warlock
60: The Last Voyage
61: The Last Sunset
63: Beach Party
64: Fate Is the Hunter
69: The Exhibition

Eily Malyon
1935: Clive of India
The Florentine Dagger
The Flame Within
Les Miserables
The Melody Lingers on
A Tale of Two Cities
Kind Lady
The Widow from Monte
Carlo
36: One Rainy Afternoon
Anthony Adverse
Dracula's Daughter
The White Angel
Cain and Mabel
A Woman Rebels
Three Men on a Horse
Career Woman
God's Country and the
Woman
37: Night Must Fall
Another Dawn
38: Rebecca of Sunnybrook
Farm
Kidnapped

The Young at Heart
39: The Hound of the Basker-
villes
The Little Princess
Confessions of a Nazi Spy
On Borrowed Time
We Are not Alone
Barricade
40: Young Tom Edison
Untamed
Foreign Correspondent
41: Arkansas Judge
Man Hunt
Hit the Road
42: The Man in the Trunk
The Undying Monster
Scattergood Survives a
Murder
I Married a Witch
43: Jane Eyre
Going My Way
44: The Seventh Cross
Roughly Speaking
Scared Stiff
Grissly's Millions
Son of Lassie
Paris Underground
46: She Wolf of London
Devotion
The Scarlet Heart
48: The Challenge

Miles Mander (1888-1946)
1929: Doctors' Women   S
The Physician   S
30: Loose Ends
Murder
32: Lily Christine
35: The Three Musketeers
36: Here's to Romance
Lloyds of London
37: Wake Up and Live
Slave Ship
Youth on Parole
38: Kidnapped
The Mad Miss Manton
39: The Little Princess
Wuthering Heights
The Man in the Iron Mask
Stanley and Livingstone

897

39: Tower of London
40: Road to Singapore
Primrose Path
The House of Seven Gables
Babies for Sale
Captain Caution
Laddie
South of Suez
41: That Hamilton Woman
Shadows on the Stairs
Dr. Kildare's Wedding Day
42: Fingers at the Window
Fly by Night
A Tragedy at Midnight
To be or not to be
Tarzan's New York
Adventure
Apache Trail
The War Against Mrs.
Hadley
43: Assignment in Brittany
Secrets of the Underground
Five Graves to Cairo
Guadalcanal Diary
44: Enter Arsene Lupin
Four Jills in a Jeep
Sherlock Holmes and the
Pearl of Death
The Return of the Vampire
The Scarlet Claw
45: The Brighton Strangler
Confidential Agent
Murder My Sweet
The Picture of Dorian
Gray
Weekend at the Waldorf
46: The Crime Doctor's
Warning
The Walls Came Tumbling
Down
47: The Imperfect Lady

Silvana Mangano (1925-
1949: L'Elisir D'Amore
51: Bitter Rice
53: The Lure of Sila
54: Anna
The Brigand
Mussolini
55: Mambo

Ulysses
57: The Sea Wall
Gold of Naples
58: This Angry Age
59: The Tempest
60: Five Branded Women
61: The Great War
62: Barabbas
64: And Suddenly it's Summer!
65: Flying Saucers
68: Me Me Me and the Others
(Theorem)
69: The Witches (5 diff. seq.)

Hank Mann (1888-
1929: Morgan's Last Raid   S
Donovan Affair
Fall of Eve
30: The Arizona Kid
Sinners' Holliday
Dawn Trail
31: City Lights
Annabelle's Affairs
32: Ridin' for Justice
Strange Love of Molly
Louvain
Million Dollar Legs
33: The Big Chance
34: Dawn Trail
Fugitive Road
Smoky
35: The Devil Is a Woman
36: Call of the Prairie
Modern Times
Reunion
38: Stranger from Arizona
39: Hollywood Cavalcade
40: The Great Dictator
41: Bullets for O'Hara
42: Bullet Scars
43: The Mysterious Doctor
44: Crime by Night
47: The Perils of Pauline
Jiggs and Maggie in Jack-
pot Jitters
50: Joe Palooka in Humphrey
Takes a Chance
53: The Caddy
55: Abbott & Costello Meet the
Keystone Kops

57: Man of a Thousand Faces

David Manners (1900-
1929: The Journey's End
30: The Truth about Youth
Troopers Three
Kismet
Mother's Cry
The Right to Love
He Knew Women
Sweet Mama
31: The Millionaire
Dracula
The Ruling Voice
The Miracle Woman
The Last Flight
Upper Underworld
32: The Greeks Had a Word
for Them
The Lady with a Past
The Crooner
The Death Kiss
Beauty and the Boss
Man Wanted
Stranger in Town
Bill of Divorcement
The Way of Life
Im-Ho-Tep
Cock of the Air
They Call it Sin
The Mummy
33: The Warrior's Husband
The Girl in 419
Torch Singer
The Devil's in Love
Romance Scandal
From Hell to Heaven
34: The Black Cat
The Great Flirtation
The Moonstone
35: The Perfect Clue
The Mystery of Edwin
Drood
Jalna
36: Hearts in Bondage
A Woman Rebels
Reputation

Irene Manning (1916-
1942: The Big Shot

Yankee Doodle Dandy
Spy Ship
43: The Desert Song
44: Shine on Harvest Moon
Doughgirls
Henrietta the 8th
Strangers in Our Midst
Make Your Own Bed
Hollywood Canteen
45: Escape in the Desert
I Live on Grosvenor
Square
48: Bonnie Prince Charlie

Knox Manning
1941: Meet John Doe
Cheers for Miss Bishop
Tanks a Million
42: A Yank on the Burma
Road
46: The Kid from Brooklyn
47: Hit Parade of 1947
48: The Babe Ruth Story

Jayne Mansfield (1930-1967)
1955: Illegal
Pete Kelly's Blues
56: Female Jungle
The Girl Can't Help it
Hell on Frisco Bay
57: The Burglar
The Wayward Bus
Will Success Spoil Rock
Hunter?
Kiss Them for Me
The James Dean Story
(clips)
58: The Sheriff of Fractured
Jaw
59: The Loves of Hercules
(not rel.)
60: Play Girl after Dark (or,
Too Hot to Handle)
It Takes a Thief (or, The
Challenge)
61: The George Raft Story
62: It Happened in Athens
63: Promises! Promises!
Heimweh Nach St. Paul
(Ger.)

899

63: When Strangers Meet
The Bernde and the
Psychiatrist (Ital.)
64: Panic Button
65: The Loved One
66: Dog Eat Dog
Las Vegas Hillbillies
The Fat Spy
Primitive Love
67: A Guide for the Married
Man
Spree
68: Single Furnished Room

Paul Mantee
1964: Robinson Crusoe on Mars
Blood on the Arrow
66: An American Dream
67: A Man Called Dagger

Joe Mantell
1955: Marty
56: Storm Center
57: Beau Brummel
The Sad Sack
58: Onionhead
59: Guns of Zangara
60: The Crowded Sky
63: The Birds
66: Mr. Buddwing

Adele Mara (1923-
1942: Alias Boston Blackie
Blondie Goes to College
Shut My Big Mouth
You Were Never Lovelier
43: Reveille with Beverly
44: Atlantic City
Call of the South Seas
Faces in the Fog
45: Bells of Rosarita
Girls of the Big House
Grissly's Millions
Song of Mexico
Thoroughbreds
The Tiger Woman
The Vampire's Ghost
46: The Magnificent Rogue
Passkey to Danger
Traffic in Crime

The Catman of Paris
A Guy Could Change
The Inner Circle
The Invisible Reformer
I've Always Loved You
The Night Train to
Memphis
47: The Last Crooked Mile
Exposed
The Trespasser
Blackmail
Twilight on the Rio Grande
The Web of Danger
48: Campus Honeymoon
Wake of the Red Witch
Gallant Legion
The Main Street Kid
Night Time in Nevada
I, Jane Doe
Angel in Exile
Riders of the Northwest
Mounted
49: Sands of Iwo Jima
50: The Avengers
Rock Island Trail
California Passage
51: The Sea Hornet
53: Count the Hours
56: Back from Eternity
57: The Black Whip
58: The Curse of the Faceless
Man
59: The Big Show

Jean Marais (1913-
1943: L'Eternal Retour
45: La Belle et La Bête
47: L'Aigle à Deux Têtes
48: Les Parents Terribles
50: Orpheus
57: Paris Does Strange Things
Royal Affairs in Versailles
Julietta
59: Typhoon over Nagasaki
60: Girl in His Pocket
61: Rape of the Sabines
The Hunchback of Notre
Dame
62: The Man in the Iron Mask
63: Blood on the Sword (or,
The Invincible Sword)

64: Napoleon (L'Aiglon)
65: The Reluctant Spy
66: Fantomas
    Friend of the Family
    Man from Cocody

Fredric March (1897-

1929: The Dummy
      Jealousy
      Paris Bound
      Marriage Playground
      The Wild Party
      The Studio Murder
        Mystery
      Footlights and Fools
30: Sarah and Son
    Royal Family of Broadway
    Manslaughter
    Laughter
    Paramount on Parade
    True to the Navy
31: Honor Among Lovers
    My Sin
    Night Angel
32: Dr. Jekyll and Mr. Hyde
      (OSCAR)
    Sign of the Cross
    Smilin' Through
    Strangers in Love
    Merrily We Go to Hell
    If I Had a Million
33: The Eagle and the Hawk
    Design for Living
    Tonight Is Ours
34: Death Takes a Holiday
    Affairs of Cellini
    The Barretts of Wimpole
      Street
    Good Dame
    All of Me
    We Live Again
35: Les Miserables
    Dark Angel
    Anna Karenina
36: Mary of Scotland
    Ladies Love Brutes
    Anthony Adverse
37: A Star Is Born
    Nothing Sacred
38: Trade Winds

      Road to Glory
      There Goes My Heart
      The Buccaneer
39: 400 Millions (narr.)
40: Susan and God
    Lights Out in Europe
      (short)
    Victory
41: One Foot in Heaven
    So Ends Our Night
    Bedtime Story
42: I Married a Witch
    Lake Carrier (short)
44: Salute to France (short)
    Adventures of Mark Twain
    Tomorrow the World!
46: The Best Years of Our
      Lives (OSCAR)
48: An Act of Murder
    Another Part of the Forest
49: Christopher Columbus
51: It's a Big Country
    Death of a Salesman
53: Man on a Tightrope
54: Executive Suite
    The Bridges at Toko-Ri
55: Desperate Hours
56: Alexander the Great
    The Man in the Gray
      Flannel Suit
57: Albert Schweitzer (narr.
      doc.)
59: Middle of the Night
60: Inherit the Wind
61: The Young Doctors
62: The Interns
63: The Condemned of Altona
64: Seven Days in May
67: Hombre
69: Tick, Tick, Tick

Hal March (1920-1970)

1950: Ma and Pa Kettle Go to
        Town (or, ...In New York)
      The Outrage
53: The Eddie Cantor Story
    Combat Squad
54: Yankee Pasha
    The Atomic Kid
55: My Sister Eileen

901

55: It's Always Fair Weather
57: Hear Me Good
64: Send Me no Flowers
67: A Guide for the Married
Man

Margo (1918-
1934: Crime Without Passion
35: Rumba
36: Robin Hood of El Dorado
Winterset
37: Lost Horizon
40: A Miracle on Main Street
43: The Leopard Man
Behind the Rising Sun
Gangway for Tomorrow
44: The Falcon in Mexico
52: Viva Zapata!
55: I'll Cry Tomorrow
58: From Hell to Texas
62: Who's Got the Action?
65: Taffy and the Jungle
Hunter

Janet Margolin (1943-
1963: David and Lisa
65: Bus Riley's Back in Town
The Greatest Story Ever
Told
Morituri--The Saboteur
Code Name
66: Nevada Smith
The Eavesdropper
67: Enter Laughing
69: Take the Money and Run
Buona Sera, Mrs. Camp-
bell

Tammy Marihugh
1960: The Last Voyage
The Snow Queen (cartoon
voice)
61: A Thunder of Drums
Back Street
62: The Wonderful World of
the Brothers Grimm

George Marion (1860-1945)
1929: Evangeline   PT
The Bishop Murder Case

30: Anna Christie
The Sea Bat
The Big House
The Benson Murder Case
Pay Off
A Lady's Morals
Soul Kiss
31: Man to Man
Hook, Line, and Sinker
Laughing Sinners
32: Six Hours to Live
33: Her First Mate
35: Port of Lost Dreams

Mona Maris (1903-
1928: Die Drei Frauen Von Urban
Hell
La Bonne Botesse
Die Leibenen
Der Marquis D'Eon
29: Under a Texas Moon
The Spy of Mme.
Pompadour
Romance of the Rio Grande
30: The Arizona Kid
One Mad Kiss
A Devil with Women
On the Make
31: Cuando el Amor Rie
The Sea Beneath
32: The Passionate Plumber
South of the Rio Grande
The Man Who Called Back
Once in a Lifetime
33: The Death Kiss
Secrets
34: White Heat
Kiss and Make Up
40: Flight from Destiny
41: Underground
Law of the Tropics
A Date with the Falcon
42: My Gal Sal
I Married an Angel
Pacific Rendezvous
Cairo
Berlin Correspondent
44: Desert Hawk (ser.)
Tampico
The Falcon in Mexico

46:   Monsieur Beaucaire
       Heartbeat
49:   Los Vengadores
50:   The Avengers
52:   La Mujer de las Camelias

Sari Maritza
1932: Forgotten Commandments
       Evenings for Sale
33:   A Lady's Profession
       International House
       Right to Romance
       Her Secret
34:   Crimson Romance

Enid Markey (1896-
1946: Snafu
48:   The Naked City

Melinda Markey
1954: Adventures of Hajji Baba
       The Other Woman
55:   Prince of Players
       Crashout

Monte Markham (1935-
1967: Hour of the Gun
68:   Guns of the Magnificent
       Seven
       Project X

Lucy Marlow
1954: A Star Is Born
55:   Bring Your Smile Along
       My Sister Eileen
       Queen Bee
       Tight Spot
56:   He Laughed Last

Hugh Marlowe (1911-
1936: It Could Have Happened
37:   Married Before Breakfast
       Between Two Women
44:   Marriage Is a Private
       Affair
       Meet Me in St. Louis
       Mrs. Parkington
       Murder in the Blue Room
45:   Identity Unknown
49:   Come to the Stable

       12 O'Clock High
50:   Night and the City
       All About Eve
51:   Rawhide
       Mr. Belvedere Rings the
       Bell
       The Day the Earth Stood
       Still
52:   Wait till the Sun Shines
       Nellie
       Bugles in the Afternoon
       Way of a Gaucho
       Monkey Business
53:   The Stand at Apache River
54:   Casanova's Big Night
       Garden of Evil
55:   Illegal
56:   Earth vs the Flying Saucers
       World Without End
57:   The Black Whip
60:   Elmer Gantry
61:   The Lone Rope
62:   Birdman of Alcatraz
63:   Thirteen Frightened Girls
64:   Seven Days in May
67:   Castle of Evil
69:   The Last Shot You Hear

Jo Ann Marlowe
1945: Dangerous Intruder
       Mildred Pierce
       Roughly Speaking
46:   Joe Palooka--Champ
       Little Iodine
       The Man from Rainbow
       Valley
47:   A Scandal in Paris
       Rolling Home
       Keeper of the Bees

June Marlowe (1907-
1928: Their Hour   S
       The Branded Man   S
       Foreign Legion   S
       Grip of the Yukon S
       Free Lips   S
31:   Pardon Us
32:   Devil on Deck
35:   Riddle Ranch
47:   Slave Girl

Scott Marlowe
1956: Gaby
       The Scarlet Hour
       The Young Guns
  57: Men in War
       The Restless Breed
  58: The Cool and the Crazy
       Young and Wild
  59: Riot in Juvenile Prison
  60: The Subterraneans
  61: A Cold Wind in August

Florence Marly (c1915-
1948: Sealed Verdict
  49: Tokyo Joe
  51: Tokyo File No. 212
  52: Gobs and Gals
  57: Undersea Girl
  66: Queen of Blood (re. rel. in
       '69 as Planet of Blood)
  67: Games

Percy Marmont (1883-
1928: San Francisco Nights   S
       Stronger Will   S
  29: Silver King   S
  30: Lady of the Lake   S
  36: Secret Agent
  38: Action for Slander
  41: I'll Walk Beside You
  45: Loyal Heart
  48: No Orchids for Miss
       Blandish
  53: Four-Sided Triangle
  56: Lisbon

Christian Marquand
1957: And God Created Woman
  58: No Sun in Venice
  59: Sgt. X of the Foreign
       Legion
  62: The Longest Day
       End of Desire
       Crime Does not Pay
  63: Temptation
       I Spit on Your Grave
  64: Behold a Pale Horse
  65: The Flight of the Phoenix
       Lord Jim
  67: The Corrupt Ones

  68: Candy (dir.)

Tina Marquand (1946-
1966: Modesty Blaise
       Texas Across the River
  67: The Game Is Over

Maurice Marsac
1944: This Is the Life
  47: Crime Doctor's Gamble
  48: Woman from Tangier
  49: Secret of St. Ives
  50: Tyrant of the Sea
  52: The Happy Time
  53: The Caddy
  55: Jump into Hell
  56: Four Girls in Town
  57: China Gate
  58: Lafayette Escadrille
       Twilight for the Gods
       Me and the Colonel
  60: Scent of Mystery
  61: The Armored Command
       King of Kings
  63: Take Her She's Mine
       Captain Sinbad
       Werewolf in a Girls'
       Dormitory
  64: What a Way to Go!
       The Pleasure Seekers
       Wild and Wonderful
  65: Clarence, the Cross-Eyed
       Lion
       The Art of Love
  66: Gambit
  67: Caprice
       Monkeys, Go Home!
       Double Trouble
  69: How Do I Love Thee?

Joan Marsh (1915-
1931: Shipmates
       A Tailor Made Man
       Three Girls Lost
       Inspiration
       Dance, Fools, Dance
       Meet the Wife
       Politics
  32: Are You Listening?
       Wet Parade

904

32:	Bachelor Affairs		Impact
33:	Speed Demon	50:	When Willie Comes March-
	High Gear		ing Home
	Daring Daughters		The Gunfighter
	It's Great to be Alive	52:	Night Without Sleep
	The Man Who Dared		The Sun Shines Bright
	Three-Cornered Moon	53:	Blueprint for Murder
	Rainbow over Broadway		The Robe
34:	You're Telling Me	55:	Tall Men
	Many Happy Returns		Prince of Players
	We're Rich Again		Hell on Frisco Bay
35:	Anna Karenina	56:	Julie
	Champagne for Breakfast	57:	Wings of Eagles
36:	Dancing Feet	58:	Cry Terror
	Brilliant Marriage	60:	Sgt. Rutledge
37:	Life Begins in College		From the Terrace
	Charlie Chan on Broadway	61:	Two Rode Together
	Hot Water		
38:	The Lady Objects	Marion Marsh (1913-
39:	Fast and Loose	1930:	Hell's Angels
41:	Road to Zanzibar		Whoopee
42:	The Man in the Trunk	31:	50 Million Frenchmen
	Police Bullets		The Devil Was Sick
43:	Keep 'em Slugging		Svengali
44:	Follow the Leader		Five Star Final
			The Mad Genius

Mae Marsh (1895-1968)

1928:	Racing Through		Road to Singapore
31:	Over the Hill	32:	Alias the Doctor
32:	That's My Boy!		Beauty and the Boss
	Rebecca of Sunnybrook		Under Eighteen
	Farm		The Sport Parade
33:	Alice in Wonderland		Without Consent
34:	Little Man, What Now?		Free, White, and 21
	Bachelor of Arts		Strange Justice
35:	Black Fury	33:	The 11th Commandment
36:	Hollywood Boulevard		Man of Sentiment
40:	The Man Who Wouldn't		Daring Daughters
	Talk		Notorious but Nice
	Young People	34:	Love at Second Sight
41:	Great Guns		Over the Garden Wall
	Blue, White, and Perfect		I Like it that Way
42:	Tales of Manhattan		Girl on the Limberlost
43:	Dixie Dugan	35:	In Spite of Danger
44:	Jane Eyre		Black Room Mystery
	In the Meantime, Darling		The Prodigal Son
45:	A Tree Grows in Brooklyn		Unknown Woman
48:	Deep Waters		Crime and Punishment
	Three Godfathers	36:	Come Closer, Folks!
49:	The Fighting Kentuckian		The Man Who Lived Twice
			Lady of Secrets

36: Counterfeit
37: Saturday's Heroes
When's Your Birthday?
The Great Gambini
Youth on Parole
38: Prison Nurse
A Desperate Adventure
39: Missing Daughters
The Hound of the Basker-
villes
Elsa Maxwell's Hotel for
Women
Day Time Wife
40: Star Dust
The Man I Married
Fugitive from a Prison
Camp
Hudson's Bay
41: Adam Had Four Sons
Sleepers West
Murder by Invitation
Gentleman from Dixie
42: House of Errors

Alan Marshal (1909-1961)
1936: Garden of Allah
After the Thin Man
37: Parnell
Night Must Fall
Conquest
38: I Met My Love Again
Dramatic School
Invisible Enemy
Road to Reno
39: Four Girls in White
Adventures of Sherlock
Holmes
Exile Express
The Hunchback of Notre
Dame
40: Married and in Love
Irene
He Stayed for Breakfast
The Howards of Virginia
41: Tom, Dick, and Harry
Lydia
44: The White Cliffs of Dover
Bride by Mistake
49: The Barkleys of Broadway
56: The Opposite Sex

58: The House on Haunted Hill
59: Day of the Outlaw

Brenda Marshall (1915-
1939: Espionage Agent
40: The Man Who Talked too
Much
The Sea Hawk
Money and the Woman
East of the River
South of Suez
41: Footsteps in the Dark
Singapore Woman
Highway West
The Smiling Ghost
42: Captains of the Clouds
You Can't Escape Forever
43: The Constant Nymph
Paris After Dark
Background to Danger
44: Something for the Boys
46: Strange Impersonation
48: Whispering Smith
50: Iroquois Trail

E. G. Marshall (1910-
1945: The House on 92nd Street
46: 13 Rue Madeleine
47: Untamed Fury
48: Call Northside 777
54: The Caine Mutiny
The Pushover
The Bamboo Prison
Broken Lance
The Silver Chalice
55: The Left Hand of God
56: The Scarlet Hour
The Mountain
57: Twelve Angry Men
The Bachelor Party
Man on Fire
58: The Buccaneer
59: The Journey
Compulsion
Cash McCall
61: Town Without Pity
66: The Chase
Is Paris Burning?
The Poppy Is Also a
Flower (TV)

69:   The Bridge at Remagen
     Tora! Tora! Tora!

Everett Marshall (1901-
1930: Dixiana
31: George White's Scandals
33: Melody
35: I Live for Love

Herbert Marshall (1891-1966)
1929: Mumsie
     The Letter
30: Murder
31: Secrets of a Secretary
32: The Calendar
     Michael and Mary
     Blonde Venus
     Trouble in Paradise
     Evenings for Sale
33: The Solitaire Man
     White Woman
     Clear All Wires
     Faithful Heart
34: I Was a Spy
     Four Frightened People
     Outcast Lady
     Painted Veil
     Rip Tide
35: The Good Fairy
     The Flame Within
     Accent on Youth
     The Dark Angel
     If You Could only Cook
     Morning, Noon, and Night
36: The Lady Consents
     A Woman Rebels
     Make Way for a Lady
     Till We Meet Again
     Forgotten Faces
     Girls Dormitory
     Crack-Up
37: Angel
     Breakfast for Two
     Fight for Your Lady
38: Mad About Music
     Always Goodbys
     Woman Against Woman
     Behind the Bridegroom
     Marie Antoinette
39: Zaza

40: A Bill of Divorcement
     Foreign Correspondent
     The Letter
     The Honest Finder
41: Adventure in Washington
     The Little Foxes
     When Ladies Meet
     Kathleen
42: The Moon and Sixpence
     Portrait of a Rebel
43: Forever and a Day
     Young Ideas
     Flight for Freedom
44: Andy Hardy's Blonde
      Trouble
45: The Unseen
     The Enchanted Cottage
46: The Razor's Edge
     Crack-Up
     Duel in the Sun
47: High Wall
     Ivy
49: The Secret Garden
50: The Underworld Story
51: Anne of the Indies
     The Whipped (or, The
      Unexpected)
     Captain Black Jack
52: Angel Face
54: Riders to the Stars
     Gog
     The Black Shield of Fal-
      worth
55: The Virgin Queen
56: Portrait in Smoke
57: Wicked as They Come
     The Weapon
58: The Fly
     Stage Struck
60: Midnight Lace
     College Confidential
61: A Fever in the Blood
62: Five Weeks in a Balloon
63: The Caretakers
     The List of Adrian
      Messenger
     Honest Finder
65: The Third Day

Marion Marshall
1948: Sitting Pretty
Street with no Name
Unfaithfully Yours
Apartment for Peggy
49: I Was a Male War Bride
50: Ticket to Tomahawk
Stella
My Blue Heaven
51: I Can Get it for You
Wholesale
That's My Boy!
52: The Stooge
67: Gunn

Trudy Marshall
1936: Boston Blackie and the
Law
42: Girl Trouble
43: Heaven can Wait
The Dancing Masters
44: Ladies in Washington
The Purple Heart
Roger Touhy--Gangster
The Sullivan
45: Circumstantial Evidence
The Dolly Sisters
46: Alias Mr. Twilight
Blackie and the Law
Dragonwyck
Sentimental Journey
47: Too Many Winners
Beyond Our Own
Joe Palooka in The Knock-
out
Key Witness
48: The Fuller Brush Man
Disaster
49: Shamrock Hill
Barbary Pirate
50: Mark of the Gorilla

Tully Marshall (1865-1943)
1929: Redskin   SSE
Conquest
Bridge of San Luis Rey PT
Thunderbolt
Skin Deep
Alias Jimmy Valentine
Tiger Rose

The Show of Shows
The Mysterious Dr. Fu
Manchu
30: She Couldn't Say No
Burning Up
Mammy
Redemption
Murder Will Out
Numbered Men
Common Clay
Dancing Sweeties
The Big Trail
Tom Sawyer
One Night at Susie's
Under a Texas Moon
31: Virtuous Husbands
Fighting Caravans
The Millionaire
The Unholy Garden
32: Broken Lullaby
The Hatchet Man
Arsene Lupin
The Beast of the City
Scarface
Grand Hotel
Night Court
Scandal for Sale
Strangers of the Evening
Two-Fisted Law
Exposure
Klondike
Cabin in the Cotton
Red Dust
Afraid to Talk
Hurricane Express (ser.)
33: Night of Terror
Corruption
Laughing at Life
34: Massacre
Murder on the Blackboard
35: Black Fury
Diamond Jim
A Tale of Two Cities
37: California Straight Ahead
She Asked for it
Souls at Sea
Stand-In
Hold 'em, Navy!
38: House of Mystery
A Yank at Oxford

908

38: Mr. Boggs Steps Out
Arsene Lupin Returns
Making the Headlines
College Swing
39: The Kid from Texas
Blue Montana Skies
40: Invisible Stripes
Brigham Young--Frontiers-
man
You Will be Served
Go West
Chad Hanna
41: For Beauty's Sake
Ball of Fire
42: This Gun for Hire
Moontide
Ten Gentlemen from West
Point
43: Behind Prison Walls
Hitler's Hangman

Joel Marston (1922-
1960: The Last Voyage
61: Ring of Fire

Gregg Martell
1950: Double Crossbones
I Was a Shoplifter
Ma and Pa Kettle Go to
Town (or, ...In New
York)
Under the Gun
Leave it to the Marines
52: Affair in Trinidad
53: The Glory Brigade
54: Masterson of Kansas
56: Between Heaven and Hell
58: Space Master X-7
Tonka
59: Alaska Passage
60: Dinosaurus
Cage of Evil
61: The Sgt. Was a Lady
Valley of the Dragons
62: The Three Stooges Meet
Hercules

Andra Martin
1958: The Lady Takes a Flyer
The Big Heat

The Thing that Couldn't Die
59: Up Periscope!
Yellowstone Kelly
61: A Fever in the Blood

Cris-Pin Martin (1894-1953)
1931: The Squaw Man
The Cisco Kid
32: South of Santa Fe
Girl Crazy
The Stoker
Painted Woman
33: Outlaw Justice
California Trail
34: Four Frightened People
35: Bordertown
39: Stagecoach
Return of the Cisco Kid
The Fighting Gringo
40: Charlie Chan in Panama
The Cisco Kid and the Lady
The Llano Kid
Viva, Cisco Kid!
Down Argentine Way
The Gay Caballero
The Mark of Zorro
41: Romance of the Rio Grande
The Bad Man
Ride on, Vaquero!
Week-end in Havana
42: Undercover Man
Tombstone, the Town too
Tough to Die
American Empire
43: The Ox-Bow Incident
The Sultan's Daughter
44: Ali Baba and the Forty
Thieves
Tampico
45: Along Came Jones
San Antonio
46: Gallant Journey
47: Robin Hood of Monterey
The Fugitive
King of the Bandits
48: Belle Starr's Daughter
Mexican Hayride
The Return of Wildfire
49: The Beautiful Blonde from
Bashful Bend

909

49: Rimfire
50: The Arizona Cowboy
51: A Millionaire for Christy
   The Lady from Texas
52: Ride the Man Down

Dean Martin (1917-
(with Jerry Lewis through '56)
1949: My Friend Irma
50: My Friend Irma Goes
   West
   At War with the Army
51: That's My Boy!
   Sailor, Beware!
52: The Stooge
   Jumping Jacks
53: The Caddy
   Scared Stiff
   Money from Home
54: Living it Up
   Three-Ring Circus
55: You're Never too Young
   Artists and Models
56: Pardners
   Hollywood or Bust
57: 10,000 Bedrooms
58: The Young Lions
   Some Came Running
59: Rio Bravo
   Career
60: Who Was that Lady?
   Bells Are Ringing
   Ocean's Eleven
61: Ada
   All in a Night's Work
62: Sergeants Three
   Who's Got the Action?
63: Toys in the Attic
   Four for Texas
   Who's Been Sleeping in
   My Bed?
64: Robin and the Seven Hoods
   Kiss Me, Stupid!
   What a Way to Go!
65: The Sons of Katie Elder
   Marriage on the Rocks
66: The Silencers
   Murderers' Row
   Texas Across the River
67: Rough Night in Jericho

The Ambushers
The Man Called Gringo
68: Bandolero
   How to Save a Marriage
   and Ruin Your Life
   Five Card Stud
69: The Wrecking Crew
   House of Seven Joys
   Airport

Dewey Martin (1923-
1949: Knock on Any Door
50: The Golden Gloves Story
   Kansas Raiders
51: The Thing
52: The Big Sky
54: Tennessee Champ
   Prisoner of War
   Men of the Fighting Lady
55: Land of the Pharaohs
   Desperate Hours
56: The Proud and Profane
57: 10,000 Bedrooms
62: The Longest Day
63: Savage Sam
64: Flight to Fury

Dick Martin
1958: Once Upon a Horse
66: The Glass Bottom Boat
see also: Dan Rowan

Dino Martin, Jr. (1951-
1967: Rough Night in Jericho
69: A Boy, a Girl

Marion Martin (1916-
1939: Sergeant Madden
   Invitation to Happiness
   Man in the Iron Mask
40: Boom Town
   Ellery Queen, Master
   Detective
41: Blonde Inspiration
   The Lady from Cheyenne
   The Big Store
   New Wine
   Lady Scarface
   Mexican Spitfire's Baby
   Week-End for Three

910

42: They Got Me Covered
Tales of Manhattan
Mexican Spitfire at Sea
Powder Town
The Big Street
Mexican Spitfire's Elephant
43: The Lady of Burlesque
Woman of the Town
44: Gildersleeve's Ghost
The Great Mike
Irish Eyes Are Smiling
It Happened Tomorrow
The Merry Monahans
Sweethearts of the U.S.A.
Swingtime Johnny
45: Abbott & Costello in
Hollywood
Eadie Was a Lady
Gangs of the Waterfront
Penthouse Rhythm
The Phantom Speaks
46: Angel on My Shoulder
Cinderella Jones
Deadline for Murder
That Brennan Girl
47: That's My Gal!
49: Come to the Stable
Thunder in the Pines
Oh, You Beautiful Doll!
50: Key to the City
Dakota Lil

Mary Martin (1913-
1939: The Great Victor Herbert
40: Rhythm on the River
Love Thy Neighbor
41: New York Town
Kiss the Boys Goodbye
Birth of the Blues
42: Star-Spangled Rhythm
43: True to Life
Happy Go Lucky
46: Night and Day
53: Main Street to Broadway

Millicent Martin (1934-
1960: Horsemasters
61: Invasion Quartet
62: The Girl on the Boat
64: Nothing but the Best

65: Those Magnificent Men in
Their Flying Machines
66: Stop the World I Want to
Get Off!
Alfie

Ross Martin (1920-
1955: Conquest of Space
58: Underwater Warrior
The Colossus of New York
62: Geronimo
Experiment in Terror
63: The Ceremony
65: The Great Race

Strother Martin (1920-
1952: Storm over Tibet
55: Strategic Air Command
The Big Knife
Target Zero
56: Attack!
57: The Black Patch
Copper Sky
59: The Shaggy Dog
The Wild and the Innocent
61: Sanctuary
The Deadly Companions
62: The Man Who Shot Liberty
Valance
63: McLintock!
Showdown
64: Invitation to a Gunfighter
65: Shenandoah
The Sons of Katie Elder
Brainstorm
66: Harper
An Eye for an Eye
67: Cool Hand Luke
The Flim-Flam Man
68: The Wild Bunch
69: True Grit
Butch Cassidy and the
Sundance Kid
Come in, Children

Tony Martin (1913-
1936: Sing, Baby, Sing
Educating Father
Pigskin Parade
Banjo on My Knee

36: Follow the Fleet
    Back to Nature
37: Sing and be Happy
    The Holy Terror
    You Can't Have Everything
    Life Begins in College
    Ali Baba Goes to Town
38: Sally, Irene, and Mary
    Kentucky Moonshine
    Up the River
    Thanks for Everything
38: Winner Take All
40: Music in My Heart
41: Ziegfeld Girl
    The Big Store
47: Till the Clouds Roll By
48: Casbah
51: Two Tickets to Broadway
53: Here Come the Girls
    Easy to Love
54: Deep in My Heart
55: Hit the Deck
56: Quincannon, Frontier
    Scout
57: Let's be Happy

Edward Martindel (1876-1955)
1929: The Devil's Apple Tree S
    Why be Good? S
    Desert Song
    Hard-Boiled Rose
    The Singing Fool
    Modern Love
    Footlights and Fools
    The Aviator
30: Second Choice
    Song of the West
    Song o' My Heart
    Mamba
    Rain or Shine
    Golden Dawn
    Check and Double Check
31: Divorce Among Friends
    High Stakes
    Woman Pursued
    Gay Diplomat
32: American Madness
    False Faces
    Afraid to Talk
33: By Appointment Only

34: Two Heads on a Pillow
35: Champagne for Breakfast
    The Girl Who Came Back

Elsa Martinelli (1933-
1955: The Indian Fighter
56: Four Girls in Town
57: Manuela
    The Stowaway Girl
60: Prisoner of the Volga
61: Blood and Roses
    La Notte Brava
62: Hatari!
    Wildcats on the Beach
    The Pigeon that Took
     Rome
63: Rampage
    Rice Girl
    The Trial
    The Invisible Swordsman
    The VIP's
65: De L'Amour
    The Tenth Victim
    Bad Girls Don't Cry
66: Marco Polo, the Magnificent
67: Woman Times Seven (Super
    Simone seq.)
    Maroc 7
    Every Man Is My Enemy
68: Candy
69: If It's Tuesday, This Must
    be Belgium
    Devil's Dolls
    Maldonne (Fr; Misdeal)

Nino Martini (1904-
1930: Paramount on Parade
35: Here's to Romance
36: The Gay Desperado
37: Music for Madame
48: One Night with You

Lee Marvin (1924-
1946: The Killers
51: You're in the Navy Now
    (or, U.S.S. Tea Kettle)
52: Diplomatic Courier
    We're not Married
    Eight Iron Men
    Duel at Silver Creek

52:	Hangman's Knot	1929:	The Cocoanuts
	Hong Kong	30:	Animal Crackers
53:	Seminole	31:	Monkey Business
	The Glory Brigade	32:	Horsefeathers
	Down Among the Shelter-	33:	Duck Soup
	ing Palms	35:	A Night at the Opera
	The Stranger Wore a Gun	37:	A Day at the Races
	The Big Heat	38:	Room Service
	Gun Fury	39:	At the Circus
54:	The Wild One	40:	Go West
	The Caine Mutiny	41:	The Big Store
	Gorilla at Large	46:	Night in Casablanca
	The Raid	50:	Love Happy
	Bad Day at Black Rock	57:	Story of Mankind
55:	A Life in the Balance		
	Violent Saturday		Harpo Alone
	Not as a Stranger		1943: Stage Door Canteen

Harpo Alone
1943:   Stage Door Canteen

Groucho Alone
1947:   Copacabana

	Pete Kelly's Blues		
	I Died a Thousand Times		
	Shack Out on 101	50:	Mr. Music
56:	The Rack	51:	Double Dynamite
	Seven Men from Now	52:	A Girl in Every Port
	Pillars of the Sky		Will Success Spoil Rock
	Attack!		Hunter?
57:	Raintree County	68:	Skidoo!
58:	The Missouri Traveler		
61:	The Comancheros		
62:	The Man Who Shot Liberty		James Mason (Amer.)

James Mason (Amer.)

	Valance	1929:	Phantom City	S
63:	Donovan's Reef		Flying Marine	PT
64:	The Killers		Show of Shows	
65:	Ship of Fools		Dark Skies	
	Cat Ballou (OSCAR)	30:	Last of the Duanes	
66:	The Professionals		The Concentratin' Kid	
67:	The Dirty Dozen	31:	The Painted Desert	
	Point Blank		Caught	
68:	Hell in the Pacific		Border Love	
	Sgt. Ryker ('63 TV re-	32:	Texas Gun-Fighter	
	rel.)	33:	Renegades of the West	
69:	Paint Your Wagon		Drum Taps	
	The Diehard		The Story of Temple	
	Monte Walsh		Drake	
			Sunset Pass	

The Marx Brothers (Groucho, 1890-; Chico, 1891-1961; Harpo, 1893-1964; Gummo, 1894- (appeared only through 1933); the 5th, Zeppo, 1901-, was in only one movie*.)

34:	Last Round Up
	Dude Ranger
35:	Hopalong Cassidy
36:	Call of the Prairie
39:	The Renegade Stranger
	I Met a Murderer

James Mason (Eng.)
1935: Late Extra
  36: Prison Breakers
  37: Fire over England
  38: The Mill on the Floss
       The Return of the Scarlet
       Pimpernel
  39: This Man Is Dangerous
       The High Command
       Catch as Catch can
       Secret of Stamboul
  41: Hatter's Castle
       The Patient Vanishes
  42: Secret Mission
       Thunder Rock
  43: Alibi
       The Bells Go Down
  44: Candlelight in Algeria
  45: The Man in Grey
       They Met in the Dark
       Fanny by Gaslight
  46: Hotel Reserve
       A Place of One's Own
       They Were Sisters
       The Seventh Veil
       Wicked Lady
  47: Odd Man Out
       Upturned Glass
  48: Man of Evil
       Hatter's Castle
  49: Caught
       East Side, West Side
       The Reckless Moment
       Madame Bovary
       Troubled Waters
       Twice Branded
       Prison Breakers
       Blindman's Bluff
  50: One Way Street
  51: Pandora and the Flying
       Dutchman
       The Desert Fox
  52: The Lady's Possessed
       Five Fingers
       Face to Face
       The Prisoner of Zenda
  53: Julius Caesar
       Desert Rats
       Tell-Tale Heart (cartoon
       narr.)
       Story of Three Loves

       Botany Bay
  54: Prince Valiant
       A Star Is Born
       20,000 Leagues Under the
       Sea
  56: Forever Darling
       Bigger than Life
  57: Island in the Sun
  58: The Decks Ran Red
       Cry Terror
  59: North by Northwest
       Journey to the Center of
       the Earth
  60: A Touch of Larceny
       The Green Carnation
       Marriage-Go-Round
  62: Lolita
       Torpedo Bay
       Escape from Zahrain
       Hero's Island
  63: Tiara Tahiti
  64: The Fall of the Roman
       Empire
       The Pumpkin Eater
  65: Lord Jim
       The Piano Player
       Genghis Khan
       Terror at Sea
  66: Georgy Girl
       The Blue Max
  67: The Deadly Affair
       The Uninhibited
  68: Stranger in the House
       The London Nobody Knows
       Mayerling
       Age of Consent
  69: The Sea Gull
       Duffy
       Dance to Your Daddy
       Spring and Port Wine
       The Night Has Eyes

Leroy Mason (1903-1947)
1939: Mexicali Rose
       West of Santa Fe
       Wyoming Outlaw
       Sky Patrol
       New Frontier
       The Fighting Gringo
  40: Killers of the Wild
       Ghost Valley Raiders

40: Rocky Mountain Rangers
    The Range Busters
    Triple Justice
41: Silver Stallion
    Robbers of the Range
    Across the Sierras
    The Apache Kid
    The Perfect Snob
42: Sundown Jim
    The Man Who Wouldn't
     Die
    It Happened in Flatbush
    The Silver Bullet
    Time to Kill
43: Chetniks
    Blazing Guns
    Hands Across the Border
44: Beneath Western Skies
    Firebrands of Arizona
    Hidden Valley Outlaws
    The Rockies
    Call of the South Seas
    None Shall Escape
    The Silver City Kid
    Marshal of Reno
    The Mojave Firebrand
    Outlaws of Santa Fe
    The San Antonio Kid
    Song of Nevada
    Stagecoach of Monterey
    Tucson Raiders
    Vigilantes of Dodge City
45: Home on the Range
46: Heldorado
    Murder in the Music Hall
    My Pal Trigger
    Night Train to Memphis`
    Red River Renegades
    Under Nevada Skies
    Valley of the Zombies
47: Apache Rose
    Along the Oregon Trail
    Bandits of Dark Canyon
    Under Colorado Skies
48: California Firebrand
    The Gay Ranchero

Pamela (Kellino) Mason (1918-
1934: Jew Süss
  38: I Met a Murderer

45: They Were Sisters
47: The Upturned Glass
51: Lady Possessed
60: Sex Kittens Go to College
    College Confidential
66: Door to Door Maniac
69: Voices

Osa Massen (1916-
1940: Honeymoon in Bali
  41: Honeymoon for Three
    A Woman's Face
    Accent on Love
    You'll Never Get Rich
    The Devil Pays Off
  42: Iceland
  43: Background to Danger
    Jack London
  44: Black Parachute
    The Master Race
    Cry of the Werewolf
  45: Tokyo Rose
  46: The Gentleman Misbehaves
    Strange Journey
    Deadline at Dawn
  48: Million Dollar Weekend
  49: Night unto Night
  50: Rocketship XM
  58: Outcasts of the City

Daniel Massey (1933-
1957: Girls at Sea
  58: Upstairs and Downstairs
  59: Girls in Arms
    The Entertainer
  60: The Queen's Guards
  61: Go to Blazes
  65: The Amorous Adventures
     of Moll Flanders
  67: The Jokers
  68: Star! (or, Those Were
     the Happy Years)
  69: Madame Solario
    Fragment of Fear

Ilona Massey (1910-
1937: Rosalie
  39: Balalaika
  41: New Wine
    International Lady
  42: Invisible Agent

915

43: Frankenstein Meets the
   Wolf Man
45: Tokyo Rose
46: Holiday in Mexico
47: Northwest Outpost
48: The Plunderers
49: Love Happy
60: Jet over the Atlantic

Raymond Massey (1896-
1931: The Speckled Band
   Face at the Window
32: The Old Dark House
35: The Scarlet Pimpernel
36: Things to Come
37: Dreaming Lips
   The Prisoner of Zenda
   The Hurricane
   Fire over England
   Under the Red Robe
38: Drums
39: Black Limelight (short)
40: Abe Lincoln in Illinois
   Santa Fe Trail
41: The Invaders (or, The
   49th Parallel)
   Reap the Wild Wind
   Desperate Journey
43: Action in the North
   Atlantic
44: The Woman in the Window
   Arsenic and Old Lace
45: Hotel Berlin
   God Is My Co-Pilot
46: Stairway to Heaven (or,
   A Matter of Life and
   Death)
47: Possessed
   Mourning Becomes Electra
48: The Plunderers
49: The Fountainhead
   Roseanna McCoy
50: Dallas
   Chain Lightning
   Barricade
   A Swirl of Glory
51: Sugarfoot
   David and Bathsheba
   Come Fill the Cup
52: Carson City

53: The Desert Song
   The Man with a Thousand
   Hands
55: Prince of Players
   Battle Cry
   East of Eden
   Seven Angry Men
57: Omar Khayyam
58: The Naked and the Dead
60: The Great Impostor
61: The Fiercest Heart
62: How the West Was Won
63: The Queen's Guards
   Report on China (narr.)
69: Mackenna's Gold

Paul Massie (1932-
1958: Orders to Kill
   High Tide at Noon
59: Sapphire
   Intent to Kill
   Libel
60: The Rebel
61: 20,000 Eyes
   Call Me Genius
   House of Fright (or, The
   Two Faces of Dr. Jekyll)
62: The Pot Carriers
   Raising the Wind

Marcello Mastroianni (1924-
1947: I Miserabili
49: Sunday in August
51: Girls of the Spanish Steps
55: Too Bad She's Bad
56: House of Ricordi
57: The Miller's Beautiful Wife
   White Nights
58: The Bigamist
   I Soliti Ignoti
59: The Most Wonderful Moment
   The Tailor's Maid
   Anatomy of Love
60: Where the Hot Wind Blows
   The Big Deal on Madonna
   Street
61: La Dolce Vita
   The Ghosts of Rome (dual
   role)
   La Notte Brava

62: Divorce Italian Style
   Bell' Antonio
   A Very Private Affair
63: 8 1/2
   Family Diary
64: The Organizer
   Yesterday, Today, and
   Tomorrow
   Marriage--Italian Style
   Love on the Riviera
65: Casanova '70
   The Tenth Victim
   Love a La Carte
   Paranoia
66: The Poppy Is Also a
   Flower (TV)
67: Shout Loud...Louder...
   I Don't Understand
   The Stranger
68: A Place for Lovers
   Me Me Me and the Others
   Kiss the Other Sheik
   Man with the Balloons
69: Diamonds for Breakfast
   Giovanni
   99 ^{44}/100% Dead
   Sunflowers
   Honorable Picnic
   Leo the Last
   Absurd Universe

Jack Mather (1908-1966)
1954: River of no Return
   Broken Lance
55: How to be Very, Very
   Popular
   The View from Pompey's
   Head
56: The Man in the Gray
   Flannel Suit
   The Revolt of Mamie
   Stover
58: The Bravados
59: This Earth Is Mine

Jerry Mathers
1954: This Is My Love
55: The Trouble with Harry
56: That Certain Feeling
   Bigger than Life

57: Shadow on the Window

Carole Mathews (1920-
1944: The Girl in the Case
   Swing in the Saddle
45: The Missing Juror
   She's a Sweetheart
   Strange Affair
   The Monster and the Ape
   (ser.)
   Tahiti Nights
   Love Is a Mystery
   A Thousand and One Nights
46: Stars over Texas
   Blazing the Western Trail
   I Love a Mystery
   Outlaws of the Rockies
   Sing Me a Song of Texas
   10¢ a Dance
48: Massacre River
   The Accused
49: The Great Gatsby
   Special Agent
   Amazone Quest
50: No Man of Her Own
   Cry Murder
51: The Man with My Face
52: Red Snow
   Meet Me at the Fair
   Swamp Woman
53: City of Bad Men
   Shark River
54: Port of Hell
55: Treasure of Ruby Hills
   Requirement for a Redhead
   Look in any Window
   Thirteen Men
   Female Fiend
   Tender Is the Night
56: Betrayed Women
58: Showdown at Boot Hill
59: The Strange Awakening
60: Thirteen Fighting Men
69: Rabbit, Run

Joyce Mathews (1919-
1937: Artists and Models
   This Way, Please
   Big Broadcast of 1938
38: Tip-Off Girls

38: Artists and Models A-
    Broad
39: Boy Trouble
    Sudden Money
    Night Work
    Million Dollar Legs
    $1000 a Touchdown
40: All Women Have Secrets
51: Mr. Universe

Kerwin Mathews (1926-
1955: Five Against the House
57: The Garment Jungle
58: The 7th Voyage of Sinbad
    Tarawa Beachhead
    The Last Blitzkrieg
60: The Three Worlds of
    Gulliver
    Man on a String
61: The Warrior Empress
    The Devil at Four O'Clock
62: Jack, the Giant Killer
    Pirates of Blood River
63: Maniac
67: The Battle Beneath the
    Earth
68: The Viscount
69: A Boy, a Girl
    Barquero

Lester Mathews (1900-
1938: There's Always a Woman
    Adventures of Robin Hood
    Meridian 7-1212
    Three Loves Has Nancy
    Mysterious Mr. Moto of
    Devil's Island
    I Am a Criminal
    If I Were King
    Time Out for Murder
39: The Three Musketeers
    Susannah of the Mounties
    Should a Girl Marry?
    Conspiracy
    Rulers of the Sea
    Everything Happens at
    Night
40: Northwest Passage
    British Intelligence
    The Biscuit Eater

Gaucho Serenade
Women in War
Sing, Dance, Plenty Hot
41: The Lone Wolf Keeps a
    Date
    Man Hunt
42: Son of Fury
    The Pied Piper
    Desperate Journey
    Across the Pacific
    Manila Calling
    London Blackout Murders
43: Tonight We Raid Calais
    The Mysterious Doctor
    Corvette K-225
44: Invisible Man's Revenge
    Four Jills in a Jeep
    Between Two Worlds
    Nine Girls
    Ministry of Fear
    Shadows in the Night
45: Objective, Burma!
    Salty O'Rourke
    Two O'Clock Revenge
    I Love a Mystery
    The Beautiful Cheat
47: Dark Delusion
    Bulldog Drummond at Bay
48: Fighting Father Dunne
50: Tyrant of the Sea
    Montana
    Rogues of Sherwood Forest
51: Son of Dr. Jekyll
    Lorna Doone
    Corky of Gasoline Alley
    Tales of Robin Hood
52: Jungle Jim and the
    Forbidden Island
    The Brigand
    Captain Pirate
    Operation Secret
    Lady in the Iron Mask
    The Stars and Stripes
    Forever
53: Savage Mutiny
    Niagara
    Jamaica Run
    Fort Ti
    Sangaree
    Bad for Each Other

918

53: Trouble Along the Way
54: Charge of the Lancers
    King Richard and the
      Crusaders
    Desiree
    Jungle Man-Eaters
55: Ten Wanted Men
    Moonfleet
    The Far Horizons
    Flame of the Island
59: The Miracle

Otto Matieson (1873-
1929: Strange Cargo
    Behind Closed Doors   S
    Prisoners   PT
    General Crack
    Show of Shows
30: Golden Dawn
    Last of the Lone Wolf
    Conspiracy
31: Beau Ideal
    The Maltese Falcon
    Soldiers Plaything
    Men of the Sky

Walter Matthau (1923-
1955: The Kentuckian
    The Indian Fighter
56: Bigger than Life
57: A Face in the Crowd
    Slaughter on Tenth Avenue
58: King Creole
    Voice in the Mirror
    Ride a Crooked Trail
    Onionhead
60: Strangers When We Meet
    The Ganster's Story
62: Lonely Are the Brave
    Who's Got the Action?
63: Island of Love
    Charade
64: Ensign Pulver
    Fail Safe
    Goodbye, Charlie
65: Mirage
66: Fortune Cookie (OSCAR)
67: A Guide for the Married
    Man
68: The Odd Couple

    The Secret Life of an
      American Wife
    Candy
69: Hello Dolly!
    The Cactus Flower
    A New Leaf

Martha Mattox (d. 1933)
1929: Big Diamond Robbery   S
    Montmartre Rose   S
30: The Love Racket
    Night Work
    Extravagance
31: Misbehaving Ladies
    Murder by the Clock
32: Murder at Dawn
    The Silver Lining
    The Monster Walks
    Careless Lady
    So Bug
    No Greater Love
    Dynamite Ranch
33: Haunted Gold
    Bitter Tea of General Yen

Matt Mattox (1921-
1945: Yolanda and the Thief
46: Easy to Wed
    Till the Clouds Roll by
47: Good News
    Something in the Wind
52: The Merry Widow
53: The I Don't Care Girl
    Gentlemen Prefer Blondes
    The Band Wagon
54: Seven Brides for Seven
      Brothers
    Brigadoon
60: Pepe

Victor Mature (1915-
1939: To Quito and Back
    The Housekeeper's Daughter
40: One Million B. C.
    Captain Caution
    No, No, Nanette
41: I Wake Up Screaming
    (or, Hot Spot)
    Shanghai Gesture
42: Song of the Islands

Victor Mature as "Chief Crazy Horse"

42: My Gal Sal
Footlight Serenade
Seven Days' Leave
46: My Darling Clementine
47: Moss Rose
Kiss of Death
48: Cry of the City
Martin Rome
Interference
Fury at Furnace Creek
49: Red, Hot, and Blue
Samson and Delilah
Easy Living
50: Wabash Avenue
Stella
Gambling House
52: The Las Vegas Story
Androcles and the Lion
Million Dollar Mermaid
Something for the Birds
53: Glory Brigade
Affair with a Stranger
The Robe
Veils of Bagdad
54: Dangerous Mission
Betrayed
Demetrius and the
Gladiators
The Egyptian
55: Chief Crazy Horse (or,
Valley of Fury)
Violent Saturday
The Last Frontier
Savage Wilderness
56: Safari
The Sharkfighters
57: Zarak
The Long Haul
Pickup Alley
58: Tank Force
China Doll
59: Bandit of Zhobe
The Big Circus
Timbuktu
Escort West
60: Hannibal
62: The Tartars
66: After the Fox
68: Head

Billy & Bobby Mauch (Billy only*)
1936: Anthony Adverse *
37: Penrod and Sam *
White Angel *
The Prince and the Pauper
38: Penrod and His Twin
Brother
Penrod's Double Trouble
48: Street with no Name*
The Accused*
49: Roseanna McCoy*
51: Bedtime for Bonzo*

Nicole Maurey (1925-
1953: Little Boy Lost
54: Secret of the Incas
L'Aiglon (Napoleon II)
Diary of a Country Priest
Companions of the Night
56: The Bold and the Brave
57: The Weapon
The Rogue's Yarn
58: Me and the Colonel
59: The Scapegoat
The Jaywalkers
House of Seven Hawks
60: High Time
62: The Most Wanted Man in
the World
63: Day of the Triffids
64: Why Bother to Knock?
69: His and Hers

Paul Maxey (1908-1963)
1941: Father Steps Out
I'll Sell My Life
City Limits
Let's Go Collegiate
46: Below the Deadline
Personality Kid
Till the Clouds Roll By
47: Millie's Daughter
Brasher Doubloon
Philo Vance's Secret
Mission
48: Winter Meeting
49: Sky Dragon
Fighting Fools
Mississippi Rhythm

49: Bride for Sale
50: The Reformer and the
    Redhead
    Return of Jesse James
51: Casa Manana
52: The Narrow Margin
    Kid Monk Baroni
    Here Come the Marines!
54: Black Tuesday
57: High Tide at Noon
58: Showdown at Boot Hill
61: 20,000 Eyes

Edwin Maxwell (d. 1948)
1928: Easy Come, Easy Go
    John Ferguson   S
29: The Taming of the Shrew
    The Donovan Affair
    The Doctor's Secret
30: All Quiet on the Western
    Front
    Top Speed
    The Gorilla
31: Kiki
    Inspiration
    Daybreak
    Daddy Long Legs
    Men of the Sky
    Yellow Ticket
32: Two Kinds of Women
    Shopworn
    Scarface
    Grand Hotel
    American Madness
    Those We Love
    Six Hours to Live
    You Said a Mouthful
    The Girl from Calgary
33: State Trooper
    Fog
    Mayor of Hell
    Heroes for Sale
    Dinner at Eight
    Gambling Ship
    Duck Soup
    Emergency Call
    The Woman I Stole
    Mystery of the Wax
    Museum
    Tonight Is Ours

Night of Terror
Police Car 17
Big Time or Bust
34: Miss Fane's Baby Is
    Stolen
    The Dancing Man
    Happiness C.O.D.
    Cleopatra
    Gift of Gab
    The Ninth Guest
    Mystery Liner
35: Burn 'em Up Barnes (ser.)
    Men of Action
    The Devil Is a Woman
    All the King's Horses
    The Great God Gold
    Motive for Revenge
    The Crusades
    Thanks a Million
36: Dangerous Waters
    Big Brown Eyes
    The Plainsman
    Panic on the Air
    Fury
    Come and Get it
37: A Man Betrayed
    Night Key
    The Road Back
    Slave Ship
    Love Takes Flight
    Love Is News
38: Romance on the Run
39: Young Mr. Lincoln
    Drums Along the Mohawk
    Way Down South
    Ninotchka
40: The Shop Around the
    Corner
    His Girl Friday
    The Blue Bird
    New Moon
    Kit Carson
    Brigham Young--Frontiers-
    man
41: The Devil and Miss Jones
    Ride on, Vaquero!
    Midnight Angel
42: Ten Gentlemen from West
    Point
    I Live on Danger

922

43: Behind Prison Walls
     Holy Matrimony
44: Waterfront
     The Great Moment
     Wilson
     Since You Went Away
45: Mama Loves Papa
46: The Jolson Story
     Swamp Fire
47: Second Chance
49: Ride, Ryder, Ride!
     The Set Up
     Follow Me Quietly
     Thieves' Highway
     Law of the Barbary Coast
     Side Street

John Maxwell
1942: Murder in the Big House
     Man from Headquarters
     Arizona Terrors
     Mystery of Marie Roget
     Spy Ship
     Ross of Big Town
     The Pay-Off
43: Silver Skates
     Truck Busters
     Rhythm of the Islands
     Mission to Moscow
     Murder on the Waterfront
44: Lady in the Death House
     The Last Horseman
     Alaskan

Lois Maxwell (1927-
1947: That Hagen Girl
48: The Big Punch
     The Decision of Chris-
      topher Blake
49: The Dark Past
     Corridor of Mirrors
     The Crime Doctor's
      Diary
     Kazan
53: Twilight Women
     Another Chance
     Man in Hiding
     Scotland Yard Inspector
54: Aida
     Submarine Attack

55: Passport to Treason
56: High Terrace
     Satellite in the Sky
58: Kill Me Tomorrow
59: Face of Fire
62: Lolita
63: Dr. No
     The Haunting
64: From Russia with Love
     Goldfinger
65: Thunderball
67: You Only Live Twice
68: Operation, Kid Brother

Marilyn Maxwell (1921-
1942: Stand by for Action
43: Du Barry Was a Lady (bit)
     Presenting Lily Mars
     Salute to the Marines
     Dr. Gillespie's Criminal
      Case
     Right about face
     Swing Fever
     Crazy to Kill
     Thousands Cheer
44: Lost in a Harem
     Music for Millions
     Ziegfeld Follies
     Between Two Women
     Three Men in White
46: The Show-Off
47: High Barbaree
48: Summer Holiday
     Race Street
49: The Champion
50: Outside the Wall
     Key to the City
51: New Mexico
     The Lemon Drop Kid
53: Off Limits
     East of Sumatra
     Paris Model
55: New York Confidential
58: Rock-A-Bye Baby
63: Critic's Choice
64: Stagecoach to Thunder Rock
     The Lively Set
68: Arizona Bushwackers
69: The Phynx

Donald May
1964: A Tiger Walks
Kisses for My President
66: Follow Me, Boys!

Elaine May
1967: Enter Laughing
Luv
69: A New Leaf

Eddie Mayehoff (1911-
1951: That's My Boy!
52: The Stooge
53: Off Limits
55: Artists and Models
65: How to Murder Your Wife
67: Luv
68: The Military Policeman

Ken Maynard (1895-
1928: Glorious Trail   S
29: California Mail   S
Cheyenne   S
Lawless Legion   S
Royal Rider   S
Wagon Master   PT
Phantom City   S
30: Senor Americano
Kettle Creek
Lucky Larkin
Mountain Justice
Parade of the West
Sons of the Saddle
Fighting Through
The Fighting Legion
Song of the Caballero
31: Two-Gun Men
Arizona Terror
Branded Men
The Pocatello Kid
Range Law
Alias the Bad Man
32: Sunset Trail
Death Rides the Range
Texas Gunfighter
Whistling Dan
King of the Range
Hell Fire Austin
Dynamite Ranch
33: Come on, Tarzan!

Between Fighting Men
Fargo Express
Tombstone Canyon
Drum Taps
Lone Avenger
Phantom Thunderbolt
Strawberry Roan
King of the Arena
Fiddlin' Buckaroo
34: Trail Drive
Gun Justice
Mystery Mountain (ser.)
Wheels of Destiny
Doomed to Die
Smoking Guns
Honor of the Range
In Old Santa Fe
35: Heir to Trouble
Lawless Riders
Western Courage
Western Frontier
36: Heroes of the Range
Avenging Waters
Cattle Thief
Fugitive Sheriff
37: Trailin' Trouble
Boots of Destiny
38: Six-Shootin' Sheriff
Whirlwind Horseman
Phantom Ranger
43: Wild Horse Stampede
The Law Rides Again
Blazing Guns
44: Arizona Whirlwind
Westward Bound
69: Bigfoot

Kermit Maynard (1902-
1933: Drum Taps
Outlaw Justice
34: The Fighting Trooper
Sandy of the Mounted
35: Northern Frontier
Code of the Mounted
Red Blood of Courage
Wilderness Mail
His Fighting Blood
Trails of the Wild
36: Timber War
Song of the Trail

924

36: Phantom Patrol
Wildcat Trooper
Wild Horse Roundup
Valley of Terror
Whistling Bullets
The Fighting Texan
37: Galloping Dynamite
Roaring Six-Guns
38: Wild Bill Hickok (ser.)
Western Jamboree
39: The Night Riders
Colorado Sunset
40: The Showdown
The Range Busters
Pony Post
41: Billy the Kid
The Man from Montana
Sierra Sue
42: Rock River Renegades
43: The Mysterious Rider
Fugitive of the Plains
Beyond the Last Frontier
44: The Drifter
Gunsmoke Mesa
Frontier Outlaws
Thundering Gunslingers
Brand of the Devil
45: Devil Riders
Enemy of the Law
Fighting Bill Carson
Gangsters
Stagecoach Outlaws
Wild Horse Phantom
46: Oath of Vengeance
Ambush Trail
Galloping Thunder
Prairie Badmen
Prairie Rustlers
Under Arizona Skies
Stars over Texas
Terror on Horseback
47: Buckaroo from Powder
River
Ridin' Down the Trail
Raiders of Red Rock
Frontier Fighters
Panhandle Trail
48: Tumbleweed Trail
49: Massacre River
51: Three Desperate Men

Fort Dodge Stampede
Golden Girl
58: Once Upon a Horse
60: Noose for a Gunman

Frank Mayo (1889-1963)
1930: Dough Boy
Big Shot
31: Alias the Bad Man
Range Law
Chinatown After Dark
32: The Last Ride
Hell's Headquarters
The Last Ride
35: One Hour Late
36: Desert Gold
Burning Gold
Hollywood Boulevard
39: Confessions of a Nazi Spy
Nancy Drew and the Hidden
Staircase
40: British Intelligence
Torrid Zone
Flowing Gold
41: She Couldn't Say No
The Bride Came C.O.D.
The Wagons Roll at Night
Bullets for O'Hara
42: Lady Gangster
The Male Animal
Gentleman Jim
The Gorilla Man
43: The Mysterious Doctor
Murder on the Waterfront
44: The Last Ride
Adventures of Mark Twain
45: The Great Mystic
46: The Strange Mr. Gregory
The Devil's Mask
47: Her Husband's Affair

Virginia Mayo (1922-
1942: Stand by for Action
43: Salute to the Marines
Swing Fever
Dr. Gillespie's Criminal
Case
Jack London
44: Lady in the Death House
Up in Arms

925

44: Lost in a Harem
The Princess and the
Pirate
Three Men in White
Seven Days Ashore
45: Billy Rose's Diamond
Horseshoe
The Wonder Man
46: The Kid from Brooklyn
The Best Years of Our
Lives
47: The Secret Life of Walter
Mitty
Out of the Blue
48: Smart Girls Don't Talk
A Song Is Born
49: The Girl from Jones
Beach
Flaxy Martin
Colorado Territory
Always Leave Them
Laughing
Red Light
White Heat
50: Backfire
The Flame and the Arrow
The West Point Story
51: Along the Great Divide
Captain Horatio Horn-
blower
Painting the Clouds with
Sunshine
Starlift
52: She's Working Her Way
Through College
The Iron Mistress
Adventure
53: She's Back on Broadway
South Sea Woman
Devil's Canyon
54: King Richard and the
Crusaders
The Silver Chalice
55: Pearl of the South Pacific
56: Great Day in the Morning
The Proud Ones
Congo Crossing
57: The Tall Stranger
The Big Land
The Story of Mankind

58: Fort Dobbs
59: Westbound
60: Jet over the Atlantic
61: Revolt of the Mercenaries
65: Young Fury
67: Fort Utah
Castle of Evil

Mike Mazurki (1909-
1941: The Shanghai Gesture
43: Farewell My Lovely
Henry Aldrich Haunts a
House
Taxi, Mister!
Mission to Moscow
Bomber's Moon
Behind the Rising Sun
44: The Missing Juror
Summer Storm
The Canterville Ghost
45: Abbott & Costello in
Hollywood
Dakota
Dick Tracy
The Horn Blows at
Midnight
Murder, My Sweet
The Spanish Main
46: The French Key
Live Wires
Mysterious Intruder
47: Killer Dill
Sinbad the Sailor
I Walk Alone
Nightmare Alley
Unconquered
48: Relentless
The Noose Hangs High
49: Come to the Stable
Neptune's Daughter
Rope of Sand
The Devil's Henchmen
Samson and Delilah
Abandoned
50: Night and the City
The Dark City
He's a Cockeyed Wonder
51: Pier 23
Criminal Lawyer
My Favorite Spy

926

51: Ten Tall Men
   The Light Touch
54: The Egyptian
55: New York Confidential
   New Orleans Uncensored
   Davy Crockett--King of
   the Wild Frontier
   Blood Alley
   Kismet
56: Comanche
   Man in the Vault
   Around the World in 80
   Days
57: Hell Ship Mutiny
58: The Buccaneer
   The Man Who Died Twice
59: Some Like it Hot
60: The Facts of Life
61: Pocketful of Miracles
   Double Trouble
62: Five Weeks in a Balloon
   Zotz!
63: Donovan's Reef
   It's a Mad Mad Mad Mad
   World
   Four for Texas
64: Cheyenne Autumn
65: Requiem for a Gunfighter
   Seven Women
67: The Adventures of Bull
   Whip Griffin

Claude McAllister
1929: Trial of Mary Dugan
   Bulldog Drummond
   Three Live Ghosts
   Charming Sinners

May McAvoy (1901-
1928: The Terror
29: Stolen Kisses   PT
   No Defense   PT

Diane McBain (1941-
1960: Ice Palace
61: Parrish
   Claudelle Inglish
63: The Caretakers
   Mary Mary
   Black Gold

64: A Distant Trumpet
66: Spin-Out
67: Thunder Alley
68: Maryjane
   The Mini-Skirt Mob
69: The Savage Season
   The Delta Factor

Donald McBride (1889-1957)
1932: Misleading Lady
33: Get that Venus
36: The Chemist
38: Annabel Takes a Tour
   Room Service
39: The Great Man Votes
   Twelve Crowded Hours
   The Girl and the Gambler
   The Flying Irishman
   The Story of Vernon
   and Irene Castle
   The Girl from Mexico
   The Gracie Allen Murder
   Case
   Blondie Takes a Vacation
   The Amazing Mr. Williams
   Charlie Chan at Treasure
   Island
40: The Saint's Double Trouble
   Northwest Passage
   Murder over New York
   Michael Shayne, Private
   Detective
   Curtain Call
   My Favorite Wife
   Hit Parade of 1941
41: The Invisible Woman
   Footlight Fever
   Topper Returns
   High Sierra
   Love Crazy
   Here Comes Mr. Jordan
   You'll Never Get Rich
   Rise and Shine
   You're in the Navy Now
   Louisiana Purchase
42: Two Yanks in Trinidad
   Juke Girl
   The Mexican Spitfire Sees
   a Ghost
   The Glass Key

927

42: My Sister Eileen
43: A Night to Remember
    They Got Me Covered
    Best Foot Forward
    Lady Bodyguard
    A Stranger in Town
44: Doughgirls
    The Thin Man Goes Home
45: Penthouse Rhythm
    Hold that Blonde
    Out of this World
    Girl on the Spot
    She Gets Her Man
    Abbott & Costello in
     Hollywood
    Doll Face
46: Blonde Alibi
    Little Giant
    The Killers
    The Time of Their Lives
    The Dark Horse
    The Brute Man
47: Beat the Band
    The Old Gray Mayor
    Joe Palooka in The
     Knockout
    Hal Roach Comedy
     Carnival
    Good News
    Buck Privates Come
     Home
    The Egg and I
    The Fabulous Joe
48: Campus Sleuth
    Jinx Money
    Smart Politics
49: The Story of Seabiscuit
    Challenge to Lassie
50: Joe Palooka Meets
     Humphrey
    Holiday Rhythm
51: Cuban Fireball
    Bowery Battalion
    Texas Carnival
52: Gobs and Gals
55: The Seven Year Itch

Irish McCalla (1928-
1959: She Demons
    Beat Generation

     Five Gates to Hell
60: Five Bold Women
62: Hands of a Stranger

Lon McCallister (1923-
1936: Romeo and Juliet
37: Souls at Sea
39: Babes in Arms
    Joe and Ethel Turp Visit
     the President
41: Henry Aldrich for
     President
    Summer Lightning
43: Stage Door Canteen
44: Home in Indiana
    Winged Victory
47: Thunder in the Valley (or,
     Bob, Son of Battle)
    The Red House
48: Scudda Hoo! Scudda Hay!
49: Story of Seabiscuit
50: The Boy from Indiana
51: A Yank in Korea
52: Montana Territory
53: Combat Squad

David McCallum (1933-
1956: The Dangerous Years
     (narr.)
    The Secret Plan
    Hell Drivers
57: Robbery Under Arms
    The Violent Playground
58: A Night to Remember
    To Trap a Spy
61: The Long, the Short, and
     the Tall
    Jungle Fighters
62: Freud (or, The Secret
     Passion)
    Billy Budd
63: The Great Escape
    Jungle Street Girls
65: The Greatest Story Ever
     Told
66: Around the World Under
     the Sea
    The Big T. N. T. Show
    One Spy too Many
    To Trap a Spy

67: The Spy with My Face
68: Three Bites of the Apple
69: Mosquito Squadron
    The Ravine

Mercedes McCambridge (1918-
1949: All the King's Men
      (OSCAR)
51: Lightning Strikes Twice
    Inside Straight
    The Scarf
54: Johnny Guitar
56: Giant
57: A Farewell to Arms
58: Touch of Evil
59: Suddenly Last Summer
60: Cimarron
61: Angel Baby
65: Run Home Slow
68: The Counterfeit Killer
    99 Women
69: Justine

Kevin McCarthy (1914-
1951: Death of a Salesman
54: Drive a Crooked Road
    Gambler from Natchez
55: Stranger on Horseback
    An Annapolis Story
56: Nightmare
    Invasion of the Body
    Snatchers
58: Diamond Safari
61: The Misfits
62: Forty Pounds of Trouble
63: Gathering of Eagles
    The Prize
64: The Best Man
    An Affair of the Skin
65: Mirage
66: Three Sisters
    A Big Hand for the Little
    Lady
67: Hotel
    A Time for Heroes
68: Night Hunt
    The Hell with Heroes
69: If He Hollers, Let Him Go
    UMC
    Shadow on the Land (TV)

Nobu McCarthy
1958: The Geisha Boy
59: Tokyo after Dark
    Five Gates to Hell
60: Wake Me When it's Over
    Walk Like a Dragon
61: Two Loves

Paul McCartney: see The Beatles

Sean McClory (1924-
1949: Beyond Glory
50: Daughter of Rosie O'Grady
    The Glass Menagerie
    Storm Warning
51: Lorna Doone
    Anne of the Indies
    Rommel--Desert Fox
52: The Quiet Man
    Les Miserables
    What Price Glory?
53: Botany Bay
    Plunder of the Sun
    Island in the Sky
54: Man in the Attic
    Them
    Ring of Fear
55: The Long Gray Line
    I Cover the Underworld
    Diane
    The King's Thief
    Moonfleet
57: Guns of Fort Petticoat
61: Valley of the Dragons
64: Cheyenne Autumn
65: Mara of the Wilderness
66: Follow Me, Boys!
67: The King's Pirate
    The Gnome-Mobile
    The Happiest Millionaire
68: Bandolero

Doug McClure (1934-
1957: The Enemy Below
59: Gidget
60: Because They're Young
    The Unforgiven
64: The Lively Set
65: Shenandoah
66: Beau Geste

66: The Longest One Hundred
Miles (TV)
67: The King's Pirate
68: Nobody's Perfect
69: Backtrack

Gregg McClure (1918-
1945: The Great John L.
47: Bury Me Dead
48: Lulu Belle
49: Joe Palooka in The Big
Fight
The Golden Stallion
50: Breakthrough
51: Stop that Cab!
The Roaring City
67: Adventures of Batman
and Robin

Patty McCormack (1945-
1951: Two Gals and a Guy
56: The Bad Seed
57: All Mine to Give
58: Kathy O'
60: The Snow Queen (cartoon
voice)
The Adventures of Huckle-
berry Finn
61: The Explosive Generation
Jacktown
68: Maryjane
The Mini-Skirt Mob
Born Wild
69: Blow-Off
The Young Runaways
The Phynx

Myron McCormick (1908-1962)
1937: Winterset
39: One Third of a Nation
40: The Fight for Life
49: Jigsaw
Jolson Sings Again
Gun Moll
55: Three for the Show
Not as a Stranger
58: No Time for Sergeants
59: The Man Who Understood
Women
61: The Hustler

Tim McCoy (1891-
1928: Law of the Range   S
Wyoming   S
Riders of the Dark   S
The Adventurer   S
Beyond the Sierras   S
Bushranger   S
29: Morgan's Last Raid   S
The Overland Telegraph S
Sioux Blood   S
Desert Rider   S
A Night on the Range
(musical short)
30: The Indians Are Coming
(ser.)
31: The One Way Trail
Heroes of the Flames
(ser.)
Long Loop Laramie
32: The Fighting Fool
The Fighting Marshal
The Texas Cyclone
The Riding Tornado
Shotgun Pass
Daring Danger
The Bullet Trail
Texas Keane's Return
Two-Fisted Law
The End of the Trail
The Western Code
33: Silent Men
The Whirlwind
Police Car 17
Hold the Press
Rusty Rides Alone
Cornered
Man of Action
Fighting for Justice
34: Straightaway
Speed Wings
Beyond the Law
Hell Bent for Love
A Man's Game
The Prescott Kid
Voice in the Night
35: The Westerner
Square Shooter
Revenge Rider
Outlaw Law
Riding Wild

35: Fighting Shadows
Range Raiders
Law Beyond the Range
Justice of the Range
Range Man
Man from Guntown
The Outlaw Deputy
36: Bulldog Courage
Border Caballero
Aces and Eights
Ghost Patrol
Lightnin' Bill Carson
The Lion's Den
Roarin' Guns
The Traitor
38: Code of the Rangers
Phantom Ranger
Two-Gun Justice
Lightning Bill Carson
Rides Again
39: Texas Wildcats
40: Frontier Crusader
West of Rainbow's End
Gun Code
Arizona Gang Busters
Riders of Black Mountain
Straight Shooter
41: Texas Marshal
Outlaws of the Rio Grande
Arizona Bound
Gunman from Bodie
42: Forbidden Trails
Below the Border
Ghost Town Law
Down Texas Way
Riders of the West
West of the Law
55: Injun Talk
56: Around the World in 80
Days
57: Run of the Arrow
65: Requiem for a Gunfighter

Ann McCrea
1955: Artists and Models
57: Will Success Spoil Rock
Hunter?
Kiss Them for Me
58: China Doll
61: The Ladies' Man

62: Girls! Girls! Girls!
67: Welcome to Hard Times

Joel McCrea (1905-
1929: Jazz Age   S
Five O'Clock Girl
Dynamite
So This Is College?
The Single Standard   S
30: Lightnin'
The Silver Horde
31: The Common Law
Once a Sinner
Kept Husbands
Born to Love
The Plutocrat
Girls About Town
32: Lost Squadron
Business and Pleasure
Hounds of Zaroff
Free, White, and 21
Tess of the Storm Country
Bird of Paradise
The Most Dangerous Game
Rockabye
Sport Parade
33: Our Betters
Bed of Roses
The Silver Cord
One Man's Journey
Chance at Heaven
34: Gambling Lady
Half a Sinner
The Richest Girl in the
World
35: Splendor
Private Worlds
Our Little Girl
Woman Wanted
Barbary Coast
36: These Three
Come and Get it
Two in a Crowd
Adventure in Manhattan
Banjo on My Knee
37: Interns Can't Take Money
Woman Chases Man
Dead End
Wells Fargo
38: Three Blind Mice

38: Youth Takes a Fling
39: Union Pacific
They Shall Have Music
Espionage Agent
40: He Married His Wife
The Primrose Path
Foreign Correspondent
41: Reaching for the Sun
Pioneer Woman
Sullivan's Travels
42: The Great Man's Lady
Palm Beach Story
43: The More the Merrier
44: Buffalo Bill
The Great Moment
45: The Unseen
46: The Virginian
47: Ramrod
48: Four Faces West (or,
They Passed this Way)
49: South of St. Louis
Colorado Territory
50: Stars in My Crown
Saddle Tramp
Frenchie
The Outriders
51: Cattle Drive
52: The San Francisco Story
53: Lone Hand
Shoot First
54: Border River
Black Horse Canyon
55: Wichita
Stranger on Horseback
56: The First Texan
57: Gunsight Ridge
The Oklahoman
Trooper Hook
The Tall Stranger
58: Fort Massacre
Cattle Empire
59: Gunfight at Dodge City
62: Ride the High Country
Guns in the Afternoon
69: Born Wild

Jody McCrea
1956: The First Texan
The Naked Gun
57: Gunsight Ridge

The Monster that Challenged
the World
58: Lafayette Escadrille
The Restless Years
61: Force of Impulse
All Hands on Deck
62: The Broken Land
The Young Guns of Texas
63: Beach Party
Operation Bikini
64: Law of the Lawless
Muscle Beach Party
Bikini Beach
Pajama Party
65: How to Stuff a Wild Bikini
Young Fury
Beach Blanket Bingo
67: The Glory Stompers
69: Free Grass

Philo McCullough (1893-
1929: Untamed Justice   S
The Leatherneck   PT
Show of Shows
30: On the Border
Spurs
31: Swanee River
Sheer Luck
Defenders of the Law
Sky Spider
Branded
32: Sunset Trail
South of the Rio Grande
Breach of Promise
33: Laughing at Life
Tarzan the Fearless
34: Riding Through
Wheels of Destiny
I Hate Women
Inside Information
Thunder over Texas
Outlaws' Highway
35: Captured in Chinatown
37: On Such a Night
Texas Trail
38: The Buccaneer
47: That Way with Women
49: Stampede
69: They Shoot Horses, Don't
They?

Hattie McDaniel (1895-1952)

1932: The Golden West
33: The Story of Temple Drake
Blonde Venus
I'm No Angel
34: Operator 13
Judge Priest
Little Men
Lost in the Stratosphere
35: The Little Colonel
Alice Adams
Another Face
China Seat
Music Is Magic
36: Gentle Julia
The First Baby
High Tension
Star for a Night
Can This Be Dixie?
The Bride Walks Out
Reunion
Hearts Divided
Valiant Is the Word for
Carrie
Showboat
Postal Inspector
37: Racing Lady
Don't Tell the Wife
The Crime Nobody Saw
True Confession
Saratoga
Over the Goal
45 Fathers
Nothing Sacred
38: Battle on Broadway
Everybody's Baby
Shopworn Angel
The Shining Hour
The Mad Miss Manton
39: Zenobia
Gone with the Wind
(OSCAR)
40: Maryland
41: Affectionately Yours
The Great Lie
They Died with Their
Boots on
42: The Male Animal
George Washington Slept
Here

In This Our Life
43: Thank Your Lucky Stars
Johnny Come Lately
44: Janie
Three Is a Family
45: Hi Beautiful!
46: Margie
Never Say Goodbye
Song of the South
Janie Gets Married
47: The Flame
48: Mr. Blanding Builds His
Dream House
49: The Big Wheel

Sam McDaniel (1887-1963)

1934: The Lemon Drop Kid
35: George White's Scandals
of 1935
Unwelcome Stranger
Lady Tubbs
The Virginia Judge
36: Hearts Divided
37: Captains Courageous
38: Sergeant Murphy
Gambling Ship
39: Pride of the Bluegrass
40: Calling All Husbands
41: The Great Lie
South of Panama
Broadway Limited
New York Town
Bad Men of Missouri
Louisiana Purchase
42: All Through the Night
Johnny Doughboy
The Traitor Within
I Was Framed
Mokey
43: Dixie Dugan
The Ghost and the Guest
Gangway for Tomorrow
44: Adventures of Mark Twain
Home in Indiana
Three Little Sisters
45: A Guy, a Gal, and a Pal
46: Joe Palooka--Champ
Gentleman Joe Palooka
47: I Wonder Who's Kissing
Her Now

933

48: Heart of Virginia
Secret Service Investigator
49: Flamingo Road
50: Girls' School

Ruth McDevitt (1895-
1951: The Guy Who Came Back
61: The Trap
62: Boys' Night Out
63: Love Is a Ball
The Birds
64: Dear Heart
The Out-Of-Towners
68: The Shakiest Gun in the
West
An Angel in My Pocket
69: The Love God?
Change of Habit

Francis McDonald (1891-1968)
1928: Legion of the
Condemned   S
29: Blockade   PT
30: Girl Overboard
Burning Up
Morocco
Gang Busters
The Woman from Monte
Carlo
Forbidden Paradise
Brothers
Dangerous Paradise
Safety in Numbers
The Runaway Bride
31: The Lawyer's Secret
In Line of Duty
32: Honor of the Mounted
Texas Buddies
Trailing the Killer
The Devil Is Driving
33: Terror Trail
Broadway Bad
34: Straightaway
The Trumpet Blows
The Line-Up (ser.)
Burn 'em Up Barnes
(ser. & feature)
Voice in the Night
Girl in Danger
35: Red Morning

Mississippi
Marriage Bargain
Star of Midnight
Mummy's Boys
Ladies Crave Excitement
36: Prisoner of Shark Island
Under Two Flags
Big Brown Eyes
The Plainsman
Robin Hood of El Dorado
37: The Devil's Playground
Parole Racket
Born Reckless
Love Under Fire
Every Day's a Holiday
38: Gun Law
If I Were King
39: Range War
Bad Lands
Union Pacific
The Light that Failed
40: The Carson City Kid
Green Hell
The Sea Hawk
Northwest Mounted Police
The Devil's Pipeline
41: The Sea Wolf
Men of Timberland
The Kid from Kansas
42: The Girl from Alaska
43: The Kansan
Buckskin Frontier
Bar-20
44: Lumberjack
Mystery Man
Texas Masquerade
Border Town Trail
Cheyenne Wildcat
45: Corpus Christi Bandits
The Great Stagecoach
Robbery
South of the Rio Grande
Strange Confessions
46: Bad Men of the Border
Canyon Passage
The Devil's Playground
The Catman of Paris
The Invisible Informer
Tangier
My Pal Trigger

934

46: Roll on Texas Moon
Right Train to Memphis
The Magnificent Doll
47: Dangerous Venture
Spoilers of the North
Perils of Pauline
Duel in the Sun
Saddle Pals
48: Panhandle
Desert Passage
Bandits of Corsica
Bold Frontiersman
The Paleface
An Act of Murder
49: Son of God's Country
Brothers of the Saddle
Daughter of the Jungle
Rose of the Yukon
Son of the Badman
Apache Chief
Samson and Delilah
Strange Gamble
Rim of the Canyon
50: California Passage
52: Rancho Notorious
The Raiders
54: Three Hours to Kill
55: Ten Wanted Men
56: Thunder over Arizona
The Ten Commandments
57: Duel at Apache Wells
Pawnee
Last Stagecoach West
58: Saga of Hemp Brown
Fort Massacre
59: The Big Fisherman

Grace McDonald
1942: What's Cooking?
Give Out, Sisters
Behind the Eighth Ball
43: It Ain't Hay
Strictly in the Groove
How's About it?
Mug Town
Gals, Inc.
Get Going!
Flesh and Fantasy
Always a Bridesmaid
Crazy House

She's For Me
Gung Ho!
44: Follow the Boys
Hat Check Honey
Murder in the Blue Room
My Gal Loves Music
Destiny

Ian McDonald (1914-
1941: Secrets of the Wasteland
They Died with Their Boots
On
42: The Adventures of Martin
Eden
Swamp Woman
47: Pursued
Ramrod
48: The Man from Colorado
50: Montana
Colt .45
Comanche Territory
The Desert Hawk
51: Thunder in God's Country
New Mexico
The Texas Rangers
Ten Tall Men
Flaming Feather
52: This Woman Is Dangerous
High Noon
The Brigand
The Savage
Toughest Man in Arizona
Hiawatha
53: Silver Whip
A Perilous Journey
Blowing Wild
54: Taza, Son of Cochise
Apache
Johnny Guitar
The Egyptian
55: Timberjack
The Lonesome Trail
Son of Sinbad
56: Two-Gun Lady
Stagecoach to Fury
Accused of Murder
57: Duel at Apache Wells
58: Money, Women, and Guns
59: Warlock

Marie McDonald (1923-1965)
1941: It Started with Eve
You're Telling Me
  42: Pardon My Sarong
Lucky Jordan
  43: Tornado
Riding High
  44: I Love a Soldier
Standing Room Only
Guest in the House
  45: Getting Gertie's Garter
It's a Pleasure
  47: Living in a Big Way
  49: Tell it to the Judge
  50: The Song Parade
Hit Parade of 1951
Once a Thief
  58: Geisha Boy
  63: Promises, Promises!

Roddy McDowall (1928-
1936: Murder in the Family
You Will Remember
  37: Scruffy
I See Ice
Just William
  38: The Outsider
Hey! Hey! U.S.A.
John Halifax--Gentleman
Convict 99
Sarah Seddons
Poison Pen
Dead Man's Shoes
  39: His Brother's Keeper
Dirt
Saloon Bar
  40: This England
  41: How Green Was My Valley
Confirm or Deny
Man Hunt
  42: Son of Fury
The Pied Piper
On the Sunny Side
  43: My Friend Flicka
Lassie Come Home
  44: White Cliffs of Dover
Keys of the Kingdom
  45: Molly and Me
Thunderhead, Son of Flicka
  46: Holiday in Mexico

  48: Green Grass of Wyoming
Rocky
Kidnapped
Macbeth
  49: Tuna Clipper
Black Midnight
  50: Big Timber
Killer Shark
  52: The Steel Fist
  60: The Subterraneans
Midnight Lace
  61: The Power and the Glory
  62: The Longest Day
  63: Cleopatra
  64: Shock Treatment
  65: The Greatest Story Ever
Told
The Third Day
That Darn Cat
The Loved One
Inside Daisy Clover
  66: Lord Love a Duck
The Defector
  67: The Adventures of Bullwhip
Griffin
The Cool Ones
  68: Planet of the Apes
The Midas Run
Five Card Stud
  69: Giovanni
Angel, Angel, Down We Go
Hello Down There

Claire McDowell (1877-1967)
1928: The Viking   S
  29: When Dreams Come
True   S
Silks and Saddles   S
The Quitter   S
Whispering Winds   PT
  30: Redemption
Second Floor Mystery
Young Desire
The Big House
Wild Company
Mothers Cry
  31: An American Tragedy
  32: Manhattan Parade
It's Tough to be Famous
Strange Love of Molly
Louvain

32: Phantom Express
    Rebecca of Sunnybrook
    Farm
33: Cornered
    Central Airport
    The Working Man
    By Appointment Only
    Paddy, the Next Best
    Thing
    Wild Boys of the Road
    Two Heads on a Pillow
35: August Week-End
37: Two-Fisted Sheriff
38: several shorts
44: Are These Your Parents?
    Men on Her Mind

Peter McEnery (1940-
1960: Tunes of Glory
62: Victim
64: The Moonspinners
66: The Fighting Prince of
    Donegal
67: The Game Is Over
68: Better a Widow (Ital.)
    I Love You, I Hate You!
    Negatives
69: The Adventures of Gerard

Spanky McFarland (1928-
1930: "Our Gang" Comedies
34: Kidnapped
36: Trail of the Lonesome
    Pine
43: Johnny Doughboy

Darren McGavin (1922-
1945: A Song to Remember
    Kiss and Tell
    She Wouldn't Say Yes
    Counter-Attack
    Fear
51: Queen for a Day
55: Summertime
    The Man with the Golden
    Arm
    The Court-Martial of
    Billy Mitchell
57: Beau James
    The Delicate Delinquent
58: The Case Against Brook-
    lyn

64: Bullet for a Badman
65: The Great Sioux Massacre
66: Ride the High Wind
67: The Outsider (TV pilot)
68: Mission: Mars
69: The Challengers

John McGiver (1913-
1957: Love in the Afternoon
58: Man in the Raincoat
    I Married a Woman
    Once Upon a Horse
59: The Gazebo
61: Love in a Goldfish Bowl
    Breakfast at Tiffany's
    Bachelor in Paradise
62: Mr. Hobbs Takes a
    Vacation
    The Manchurian Candidate
    Period of Adjustment
    Who's Got the Action?
63: My Six Loves
    Johnny Cool
    Take Her She's Mine
    Who's Minding the Store?
64: A Global Affair
    Man's Favorite Sport?
65: Marriage on the Rocks
66: Made in Paris
    The Glass Bottom Boat
67: The Spirit Is Willing
    Fitzwilly
69: Midnight Cowboy

Frank McGlynn (1867-1951)
1934: Search for Beauty
    Little Miss Marker
    Are We Civilized?
    Lost in the Stratosphere
35: Folies Bergère
    It's a Small World
    Outlawed Guns
    The Littlest Rebel
    Captain Blood
36: Prisoner of Shark Island
    For the Service
    Parole!
    The Last of the Mohicans
    King, of the Royal Mounted
    North of Nome
    Career Woman
37: Silent Barriers

937

37: Sing and be Happy
    Western Gold
    Wells Fargo
38: Sudden Bill Dorn
39: Juarez and Maximilian
40: Hi-Yo, Silver!
    Boom Town
41: A Girl, a Guy, and a
      Gob
    Marry the Boss's Daughter
    Three Girls in Town
44: Delinquent Daughters
45: Rogues' Gallery
47: Hollywood Barn Dance

Patrick McGoohan (1928-
1955: Passage Home
    I Am a Camera
56: High Tide at Noon
57: Zarak
58: Hell Drivers
    The Gypsy and the
      Gentleman
59: The Elephant Gun
61: All Night Long
    Two Living, One Dead
62: The Quare Fellow
63: Three Lives of Thomasina
66: Walk in the Shadow
68: Ice Station Zebra
69: Moonshine War

J.P. McGowan (1880-1952)
1929: The Cleanup   S
    Lawless Legion   S
    Plunging Hoofs   S
    Headin' Westward   S
    Law of the Mounted   S
    Bad Men's Money   S
    Arizona Days   S
    Below the Deadline   S
    Golden Bridle   S
    The Last Roundup   S
    West of Santa Fe   S
    Texas Tommy   S
    Phantom Rider   S
    The Invaders   SSE
    Fighting Terror   S
    The Oklahoma Kid   S

    Lone Horseman   S
30: Señor Americano
    'Neath Western Skies   S
    Cowboy and the Outlaw   S
    Pioneers of the West   S
    Canyon of Missing Men   S
    Covered Wagon Trails   S
33: Somewhere in Arizona
34: No More Women
    Wagon Wheels
    Fighting Hero
35: Mississippi
    Border Brigands
    Bar-20 Rides Again
    Secret Patrol
36: The Three Mesquiteers
    Ride 'em, Cowboy!
    Stampede
    Guns and Guitars
37: Fury and the Woman
38: The Buccaneer
39: In Old Montana
    Code of the Fearless
    Calling All Marines
    Stagecoach

Walter McGrail (1889-
1929: Confessions of a Wife   S
    Veiled Woman   S
    River of Romance
30: Men Without Women
    Lone Star Ranger
    Anybody's War
    Women Everywhere
    Soldiers and Women
    Last of the Duanes
    Pay-Off
    River's End
    Part Time Wife
31: The Seas Beneath
    Murder by the Clock
32: Night Beat
    Under Eighteen
    McKenna of the Mounted
    Exposed
33: State Trooper
    Robbers' Roost
    Sing, Sinner, Sing!
    Police Call
34: The World Moves On

34: Demon for Trouble
The Lemon Drop Kid
35: Men of the Night
All the King's Horses
Sunset Range
37: The Shadow Strikes
38: Held for Ransom
40: My Little Chickadee
42: Billy the Kid Trapped
Riders of the West

Frank McGrath (1903-1967)
1942: Sundown Jim
53: Ride On, Vaquero!
57: Hell Bound
The Tin Star
65: The Sword of Ali Baba
67: The Last Challenge
The War Wagon
The Shakiest Gun in the West
Gunfight in Abilene
The Reluctant Astronaut
Tammy and the Millionaire

Paul McGrath (1904-
1940: The Parole Fixer
Wildcat Bus
41: This Thing Called Love
Dead Men Tell
We Go Fast
Marry the Boss's Daughter
43: No Time for Love
57: A Face in the Crowd
62: Advise and Consent
68: Pendulum

Charles McGraw (1914-
1943: The Moon Is Down
They Came to Blow Up America
The Mad Ghoul
44: The Impostor
46: The Killers
47: On the Old Spanish Trail
Roses Are Red
The Big Fix
The Long Night
T-Men
48: The Hunted

Hazard
Blood on the Moon
49: Once More, My Darling
The Threat
Border Incident
Reign of Terror (or, The Black Book)
The Story of Molly X
Side Street
50: Armed Car Robbery
Double Crossbones
51: The Back Road
52: The Narrow Margin
One Minute to Zero
53: War Paint
Thunder over the Plains
54: Loophole
The Bridges at Toko-Ri
56: Toward the Unknown
Away All Boats
The Cruel Tower
57: Joe Butterfly
Joe Dakota
Slaughter on Tenth Avenue
58: Saddle the Wind
Twilight for the Gods
The Defiant Ones
59: Man in the Net
The Wonderful Country
60: Spartacus
Cimarron
62: The Horizontal Lieutenant
63: The Birds
It's a Mad Mad Mad Mad World
67: In Cold Blood
The Busy Body
68: Hang 'em High
Pendulum
69: Willie Boy

Malcolm McGregor (1892-1945)
1928: Freedom of the Press   S
29: Girl on the Barge   PT
30: Murder Will Out
35: Happiness C.O.D.

Don McGuire (1919-
1945: Pillow to Post
Pride of the Marines
Too Young to Know

46: Shadow of a Woman
47: Always Together
My Wild Irish Rose
Love and Learn
The Man I Love
Nora Prentiss
Possessed
That Way with Women
48: The Fuller Bush Man
Wallflower
Whiplash
I Surrender Dear
49: Sky Liner
Boston Blackie's Chinese
Venture
The Threat
50: Joe Palooka Meets
Humphrey
Armed Car Robbery
Sideshow
51: Three Guys Named Mike
Double Dynamite

Dorothy McGuire (1919-
1943: Claudia
45: A Tree Grows in Brooklyn
Enchanted Cottage
46: Spiral Staircase
Claudia and David
Till the End of Time
47: A Gentleman's Agreement
50: Mother Didn't Tell Me
Mr. 880
51: Callaway Went Thataway
I Want You
52: Invitation
53: Make Haste to Live
54: Three Coins in a Fountain
55: Trial
56: Friendly Persuasion
57: Old Yeller
59: The Remarkable Mr.
Pennypacker
This Earth Is Mine
A Summer Place
60: The Dark at the Top of
the Stairs
The Swiss Family Robin-
son
61: Susan Slade

63: Summer Magic
65: The Greatest Story Ever
Told

Kathryn McGuire (1897-
1929: Children of the Ritz   SSE
Synthetic Sin   S
Big Diamond Robbery   S
Border Wildcat   S
The Long, Long Trail

Frank McHugh (1898-
1928: If Men Played Cards as
Women Do (short)
30: Top Speed
Bright Lights
Mlle Modiste
The Dawn Patrol
Toast of the Legion
College Lovers
Flight Command
The Widow from Chicago
Little Caesar
31: Going Wild
Millie
Corsair
Traveling Husbands
Men of the Sky
Gentleman for a Day
Bad Company
Front Page
Fires of Youth
Up for Murder
Kiss Me Again
32: High Pressure
Strange Love of Molly
Louvain
One Way Passage
Life Begins
Blessed Event
Dark Horse
Union Depot
The Crowd Roars
33: The Mystery of the Wax
Museum
42nd Street
Parachute Jumper
Elmer the Great
Convention City
Son of a Sailor

940

33: Lilly Turner
Havana Widows
Private Jones
Professional Sweetheart
Tomorrow at Seven
Hold Me Tight
Not Tonight, Josephine
The Mad Game
Footlight Parade
The House on 56th Street
Ex-Lady
Grand Slam
Telegraph Trail
34: Fashions of 1934
Happiness Ahead
Maybe It's Love
Merry Wives of Reno
Heat Lightning
Smarty
Here Comes the Navy
Let's be Ritzy
Return of the Terror
Six Day Bike Race
35: Devil Dogs of the Air
A Midsummer Night's
  Dream
Page Miss Glory
Stars over Broadway
Gold Diggers of 1935
The Irish in Us
Three Kids and a Queen
36: Freshman Love
Snowed Under
Bullets or Ballots
Stage Struck
Three Men on a Horse
Moonlight Murder
37: Ever Since Eve
Mr. Dodd Takes the Air
Marry the Girl
Submarine D-1
38: Swing Your Lady
He Couldn't Say No
Little Miss Thoroughbred
Boy Meets Girl
Four Daughters
Valley of the Giants
39: Wings of the Navy
Daughters Courageous
Indianapolis Speedway

Dust be My Destiny
The Roaring Twenties
Four Wives
On Your Toes
40: The Fighting 69th
Virginia City
Saturday's Children
Till We Meet Again
City for Conquest
Here Comes the Navy
41: Four Mothers
I Love You Again
Back Street
Manpower
42: All Through the Night
Her Cardboard Lover
43: Marine Raiders
44: Going My Way
Bowery to Broadway
45: A Medal for Benny
State Fair
Third Avenue
46: Deadline for Murder
The Hoodlum Saint
Little Miss Big
The Runaround
47: Carnegie Hall
Easy Come, Easy Go
48: The Velvet Touch
Bitter Victory
49: Paid in Full
Miss Grant Takes Rich-
  mond
The Mighty Joe Young
50: The Tougher They Come
Crackdown
52: The Pace that Thrills
My Son John
53: It Happens Every Tuesday
A Lion Is in the Streets
54: There's no Business like
  Show Business
58: The Last Hurrah
59: Say One for Me
64: A Tiger Walks

John McIntire (1907-
1948: Call Northside 777
Black Bart
River Lady

941

48: Street with no Name
Command Decision
An Act of Murder
49: Top O' the Morning
Down to the Sea in Ships
Red Canyon
Francis
Ambush
Scene of the Crime
50: Saddle Tramp
Under the Gun
Winchester 73
Asphalt Jungle
Shadow on the Wall
No Sad Songs for Me
51: The Raging Tide
Westward the Women
That's My Boy!
You're in the Navy Now
(or, U. S. S. Tea Kettle)
52: The World in His Arms
Glory Alley
Sally and St. Anne
Horizons West
The Lawless Breed
53: Mississippi Gambler
The President's Lady
A Lion Is in the Streets
War Arrow
54: Apache
Four Guns to the Border
The Yellow Mountain
55: The Far Country
Stranger on Horseback
The Scarlet Coat
The Phenix City Story
The Spoilers
The Kentuckian
56: The World in My Corner
I've Lived Before
Backlash
Away all Boats
57: The Tin Star
58: The Light in the Forest
Sing, Boy, Sing!
Mark of the Hawk
Gunfight at Dodge City
60: Elmer Gantry
Seven Ways from Sundown
Who Was that Lady?

Flaming Star
Psycho
61: Two Rode Together
Summer and Smoke
67: Rough Night in Jericho

Wanda McKay
1940: All Women Have Secrets
41: Dancing on a Dime
The Pioneers
Twilight on the Trail
42: One Thrilling Night
Bowery at Midnight
Law and Order
43: Corregidor
Danger: Women at Work!
The Deerslayer
What a Man!
The Black Raven
44: Belle of the Yukon
Leave it to the Irish
The Monster Maker
Smart Guy
The Voodoo Man
45: Hollywood and Vine
There Goes Kelly
46: Kilroy Was Here
47: Jiggs and Maggie in
Society
Jinx Money
Stage Struck
Story of Life
The Golden Eye
48: Jungle Goddess
50: A Woman of Distinction
51: Roaring City

"Lafe" McKee (1872-
1930: Under Montana Skies
The Rainbow's End
Lonesome Trail
Code of Honor
The Utah Kid
Hell's Valley
31: Red Fork Range
Alias the Bad Man
Two-Gun Man
Grief Street
Partners of the Trail
Hurricane Horseman

942

31: Range Law
Neck and Neck
Lariats and Six-Shooters
The Cyclone Kid
32: The Fighting Marshal
Without Honor
The Gay Buckaroo
Mark of the Spur
Spirit of the West
Hell-Fire Austin
The Riding Tornado
The Man from New
Mexico
Klondike Gold
The Boiling Point
Hello Trouble
The Fighting Champ
33: Tombstone Canyon
Self Defense
Young Blood
Terror Trail
Deadwood Pass
End of the Trail
Fighting for Justice
Dude Bandit
Man from Monterey
Crossfire
Fighting Texans
Galloping Romeo
War of the Range
Under Secret Orders
34: Gun Justice
Riding Through
The Quitter
Trail Drive
West of the Divide
Riders of Destiny
Straightaway
Tracy Rides
Hell Bent for Love
The Man from Utah
Demons for Trouble
Outlaws' Highway
Frontier Days
35: Port of Lost Dreams
Keeper of the Bees
What Price Crime?
Kid Courageous
The Hawk
Desert Trail

The Ivory-Handled Gun
36: Swifty
Roaming Wild
Bridge of Sighs
The Cowboy and the Kid
The Last of the Warrens
The Idaho Kid
Men of the Plains
37: Melody of the Plains
Law of the Ranger
Mystery of the Hooded
Horsemen
38: Rawhide
I'm from the City
40: Pioneers of the Frontier
Covered Wagon Trails
Riders of the Pasco Basin
The Bad Man from Red
Butte
Son of the Roaring Dan
42: Inside the Law

Siobhan McKenna (1922-
1946: Hungry Hill
48: Daughter of Darkness
49: The Last People
50: The Adventurers
61: King of Kings
62: Playboy of the Western
World
64: Of Human Bondage
66: Dr. Zhivago

Virginia McKenna (1931-
1953: Father's Doing Fine
The Cruel Sea
55: Simba
56: A Town Like Alice
The Ship that Died of
Shame
57: Carve Her Name with
Pride
The Smallest Show on
Earth
The Barretts of Wimpole
Street
59: The Wreck of the Mary
Deare
Passionate Summer
62: Two Living, One Dead

66: Born Free
68: The Lions Are Free
69: Ring of Bright Water
    Waterloo

Fay McKenzie
1941: Down Mexico Way
      Sierra Sue
  42: Cowboy Serenade
      Heart of the Rio Grande
      Remember Pearl Harbor
  44: The Singing Sheriff
  46: Murder in the Music Hall
  68: The Party

Robert McKenzie
1939: Death of a Champion
  40: Buried Alive
      Dreaming Out Loud
      Triple Justice
  41: Citadel of Crime
      Death Valley Outlaws
  42: In Old California
      The Sombrero Kid
  43: Jive Junction
  44: Texas Masquerade
      Three of a Kind
      Tall in the Saddle
  46: Romance of the West
      Colorado Serenade

Victor McLaglen (1886-1959)
1928: Mother Machree   SSE
      A Girl in Every Port   S
      Hangman's House   S
      River Pirate   SSE
  29: Captain Lash   SSE
      Strong Boy   SSE
      Not for Paris
      The Cockeyed World
      Sez You, Sez Me
      Black Watch
  30: A Devil with Women
      On the Level
      King of the Khyber Rifles
      Happy Days
  31: Dishonored
      Wicked
      Annabelle's Affairs
      Women of all Nations

      Three Rogues
      Not Exactly Gentlemen
  32: Guilty as Hell
      The Devil's Lottery
      The Gay Caballero
      While Paris Sleeps
      Rackety Rax
  33: Hot Pepper
      Laughing at Life
      Dick Turpin
  34: Murder at the Vanities
      The Captain Hates the Sea
      Lost Patrol
      No More Women
      Wharf Angel
  35: Under Pressure
      The Great Hotel Murder
      The Informer (OSCAR)
      Professional Soldier
  36: Under Two Flags
      Mary of Scotland
      Klondike Annie
      The Magnificent Brute
  37: Sea Devils
      Nancy Steele Is Missing
      This Is My Affair
      Wee Willie Winkie
  38: Battle of Broadway
      We're Going to be Rich
      The Devil's Party
  39: Pacific Liner
      Gunga Din!
      Full Confession
      Let Freedom Ring
      Captain Fury
      Ex-Champ
      Rio
  40: The Big Guy
      South of Pago Pago
      Diamond Frontier
  41: Broadway Limited
  42: Call Out the Marines
      Powder Town
      China Girls
  43: Forever and a Day
  44: Roger Touhy--Gangster
      Tampico
      The Princess and the
        Pirate
  45: Rough, Tough, and Ready

944

45: Love, Honor, and Goodbye
46: Whistle Stop
47: The Michigan Kid
    The Foxes of Harrow
    The Calendar Girl
48: Fort Apache
49: She Wore a Yellow Ribbon
50: Rio Grande
52: The Quiet Man
53: Fair Wind to Java
54: Prince Valiant
    Trouble in the Glen
55: Many Rivers to Cross
    Bengazi
    Lady Godiva
    City of Shadows
56: Around the World in 80
    Days
57: The Abductors
59: Sea Fury

David McLean
1961: The Right Approach
    The Silent Call
    Voyage to the Bottom of
    the Sea
    X-15
64: The Strangler
66: Nevada Smith

Catherine McLeod (c1924-
1945: They Shall Have Faith
46: Courage of Lassie
    I've Always Loved You
47: That's My Man
    The Fabulous Texan
48: Old Los Angeles
50: So Young, So Bad
52: My Wife's Best Friend
53: A Blueprint for Murder
    Sword of Venus
54: The Outcast
58: Return to Warbow
61: Tammy Tell Me True
    The Sergeant and the Lady
64: Ride the Wild Surf

Allyn McLerie (1926-
1948: Words and Music
52: Where's Charley?

53: The Desert Song
    Calamity Jane
54: Phantom of the Rue Morgue
55: Battle Cry
69: The Reivers

Horace McMahon (1907-
1937: Navy Blues
    Exclusive
    The Wrong Road
    A Girl with Ideas
    They Gave Him a Gun
    Double Wedding
    Kid Galahad
38: King of the Newsboys
    When G-Men Step In
    Fast Company
    Ladies in Distress
    Tenth Avenue Kid
    Secrets of a Nurse
    Broadway Musketeers
    Pride of the Navy
39: Sergeant Madden
    The Gracie Allen Murder
    Case
    Rose of Washington Square
    I Was a Convict
    Federal Man-Hunt
    Laugh it Off
    Big Town Czar
    For Love or Money
    She Married a Cop
    Quick Millions
    Sabotage
40: The Marines Fly High
    Dr. Kildare's Strange Case
    I Can't Give You Anything
    but Love, Baby
    Gangs of Chicago
    Millionaires in Prison
    Oh Johnny, How You can
    Love!
    We Who Are Young
    The Leather Pushers
    Melody Ranch
    Dr. Kildare's Crisis
41: Come Live with Me
    Rookies on Parade
    The Bride Wore Crutches
    Lady Scarface

41: Buy Me that Town
Birth of the Blues
The Stork Pays Off
42: Jail House Blues
44: Roger Touhy--Gangster
Timber Queen
48: Smart Woman
Fighting Mad
Waterfront at Midnight
The Return of October
51: Detective Story
53: Abbott & Costello Go to
Mars
Man in the Dark
Fast Company
Champ for a Day
54: Duffy of San Quentin
Susan Slept Here
55: Blackboard Jungle
My Sister Eileen
Texas Lady
57: The Delicate Delinquent
Beau James
59: Never Steal Anything
Small
66: The Swinger
68: The Detective

Barbara McNair (1939-
1968: If He Hollers, Let Him Go
69: Venus in Furs
Stiletto
Change of Habit
The Savarona Syndrome

Horace McNally
1942: The War Against Mrs.
Hadley
Eyes in the Night
For Me and My Gal
Dr. Gillespie's New
Assistant
Keeper of the Flame
43: Air Raid Wardens
44: An American Romance
Thirty Seconds over Tokyo
45: Bewitched

Stephen McNally (1913-
1942: Grand Central Murder

43: The Man from Down Under
45: The Harvey Girls
46: The Magnificent Doll
48: Johnny Belinda
Rogues' Regiment
49: City Across the River
Criss Cross
The Lady Gambles
Woman in Hiding
Sword in the Desert
50: Winchester 73
Wyoming Mail
No Way Out
51: Air Cadet
Apache Drums
The Raging Tide
The Lady Pays Out
Iron Man
52: Duel at Silver Creek
Diplomatic Courier
Black Castle
Battle Zone
53: Split Second
The Stand at Apache River
Devil's Canyon
54: Make Haste to Live
A Bullet Is Waiting
55: The Man from Bitter Ridge
Violent Saturday
56: Tribute to a Bad Man
57: Hell's Crossroads
58: Hell's Five Hours
The Fiend Who Walked the
West
Johnny Rocco
60: Hell Bent for Leather
65: Requiem for a Gunfighter
68: Sudden Death
69: Panic in the City
The Savarona Syndrome
The Whole World Is Talking

Maggie McNamara (1928-
1954: Three Coins in the Fountain
55: Prince of Players
63: The Cardinal

Howard McNear (1905-1969)
1954: Drums Across the River
56: You Can't Run Away from
it

946

56: Bundle of Joy
57: Public Pigeon No. 1
Affair in Reno
58: Bell, Cook, and Candle
Good Day for a Hanging
59: The Big Circus
Anatomy of a Murder
61: Voyage to the Bottom of
the Sea
Bachelor Flat
Blue Hawaii
62: The Errand Boy
Follow that Dream
63: Irma La Douce
64: Kiss Me, Stupid!
65: My Blood Runs Cold
Love and Kisses
66: The Fortune Cookie

Douglas McPhail (d. 1942)
1936: Born to Dance
37: Maytime
38: Test Pilot
Toy Wife
Sweethearts
39: Babes in Arms
40: Broadway Melody of 1940
Little Nellie Kelly
42: Born to Sing

Butterfly McQueen
1939: Gone With the Wind
41: Affectionately Yours
43: Cabin in the Sky
I Dood it
45: Flame of Barbary Coast
Mildred Pierce
46: Duel in the Sun
69: The Phynx

Steve McQueen (1930-
1956: Somebody Up There Likes
Me
Beyond a Doubt
58: Never Love a Stranger
The Blob
59: Never so Few
The Great St. Louis Bank
Robbery
60: The Magnificent Seven

61: The Honeymoon Machine
62: Hell Is for Heroes!
The War Lover
63: The Great Escape
Soldier in the Rain
Love with a Proper
Stranger
65: Baby, the Rain Must Fall
The Cincinnati Kid
66: Nevada Smith
The Sand Pebbles
67: The Traveling Saleslady
The Day of the Champion
The Curse of the Mummy's
Tomb
68: The Thomas Crown Affair
Bullitt
69: The Reivers
The Phynx (cameo)
Le Mans
Yucatan

Paul McVey
1936: The Country Beyond
Half Angle
The Crime of Dr. Forbes
Sing, Baby, Sing!
37: Love Is News
Fair Warning
This Is My Affair
One Mile from Heaven
38: Passport Husband
Night Hawk
Meet the Girls
39: Stagecoach
Panama Patrol
Inside Information
Drums Along the Mohawk
40: Slightly Honorable
Buried Alive
42: The Yukon Patrol
The Living Ghost
43: Silver Skates
Happy Go Lucky
You Can't Beat the Law
The Mystery of the 13th
Guest
Henry Aldrich Haunts a
House
44: Lady in the Dark

947

44: Smart Guy
48: Force of Evil
50: Perfect Strangers
    Ma and Pa Kettle Go to
    Town
52: No Room for the Groom
    Bwana Devil
53: Shane

Tyler McVey
1951: The Day the Earth Stood
    Still
52: The Confidence Girl
    O. Henry's Full House
    (The Clarion Call seq.)
53: A Blueprint for Murder
54: Day of Triumph
56: The Come On
58: Hot Car Girl
    Terror in a Texas Town
59: The Giant Leeches
60: The Gallant Hours
    Louisiana Hussey
64: Man's Favorite Sport?
    The Best Man
66: Lt. Robin Crusoe, U.S.N.
    Dead Heat on a Merry-Go-
    Round

Julia Meade (1928-
1959: Pillow Talk
61: Tammy Tell Me True
62: Zotz!

George Meader
1940: Courageous Dr. Christian
    Gambling on the High
    Seas
41: The Man-Made Monster
    Petticoat Politics
    Dancing on a Dime
    New York Town
    Father Takes a Wife
    Bachelor Daddy
    The Smiling Ghost
42: The Glass Key
45: A Tree Grows in Brooklyn
    Roughly Speaking
    Boston Blackie Booked on
    Suspicion

    Spellbound
46: Betty Co-Ed
47: Too Many Winners
    For the Love of Rusty
    Keeper of the Bees
49: That Midnight Kiss
    On the Town
51: The Groom Wore Spurs

Audrey Meadows (1924-
1962: That Touch of Mink
63: Take Her She's Mine
67: Rosie

Jayne Meadows (1923-
1946: Undercurrent
47: Dark Delusion
    Lady in the Lake
    Song of the Thin Man
    Cynthia
48: Luck of the Irish
    Enchantment
51: The Fat Man
    David and Bathsheba
59: It Happened to Jane
60: College Confidential
68: Now You See it, Now You
    Don't (TV)

Joyce Meadows
1958: Frontier Gun
60: Walk Tall
    The Girl in Lover's Lane
65: Zebra in the Kitchen
67: I Saw What You Did
    The Busy Body

Kay Medford (1920-
1942: The War Against Mrs.
    Hadley
43: Swing Shift Maisie
45: Adventure
50: Guilty Bystander
57: A Face in the Crowd
    Jamboree
60: The Rat Race
    Girl of the Night
    Butterfield 8
62: Two Tickets to Paris
64: Ensign Pulver

66: A Fine Madness
68: Funny Girl
69: Angel in My Pocket
Twinky

Patricia Medina (1920-
1938: Simply Terrific
Double or Quit
42: Secret Journey
The Avengers
43: They Met in the Dark
Kiss the Bride Goodbye
The Day Will Dawn
44: Hotel Reserve
Don't Take It to Heart
45: Waltz Time
46: A Secret Heart
47: Moss Rose
The Foxes of Harrow
The Beginning or the End?
48: The Three Musketeers
49: The Fighting O'Flynn
Francis
50: Abbott & Costello in the
Foreign Legion
The Jackpot
51: The Magic Carpet
The Lady and the Bandit
Valentino
52: Aladdin and His Lamp
Captain Pirate
Lady in the Iron Mask
Desperate Search
53: Botany Bay
Siren of Bagdad
Plunder of the Sun
Sangaree
54: Drums of Tahiti
Phantom of the Rue
Morgue
The Black Knight
55: Pirates of Tripoli
Duel on the Mississippi
Il Mantello Rosso
56: Uranium Boom
Miami Exposé
Stranger at My Door
The Beast of Hollow
Mountain
57: The Buckskin Lady

59: Count Your Blessings
61: Snow White and the Three
Stooges
62: Mr. Arkadin
68: Killing of Sister George
69: Latitude Zero
Keene

Donald Meek (1880-1946)
1929: Hole in the Wall
30: The Love Kiss
31: Girl Habit
32: S.S. Van Dyne Mystery
series
33: Love, Honor, and Oh
Baby!
College Coach
34: The Defense Rests
Hi Nellie!
Bedside
Mrs. Wiggs of the Cabbage
Patch
Murder at the Vanities
Merry Widow
The Last Gentleman
The Captain Hates the Sea
35: Biography of a Bachelor
Girl
The Whole Town's Talking
The Informer
The Village Tale
The Return of Peter Grimm
Old Man Rhythm
The Gilded Lady
Accent on Youth
The Bride Comes Home
Society Doctor
Mark of the Vampire
Baby Face Harrington
King Lady
Barbary Coast
She Couldn't Take it
Captain Blood
Only Eight Hours
China Seas
Peter Ibbetson
Happiness C.O.D.
36: Everybody's Old Man
And So They Were Married
Pennies from Heaven

36: One Rainy Afternoon
Three Wise Guys
Old Hutch
Love on the Run
Three Married Men
Two in a Crowd
37: Maid of Salem
Artists and Models
Parnell
Three Legionnaires
Behind the Headlines
The Toast of New York
Make a Wish
Breakfast for Two
You're a Sweetheart
38: Double Danger
Having a Wonderful Time
Adventures of Tom
Sawyer
Goodbye Broadway
Little Miss Broadway
Hold that Coed!
You Can't Take it with
You
39: Jesse James
Young Mr. Lincoln
Hollywood Cavalcade
Stagecoach
Blondie Takes a Vacation
The Housekeeper's
Daughter
Nick Carter, Master
Detective
40: My Little Chickadee
Dr. Ehrlich's Magic
Bullet
Turnabout
The Man from Dakota
The Ghost Comes Home
Oh Johnny, How You can
Love!
Phantom Riders
Sky Murder
Third Finger, Left Hand
Hullabaloo
Star Dust
Return of Frank James
41: A Woman's Face
Wild Man of Borneo
Blonde Inspiration

Come Live with Me
Rise and Shine
Babes on Broadway
The Feminine Touch
Barnacle Bill
42: Tortilla Flat
Maisie Gets Her Man
Seven Sweethearts
The Omaha Trail
Keeper of the Flame
43: Air Raid Wardens
They Got Me Covered
Du Barry Was a Lady
Lost Angel
The Honest Thief
44: Rationing
Two Girls and a Sailor
Bathing Beauty
Barbary Coast Gent
Maisie Goes to Reno
The Thin Man Goes Home
45: Col. Effingham's Raid
State Fair
46: Because of Him
Janie Gets Married
Affairs of Geraldine
47: The Fabulous Joe
Magic Town

George Meeker (1904-
1932: Fireman, Save My Child!
Emma
A Fool's Advice
Misleading Lady
The Famous Ferguson
Case
The First Year
Vanity Street
Tess of the Storm Country
The Match King
Back Street
Afraid to Talk
33: Pick Up
Sweepings
Night of Terror
The Life of Jimmy Dolan
Double Harness
Only Yesterday
King for a Night
A Chance at Heaven

34: Ever Since Eve
Dark Hazard
Hips Hips Hooray!
I Believed in You
Melody in Spring
Uncertain Lady
Little Man, What now?
Paris Interlude
The Dragon Murder Case
Richest Girl in the World
Against the Law
Bachelor of Arts
35: Murder on a Honeymoon
Oil for the Lamps of
China
Manhattan Butterfly
Welcome Home
The Rainmakers
Remember Last Night
36: Gentle Julia
The Country Doctor
Tango
Don't Get Personal
In Paris A.W.O.L.
Neighborhood House
Walking on Air
Wedding Present
Career Woman
37: Beware of Ladies
History Is Made at Night
On Again, Off Again
Escape by Night
The Westland Case
38: Tarzan's Revenge
Marie Antoinette
Danger on the Air
Slander House
Meet the Mayor
Long Shot
39: Rough Riders' Roundup
The Lady and the Mob
Undercover Doctor
Stunt Pilot
The Roaring Twenties
Everything's on Ice
Gone With the Wind
Swanee River
40: A Night at Earl Carroll's
Michael Shayne, Private
Detective
Yesterday's Heroes

41: High Sierra
The Singing Hill
Mountain Music
Marry the Boss's Daughter
You're in the Army Now
42: Larceny, Inc.
Murder in the Big House
Wings for the Eagle
Spy Ship
The Busses Roar
Secret Enemies
You Can't Escape Forever
43: The Ox-Bow Incident
44: Take it Big
Seven Doors to Death
Dead Man's Eyes
The Port of Forty Thieves
I Accuse My Parents
Silent Partner
Up in Arms
45: Big Show-Off
Black Market Babies
Blonde Ransom
Come Out Fighting
Crime, Inc.
Docks of New York
A Guy, a Gal, and a Pal
Mr. Muggs Rides Again
Northwest Trail
46: Angel on My Shoulder
Below the Deadline
Home in Oklahoma
Murder Is My Business
Red Dragon
The People's Choice
47: Apache Rose
Smash-Up, the Story of
a Woman
Case of the Baby-Sitter
48: The Dude Goes West
The Gay Ranchero
King of the Gamblers
The Denver Kid
49: Omoo-Omoo, the Shark
God
Sky Liner
The Crime Doctor's Diary
Ranger of Cherokee Strip
50: Twilight in the Sierras
51: Spoilers of the Plains
Wells Fargo Gunmaster

Ralph Meeker (1920-
1951: Teresa
Four in a Jeep
52: Shadow in the Sky
Somebody Loves Me
Glory Alley
53: The Naked Spur
Jeopardy
Code Two
55: Big House U. S. A.
Kiss Me Deadly
Desert Sands
56: Battle Shock
A Woman's Devotion
57: Run of the Arrow
The Fuzzy Pink Nightgown
Paths of Glory
61: Ada
Something Wild
63: Wall of Noise
67: Gentle Ben (or, Gentle
Giant)
The Dirty Dozen
The St. Valentine's Say
Massacre
68: The Detective
69: Inferno Road
Lost Flight (TV)
The Devil's Eight

Don Megowan
1951: The Kid from Amarillo
55: Davy Crockett--King of
the Wild Frontier
A Lawless Street
56: The Werewolf
The Creature Walks
Among Us
The Great Locomotive
Chase
Gun the Man Down
57: The Story of Mankind
Hell Canyon Outlaws
58: Snowfire
The Man Who Died Twice
61: Guns of the Black Witch
62: Valley of the Doomed
Creation of the Humanoids
63: For Love or Money

Thomas Meighan (1879-1936)
1931: Young Sinners
32: Cheaters at Play
Madison Square Garden
34: Peck's Bad Boy

Lauritz Melchior (1890-
1945: Thrill of a Romance
The Red Mill
46: Two Sisters from Boston
47: This Time for Keeps
48: Luxury Liner

George Melford (d. 1961)
1939: Ambush
Rulers of the Sea
40: My Little Chickadee
Safari
Brigham Young--Frontiers-
man
41: Robbers of the Range
42: The Lone Star Ranger
That Other Woman
43: Dixie Dugan
44: The Miracle of Morgan's
Creek
Hail the Conquering Hero
45: A Tree Grows in Brooklyn
Billy Rose's Diamond
Horseshoe
Col. Effingham's Raid
53: A Blueprint for Murder
The Robe
54: The Egyptian
Woman's World
55: Prince of Players

James Melton (1904-1961)
1935: Stars over Broadway
36: Sing Me a Love Song
37: Melody for Two
45: Ziegfeld Follies

Sidney Melton
1942: Blondie Goes to College
Dr. Broadway
43: Girls in Chains
46: Suspense
47: Kilroy Was Here

48: Close-Up
49: Knock on Any Door
Tough Assignment
Treasure of Monte Cristo
50: Western Pacific Agent
Hi-Jacked
Motor Patrol
Radar Secret Service
Return of Jesse James
Holiday Rhythm
51: The Steel Helmet
The Lemon Drop Kid
Savage Drums
Mask of the Dragon
Stop that Cab!
Three Desperate Men
Fingerprints Don't Lie
Leave it to the Marines
Sky High
The Lost Contiment
56: Edge of Hell
57: Beau James
Under Fire
58: Thundering Jets
59: The Atomic Submarine
68: It Takes All Kinds
69: The Girl from Peking

Adolphe Menjou (1890-1963)
1927: Gentlemen of Paris   S
29: Bachelor Girl   PT
Marquis Preferred   S
The Kiss
Fashions in Love
30: Morocco
The Front Page
Diamond Cut Diamond
New Moon
Mysterious Mr. Parkes
31: The Great Lover
The Easiest Way
The Marriage Interlude
A Gust of Wind
Men Call it Love
32: Forbidden
Front Page
Friends and Lovers
Two White Arms
Bachelor's Affair
Night Club Lady

Blame the Woman
Farewell to Arms
A Communist Henchman
Prestige
Man from Yesterday
33: The Circus Queen Murder
Morning Glory
Convention City
The Worst Woman in
Paris?
34: The Trumpet Blows
Little Miss Marker
The Great Flirtation
Easy to Love
Journal of a Crime
The Human Side
The Mighty Barnum
35: Gold Diggers of 1935
Broadway Gondolier
36: The Milky Way
Wives Never Know
Sing, Baby, Sing!
One in a Million
37: A Star Is Born
Cafe Metropole
One Hundred Men and a
Girl
Stage Door
38: Goldwyn Follies
Thanks for Everything
A Letter of Introduction
39: King of the Turf
Golden Boy
The Housekeeper's Daughter
That's Right, You're Wrong
40: A Bill of Divorcement
Turnabout
41: Road Show
Father Takes a Wife
42: Roxie Hart
Syncopation
You Were Never Lovelier
43: Sweet Rosie O'Grady
Hi Diddle Diddle
44: Step Lively
45: Man Alive
46: Dancing in the Dark
The Bachelor's Daughters
Heartbeat
47: I'll be Yours

47: Mr. District Attorney
The Hucksters
48: State of the Union
49: My Dream Is Yours
50: To Please a Lady
51: Across the Wide Missouri
Tall Target
52: The Sniper
53: Man on a Tightrope
55: Timberjack
56: The Ambassador's
Daughter
Bundle of Joy
57: Paths of Glory
58: I Married a Woman
60: Pollyanna

Shephard Menken
1951: The Great Caruso
52: Harem Girl
The Merry Widow
53: Man in the Dark
Tangier Incident
Captain John Smith and
Pocahontas
54: Killers from Space

Doro Merande
1939: The Star Maker
40: Our Town
49: The Cover Up
51: Mr. Belvedere Rings the
Bell
The Whistle at Eaton
Falls
55: The Seven Year Itch
The Man with the Golden
Arm
59: The Remarkable Mr.
Pennypacker
The Gazebo
63: The Cardinal
64: Kiss Me, Stupid!
66: The Russians Are Coming,
The Russians Are Coming!
67: Hurry Sundown
68: Skidoo!
69: Change of Habit

Beryl Mercer (1882-1939)
1928: We Americans   S
29: Mother's Boy
Three Live Ghosts
Seven Days' Leave
30: In Gay Madrid
All Quiet on the Western
Front
Dumb-Bells in Ermine
Matrimonial Bed
Common Clay
Outward Bound
31: East Lynne
Public Enemy
Inspiration
Always Goodbye
Merely Mary Ann
The Miracle Woman
Man in Possession
Sky Spider
Are These Our Children?
32: The Devil's Lottery
Forgotten Women
Lovers Courageous
Lena Rivers
Young America
No Greater Love
Unholy Love
Midnight Morals
Smilin' Through
Six Hours to Live
33: Cavalcade
Supernational
Berkeley Square
Her Splendid Folly
Blind Adventure
Broken Dreams
34: Change of Heart
Jane Eyre
Little Minister
Richest Girl in the World
35: Age in Indiscretion
My Marriage
Hitchhike Lady
Three Live Ghosts
Magnificent Obsession
36: Forbidden Heaven
37: Call it a Day

37: Night Must Fall
39: Hound of the Baskervilles
    The Little Princess
    A Woman Is the Judge

Melina Mercouri (1925-
1957: Stella
58: He Who Must Die
    The Gypsy and the Gentle-
    man
60: Where the Hot Wind Blows
    Never on Sunday
62: Phaedra
63: The Victors
64: Topkapi
66: Ten Thirty P. M. --Summer
    A Man Could Get Killed
67: The Uninhibited
68: Gaily, Gaily
69: Promise at Dawn

Burgess Meredith (1908-
1936: Winterset
37: There Goes the Groom
38: Spring Madness
39: Idiot's Delight
    Of Mice and Men
40: Second Chorus
    Castle on the Hudson
41: That Uncertain Feeling
    Tom, Dick, and Harry
    San Francisco Docks
    Forgotten Village
42: Street of Chance
43: Welcome to Britain
44: Salute to France (Army
    short)
45: The Story of G.I. Joe
    A Miracle can Happen
46: Diary of a Chambermaid
    The Magnificent Doll
48: Mine Own Executioner
    On Our Merry Way
49: The Man on the Eiffel
    Tower
53: The Gay Adventure
57: Joe Butterfly
61: Universe (narr. doc.)
62: Advise and Consent
63: The Cardinal

64: Fanfare for a Death Scene
65: In Harm's Way
    The Crazy Quiet
    (commentary)
66: Madame X
    A Big Hand for the Little
    Lady
    Batman
67: Hurry Sundown
68: Stay Away, Joe!
69: Mackenna's Gold
    Torture Garden
    Skidoo
    The Hard Contract
    There Was a Crooked Man
    Touch and Go (act., dir.)

Charles Meredith (1894-1964)
1950: Perfect Strangers
    The Sun Sets at Dawn
    Counterspy Meets Scotland
    Yard
51: Al Jennings of Oklahoma
    Along the Great Divide
    Submarine Patrol
52: The Big Trees
    Cattle Town
56: The Lone Ranger
57: Chicago Confidential
58: The Buccaneer
60: Twelve Hours to Kill
64: The Incredible Mr. Limpet
    The Quick Gun

Cheerio Meredith (1890-1964)
1958: The Case Against Brooklyn
    I Married a Woman
59: The Legend of Tom Dooley
62: The Wonderful World of
    the Brothers Grimm
    The Three Stooges in
    Orbit

Iris Meredith
1939: West of Santa Fe
    Spoilers of the Range
    Western Caravans
    Riders of the Black River
    Mad from Sundown
    Those High Grey Walls

39: Taming of the West
    Outposts of the Mounties
40: Convicted Woman
    Two-Fisted Rangers
    Blazing Six-Shooters
    Texas Stagecoach
    The Man from Tumble-
    weeds
    The Return of Wild Bill
    Thundering Frontier
41: Caught in the Act
    Son of Davy Crockett
    Louisiana Purchase
43: The Rangers Take Over

John Merivale (1917-
1933: The Invisible Man
47: If Winter Comes
55: Battle of the River Plate
58: A Night to Remember
60: Caltiki, the Immortal
    Monster
    Circus of Horrors
63: The List of Adrian
    Messenger
    80,000 Suspects

Philip Merivale (1880-1946)
1935: Passing of the Third
    Floor Back
36: Give Us this Night
41: Mr. and Mrs. Smith
    Rage in Heaven
    Midnight Angel
    Lady for a Night
42: This Above All
    Crossroads
43: This Land Is Mine
    Lost Angel
44: The Hour Before the
    Dawn
    Nothing but Trouble
45: Tonight and Every Night
46: Adventure
    Sister Kenny
    The Stranger

Lee Meriwether
1959: The 4-D Man
66: Batman

Namu, the Killer Whale
68: The Legend of Lylah
    Clare
69: Angel in My Pocket
    The Undefeated

Una Merkel (1903-
1930: Abraham Lincoln
    Eyes of the World
31: The Bat Whispers
    Command Performance
    Don't Bet on Women
    The Maltese Falcon
    The Bargain (or, You and
    I)
    Daddy Long Legs
    The Secret Witness
    Six-Cylinder Love
    Wicked
    Terror by Night
    Private Lives
32: The Impossible Lover
    Red-Headed Woman
    The Way of Life
    Second Fiddle
    The Silent Witness
    She Wanted a Millionaire
    Men Wanted
    Huddle
    They Call it Sin
33: Whistling in the Dark
    Impatient Maiden
    42nd Street
    Reunion in Vienna
    Midnight Mary
    Beauty for Sale
    Broadway to Hollywood
    Bombshell
    Day of Reckoning
    Her First Mate
    Clear All Wires
    The Secret of Madame
    Blanche
    Men Are Such Fools
    Lady of the Night
34: This Side of Heaven
    The Women in His Life
    Murder in the Private Car
    Have a Heart
    Paris Interlude

34: Merry Widow
    Evelyn Prentice
    Bulldog Drummond Strikes
      Back
    The Cat's Paw
35: The Night Is Young
    Biography of a Bachelor
      Girl
    One New York Night
    Baby Face Harrington
    Murder in the Fleet
    Broadway Melody of 1936
    It's in the Air
36: Riffraff
    Speed
    We Went to College
    Born to Dance
37: Don't Tell the Wife
    The Good Old Soak
    Saratoga
    True Confession
    Checkers
38: Test Pilot
39: Some Like it Hot
    Four Girls in White
    On Borrowed Time
    Destry Rides Again
40: Saturday's Children
    The Bank Dick
    Sandy Gets Her Man
    Comin' Round the Mountain
41: Road to Zanzibar
    Double Date
42: Mad Doctor of Market
      Street
    Twin Beds
43: This Is the Army
44: Sweethearts of the U.S.A.
    To Heir Is Human (short)
47: It's a Joke, Son!
48: The Bride Goes Wild
    The Man from Texas
50: Emergency Wedding
    My Blue Heaven
    Kill the Umpire
51: Rich, Young, and Pretty
    Golden Girl
    Millionaire for Christy
52: With a Song in My Heart
53: I Love Melvin

55: The Kentuckian
56: The Merry Widow
    The Kettles in the Ozarks
    Bundle of Joy
57: The Girl Most Likely
    The Fuzzy Pink Nightgown
59: The Mating Game
61: Summer and Smoke
    The Parent Trap
63: Summer Magic
64: A Tiger Walks
67: Spin-Out

Jan Merlin
1955: Six Bridges to Cross
    Illegal
    Running Wild
56: A Day of Fury
    Screaming Eagles
    A Strange Adventure
    The Peacemaker
58: Cole Younger--Gunfighter
60: Hell Bent for Leather
63: Gunfight at Comanche
    Creek
67: The St. Valentine's Day
    Massacre

Ethel Merman (1909-
1932: Big Broadcast of 1932
34: Shoot the Works
    We're Not Dressing
    Kid Millions
    Happy Landing
35: The Big Broadcast of 1936
36: Strike Me Pink
    Tops Is the Limit
38: Alexander's Ragtime Band
    Straight Place and Show
43: Stage Door Canteen
53: Call Me Madam
54: There's No Business Like
    Show Business
63: It's a Mad Mad Mad Mad
    World
65: The Art of Love

Lynn Merrick
1941: Death Valley Outlaws
    A Missouri Outlaw

41: Sis Hopkins
    Two-Gun Sheriff
    Desert Bandit
    The Gay Vagabond
    The Kansas Cyclone
    The Apache Kid
42: Arizona Terrors
    Jesse James, Jr.
    Stagecoach Express
    The Cyclone Kid
    Youth on Parade
    The Sombrero Kid
    Mountain Rhythm
    Outlaws of Pine Ridge
43: Dead Man's Gulch
    Fugitive from Sonora
44: The Crime Doctor's
    Strangest Case
    Swing Out the Blues
    Meet Miss Bobby-Socks
    Nine Girls
    Stars on Parade
45: The Blonde from Brooklyn
    Boston Blackie Booked on
    Suspicion
    A Guy, a Gal, and a Pal
    The Voice of the Whistler
46: A Close Call for Boston
    Blackie
    Dangerous Business
47: I Love Trouble

Dina Merrill (1928-
1957: Desk Set
58: A Nice Little Bank that
    Should be Robbed
    Mr. Pharaoh and
    Cleopatra
59: Don't Give Up the Ship
    Operation Petticoat
60: Butterfield 8
    The Sundowners
61: The Young Savages
    Twenty Plus Two
63: The Courtship of Eddie's
    Father
64: The Pleasure Seekers
65: I'll Take Sweden
68: The Sunshine Patriot (TV)
69: The Savarona Syndrome

    Against Heaven's Hand
    (TV)
    The Big Blast

Gary Merrill (1915-
1948: Strange Victory
49: Slattery's Hurricane
    Twelve O'Clock High
50: Where the Sidewalk Ends
    Mother Didn't Tell Me
    All About Eve
51: The Frogmen
52: Devision Before Dawn
    Another Man's Poison
    Phone Call from a
    Stranger
    Girl in White
    Night Without Sleep
53: Blueprint for Murder
54: The Black Dakotas
    Witness to Murder
    The Human Jungle
56: Navy Wife
58: Crash Landing
    The Missouri Traveler
59: The Wonderful Country
60: The Savage Eye
    The Great Impostor
61: Jules Verne's Mysterious
    Island
    The Pleasure of His
    Company
    Farewell to Hong Kong
    (Ital.)
62: A Girl Named Tamiko
65: The Woman Who Wouldn't
    Die
66: Dangerous Days of Kiowa
    Jones (TV)
    Catacombs
    Around the World Under
    the Sea
    Cast a Giant Shadow
    Ride Beyond Vengeance
    Destination Inner Space
67: The Incident
    The Last Challenge
    Clambake
    Run, Psyche, Run
68: The Power

958

69: Then Came Bronson (TV pilot)
A Wrong Kind of Love (Ital.)

Gertrude Messenger (1911-
1934: Love Past Thirty
Anne of Green Gables
35: Social Error
The Fighting Pilot
Wagon Train
Roaring Roads
Rustlers' Paradise
Adventurous Knight
Melody Trail
Rider of the Law
36: Blazing Justice
37: Aces Wild
41: Gambling Daughters
42: The Miracle Kid
49: Joe Palooka in The Counterspy

Mayo Methot (1904-1951)
1931: Corsair
32: Night Club Lady
Virtue
Vanity Street
Afraid to Talk
33: Mind Reader
Lilly Turner
Counsellor-at-Law
34: Harold Teen
Goodbye Love
Jimmy the Gent
Side Streets
35: Mills of the Gods
The Case of the Curious Bride
Dr. Socrates
36: Mr. Deeds Goes to Town
The Case Against Mrs. Ames
37: Marked Woman
38: Women in Prison
Numbered Woman
The Sisters
39: Should a Girl Marry?
Unexpected Father
A Woman Is the Judge

40: Brother Rat and a Baby

Emile Meyer
1953: Shane
54: Silver Lode
Riot in Cell Block 11
The Human Jungle
Drums Across the River
55: The Blackboard Jungle
White Feather
Stranger on Horseback
The Tall Men
Girl in the Red Velvet Swing
Man with the Gun
Man with the Golden Arm
56: The Maverick Queen
Raw Edge
Gun the Man Down
57: Badlands of Montana
Sweet Smell of Success
Baby Face Nelson
Paths of Glory
58: The Line-Up
The Case Against Brooklyn
The Fiend Who Walked the West
Revolt in the Big House
Good Day for a Hanging
59: King of the Wild Stallion
60: The Threat
The Girl in Lover's Lane
Young Jesse James
64: Taggart
65: Young Dillinger
67: Hostile Guns
A Time for Killing

Greta Meyer
1932: Flesh
The Match King
33: The Nuisance
Jennie Gerhardt
34: Let's Fall in Love
Young and Beautiful
Line-Up
Servants' Entrance
35: Forsaking All Others
Naughty Marietta
Biography of a Bachelor Girl

959

35: Laddie
  Mr. Dynamite
  Return of Peter Grimm
  Smart Girl
36: Suzy
  Libeled Lady
  The Gorgeous Hussy
37: Bill Cracks Down
  When Love Is Young
  Damaged Goods
  Thin Ice
38: The Great Waltz
  Torchy Gets Her Man
39: No Place to Go
40: Four Sons
  Bitter Sweet
41: Come Live With Me
42: Friendly Enemies

Gertrude Michaels (1911-1964)
1932: Wayward
  Unashamed
33: I'm No Angel
  Sailor be Good
  A Bedtime Story
  The Cradle Song
  A Night of Terror
  Ann Vickers
34: Cleopatra
  She Was a Lady
  Murder on the Blackboard
  Notorious Sophie Lang
  Bolero
  The Witching Hour
  Murder at the Vanities
  The Menace
  George White's Scandals
    of 1934
  I Believed in You
  Search for Beauty
  Hold that Girl!
35: The Last Outpost
  Father Brown, Detective
  It Happened in New York
  Four Hours to Kill
36: Till We Meet Again (or,
    Forgotten Faces)
  Make Way for a Lady
  Woman Trap
  Second Wife

  The Return of Sophie Lang
37: Just Like a Woman
  Sins of the Fathers
  Mr. Dodd Takes the Air
39: Hidden Power
40: Parole Fixer
  The Hidden Menace
  The Farmer's Daughter
  I Can't Give You Anything
    but Love, Baby
40: Slightly Tempted
42: Prisoner of Japan
43: Women in Bondage
  Where Are Your Children?
  Behind Prison Walls
44: Faces in the Fog
45: Club Havana
  Allotment Wives
  Three's a Crowd
48: That Wonderful Urge
49: Flamingo Road
50: Caged
51: Darling, How Could You?
52: Bugles in the Afternoon
53: No Escape
55: Women's Prison
62: Twist All Night

Beverly Michaels
1949: East Side, West Side
51: Pickup
  The Girl on the Bridge
53: Wicked Woman
55: Crashout
  Betrayed Women
56: Blonde Bait

Dolores Michaels
1957: The Wayward Bus
  Time Limit
  April Love
58: Fraulein
  The Fiend Who Walked
    the West
59: Warlock
  Five Gates to Hell
60: One Foot in Hell
61: Battle at Bloody Beach

960

Robert Middlemass (1885-
1936:   I Loved a Soldier
  38:   Blondes at Work
        Highway Patrol
        Spawn of the North
        I Am the Law
        Kentucky
        I Stand Accused
  39:   Stand Up and Fight
        The Magnificent Fraud
        Coast Guard
        Stanley and Livingstone
        Blondie Brings Up Baby
  40:   Little Old New York
        Slightly Honorable
        The Saint Takes Over
        Pop Always Pays
  43:   Truck Busters
        The Black Raven
  44:   Lady in the Death House
        Wilson
  45:   A Sporting Chance
        The Dolly Sisters

Charles Middleton (1879-1949)
1929:   The Bellamy Trial
        The Far Call
        Welcome Danger
  30:   Beau Bandit
        Way Out West
        Framed
        Christmas Knight
  31:   An American Tragedy
        Beau Hunks
        Full of Notions
        Ships of Hate
        Caught Plastered
        Miracle Woman
        Palmy Days
        Alexander Hamilton
        A Dangerous Affair
  32:   High Pressure
        The Hatchet Man
        Manhattan Parade
        Strange Love of Molly
          Louvain
        Pack Up Your Troubles
        Hell's Highway
        Mystery Ranch
        Silver Dollar

        Breach of Promise
        Rockabye
  33:   Tomorrow at Seven
        Sunset Pass
        Pickup
        Destination Unknown
        Disgraced!
        This Day and Age
        Big Executive
        White Woman
        Duck Soup
  34:   Lone Cowboy
        The Last Roundup
        Murder at the Vanities
        Behold My Wife
        Massacre
        David Harum
        Mrs. Wiggs of the Cabbage
          Patch
        When Strangers Meet
  35:   Special Agent
        The Fixer-Uppers
        Steamboat 'Round the
          Bend
        County Chairman
        Hopalong Cassidy
        Square Shooter
        In Spite of Danger
        Red Morning
        The Virginia Judge
  36:   Texas Rangers
        Road Gang
        Trail of the Lonesome
          Pine
        Flash Gordon (ser.)
        Space Soldiers
        Empty Saddles
        Sunset of Power
        Showboat
        Song of the Saddle
        Jailbreak
        A Son Comes Home
        Career Woman
  37:   We're on the Jury
        Two-Gun Law
        Hollywood Cowboy
        Yodelin' Kid from Pine
          Ridge
  38:   Flaming Frontiers (ser.)
        Mars Attacks the World
          (or, Flash Gordon's Trip
          to Mars [ser.])

38: Dick Tracy, Detective (ser.)	Robert Middleton (1911–
Outside the Law	1954: The Silver Chalice
Kentucky	55: The Big Combo
39: Jesse James	Desperate Hours
Captain Fury	Trial
The Oklahoma Kid	56: Friendly Persuasion
Blackmail	The Court Justice
Daredevils of the Red Circle (ser.)	Red Sundown
Wyoming Outlaw	The Proud Ones
Cowboys from Texas	Love Me Tender
Slave Ship	Pylon
Juarez	57: The Tarnished Angels
Way Down South	The Lonely Man
The Flying Deuces	58: Day of the Bad Man
$1000 a Touchdown	Law of Jake Wade
40: Thou Shalt Not Kill	No Place to Land
Abe Lincoln in Illinois	59: Gun of Zangara
Chad Hanna	Career
The Grapes of Wrath	Don't Give Up the Ship
Shooting High	60: Hell Bent for Leather
Charlie Chan's Murder Cruise	61: Gold of the Seven Saints
Virginia City	The Great Impostor
Santa Fe Trail	63: Cattle King
Island of Doomed Men	64: For Those Who Think Young
Flash Gordon Conquers the Universe (ser.)	66: Big Hand for the Little Lady
41: Jungle Man	
Western Union	Toshiro Mifune (1920–
Wild Geese Calling	1948: The Drunken Angel
Belle Starr	49: The Stray Dog
Wild Bill Hickok Rides	50: Roshomon
42: Mystery of Marie Roget	54: Seven Samurai (Pt. 1 Legend of Murashi)
Men of San Quentin	57: The Lower Depth
43: Two Weeks to Live	61: Yojimbo
The Black Raven	Thrown of Blood
44: The Town Went Wild	62: I Bombed Pearl Harbor
45: How Do You Do?	63: The Bad Sleep Well
Our Vines Have Tender Grapes	Chushingura (or, High and Low)
Strangler of the Swamp	The Important Man
46: Spook Busters	Sanjuro
47: The Pretender	64: Red Beard
48: Station West	The Lost World of Sinbad
Jiggs and Maggie in Court	Duel at Ichijoje Temple, (Pt. 2)
49: The Last Bandit	The Last Gun Fight
Black Arrow	65: Grand Prix

65: Samurai Assassin, Pt. 3
 (or, Duel at Ganryu
 Island)
66: The Hidden Fortress
67: The Rikishaman--Muko-
 matsu
 The Secret Scrolls, Pt. 2
 The Mad Atlantic
 Sword of Doom
 I Live in Fear
68: Samurai, Pt. 3 (Ketto
 Ganryn Kjima)
 Judo Saga
 Admiral Yamamoto
 Tunnel to the Sun
 Adventures of Taklamakan
 The Emperor and the
 General
 Whirlwind
 Red Beard
69: Ninjutsu
 Furin Kazan
 Hell in the Pacific
 The Red Sun
 Seven Samurai
 Under the Banner of
 Samurai
 Daredevil of the Castle

Lita Milan
1955: The Toughest Man Alive
 The Violent Men
 Desert Sands
56: Gun Brothers
57: The Ride Back
 Naked in the Sun
 Bayou
58: Girls on the Loose
 The Left-Handed Gun
 Never Love a Stranger
 I, Mobster

Sarah Miles (1941-
1962: Term of Trial
63: The Ceremony
65: The Servant
 Those Magnificent Men in
 Their Flying Machines
66: Blow-Up
 Time Lost and Time
 Remembered

69: Ryan's Daughter

Vera Miles (1929-
1952: For Men Only
 The Rose Bowl Story
53: Charge at Feather River
54: Pride of the Blue Grass
55: Tarzan's Hidden Jungle
 Wichita
56: The Searchers
 23 Pages to Baker Street
 Autumn Leaves
57: The Wrong Man
 Beau James
59: Web of Evidence
 The FBI Story
60: A Touch of Larceny
 Five Branded Women
 Psycho
 Beyond this Place
61: Back Street
62: The Man Who Shot Liberty
 Valance
64: A Tiger Walks
 Those Calloways
65: The Hanged Man
66: Follow Me, Boys!
67: Gentle Ben
 The Spirit Is Willing
68: Sgt. Ryker ('63 re-rel.)
 It Takes All Kinds
 Kona Coast
69: Mission: Batangas (TV)
 The Hellfighters

John Miljan (1893-1960)
1928: Glorious Betsy   PT
 Tenderloin   PT
 Land of the Silver Fox   S
 Women They Talk About PT
 The Terror   PT
 The Home Towners   PT
29: Stark Mad
 The Painted Lady
 Queen of the Night Clubs
 Desert Song
 Hard-Boiled Rose
 Speedway
 Voice of the City
 Eternal Woman
 Times Square

29: Fashions of Paris
Untamed
Unholy Night
30: The Devil May Care
Sea Bat
The Woman Racket
Show Girl in Hollywood
a short
His Night Out
Our Blushing Brides
The Unholy Three
Within the Law
Lights and Shadows
Remote Control
Not so Dumb
Free and Easy
Paid
31: Inspiration
The Iron Man
The Secret Six
A Gentleman's Fate
Son of India
Rise of Helga
The Great Meadow
War Nurse
Politics
Hell Divers
Susan Lennox
Possessed
32: Emma
Sky Devils
West of Broadway
Beast of the City
Arsene Lupin
Wet Parade
Are You Listening?
Justice for Sale
Grand Hotel
The Rich Are Always
  with Us
Unashamed
Flesh
Night Court
Prosperity
The Kid from Spain
33: The Nuisance
King for a Night
Blind Adventure
The Way to Love
What! No Beer?

Whistling in the Dark
The Mad Game
The Sin of Nora Moran
34: The Poor Rich
Madame Spy
Whirlpool
Line-Up
Belle of the Nineties
Young and Beautiful
Unknown Blonde
Twin Husbands
35: Mississippi
Charlie Chan in Paris
Under the Pampas Moon
The Ghost Walks
Tomorrow's Youth
Three Kids and a Queen
36: Sutter's Gold
Criminal Within
Private Number
Murder at Glen Athol
The Gentleman from
  Louisiana
North of Nome
The Plainsman
37: Arizona Mahoney
38: Man Proof
a short
Pardon Our Nerve
Border G-Man
If I Were King
Juarez
Ride a Crooked Mile
39: Torchy Runs for Mayor
Fast and Furious
The Oklahoma Kid
40: Emergency Squad
Women Without Names
Queen of the Mob
New Moon
Young Bill Hickok
41: Texas Rangers Ride Again
The Cowboy and the Blonde
The Deadly Game
Forced Landing
Riot Squad
Double Cross
42: True to the Army
The Big Street
Scattergood Survives a
  Murder

42: Boss of Big Town
Criminal Investigator
43: Bombardier
Submarine Alert
The Fallen Sparrow
44: Bride by Mistake
I Accuse My Parents
The Merry Monahans
45: It's in the Bag
46: The Last Crooked Mile
The Killers
White Tie and Tails
Gallant Men
Unconquered
47: Sinbad the Sailor
Queen of the Amazons
In Self Defense
That's My Man!
The Quest of Willie
Hunter
48: The Flame
Perilous Waters
49: Samson and Delilah
Stampede
Adventure in Baltimore
Mrs. Mike
50: Mule Train
52: Savage
Bonzo Goes to College
55: Pirates of Tripoli
Run for Cover
56: The Ten Commandments
57: Apache Warrior
58: The Lone Ranger and the
Lost City of Gold

Ray Milland (1905-
1929: The Informer
The Plaything
The Flying Scotsman
31: Bought
Ambassador Bill
Blonde Crazy
32: Polly of the Circus
Larceny Lane
Payment Deferred
33: This Is the Life
Orders Is Orders
34: We're Not Dressing
Many Happy Returns

The Menace
Charlie Chan in London
Bolero
35: One Hour Late
The Gilded Lily
Four Hours to Kill
The Glass Key
Alias Mary Dow
36: Next Time We Love
Return of Sophie Lang
Big Broadcast of 1937
Jungle Princess
37: Three Smart Girls
Wings over Honolulu
Bulldog Drummond Escapes
Easy Living
Ebb Tide
Wise Girl
38: Her Jungle Love
Tropic Holiday
Men with Wings
Say it in French
39: Hotel Imperial
Beau Geste
Everything Happens at
Night
40: French Without Tears
Irene
The Doctor Takes a Wife
Untamed
Arise My Love
41: Skylark
I Wanted Wings
42: The Lady Has Plans
Reap the Wild Wind
Are Husbands Necessary?
The Major and the Minor
Star Spangled Rhythm
43: The Crystal Ball
Forever and a Day
44: The Uninvited
Lady in the Dark
Ministry of Fear
Till We Meet Again
45: Lost Weekend (OSCAR)
Kitty
46: The Well-Groomed Lady
California
47: Imperfect Lady
The Trouble with Women

965

47: Golden Earrings
Variety Girl
48: So Evil My Love
The Sealed Verdict
The Big Clock
Wings over Honolulu
Miss Tatlock's Millions
(bit)
49: Alias Nick Beal
It Happens Every Spring
50: A Life of Her Own
Copper Canyon
A Woman of Distinction
51: Night into Morning
Rhubarb
Close to My Heart
Circle of Danger
52: Something to Live For
Bugles in the Afternoon
The Thief
53: Jamaica Run
Let's Do it Again
54: Dial M for Murder
55: A Man Alone
Girl in the Red Velvet
Swing (act., dir.)
56: Lisbon (act., dir.)
57: Three Brave Men
The River's Edge
58: The Safecracker
High Flight
62: Panic in the Year Zero
(act., dir.)
The Premature Burial
63: X--The Man with the
X-Ray Eyes
65: The Confession
Hostile Witness
69: Daughter of the Mind (TV)

Marjie Millar (1930-
1953: Money from Home
54: About Mrs. Leslie
56: When Gangland Strikes

Ann Miller (1919-
1937: New Faces of 1937
Life of the Party
Stage Door
38: Radio City Revels

Having a Wonderful Time
Room Service
Tarnished Angel
You Can't Take it with
You
40: Too Many Girls
The Hit Parade of 1941
Melody Ranch
41: Time Out for Rythm
Go West Young Lady
42: True to the Army
Priorities on Parade
43: Reveille with Beverly
What's Buzzin' Cousin?
44: Jam Session
Hey Rookie!
Carolina Blues
45: Eadie Was a Lady
Eve Knew Her Apples
46: The Thrill of Brazil
47: The Petty Girl
48: Easter Parade
49: The Kissing Bandit
On the Town
50: Watch the Birdie
51: Texas Carnival
Two Tickets to Broadway
52: Lovely to Look at
53: Small Town Girl
Kiss Me Kate
54: Deep in My Heart
55: Hit the Deck
56: The Opposite Sex
The Great American
Pastime

Colleen Miller (1932-
1952: The Las Vegas Story
54: Playgirl
Man Crazy
Beat the Devil
Four Guns to the Border
55: The Purple Mask
56: The Rawhide Years
57: Hot Summer Night
The Night Runner
Man in the Shadow
58: Step Down to Terror
63: Gunfight at Comanche
Creek

966

Dean Miller
1952: Skirts Ahoy!
Because You're Mine
Everything I Have Is
Yours
53: Dream Wife
Small Town Girl

Dennis Miller (1935-
1959: Tarzan of the Apes
61: Love in a Goldfish Bowl
68: The Party
69: Armageddon

Eve Miller (1925-
1947: I Wonder Who's Kissing
Her Now
48: Buckaroo from Powder
River
Inner Sanctum
49: Arctic Fury
50: Never Fear
51: Pier 23
52: The Big Trees
The Winning Team
The Will Rogers Story
April in Paris
53: Kansas Pacific
54: There's no Business like
Show Business
55: The Big Bluff

Kristine Miller
1947: Desert Fury
I Walk Alone
48: Jungle Patrol
49: Paid in Full
Too Late for Tears
50: Shadow on the Wall
Young Daniel Boone
High Lonesome
52: The Steel Fist
Tropical Heat Wave
53: Flight Nurse
Geraldine
55: Hell's Outpost
56: Thunder over Arizona
57: The Persuader
The Domino Kid

Mark Miller
1963: The Hook
64: Youngblood Hawke

Marvin Miller (1913-
1945: Blood on the Sun
Johnny Angel
46: Deadline at Dawn
Just Before Dawn
A Night in Paradise
The Phantom Thief
47: The Brasher Doubloon
Dead Reckoning
The Corpse Came C.O.D.
Intrigue
51: Smuggler's Island
Peking Express
The Prince Who Was a
Thief
The Golden Horde
Hong Kong
52: Red Planet Mars
53: Forbidden
Off Limits
54: Jivaro
The Shanghai Story
57: The Story of Mankind
58: Man Hunt in the Jungles
(narr.)
64: Malamondo (narr.)
The Day the Earth Froze
65: Saturday Night in Apple
Valley
66: Macabro (narr.)
67: A Trip to Terror
69: Is This Trip Necessary?

Marilyn Miller (1899-1936)
1930: Sunny
31: Her Majesty Love

Patsy Ruth Miller (1904-
1929: The Hottentot
Twin Beds
Whispering Winds   PT
The Sap   PT
Fall of Eve
Show of Shows
The Aviator

967

29: So Long Letty
30: Wide Open
Last of the Lone Wolf
31: Lonely Wives
32: Night Beat
51: Quebec

Scott Miller
1968: Run Like a Thief
69: Play Dirty

Sidney Miller
1933: Mayor of Hell
34: Rafter Romance
When Strangers Meet
The Band Plays on
35: Dinky
One Hour Late
38: Boys Town
Cipher Bureau
39: Panama Patrol
Streets of New York
Andy Hardy Gets Spring
Fever
20,000 Men a Year
What a Life
40: Golden Gloves
41: Men of Boys Town
42: Mr. Wise Guy
43: Here Comes Kelly
Moonlight in Vermont
44: Babes on Swing Street
Hot Rhythm
45: She Gets Her Man
There Goes Kelly
49: The Lucky Stiff
52: The Sniper
53: Walking My Baby Back
Home
62: Experiment in Terror

Walter Miller (1893-1940)
1929: Hawk of the Hills (ser.)
Queen of the North Woods
(ser.)
King of the Congo (ser.)
30: Rough Waters
Lone Defender (ser.)
On the Border
The Utah Kid

Rogue of the Rio Grande
31: Hell's Valley
Sky Raiders
Swanee River
Street Scene
Hurricane Horseman
King of the Wild (ser.)
32: Manhattan Parade
The Famous Ferguson
Case
Ridin' for Justice
Ghost City
Face on the Barroom Floor
Three Wise Girls
Heart Punch
33: Gordon of Ghost City (ser.)
Maisie
Sin of a Sailor
Behind Jury Doors
Parachute Jumper
34: Rocky Rhodes
Fighting Trooper
Gun Justice
Pirate Treasure (ser.)
The Red Rider (ser.)
Smoking Guns
The Vanishing Shadow (ser.)
35: Alias Mary Dow
Gun Valley
Valley of Wanted Men
Rustlers of Red Gap (ser.)
Roaring West (ser.)
Stormy
Call of the Savage (ser.)
36: Heart of the West
Desert Gold
The Fugitive Sheriff
Ghost Patrol
Without Orders
Night Waitress
37: Draegerman Courage
Boss of Lonely Valley
Midnight Court
Slim
Border Cafe
Flight from Glory
Saturday's Heroes
Danger Patrol
Wild West Days (ser.)
38: Secret of a Treasure
Island (ser.)

968

38: Wild Horse Rodeo
    Blind Alibi
    Crime Ring
    Lawless Valley
    Come on, Leathernecks!
    Down in Arkansas
39: Home on the Prairie
40: Bullet Code
    Grandpa Goes to Town

James Millican
1943: So Proudly We Hail!
  44: The Story of Dr. Wassell
  45: Tokyo Rose
      The Affairs of Susan
      Love Letters
  46: Trouble with Women
      Stepchild
      The Tender Years
  48: Hazard
      Mr. Reckless
      Let's Live Again
      Disaster
      Man from Colorado
      Return of Wildfire
      Last of the Wild Horses
      Command Decision
      Rogues' Regiment
      In this Corner
  49: Rimfire
      The Dalton Gang
      Fighting Man of the Plains
      The Gal Who Took the
        West
      Grand Canyon
  50: Military Academy with
        that Tenth Avenue Gang
      The Devil's Doorway
      Winchester 73
      Beyond the Purple Hills
      Mr. 880
      The Great Missouri Raid
  51: I Was a Communist for
        the FBI
      Al Jennings of Oklahoma
      Rawhide
      Fourteen Hours
      Missing Women
      Warpath
      Cavalry Scout

53: Gun Belt
54: Riding Shot Gun
    Jubilee Trail
    The Long Wait
    Dawn at Socorro
    The Outcast
55: Strategic Air Command
    The Big Tip-Off
    Chief Crazy Horse
    Las Vegas Shakedown
    The Man from Laramie
    I Died a Thousand Times
    The Vanishing American
    Top Gun
56: Red Sundown

Carl Millitaire
1950: Black Hand
      511 Ocean Drive
  51: The Great Caruso
      Miracle of Our Lady of
        Fatima
      Young Man with Ideas
  53: Siren of Bagdad
      Not News
  54: The Adventures of Hajji
        Baba
  55: New York Confidential
      The Fighting Chance
  57: Shadow on the Window
  59: Inside the Mafia
  60: The Music Box Kid

Hayley Mills (1945-
1959: Tiger Bay
  60: Polyanna
      (SPECIAL AWARD)
  61: The Parent Trap (dual Role)
  62: Whistle Down the Wind
      In Search of the Castaways
  63: Summer Magic
  64: The Moonspinners
      The Chalk Garden
  65: The Truth about Spring
      That Darn Cat
  66: The Trouble with Angels
      Gypsy Girl
      Bats with Baby Faces
      The Daydreamer
  67: The Family Way

969

68: A Nice Girl Like Me
Pretty Polly
A Matter of Innocence
Twisted Nerve
69: Take a Girl Like You

John Mills (1908-
1932: Midshipmaid Gob
33: Britannia of Billingsgate
The Ghost Camera
The Cavalcade
34: The River Wolves
A Political Party
Those Were the Days
35: Forever England
Car of Dreams
Doctor's Orders
Born for Glory
Blind Justice
36: First Offense
Nine Days a Queen
Charing Cross
37: Heidi
O.H.M.S.
39: Goodbye, Mr. Chips
40: Old Bill and Son
41: Cottage to Let
The Goose Steps Out
42: The Black Sheep of
Whitehall
The Big Stockade
Young Mr. Pitt
In Which We Serve
43: We Dive at Dawn
44: This Happy Breed
Blue for Waterloo
45: The Way to the Stars
Johnny in the Clouds
46: Great Expectations
47: So Well Remembered
The Vicious Circle
48: The October Man
49: Scott of the Antarctic
The History of Mr. Polly
(act., prod.)
50: Morning Departure
The Rocking Horse Winner
51: Operation, Disaster
52: The Long Memory
53: The Colditz Story

Mr. Denning Drives North
The Gentle Gunman
54: Hobson's Choice
55: The End of the Affair
56: War and Peace
Around the World in 80
Days
Above Us the Waves
57: The Baby and the Battle-
ship
Town on Trial
Escapade
58: Dunkirk
It's Great to be Young
Ice Cold in Alex
59: I Was Monty's Double (or,
Hell, Heaven, or Hoboken)
The Circle
Tiger Bay
60: The Swiss Family Robinson
Tunes of Glory
Desert Hawk
61: Season of Passion
The Singer not the Song
62: The Valiant
Flame in the Streets
63: Tiara Tahiti
64: The Chalk Garden
65: The Truth about Spring
Operation Crossbow (or,
The Great Spy Mission)
King Rat
66: The Wrong Box
Gypsy Girl
67: Bats with Baby Faces (dir.)
The Family Way
Africa--Texas Style!
Chuka
68: Nights of Lady Hamilton
Showdown
A Black Veil for Lisa
69: Oh, What a Lovely War!
The White Colt
The Making of a Lady
Ryan's Daughter
Return of Boomerang
Philip

Juliet Mills (1941-
1961: No, My Darling Daughter

61: Around the Daffodils
    Dangerous Hideaway
62: Nurse on Wheels
63: Carry On, Jack
66: The Rare Breed
67: Wings of Fire
68: Oh, What a Lovely War!
69: The Challengers

Martin Milner (1927-
1947: Life with Father
48: Wreck of the Hesperus
49: Sands of Iwo Jima
50: Louisa
    The Halls of Montezuma
    Our Very Own
51: I Want You
    Operation Pacific
52: The Captive City
    My Wife's Best Friend
    Battle Zone
    Last of the Comanches
53: Destination Gobi
55: Pete Kelly's Blues
    The Long Gray Line
    Francis in the Navy
56: On the Threshold of Space
    Screaming Eagles
    Pillars of the Sky
57: Sweet Smell of Success
    Gun Fight at the O.K.
    Corral
    Man Afraid
58: Marjorie Morningstar
    Too Much Too Soon
59: Compulsion
60: Thirteen Ghosts
    Sex Kittens Go to College
    Private Lives of Adam
    and Eve
63: 55 Days at Peking
    The VIP's
64: The Pink Panther
    Children of the Damned
65: Zebra in the Kitchen
67: Valley of the Dolls
    Sullivan's Empire
68: Three Guns for Texas
69: Ski Fever

Yvette Mimieux (1939-
1960: Platinum High School
    The Time Machine
    Where the Boys Are
62: Light in the Piazza
    The Four Horsemen of the
    Apocalypse
    The Wonderful World of
    the Brothers Grimm
    Diamond Head
63: Toys in the Attic
64: Looking for Love
65: Joy in the Morning
66: The Reward
67: Monkeys, Go Home!
    The Caper of the Golden
    Bulls
68: The Mercenaries
    Dark of the Sun
    Three in the Attic
69: The Picasso Summer
    The Jolly Girls
    The Delta Factor

Nico Minardos
1955: Desert Sands
57: Ghost Diver
    Istanbul
    Under Fire
59: Holiday for Lovers
60: Twelve Hours to Kill
62: It Happened in Athens
    Samar
68: Day of the Evil Gun
    The Daring Game
    A River of Diamonds (TV)
69: The Challengers
    Cannon for Cordoba

Sal Mineo (1939-
1955: Six Bridges to Cross
    The Private War of Major
    Benson
    Rebel Without a Cause
56: Giant
    Crime in the Streets
    Somebody Up There Likes
    Me
    Rock, Pretty Baby!

971

52: Los Tres Perfectas
Casadas
The Bullfighter and the
Lady
53: Reportaje
54: La Visita Que no Toco
el Timbre
Escuella de Vagabundos
55: Ensayo de un Crimen
Stranger on Horseback

Cameron Mitchell (1918-
1945: The Hidden Eye
They Were Expendable
What Next, Corporal
Hargrove?
46: Tenth Avenue Angel
The Mighty McGuirke
47: High Barbaree
Cass Timberlane
48: Leather Gloves
Homecoming
Command Decision
51: The Sellout
Smuggler's Gold
Death of a Salesman
Man in the Saddle
52: Japanese War Bride
Flight to Mars
Outcasts of Poker Flat
Okinawa
Les Miserables
Pony Soldier
The Jungle
53: The Robe (voice of Christ)
Powder River
Man on a Tightrope
How to Marry a Millionaire
54: Hell and High Water
Gorilla at Large
Garden of Evil
Desiree
55: Strange Lady in Town
Love Me or Leave Me
House of Bamboo
The Tall Men
The View from Pompey's
Head
56: Carousel
Tension at Table Rock

57: Monkey on My Back
All Mine to Give
Escape in Japan
No Down Payment
59: Face of Fire
Inside the Mafia
Pier 5--Havana
60: Three Came to Kill
The House on Airport
Drive
As the Sea Rages
61: The Unstoppable Man
62: The Last of the Vikings
Attack of the Normans
63: Caesar the Conqueror
65: Blood and Black Lace
The Black Duke
66: Minnesota Clay
Dog Eat Dog
67: Hombre
The Treasure of Makuba
Monster of the Black
Museum
68: Knives of the Avenger
Island of the Doomed
69: Nightmare in Wax

Grant Mitchell (1875-1957)
1931: Man to Man
Star Witness
32: The Famous Ferguson Case
Week-End Marriage
No Man of Her Own
Big City Blues
20,000 Years in Sing Sing
Three on a Match
M. A. R. S.
33: He Learned about Women
Central Airport
Lilly Turner
Heroes for Sale
I Love that Man
Tomorrow at Seven
Dinner at Eight
The Stranger's Return
Dancing Lady
Saturday's Millions
King for a Night
Wild Boys of the Road
Convention City

973

33: Our Betters
34: Shadows of Sing Sing
The Poor Rich
Show-Off
We're Rich Again
The Gridiron Flash
Twenty Million Sweet-
hearts
Secret Bride
The Cat's Paw
The Case of the Howling
Dog
365 Nights in Hollywood
One Exciting Adventure
35: One More Spring
Traveling Saleslady
Gold Diggers of 1935
Straight from the Heart
Men Without Names
Broadway Gondolier
A Midsummer Night's
Dream
In Person
It's in the Air
Seven Keys to Baldpate
36: Next Time We Love
The Garden Murder Case
Moonlight Murder
Piccadilly Jim
The Devil Is a Sissy
Her Master's Voice
My American Wife
The Ex-Mrs. Bradford
Parole!
37: The Life of Emile Zola
First Lady
Hollywood Hotel
Music for Madame
The Last Gangster
38: Lady Behave
The Headleys at Home
Women Are Like that
Peck's Bad Boy at the
Circus
Reformatory
Youth Takes a Fling
That Certain Age
39: 6000 Enemies
Juarez
On Borrowed Time

The Secret of Dr. Kildare
Hell's Kitchen
Mr. Smith Goes to
Washington
a short
40: The Grapes of Wrath
It All Came True
My Love Came Back
Edison the Man
New Moon
We Who Are Young
Father Is a Prince
41: Tobacco Road
Footsteps in the Dark
The Bride Wore Crutches
Nothing but the Truth
Skylark
One Foot in Heaven
The Feminine Touch
The Penalty
The Great Lie
The Man Who Came to
Dinner
42: Larceny, Inc.
Meet the Stewarts
My Sister Eileen
The Gay Sisters
Cairo
Orchestra Wives
43: The Gold Tower
The Amazing Mrs. Holiday
Dixie
All by Myself
44: See Here, Private Har-
grove!
Step Lively
Arsenic and Old Lace
When the Lights Go on
Again
And Now Tomorrow
The Impatient Years
Laura
45: A Medal for Benny
Crime, Inc.
Bring on the Girls
Bedside Manner
Conflict
Guest Wife
Col. Effingham's Raid
Leave Her to Heaven

46: Easy to Wed
Cinderella Jones
47: Blondie's Holiday
Honeymoon
Blondie's Anniversary
It Happened on Fifth
Avenue
The Corpse Came C.O.D.
48: Who Killed Cock Robin?

James Mitchell (1920-
1949: Colorado Territory
Border Incident
50: Stars in My Crown
53: The Band Wagon
54: Deep in My Heart
55: The Prodigal
Oklahoma!
56: The Peacemaker

Millard Mitchell (1903-1953)
1940: Mr. and Mrs. Smith
42: The Mayor of 44th Street
Grand Central Murder
The Big Street
Get Hep to Love
43: Slightly Dangerous
46: Swell Guy
47: Kiss of Death
48: A Double Life
A Foreign Affair
49: Everybody Does It
Thieves' Highway
Twelve O'Clock High
50: The Gunfighter
Winchester 73
Mr. 880
51: You're in the Navy Now
Strictly Dishonorable
52: My Six Convicts
Singin' in the Rain
53: The Naked Spur
Here Come the Girls!

Thomas Mitchell (1893-1962)
1930: Little Accident (collab.)
34: All of Me (collab.)
36: Craig's Wife
Adventures in Manhattan
Theodora Goes Wild

37: Man of the People
When You're in Love
Lost Horizon
The Hurricane
I Promise to Pay
Life Begins with Love
(collab.)
Make Way for Tomorrow
38: Love, Honor, and Behave
Trade Winds
39: Only Angels Have Wings
Stagecoach (OSCAR)
Mr. Smith Goes to
Washington
The Hunchback of Notre
Dame
Gone with the Wind
40: Swiss Family Robinson
Three Cheers for the Irish
Our Town
The Long Voyage Home
Angels over Broadway
41: Flight from Destiny
Out of the Fog
42: Joan of Paris
Song of the Islands
This Above All
Moontide
Tales of Manhattan
The Black Swan
43: The Immortal Sergeant
The Outlaw
Bataan
Flesh and Fantasy
44: The Sullivans
Wilson
Dark Waters
Buffalo Bill
45: Keys of the Kingdom
Within These Walls
Captain Eddie
46: Adventure
Three Wise Fools
The Dark Mirror

Jim Mitchum (1938
1958: Thunder Road
59: The Beat Generation
Girls Town
60: The Night Fighters

61: The Last Time I Saw
    Archie
62: The Young Guns of Texas
63: The Victors
64: Ride the Wild Surf
65: In Harm's Way
66: Ambush Bay
    The Money Trap
    The Tramplers
68: The Heroes
69: Bigfoot

John Mitchum
1962: Hitler
  63: Cattle King

Robert Mitchum (1917-
1935: Hopalong Cassidy Series
  43: False Colors
      Border Patrol
      Minesweeper
      The Leather Burners
      Colt Comrades
      Riders of the Deadline
      The Lone Star Trail
      We've Never Been Licked
      Corvette K-225
      Beyond the Last Frontier
      Hoppy Serves a Writ
      Follow the Band
      Bar-20
      The Dancing Masters
      Gung Ho!
  44: Girl Rush
      Nevada
      And so They Were Married
      Johnny Doesn't Live Here
        Anymore
      When Strangers Marry
      30 Seconds over Tokyo
  45: The Story of G.I. Joe
      West of the Pecos
  46: Undercurrent
      The Locket
      Till the End of Time
  47: Pursued
      Desire Me
      Crossfire
      Out of the Past
      Build My Gallows High

48: Rachel and the Stranger
    Blood on the Moon
49: The Red Pony
    The Big Steal
    Holiday Affair
50: Where Danger Lives
51: His Kind of Woman
    My Forbidden Past
    The Racket
52: Macao
    One Minute to Zero
    The Lusty Men
    Angel Face
53: White Witch Doctor
    Second Chance
54: She Couldn't Say No
    River of No Return
    Track of the Cat
55: Night of the Hunter
    Man with the Gun (or,
      The Trouble Shooter)
56: Foreign Intrigue
    Bandido
57: The Enemy Below
    Heaven Knows, Mr. Allison
    Fire Down Below
58: Home Before Dark
    Thunder Road
    The Hunters
59: The Wonderful Country
    The Angry Hills
60: Home from the Hill
    The Sundowners
    The Night Fighters
    The Grass Is Greener
61: The Last Time I Saw
    Archie
62: Cape Fear
    The Longest Day
    Two for the Seesaw
63: The List of Adrian
      Messenger
    Rampage
64: Man in the Middle
    What a Way to Go!
65: Mr. Moses
67: The Way West
    El Dorado
68: Anzio
    Five Card Stud

68: Secret Ceremony
69: Villa Rides
Coming of Age
Young Billy Young
The Good Guys and the
Bad Guys
Ryan's Daughter

Tom Mix (1881-1940)
1928: The Devil's Reward   S
Horseman of the Plains S
Hello Cheyenne   S
Painted Post   S
Son of the Golden West S
Arizona Wildcat   S
King Cowboy   S
29: Outlawed   S
Big Diamond Robbery S
The Drifter   S
32: Destry Rides Again
The Fourth Horseman
My Pal, the King
Texas Bad Man
Rider of Death Valley
33: The Terror Trail
Hidden Gold
Flaming Guns
Rustlers' Roundup

Ruth Mix
1931: Red Fork Range
35: Fighting Pioneers
Saddle Aces
36: The Riding Avenger

Mary Ann Mobley (1939-
1964: Get Yourself a College
Girl
65: Girl Happy
Harum Scarum
Young Dillinger
66: Three on a Couch
67: The King's Pirate
68: A Dandy in Aspic
For Singles Only
Istanbul Express (TV)

Roger Mobley
1960: A Dog's Best Friend
61: The Comancheros

The Silent Call
The Boy Who Caught a
Crook
62: Jack, the Giant Killer
63: Dime with a Halo
64: Emil and the Detectives

Gerald Mohr (1914-1968)
1941: The Monster and the Girl
We Go Fast
42: The Lady Has Plans
43: King of the Cowboys
Lady of Burlesque
One Dangerous Night
The Desert Song
Murder in Times Square
46: A Guy Could Change
The Catman of Paris
The Magnificent Rogue
Passkey to Danger
The Invisible Informer
Gilda
The Notorious Lone Wolf
The Truth about Murder
Dangerous Business
47: The Lone Wolf in Mexico
Heaven Only Knows
The Lone Wolf in London
48: Two Guys from Texas
50: Undercover Girl
Hunt the Man Down
51: Ten Tall Men
Detective Story
Sirocco
52: The Sniper
Son of Ali Baba
The Ring
Duel at Silver Creek
Invasion U.S.A.
53: Raiders of the Seven Seas
Money from Home
The Eddie Cantor Story
54: Dragonfly Squadron
57: The Buckskin Lady
58: Terror in the Haunted
House
59: Guns, Girls, and Gangsters
60: This Rebel Breed
The Angry Red Planet
68: Funny Girl

977

Georgia Moll
1960: The Cossacks
Lipstick
Thief of Baghdad
61: The White Warrior
63: Island of Love
Sulemein the Conqueror
64: Dark Purpose
Contempt
68: The Devil in Love
Misunderstood
Italian Secret Service
69: The Crime Thief (Fr.)

William V. Mong (1875-1940)
1929: Noah's Ark   PT
Seven Footprints to
Satan   SSE
House of Horror   PT
Should a Girl Marry? PT
Dark Skies
30: Double Cross Roads
The Girl Said No
In Gay Madrid
Murder on the Roof
Big Trail
31: The Flood
Gun Smoke
Bad Company
A Dangerous Affair
32: Cross Examination
By Whose Hands?
Fighting Fool
Widow in Scarlet
Dynamite Denny
Sign of the Cross
No More Orchids
33: Women Won't Tell
Strange Adventure
Vampire Bat
The 11th Commandment
Fighting for Justice
Narrow Corner
I Loved a Woman
Silent Men
Her Forgotten Past
34: Dark Hazard
Massacre
Treasure Island
35: County Chairman

The Hoosier Schoolmaster
Last Days of Pompeii
Whispering Smith Speaks
36: The Dancing Pirate
Last of the Mohicans
The Dark Hour
37: Stand-In
38: The Painted Desert

Marilyn Monroe (1928-1962)
1947: Dangerous Years
48: Scudda Hoo! Scudda Hay!
Ladies of the Chorus
50: Love Happy
Light Cross
The Asphalt Jungle
All About Eve
The Fireball
A Ticket to Tomahawk
51: Hometown Story
As Young as You Feel
Let's Make it Legal
Love Nest
52: Clash by Night
We're not Married
Don't Bother to Knock
Monkey Business
O. Henry's Full House
(The Cop and The
Anthem seq.)
53: Niagara
Gentlemen Prefer Blondes
How to Marry a Millionaire
54: River of No Return
There's no Business Like
Show Business
55: The Seven Year Itch
56: Bus Stop
57: The Prince and the Show-
girl
59: Some Like it Hot
60: Let's Make Love
61: The Misfits
63: Marilyn (doc.)

Ricardo Montalban (1920-
1941: The Three Musketeers
El Verdugo de Sevilla
Santa
42: La Fuga

42: La Hora de la Verdad

43: La Casa de la Zorro

44: Nosotros

46: Pepita Jimenez

47: Fiesta

48: On an Island with You
His Only Song
The Kissing Bandit

49: Neptune's Daughter
Battleground
Border Incident

50: Mystery Street
Right Cross
Two Weeks with Love

51: Across the Wide Missouri
Mark of the Renegade

52: My Man and I

53: Sombrero
Latin Lovers

54: The Saracen Blade
Sombre Verde

55: A Life in the Balance
Semiramis (Ital.)

56: Three for Jamie Dawn
Queen of Babylon
Untouched

57: Sayonara
Son of the Sheik (Ital.-
Span.)

60: Let no Man Write My
Epitaph

61: Desert Warrior
The Black Pirate (Ital.)

62: Hemingway's Adventures
of a Young Man
The Reluctant Saint
Rage of the Buccaneers

63: Love Is a Ball
The Long Flight

64: Cheyenne Autumn

65: The Money Trap

66: The Singing Nun
Madame X

67: The Longest Hundred Miles
(TV)

68: Blue

69: Sweet Charity
Code Name: Heraclitus
Joaquin Murietta (TV)

Yves Montand (1921-

1946: Les Portes de la Nuit

50: Lost Property

53: The Wages of Fear

54: Napoleon

55: The Heroes Are Tired

58: Where the Hot Wind Blows!
Premier May
Witches of Salem
Man-to-Man Talk
The Crucible

59: Heroes and Sinners
The Wide Blue Road

60: Let's Make Love
Sanctuary
Goodbye Again

62: My Geisha

66: The Sleeping Car Murder
Is Paris Burning?

67: Grand Prix
Live for the Living
La Guerre Est Finis

68: A Night a Train

69: Le Joli Mai (narr.)
"Z"
The Son
The Tiger by the Tail
On a Clear Day You can
See Forever
Last Known Address

Lisa Montell

1955: Escape to Burma
Pearl of the South Pacific

56: World Without End
Gaby

57: Tomahawk Trail
10,000 Bedrooms

58: The Lone Ranger and the
Lost City of Gold

61: The Long Rope

62: The Firebrand

Conchita Montenegro (1912-

1931: Strangers May Kiss
Never the Twain Shall
Meet
Paid to Love
The Cisco Kid

32: The Gay Caballero
33: Laughing at Life
34: Hell in the Heavens
    Handy Andy
35: He Trusted His Wife

Liliane Montevecchi
1955: Moonfleet
    The Glass Slipper
56: Meet Me in Las Vegas
57: The Living Idol
    The Sad Sack
58: The Young Lions
    King Creole
    Me and the Colonel

Maria Montez (1918-1951)
1941: The Invisible Woman
    That Night in Rio
    Boss of Bullion City
    Raiders of the Desert
42: Moonlight in Hawaii
    South of Tahiti
    Bombay Clipper
    The Mystery of Marie
    Roget
    Arabian Nights
43: White Savage
44: Ali Baba and the Forty
    Thieves
    Follow the Boys
    Cobra Woman
    Gypsy Wildcat
    Bowery to Broadway
45: Sudan
46: Tangier
47: Exile
    Pirates of Monterey
48: Siren of Atlantis
51: Wicked City
    The Pirate's Revenge
52: The Thief of Venice

Douglass Montgomery [Kent
Douglas] (1912-1966)
1931: Paid
    Five and Ten
    Waterloo Bridge
33: Little Women
34: A House Divided

Eight Girls in a Boat
Little Man, What Now?
Music in the Air
35: Tropical Trouble
    The Mystery of Edwin
    Drood
    Harmony Lane
    Lady Tubbs
36: Everything Is Thunder
37: Counsel for Crime
    Life Begins with Love
39: Cat and the Canary
45: Johnny in the Clouds
    The Way to the Stars
46: Woman to Woman
48: Forbidden
52: When in Rome

Elizabeth Montgomery (1933-
1963: Johnny Cool
    Who's Been Sleeping in
    My Bed?
65: The Court-Martial of
    Billy Mitchell

George Montgomery (1916-
1937: Conquest
40: The Cisco Kid and the
    Lady
    Star Dust
    Young People
    Charter Pilot
    Jennie
41: The Cowboy and the
    Blonde
    Accent on Love
    Riders of the Purple Sage
    Last of the Duanes
    Cadet Girl
42: Roxie Hart
    Ten Gentlemen from West
    Point
    Orchestra Wives
    China Girl
43: Bomber's Moon
    Coney Island
46: Three Little Girls in Blue
47: The High Window
    Brasher Doubloon
48: Lulu Belle

980

48: Belle Starr's Daughter
    Girl from Manhattan
50: Davy Crockett--Indian
    Scout
    Dakota Lil
    The Iroquois Trail
    Tomahawk Trail
51: Sword of Monte Cristo
    The Texas Rangers
52: Indian Uprising
    Cripple Creek
    The Pathfinder
53: Jack McCall--Desperado
    Fort Ti
    Gun Belt
54: Battle of Rogue River
    The Lone Gun
    Masterson of Kansas
55: Robbers' Roost
    Seminole Uprising
56: Canyon River
    Huk
57: Pawnee
    Pale Arrow
    Street of Sinners
    Last of the Badmen
    Black Patch
    Gun Duel in Durango
58: Badman's Country
    Man from God's Country
    Toughest Gun in Tomb-
    stone
59: King of the Wild Stallions
    Too Many Crooks
    Stallion Trail
    Watusi
61: The Steel Claw (act.,dir.)
62: Samar (act.,dir.)
64: Guerrillas in Pink Lace
    From Hell to Borneo
65: Battle of the Bulge
66: Outlaw of Red River
    Generation
    Hallucination
67: The Outlaw
    The Lone Ranger (ser.)
    Hostile Guns
68: Warkill
    Bomb at 10:10
69: The Last of the
    Comancheros

Strangers at Sunrise
Satan's Harvest

Ray Montgomery
1942: The Hard Way
43: Action in the North
    Atlantic
48: June Bride
    Johnny Belinda
49: The House Across the
    Street
    Task Force
51: People Will Talk
52: The Las Vegas Story
53: Down Among the Shelter-
    ing Palms
    Bandits of the West
    Eyes of the Jungle
    Ramar and the Jungle
    Secrets
    White Goddess
55: Phantom of the Jungle
    Thunder over Sangaland
57: Ramar and the Burning
    Barrier
    Three Brave Men
    Bombers B-52
59: Ramar and the Savage
    Challenger
    A Private Affair
60: Ramar and the Deadly
    Females
    Ramar and the Unknown
    Terror
63: A Gathering of Eagles
64: Ramar's Mission to India

Robert Montgomery (1904-
1929: College Days   S
    So This Is College?
    Untamed
    On the Set
    Father's Day
    The Single Standard   S
    Three Live Ghosts
30: Their Own Desire
    The Divorcee
    Free and Easy
    Our Blushing Brides
    Sins of the Children
    Inspiration

30: War Nurse
The Richest Man in the
World
Love in the Rough
Let Us be Gay
Courage
31: The Big House
Transatlantic
The Easiest Way
Strangers May Kiss
Shipmates
Man in Possession
32: But the Flesh Is Weak
Lovers Courageous
Letty Lynton
Faithless
Blondie of the Follies
Pig Boat
33: Tinfoil
Hell Below
Made on Broadway
When Ladies Meet
Another Language
Night Flight
34: Private Lives
Fugitive Lovers
The Mystery of Mr. X
Riptide
Hide-Out
Forsaking All Others
35: Vanessa--Her Love Story
No More Ladies
The Man I Made
Biography of a Bachelor
Girl
Suicide Club
36: Petticoat Fever
Trouble for Two
Piccadilly Jim
37: The Last of Mrs. Cheyney
Night Must Fall
Live, Love, and Learn
Ever Since Eve
38: The First Hundred Years
Yellow Jack
Three Loves Has Nancy
39: Fast and Loose
40: The Earl of Chicago
Haunted Honeymoon
41: Mr. and Mrs. Smith

The Rage of Heaven
Unfinished Business
Here Comes Mr. Jordan
45: They Were Expendable
46: Lady in the Lake (act.,
dir.)
47: Desire Me
Ride the Pink Horse
48: The Saxon Charm
Secret Land (narr.)
June Bride
49: Once More My Darling
(act., dir.)
50: Eye Witness (dir.)
60: The Gallant Hours (dir.,
pro.)

Sarita Montiel
1951: Carcel de Mujeres
54: Vera Cruz
56: Serenade
57: Run of the Arrow
60: Circle of Death
63: A Girl Against Napoleon

Alex Montoya
1954: Three Young Texans
Passion
55: Escape to Burma
Hell's Island
Apache Ambush
56: War Drums
57: Stagecoach to Fury
58: Toughest Gun in Tombstone
59: Ghost of Zorro
64: Island of the Blue Dolphins
65: The Flight of the Phoenix
66: The Appaloosa
67: Daring Game
The King's Pirate

Ralph Moody
1948: Man-Eater of Kumaon
49: Square Dance Jubilee
51: Red Mountain
52: Affair in Trinidad
Road to Bali
53: Seminole
Column South
Tumbleweed

55: Many Rivers to Cross
Strange Lady in Town
Rage at Dawn
Far Horizons
I Died a Thousand Times
56: The Last Hunt
The Steel Jungle
Toward the Unknown
Reprisal!
57: The Monster that
Challenged the World
Pawnee
58: Going Steady
The Lone Ranger and the
Lost City of Gold
59: The Legend of Tom Dooley
The Big Fisherman
60: The Story of Ruth
61: Homicidal
The Outsider

Ron Moody (1923-
1964: Every Day's a Holiday
Murder Most Foul
65: Seaside Swingers
68: Oliver!
69: David Copperfield (TV)

Alvy Moore
1952: Okinawa
53: The Glory Brigade
China Venture
54: Riot in Cell Block 11
Susan Slept Here
Return from the Sea
55: An Annapolis Story
Five Against the House
56: Screaming Eagles
57: Designing Woman
The Persuader
58: Perfect Furlough
60: The Wackiest Ship in the
Army
61: Everything's Ducky
Twist Around the Clock
64: Move Over, Darling
For Love or Money
Three Nuts in Search of a
Bolt
65: Love and Kisses

One Way Wahini
69: Come in, Children
Suicide for Six
The Witchmaker

Clayton Moore
1940: Kit Carson
Son of Monte Cristo
41: International Lady
Tuxedo Junction
42: Perils of Nyoka (ser.)
Black Dragons
46: The Crimson Ghost (ser.)
The Bachelor's Daughter
Cyclotrode X
47: Jesse James Rides Again
(ser.)
Along the Oregon Trail
48: G-Men Never Forget
Adventures of Frank and
Jesse James (ser.)
Marshal of Amarillo
49: The Ghost of Zorro (ser.)
The Far Frontier
Frontier Investigator
Sheriff of Wichita
The Gay Amigo
South of Death Valley
Riders of the Whistling
Pines
Masked Raiders
Bandits of El Dorado
Cowboy and the Indians
51: Cyclone Fury
52: Nyoka and the Tigerman
(ser.)
Night Stage to Galveston
Mutiny
Hawk of Wild River
Buffalo Bill in Tomahawk
Territory
Desert Passage
Montana Territory
Barbed Wire
Captive of Billy the Kid
Son of Geronimo (ser.)
53: Jungle Drums of Africa
(ser.)
Kansas Pacific
Down Laredo Way

53: 238 and the Witch Doctor
54: The Black Dakotas
56: The Lone Ranger
58: The Lone Ranger and the
    Lost City of Gold
59: The Ghost of Zorro

Cleo Moore (1930-
1948: Congo Bill (ser.)
50: This Side of the Law
    Gambling House
    Dynamite Pass
    Rio Grande Patrol
    Hunt the Man Down
51: On Dangerous Ground
52: Strange Fascination
    The Pace that Thrills
53: One Girl's Confession
    Thy Neighbor's Wife
54: The Other Woman
    Bait
55: Hold Back Tomorrow
    Women's Prison
56: Over-Exposed
57: Hit and Run

Colleen Moore (1900-
1929: Synthetic Sin   S
    Why be Good?   S
    Smiling Irish Eyes
    Footlights and Fools
33: The Power and the Glory
34: Social Register
    Success at Any Price
    The Scarlet Letter

Constance Moore (1920-
1938: State Police
    Border Wolves
    The Last Stand
    The Crime of Dr. Hallet
    Wives Under Suspicion
    Prison Break
    A Letter of Introduction
    The Missing Guest
    Freshman Year
    Swing that Cheer
39: Buck Rogers (ser. re-edit.
    as feature: Planet Out-
    laws)

You Can't Cheat an
    Honest Man
Ex-Champ
Mutiny on the Blackhawk
Hawaiian Nights
Charlie McCarthy, Detec-
    tive
Laugh it Off
40: Framed
    Ma, He's Making Eyes at
    Me
    La Conga Nights
    I'm Nobody's Sweetheart
    Now
    Argentine Nights
41: I Wanted Wings
    Las Vegas Nights
    Buy Me that Town
42: Take a Letter, Darling
44: Show Business
    Atlantic City
45: Delightfully Dangerous
    Mexicana
    Earl Carroll's Vanities
46: Earl Carroll's Sketchbook
    In Old Sacramento
47: Hit Parade of 1947
    High and Happy
48: Hats Off to Rhythm
51: The 13th Letter
67: Spree

Del Moore
1961: The Last Time I Saw
    Archie
62: The Errand Boy
    Stagecoach to Dancers' Rock
63: The Nutty Professor
64: The Patsy
    The Disorderly Orderly
67: The Big Mouth
68: The Catalina Caper

Dickie Moore (1925-
1929: Timothy's Quest   S
    Object: Alimony
30-32: Our Gang Comedies
    Lawful Larceny
    Son of the Gods
    Let Us be Gay

984

32: The Passion Flower
31: Star Witness
      Aloha
      Seed
      The Squaw Man
      Three Who Loved
32: And God Smiles
      Husband's Holiday
      Manhattan Parade
      The Expert
      So Big
      Disorderly Conduct
      Winner Takes All
      The Blonde Venus
      No Greater Love
      Million Dollar Legs
      The Racing Strain
      Fireman, Save My Child!
      Cauliflower Alley
      Union Depot
      When a Fellow Needs a
        Friend
      The Devil Is Driving
33: Oliver Twist
      Gabriel over the White
        House
      The Cradle Song
      Gallant Lady
      A Man's Castle
      Deception
      Obey the Law
      Swell Head
34: The Human Side
      This Side of Heaven
      The Upper World
      In Love with Life
      Little Men
35: The World Accuses
      Peter Ibbetson
      So Red the Rose
      The Story of Louis
        Pasteur
      Tomorrow's Youth
36: Timothy's Quest
      Little Red Schoolhouse
37: The Life of Emile Zola
      The Bride Wore Red
38: Love, Honor, and Behave
      The Arkansas Traveler
      My Bill

      The Gladiator
39: a short
      The Hidden Power
40: A Dispatch from Reuter's
41: Sergeant York
      The Great Mr. Nobody
42: Adventures of Martin Eden
      Are These Our Children?
      Miss Annie Rooney
43: Heaven can Wait
      Song of Bernadette
      Happy Land
      Jive Junction
44: Youth Runs Wild
      The Eve of St. Mark
      Sweet and Low Down
      Divine Love
      Together Again
      Gentleman for a Day
47: Dangerous Years
      Out of the Past
48: 16 Fathoms Deep
      Behind Locked Doors
49: Bad Boy
      Tuna Clipper
      The Boy and the Eagle
50: Cody of the Pony Express
      (ser.)
      Killer Shark
52: Eight Iron Men
      Member of the Wedding

Grace Moore (1902-1947)
1930: A Lady's Morals
      Soul Kiss
      New Moon
34: One Night of Love
35: Love Me Forever
36: The King Steps Out
37: I'll Take Romance
      When You're in Love
40: Louise

Ida Moore (1883-1964)
1944: Riders of the Santa Fe
      The Ghost Walks Alone
      She's a Soldier Too
45: Girls of the Big House
      Her Lucky Night
      Rough, Tough, and Ready

46: To Each His Own
47: Easy Come, Easy Go
The Egg and I
It's a Joke, Son!
48: Rusty Leads the Way
Good Sam
Money Madness
Johnny Belinda
Manhattan Angel
49: Ma and Pa Kettle
Leave it to Henry
Hold that Baby!
Paid in Full
50: Backfire
Mr. Music
Harvey
51: The Lemon Drop Kid
Comin' Round the Mountain
Honeychile
Leave it to the Marines
52: Scandal Sheet
Rainbow 'Round My
Shoulders
54: The Country Girl
55: Ma and Pa Kettle at
Waikiki
57: Desk Set
58: Rock-a-Bye Baby

Joanna Moore
1957: Slim Carter
58: Flood Tide
Touch of Evil
Ride a Crooked Trail
Appointment with a
Shadow
59: Monster on the Campus
The Last Angry Man
62: Walk on the Wild Side
Follow that Dream
63: Son of Flubber
64: The Man from Galveston
67: Moon Shot
68: Countdown
Never a Dull Moment

Juanita Moore
1952: Lydia Bailey
Affair in Trinidad
54: Witness to Murder

55: Women's Prison
56: Ransom
The Girl Can't Help it
57: The Green-Eyed Blonde
59: Imitation of Life
61: Tammy Tell Me True
Raisin in the Sun
62: Walk on the Wild Side
63: Papa's Delicate Condition
66: The Singing Nun
67: Rosie
68: Betrayal
69: Up Tight!

Kieron Moore (1925-
1944: The Voice Within
47: A Man about the House
48: Anna Karenina
Mine Own Executioner
49: Saints and Sinners
51: Ten Tall Men
David and Bathsheba
53: Man in Hiding (or, Man
Trap)
54: Recoil
55: The Naked Heart
Honeymoon Deferred
Conflict of Wings (or,
Fuss over Feathers)
The Green Scarf
56: Satelite in the Sky
Three Sundays to Live
57: Blue Peter
58: The Key
Steel Bayonet
59: The Angry Hills
Darby O'Gill and the Little
People
60: The Day They Robbed the
Bank of England
Siege of Sidney Street
61: League of Gentlemen
Dr. Blood's Coffin
The Siege of Sidney Street
Facts of Evil
Lion of Sparta
62: I Thank a Fool
Double Twist
Three Hundred Spartans
63: Day of the Triffids

63: The Main Attraction
    The Model Murder Case
64: The Thin Red Line
    Hide and Seek
65: Crack in the World
66: Arabesque
    Son of a Gunfighter
67: Bikini Paradise
68: Run Like a Thief
    Custer of the West

Mary Tyler Moore (1938-
1961: X-15
67: Thoroughly Modern Millie
68: Don't Just Stand There!
    What's so Bad about
    Feeling Good?
69: A Change of Habit
    Run a Crooked Mile

Matt Moore (1888-1960)
1929: Coquette
    Side Street
    King of Kings   SSE
30: Call of the West
    The Squealer
31: Penrod and Sam
    The Front Page
    Married in Haste
    Consolation Marriage
32: Cock of the Air
    Rain
    Pride of the Legion
    Little Orphan Annie
33: The Deluge
34: All Men Are Enemies
    Such Women Are
    Dangerous
36: Absolute Quiet
    Anything Goes
39: Range War
    Bad Boy
41: My Life with Caroline
42: Mokey
43: Happy Land
44: Wilson
45: Spellbound
46: Good Sam
49: That Forsyte Woman
50: The Big Hangover

52: Plymouth Adventure
    Invitation
54: Seven Brides for Seven
    Brothers
56: The Birds and the Bees
57: An Affair to Remember

Owen Moore (1886-1939)
1929: Stolen Love   S
    High Voltage
    Side Street
30: Outside the Law
    Extravagance
    What a Widow!
31: Hush Money
32: As You Desire Me
33: She Done Him Wrong
    Man of Sentiment
37: A Star Is Born

Roger Moore (1930-
1945: Perfect Strangers (or,
    Vacation from Marriage)
46: Caesar and Cleopatra
48: The Fuller Brush Man
51: As Young as You Feel
54: The Last Time I Saw Paris
55: Interrupted Melody
    The King's Thief
56: Diane
61: Gold of the Seven Saints
    The Sins of Rachel Cade
    Rape of the Sabines
68: Crossplot
    The Patterson Report
    The Wrecking of Off-
    Shore No. 5
    Jazz Baby
69: The Vanishing Point
    Crossfire
    Girl from Paradise

Terry Moore (1929-
1944: Gaslight
45: Son of Lassie
46: Sweet and Low Down
    Shadowed
47: The Devil on Wheels
48: Return of October
49: Mighty Joe Young

50:	The Great Rupert	Victor Moore (1876-1962)	
	He's a Cockeyed Wonder	1930:	Heads Up!
	Gambling House		Dangerous Nan McGrew
51:	Two of a Kind	32:	1-reel comedies
	On the Sunny Side of the	34:	Romance in the Rain
	Street		Gift of Gab
	The Barefoot Mailman	36:	Swing Time
52:	Come Back Little Sheba		Gold Diggers of 1937
53:	Man on a Tightrope	37:	We're on the Jury
	Beneath the Twelve-Mile		Meet the Missus
	Reef		Life of the Party
	King of the Khyber Rifles		Make Way for Tomorrow
54:	The Black Knight	38:	Radio City Revels
55:	Daddy Long Legs		This Marriage Business
	Shack Out on 101	41:	Louisiana Purchase
56:	Postmark for Danger	42:	Star-Spangled Rhythm
	Between Heaven and Hell	43:	True to Life
57:	Bernadine		Riding High
	Girl on Death Row		The Heat's On
	Peyton Place	44:	Carolina Blues
59:	A Private's Affair	45:	It's in the Bag
	Cast a Long Shadow		Duffy's Tavern
60:	Why Must I Die?	46:	Ziegfeld Follies
	Platinum High School	47:	It Happened on Fifth Avenue
65:	City of Fear	48:	On Our Merry Way (or,
	Black Spurs		A Miracle can Happen)
	Town Tamer	49:	A Kiss in the Dark
66:	Waco	52:	We're not Married
67:	A Man Called Dagger	55:	The Seven Year Itch

Tom Moore (1885-1955)		Agnes Moorehead (1906-	
1929:	The Yellowback	1941:	Citizen Kane
	Side Street	42:	The Magnificent Ambersons
30:	The Woman Racket		Journey into Fear
	The Costello Case		The Big Street
31:	Last Parade		Mrs. Miniver
32:	Cannonball Express	43:	The Youngest Profession
33:	Men Are Such Fools		Government Girl
	Neighbors' Wives	44:	The Seventh Cross
	Mr. Broadway		Jane Eyre
34:	Bombay Mail		Dragon Seed
36:	Reunion		Since You Went Away
	Trouble for Two		Mrs. Parkington
46:	Behind Green Lights		Tomorrow the World!
47:	Moss Rose		Dangerous Journey
	Forever Amber	45:	Keep Your Powder Dry
48:	Scudda-Hoo! Scudda-Hay!		Our Vines Have Tender
49:	The Fighting O'Flynn		Grapes
50:	The Redhead and the		Her Highness and the
	Cowboy		Bellboy

47: The Beginning or the End?
Lost Moment
Dark Passage
48: Woman in White
Tish
Summer Holiday
Station West
Johnny Belinda
49: The Great Sinner
The Stratton Story
Without Honor
50: Caged
51: Fourteen Hours
Show Boat
Adventures of Captain
Fabian
The Blue Veil
52: The Blazing Forest
Three Loves
Captain Black Jack
53: Scandal at Scourie
Main Street to Broadway
Those Redheads from
Seattle
54: Magnificent Obsession
55: Untamed
All that Heaven Allows
The Left Hand of God
56: Pardners
Meet Me in Las Vegas
The Revolt of Mamie
Stover
The Conqueror
The Swan
The Opposite Sex
57: The True Story of Jesse
James
Raintree County
The Story of Mankind
Jeanne Eagels
59: The Bat
Night of the Quarter Moon
Tempest
60: Pollyanna
61: Twenty Plus Two
Bachelor in Paradise
62: Jessica
How the West Was Won
63: Who's Minding the Story?
65: Hush, Hush, Sweet
Charlotte!

66: The Singing Nun
69: The Magic Pear Tree
(cartoon voice)

Natalie Moorhead
1929: Through Different Eyes
Unholy Night
Girl from Havana
30: My Past
The Benson Murder Case
The Furies
Shadow of the Law
Hot Curves
Runaway Bride
Manslaughter
Ladies Must Play
Illicit
Office Wife
Hook, Line, and Sinker
31: Divorce Among Friends
Women Men Marry
Parlor, Bedroom, and Bath
Dance, Fools, Dance
Captain Thunder
The Phantom of Paris
Morals for Women
The Deceiver
Maker of Men
32: Discarded Lovers
The Menace
Cross Examination
Three Wise Girls
The Stoker
The Fighting Gentleman
The King Murder
33: Mind Reader
Forgotten
Corruption
Private Detective 62
Gigolettes of Paris
Big Chance
Dance Hall Hostess
Only Yesterday
34: Curtain at Eight
The Thin Man
Secret Sinners
Dancing Man
Fifteen Wives
The Curtain Falls
37: The Adventurous Blonde
38: Heart of Arizona

38: Beloved Brat
39: Lady of the Tropics
40: Flight Angels

Dolores Moran (1926-
1941: Yankee Doodle Dandy
42: The Hard Way
43: Old Acquaintance
44: To Have and Have not
Hollywood Canteen
45: The Horn Blows at
Midnight
Too Young to Know
46: The Man I Love
47: Christmas Eve
50: Johnny One-Eye
53: Count the Hours
54: The Silver Lode

Jackie Moran (1925-
1936: And so They Were
Married
Valiant Is the Word for
Carrie
37: The Outcast
Michael O'Halloran
38: Adventures of Tom
Sawyer
Mad About Music
Arson Gang Busters
Mother Carey's Chickens
Barefoot Boy
39: Everybody's Hobby
a short
Spirit of Culver
Meet Dr. Christian
Gone with the Wind
40: Tomboy
The Haunted House
The Ol' Swimmin' Hole
Anne of Windy Poplars
41: The Gang's all Here
Let's Go Collegiate!
43: Nobody's Darling
Henry Aldrich Haunts a
House
44: Song of the Open Road
Three Little Sisters
Since You Went Away
Janie
45: There Goes Kelly

Let's Go Steady
46: Freddie Steps Out
High School Hero
Junior Prom
Specter of the Rose
Her Sister's Secret
47: Betty Coed

Lee Moran (1888-1961)
1929: Children of the Ritz   SSE
On with the Show   PT
Glad Rag Doll
Gold Diggers of Broadway
Madonna of Avenue A   PT
Show of Shows
No Defense   PT
The Aviator
Dance Hall
30: Hideout
Pardon My Gun
Golden Dawn
Sweet Mama
31: Soldiers' Plaything
32: Stowaway
Exposure
Racetrack
The Fighting Gentleman
Uptown New York
The Death Kiss
33: Sister of Judas
Grand Slam
High Gear
The 11th Commandment
Goldie Gets Along
34: Circus Clown
35: Circumstantial Evidence
36: The Calling of Dan
Matthews

Lois Moran (1908-
1929: True Heaven   S
Making the Grade   PT
Joy Street   SSE
Behind that Curtain
Words and Music
Song of Kentucky
30: Mammy
Not Damaged
Dancers
Under Suspicion
31: Transatlantic

990

31: The Spider
    Men in Her Life
32: West of Broadway

Peggy Moran (1918-
1939: Little Accident
    The Big Guy
    Girls' School
40: Oh Johnny, How You can
    Love!
    Danger on Wheels
    West of Carson City
    Alias the Deacon
    I Can't Give You Anything
      but Love, Baby!
    Hot Steel
    Trail of the Vigilantes
    The Mummy's Hand
    Argentine Nights
    Spring Parade
    Slightly Tempted
    One Night in the Tropics
41: Horror Island
    Double Date
    Hello Sucker
    Flying Cadets
42: Treat 'em Rough
    Drums of the Congo
    Seven Sweethearts
    There's One Every Minute
43: King of the Cowboys

Polly Moran (1884-1952)
1929: Honeymoon   S
    China Bound   S
    Dangerous Females
    Hollywood Revue of 1929
    Hot for Paris
    Unholy Night
    It's a Wise Child
30: Paid
    Chasing Rainbows
    The Bishop Murder Case
    Caught Short
    Those Three French Girls
    a short
    Remote Control
    Way for a Sailor
    Way Out West
    The Girl Said No

31: Guilty Hands
    Reducing
    Politics
32: Prosperity
    The Passionate Plumber
33: Alice in Wonderland
34: Hollywood Party
36: a short
37: Two Wise Maids
38: Ladies in Distress
    Down to Their Last Yacht
39: Ambush
40: Tom Brown's School Days
    Meet the Missus
41: Petticoat Politics
49: Adam's Rib
50: The Yellow Cab Man
64: Big Parade of Comedy
    (doc.)

Milburn Morante (1888-1964)
1941: Buzzy and the Phantom
    Pinto
42: West of the Law
43: The Ghost Rider
50: West of Wyoming
    Over the Border
    Outlaw Gold
    Law of the Panhandle
    Six-Gun Men
51: Blazing Bullets
    Abilene Trail

S Kenneth More (1914-
1948: Scott of the Antarctic
    Now Barabbas
    The Clouded Yellow
49: The Chance of a Lifetime
50: No Highway
51: Appointment with Venus
    The Franchise Affair
52: Brandy for the Parson
    Yellow Balloon
53: Never Let Me Go
54: Genevieve
55: Our Girl Friday (or,
    Adventures of Sadie)
    Doctor in the House
    The Deep Blue Sea
57: Raising a Riot

57: Reach for the Sky
    Paradise Lagoon (or, The
      Admirable Crichton)
58: A Night to Remember
    Northwest Frontier
59: Sheriff of Fractured Jaw
60: Next to No Time
    The 39 Steps
    Sink the Bismarck!
    Flame over India
51: The Greengage Summer
    We Joined the Navy
    Loss of Innocence
    The Man in the Moon
62: The Comedy Man
    The Longest Day
64: Some People
65: The Collector
68: The Mercenary
    Dark of the Sun
69: Oh, What a Lovely War!
    The Battle of Britain
    The Betrayal
    The Fraulein Doktor

Jeanne Moreau (1928-
1953: Woman of Evil
55: The She-Wolves
56: Fountain of Youth (short)
57: Lift to the Scaffold
    Julietta
58: Demoniaque
59: The Lovers
    La Dialogue des Carmelites
    Back to the Wall
60: Moderato Cantabile
    Five Branded Women
61: Les Liaisons Dangereuses
    Frantic
    La Notte Brava
    Jules et Jim
62: Eva
63: The Trial
    The Victors
64: Le Feu Follet
    Bay of Angels
65: The Diary of a Chamber-
    maid
    The Yellow Rolls-Royce
    Mata Hari!

Banana Peel
The Train
66: Viva Maria!
    Mademoiselle
67: The Oldest Profession in
    the World (Mlle. Mimi
    seq.)
    The Sailor from Gibraltar
    Falstaff
    The Great Catherine
68: La Mariêe Etait en Noire
    (The Bride Wore Black)
    An Immortal Story
69: The Fire Within
    Monte Walsh
    Jealousy
    Diane's Body (Fr.)

Mantan Moreland
1937: Spirit of Youth
38: Next Time I Marry
    Frontier Scout
    There's that Woman Again
39: Irish Luck
    Tell No Tales
    One Dark Night
    Riders of the Frontier
40: Millionaire Playboy
    Chasing Trouble
    Pier 13
    The City of Chance
    The Man Who Wouldn't
      Talk
    Star Dust
    Maryland
    Viva Cisco Kid!
    On the Spot
    Laughing at Danger
    Drums of the Desert
41: Ellery Queen's Penthouse
    Mystery
    Cracked Nuts
    Up in the Air
    King of the Zombies
    The Gang's all Here
    Hello, Sucker!
    Dressed to Kill
    Four Jacks and a Jill
    Footlight Fever
    You're Out of Luck

41: Sign of the Wolf
Let's Go Collegiate!
Sleepers West
Marry the Boss's
Daughter
World Premiere
42: Professor Creeps
Andy Hardy's Double Life
The Strange Case of Dr.
RX
Treat 'em Rough
Mexican Spitfire Sees a
Ghost
Palm Beach Story
Footlight Serenade
Phantom Killer
Eyes in the Night
Girl Trouble
Tarzan's New York
Adventure
43: Hit the Ice
Cabin in the Sky
Cosmo Jones--Crime
Smasher
Sarong Girl
Revenge of the Zombies
Melody Parade
She's for Me
My Kingdom for a Cook
Slightly Dangerous
Swing Fever
You're a Lucky Fellow,
Mr. Smith
We've Never Been Licked
44: This Is the Life
The Mystery of the River
Boat (ser.)
The Chinese Cat
Moon Over Las Vegas
Chip Off the Old Block
Pin-Up Girl
South of Dixie
Black Magic
Bowery to Broadway
Charlie Chan in the Secret
Service
See Here, Private Har-
grove!
46: She Wouldn't Say Yes
The Scarlet Clue

The Jade Mask
The Shanghai Cobra
The Spider
Captain Tugboat Annie
46: Mantan Messes Up
Mantan Runs for Mayor
Dark Alibi
Shadows over Chinatown
47: The Trap
The Chinese Ring
48: Docks of New Orleans
The Mystery of the Golden
Eye
The Feathered Serpent
The Shanghai Chest
Best Man Wins
49: Sky Dragon
56: Rockin' the Blues
Rock 'n' Roll Revue
57: Rock 'n' Roll Jamboree
67: Enter Laughing

Andre Morell (1909-
1948: Thirteen Men and a Gun
49: No Time for Jennifer
50: Seven Days to Noon
Trio (Sanatorium Seq.)
51: High Treason
54: The Black Night
55: Three Cases of Murder
Summertime
56: The Baby and the Battle-
ship
The Man Who Never Was
57: The Black Tent
Pickup Alley
The Bridge on the River
Kwai
The Vengeance of She
58: Diamond Safari
Paris Holiday
The Camp on Blood Island
59: The Giant Behemoth
The Hound of Baskervilles
Ben-Hur
60: Cone of Silence
61: Mysterious Island
The Shadow of the Cat
62: Cash on Demand
64: The Moonspinners

65: She
66: Judith
The Wrong Box
The Plague of the Zombies
67: The Mummy's Shroud
68: The Mercenary

Antonio Moreno (1887-1967)
1929: Romance of the Rio
Grande   PT
Careers   PT
Synthetic Sin
Air Legion
30: The Benson Murder Case
El Cuerpo Del Delito
One Mad Kiss
Rough Romance
El Hombre Male
The Cat Creeps
Desire of Death (or, Will
of the Deceased)
31: Las Que Danzan (Those
Who Dance)
Santa
32: Wide Open Spaces (2 reels)
Aguilas Frente al Sol
(Eagles Across the Sun)
Primavera en Otono
(Springtime in Autumn)
La Cuidad de Carton
(The Cardboard City)
34: Asegure
Senora Casada Necessita
Maredo (My Second Wife)
35: Storm over the Andes
He Trusted His Wife
Rosa de Feancia
36: The Bohemian Girl
Maria de la O.
38: Rose of the Rio Grande
39: Ambush
40: Seven Sinners
41: They Met in Argentina
Two Latins from Manhattan
The Kid from Kansas
42: Fiesta
Undercover Man
The Valley of the Giants
44: Tampico
45: The Spanish Main

46: Notorious
47: Captain from Castile
49: Lust for Gold
For Those Who Dare
50: Saddle Tramp
The Crisis
Dallas
51: Mark of the Renegade
52: Untamed Frontier
53: Wings of the Hawk
Thunder Bay
54: The Creature from the
Black Lagoon
Saskatchewan
56: The Searchers
58: El Senor Faron y la
Cleopatra (Mr. Pharaoh
and Cleopatra)

Rita Moreno (1931-
1950: Pagan Love Song
Toast of New Orleans
52: Singin' in the Rain
The Ring
Cattle Town
The Fabulous Senorita
53: Latin Lovers
Fort Vengeance
El Alamein
54: Jivaro
Yellow Tomahawk
Garden of Evil
Tales of Adventure
55: Untamed
Seven Cities of Gold
56: The Vagabond King
The Lieutenant Wore Skirts
The King and I
57: The Deerslayer
60: This Rebel Breed
61: The West Side Story (OSCAR)
Summer and Smoke
62: Samar
63: Cry of Battle
68: Popi
69: The Little Sister
The Night of the Following
Day

Claudia Morgan (1912-
1932: Vanity Street
Once in a Lifetime
38: That's My Story
39: Stand Up and Fight
63: The World of Henry
Orient

Dennis Morgan (1910-
1936: Suzy
The Great Ziegfeld
I Conquer the Sea
37: Song of the City
Mama Steps Out
Navy Blue and Gold
39: Return of Dr. X
Waterfront
No Place to Go
Ride, Cowboy, Ride!
40: The Fighting 69th
Three Cheers for the
Irish
Flight Angels
Tear Gas Squad
River's End
Kitty Foyle
The Male Animal
41: Affectionately Yours
Bad Men of Missouri
Kisses for Breakfast
42: In this Our Life
Captains of the Clouds
Wings for the Eagle
The Hard Way
43: The Desert Song
Thanks Your Lucky Stars
44: Hollywood Canteen
Shine on Harvest Moon
The Very Thought of You
Henrietta the Eighth
Sometimes I'm Happy
45: Christmas in Connecticut
God Is My Co-Pilot
46: One More Tomorrow
The Time, the Place,
and the Girl
Two Guys from Milwaukee
47: My Wild Irish Rose
Cheyenne
The Wyoming Kid

Royal Flush
48: Two Guys from Texas
To the Victor
One Sunday Afternoon
49: It's a Great Feeling
The Lady Takes a Sailor
50: Perfect Strangers
Pretty Baby
51: Raton Pass (or, Canyon
Pass)
Painting the Clouds with
Sunshine
52: This Woman Is Dangerous
Cattle Town
55: The Gun that Won the
West
Star of Tomorrow
Pearl of the South Pacific
56: Uranium Boom

Frank Morgan (1890-1949)
1929: Belle of the Night
30: Dangerous Nan McGrew
Queen High
Laughter
Fast and Loose
32: The Half-Naked Truth
Secrets of the French
Police
33: Luxury Liner
Hallelujah, I'm a Bum!
Reunion in Vienna
The Nuisance
When Ladies Meet
Broadway to Hollywood
Bombshell
The Best of Enemies
Billion Dollar Scandal
Sailor's Luck
Kiss Before the Mirror
34: Cat and the Fiddle
Affairs of Cellini
There's Always Tomorrow
By Your Leave
Success at Any Price
Sisters Under the Skin
Lost Lady
35: The Good Fairy
Naughty Marietta
Escapade

995

35: I Live My Life
Perfect Gentleman
Enchanted April
36: The Dancing Pirate
The Great Ziegfeld
Trouble for Two
Piccadilly Jim
Dimples
37: The Last of Mrs. Cheyney
The Emperor's Candle-
sticks
Saratoga
Beg, Borrow, or Steal
Rosalie
38: Paradise for Three
Port of Seven Seas
The Crowd Roars
Sweethearts
39: Broadway Serenade
The Wizard of Oz
Balalaika
40: The Shop Around the
Corner
Broadway Melody of 1940
The Ghost Comes Home
The Mortal Storm
Boom Town
Hullabaloo
41: Keeping Company
Washington Melodrama
Wild Man of Borneo
Honky Tonk
The Vanishing Virginian
42: Tortilla Flat
White Cargo
43: A Stranger in Town
Human Comedy
Thousands Cheer
44: The White Cliffs of Dover
Hail the Conquering Hero
Return of the Ape Man
Miracle of Morgan's Creek
Casanova Brown
Dear Barbara
45: Yolanda and the Thief
Courage of Lassie
46: The Cockeyed Miracle
Lady Luck
The Great Morgan
Mr. Griggs Returns

47: Green Dolphin Street
48: Summer Holiday
The Three Musketeers
49: Any Number can Play
The Great Sinner
The Stratton Story
50: Key to the City

Helen Morgan (1900-1941)
1929: Glorifying the American
Girl
30: Roadhouse Nights
Applause
34: Marie Galante
35: Sweet Music
Go Into Your Dance
Frankie and Johnnie
36: Showboat
40: Henry Goes Arizona

Henry (Harry) Morgan (1915-
1942: The Omaha Trail
To the Shores of Tripoli
Loves of Edgar Allan Poe
Orchestra Wives
A-Haunting We Will Go
43: Crash Dive
The Ox-Bow Incident
Happy Land
44: Roger Touhy--Gangster
The Eve of St. Mark
Wing and a Prayer
Gentle Annie
45: A Bell for Adano
State Fair
46: Dragonwyck
Johnny Comes Flying Home
It Shouldn't Happen to a
Dog
Somewhere in the Night
From this Day Forward
47: The Gangster
48: The Big Clock
All My Sons
Race Street
Yellow Sky
The Saxon Charm
Moonrise
49: Down to the Sea in Ships

49: Madame Bovary
    Holiday Affair
    Red Light
    Strange Bargain
50: Outside the Wall
    The Showdown
    The Dark City
51: Belle Le Grande
    Appointment with Danger
    The Highwayman
    When I Grow Up
    The Well
    The Blue Veil
52: Bend of the River
    Scandal Sheet
    My Six Convicts
    Boots Malone
    High Noon
    Apache War Smoke
    The Toughest Man in
      Arizona
    What Price Glory?
    Stop, You're Killing Me!
53: Arena
    Torch Song
    Thunder Bay
    Champ For a Day
54: The Glenn Miller Story
    About Mrs. Leslie
    The Forty-Niners
    Prisoner of War
55: The Far Country
    Not as a Stranger
    Strategic Air Command
56: Backlash
    The Teahouse of the
      August Moon
57: Under Fire
59: It Started with a Kiss
60: Inherit the Wind
    Murder, Inc.
    Cimarron
    Mountain Road
62: How the West Was Won
64: Johnny Goldfarb, Please
      Come Home
66: Frankie and Johnny
    What Did You Do in the
      War, Daddy?
67: The Flim Flam Man

68: Support Your Local Sheriff
69: Dragnet ('66 TV rel.)
    Viva Max!

Michèle Morgan (1920-
1937: Gribouille (Lady in
      Question)
    The Storm
    Remarque
    Le Roi du Nord
38: Le Quai des Brumes
    (The Foggy Quay)
39: Le Recif de Corail
    The Heart of Paris
42: Joan of Paris
43: Heart of a Nation
    Higher and Higher
    Two Tickets to London
44: Passage to Marseilles
46: The Case
47: The Storm Waters
    The Lost Illusion
48: Le Symphonie Pastorale
49: The Fallen Idol
50: Les Orgenilleux
51: Fabiola
53: Seven Deadly Sins
54: Moment of Truth
    Daughters of Destiny
    Napoleon
55: The Naked Heart
56: The Proud and the
      Beautiful
    Grand Maneuver
    Marguerite de la Nuit
57: Oasis
    The Vintage
58: There's Always a Price
      Tag
59: The Mirror Has Two
      Faces
60: Marie Antoinette
62: Crime Does not Pay (The
      Hugues Case seq.)
    Gentle Art of Murder (or,
      The Spider's Web)
    Maxime
63: Landru (or, Bluebeard)
64: Love on the Riviera
66: The Lost Command

66: The Winner
68: Benjamin (or, Memoirs
of a Virgin)

Ralph Morgan (1882-1956)
1931: Honor Among Lovers
Charlie Chan's Chance
32: Dance Team
Strange Interlude
Rasputin and the Empress
Cheaters at Play
Disorderly Conduct
The Devil's Lottery
The Son-Daughter
33: Humanity
Trick for Trick
The Power and the Glory
Shanghai Madness
Walls of Gold
Dr. Bull
The Mad Game
The Kennel Murder Case
34: Little Men
Orient Express
The Cat and the Fiddle
Stand Up and Cheer
She Was a Lady
No Greater Glory
Transatlantic Merry-Go-
Round
Girl of the Limberlost
The Last Gentleman
Their Big Moment
Hell in the Heavens
35: Star of Midnight
Unwelcome Stranger
Condemned to Live
Calm Yourself
I've Been Around
Magnificent Obsession
36: Yellowstone
Muss 'em Up
The Ex-Mrs. Bradford
Little Miss Nobody
Human Cargo
Speed
General Spanky
Anthony Adverse
37: Crack-Up
The Man in Blue

The Life of Emile Zola
Exclusive
Wells Fargo
Behind Prison Bars
38: Love Is a Headache
Out West with the Hardys
Army Girl
Mannequin
Wives Under Suspicion
Orphans of the Street
Mother Carey's Chickens
Barefoot Boy
Shadows over Shanghai
That's My Story
39: Off the Record
Fast and Loose
Man of Conquest
Smuggled Cargo
Way Down South
Geronimo
Trapped in the Sky
The Lone Spy Hunt
40: Forty Little Mothers
I'm Still Alive
41: The Mad Doctor
Adventure in Washington
42: A Close Call for Ellery
Queen
Klondike Fury
The Traitor Within
Night Monster
43: Hitler's Hangman
The Monster Maker
Stage Door Canteen
Jack London
44: Trocadero
Weird Woman
The Impostor
The Great Alaskan
Mystery (ser.)
Double Furlough
I'll be Seeing You
Enemy of Women
45: Hollywood and Vine
This Love of Ours
Black Market Babies
47: Mr. District Attorney
Song of the Thin Man
The Last Roundup
48: Sleep My Love

48: The Creeper
Sword of the Avenger
50: Blue Grass of Kentucky
51: Heart of the Rockies
52: Gold Fever
Dick Tracy vs the
Phantom Empire (ser.)

Terence Morgan (1921-
1948: Hamlet
52: The Story of Mandy
Encore (Gigolo and
Gigolette seq.)
53: Turn the Key Softly
54: Both Sides of the Law
Always a Bride
55: Svengali
They Can t Hang Me
Dance, Little Lady
56: The Scamp
57: Strange Affection
Forbidden Cargo
59: Tread Softly, Stranger
60: The Shakedown
61: Piccadilly Third Stop
62: Raiders of the Spanish
Main
Mission of the Sea Hawk
63: The Flame and the Sword
65: Curse of the Mummy's
Tomb
67: The Penthouse
The Sea Pirate

Patricia Morison (1915-
1938: Persons in Hiding
39: I'm from Missouri
The Magnificent Fraud
40: Untamed
Rangers of Fortune
41: Romance of the Rio
Grande
The Roundup
One Night in Lisbon
42: Night in New Orleans
Beyond the Blue Horizon
Are Husbands Necessary?
43: Silver Skates
Song of Bernadette
Where Are Your Children?

Hitler's Hangman
The Fallen Sparrow
Calling Dr. Death
45: Without Love
Lady on a Train
46: Dressed to Kill
Danger Woman
47: Tarzan and the Huntress
Queen of the Amazons
Song of the Thin Man
Kiss of Death
48: Return of Wild Fire
Sofia
Prince of Thieves
60: Song Without End

Karen Morley (1905-
1931: Never the Twain Shall
Meet
Inspiration
Politics
Daybreak
High Stakes
Cuban Love Song
Lullaby
The Sin of Madelon Claudet
32: Scarface
Arsene Lupin
Phantom of Crestwood
The Fast Life
Mata Hari
Are You Listening?
Man About Town
Washington Masquerade
The Mask of Fu Manchu
Flesh
33: Gabriel over the White
House
Dinner at Eight
34: The Crime Doctor
Wednesday's Child
Our Daily Bread
Straight Is the Way
35: Ten Dollar Raise
The Healer
Black Fury
Thunder in the Night
The Littlest Rebel
36: The Devil's Squadron
Beloved Enemy

37: Outcast
Last Train from Madrid
On Such a Night
Girl from Scotland Yard
38: Kentucky
40: Pride and Prejudice
45: Jealousy
46: Unknown
47: The 13th Hour
Framed
Six-Gun Serenade
Code of the Saddle
51: M

Robert Morley (1908-
1938: Marie Antoinette
You Will Remember Me
41: Major Barbara
The Big Blockade
42: This Was Paris
The Foreman Went to
France
Young Mr. Pitt
45: I Live in Grosvenor
Square
47: No Nightingales
49: Edward, My Son
Six Months' Grace
Full Treatment
Hippo Dancing
51: African Queen
Curtain Up
52: Outcast of the Islands
53: Melba
Gilbert & Sullivan
54: The Final Test
Beat the Devil
Beau Brummel
Rainbow Jacket
55: The Good Die Young
Quentin Durward
56: Around the World in 80
Days
57: Loser Takes All
58: Law and Disorder
Sheriff of Fractured Jaw
The Doctor's Dilemma
59: Libel
The Journey
60: The Battle of the Sexes

Oscar Wilde
Go to Blazes
61: The Young One (or,
The Boys)
62: Road to Hong Kong
Wonderful to be Young
Joseph and His Brethren
63: Nine Hours to Rama
Murder at the Gallop
Take Her She's Mine
Ladies Who Do
The Old Dark House
64: Topkapi
Of Human Bondage
65: Those Magnificent Men in
Their Flying Machines
Genghis Khan
The Loved One
Agent 8 3/4
Life at the Top
66: A Study in Terror
Hotel Paradiso
Way, Way Out
The Alphabet Murders
67: Finders Keepers
Tender Scoundrel
Woman Times Seven
(Super Simone seq.)
68: Sinful Davey
Hot Millions
69: The Trygon Factor
Some Girls Do
Song of Norway
How Did a Nice Girl Like
You Get into this Business?
Twinky

Adrian Morris (d. 1940)
1936: The Petrified Forest
Poppy
My American Wife
Rose Bowl
37: Her Husband Lies
The Woman I Love
There Goes the Groom
Every Day's a Holiday
38: You and Me
If I Were King
Angels with Dirty Faces
39: Return of the Cisco Kid

1000

39: 6000 Enemies
Wall Street Cowboy
Gone with the Wind
40: The Grapes of Wrath
Florian

Chester Morris (1901-
1929: Fast Life
Woman Trap
Second Choice
Show of Shows
Alibi
30: Playing Around
The Big House
The Divorcee
The Case of Sgt. Grischa
She Couldn't Say No
31: The Bat Whispers
Corsair
32: Cock of the Air
The Miracle Man
Breach of Promise
Sinners in the Sun
Red-Headed Woman
33: Blondie Johnson
The Infernal Machine
Tomorrow at Seven
Golden Harvest
King for a Night
34: Let's Talk it Over
Embarrassing Moments
Gift of Gab
The Gay Bride
35: I've Been Around
Princess O'Hara
Public Hero No. 1
Society Doctor
Pursuit
Frankie and Johnnie
36: Three Godfathers
Moonlight Murder
They Met in a Taxi
Counterfeit
37: I Promise to Pay
The Devil's Playground
Flight from Glory
38: Law of the Underworld
Sky Giant
Smashing the Racket
39: Pacific Liner

Five Came Back
Thunder Afloat
Blind Alley
40: The Marines Fly High
Wagons Westward
The Girl from God's
Country
41: Meet Boston Blackie
Confessions of Boston
Blackie
No Hands on the Clock
The Phantom Thief
42: Canal Zone
I Live on Danger
The Wrecking Crew
Boston Blackie Goes to
Hollywood
43: After Midnight with Boston
Blackie
High Explosive
Aerial Gunner
Tornado
Thunderbolt
44: Derelict Ship
Dark Mountain
One Mysterious Night
Gambler's Choice
The Awakening of Jim
Burke
Secret Command
Double Exposure
Men of the Deep
45: Rough, Tough, and Ready
Boston Blackie's Rendezvous
Boston Blackie Booked on
Suspicion
The Blonde from Brooklyn
One Way to Love
46: A Close Call for Boston
Blackie
Boston Blackie and the
Law
47: Blind Spot
48: Trapped by Boston Blackie
49: Boston Blackie's Chinese
Venture
55: Unchained
56: The She-Creature
64: Big Parade of Comedy (doc.)

Howard Morris (1919-
1962: Boys' Night Out
Forty Pounds of Trouble
63: The Nutty Professor
65: Fluffy
66: Way Way Out!

Wayne Morris (1914-1959)
1936: China Clipper
King of Hockey
Here Comes Carter!
37: Don't Pull Your Punches
Kid Galahad
Submarine D-1
38: Love, Honor, and Behave
Men Are Such Fools
Valley of the Giants
The Kid Comes Back
Brother Rat
39: The Kid from Kokomo
Return of Dr. X
40: Brother Rat and a Baby
Flight Angels
An Angel from Texas
Ladies Must Live
Double Alibi
The Quarterback
Gambling on the High
Seas
41: I Wanted Wings
Bad Men of Missouri
The Smiling Ghost
Three Sons o' Guns
47: Voice of the Turtle
Deep Valley
48: The Time of Your Life
The Big Punch
49: The Younger Brothers
The House Across the
Street
John Loves Mary
A Kiss in the Dark
Task Force
50: The Tougher They Come
Johnny One-Eye
Stage to Tucson
51: Sierra Passage
Yellow Fin
Big Gusher
52: Desert Pursuit

Arctic Flight
The Bushwackers
53: The Marksman
Star of Texas
The Fighting Lawman
54: Riding Shotgun
The Desperado
Two Guns and a Badge
Port of Hell
55: Lord of the Jungle
Green Buddha
Cross Channel
Master Plan
The Lonesome Trail
56: The Dynamiters
The Crooked Sky
57: Paths of Glory
Plunder Road
58: Buffalo Gun

Jeff Morrow (1913-
1953: The Robe
Flight to Tangier
54: Siege of Red River
Tanganyika
Sign of the Pagan
55: Captain Lightfoot
This Island Earth
Hour of Decision
56: The World in My Corner
The Creature Walks
Among Us
Pardners
The First Texan
57: The Giant Claw
Copper Sky
Kronos
60: Five Bold Women
The Story of Ruth
63: Harbor Lights

Jo Morrow
1959: Juke Box Rhythm
60: Our Man in Havana
Thirteen Ghosts
The Three Worlds of
Gulliver
64: The Strangler

Susan Morrow (1932-
1951: Gasoline Alley
On the Loose
Corky of Gasoline Alley
52: The Savage
Blazing Forest
53: Problem Girls
Man of Conflict
Missile Base at Taniak
58: Macabre

Vic Morrow (1932-
1955: The Blackboard Jungle
Survival
56: Tribute to a Bad Man
57: Men in War
58: God's Little Acre
Hell's Five Hours
King Creole
60: Cimarron
61: Portrait of a Mobster
Last Year at Malibu
Posse from Hell
66: Dead Watch (prod., dir.,
sc., act.)
69: A River of Diamonds
"A Western" (dir.)

Robert Morse (19131-
1956: The Proud and Profane
58: The Matchmaker
63: The Cardinal
64: Quick Before it Melts
Honeymoon Hotel
65: The Loved One
67: How to Succeed in
Business Without Really
Trying
Oh, Dad, Poor Dad,
Mama's Hung You in the
Closet and I am Feeling
so Sad
A Guide for the Married
Man
68: Where Were You When
the Lights Went Out?

Charles Morton (1907-
1928: Four Sons   SSE
None but the Brave   S

29: The Four Devils   PT
Christina   PT
New Year's Eve   SSE
The Far Call   SSE
30: Cameo Kirby
Caught Short
Check and Double Check
32: The Last Ride
33: Goldie Gets Along
34: Dawn Trail
36: Hollywood Boulevard
39: Stunt Pilot

James Morton
1940: My Little Chickadee
41: Never Give a Sucker an
Even Break

Arnold Moss (1910-
1946: Temptation
48: The Loves of Carmen
49: Border Incident
Reign of Terror (or, The
The Black Book)
50: Kim
Salome
51: Quebec
Mask of the Avenger
My Favorite Spy
52: Viva Zapata!
54: Casanova's Big Night
Bengal Brigade
55: Jump into Hell
Hell's Island
57: The 27th Day
65: The Fool Killer
66: Gambit
67: Caper of the Golden Bulls

Zero Mostel (1915-
1943: Du Barry Was a Lady
50: Panic in the Streets
51: The Enforcer
Sirocco
The Guy Who Came Back
Mr. Belvedere Rings the
Bell
The Model and the Marriage
Broker
59: Zero

66: A Funny Thing Happened
    on the Way to the Forum
67: The Great Catherine
    The Producers
69: The Great Bank Robbery
    Mastermind
    The Angel Levine

Mickey Mouse (1927-

1928: Steamboat Willie
29: Barnyard Battle
    When the Cat's Away
    Karnival Kid
    Opry House
    Jass Fool
    Jungle Rhythm
30: Wild Waves
    Haunted House
    Barnyard Concert
    Fiddling Around Fire
    Fighters
    The Shindig
    Plow Boy
    The Chain Gang
    The Cactus Kid
    Gallopin' Gaucho
    Plane Crazy
    Gorilla Mystery
    Pickey's Choochoo
    Pioneer Days
31: Birthday Party
    Traffic Troubles
    The Castaways
    The Moose Hunt
    Delivery Boy
    Blue Rhythm
    Mickey Steps Out
    Fishin' Around
    Barnyard Broadcast
    The Beach Party
    Mickey Cuts Up
    Mickey's Orphans
32: Duck Hunt
    Grocery Boy
    Mad Dog
    Barnyard Olympics
    Mickey's Revue (OSCAR)
    Musical Farmer
    Mickey in Arabia
    Mickey's Nightmare

    Trader Mickey
    The Whoopee Party
    Touchdown Mickey
    The Wayward Canary
33: Mickey Shanghaied
    The Mad Doctor
    Mickey's Pal Pluto
    The Mellerdrammer
    The Mail¯Pilot
    Ye Olden Days
    Mickey's Mechanical Man
    Mickey's Gala Premiere
    Puppy Love
    Steeple Chase
    The Pet Shop
    Giant Land
34: Playful Pluto
    Camping Out
    Gulliver Mickey
    Mickey's Steam Roller
    Orphan's Benefit
    Mickey Plays Papa
    The Dognappers
    Two-Gun Mickey
35: Mickey's Man Friday (color)
    Band Concert (OSCAR)
    Mickey's Service Station
    Mickey's Kangaroo
    Mickey's Garden
    Mickey's Fire Brigade
    Pluto's Judgment Day
    On Ice
36: Polo Team
    Mickey's Grand Opera
    Through the Mirror
    Moving Day
    Mickey's Rival
    Alpine Climbers
    Mickey's Circus
37: Mickey's Elephant
    The Worm Turns
    Mickey's Amateurs
    Moose Hunter
    The Clock Cleaners
    The Old Milk (OSCAR)
38: Mickey's Trailer
    Mickey's Parrot
    Farmyard Symphony
39: Society Dog Show
    Autograph Hound

39: Standard Parade for 1939
40: Tugboat Mickey
Mickey's Magic Lamp
Mr. Mouse Takes a Trip
Fire Chief
Volunteer Worker
41: Lend a Paw (OSCAR)
42: Mickey's Birthday Party
47: Mickey's Delayed Date
48: Mickey Down Under
Mickey and the Seal
54: Mickey Mouse March of
Dimes

Movita (1917-
1935: Mutiny on the Bounty
36: Captain Calamity (or,
Captain Hurricane)
37: Paradise Isle
38: Rose of the Rio Grande
39: Wolf Call
The Girl from Rio
52: Wild Rose Ambush
53: Dream Wife
55: Apache Ambush

Alan Mowbray (1896-1969)
1931: God's Gift to Women
Man in Possession
Alexander Hamilton
Guilty Hands
Honor of the Family
32: Silent Witness
Nice Women
Lovers Courageous
The World and the Flesh
Man about Town
Winner Take All
Jewel Robbery
Two Against the World
The Man from Yesterday
The Man Called Back
Sherlock Holmes
Hotel Continental
Left over Ladies
33: Peg o' My Heart
A Study in Scarlet
Voltaire
Berkeley Square
Midnight Club

The World Changes
Roman Scandals
Our Betters
Her Secret
34: Long Lost Father
Where Sinners Meet
Girl from Missouri
Charlie Chan in London
House of Rothschild
Cheaters
Little Man, What Now?
One More River
Embarrassing Moments
35: Night Life of the Gods
Lady Tubbs
Becky Sharp
Gay Deception
In Person
She Couldn't Take It
36: Rose Marie
Muss 'em Up!
Mary of Scotland
Desire
Give Us this Night
The Case Against Mrs.
Ames
Fatal Lady
My Man Godfrey
Ladies in Love
37: Four Days' Wonder
As Good as Married
Topper
Vogues of 1938
Stand-In
On Such a Night
Music for Madame
Rainbow on the River
On the Avenue
The King and the Chorus
Girl
Marry the Girl
Hollywood Hotel
38: Merrily We Live
There Goes My Heart
39: Topper Takes a Trip
Never Say Die
The Llano Kid
Way Down South
40: Music in My Heart
Curtain Call

40: The Villain Still Pursued
    Her
    Scatterbrain
    The Boys from Syracuse
    The Quarterback
41: That Hamilton Woman
    That Uncertain Feeling
    Footlight Fever
    The Cowboy and the
    Blonde
    I Wake Up Screaming
    Moon over Her Shoulder
    Ice-Capades Revue
    Hot Spot
    The Perfect Snob
42: The Mad Martindales
    Panama Hattie
    A Yank at Eton
    Isle of Missing Men
    Yokel Boy
    The Devil with Hitler
    So This Is Washington
    The Powers Girl
43: Slightly Dangerous
    His Butler's Sister
    Holy Matrimony
    Stage Door Canteen
44: Doughgirls
    My Gal Loves Music
    Ever Since Venus
45: The Phantom of 42nd
    Street
    Bring on the Girls
    Men in Her Diary
    Sunbonnet Sue
    Earl Carroll's Vanities
    Tell it to a Star
    Where Do We Go from
    Here?
46: Terror by Night
    My Darling Clementine
    Idea Girl
47: Lured
    Merton of the Movies
    The Pilgrim Lady
    Man about Town
    Captain from Castile
48: Prince of Thieves
    The Main Street Kid
    My Dear Secretary

An Innocent Affair
Every Girl Should be
Married
49: You're My Everything
    Abbott & Costello Meet
    the Killer--Boris Karloff
    The Lovable Cheat
    The Lone Wolf and His
    Lady
50: Jackpot
    Wagonmaster
51: The Lady and the Bandit
    Crosswinds
52: Just Across the Street
    Androcles and the Lion
    Blackbeard the Pirate
54: Ma and Pa Kettle at Home
    Steel Cage
55: The King's Thief
56: The King and I
    The Man Who Knew too
    Much
    Around the World in 80
    Days

Jack Mower (1890-1965)

1927:	Uncle Tom's Cabin	S
	Pretty Clothes	S
28:	Sailors' Wives	S
	Air Patrol	S
	Sinners' Parade	S
	Water Hole	S
29:	Anne Against the World	S
	Ships of the Night	S
30:	Ridin' Law	
32:	Lone Trail	
	Midnight Patrol	
	Phantom Express	
33:	Come on, Tarzan!	
	Law and the Lawless	
	King of the Arena	
	Fiddlin' Buckaroo	
35:	Revenge Rider	
36:	Hollywood Boulevard	
37:	Missing Witness	
	White Bondage	
	Love Is in the Air	
	Without Warning	
38:	Penrod and His Twin	
	Brother	

38: Crime School
Hard to Get
Comet over Broadway
Tarzan and the Green
Goddess
39: The Return of Dr. X
Confessions of a Nazi Spy
Code of the Secret
Service
Smashing the Money Ring
Private Detecgive
Everybody's Hobby
40: King of the Lumberjacks
Torrid Zone
Tugboat Annie Sails Again
Always a Bride
41: The Bride Came C.O.D.
Bullets for O'Hara
The Wagons Roll at Night
42: Murder in the Big House
Spy Ship
43: The Mysterious Doctor
44: Adventures of Mark Twain
The Last Ride
47: Shadows over Chinatown
That Way with Women
48: Fighting Mad
49: Angels in Disguise
50: County Fair

Leonard Mudie (1883-1965)
1932: The Mummy
33: Voltaire
34: Mystery of Mr. X
House of Rothschild
Cleopatra
35: The Great Impersonator
Clive of India
Cardinal Richelieu
Becky Sharp
Rendezvous
Captain Blood
Magnificent Obsession
36: Anthony Adverse
Mary of Scotland
His Brother's Wife
37: Lancer Spy
The King and the Chorus
Girl
They Won't Forget

The League of Frightened
Men
London by Night
38: Adventures of Robin Hood
Kidnapped
Suez
The Jury's Secret
When Were You Born?
39: Tropic Fury
Arrest Bulldog Drummond!
Dark Victory
Don't Gamble with Strangers
40: Devil's Island
Congo Maisie
British Intelligence
Charlie Chan's Murder
Cruise
South of Suez
41: Shining Victory
The Nurse's Secret
42: Berlin Correspondent
43: Appointment in Berlin
45: Divorce
My Name Is Julia Ross
47: Bulldog Drummond at Bay
Private Affairs of Bel Ami
Song of My Heart
48: The Checkered Coat
51: Bomba and the Elephant
Stampede
52: Bomba and the Jungle Girl
African Treasure
53: The Magnetic Monster
Safari Drums
54: Killer Leopard
55: Lord of the Jungle
56: Autumn Leaves
57: The Story of Mankind
59: Timbuktu
The Big Fisherman
65: The Greatest Story Ever
Told

Esther Muir (1895-
1931: Dangerous Affair
33: The Bowery
37: On Again, Off Again
Under Suspicion
City Girl
I'll Take Romance

1007

38: Romance in the Dark
Battle of Broadway
The Law West of Tomb-
stone
Western Jamboree
A Day at the Races
40: Misbehaving Husbands
41: Stolen Paradise
42: The Mayor of 44th Street
X Marks the Spot

Gavin Muir (1909-
1936: Half Angel
Mary of Scotland
Charlie Chan at the Race-
track
Lloyds of London
37: Wee Willie Winkie
The Holy Terror
Fair Warning
42: Eagle Squadron
Nightmare
43: Sherlock Holmes in
Washington
Passport to Suez
Hitler's Children
44: The Merry Monahans
Passport to Adventure
The Master Race
45: Tonight and Every Night
Salome Where She Danced
The House of Fear
Patrick the Great
46: O.S.S.
California
Temptation
47: Ivy
Unconquered
48: The Prince of Thieves
Calcutta
49: Chicago Deadline
50: Rogues of Sherwood Forest
57: Johnny Trouble
The Abductors
59: Island of Lost Women
63: Night Tide

Jean Muir (1911-
1933: The World Changes
Son of a Sailor

34: As the Earth Turns
Desirable
Female
Dr. Monica
Gentlemen Are Born
Bedside
A Modern Hero
35: The White Cockatoo
Oil for the Lamps of
China
A Midsummer Night's
Dream
Stars over Broadway
Orchids to You
36: White Fang
Lloyds of London
37: Draegerman Courage
Fugitive in the Sky
Her Husband's Secretary
Once a Doctor
White Bondage
Dance, Charlie, Dance
Outcasts of Poker Flat
40: And One Was Beautiful
The Lone Wolf Meets a
Lady
43: The Constant Nymph

Jack Mulhall (1894-
1929: Children of the Ritz   SSE
Dark Streets
Twin Beds
Two Weeks Off   PT
Show of Shows
Naughty Baby
30: In the Next Room
Murder Will Out
Road to Paradise
Show Girl in Hollywood
The Golden Calf
The Fall Guy
For the Love of Lil
Death Ray
Second Choice
31: Reaching for the Moon
Lover Come Back
Murder at Dawn
32: Passport to Paradise
Night Beat
Sally of the Subway

32: Lovebound
   Hell's Headquarters
   Mystery Squadron (ser.)
   Sinister Hands
33: Secret Sinners
34: Notorious Sophie Lang
   Curtain at Eight
   Many Happy Returns
   The Old-Fashioned Way
   Burn 'em Up Barnes (ser.)
35: Love in Bloom
   People Will Talk
   Paris in Spring
   Big Broadcast of 1936
   George White's 1935
    Scandals
   Headline Woman
   His Night Out
   Custer's Last Stand (ser.)
   Chinatown Squad
   Sweet Adeline
   Mississippi
   Fighting Lady
   Roaring Roads
   What Price Crime?
   Skull and Crown
36: Rogues' Tavern
   Kelly of the Secret
    Service
   Preview Murder Mystery
   13 Hours by Air
   Hollywood Boulevard
   Wedding Present
   The Clutching Hand (ser.)
   Beloved Enemy
37: Secret Valley
   History Is Made at Night
   Dangerous Holiday
   One Hundred Men and a
    Girl
   a short
   Tim Tyler's Luck (ser.)
38: The Spy Ring
   The Storm
   Outlaws of Sonora
   Crime Ring
   The Chaser
   You and Me
   Held for Ransom
39: Home on the Prairie

   First Love
   a short
40: Black Friday
   Son of Monte Cristo
41: Desperate Cargo
   Hard Guy
   Cheers for Miss Bishop
   Invisible Ghost
   Dangerous Lady
   Bowery Blitzkrieg
   I Killed that Man
42: Saddle Mountain Roundup
   Foreign Agent
   Mr. Wise Guy
   Queen of Broadway
   Sin Town
   'Neath Brooklyn Bridge
   Silent Witness
   Man from Headquarters
43: Kid Dynamite
   The Ape Man
   Ghosts on the Loose
44: South of Dixie
   A Wave, a Wac, and a
    Marine
45: The Phantom of 42nd
    Street
   The Man Who Walked
    Alone
46: Deadline for Murder
49: Sky Liner
56: Around the World in 80
    Days
57: Up in Smoke
59: The Atomic Submarine

Edward Mulhare (1923-
1955: Hill 24 Doesn't Answer
64: Signpost to Murder
65: Von Ryan's Express
66: Our Man Flint
67: Eye of the Devil
   Caprice

Jack Mullaney
1957: The Young Stranger
   The Vintage
   Kiss Them for Me
58: South Pacific

1009

60: All the Fine Young
     Cannibals
61: The Absent-Minded
     Professor
     The Honeymoon Machine
64: Seven Days in May
65: Tickle Me
     Dr. Goldfoot and the
       Bikini Machine
66: Spin-Out

Billy Mumy
1963: Palm Springs Weekend
       A Ticklish Affair
65: Dear Brigitte
69: Rascal

Herbert Mundin (1889-1939)
1931: Enter the Queen
       The Wrong Mr. Perkins
       We Dine at Seven
       Peace and Quiet
       East Lynne on the
         Western Front
32: The Devil's Lottery
     Trial of Vivienne Ware
     Silent Witness
     Almost Married
     Life Begins
     The Bachelor's Affairs
     One Way Passage
     Chandu the Magician
     Sherlock Holmes
33: Dangerously Yours
     Pleasure Cruise
     Adorable
     Cavalcade
     It's Great to be Alive
     Arizona to Broadway
     Shanghai Madness
     The Devil's in Love
34: Ever Since Eve
     Hell in Heavens
     Orient Express
     Bottoms Up
     All Men Are Enemies
     Springtime for Henry
     Call it Luck
     Such Women Are Dangerous
     Love Time

35: David Copperfield
     Mutiny on the Bounty
     The Widow from Monte
       Carlo
     Ladies Love Danger
     Black Sheep
     The Perfect Gentleman
     King of Burlesque
36: Charlie Chan's Secret
     A Message to Garcia
     Under Two Flags
     Champagne Charlie
     Tarzan Escapes
37: Another Dawn
     You Can't Beat Love
     Angel
38: Adventures of Robin Hood
     Invisible Enemy
     Lord Jeff
     Exposed
39: Society Lawyer

Paul Muni (1895-1967)
1929: The Valiant
       Seven Faces
32: Scarface
     I Am a Fugitive from a
       Chain Gang
33: The World Changes
34: Hi Nellie!
35: Bordertown
     Dr. Socrates
     Black Fury
     The Story of Louis Pasteur
       (OSCAR)
37: The Good Earth
     The Woman I Love
     The Life of Emile Zola
38: For Auld Lang Syne (short)
39: Juarez
     We Are not Alone
40: Hudson's Bay
43: Commandos Strike at Dawn
     Stage Door Canteen
45: A Song to Remember
     Counter-Attack
46: Angel on My Shoulder
50: Embarkation at Midnight
53: Stranger on the Prowl
59: The Last Angry Man

Janet Munro (1934-
1957: The Young and the
Guilty
The Trollenberg Terror
58: Creatures from Another
World
59: Darby O'Gill and the
Little People
Third Man on the Mountain
Tommy the Toreador
60: The Swiss Family Robinson
62: The Day the Earth Caught
Fire
Life for Ruth
The Horsemasters
63: Bitter Harvest
64: Hide and Seek
A Jolly and Bad Fellow
66: Walk in the Shadow
68: Sebastian

Jules Munshin (1915-
1948: Easter Parade
49: On the Town
Take Me Out to the Ball
Game
That Midnight Kiss
57: 10,000 Bedrooms
Silk Stockings
64: Wild and Wonderful
Monte Carlo Baby
67: Monkeys, Go Home!

Ona Munson (1903-1955)
1928: Head of the Family
30: Going Wild
31: Hot Heiress
Collegiate Model
Broadminded
Five-Star Final
38: His Exciting Night
39: Gone with the Wind
Legion of Lost Flyers
40: The Big Guy
Wagons Westward
Scandal Sheet
41: Lady from Louisiana
Wild Geese Calling
Shanghai Gesture

42: Drums of the Congo
43: Idaho
45: Dakota
46: The Cheaters
47: The Red House

Audie Murphy (1924-
1940: Guns to Apache Pass
48: Texas, Brooklyn, and
Heaven
Beyond Glory
49: Bad Boy
50: Sierra
The Kid from Texas
Kansas Raiders
51: The Cimarron Kid
The Red Badge of Courage
52: Duel at Silver Creek
53: Gunsmoke
Column South
Tumbleweed
54: Ride Clear of Diablo
Drums Across the River
Destry
55: To Hell and Back
56: The World in My Corner
Walk the Proud Land
57: Guns of Fort Petticoat
Joe Butterfly
Night Passage
58: Ride a Crooked Trail
The Gun Runners
The Quiet American
59: No Name on the Bullet
Cast a Long Shadow
The Wild and the Innocent
60: Hell Bent for Leather
The Unforgiven
Seven Ways from Sundown
61: Posse from Hell
Battle at Bloody Beach
62: Six Black Horses
63: Showdown
Gunfight at Comanche
Creek
64: The Quick Gun
Bullet for a Badman
Apache Rifles
66: Arizona Raiders
Gunpoint

```
66:  The Texican                        Tom, Dick, and Harry
67:  Forty Guns to Apache               Ringside Maisie
     Pass                          42:  The Mayor of 44th Street
     Trunk to Cairo                     For Me and My Gal
69:  A Time for Dying (cameo)           The Powers Girl
                                        The Navy Comes Through
Edna Murphy (1904-                      Hello Beautiful!
1928:  My Man              PT           The Rich Full Life
29:  Greyhound Limited     PT      43:  This Is the Army
     Stolen Kisses         PT           Bataan
     The Sap               PT      44:  Broadway Rhythm
     Show of Shows                      Step Lively
30:  Little Johnny Jones                Show Business
     The Lummox                    45:  Having a Wonderful Crime
     Second Choice                 46:  Up Goes Maisie
     Wide Open                     47:  The Arnelo Affair
     Dancing Sweeties                   Cynthia
31:  Behind Office Doors           48:  Tenth Avenue Angel
     Anybody's Blonde                   Bit City
32:  Forgotten Women               49:  Battleground
     Girl of the Rio                    Border Incident
                                   50:  (SPECIAL AWARD)
George Murphy (1904-              51:  No Questions Asked
1934:  Kid Millions                     It's a Big Country
     Jealousy                      52:  Talk about a Stranger
35:  The Public Menace                  Walk East on Beacon
     I'll Love You Always          57:  Jamboree
     After the Dance
     Choose Your Partner           Mary Murphy
     Cash and Carry                1949:  The Lemon Drop Kid
     The Navy Steps Out            50:  Make Haste to Live
     Rise and Shine                51:  When World Collide
36:  Woman Trap                         How Could You, Darling?
37:  Top of the Town               52:  The Plymouth Adventure
     You're a Sweetheart                Carrie
     London by Night                    Come Back, Little Sheba
     Broadway Melody of 1938       53:  Off Limits
     The Women Men Marry                Houdini
38:  Little Miss Broadway               Main Street to Broadway
     Hold that Coed!               54:  The Wild One
     A Letter of Introduction           Beachhead
39:  Risky Business                     The Mad Magician
40:  Broadway Melody of 1940            Sitting Bull
     Two Girls on Broadway         55:  Hell's Island
     Little Nellie Kelly                Desperate Hours
     Elsa Maxwell's Public              A Man Alone
     Deb No. 1                     56:  Maverick Queen
41:  Rise and Shine                     Zex
     A Girl, A Guy, and A               The Intimate Stranger
     Gob                                Finger of Guilt
```

57: Escapement
58: Live Fast, Die Young
59: Crime and Punishment,
U. S. A.
60: The Electronic Monster
63: Forty Pounds of Trouble
65: Harlow (Para.)

Charlie Murray (1872-1941)
1930: The Cohens and the
Kellys in Scotland
Clancy in Wall Street
Around the Corner
31: The Cohens and the
Kellys in Africa
Caught Cheating
32: The Cohens and the
Kellys in Hollywood
33: The Cohens and the
Kellys in Trouble
36: Dangerous Waters
37: Circus Girl
38: The Road to Reno
Breaking the Ice
46: Two-Fisted Stranger

Don Murray (1929-
1956: Bus Stop
57: Bachelor Party
A Hatful of Rain
58: From Hell to Texas
59: These Thousand Hills
Shake Hands with the
Devil
60: One Foot in Hell
61: The Hoodlum Priest
The Hustler
62: Advise and Consent
Escape from East Berlin
Tunnel 6 (also co-prod.)
64: One Man's Way
65: Baby, the Rain Must Fall
66: Kid Rodelo
The Plainsman
Tale of the Cock
67: The Borgia Stick (TV)
Beyond the Night
Sweet Love Bitter
The Viking Queen
68: Jean Christophe

A Certain Rapture
The Hidden Face of Love
69: Childish Things

James Murray (1901-
1929: Little Wildcat   PT
The Shakedown   PT
Thunder   S
Shanghai Lady
30: Rampant Age
Hideout
31: Bright Lights
Kick in
In Line of Duty
32: The Reckoning
Bachelor Mother
33: Air Hostess
Frisco Jenny
High Gear
Central Airport
Heroes for Sale
35: $20 a Week
Skull and Crown

Jan Murray
1965: Who Killed Teddy Bear?
67: Tarzan and the Great
River
Thunder Alley
68: The Angry Breed
A Man Called Dagger

Ken Murray (1903-
1932: The Crooner
33: Disgraced!
37: You're a Sweetheart
38: Swing, Sister, Swing!
40: A Night at Earl Carroll's
42: Juke Box Jenny
47: Bill and Coo
53: The Marshal's Daughter
62: The Man Who Shot
Liberty Valance
63: Son of Flubber
66: Follow Me, Boys!
67: The Way West
68: The Power

Mae Murray (1890-1965)
1930: Peacock Alley

1013

31: Bachelor Apartment
    High Stakes
Clarence Muse (1889-
1928; Hearts in Dixie
30: Guilty?
    Royal Romance
    Rain or Shine
31: The Last Parade
    The Fighting Sheriff
    Huckleberry Finn
    Secret Witness
    Terror by Night
32: Woman from Monte Carlo
    Prestige
    Lena Rivers
    Night World
    Wet Parade
    Winner Take All
    Attorney for the Defense
    Is My Face Red?
    White Zombie
    Hell's Highway
    Washington Merry-Go-Round
    Cabin in the Cotton
    Laughter in Hell
    Man Against Woman
33: From Hell to Heaven
    The Mind Reader
    The Wrecker
34: Massacre
    Fury in the Jungle
    Black Moon
    The Personality Kid
    The Count of Monte Cristo
    Broadway Hill
35: Alias Mary Dow
    O'Shaughnessy's Boy
    So Red the Rose
    East of Java
36: Laughing Irish Eyes
    Muss 'em Up!
    Showboat
    Follow Your Heart
    Daniel Boone
37: Mysterious Crossing
    Spirit of Youth
38: The Toy Wife
    Prison Train
    Secrets of a Nurse
39: Way Down South
40: Broken Strings
    Zanzibar
    Maryland
    Sporting Blood
    That Gang of Mine

    Murder over New York
41: Adam Had Four Sons
    Invisible Ghost
    Love Crazy
    Gentleman from Dixie
42: Tales of Manhattan
    The Black Swan
43: Watch on the Rhine
    Shadow of a Doubt
    Heaven Can Wait
    Flesh and Fantasy
    Johnny Come Lately
44: Follow the Boys
    In the Meantime Darling
    Jam Session
    The Racket Man
46: Night and Day
    Two Smart People
47: Joe Palooka in The Knockout
48: An Act of Murder
49: The Great Dan Patch
50: Riding High
    County Fair
51: My Forbidden Past
    Apache Drums
52: Caribbean
    So Bright the Flame
53: Jamaica Run
59: Porgy and Bess

Carmel Myers (1899-1966)
1928: Dream of Love   S
29: Red Sword   S
    Careers   PT
    Careless Age
    Ghost Talks
30: Ship from Shanghai
31: Svengali
    The Lion and the Lamb
    Mad Genius
32: Nice Women
    Pleasure
    No Living Witness
33: Countess of Monte Cristo
41: Lady for a Night
46: Whistle Stop

Harry Myers (1886-1938)
1928: Dream of Love   S
29: The Clean-Up   S
    Montmartre Rose   S
    Wonder of Women
31: City Lights
    Meet the Wife
32: The Savage Girl
33: Strange Adventure

1014

Police Call
35: Mississippi
36: Hollywood Boulevard

Odette Myrtil (1898-
1936: Dodsworth
37: Girl from Scotland Yard
40: Kitty Foyle
41: Out of the Fog
42: I Married an Angel
    Yankee Doodle Dandy
    The Pied Piper
    Reunion in France
43: Forever and a Day
44: Dark Waters
    Uncertain Glory
46: Devotion
49: The Fighting Kentuckian
51: Here Comes the Groom

George Nader (1921-
1950: Rustlers on Horseback
51: Overland Telegraph
    Take Care of My Little
    Girl
    Han Glomde Henne Aldrig
53: Monsoon
    Miss Robin Crusoe
    Sins of Jezebel
    Robot Monster
    Down Among the Sheltering
    Palms
54: The Carnival Story
    Four Guns to the Border
55: Six Bridges to Cross
56: The Unguarded Moment
    Four Girls in Town
57: Man Afraid
    Joe Butterfly
58: Appointment with a Shadow
    The Female Animal
    Flood Tide
59: Nowhere to Go
63: The Secret Mark of
    D'Artegnon
    The Great Space
    Adventure
    Zigzag
    Walk by the Sea (dir.)
65: The Human Duplicators
    Alarm on 84th Street
    The Violin Case Murderer
67: Million Eyes of Su-Muru
    House of a Thousand Dolls
68: Death in a Red Jaguar
    Murder Club from Brooklyn

Dynamite in Green Silk
Operation Hurricane
69: Countdown for Manhattan (or,
    Deadly Shots on Broadway)
    (Ger.)

Anne Nagel (1916-1966)
1933: I Loved You Yesterday
34: Stand Up and Cheer
36: Hot Money
    China Clipper
    King of Hockey
    Here Comes Carter!
    Love Begins at Twenty
37: Three Legionnaires
    Hoosier Schoolboy
    A Bride for Henry
    She Loved a Fireman
    Guns of the Pecos
    Escape by Night
    The Case of the Stuttering
    Bishop
    Footloose Heiress
    The Adventurous Blonde
38: Saleslady
    Under the Big Top
    Gang Bullets
    Mystery House
39: Convict's Code
    Unexpected Father
    Call a Messenger
    Legion of Lost Flyers
    Should a Girl Marry?
40: Black Friday
    Ma, He's Making Eyes at Me
    Winners of the West (ser.)
    The Green Hornet (ser.)
    Not Steel
    My Little Chickadee
    Argentine Nights
    Diamond Frontier
    The Green Hornet Strikes
    Again (ser.)
41: The Invisible Woman
    Meet the Chump
    Man-Made Monster
    Mutiny in the Arctic
    Don Winslow of the Navy(ser.)
    Sealed Lips
    Never Give a Sucker an Even
    Break
    Road Agent
42: Nazi Spy Ring
    Stagecoach Buckaroo
    The Secret Code (ser.)

42: The Mad Monster
    Dawn Express
43: Women in Bondage
46: Murder in the Music Hall
    Traffic in Crime
47: Spirit of West Point
    The Trap
    Blondie's Holiday
48: Innocent Affair
49: Prejudice

Conrad Nagel (1897-
1928: Glorious Betsy   PT
    Caught in The Fog   PT
29: Redeeming Sin
    Red Wine
    Kid Gloves
    The Idle Rich
    Dynamite
    The Sacred Flame
    The Kiss
    Hollywood Revue of 1929
    The 13th Chair
30: The Ship from Shanghai
    Redemption
    Second Wife
    One Romantic Night
    The Divorcee
    Numbered Men
    Today
    Du Barry--Woman of
      Passion
    A Lady Surrenders
    Free Love
31: East Lynne
    The Right of Way
    The Reckless Hour
    Son of India
    Three Who Loved
    Pagan Lady
    The Bad Sister
    Hell Divers
32: Divorce in the Family
    The Man Called Back
    Kongo
    Fast Life
33: Ann Vickers
    The Constant Woman
34: Dangerous Corner
    The Marines Are Coming!
35: One Hour Late
    Death Flies East
    One New York Night
36: Girl from Mandalay
    Yellow Cargo

Wedding Present
37: Bank Alarm
    Navy Spy
    The Gold Racket
    Love Takes Flight (dir.)
    Forever Yours
39: Juarez and Maximilian
40: I Want a Divorce
    One Million B.C. (narr.)
44: They Shall Have Faith
    Dangerous Money (narr.)
45: The Adventures of Rusty
47: The Vicious Circle
48: Stage Struck
49: Dynamite
54: Tide a Tiger
55: All that Heaven Allows
56: The Swan
57: Hidden Fear
59: Stranger in My Arms
    The Man Who Understood
      Women

J. Carrol Naish (1900-
1930: The Queen's Husband
    Cheer Up and Smile
    Double Cross Roads
    Good Intentions
    Scotland Yard
31: Homicide Squad
    Kick In
    Tonight or Never
    Gun Smoke
    The Honorable Mr. Wong
    The Royal Bed
32: The Kid from Spain
    Beast of the City
    Ladies of the Big House
    Lost Men
    The Mouthpiece
    Two Seconds
    It's Tough to be Famous
    The Famous Ferguson Case
    Tiger Shark
    Merry-Go-Round
    The Crooner
    No Living Witness
    The Hatchet Man
33: Elmer the Great
    The Infernal Machine
    The Devil's in Love
    The Mad Game
    Arizona to Broadway
    The World Gone Mad
    The Whirlwind

1016

33: The Past of Mary Holmes
Captured
The Avenger
Notorious but Nice
Silent Men
The Last Trail
No Other Woman
Frisco Jenny
Big Chance
34: What's Your Racket?
Upperworld
Murder in Trinidad
One Is Guilty
The Hell Cat
Sleepers East
Girl in Danger
The Defense Rests
Hell in the Heavens
35: Lives of a Bengal Lancer
The Crusades
Behind Green Lights
Confidential
Black Fury
Captain Blood
Under the Pampas Moon
Front Page Woman
Little Big Shot
Special Agent
36: Two in the Dark
Special Investigator
We Who Are About to Die
Exclusive Story
Return of Jimmy Valentine
The Leathernecks Have
  Landed
Robin Hood of El Dorado
Moonlight Murder
Absolute Quiet
Charlie Chan at the Circus
Ramona
Anthony Adverse
Charge of the Light Brigade
Crack-Up
37: Think Fast, Mr. Moto
Song of the City
Border Cafe
Hideaway
See Racketeers
Bulldog Drummond Comes
  Back
Thunder Trail
Night Club Scandal
Daughter of Shanghai

  a short
38: Tip-Off Girls
Her Jungle Love
The Hunted Man
Prison Farm
Bulldog Drummond in Africa
King of Alcatraz
Illegal Traffic
39: Persons in Hiding
Hotel Imperial
Undercover Doctor
Beau Geste
King of Chinatown
Island of Lost Men
40: Typhoon
Queen of the Mob
Golden Gloves
A Night at Earl Carroll's
Down Argentine Way
41: That Night in Rio
Mr. Dynamite
Blood and Sand
Accent on Love
Forced Landing
Birth of the Blues
The Corsican Brothers
42: A Gentleman at Heart
Dr. Broadway
Jackass Mail
The Pied Piper
Tales of Manhattan
The Man in the Trunk
Dr. Renault's Secret
43: Harrigan's Kid
Good Morning, Judge
Sahara
Behind the Rising Sun
Batman (ser.)
Gung Ho!
Calling Dr. Death
44: The Monster Maker
Waterfront
The Whistler
Two-Man Submarine
The Devil's Brood
Voice in the Wind
Jungle Woman
Dragon Seed
Mark of the Whistler
Enter Arsene Lupin
45: A Medal for Benny
The Southerner
A Strange Confession

1018

40: The Invisible Man Returns
    The House of Seven
      Gables
42: Eagle Squadron
    A Yank at Eton
    Random Harvest
    The Cat People
43: Appointment in Berlin
    Lassie Come Home
    Lost Angel
    The Song of Bernadette
44: Ministry of Fear
    The Uninvited
    Action in Arabia
    The Hairy Ape
    Mademoiselle Fifi
    Dark Waters
    30 Seconds over Tokyo
45: Hangover Square
    Isle of the Dead
46: Three Strangers
    House of Mirrors
    A Scandal in Paris
47: High Conquest
    Driftwood
    Forever Amber
    Sinbad the Sailor
    Fiesta
    The Strange Woman
    Adventure Island
    The Lone Wolf in London
    Unconquered
48: Macbeth
    Joan of Arc
    The Hills of Home
    Tripoli
    My Own True Love
    Johnny Belinda
49: Criss Cross
    A Connecticut Yankee in
      King Arthur's Court
    Manhandled
    The Red Danube
    Challenge to Lassie
    Tarzan's Magic Fountain
    Master Minds
50: Double Crossbones
51: The Great Caruso
    Tarzan's Peril
    The Highwayman

Strange Door
The Blue Veil
Across the Wide Missouri
52: Big Jim McLain
53: Young Bess
    Julius Caesar
54: Desiree
55: Moonfleet
56: The Court Jester
    Miami Exposé
    The Mole People
57: Until They Sail
59: Journey to the Center of
      the Earth
    Island of Lost Women
61: Wild in the Country
62: Tender Is the Night
    The Premature Burial
63: Sword in the Stone (voice)
64: Marnie
    36 Hours
    Signpost to Murder
65: The Loved One
66: Batman

Mary Nash (1885-1965)
1934: Uncertain Lady
35: College Scandal
36: Come and Get It
37: The King and the Chorus
      Girl
    Easy Living
    Heidi
    Wells Fargo
39: The Little Princess
    The Rains Came
40: Charlie Chan in Panama
    Sailor's Lady
    Gold Rush Maisie
    The Philadelphia Story
41: Men of Boys Town
42: Calling Dr. Gillespie
43: The Human Comedy
44: In the Meantime Darling
    Cobra Woman
    The Lady and the Monster
45: Yolanda and the Thief
46: Monsieur Beaucaire
    Swell Guy
    Till the Clouds Roll By

Noreen Nash
1945: The Southerner
47: The Big Fix
The Devil on Wheels
The Red Stallion
The Tender Years
48: Adventures of Casanova
Assigned to Danger
The Checkered Coat
Assignment to Danger
50: Storm over Wyoming
52: Aladdin and His Lamp
53: Phantom from Space
56: Giant
58: The Lone Ranger and the
Lost City of Gold
60: Wake Me When It's Over

Mildred Natwick (1908-
1940: The Long Voyage Home
45: The Enchanted Cottage
Yolanda and the Thief
47: The Late George Apley
A Woman's Vengeance
48: Three Godfathers
The Kissing Bandit
49: She Wore a Yellow Ribbon
50: Cheaper by the Dozen
52: The Quiet Man
Against All Flags
55: The Trouble with Harry
56: The Court Jester
Teenage Rebel
57: Tammy and the Bachelor
64: Youngblood Hawke
67: Barefoot in the Park
69: If It's Tuesday, This Must
Be Belgium
The Maltese Bippy

Alla Nazimova (1879-1945)
1940: Escape
41: Blood and Sand
44: Since You Went Away

Cliff Nazarro
1942: Pardon My Stripes
Call of the Canyon
Hillbilly Blitzkrieg
Rhythm Parade

43: Shantytown
44: Trocadero
I'm from Arkansas
Swing Hostess

Dame Anna Neagle (1904-
1930: Should Doctors Tell?
The Chinese Bungalow
Goodnight Vienna
Flag Lieutenant
The Little Damozel
32: The Magic Night
33: Bitter Sweet
34: The Queen's Affair
Nell Gwynne
35: Limelight
Peg of Old Drury
Three Maxims
36: London Melody (or, The
Street Singer)
37: Victoria the Great
38: 60 Glorious Years
Girl in the Streets
39: Edith Cavell, Nurse
40: No, No, Nanette
Irene
41: Sunny
42: Wings and the Woman
43: Forever and a Day
44: The Yellow Canary
45: I Live on Grosvenor Square
46: A Yank in London
47: The Courtneys of Curzon
Street
48: Piccadilly Incident
49: Spring in Park Lane
Elizabeth of Ladymead
51: Odette
The Lady with a Lamp
Derby Day
52: Maytime in Mayfair
54: Lilacs in the Spring
The King's Rhapsody
55: Let's Make Up
56: My Teenage Daughter
No Time for Tears
Wonderful Things
58: Teenage Bad Girl
Yangtse Incident
These Dangerous Years

1020

60: The Man Who Wouldn't
     Talk
     The Lady Is a Square
     (prod.)
     The Heart of a Man

Patricia Neal (1926-
1949: John Loves Mary
     The Fountainhead
     The Hasty Heart
50: Bright Leaf
     Three Secrets
     The Breaking Point
51: Raton Pass
     Operation Pacific
     The Day the Earth Stood
       Still
     Weekend with Father
52: Diplomatic Courier
     The Washington Story
     Something for the Birds
55: La Tua Donna (Ital.)
57: A Face in the Crowd
61: Breakfast at Tiffany's
63: Hud (OSCAR)
64: Psycho '59
65: In Harm's Way
68: The Subject Was Roses

Tom Neal (1914-
1938: Out West with the Hardys
39: Burn 'em Up O'Connor
     Four Girls in White
     Another Thin Man
     6000 Enemies
     Within the Law
     They All Came Out
     Joe and Ethel Turp Call
       on the President
40: Courageous Dr. Christian
     Sky Murder
41: Under Age
     Top Sergeant Mulligan
42: The Miracle Kid
     China Girl
     Ten Gentlemen from West
       Point
     One Thrilling Night
     Flying Tigers
     The Bowery at Midnight

43: Behind the Rising Sun
     Good Luck, Mr. Yates
44: The Racket Man
     Unwritten Code
     Two-Man Submarine
45: Thoroughbreds
     Crime, Inc.
     First Yank in Tokyo
46: The Unknown
     Detour
     Club Havana
     Blonde Alibi
     The Brute Man
47: The Hat Box Mystery
     The Case of the Baby-
       Sitter
48: Beyond Glory
     My Dog Shep
49: Amazon Quest
     Bruce Gentry (ser.)
     Apache Chief
     Red Desert
50: Radar Secret Service
     Joe Palooka in Humphrey
       Takes a Chance
     Call of the Klondike
     Train to Tombstone
     Everybody's Dancing
51: Danger Zone
     Navy Bound
     Stop that Cab!
     Fingerprints Don't Lie
     G.I. Jane
     Let's Go Navy!
     Varieties on Parade

Hildegarde Neff (1925-
1946: Murderers Among Us
     Between Yesterday and
       Tomorrow
47: The Film Without a Title
50: The Sinner
51: Decision Before Dawn
52: Diplomatic Courier
     The Snows of Kilimanjaro
     Holiday for Henrietta
     Night Without Sleep
55: Svengali
     None but the Lonely Spy
57: The Girl from Hamburg

58: A Love Story
60: Port of Desire
62: Mark of the Tortoise
Catherine of Russia
Valley of the Doomed
63: Landru
Threepenny Opera
Gilbraltar
Escape from Sahara
65: And so to Bed
66: Mozambique

Pola Negri (1897-
1928: Three Sinners   S
Secret Hour   S
Loves of an Actress SSE
Woman from Moscow   S
32: A Woman Commands
35: Madame Bovary
43: Hi Diddle Diddle
64: The Moonspinners

Barry Nelson (1920-
1941: Shadow of the Thin Man
Johnny Eager
Dr. Kildare's Victory
The Doctor and the
Debutante
42: Stand by for Action
China Caravan
Once Upon a Thursday
Rio Rita
Eyes in the Night
A Yank on the Burma Road
43: The Human Comedy
Bataan
44: A Guy Named Joe
Winged Victory
47: The Beginning or the End?
Undercover Maisie
48: Tenth Avenue Angel
50: Undercover Girl
51: The Man with My Face
56: First Traveling Saleslady
57: Forty Guns
63: Mary, Mary
66: The Borgia Stick (TV)
68: The Only Game in Town
69: Airport

David Nelson (1936-
1952: Here Come the Nelsons
57: Peyton Place
59: The Remarkable Mr. Pennypacker
Thirty
The Big Circus
61: The Big Show

Ed Nelson (1928-
1955: New Orleans Uncensored
57: Bayou
Hell on Devil's Island
Invasion of the Saucer Men
Teenage Doll
58: Hot Car Girl
The Cry Baby Killer
The Brain Eaters
Street of Darkness
59: The Young Captives
A Bucket of Blood
60: Valley of the Redwoods
63: Soldier in the Rain
64: The Man from Galveston
Code of Silence

Gene Nelson (1920-
1943: This Is the Army
47: I Wonder Who's Kissing Her
Now
48: Apartment for Peggy
50: Daughter of Rosie O'Grady
Tea for Two
The West Point Story
51: Lullaby of Broadway
Painting the Clouds with
Sunshine
Starlift
52: She's Working Her Way
Through College
53: She's Back on Broadway
Three Sailors and a Girl
54: Crime Wave
So This Is Paris
55: Oklahoma!
Hit the Deck
56: The Way Out
Atomic Man
61: 20,000 Eyes

1022

61: The Purple Hills
63: Hootenanny Hoot (dir.)
    Thunder Island
64: Your Cheatin' Heart (dir.)
    Kissin' Cousins (dir.)
65: Harum Scarum (dir.)
67: The Perils of Pauline
    (dir.)

Harriet Nelson: see Harriet
Hilliard (Welson)

Lori Nelson (1933-
1952: Ma and Pa Kettle at the
    Fair
    Bend of the River
    Francis Goes to West
    Point
53: All I Desire
    The All-American
    Walking My Baby Back
    Home
54: Tumbleweed
    Underwater
    Destry
55: Ma and Pa Kettle at
    Waikiki
    Revenge of the Creature
    I Died a Thousand Times
    Sincerely Yours
    The Day the World Ended
56: Mohawk
    Pardners
    Hot Rod Girl
57: Untamed Youth
    The Outlaw's Son

Ozzie Nelson (1907-
1941: Sweetheart of the Campus
42: The Big Street
43: Strictly in the Groove
    Honeymoon Lodge
44: Hi Good Lookin'!
    Take it Big
46: People Are Funny
52: Here Come the Nelsons
69: The Impossible Years

Ricky Nelson (1940-
1952: Here Come the Nelsons

59: Rio Bravo
61: The Wackiest Ship in the
    Army
65: Love and Kisses

Franco Nero
1966: The Tramplers
    The Bible
67: The Hired Killer
    Camelot
    Wild Wild Planet
68: The Day of the Owl (Ital.)
    A Quiet Place in the
    Country
    Sardinia: Ransom (Ital.)
69: The Mercenary
    Cyril
    The Battle on the River
    Neretva
    Mafia
    The Brute and the Beast
    (Ital.)
    The Virgin and the Gypsy

Cathleen Nesbitt (1888-
1932: Case of the Frightened
    Lady
43: Fanny by Gaslight
47: Nicholas Nickleby
54: Three Coins in the Fountain
    Desiree
    Black Widow
    A Day at the Fair
57: An Affair to Remember
58: Separate Tables
61: The Parent Trap
62: Men of Two Worlds
66: Promise Her Anything
68: The Trygon Factor
69: Staircase

Ottola Nesmith
1928: The Girl Shy Cowboy   S
35: Becky Sharp
36: Three Men on a Horse
37: Nobody's Baby
38: Fools for Scandal
39: The Star Maker
40: Lillian Russell
    Her First Romance

40: The Letter
41: The Invisible Ghost
    The Deadly Game
44: The Return of the Vampire
45: Molly and Me
    My Name Is Julia Ross
46: Cluny Brown
47: The Late George Apley
54: Man Crazy
57: Witness for the
    Prosecution
60: From the Terrace
65: Inside Daisy Clover
69: Billy Bright

Lois Nettleton
1962: Period of Adjustment
63: Come Fly with Me
64: The Mail Order Bride
68: Valley of Mystery
    The Bamboo Saucer
69: Any Second Now (TV)

Dorothy Neumann
1948: Sorry, Wrong Number
    Luck of the Irish
50: My Blue Heaven
    Wabash Avenue
53: Take Me to Town
    Latin Lovers
54: Desiree
55: A Man Called Peter
56: Anything Goes
57: Spring Reunion
    Teenage Doll
59: The Ghost of Dragstrip
    Hollow
63: The Thrill of it All
    The Man from the Diner's
    Club
    The Terror
64: Get Yourself a College
    Girl

William Newell (1894-1967)
1936: Riffraff
    Libeled Lady
40: The Invisible Killer
    Fugitive from Justice
    Slightly Tempted

Hold that Woman!
41: Caugh in the Act
    The Bride Came C.O.D.
    Miss Polly
42: A Tragedy at Midnight
    Who Is Hope Schuyler?
    Keeper of the Flame
44: Sing a Jingle
    Kansas City Kitty
45: The Lucky Night
    Captain Eddie
57: Short Cut to Hell
58: The Missouri Traveler
59: High Flight
    Tank Force
    The Man Inside
60: Who Was that Lady?

Bob Newhart (1929-
1968: Hot Millions
69: On a Clear Day You can
    See Forever
    Catch 22
    Cold Turkey

James Newill (1911-
1937: Something to Sing About
    Renfrew of the Royal
    Mounted
38: On the Great White Trail
39: Crashing Through
40: Young People
    Danger Ahead
    Murder on the Yukon
41: The Great American
    Broadcast
42: The Falcon's Brother
43: The Rangers Take Over
    Guns of the Lawless
    Riders of Mystery Mountain
44: Trail of Terror
    Return of the Rangers
    Boss of Rawhide
    Brand of the Devil
45: Outlaw Roundup
    The Pinto Bandit
    Gunsmoke Mesa
    Spook Town
47: Shootin' Irons

1024

Anthony Newley (1931-

1946: Adventures of Dusty Bates
47: Little Ballerina
48: The Guinea Pig
Oliver Twist
Vice Versa
49: Vote for Huggett
Don't Ever Leave Me
A Boy, a Girl, and a
Bike
50: Golden Salamander
Madeleine
Highly Dangerous
52: Those People Next Door
53: Top of the Form
54: The Weak and the Wicked
Up to His Neck
55: Above Us the Waves
Blue Peter
56: Last Man to Hang
Battle of the River Plate
Cockleshell Heroes
X the Unknown
Port Afrique
57: The Good Companions
Fire Down Below
How to Marry a Rich
Uncle
58: High Flight
No Time to Die
Task Force
The Man Within
59: Idle on Parade
The Bandit of Zhoke
The Lady Is a Square
The Heart of a Man
60: In the Nick
Killers of Kilimanjaro
Let's Get Married
Jazz Boat
61: Play it Cooler
63: The Small World of
Sammy Lee
64: Goldfinger (sang title)
67: Dr. Dolittle
68: Sweet November
Can Heironymus Merkin
Ever Forget Mercy
Humppe and Find True
Happiness?

Paul Newman (1925-

1955: The Silver Chalice
56: The Rack
Somebody Up There Likes
Me
57: The Helen Morgan Story
Until They Sail
The Tijuana Story
58: The Long Hot Summer
Cat on a Hot Tin Roof
Rally 'Round the Flag,
Boys!
The Left-Handed Gun
59: The Young Philadelphians
60: Exodus
From the Terrace
61: The Hustler
Paris Blues
62: Sweet Bird of Youth
Hemingway's Adventures
of a Young Man
63: Hud
A New Kind of Love
The Prize
64: The Outrage
What a Way to Go!
65: The Slender Thread
66: Harper
Torn Curtain
The Moving Target
Lady L
67: Hombre
Cool Hand Luke
68: The Secret War of Harry
Frigg
Bye Bye, Braverman
69: Winning
Butch Cassidy and the
Sundance Kid
A Hall of Mirrors

Phyllis Newman (1935-

1956: The Vagabond Kind
58: Let's Rock
68: Bye Bye, Braverman

Julie Newmar (1935-

1954: Seven Brides for Seven
Brothers
59: Lil Abner

59: The Rookie
60: The Marriage-Go-Round
63: For Love or Money
69: MacKenna's Gold
The Maltese Bippy

Robert Newton (1905-1956)
1937: Fire over England
Dark Journey
Farewell Again
38: The Beachcomber
39: Jamaica Inn
Dead Men Are Dangerous
21 Days Together
Yellow Sands
40: Hell's Cargo
41: Major Barbara
Hatter's Castle
42: Wings and the Woman
44: Gaslight
Henry V
46: Night Boat to Dublin
47: This Happy Breed
Odd Man Out
Snowbound
Oliver Twist
The Deep End
48: Kiss the Blood off My
Hands
49: Temptation Harbor
50: Treasure Island
Waterfront
Obsession
51: Soldiers Three
Robin Hood
Tom Brown's School Days
52: Androcles and the Lion
Les Miserables
Blackbeard the Pirate
53: Desert Rats
54: The High and the Mighty
55: Long John Silver
56: Around the World in 80
Days

Theodore Newton (1905-1963)
1933: The Working Man
The Sphinx
Voltaire
The World Changes

Ace of Aces
From Headquarters
The House on 56th Street
34: Heat Lightning
A Modern Hero
Now I'll Tell
Upper World
Let's Try Again
Blind Date
Gambling
35: Jalna
45: The Hidden Eye
What Next, Corporal
Hargrove?
46: Miss Susie Slagle's
Two Years Before the
Mast
56: The Come On
The Proud and Profane
Somebody Up There Likes
Me
Friendly Persuasion
58: The Sage of Hemp Brown
59: The Story on Page One
63: Dime with a Halo

Richard Ney (1918-
1942: Mrs. Miniver
The War Against Mrs.
Hadley
47: The Late George Apley
Ivy
48: Joan of Arc
49: The Fan
The Secret of St. Ives
The Lovable Cheat
52: Babes in Bagdad
Miss Italia
The Sergeant and the Spy
60: Midnight Lace
62: Premature Burial

Barbara Nichols (1932-
1956: Manfish
Miracle in the Rain
Beyond a Reasonable Doubt
The King and Four Queens
57: Sweet Smell of Success
Pal Joey
The Pajama Game

58: 10 North Frederick
    The Naked and the Dead
59: Woman Obsessed
    That Kind of Woman
60: Who Was that Lady?
    Where the Boys Are
61: The George Raft Story
62: The Scarface Mob
    House of Women
64: Looking for Love
    The Disorderly Orderly
    Dear Heart
65: The Loved One
    The Human Duplicators
66: The Swinger
68: The Power

Alex Nicol (1919-
1950: The Sleeping City
51: Target Unknown
    Air Cadet
    The Raging Tide
    Tomahawk
52: Meet Danny Wilson
    Red Ball Express
    Because of You
    The Redhead from
     Wyoming
53: Lone Hand
    Champ for a Day
    Law and Order
54: Black Glove
    Heat Wave
    About Mrs. Leslie
    Dawn at Socorro
55: Strategic Air Command
    The Man from Laramie
    Sincerely Yours
56: Stranger in Town
    Great Day in the Morning
    The Screaming Skull (dir.)
    Air Force training films
60: Five Branded Women
    Via Margutta
    Gunfight at Casa Grande
    Under Ten Flags
61: Look in Any Window
    The Sleeping Skull
62: Then There Were Three
    Everybody, Go Home!

The Savage Guns
A Matter of Who
63: Rise and Kill
    Run with the Devil

Leslie Nielsen (1926-
1956: Ransom!
    The Vagabond Kind
    Forbidden Planet
    The Opposite Sex
57: Hot Summer Night
    Tammy and the Bachelor
58: The Sheepman
64: Night Train to Paris
65: See How They Run
    Dark Intruder
    Harlow (Para.)
66: Beau Geste
    The Plainsman
67: Rosie
    Gunfight in Abilene
    The Reluctant Astronaut
68: Counterpoint
    Hawaii 5-0 (TV)
    Code Name: Heraclitus
    Shadow over Elveron (TV)
    Dayton's Devils
69: How to Commit Marriage
    Four Rode Out
    Change of Mind
    Trial Run (TV)
    Deadlock

Gertrude Neisen (1910-
1937: Top of the Town
38: Start Cheering
41: Rookies on Parade
43: He's My Guy
    Thumbs Up
    This Is the Army
48: The Babe Ruth Story

Jane Nigh (1926-
1944: Something for the Boys
45: State Fair
46: Dragonwyck
    Whistle Stop
47: Unconquered
48: Give My Regards to
    Broadway

1027

48: Leather Gloves
49: Red, Hot, and Blue
    Fighting Man of the Plains
50: Blue Grass of Kentucky
    Operation Haylift
    Border Treasure
    Motor Patrol
    Rio Grande Patrol
    County Fair
    Captain Carey, U.S.A.
51: Blue Blood
    Disc Jockey
    Fort Osage
    Rodeo
57: Hold that Hypnotist

Anna Q. Nilsson (1893-
1928: The Whip   S
    Blockade   PT
33: The World Changes
34: School for Girls
35: Wanderer of the Waste-
    land
38: Prison Farm
41: Riders of the Timberland
42: Girls' Town
43: Headin' for God's Country
47: The Farmer's Daughter
    Cynthia
48: Fighting Father Dunne
    Every Girl Should be
    Married
50: Sunset Boulevard

Leonard Nimoy (1932-
1951: Queen for a Day
    Rhubarb
52: Kid Monk Baron
    Francis Goes to West
    Point
53: Old Overland Trail
58: Satan's Satellites
63: The Balcony
67: Deathwatch (act., prod.)

Greta Nissen (1906-
1931: Women of All Nations
    Transatlantic
    Ambassador Bill
    Good Sport

32: Silent Witness
    Rackety Rax
    The Unwritten Law
33: The Circus Queen Murder
    Melody Cruise
    Best of Enemies
    Life in the Raw
34: Hired Wife
36: Spy 77

David Niven (1910-
1935: A Feather in Her Hat
    Splendor
    Barbary Coast
    Without Regret
36: Rose Marie
    Palm Springs
    Thank You, Jeeves
    Dodsworth
    Beloved Enemy
    The Charge of the Light
    Brigade
37: We Have Our Moments
    The Prisoner of Zenda
    Dinner at the Ritz
38: Four Men and a Prayer
    Three Blind Mice
    Dawn Patrol
    Bluebeard's Eighth Wife
39: Bachelor Mothers
    Eternally Yours
    Wuthering Heights
    The Real Glory
40: Raffles
43: Spitfire (or, First of the
    Few)
45: The Way Ahead
    A Matter of Life and Death
46: Perfect Marriage
    Stairway to Heaven
    Josephine
    The Magnificent Doll
47: La Citta Frogiomera
    The Other Love
    The Bishop's Wife
    The Elusive Pimpernel
48: Bonnie Prince Charlie
    Enchantment (dual role)
49: Kiss in the Dark
    A Kiss for Corliss

50: Toast of New Orleans
51: Happy Go Lovely
Soldiers Three
The Lady Says No
52: Island Rescue
53: The Moon Is Blue
Love Lottery
54: Tonight's the Night (or,
O'Leary Night)
55: The King's Thief
Court Martial
56: The Birds and the Bees
Around the World in 80
Days
57: Oh Men! Oh Women!
The Little Hut
My Man Godfrey
The Silken Affair
58: Bonjour Tristesse
Separate Tables (OSCAR)
59: Ask Any Girl
Happy Anniversary
60: Please Don't Eat the
Daisies
61: The Guns of Navarone
The Road to Hong Kong
(cameo)
62: Guns of Darkness
The Best of Enemies
63: 55 Days at Peking
64: Bedtime Story
The Pink Panther
King of the Mountain
65: Where the Spies Are
The Conquered City
66: Lady L
67: Island of the Blue Dolphin
Casino Royale
Eye of the Devil
68: The Impossible Years
Prudence and the Pill
Green Eyes
Before Winter Comes
69: The Brain
The Extraordinary Sea-
man
Man's Fate
Barbary Lights
The Kremlin Letter

Marian Nixon (1904-
1929: Show of Shows
Young Nowheres
The Rainbow Man
In the Headlines
Little Pal
General Crack
Geraldine
Silks and Saddles
Man, Woman, and Wife
Red Sword
Say it with Songs
30: Courage
Mixed Doubles
Pay Off
Jubilo
College Lovers
Scarlet Pages
31: The Lash
Sweepstakes
Women Go on Forever
Private Scandal
Ex-Flame
32: Charlie Chan's Chance
After Tomorrow
Amateur Daddy
Rebecca of Sunnybrook
Farm
Winner Take All
Too Busy to Work
Madison Square Garden
33: Face in the Sky
The Best of Enemies
Dr. Bull
Pilgrimage
Chance at Heaven
34: The Line Up
We're Rich Again
Strictly Dynamite
Once to Every Bachelor
Embarrassing Moments
By Your Leave
35: Sweepstakes Annie
36: Tango
Captain Calamity (or,
Captain Hurricane)
The Dragnet

Chris Noel (1941-
1963: Soldier in the Rain
64: Honeymoon Hotel
Diary of a Bachelor
Get Yourself a College
Girl
65: Joy in the Morning
Beach Ball
Girl Happy
John Goldfarb, Please
Come Home
66: Wild Wild Winter
67: The Glory Stompers
68: For Singles Only

Bob Nolan: see Sons of the
Pioneers

Doris Nolan (1916-
1936: The Man I Married
37: As Good as Married
Top of the Town
38: Holiday
39: One Hour to Live
40: Irene
Moon over Burma
44: Follies Girl

James Nolan
1938: Torchy Blane in Panama
Little Miss Thoroughbred
Girls on Probation
46: Little Miss Big
47: Dick Tracy Meets Grue-
some
48: Miracle of the Bells
The Arizona Rangers
Guns of Hate
Fighting Father Dunne
Nighttime in Nevada
Son of God's Country
Death Valley Gunfighter
49: Daughter of the Jungle
Bandit King of Texas
Alias the Champ
50: Mary Ryan, Detective
57: The Big Caper
60: Portrait in Black

Jeanette Nolan
1948: Words and Music

Macbeth
49: Abandoned
50: Saddle Tramp
No Sad Songs for Me
51: Secret of Convict Lake
52: The Happy Time
The Hangman's Knot
53: The Big Heat
A Lawless Street
56: Tribute to a Badman
Everything but the Truth
The Seventh Cavalry
57: The Halliday Brand
Guns of Fort Petticoat
April Love
58: The Deep Six
Wild Heritage
59: The Rabbit Trap
60: The Great Impostor
61: Two Rode Together
62: The Man Who Shot Liberty
Valance
63: The Twilight Hour
65: My Blood Runs Cold
66: Chamber of Horrors
67: Sullivan's Empire
The Reluctant Astronaut
68: Sgt. Ryker ('63 TV re-rel.)
Did You Hear the One about
the Traveling Saleslady?

Kathy Nolan
1956: The Desperados Are in
Town
57: The Iron Sheriff
No Time to be Young

Lloyd Nolan (1902-
1934: Atlantic Adventure
35: One Way Ticket
Stolen Harmony
The G-Men
She Couldn't Take It
36: You May be Next
The Devil's Squadron
Big Brown Eyes
Texan Rangers
15 Maiden Lane
Counterfeit
Lady Secrets
37: Interns Can't Take Money

37: King of the Gamblers
Exclusive
Ebb Tide
Wells Fargo
Every Day's a Holiday
38: Dangerous to Know
Hunted Men
Prison Farm
Tip-Off Girls
King of Alcatraz
39: Ambush
St. Louis Blues
Undercover Doctor
The Magnificent Fraud
40: The Man Who Wouldn't
Talk
Michael Shayne, Private
Detective
The Man I Married
The House Across the Bay
Gangs of Chicago
Behind the News
The Golden Fleecing
Johnny Apollo
Pier No. 13
Charter Pilot
41: Mr. Dynamite
Sleepers West
Dressed to Kill
Buy Me that Town
Blues in the Night
Steel Against the Sky
Blue, White, and Perfect
42: The Man Who Wouldn't Die
It Happened in Flatbush
Just Off Broadway
Manila Calling
Apache Trail
Time to Kill
43: Guadalcanal Diary
Bataan
44: A Tree Grows in Brooklyn
45: Circumstantial Evidence
Captain Eddie
Sunset in Eldorado
House on 92nd Street
46: Lady in the Lake
Somewhere in the Night
Two Smart People
47: Wild Harvest

48: Green Grass of Wyoming
Street with No Name
Interference
49: The Sun Comes Up
Bad Boy
Easy Living
51: The Lemon Drop Kid
53: Island in the Sky
Crazylegs--All American
56: The Last Hunt
Santiago
Toward the Unknown
57: Abandon Ship!
A Hatful of Rain
Peyton Place
60: A Portrait in Black
Girl of the Night
61: Susan Slade
62: We Joined the Navy
63: The Girl Hunters
64: Circus World
65: Never too Late
66: The American Dream
67: Wings of Fire
The Double Man
68: Sgt. Ryker ('63 TV re-rel.)
Triple Cross
69: Ice Station Zebra

Mary Nolan (1905-1940)
1928: Silks and Saddles   S
29: Eleven Who Were Loyal S
Desert Nights   SSE
Charming Sinners
Shanghai Lady
30: Undertow
Young Desire
Outside the Law
31: Enemies of the Law
X Marks the Spot
32: The Big Shot
Docks of San Francisco
File No. 113
Midnight Patrol

Tommy Noonan (1922-1968)
1946: The Bamboo Blonde
Ding Dong Williams
The Truth about Murder
47: The Big Fix

1031

48: Open Secret
Jungle Patrol
49: I Shot Jesse James
I Cheated the Law
50: The Return of Jesse
James
Holiday Rhythm
51: Starlift
F.B.I. Girl
53: Gentlemen Prefer Blondes
54: A Star Is Born
55: Violent Saturday
How to be Very, Very
Popular
56: The Ambassador's
Daughter
The Best Things in Life
Are Free
Bundle of Joy
57: The Girl Most Likely
59: The Rookie
61: Double Trouble
62: Swingin' Along
63: Promises! Promises!
64: Three Nuts in Search of
a Bolt

Lucille Norman
1942: For Me and My Gal
51: Painting the Clouds
with Sunshine
Starlift
52: Carson City
53: Sweethearts on Parade

Eduardo Noriego
1950: The Eagle and the Hawk
55: Hell's Island
The Magnificent Matador
Far Horizons
Seven Cities of Gold
56: Serenade
The Beast of Hollow
Mountain
Daniel Boone, Trail
Blazer
57: The Living Doll
The Sun Also Rises
58: The Last of the Fast Guns
59: Pier 5--Havana
62: Geronimo

63: Of Love and Desire
66: Tarzan and the Valley of
Gold

Edward Norris (1910-
1934: Queen Christina
35: Murder in the Fleet
Wagon Trail
Show Them no Mercy
Alibi Racket
short from ser.: Crime
Doesn't Pay
36: Small Town Girl
The Magnificent Brute
37: Mama Steps Out
Song of the City
Between Two Women
Bad Guy
They Won't Forget
38: Boys' Town
39: Tail Spin
The Gorilla
Frontier Marshal
Here I Am a Stranger
The Escape
On Trial
Newsboys' Home
40: The Story of Dr. Ehrlich's
Magic Bullet
Scandal Sheet
Ski Patrol
Lady in Question
41: Road Show
Back in the Saddle
Here Comes Happiness
Angels with Broken Wings
Doctors Don't Tell
42: The Man with Two Lives
Mystery of Marie Roget
The Lady Has Plans
Sabotage Squad
I Live on Danger
The Great Impersonation
43: Mug Town
You Can't Beat the Law
Career Girl
The Sultan's Daughter
44: Men on Her Mind
Sing a Jingle
The Singing Sheriff
End of the Road

44: Shadows in the Night
45: Night Club Girl
    Penthouse Rhythm
46: Murder in the Music Hall
    The Truth about Murder
    Decoy
47: Heartaches
48: Trapped by Boston Blackie
49: Forgotten Women
    The Mysterious Desperado
    Wolf Hunters
50: Killer Shark
    Breakthrough
    The Blazing Sun
    Surrender
51: I Was a Communist for
    the FBI
53: Murder Without Tears
55: The Kentuckian

Jay North (1951-
1959: The Big Operator
    Miracle of the Hills
65: Zebra in the Kitchen
66: Maya

Sheree North (1930-
1945: An Angel Comes to
    Brooklyn
51: Excuse My Dust
54: Living it Up
55: How to be Very, Very
    Popular
56: The Lieutenant Wore
    Skirts
    The Best Things in Life
    Are Free
57: Way to the Gold
    No Down Payment
58: In Love and War
    Mardi Gras
66: Destination Inner Space
67: Code Name: Heraclitus
68: Madigan
69: The Gypsy Moths
    Then Came Bronson (TV
    pilot)
    The Trouble with Girls
    (or, The Chautauqua)

Ted North
1940: Chad Hanna
    Yesterday's Heroes
41: The Bride Wore Crutches
    For Beauty's Sake
    Charlie Chan in Rio
42: Syncopation
    Manila Calling
    Girl Trouble
    Thunder Birds
    Roxie Hart
43: Margin for Error
    The Ox-Bow Incident
44: Men on Her Mind

Barry Norton (1905-1956)
1928: Mother Knows Best   PT
    Legion of the Condemned S
    Fleetwing
29: The Four Devils   PT
    Exalted Flapper   SSE
    Sins of the Fathers   S
30: The Benson Murder Case
    Slightly Scarlet
31: Dishonored
33: The Cocktail Hour
    Only Yesterday
    Lady for a Day
34: Nana
    Unknown Blonde
    The World Moves On
    Grand Canary
35: Storm over the Andes
36: Murder at Glen Athol
    Captain Calamity
    The Criminal Within
37: History Is Made at Night
    I'll Take Romance
    Timberesque
38: The Buccaneer
    Radio Troubador
39: Should Husbands Work?
46: Devil Monster
56: Around the World in 80
    Days

Jack Norton (1889-1958)
1934: Counsel on De Fence
    Sweet Music

1033

35: Calling All Cars
Stolen Harmony
Don't Bet on Blondes
His Night Out
Bordertown
Ship Cafe
36: Too Many Parents
37: a short
Marked Woman
Meet the Missus
38: Meet the Girls
Thanks for the Memory
39: Grand Jury Secrets
Joe and Ethel Turp Call
on the President
40: The Farmer's Daughter
Opened by Mistake
A Night at Earl Carroll's
The Bank Dick
41: Louisiana Purchase
42: The Spoilers
Moonlight in Havana
Dr. Renault's Secret
Palm Beach Story
The Fleet's In
Brooklyn Orchid
43: Lady Bodyguard
Taxi, Mister!
Prairie Chickens
44: The Chinese Cat
Hail the Conquering Hero
The Big Noise
45: Wonder Man
Her Highness and the
Bellboy
The Scarlet Clue
A Guy, a Gal, and a Pal
Flame of the Barbary
Coast
Man Alive
Strange Companions
Captain Tugboat Annie
46: The Strange Mr. Gregory
Blue Skies
No Leave No Love
The Kid from Brooklyn
Rendezvous 24
Bringing Up Father
The Sin of Harold
Diddlebock (or, Mad
Wednesday)

Shadows over Chinatown
47: Linda be Good
48: Variety Time

Eva Novak (1899-
1929: For the Term of His
Natural Life   S
30: Medicine Man
45: Apology for Murder
The Topeka Terror
47: Blackmail
48: Four Faces West
57: Ride a Violent Mile
65: Wild Seed

Jane Novak (1896-
1929: Redskin   SSE
36: Hollywood Boulevard
37: Ghost Town
40: Foreign Correspondent
42: Prison Girls
The Yanks Are Coming
43: Man of Courage
47: Desert Fury
49: Paid in Full
Thelma Jordan

Kim Novak (1933-
1954: The Pushover
Phffft!
55: Five Against the House
Picnic
The Man with the Golden
Arm
56: The Eddie Duchin Story
57: Jeanne Eagels
Pal Joey
58: Bell, Book, and Candle
Vertigo
59: Middle of the Night
60: Pepe
Strangers When We Meet
62: The Notorious Landlady
Boys' Night Out
64: Of Human Bondage
Kiss Me, Stupid
65: The Amorous Adventures
of Moll Flanders
68: The Legend of Lylah
Clare
69: The Great Bank Robbery

69: Christine

Ramon Novarro (1899-1968)
1929: The Pagan
    The Devil May Care
30: In Gay Madrid
    Singer of Seville
    Call of the Flesh
31: Daybreak
    Son of India
32: Mata Hari
    The Son-Daughter
    The Huddle
33: The Barbarian
34: Cat and the Fiddle
    Laughing Boy
35: The Night Is Young
36: Contre la Corriente
    (prod., dir.)
37: The Sheik Steps Out
38: A Desperate Adventure
    Ben Hur (silent film rel.
    with sound track)
    La Comedie de Bonheur
42: La Virgen que Forjo una
    Patria
49: We Were Strangers
    The Big Steal
50: The Outriders
    Crisis
60: Heller in Pink Tights

Ivor Novello (1893-1951)
1928: When Boys Leave Home S
    The Vortex   S
    South Sea Bubble   S
29: The Constant Nymph   S
32: The Lodger
33: Sleeping Car
34: I Lived With You
    Autumn Crocus

Jay Novello (1904-
1938: Tenth Avenue Kid
    Flirting with Fate
39: Calling All Marines
    Girl from Havana
    The Border Legion
41: Robin Hood of the Pecos
    Two-Gun Sheriff

Sheriff of Tombstone
The Great Train Robbery
They Met in Bombay
Citadel of Crime
Bad Man of Deadwood
42: Sleepytime Gal
    Swamp Woman
43: The Man from Music
    Mountain
44: Phantom Lady
45: Hotel Berlin
    The Bullfighters
    The Chicago Kid
46: Perilous Holiday
48: Port Said
    Kiss the Blood Off My
    Hands
49: Tell it to the Judge
51: Smuggler's Island
    Sirocco
52: The Snipper
    The Miracle of Our Lady
    of Fatima
    Operation Secret
    Cattle Town
53: Ma and Pa Kettle on
    Vacation
    The Hindu
    Diamond Queen
    The Robe
    Beneath the Twelve-Mile
    Reef
54: Crime Wave
    The Mad Magician
    The Gambler from Natchez
55: The Prodigal
    Sabaka
    Son of Sinbad
    Bengazi
56: Lisbon
    Jaguar
57: The Pride and the Passion
58: The Perfect Furlough
60: This Rebel Breed
    The Lost World
61: Atlantis, the Lost Continent
    A Pocketful of Miracles
62: Escape from Zahrain
63: The Man from the Diner's
    Club

65: The Art of Love
Sylvia
A Very Special Favor
Harum Scarum
Zebra in the Kitchen
66: What Did You Do in the
War, Daddy?
67: Caper of the Golden Bulls
69: Billy Bright

Carol Nugent
1944: Secret Command
46: Little Mr. Jim
50: Trail of Robin Hood
Cheaper by the Dozen
52: Belles on Their Toes
The Lusty Men
53: Fast Company
59: Inside the Mafia
Vice Raid

Edward Nugent (1904-
1928: Our Dancing Daughters   S
29: Man in Hobble's   S
Vagabond Lover
Our Modern Maidens
The Duke Steps Out
Flying Feet
The Bellamy Trail
The Single Man
Untamed
30: Girl in the Show
Loose Ankles
Clancy in Wall Street
Remote Control
War Nurse
31: Girls Demand Excitement
Shipmates
Bought
Bright Lights
Young Sinners
Up Pops the Devil
Local Boy Makes Good
The Scoop
Second Fiddle
32: Behind Stone Walls
Honor of the Press
The Crooner
33: 42nd Street
Men Are Such Fools

The Past of Mary Holmes
College Humor
This Day and Age
Dance Hall Hostess
Beauty for Sale
Dance, Girl, Dance
34: This Side of Heaven
She Loves Me Not
Girl of the Limberlost
Girl o' My Dreams
Lost in the Stratosphere
35: No Ransom
Lottery Lover
Baby Face Harrington
Kentucky Blue Streak
College Scandal
The Old Homestead
Fighting Youth
Ah, Wilderness!
Forced Landing
Sky Bound
36: Dancing Feet
Just My Luck
Doughnuts and Society
The Harvester
Rio Grande Romance
Bunker Bean
Prison Shadows
The Big Game
Pigskin Parade
Put on the Spot
37: A Man Betrayed
Speed to Spare
Island Captives
Two Minutes to Play
38: Meet the Mayor

Elliott Nugent (1899-
1929: So This Is College?
The Single Standard   S
Our Modern Maidens
Wise Girls
Not so Dumb
30: Father's Day
Bright Lights
The Richest Man in the
World
The Unholy Three
Sins of the Children
For the Love of Lil

1036

30: Romance
31: The Last Flight
   Virtuous Husbands
32: Behind Stone Walls
   Cock of the Air
   The Mouthpiece (co-dir.)
   Life Begins (co-dir.)
From '33 on, as director:
33: Whistling in the Dark
   Three-Cornered Moon
   If it Were Free
34: Two Alone
   Strictly Dynamite
   She Loves Me not
35: Love in Bloom
   College Scandal
   Enter Madame
   Splendor
36: Wives Never Know
   And so They Were
   Married
38: It's All Yours
   Professor Beware
   Give Me a Sailor
39: Cat and the Canary
42: The Male Animal
43: The Crystal Ball
44: Up in Arms
47: Welcome Stranger
   The Innocent Years
   My Favorite Brunette
48: My Girl Tisa
49: The Great Gatsby
52: Just for You

J.C. Nugent (1878-1947)
1929: Wise Girls
   Navy Blues
30: They Learned about
   Women
   The Big House
   Love in the Rough
   Remote Control
31: The Millionaire
   Many a Slip
   Virtuous Husbands
35: Love in Bloom
   Men Without Names
37: A Star Is Born
   Stand-In

This Is My Affair
   Life Begins in College
38: It's All Yours
   Midnight Intruder
   Give Me a Sailor

France Nuyen (1939-
1958: South Pacific
   In Love and War
61: The Last Time I Saw
   Archie
62: Diamond Head
   Satan Never Sleeps
   A Girl Named Tamiko
64: The Man in the Middle
66: Dimension 5

Carroll Nye (1901-1968)
1929: Flying Feet   SSE
   Madame X
   Girl in the Glass Cage PT
   The Squall
   Light Fingers   PT
30: The Bishop Murder Case
   Sons of the Saddle
   Lottery Bride
31: Lawless Woman
   Hell Bent for Frisco
   Neck and Neck
   One Way Trail
35: Traveling Saleslady
38: Rebecca of Sunnybrook
   Farm
   Kentucky Moonshine
39: Gone with the Wind
40: The Trail Blazers
44: Dark Mountain

Louis Nye
1960: Sex Kittens Go to College
   The Facts of Life
   Beauty and the Robot
61: The Last Time I Saw
   Archie
63: The Wheeler Dealers
   The Stripper
   Who's Been Sleeping in
   My Bed?
64: Good Neighbor Sam
67: A Guide for the Married
   Man

O

Jack Oakie (1903-

1928:	Finders Keepers	S
	The Fleet's In	S
	Someone to Love	S
29:	Hard to Get	
	Chinatown Nights	
	Close Harmony	
	The Dummy	
	Fast Company	
	The Man I Love	
	Sweetie	
	Wild Party	
	Sin Town	
30:	Paramount on Parade	
	The Sap from Syracuse	
	Social Lion	
	Hit the Deck	
	Let's Go Native	
	Sea Legs	
31:	June Moon	
	Dude Ranch	
	The Touchdown	
	Gang Busters	
	Playing the Game	
32:	Once in a Life Time	
	Dancers in the Dark	
	Sky Bride	
	Million Dollar Legs	
	Madison Square Garden	
	Uptown New York	
	If I Had a Million	
33:	The Eagle and the Hawk	
	From Hell to Heaven	
	College Humor	
	Too Much Harmony	
	Sitting Pretty	
	Alice in Wonderland	
	Sailor be Good	
34:	Looking for Trouble	
	Murder at the Vanities	
	College Rhythm	
	Shoot the Works	
35:	Call of the Wild	
	Big Broadcast of 1936	
36:	Collegiate	
	King of Burlesque	
	Colleen	
	That Girl from Paris	
	Texas Rangers	

Florida Special

37:	Champagne Waltz
	Radio City Revels
	The Toast of New York
	Super Sleuth
	Fight for Your Lady
	Hitting a New High
38:	Affairs of Annabel
	Annabelle Takes a Tour
	Thanks for Everything
40:	The Great Dictator
	Young People
	Little Men
	Tin Pan Alley
41:	The Great American Broadcast
	Rise and Shine
	Navy Blues
42:	Song of the Islands
	Iceland
43:	Hello, Frisco, Hello
	Something to Shout About
	Wintertime
44:	It Happened Tomorrow
	The Merry Monahans
	Sweet and Low Down
	Hips, Hips, Hooray!
	Bowery to Broadway
45:	That's the Spirit
	On Stage, Everybody!
46:	She Wrote the Book
48:	When My Baby Smiles at Me
	Northwest Stampede
49:	Thieves' Highway
50:	Last of the Buccaneers
51:	Tomahawk
56:	Around the World in 80 Days
59:	The Wonderful Country
60:	The Rat Race
62:	Lover Come Back
69:	Daughter of Tugboat Annie

Simon Oakland

1958:	The Brothers Karamazov
	I Want to Live!
60:	Psycho
	Murder, Inc.
	Who's that Lady?
	The Rise and Fall of Legs Diamond

61:	West Side Story		Utah
62:	Follow that Dream	50:	Bunco Squad
	Third of a Man		
63:	Wall of Noise		**Wheeler Oakman** (1890-1949)
	The Raiders	1928:	Lights of New York
64:	Ready for the People	29:	The Shakedown PT
65:	The Satan Bug		Morgan's Last Raid S
66:	The Sand Pebbles		The Devil's Chaplain S
	The Plainsman		The Donovan Affair
67:	Tony Rome		Father and Son PT
68:	Chubasco		On with the Show
69:	Bullitt		Handcuffed
	On a Clear Day You can		Shanghai Lady
	See Forever		Show of Shows
			The Hurricane
			The Girl from Woolworth's
	Vivian Oakland (1895-1958)	30:	Little Johnny Jones
1929:	The Man in Hobble's S		Roaring Ranch
	The Time, the Place, and		The Big Fight
	the Girl		On Your Back
30:	Personality		The Costello Case
	Back Pay	31:	Lawless Woman
	Floradora Girl		The Good Bad Girl
	Matrimonial Bed		Sky Raiders
	Oh Sailor, Behave!		First Aid
	A Lady Surrenders	32:	The Devil on Deck
31:	Gold Dust Gertie		Texas Cyclone
32:	A House Divided		Two-Fisted Law
	Cock of the Air		Honor of the Press
	Scram!		Riding Tornado
	Only Yesterday		Gorilla Ship
	The Tenderfoot		Beauty Parlor
33:	They Just Had to Get		The Heart Punch
	Married		The Boiling Point
	Neighbors' Wives		Guilty or not Guilty
34:	Money Means Nothing	33:	Man of Action
	The Defense Rests		Western Code
35:	Rendezvous at Midnight		Speed Demon
	Star of Midnight		End of the Trail
36:	The Bride Walks Out		Soldiers of the Storm
	Lady Luck		Revenge at Monte Carlo
37:	Way Out West		Sundown Rider
	Mile a Minute Love		Rusty Rides Alone
38:	Double Danger		Silent Men
	Crime Afloat		Hold the Press
	Slander House	34:	One Is Guilty
	Rebellious Daughters		Lost Jungle
42:	The Man in the Trunk		Frontier Days
44:	The Girl Who Dared		In Old Santa Fe
45:	The Man Who Walked		Murder in the Clouds
	Alone		

35: Square Shooter
Motive for Revenge
Headline Woman
Code of the Mounted
Death From a Distance
Annapolis Farewell
Trails of the Wild
The Man from Guntown
36: Timber War
Song of the Trail
Darkest Africa
Aces and Eights
Roarin' Guns
The Ghost Patrol
Gambling with Souls
37: Death in the Air
Bank Alarm
38: Code of the Rangers
Mars Attacks the World
39: In Old Montana
Mutiny in the Big House
Torture Ship
40: Men with Steel Faces
41: Meet the Mob
42: Double Trouble
Bowery at Midnight
43: Fighting Buckaroo
Kid Dynamite
The Ape Man
Ghosts on the Loose
The Girl from Monterey
What a Man!
44: Bowery Champs
Riding West
Sundown West
Sundown Valley
Three of a Kind
45: Rough Ridin' Justice

Warren Oates
1959: Up Periscope!
Yellowstone Kelly
60: The Rise and Fall of Legs
Diamond
Private Property
61: Lover Come Back
62: Ride the High Country (or,
Guns in the Afternoon)
Hero's Island
64: Mail Order Bride (or,
West of Montana)

65: Major Dundee
The Rounders
66: Return of the Seven
67: The Terrornauts (or, The
Shooting)
Welcome to Hard Times
(or, Killer on a Horse)
In the Heat of the Night
68: Something for a Lonely
Man (TV)
The Wild Bunch
The Split
69: Smith!
Barquero
Crooks and Coronets
There Was a Crooked Man
Trog

Philip Ober (1902-
1934: Chloe, Love Is Calling
50: The Secret Fury
Never a Dull Moment
The Magnificent Yankee
The Dull Knife
51: The Unknown Man
52: The Washington Story
Come Back, Little Sheba
53: Scandal at Scourie
The Clown
Girls of Pleasure Island
From Here to Eternity
54: About Mrs. Leslie
Broken Lance
57: Tammy and the Bachelor
Escapade in Japan
58: The High Cost of Loving
10 North Frederick
Torpedo Run
59: North by Northwest
The Mating Game
Beloved Infidel
60: Let no Man Write My
Epitaph
Elmer Gantry
The Facts of Life
The Third Voice
The Great Impostor
61: Go Naked in the World
63: The Ugly American
64: The Brass Bottle
66: The Ghost and Mr. Chicken

68:   Assignment to Kill

Merle Oberon (1911-
1931: The Battle
      Service for Ladies
32:   Wedding Rehearsal
      Men of Tomorrow
      Dance of the Witches
33:   Thunder in the East
      The Private Life of
      Henry VIII
34:   The Private Life of Don
      Juan
      Broken Melody
35:   Folies Bergère
      Dark Angel
36:   These Three
      Beloved Enemy
37:   I, Claudius
38:   Divorce of Lady X
      The Cowboy and the Lady
39:   Wuthering Heights
40:   The Lion Has Wings
      Over the Moon
      Till We Meet Again
41:   That Uncertain Feeling
      Affectionately Yours
      Lydia
43:   Stage Door Canteen
      First Comes Courage
      Forever and a Day
44:   The Lodger
      Dark Waters
45:   A Song to Remember
      Hangover Square
      This Love of Ours
46:   Temptation
      A Night in Paradise
47:   Night Song
48:   Berlin Express
51:   Pardon My French
53:   Affair in Monte Carlo
54:   Desiree
      Deep in My Heart
56:   Price of Fear
63:   Of Love and Desire
66:   The Oscar
67:   Hotel
69:   The Private War of Mrs.
      Darling

Hugh O'Brian (1925-
1950: Buckaroo Sheriff of Texas
      Return of Jesse James
      Young Lovers
      Rocketship XM
      Never Fear
      Beyond the Purple Hills
51:   Vengeance Valley
      On the Loose
52:   Red Ball Express
      Sally and St. Anne
      The Raiders
      Meet Me at the Fair
      Battle of Apache Pass
      Stand at Apache River
      The Lawless Breed
      Seminole
      The Man from the Alamo
      Back to God's Country
53:   Riders of Vengeance
      Son of Ali Baba
54:   Saskatchewan
      Fireman, Save My Child!
      Drums Across the River
      Broken Lance
      There's No Business Like
      Show Business
55:   White Feather
      Twinkle in God's Eye
56:   The Brass Legend
      Rope Law
58:   The Fiend Who Walked the
      West
63:   Come Fly with Me
65:   Love Has Many Faces
      In Harm's Way
      Ten Little Indians
66:   Assassination in Rome
      The Ghost and Mr. Chicken
      Ambush Bay
67:   Africa--Texas Style!
68:   Strategy of Terror (TV)
69:   The Devil's Backbone

Dave O'Brien (1912-1969)
1933: Jennie Gerhardt
35:   Welcome Home
37:   Million Dollar Racket
38:   Frontier Scout
      Man's Country

38: Where the Buffalo Roam
39: Song of the Buckaroo
    Rollin' Westward
    Mutiny in the Big House
    New Frontier
    Daughter of the Tong
    Crashing Through
40: East Side Kids
    Son of the Navy
    The Cowboy from Sundown
    Yukon Flight
    Danger Ahead
    Boys of the City
    Queen of the Yukon
    That Gang of Mine
    Murder on the Yukon
    A Fugitive from Justice
    Gun Code
    The Kid from Santa Fe
    Hold that Woman!
41: Devil Bat
    Flying Wild
    Texas Marshal
    Murder by Invitation
    Buzzy and the Phantom
      Pinto
    The Deadly Game
    Gunman from Bodie
    Spooks Run Wild
    Double Trouble
    Billy the Kid Wanted
42: Down Texas Way
    Prisoner of Japan
    Billy the Kid's Smoking
      Guns
    King of the Stallions
    'Neath Brooklyn Bridge
    Bowery at Midnight
    The Yanks Are Coming
    7 Pete Smith shorts
    Captain Midnight (ser.)
43: Texas Ranger (ser.)
    The Rangers Take Over
    Border Buckaroo
44: Trail of Terror
    Gunsmoke Mesa
    Return of the Rangers
    Boss of Rawhide
    Outlaw Roundup
    Guns of the Law

    The Pinto Bandit
    Spook Town
    Dead or Alive
    The Whispering Skull
    Gangsters of the Frontier
45: Tahiti Nights
    The Man Who Walked
      Alone
    Phantom of 42nd Street
    Enemy of the Law
    Flaming Bullets
    Three in the Saddle
    Marked for Murder
46: Frontier Fugitives
47: Thundercap Outlaws
    Shootin' Irons
53: Kiss Me Kate
54: Tennessee Champ
56: The Desperadoes Are in
      Town
64: Big Parade of Comedy
      (doc.)

Edmond O'Brien (1915-
1939: The Hunchback of Notre
      Dame
41: A Girl, A Guy, and a Gob
    Parachute Battalion
    Obliging Young Lady
42: Powder Town
43: The Amazing Mrs. Holiday
44: Winged Victory
46: The Killers
47: A Double Life
    The Web
    The Hanged Man
48: Fighter Squadron
    Another Part of the Forest
    For the Love of Mary
    An Act of Murder
49: White Heat
    D.O.A. (or, Dead on
      Arrival)
50: Backfire
    The Redhead and the
      Cowboy
    The Admiral Was a Lady
    711 Ocean Drive
    Between Midnight and Dawn
51: Two of a Kind

1042

51: Silver City
    Warpath
52: The Denver and the Rio
    Grande
    The Turning Point
53: Cow Country
    The Hitchhiker
    Julius Caesar
    China Venture
    The Man in the Dark
54: Shield for Murder
    The Shanghai Story
    The Barefoot Contessa
    (OSCAR)
55: Pete Kelly's Blues
56: D-Day, the 6th of June
    The Rack
    1984
    The Girl Can't Help it
    A Cry in the Night
57: The Big Land (or,
    Stampeded)
    Stopover Tokyo
58: The Bigamist
    Sing, Boy, Sing
    The World Was His Jury
59: Up Periscope!
60: The Third Voice
    The Last Voyage
61: The Great Impostor
    Man Trap (dir.)
62: Moon Pilot
    Bird Man of Alcatraz
    The Longest Day
    The Man Who Shot
    Liberty Valance
64: Seven Days in May
    Rio Conchos
    The Climbers
65: The Hanged Man
    Synanon
    Sylvia
66: Fantastic Voyage
67: The Outsider (TV Pilot)
68: The Viscount
    The Wild Bunch
    The Love God?

Erin O'Brien
1958: Girl on the Run

59: John Paul Jones

George O'Brien (1900-
1928: Blindfold   SSE
29: Noah's Ark   PT
    Masked Emotions   SSE
    Salute
    True Heaven   S
30: The Lone Star Ranger
    Rough Romance
    Last of the Duanes
31: The Man Who Came Back
    Fair Warning
    The Seas Beneath
    A Holy Terror
    Riders of the Purple Sage
32: The Rainbow Trail
    The Gay Caballero
    Mystery Ranch
    The Golden West
33: Robbers' Roost
    Smoke Lightning
    Life in the Raw
    The Last Trail
34: Frontier Marshal
    Ever Since Eve
    The Dude Ranger
35: When a Man's a Man
    The Cowboy Millionaire
    Hard Rock Harrigan
    Thunder Mountain
    Whispering Smith Speaks
36: O'Malley of the Mounted
    Border Patrolman
    Daniel Boone
37: Park Avenue Logger
    Hollywood Cowboy
    Windjammer
38: Gun Law
    Border G-Man
    Painted Desert
    Lawless Valley
39: The Arizona Legion
    Trouble in Sundown
    The Renegade Ranger
    The Fighting Gringo
    Racketeers of the Range
    Timber Stampede
40: The Marshal of Mesa City
    Legion of the Lawless

40: Bullet Code
Prairie Law
Stage to Chino
Triple Justice
47: My Wild Irish Rose
48: Fort Apache
49: She Wore a Yellow
Ribbon
51: Gold Raiders (or, Stooges
Go West)
64: Cheyenne Autumn

Joan O'Brien
1958: Handle with Care
59: Operation Petticoat
60: The Alamo
61: The Comancheros
62: Six Black Horses
It's Only Money
Samar
63: It Happened at the World's
Fair
64: Get Yourself a College
Girl

Margaret O'Brien (1937-
1941: Babes in Arms
42: Journey for Margaret
43: Dr. Gillespie's Criminal
Case
Lost Angel
Thousands Cheer
Madame Curie
44: Jane Eyre
Canterville Ghost
Meet Me in St. Louis
Music for Millions
(SPECIAL AWARD)
45: Our Vines Have Tender
Grapes
Bad Bascomb
46: Three Wise Fools
47: Unfinished Dance
48: Tenth Avenue Angel
The Big City
49: Little Women
The Secret Garden
51: Her First Romance
56: Glory
60: Heller in Pink Tights
69: Annabelle Lee

Pat O'Brien (1899-
1929: Fury of the Wild   S
Freckled Rascal   S
Married in Haste   S
Happy Landing
Determination
31: Front Page
Personal Maid
Consolation Marriage
Flying High
Honor Among Lovers
32: Hell's House
Final Edition
Scandal for Sale
American Madness
Arm of the Law
Hollywood Speaks
Virtue
The Strange Case of
Clara Deane
Air Mail
Laughter in Hell
33: Destination Unknown
The World Gone Mad
Bureau of Missing Persons
College Coach
Bombshell
34: I've Got Your Number
The Personality Kid
Here Comes the Navy
Twenty Million Sweethearts
Flirtation Walk
I Sell Anything
Gambling Lady
Flaming Gold
35: Devil Dogs of the Air
In Caliente
Oil for the Lamps of
China
Page Miss Glory
Stars over Broadway
The Irish in Us
Outlawed Gun
Ceiling Zero
36: I Married a Doctor
Public Enemy's Wife
China Clipper
37: The Great O'Malley
San Quentin
Slim
Submarine D-1

37: Back in Circulation
38: Women Are Like That
    Boy Meets Girl
    Angels with Dirty Faces
    Cowboy from Brooklyn
    Garden of the Moon
    Bar-20 Justice
39: Off the Record
    Indianapolis Speedway
    The Kid from Kokomo
40: Night of Nights
    The Fighting 69th
    Castle on the Hudson
    Torrid Zone
    Flowing Gold
    Knute Rockne--All
      American
    Escape to Glory
    Slightly Honorable
    Till We Meet Again
41: Submarine Zone
42: Two Years in Trinidad
    Broadway
    Flight Lieutenant
    The Navy Comes Through
43: Bombardier
    The Iron Major
    His Butler's Sister
44: Marine Raiders
    The Secret Command
45: Having a Wonderful Crime
    Man Alive
46: Perilous Holiday
    Crack-Up
47: Riffraff
48: Fighting Father Dunne
    The Boy with Green Hair
49: A Dangerous Profession
50: Johnny One-Eye
    The Fireball
51: Criminal Lawyer
    The People Against
      O'Hara
52: Okinawa
54: Jubilee Trail
    Ring of Fear
55: Inside Detroit
    The Bail Bond Story
57: Kill Me Tomorrow
58: The Last Hurrah

59: Some Like it Hot
65: Town Tamer
69: The Phynx

Tom O'Brien (1898-
1929: Peacock Fan   S
      It can be Done   PT
      Last Warning   PT
      The Flying Fool
      Smiling Irish Eyes
      Untamed
      His Lucky Day   PT
      Dark Skies
      Dance Hall
32: Unexpected Father
    Phantom Express
    Night Mayor°
33: Lucky Dog
34: Woman Condemned

Virginia O'Brien (1921-
1940: Hullabaloo
      Sky Murder
41: The Big Store
    Lady be Good
    Ringside Maisie
42: Ship Ahoy!
    Panama Mattie
43: Du Barry Was a Lady
    Thousands Cheer
44: Meet the People
    Two Girls and a Sailor
    Ziegfeld Follies
45: The Harvey Girls
    The Great Morgan
46: Till the Clouds Roll by
    The Show-Off
47: Merton of the Movies

Erin O'Brien-Moore (1908-
1934: Dangerous Corner
      His Greatest Gamble
      Little Men
35: Our Little Girl
    Streamline Express
    Seven Keys to Baldpate
36: Two in the Dark
    The Leavenworth Case
    Ring Around the Moon
    The Ex-Mrs. Bradford

37: The Plough and the Stars
Black Legion
Green Light
The Life of Emile Zola
50: Destination Moon
51: The Family Secret
53: Sea of Lost Ships
54: Phantom of the Rue
Morgue
55: The Long Gray Line
57: Peyton Place
58: Girl on the Run
59: John Paul Jones
67: How to Succeed in
Business Without Really
Trying

Arthur O'Connell (1908-
1938: Murder in Soho
41: Citizen Kane (bit)
42: Law of the Jungle
Man from Headquarters
45: Having a Wonderful Crime
Man Alive
47: Riffraff
48: Open Secret
Countess of Monte Cristo
55: Picnic
56: The Solid Gold Cadillac
The Man in the Grey
Flannel Suit
The Proud Ones
Bus Stop
57: The Violators
The Monte Carlo Story
Operation Mad Ball
April Love
58: Man of the West
Voice in the Mirror
59: Gidget
Anatomy of a Murder
Hound-Dog Man
Operation Petticoat
60: Cimarron
The Great Impostor
61: A Thunder of Drums
Misty
A Pocketful of Miracles
62: Follow that Dream
64: The Seven Faces of Dr.
Lao

Kissin' Cousins
Your Cheatin' Heart
Nightmare
65: The Great Race
Nightmare in the Sun
The Third Day
Monkey's Uncle
66: The Silencers
Birds Do It
Ride Beyond Vengeance
Fantastic Voyage
67: Reluctant Astronaut
A Covenant with Death
68: The Power
If He Hollers, Let Him Go
Suppose They Gave a War
and Nobody Came
69: There Was a Crooked Man

Carroll O'Connor
1965: In Harm's Way
66: Not with My Wife, You
Don't !
Hawaii
What Did You Do in the
War, Daddy ?
67: Point Blank
Waterhole No. 3
Warning Shot
69: Marlowe
Fear No Evil
Death of a Gunfighter

Donald O'Connor (1925-
1937: Melody for Two
38: Sing, You Sinners
Sons of the Legion
Men with Wings
Tom Sawyer, Detective
39: Boy Trouble
Unmarried
Million Dollar Legs
Beau Geste
Night Work
Death of a Champion
On Your Toes
42: Get Hep to Love
Strictly in the Groove
What's Cookin' ?
Private Buckaroo
Give Out, Sisters

Donald O'Connor

43: When Johnny Comes
    Marching Home
    It Comes Up Love
    Mr. Big
    Top Man
    This Is the Life!
44: The Merry Monahans
    Chip Off the Old Block
    Follow the Boys
    Bowery to Broadway
45: Patrick the Great
47: Something in the Wind
48: Are You with it?
    Feudin', Fussin', an' A-
    fightin'
49: Yes Sir, that's My Baby
50: Francis
    The Milkman
    Curtain Call at Cactus
    Creek
    Double Crossbones
51: Francis Goes to the Races
52: Francis Goes to West
    Point
    Singin' in the Rain
53: I Love Melvin
    Call Me Madam
    Walking My Baby Back
    Home
    Francis Covers the Big
    Town
54: There's no Business like
    Show Business
    Francis Joins the Wacs
55: Francis Joins the Navy
56: Anything Goes
57: The Buster Keaton Story
61: Cry for Happy
    The Wonders of Aladdin
65: That Funny Feeling
69: The Tourist
    Do not Throw the Cushions
    into the Ring

Robert Emmett O'Connor (1885-
1962)
1928: The Singing Fool   PT
      Four Walls   S
      Freedom of the Press S
  29: Weary River   PT

Smiling Irish Eyes
The Isle of Lost Ships
30: In the Next Room
    Framed
    Up the River
    Alias French Gertie
    The Big House
    Shooting Straight
    Our Blushing Brides
31: Man to Man
    Paid
    Single Sin
    Public Enemy
    Three Who Loved
    Reckless Living
    Fanny Foley Herself
32: Two Kinds of Women
    Big Timber
    Night World
    Dark Horse
    Blonde Venus
    The Kid from Spain
33: Frisco Jenny
    The Great Jasper
    Lady of the Night
    Picture Snatchers
    Midnight Mary
    The Big Brain
    Don't Bet on Love
    Lady for a Day
    Penthouse
34: Big Shakedown
    Bottoms Up
    Return of the Terror
    White Lies
35: The Mysterious Mr. Wong
    Star of Midnight
    Let 'em Have it!
    Waterfront Lady
    A Night at the Opera
36: We Who Are about to Die
    Sing Me a Love Song
    Desire
37: Park Avenue Logger
    Girl Overboard
    The Crime Nobody Saw
    The Frame Up
    River of Missing Men
    Super Sleuth
    Boy of the Streets

1048

39: Streets of New York
Joe and Ethel Turp Call
on the President
40: Double Alibi
Hot Steel
41: Tight Shoes
43: Air Raid Wardens
Whistling in Brooklyn
44: Gentle Annie
46: Boys Ranch

Una O'Connor (1881-1959)
1929: Dark Red Roses
30: Murder
33: Cavalcade
Pleasure Cruise
The Invisible Man
Mary Stevens, M.D.
34: The Poor Rich
The Barretts of Wimpole
Street
Orient Express
All Men Are Enemies
Stingaree
Chained
35: David Copperfield
The Informer
Father Brown, Detective
Bride of Frankenstein
Thunder in the Night
The Perfect Gentleman
36: Rose Marie
Little Lord Fauntleroy
Lloyds of London
Suzy
37: The Plough and the Stars
Call it a Day
Personal Property
38: Adventures of Robin Hood
39: We Are not Alone
40: The Sea Hawk
Lillian Russell
He Stayed for Breakfast
It All Came True
All Women Have Secrets
41: Strawberry Blonde
Her First Beau
Three Girls about Town
42: Always in My Heart
My Favorite Spy

Random Harvest
43: This Land Is Mine
Forever and a Day
Holy Matrimony
Government Girl
44: My Pal Wolf
Return of Monte Cristo
45: Whispering Walls
Bells of St. Mary's
Christmas in Connecticut
46: Banjo
Child of Divorce
Cluny Brown
Of Human Bondage
Unexpected Guests
47: Lost Honeymoon
The Corpse Came C.O.D.
Ivy
48: Fighting Father Dunne
Adventures of Don Juan
57: Witness for the Prosecution

Molly O'Day (1911-
1929: Show of Shows
30: Sisters
31: Sea Devils
Sob Sister
32: Devil on Deck
33: Gigolettes of Paris
34: Hired Wife
The Life of Vergie Winters
35: Lawless Border
Skull and Crown

Doye O'Dell
1941: The Pioneers
Fugitive Valley
46: Heldorado
Man from Rainbow Valley
47: Last Frontier Uprising
48: Whirlwind Raiders
49: Son of a Badman
55: Tight Spot
68: Cross Country U.S.A.

Cathy O'Donnell (1925-
1946: The Best Years of Our
Lives
47: Bury Me Dead
48: They Live by Night

1049

48: The Twisted Road
    The Spiritualist
    Your Red Wagon
49: Side Street
50: The Miniver Story
51: Detective Story
    Never Trust a Gambler
53: Eight O'Clock Walk
55: Mad at the World
    The Man from Laramie
57: The Deerslayer
    The Story of Mankind
58: Terror in the Haunted
    House
59: Ben-Hur

Martha O'Driscoll (1922-
1935: Collegiate
37: Champagne Waltz
    She's Dangerous
    Love Is Young
38: Mad about Music
    Girls' School
39: The Secret of Dr. Kildare
    Judge Hardy and Son
40: Forty Little Mothers
    Laddie
    Wagon Train
41: The Lady Eve
    Henry Aldrich for
      President
    Pacific Blackout
    Her First Beau
    Midnight Angel
42: Reap the Wild Wind
    My Heart Belongs to
      Daddy
    Youth on Parade
43: Young and Willing
    Weekend Pass
    The Fallen Sparrow
    Crazy House
    We've Never Been Licked
44: Hi Beautiful!
    Follow the Boys
    Allergic to Love
    Ghost Catchers
45: The Daltons Ride Again
    Her Lucky Night
    Here Come the Coeds

Shady Lady
House of Dracula
46: Blonde Alibi
    Criminal Court
    Down Missouri Way
47: Carnegie Hall

Damian O'Flynn
1937: Marked Woman
41: The Gay Falcon
    Lady Scarface
42: Broadway
    Powder Town
    Wake Island
    X Marks the Spot
43: Flight for Freedom
    Sarong Girl
    So Proudly We Hail!
44: Winged Victory
46: The Bachelor's Daughters
    Crack-Up
47: The Beginning or the End?
    Desire on Wheels
    Philo Vance Returns
    Saddle Pals
    Web of Danger
48: Half Past Midnight
    A Foreign Affair
    Disaster
    The Snake Pit
49: Black Magic
    Outpost in Morocco
    Riders of the Whistling
      Pines
50: Young Daniel Boone
    Pioneer Marshal
    Gambling House
    Bomba and the Hidden City
51: The Fighting Coast Guard
    Yellow Fin
52: The Half-Breed
    Hoodlum Empire
54: The Miami Story
    Two Guns and a Badge
55: Daddy Long Legs
56: Hidden Guns
    D-Day, the 6th of June
57: Drango
    Apache Warrior
    Eighteen and Anxious

1050

63: Gunfight at Comanche
    Creek

George O'Hanlon (1917-
1941: New Wine
    The Great Awakening
42: The Man from Head-
    quarters
43: Corvette K-225
    Nearly Eighteen
47: The Hucksters
    Headin' for Heaven
    Spirit of West Point
48: Are You With It?
    The Joe Doakes series
    June Bride
51: The Tanks Are Coming
    Triple Cross
52: Park Row
    Cattle Town
    The Lion and the Horse
56: Battle Stations
57: Kronos
    Bop Girl
59: The Rookie

Maureen O'Hara (1920-
1939: Jamaica Inn
    The Hunchback of Notre
    Dame
40: A Bill of Divorcement
    Dance, Girls, Dance
41: They Met in Argentina
    How Green Was My Valley
42: To the Shores of Tripoli
    Ten Gentlemen from West
    Point
    Black Swan
43: This Land Is Mine
    The Immortal Sergeant
    The Fallen Sparrow
44: Buffalo Bill
    And Now Tomorrow
45: The Spanish Main
46: Do You Love Me?
    Sentimental Journey
47: Miracle on 34th Street
    The Foxes of Harrow
    The Homestretch
    Sinbad the Sailor

    Out of All Time
    The Big Heart
48: Sitting Pretty
49: A Woman's Secret
    Forbidden Street
    Bagdad
    Father Is a Fullback
50: Tripoli
    Rio Grande
    Comanche Territory
51: Flame of Araby
52: At Sword's Point
    Kangaroo
    The Quiet Man
    Against All Flags
    The Redhead from
    Wyoming
53: War Arrow
54: Fire over Africa
55: The Magnificent Matador
    Lady Godiva of Coventry
    The Long Gray Line
56: Everything but the Truth
    Lisbon
57: Wings of Eagles
60: Our Man in Havana
61: The Deadly Companions
    The Parent Trap
62: Mr. Hobbs Takes a
    Vacation
63: McLintock!
    Spencer's Mountain
65: The Battle of Villa Fiorita
66: The Rare Breed
69: Let Me Count the Ways

Dan O'Herlihy (1917-
1947: Odd Man Out
48: Macbeth
    Kidnapped
    Larceny
51: The Blue Veil
    Soldiers Three
    The Highwayman
52: At Sword's Point
    Actors and Sin
    Operation Secret
    Invasion U.S.A.
53: Sword of Venus
54: Adventures of Robinson
    Crusoe

54: Black Shield of Falworth
Bengal Brigade
55: The Purple Mask
The Virgin Queen
That Woman Opposite
57: Cry After Midnight
58: Home Before Dark
59: Imitation of Life
The Young Land
City After Midnight
60: One Foot in Hell
The Night Fighters
61: King of the Roaring '20s
62: The Cabinet of Dr.
Caligari
64: Fail Safe
68: 100 Rifles
69: The Big Cube
Waterloo

Carol Ohmart (1928-
1955: The Scarlet Hour
56: The Wild Party
58: The House on Haunted
Hill
59: Born Reckless
60: The Scavengers
Wild Youth
64: One Man's Way

Dennis O'Keefe (1911-1968)
1936: Born to Dance (bit)
38: Bad Man of Brimstone
Hold that Kiss
The Chaser
Vacation from Love
39: Burn 'em Up, O'Connor
The Kid from Texas
Unexpected Father
That's Right, You're
Wrong
40: Alias the Deacon
La Conga Nights
I'm Nobody's Sweetheart
Now
Pop Always Pays
You'll Find Out
Girl from Havana
Arise My Love
41: Bowery Boy

Mr. District Attorney
Topper Returns
Broadway Limited
Lady Scarface
Weekend for Three
42: The Affairs of Jimmy
Valentine
Moonlight Masquerade
43: Good Morning Judge
Hangmen Also Die
Tahiti Honey
The Leopard Man
Hi Diddle Diddle
44: Fighting Seabees
Up in Mabel's Room
Abroad with Two Yanks
The Story of Dr. Wassell
Sensations of 1945
45: Affairs of Susan
Brewster's Millions
Earl Carroll Vanities
Doll Face
Getting Gertie's Garter
46: Her Adventurous Night
Come Back to Me
47: T-Men
Dishonored Lady
Mr. District Attorney
48: Walk a Crooked Mile
Raw Deal
Siren of Atlantis
49: Cover-Up
The Great Dan Patch
Abandoned
50: The Company She Keeps
The Eagle and the Hawk
Woman on the Run
51: Passage West
Follow the Sun
52: One Big Affair
Everything I Have Is Yours
53: The Lady Wants Mink
The Fake
54: Drums of Tahiti
Diamond Wizard (dir., act.)
55: Angela
Chicago Syndicate
Las Vegas Shakedown
56: Inside Detroit
57: Dragoon Wells Massacre

57:	Lady of Vengeance		Charlie Chan at Monte
58:	Graft and Corruption		Carlo
61:	All Hands on Deck		Charlie Chan at the
			Olympics

Warner Oland (1880-1938)

1927:	The Jazz Singer PT	Edna May Oliver (1883-1942)
29:	Mysterious Dr. Fu Manchu	1929:	Saturday Night Kid
	The Studio Murder	30:	Half Shot at Sunrise
	Mystery	31:	Laugh and Get Rich
	The Faker		Fanny Foley Herself
	Chinatown Nights		Cimarron
	Dream of Love		Cracked Nuts
30:	Dangerous Paradise		Newly Rich
	Paramount on Parade	32:	Lost Squadron
	The Mighty		March of a Nation
	Return of Dr. Fu Manchu		Top of the Bill
	The Vagabond Kind		Ladies of the Jury
31:	The Big Gamble		Hold 'em Jail
	The Black Gamble		The Penguin Pool Murder
	The Black Camel		The Conquerors
	Dishonored	33:	Whoopee Cruise
	Daughter of the Dragon		The Great Jasper
	Burnt Offering		Ann Vickers
	Drums of Jeopardy		Hell Bent for Election
	Charlie Chan Carries On		It's Great to be Alive
32:	Shanghai Express		Strawberry Roan
	Charlie Chan's Chance		Only Yesterday
	A Passport to Hell		Meet the Baron
	The Son-Daughter		Little Women
33:	Charlie Chan's Greatest		Alice in Wonderland
	Case	34:	The Poor Rich
	As Husbands Go		The Last Gentleman
	Before Dawn		We're Rich Again
34:	Mandalay		Murder on the Blackboard
	Bulldog Drummond	35:	Murder on a Honeymoon
	Strikes Back		David Copperfield
	Charlie Chan's Courage		No More Ladies
	Charlie Chan in London		A Tale of Two Cities
	The Painted Veil	36:	Romeo and Juliet
35:	Charlie Chan in Paris	37:	My Dear Miss Aldrich
	Charlie Chan in Egypt		Parnell
	Werewolf of London		Rosalie
	Shanghai	38:	Paradise for Three
	Charlie Chan in Shanghai		Little Miss Broadway
	Charlie Chan's Secret	39:	The Story of Vernon and
36:	Charlie Chan at the Circus		Irene Castle
	Charlie Chan at the Race		Nurse Edith Cavell
	Track		Second Fiddle
	Charlie Chan at the Opera		Drums Along the Mohawk
37:	Charlie Chan on Broadway	40:	Pride and Prejudice

41:   Lydia

Gordon Oliver (1910-
1937: Fugitive in the Sky
      Once a Doctor
      The Go-Getter
      Draegerman Courage
      Fly-Away Baby
      White Bondage
      San Quentin
      The Case of the Stutter-
        ing Bishop
      Youth on Parole
      Over the Goal
      West of Shanghai
38:   Women Are Like that
      Alcatraz Island
      Jezebel
      The Daredevil Drivers
      The Marines Are Here
      There's that Woman
       Again
      Blondie
      Brother Rat
39:   Pride of the Navy
      My Son Is a Criminal
      Romance of the Redwoods
      A Woman Is the Judge
      Sabotage
41:   Sweetheart of the Campus
44:   Heavenly Days
      Passport to Destiny
      Seven Days Ashore
      Since You Went Away
46:   The Spiral Staircase
48:   Station West
50:   Born to be Bad
51:   My Forbidden Past
52:   The Las Vegas Story

Guy Oliver (1875-
1929: Texas Tommy   S
      Far Western Trails   S
      Fighting Terror   S
30:   Only the Brave
      Light of the Western Skies
      The Kibitzer
      Devil's Holiday
      Playboy of Paris
31:   Gun Smoke

      Skippy
      Dude Ranch
      Up Pops the Devil
      I Take this Woman
      Caught
      Huckleberry Finn
      Beloved Bachelor
      Rich Man's Folly
      Sooky

Susan Oliver (1937-
1957: The Green-Eyed Blonde
59:   The Gene Krupa Story
60:   Butterfield 8
63:   The Caretakers
64:   Looking for Love
      The Disorderly Orderly
      Your Cheatin' Heart
67:   The Love-Ins
68:   The Monitors
69:   A Man Called Gannon
      Change of Mind

Sir Laurence Olivier (1907-
1930: Too Many Crooks
31:   Yellow Ticket
      Friends and Lovers
32:   Westward Passage
33:   Perfect Understanding
34:   No Funny Business
35:   Moscow Nights
      Conquest of the Air
36:   As You Like it
37:   Fire Over England
38:   The Divorce of Lady X
      21 Days Together
39:   First and Last
      Q Planes (or, Clouds
       Over Europe)
      Wuthering Heights
40:   Rebecca
      Pride and Prejudice
41:   That Hamilton Woman
42:   The Invaders (or, The
       49th Parallel)
      Lydia
45:   Demi-Paradise
46.   Henry V
48:   Hamlet (OSCAR)
51:   The Magic Box

52: Carrie
53: A Queen Is Crowned
The Beggar's Opera
56: Richard III
57: The Prince and the Show-
girl
59: The Devil's Disciple
60: Spartacus
The Entertainer
62: Term of Trial
65: Othello
Bunny Lake Is Missing
66: Khartoum
68: The Shoes of the Fisherman
The Dance of Death
The Battle of Britain
69: Oh, What a Lovely War!

Gertrude Olmstead (1904-
1929: Passion Song   S
Sonny Boy   PT
Time, Place, and the
Girl
Show of Shows

Moroni Olsen (1889-1954)
1935: The Three Musketeers
Annie Oakley
Seven Keys to Baldpate
The Farmer in the Dell
36: Mary of Scotland
Kentucky
Air Force
We're Only Human
Yellow Dust
Two in the Dark
The Witness Chair
M'Liss
Grand Jury
37: The Plough and the Stars
Mummy's Boys
Adventure's End
Manhattan Merry-Go-Round
38: Gold Is Where You Find it
Kidnapped
Submarine Patrol
39: Homicide Bureau
Rose of Washington Square
Code of the Secret Service

Susannah of the Mounties
Allegheny Uprising
Dust be My Destiny
That's Right, You're Wrong
Barricade
40: Virginia City
Invisible Stripes
Brother Rat and a Baby
If I Had My Way
Brigham Young--Frontiers-
man
East of the River
Santa Fe Trail
41: Life with Henry
Dive Bomber
One Foot in Heaven
Three Sons o' Guns
Dangerously They Live
42: Sundown Jim
My Favorite Spy
Mrs. Wiggs of the Cabbage
Patch
The Glass Key
Reunion
43: Air Force
Mission to Moscow
The Song of Bernadette
44: Ali Baba and the Forty
Thieves
Buffalo Bill
Roger Touhy--Gangster
Cobra Woman
45: Pride of the Marines
Behind City Lights
Mildred Pierce
Don't Fence Me In
Weekend at the Waldorf
46: A Night in Paradise
Boys Ranch
The Walls Came Tumbling
Down
Notorious
The Strange Woman
47: Possessed
The Long Night
Life with Father
Black Gold
The Beginning or the End?
That Hagen Girl
High Wall

48: Call Northside 777
    Up in Central Park
    Command Decision
49: The Fountainhead
    Task Force
    Samson and Delilah
50: Father of the Bride
51: Father's Little Dividend
    No Questions Asked
    Payment on Demand
    Submarine Command
52: At Sword's Point
    Lone Star
    The Washington Story
53: Marry Me Again
54: The Long, Long Trailer
    Sign of the Pagan

Ole Olsen: see Chick Johnson &
Ole Olsen

Nancy Olson (1928-
1949: Canadian Pacific
50: Sunset Boulevard
    Union Station
    Mr. Music
51: Submarine Command
    Force of Arms
52: Big Jim McLain
53: So Big
    Donovan's Brain
54: The Boy from Oklahoma
55: Battle Cry
60: Pollyanna
61: The Absent-Minded
    Professor
63: Son of Flubber
69: Smith!

J. Pat O'Malley (1901-
1957: Four Boys and a Gun
    Courage of Black Beauty
58: The Long Hot Summer
60: Blueprint of Robbery
61: A Hundred and One
    Dalmatians (cartoon voice)
62: The Cabinet of Dr. Caligari
64: A House Is Not a Home
    Apache Rifles
67: Gunn

The Jungle Book (cartoon
    voice)
68: Star! (or, Those Were the
    Happy Times)

Pat O'Malley (1891-1966)
1929: The Man I Love
30: Alibi
    The Fall Guy
    Average Husband
    a short
    The People Versus
    Mothers Cry
31: Night Life in Reno
    Sky Spider
    Homicide Squad
    Anobody's Blonde
32: The Fighting Marshal
    The Reckoning
    High Speed
    American Madness
    Exposure
    Those We Love
    Klondike
    Speed Madness
    The Penal Code
33: Laughing at Life
    Riot Squad
    One Year Later
    Sing, Sinner, Sing
    I Love that Man
    The Whirlpool
    Frisco Jenny
    Mystery of the Wax Museum
    Sundown Rider
    Man of Sentiment
    Parachute Jumper
34: Love Past Thirty
    Crime Doctor
    Girl in Danger
35: Behind the Evidence
    Lady Tubbs
    Men of the Hour
    Man on the Flying Trapeze
    Wanderer of the Wasteland
    The Perfect Clue
    Heir to Trouble
36: Hollywood Boulevard
    Beloved Enemy
37: Mysterious Crossing
39: Wolf Call

38: Love, Honor, and Behave
Toy Wife
I Am the Law
39: The Sun Never Sets
When Tomorrow Comes
Tower of London
Gone With the Wind
40: All This and Heaven Too
41: Shining Victory
48: The Secret Beyond the
Door
I Remember Mama
49: Whirlpool
52; Angel Face
55: Flame of the Island
57: Sorority Girl
59: The Nun's Story

Nance O'Neil (1875-1965)
1929: His Glorious Night
30: The Rogue Song
Ladies of Leisure
Lady of Scandal
The Floradora Girl
Call of the Flesh
Eyes of the World
31: Royal Bed
Resurrection
Cimarron
Woman of Experience
Good Bad Girl
Their Mad Moment
Secret Service
32: False Faces
Okay, America!

Sally O'Neil (1912-1968)
1926: Mike   S
27: The Callahans and the
Murphys   S
Slide, Kelly, Slide!   S
28: Battle of the Sexes   SSE
29: On with the Show
The Sophomore
Hard-Boiled
Broadway Scandals
Girl on the Barge
Show of Shows
Broadway Fever
Jazz Heaven

30: Hold Everything
Girl of the Port
Sisters
Kathleen Mavourneen
31: Salvation Nell
The Brat
Murder by the Clock
33: By Appointment Only
Ladies Must Love
35: Convention Girl
Too Tough to Kill

Henry O'Neill (1891-1961)
1933: I Loved a Woman
The Kennel Murder Case
The World Changes
From Headquarters
Lady Killer
The House on 56th Street
34: Fog over Frisco
Fashions of 1934
Side Streets
Flirtation Walk
Murder in the Clouds
Bedside
Wonder Bar
I've Got Your Number
Journal of a Crime
Big Shakedown
Twenty Million Sweethearts
Now I'll Tell
Upper World
Madame Du Barry
The Personality Kid
Midnight Alibi
Man with Two Faces
Big-Hearted Herbert
Gentlemen Are Born
The Strong Arm
Midnight
35: Living on Velvet
Sweet Music
The Florentine Dagger
Bordertown
The Man Who Reclaimed
His Head
The Great Hotel Murder
While the Patient Slept
Secret Bride
Black Fury

35: Dinky
Alias Mary Dow
Stranded
Oil for the Lamps of
China
We're in the Money
Bright Lights
The Case of the Lucky
Legs
Special Agent
Dr. Socrates
The Story of Louis
Pasteur
36: Boulder Dam
Freshman Love
Road Gang
The Walking Dead
Bullets or Ballots
Two Against the World
The Big Noise
The Golden Arrow
Anthony Adverse
The White Angel
Rainbow on the River
37: The Great O'Malley
Marked Woman
The Go-Getter
Draegerman Courage
The Life of Emile Zola
Mr. Dodd Takes the Air
The Singing Marine
First Lady
The Great Garrick
Submarine D-1
Wells Fargo
38: The Amazing Dr. Clitter-
house
Racket Busters
Jezebel
Gold Is Where You Find It
Yellow Jack
White Banners
The Chaser
Girls on Probation
Brother Rat
39: Invisible Stripes
Torchy Blane in China-
town
Wings of the Navy
Confessions of a Nazi Spy

Juarez
Lucky Night
The Man Who Dared
Angels Wash Their Faces
Everybody's Hobby
Four Wives
40: They Drive by Night
A Child Is Born
Calling Philo Vance
The Story of Dr. Ehrlich's
Magic Bullet
Castle on the Hudson
The Fighting 69th
Till We Meet Again
Money and the Woman
Santa Fe Trail
41: Honky Tonk
Johnny Eager
The Bugle Sounds
The Trial of Mary Dugan
Men of Boys Town
Billy the Kid
Blossoms in the Dust
The Get-Away
Down in San Diego
Whistling in the Dark
Shadow of the Thin Man
42: This Time for Keeps
Born to Sing
Tortilla Flat
White Cargo
Stand By for Action
43: The Human Comedy
Air Raid Wardens
Dr. Gillespie's Criminal
Case
Whistling in Brooklyn
A Guy Named Joe
Girl Crazy
Lost Angel
The Heavenly Body
44: Rationing
Two Girls and a Sailor
Barbary Coast Gent
Nothing but Trouble
The Honest Thief
Airship Squadron No. 4
45: Anchors Aweigh
This Man's Navy
Dangerous Partners

45: Keep Your Powder Dry
46: The Virginian
The Green Years
Three Wise Fools
The Hoodlum Saint
Little Mr. Jim
Bad Bascomb
47: The Beginning or the End?
48: The Return of October
Leather Gloves
49: You're My Everything
Alias Nick Beal
Holiday Affair
The Reckless Moment
Strange Bargain
50: Convicted
The Milkman
The Flying Missile
No Man of Her Own
51: The Second Woman
The People Against
O'Hara
The Family Secret
52: Scandal Sheet
Scarlet Angel
53: The Sun Shines Bright
55: Untamed
57: Wings of Eagles

David Opatoshu (1918-
1939: The Light Ahead
48: The Naked City
49: Thieves' Highway
50: The Goldbergs
53: Public Enemy No. 1
56: Crowded Paradise
58: The Brothers Karamazov
Party Girl
60: Cimarron
Exodus
61: The Black City
King of Kings
62: The Best of Enemies
The Most Wanted Man in
the World
Guns of Darkness
Act of Mercy
65: Sands of Beersheba
66: Torn Curtain
One Spy Too Many

Tarzan and the Valley
of Gold
The Defector
67: Enter Laughing
69: Death of a Gunfighter
The Dybbuk
The Smugglers (TV)

William Orr (1917-
1939: The Hardys Ride High
40: The Mortal Storm
My Love Came Back
41: Honeymoon for Three
Thieves Fall Out
Navy Blues
Unholy Partners
Three Sons o' Guns
42: The Gay Sisters
The Big Street
43: He Hired the Boss

Frank Orth (1880-1962)
1936: Hot Money
39: Burn 'em Up, O'Connor
Broadway Serenade
Fast and Furious
Nancy Drew and the Hidden
Staircase
The Secret of Dr. Kildare
40: His Girl Friday
Dr. Kildare's Strange Case
La Conga Nights
Pier No. 13
Boom Town
Gold Rush Maisie
Let's Make Music
Dr. Kildare's Crisis
Michael Shayne, Private
Detective
Father Is a Prince
41: Come Live with Me
The Great American Broad-
cast
The People vs Dr. Kildare
Dr. Kildare's Wedding Day
Hot Spot
Dr. Kildare's Victory
Blue, White, and Perfect
42: Right to the Heart
To the Shores of Tripoli

42: Rings on Her Fingers
    My Gal Sal
    The Magnificent Dope
    Footlight Serenade
    Little Tokyo U. S. A.
    Tales of Manhattan
    Orchestra Wives
    Springtime in the Rockies
    Dr. Gillespie's New
      Assistant
    Over My Dead Body
43: Hello, Frisco, Hello
    Coney Island
    Sweet Rosie O'Grady
44: Buffalo Bill
    Carolina Blues
    Greenwich Village
    Storm over Lisbon
    Summer Storm
45: Col. Effingham's Raid
    Doll Face
    The Dolly Sisters
    The Lost Weekend
    Pillow to Post
    She Went to the Races
    Tell it to a Star
46: Blondie's Lucky Day
    It's Great to be Young
    Murder in the Music Hall
    The Strange Love of
      Martha Ivers
47: Born to Speed
    The Guilt of Janet Ames
    Heartaches
    Gas House Kids in
      Hollywood
    It Had to be You
    Mother Wore Tights
48: So this Is New York
    Fury at Furnace Creek
    The Girl from Manhattan
49: Blondie's Secret
    Red Light
    Make-Believe Ballroom
    The Great Rupert
50: Father of the Bride
    The Petty Girl
51: Double Dynamite
52: Something to Live For
53: Houdini

54: Here Come the Girls

Lyn Osborn (1923-1959)
1957: Invasion of the Saucer Men
59: The Cosmic Men
    Arson for Hire

Bud Osborne (1888-
1929: Texas Tommy   S
    Far Western Trails   S
    The Fighting Terror   S
    Days of Daring   S
    Badmen's Money   S
    The Smiling Terror   S
    The Lariat Kid   S
    The Last Roundup   S
    West of Santa Fe   S
    The Invaders   S
    On the Divide   S
30: Half Pint Polly   S
    Canyon of Missing Men   S
    O'Malley Rides Alone   S
    Call of the Desert   S
    Western Honor   S
    Code of the West   S
    Breezy Bill   S
    The Utah Kid
    The Law of the Mounted   S
31: Red Fork Range
32: Mark of the Spur
33: When a Man Rides Alone
    Diamond Trail
    Flaming Guns
    Deadwood Pass
    Rustlers Roundup
34: Riding Through
35: Outlaw Deputy
    The Crimson Trail
36: Treachery Rides the Range
    Song of the Saddle
    Heroes of the Range
    Headin' for the Rio Grande
    Roamin' Wild
37: The Californian
    Western Gold
    Boots and Saddles
    Guns of the Pecos
38: The Painted Trail
    Man's Country
    The Prairie Moon

38: The Overland Express
The Mexicali Kid
39: Racketeers of the Range
Legion of the Lawless
Across the Plains
New Frontier
40: Pioneer Days
Land of Six-Guns
West of Abilene
Lone Star Raiders
41: The Phantom Cowboy
Outlaws of the Panhandle
The Medico of Painted
Springs
Riding the Wind
The Return of Daniel
Boone
Robbers of the Range
The Bandit Trail
42: The Spoilers
Riders of the West
'Neath Brooklyn Bridge
43: Haunted Ranch
The Rangers Take Over
The Ghost Rider
The Avenging Rider
The Carson City Cyclone
Cowboy Commandos
The Stranger from Pecos
Robin Hood of the Range
44: Adventures of Mark Twain
Sonora Stagecoach
Range Law
Valley of Vengeance
Outlaw Trail
Marked Trails
Law Men
The Laramie Trail
Outlaw Roundup
Trigger Law
Dead or Alive
Song of the Range
45: The Cisco Kid Returns
The Navajo Kid
Fighting Bill Carson
His Brother's Ghost
Three in the Saddle
Flaming Bullets
Prairie Rustlers
The Cherokee Flash

46: Thundertown
Six-Gun Man
Border Bandits
Overland Riders
Outlaw of the Plains
Desert Horseman
Landrush
47: Trailing Danger
Six-Gun Serenade
Code of the Saddle
Bowery Buckaroos
Thundergap Outlaws
48: Six-Gun Law
Song of the Drifter
Blood on the Moon
Indian Agent
Crossed Trails
Courtin' Trouble
49: Gunning for Justice
Frontier Revenge
The Gay Amigo
50: Cow Town
The Cowboy and the Prize-
fighter
Hostile Country
Border Rangers
Arizona Territory
Over the Border
West of the Brazos
Marshal of Heldorado
Colorado Ranger
The Crooked River
Fast on the Draw
Outlaw Gold
Six-Gun Mesa
51: Nevada Badmen
Valley of Fire
The Whistling Hills
54: The Lawless Rider
58: Escape from Red Rock

Vivienne Osborne (1900-
1931: Beloved Bachelor
32: Husband's Holiday
Two Kinds of Women
Two Seconds
The Famous Ferguson Case
Dark Horse
Week-End Marriage
Life Begins

33: Luxury Liner
Sailor Be Good!
Men Are Such Fools
Phantom Broadcast
Supernatural
Tomorrow at Seven
The Devil's in Love
35: No More Ladies
36: Let's Sing Again
Wives Never Know
Follow Your Heart
Sinner Take All
37: Champagne Waltz
The Crime Nobody Saw
She Asked for it
40: Primrose Path
Captain Caution
So You Won't Tell
44: I Accuse My Parents
46: Dragonwyck

Michael O'Shea (1906-
1941: Mr. District Attorney
43: Lady of Burlesque
Jack London
44: The Eve of St. Mark
The Man from Frisco
Something for the Boys
45: Circumstantial Evidence
Where Do We Go from
Here?
It's a Pleasure
47: Violence
Last of the Redmen
48: Smart Woman
49: Parole, Inc.
The Threat
Captain China
The Big Wheel
50: The Underworld Story (or,
The Whipped)
51: Disc Jockey
The Model and the
Marriage Broker
Fixed Bayonets
52: Bloodhounds of Broadway
54: It Should Happen to You
55: The Sea Chase

Milo O'Shea (c1923-
1963: Carry on, Cabby
64: Never Put it in Writing
67: Ulysses
68: Barbarella
Romeo and Juliet
69: The Angel Levine

Bibi Osterwald (1921-
1961: Parrish
64: The World of Henry Orient
66: A Fine Madness
67: The Tiger Makes Out

Maureen O'Sullivan (1911-
1930: Song o' My Heart
The Princess and the
Plumber
So This Is London
Just Imagine
31: A Connecticut Yankee in
King Arthur's Court
Skyline
Thirty Days
32: The Big Shot
Tarzan the Ape Man
Skyscraper Souls
Slightly Married
Silver Lining
Payment Deferred
Okay, America!
Fast Companions
Strange Interlude
Penalty of Fame
The Information Kid
33: The Cohens and the
Kellys in Trouble
Tugboat Annie
Stage Mother
Robbers' Roost
34: Tarzan and His Mate
Hide-Out
The Barretts of Wimpole
Street
The Thin Man
35: David Copperfield
West Point of the Air
The Flame Within

35: Anna Karenina
    Woman Wanted
    The Bishop Misbehaves
    Cardinal Richelieu
36: The Voice of Bugle Ann
    The Devil Doll
    Tarzan Escapes
37: The Emperor's Candle-
    sticks
    A Day at the Races
    Between Two Women
    My Dear Miss Aldrich
38: A Yank at Oxford
    Port of Seven Seas
    Hold that Kiss
    The Crowd Roars
    Spring Madness
39: Let Us Live
    Tarzan Finds a Son
40: Pride and Prejudice
    Sporting Good
    Sterling Metal
41: Maisie Was a Lady
    Tarzan's Secret Treasure
42: Tarzan's New York
    Adventure
48: The Big Clock
50: Where Danger Lives
52: Bonzo Goes to College
53: All I Desire
    Mission over Korea
54: Duffy of San Quentin
    The Steel Cage
58: Wild Heritage
65: Never Too Late
69: The Phynx

Peter O'Toole (1933-
1960: Kidnapped
    The Day They Robbed the
    Bank of England
    Savage Innocents
62: Lawrence of Arabia
64: Becket
65: What's New Pussycat?
    Lord Jim
66: How to Steal a Million
    Dollars
    The Bible
    Will Adams (project)
67: Night of the Generals

    The Great Katherine
68: The Lion in Winter
69: Goodbye, Mr. Chips
    Country Dance

Rafaela Ottiano (1895-1942)
1932: As You Desire Me
    Grand Hotel
    Washington Masquerade
33: She Done Him Wrong
    Bondage
    Ann Vickers
    Her Man
34: Mandalay
    All Men Are Enemies
    A Lost Lady
    Great Expectations
    The Last Gentleman
35: Enchanted April
    Lottery Lovers
    The Florentine Dagger
    One Frightened Night
    Curly Top
    Remember Last Night
36: We're Only Human
    Anthony Adverse
    Riffraff
    The Devil-Doll
    Mad Holiday
    That Girl from Paris
37: Seventh Heaven
    Maytime
    League of Frightened Men
38: I'll Give a Million
    Suez
39: Paris Honeymoon
40: The Long Voyage Home
    Victory
41: Topper Returns
42: The Adventures of Martin
    Eden

Maria Ouspenskaya (1876-1949)
1936: Dodsworth
37: Conquest
39: Love Affair
    The Rains Came
    Judge Hardy's Son
40: The Story of Dr. Ehrlich's
    Magic Bullet

1064

40: Beyond Tomorrow
Dance, Girl, Dance
Waterloo Bridge
The Mortal Storm
The Man I Married
41: Shanghai Gesture
Kings Row
The Wolf Man
42: The Mystery of Marie
Roget
43: Frankenstein Meets the
Wolf Man
45: Tarzan and the Amazons
46: I've Always Loved You
47: Wyoming
49: A Kiss in the Dark

Lynne Overman (1887-1943)
1934: Midnight
Little Miss Marker
The Great Flirtation
She Loves Me Not
You Belong to Me
Broadway Bill
35: Rumba
Paris in Spring
Men Without Names
Two for Tonight
Enter Madame
36: Collegiate
Poppy
Yours for the Asking
Three Married Men
Jungle Princess
37: Partners in Crime
Nobody's Baby
Don't Tell the Wife
Murder Goes to College
Wild Money
Hotel Haywire
Night Club Scandal
True Confession
38: Big Broadcast of 1938
Her Jungle Love
Hunted Men
Spawn of the North
Sons of the Legion
Men with Wings
Ride a Crooked Mile
39: Persons in Hiding

Death of a Champion
Union Pacific
40: Edison the Man
Typhoon
Safari
Northwest Mounted Police
41: Aloma of the South Seas
Caught in the Draft
The Hard Boiled Canary
New York Town
42: Roxie Hart
Reap the Wild Wind
The Forest Ranger
Silver Queen
Star-Spangled Rhythm
43: Dixie
The Desert Song

Frank Overton (1918-1967)
1957: The True Story of Jesse
James
58: Desire Under the Elms
Lonelyhearts
59: The Last Mile
60: Wild River
The Dark at the Top of
the Stairs
61: Posse from Hell
Claudelle Inglish
62: To Kill a Mockingbird
64: Fail Safe

Catherine Dale Owen (1903-1965)
1929: His Glorious Night
30: The Rogue Song
Strictly Unconventional
Born Reckless
Such Men Are Dangerous
Today
31: Behind Office Doors
Defenders of the Law
The Circle

Reginald Owen (1887-
1929: The Letter
31: Platinum Blonde
The Man in Possession
32: A Woman Commands
Lovers Courageous
Downstairs

32: The Man Called Back
Sherlock Holmes
Bill of Divorcement
33: Robbers' Roost
A Study in Scarlet
The Big Brain
Double Harness
Voltaire
The Narrow Corner
Queen Christina
34: Fashions of 1934
Nana
House of Rothschild
Madame Du Barry
Mandalay
Countess of Monte Cristo
Where Sinners Meet
Of Human Bondage
Here Is My Heart
The Human Side
Stingaree
Music in the Air
35: The Good Fairy
Call of the Wild
Anna Karenina
Escapade
A Tale of Two Cities
The Bishop Misbehaves
Enchanted April
36: Rose Marie
Petticoat Fever
Trouble for Two
The Great Ziegfeld
Love on the Run
Girl on the Front Page
Adventure in Manhattan
Yours for the Asking
Rich and Reckless
37: Dangerous Number
Personal Property
Madame X
The Bride Wore Red
Conquest
Rosalie
38: Paradise for Three
Everybody Sing!
Three Loves Has Nancy
Vacation with Love
A Christmas Carol
The Girl Downstairs

Kidnapped
Stablemates (co-writ.)
Sweethearts
39: Balalaika
Fast and Loose
Bridal Suite
The Bad Little Angel
Remember?
Hotel Imperial
The Real Glory
40: The Earl of Chicago
The Ghost Comes Home
Florian
Hullabaloo
41: Blonde Inspiration
Free and Easy
They Met in Bombay
Lady be Good
Tarzan's Secret Treasure
A Woman's Face
Charley's Aunt
42: Mrs. Miniver
White Cargo
Random Harvest
We Were Dancing
Woman of the Year
I Married an Angel
Pierre of the Plains
Somewhere I'll Find You
Cairo
Mademoiselle France
43: Above Suspicion
Three Hearts for Julia
Forever and a Day
Salute to the Marines
Reunion
Madame Curie
Assignment in Brittany
Lassie Come Home
44: National Velvet
The Canterville Ghost
45: The Diary of a Chamber-
maid
She Went to the Races
Monsieur Beaucaire
Valley of Decision
Captain Kidd
The Sailor Takes a Wife
Kitty
46: Cluny Brown

46: Mrs. Loring's Secret
47: Thunder in the Valley
Green Dolphin Street
If Winter Comes
Imperfect Lady (or, They
Met at Midnight)
The Pirate
Julia Misbehaves
48: The Hills of Home
49: Challenge to Lassie
The Secret Garden
50: Kim
Grounds for Marriage
The Miniver Story
53: The Great Diamond
Robbery
54: Red Garters
Affairs of State
58: Darby's Rangers
62: Five Weeks in a Balloon
63: The Thrill of it All
Tammy and the Doctor
64: Mary Poppins
Voice of the Hurricane
67: Rosie

Tudor Owen
1949: Top o' the Morning
50: Montana
52: When in Rome
The Black Castle
My Cousin Rachel
53: Treasure of the Golden
Condor
Dangerous When Wet
Back to God's Country
How to Marry a Millionaire
54: Arrow in the Dust
Yankee Pasha
Brigadoon
55: The King's Thief
57: The Lonely Man
The Story of Mankind
61: Frontier Uprising
The Most Dangerous Man
Alive
A Hundred and One
Dalmatians (voice)
62: Jack, the Giant Killer

Patricia Owens
1957: Island in the Sky
No Down Payment
Sayonara
58: The Law and Jake Wade
The Fly
The Gun Runners
59: These Thousand Hills
Five Gates to Hell
60: Hell to Eternity
61: Seven Women from Hell
X-15
64: Walk a Tightrope
65: Black Spurs
67: The Destructors

P

Jack Paar (1918-
1950: Walk Softly, Stranger
51: Love Nest
53: Down Among the Sheltering
Palms

Sarah Padden
1929: Wonder of Women
The Sophomore
30: Today
31: The Great Meadow
Sob Sister
Yellow Ticket
32: Cross Examination
Young America
Midnight Lady
Blondie of the Follies
Tess of the Storm Country
Wild Girl
33: Women Won't Tell
Face in the Sky
Important Witness
The Power and the Glory
34: As the Earth Turns
Man of Two Worlds
David Harum
Finishing School
He Was Her Man
The Marrying Widow
Little Man, What Now?
Spitfire

34: The Sin of Nora Moran
The Defense Rests
Hat, Coat, and Glove
The Fountain
When Strangers Meet
35: The Hoosier School-
master
Anna Karenina
A Dog of Flanders
37: Youth on Parole
Exiled to Shanghai
38: Women in Prison
Rich Man, Poor Girl
Romance of the Limber-
lost
Woman Against Woman
Little Orphan Annie
39: Angels Wash Their Faces
Let Freedom Ring
Zero Hour
Should a Girl Marry?
40: Forgotten Girls
Son of the Navy
Lone Star Raiders
Chad Hanna
41: City of Missing Girls
The Man Who Lost
Himself
In Old Colorado
A Woman's Face
Tight Shoes
Murder by Invitation
Reg'lar Fellers
The Corsican Brothers
42: The Mad Monster
Snuffy Smith--Yard Bird
Heart of the Rio Grande
Riders of the West
Law and Order
43: Assignment in Brittany
Hangmen Also Die
So This Is Washington
Jack London
44: Ghost Guns
Girl Rush
Range Law
Summer Storm
45: Dakota
Honeymoon Ahead
Identity Unknown

Marshal of Laredo
46: Angel on My Shoulder
Joe Palooka--Champ
So Goes My Love
That Brennan Girl
Gentleman Joe Palooka
47: The Millerson Case
Joe Palooka in The Knock-
out
48: The Dude Goes West
The Return of the Whistler
Fighting Mad
My Dog Shep
49: Homicide
Frontier Revenge
50: House by the River
Gunslingers
The Missourians
51: Utah Wagon Train
52: Big Jim McLain
55: Prince of Players

Lea Padovani (1920-
1949: Give Us This Day
50: Eyes of the Sahara
Barrier of the Law
51: Three Steps North
53: Tempi Nostri
57: Angels of Darkness
Scandal in Sorrento
Montparnasse
59: The Naked Maja
Anatomy of Love
61: An Eye for an Eye
62: The Reluctant Saint
64: The Empty Canvas
68: Candy

Anita Page (1910-
1928: Our Dancing Daughters   S
While the City Sleeps   S
The Flying Ensign   S
Telling the World   S
29: Protection   SSE
Broadway Melody
Flying Feet   SSE
Hollywood Revue of 1929
Our Modern Maidens
Speedway
30: Navy Blues

30: War Nurse
    Caught Short
    Free and Easy
    Our Blushing Brides
    Little Accident
31: The Easiest Way
    Sidewalks of New York
    A Gentleman's Fate
    Reducing
32: Under Eighteen
    Are You Listening?
    Justice for Sale
    Skyscraper Souls
    Prosperity
    Night Court
33: Jungle Bride
    Soldiers of the Storm
    The Big Cage
    I Have Lived
    The Phantom Broadcast
36: Hitchhike to Heaven

Bradley Page
1934: Gentlemen Are Born
    Against the Law
35: The Best Man Wins
    Baby Face Harrington
    One Hour Late
    Shadow of Doubt
    Red Hot Tires
    The Nut Farm
    My Dynamite
    Unwelcome Stranger
    Chinatown Squad
    Champagne for Breakfast
    Cheers of the Crowd
    Cappy Ricks Returns
    King Solomon of Broad-
        way
    Public Menace
    Forced Landing
36: Six of a Kind
    Shadows of Sing Sing
    Search for Beauty
    Good Dame
    Before Midnight
    Fighting Rangers
    He Was Her Man
    Hell Bent for Love
    Name the Woman

I Hate Women
    The Crime of Helen
        Stanley
    Take the Stand
    Million Dollar Ransom
    Woman Trap
    The Princess Comes
        Across
    Three of a Kind
    Two in a Crowd
37: Don't Tell the Wife
    Outcasts of Poker Flat
    Trouble in Morocco
    Her Husband Lies
    Fifty Roads to Town
    There Goes My Girl
    You Can't Beat Love
    Hideaway
    Super Sleuth
    Music for Madame
38: Crashing Hollywood
    Night Spot
    Go Chase Yourself
    The Affairs of Annabel
    Crime Ring
    Annabella Takes a Tour
    Fugitives for a Night
    The Law West of Tomb-
        stone
39: Twelve Crowded Hours
    Fixer Dugan
40: Cafe Hostess
    Girl from Havana
    Enemy Agent
41: Footlight Fever
    Scattergood Baines
    Beyond the Sacramento
    The Big Store
    Badlands of Dakota
    Scattergood Meets Broad-
        way
    Mr. District Attorney in
        the Carter Case
42: Sons of the Pioneers
    Isle of Missing Men
    War Dogs
    Top Sergeant
    The Traitor Within
43: Sherlock Holmes in
        Washington

50: Broken Arrow
51: 14 Hours
Bird of Paradise
Anne of the Indies
52: Belles on Their Toes
Les Miserables
Stars and Stripes Forever
54: Prince Valiant
Demetrius and the
Gladiators
Princess of the Nile
The Gambler from
Natchez
55: White Feather
Seven Angry Men
56: The Last Hunt
The Ten Commandments
Love Me Tender
57: Omar Khayyam
The River's Edge
58: From the Earth to the
Moon
60: Why Must I Die?
Journey to the Lost City
61: The Most Dangerous Man
Alive
62: Tales of Terror (Case
of N. Valdemar seq.)
63: Rome 1585
The Haunted Palace

Janis Paige (1922-
1944: Bathing Beauty
Hollywood Canteen
I Won't Play
46: Of Human Bondage
The Time, the Place,
and the Girl
Two Guys from Milwaukee
Her Kind of Man
47: Cheyenne
Love and Learn
Always Together
Royal Flush
48: Wallflower
Winter Meeting
One Sunday Afternoon
Romance on the High Seas
49: The House Across the
Street

The Younger Brothers
50: This Side of the Law
51: Mr. Universe
Two Gals and a Guy
Fugitive Lady
53: Remains to be Seen
57: Silk Stockings
60: Please Don't Eat the
Daisies
61: Bachelor in Paradise
63: The Caretakers
Follow the Boys
67: Welcome to Hard Times

Mabel Paige (c1880-1953)
1942: Lucky Jordan
My Heart Belongs to Daddy
Girls' Town
Star-Spangled Rhythm
43: Young and Willing
Happy-Go-Lucky
The Crystal Ball
The Good Fellows
The Prodigal's Mother
True to Life
44: You Can't Return Love
Someone to Remember
National Barn Dance
Fun Time
Can't Help Singing
45: Kitty
Out of this World
Dangerous Partners
Murder He Says
She Wouldn't Say Yes
46: Behind Green Lights
Nocturne
47: Beat the Band
Johnny O'Clock
Her Husband's Affairs
48: The Mating of Millie
If You Knew Susie
Half Past Midnight
Johnny Belinda
Hollow Triumph
49: Roseanna McCoy
50: Edge of Doom
The Petty Girl
52: The Sniper

Robert Paige (1910-
1936: Smart Blonde
Cain and Mabel
37: Meet the Girl Friend
Murder in Swingtime
You Can't Win
Crime of the Year
38: There's Always a Woman
The Lady Objects
When G-Men Step In
Who Killed Gail Preston?
The Main Event
Highway Patrol
The Last Warning
I Stand Accused
39: Death of a Champion
Flying G-Men (ser.)
Homicide Bureau
40: Thoroughbred
Emergency Squad
Parole Fixer
Women Without Names
Opened by Mistake
Golden Gloves
41: Dancing on a Dime
The Monster and the Girl
San Antonio Rose
Melody Lane
Hellzapoppin'!
42: You're Telling Me
Don't Get Personal
Jailhouse Blues
What's Cookin'?
Almost Married
Pardon My Sarong
Get Hep to Love
43: Get Going
Crazy House
Hi Buddy!
How's About It?
Cowboy in Manhattan
Frontier Badmen
Mr. Big
Son of Dracula
Sherlock Holmes in
  Washington
Fired Wife
Hi Ya, Chum!
44: Follow the Boys
Her Primitive Man

Can't Help Singing
You Can't Ration Love
45: Shady Lady
46: Tangier
47: Red Stallion
48: Flame
Blonde Ice
49: The Green Promise
53: Abbott & Costello Go to
  Mars
Split Second
58: The Big Payoff
59: It Happened to Jane
60: Marriage-Go-Round
63: Bye Bye Birdie

Nestor Paiva (1905-1966)
1937: Ride a Crooked Mile
Beau Geste
Bachelor Mother
The Primrose Path
Northwest Mounted Police
38: Prison Trail
40: Arise My Love
Tall, Dark, and Handsome
Reap the Wild Wind
Johnny Eager
Road to Morocco
The Marines Fly High
Dark Streets of Cairo
41: Hold Back the Dawn
The Kid from Kansas
42: Fly by Night
The Girl from Alaska
Broadway
The Hard Way
Timber
43: The Crystal Ball
Rhythm of the Islands
The Dancing Masters
The Desert Song
The Song of Bernadette
44: The Purple Heart
Tampico
The Falcon in Mexico
45: A Medal for Benny
The Southerner
Salome, Where She Danced
Nob Hill
A Thousand and One Nights

45: Along the Navajo Trail
    Fear
46: Humoresque
    Road to Utopia
    Sensation Hunters
    The Last Crooked Mile
    Badman's Territory
47: The Lone Wolf in Mexico
    Ramrod
    Carnival in Costa Rica
    Shoot to Kill!
    A Likely Story
    Robin Hood of Monterey
    Road to Rio
48: Mr. Reckless
    Adventures of Casanova
    Angel's Alley
    Joan of Arc
    Mr. Blanding Builds His
      Dream House
    The Paleface
49: Bride of Vengeance
    Alias Mike Beal
    Mighty Joe Young
    Follow Me Quietly
    Oh You Beautiful Doll!
    The Inspector General
50: Young Man with a Horn
51: Flame of Stanbul
    The Great Caruso
    Jim Thorpe--All-
      American
    A Millionaire for Christy
    The Lady Pays Off
    Double Dynamite
52: Phone Call from a
      Stranger
    Five Fingers
    Mara Maru
    The Fabulous Señorita
    South Pacific Trail
53: Bandits of Corsica
    Prisoners of the Casbah
    The Killer Cop
54: Jivaro
    Four Guns to the Border
    The Creature from the
      Black Lagoon
    The Desperado
55: New York Confidential

    Revenge of the Creature
    Tarantula
    Hell on Frisco Bay
56: Comanche
    The Mole People
    Ride the High Iron
    Scandal, Inc.
57: Guns of Fort Petticoat
    Les Girls
    10,000 Bedrooms
    C.I.C.
58: The Deep Six
    The Lady Takes a Flyer
    Outcasts of the City
    The Left-Handed Gun
    The Case Against Brooklyn
59: Pier 5--Havana
    Vice Squad
    The Nine Lives of Elfredo
      Baca
60: The Purple Gang
    Can-Can
61: Frontier Uprising
62: The Three Stooges in
      Orbit
    Girls! Girls! Girls!
    The Four Horsemen of the
      Apocalypse
    The Martians
    The Wild Westerners
63: California
    The Tony Fontcune Story
64: Madmen of Mandoras
66: Jesse James Meets
      Frankenstein's Daughter
67: The Spirit Is Willing

Jack Palance (1920-
1950: Panic in the Streets
    Halls of Montezuma
52: Sudden Fear
53: Shane
    Second Chance
    Arrowhead
    Flight to Tangier
54: Man in the Attic
    Sign of the Pagan
    The Silver Chalice
55: Kiss of Fire
    A Handful of Clouds

55: The Big Knife
    I Died a Thousand Times
56: Attack!
57: House of Numbers
    The Lonely Man
58: The Man Inside
59: Ten Seconds to Hell
60: Beyond All Limits
62: Sword of the Conqueror
    Barabbas
    Warriors Five
63: The Mongols
64: Contempt
65: Once a Thief
    Night Train to Milan
66: The Professionals
67: Kill a Dragon
68: The Strange Case of
      Dr. Jekyll and Mr.
      Hyde (TV)
    The Torture Garden
    They Came to Rob Las
      Vegas
    The Desperadoes
69: The Mercenary
    Che!
    The McMasters
    Mission: Rommel
    Legion of the Damned
    Monte Walsh

Eugene Pallette (1889-1954)
1928: Lights of New York
  29: The Canary Murder Case
    The Dummy
    Men Are Like that
    The Greene Murder Case
    The Studio Murder
      Mystery
    Pointed Heels
    The Love Parade
    The Virginian
    The Kibitzer
  30: The Benson Murder Case
    Follow Through
    The Sea God
    Slightly Scarlet
    Let's Go Native
    Border Legion
    The Law Rides West

Sea Legs
Playboy of Paris
Santa Fe Trail
Paramount on Parade
31: Fighting Caravan
    It Pays to Advertise
    Gun Smoke
    Dude Ranch
    The Adventures of Huckle-
      berry Finn
    Girls about Town
32: Shanghai Express
    Dancers in the Dark
    Thunder Below
    Strangers of the Evening
    Night Mayor
    Wild Girl
    Phantom Fame
    Pig Boat
    The Half-Naked Truth
    Tom Brown of Culver
33: Made on Broadway
    Hell Below
    Storm at Daybreak
    Shanghai Express
    Mr. Skitch
    The Kennel Murder Case
    From Headquarters
    The Champs (short)
    Sailors Beware (short)
    One Awful Night (short)
34: Caravan
    Cross Country Cruise
    Friends of Mr. Sweeney
    I've Got Your Number
    The Dragon Murder Case
    Strictly Dynamite
    One Exciting Adventure
    New Dealers (short)
    Making the Rounds (short)
    News Hounds (short)
35: Bordertown
    All the King's Horses
    Baby Face Harrington
    Black Sheep
    Steamboat 'Round the Bend
36: The Ghost Goes West
    The Golden Arrow
    Easy to Take
    My Man Godfrey

36: Luckiest Girl in this
World
Stowaway
37: The Crime Nobody Saw
Clarence
Topper
She Had to Eat
Song of the City
One Hundred Men and a
Girl
38: Adventures of Robin Hood
There Goes My Heart
39: Wife, Husband, and
Friend
Mr. Smith Goes to
Washington
First Love
40: Young Tom Edison
It's a Date
Sandy Is a Lady
A Little Bit of Heaven
He Stayed for Breakfast
The Mark of Zorro
41: Ride, Kelly, Ride!
The Lady Eve
Unfinished Business
Appointment for Love
Swamp Water
World Premiere
The Bride Came C.O.D.
42: The Male Animal
Almost Married
Lady in a Jam
Are Husbands Necessary?
The Forest Rangers
The Big Street
Tales of Manhattan
Silver Queen
43: Strictly Dangerous
It Ain't Hay
Heaven Can Wait
The Gang's All Here
The Kansan
44: Laramie Trail
Pin-Up Girl
Manhattan Serenade
Heavenly Days
Sensations of 1945
Step Lively
In the Meantime, Darling

45: Lake Placid Serenade
The Cheaters
46: In Old Sacramento
47: Suspense
48: Silver River

Betsy Palmer (1929-
1955: Mr. Roberts
The Long Gray Line
Queen Bee
57: The Tin Star
58: The True Story of Lynn
Stuart
59: The Last Angry Man
It Happened to Jane

Byron Palmer
1954: Man in the Attic
55: Ma and Pa Kettle at
Waikiki
56: Emergency Hospital
Glory
The Best Things in Life
Are Free

Gregg Palmer (1927-
1951: The Cimarron Kid
52: Battle at Apache Pass
Son of Ali Baba
Red Ball Express
Francis Goes to West
Point
Sally and St. Anne
The Raiders
Back at the Front
The Redhead from Wyoming
53: Column South
Veils of Bagdad
The Golden Blade
The All-American
54: Taza, Son of Cochise
Magnificent Obsession
Playgirl
55: To Hell and Back
56: The Creature Walks
Among Us
Hilda Crane
57: Zombies of Mora-Tau
Revolt at Fort Laramie
From Hell it Came

58: Thundering Jets
The Female Animal
59: Rebel Set
61: Most Dangerous Man Alive
Five Guns to Tombstone
Gun Fight
The Cat Burglar
62: Forty Pounds of Trouble
64: The Quick Gun

Lilli Palmer (1914-
1934: Crime Unlimited
36: First Offense
Secret Agent
Good Morning, Boys!
37: The Silent Barrier
Sunset in Vienna
Command Performance
38: The Man with a Hundred
Faces
40: The Door with Seven
Locks
A Girl Must Live
41: Chamber of Horrors
42: Thunder Rock
43: The Gentle Sex
English Without Tears
44: The Rake's Progress (or,
The Notorious Gentle-
man)
46: Cloak and Dagger
My Girl Tisa
47: Beware of Pity
Body and Soul
48: No Minor Vices
49: Her Man Gilbey
51: Wicked City
The Long Dark Hall
52: The Four Poster
53: Main Street to Broadway
Is Anna Anderson
Anastasia?
58: La Vie à Deux
Tempestuous Love
59: But not for Me
The Glass Tower
60: Between Time and
Eternity
Conspiracy of Hearts
61: The Pleasure of His
Company

Modigliani of Montparnasse
62: The Counterfeit Traitor
Torpedo Bay
63: The Miracle of the White
Stallions
64: Adorable Julia
Of Wayward Love
65: The Amorous Adventures
of Moll Flanders
Operation Crossbow (or,
The Great Spy Mission)
And so to Bed
66: Maedchen in Uniform (or,
Girls in Uniform)
67: Jack of Diamonds (bit)
68: Nobody Runs Forever
Sebastian
Oedipus the King
High Commissioner
69: Hard Contract
De Sade

Maria Palmer (1924-
1943: Mission to Moscow
44: Days of Glory
45: Lady on a Train
46: Rendezvous 24
47: The Other Love
The Web
48: Thirteen Lead Soldiers
50: Surrender
51: Strictly Dishonorable
53: By the Light of the Silvery
Moon
Nostradamus and the Queen
Flight Nurse
City of Women
56: Three for Jamie Dawn
58: Outcasts of the City

Peter Palmer (1931-
1959: Li'l Abner

Luciana Paluzzi (1931-
1954: Three Coins in the Fountain
58: Tank Force
59: Sea Fury
60: Journey to the Lost City
61: Return to Peyton Place
64: Muscle Beach Party
65: Thunderball

65: Vice and Virtue
66: To Trap a Spy
67: The Venetian Affair
    Chuka
68: 99 Women
    A Black Veil for Lisa
    Showdown
    No Roses for OSS 117
    (Fr.)
    Now You See it, Now You
    Don't (TV)
69: The Green Slime

Franklin Pangborn (1889-1958)
1928: Blonde for a Night   S
    On Trial   S
    My Friend from India   S
29: The Sap   PT
    Masquerade
    The Crazy Nut
    Watch Out
30: The Lady Surrenders
    A short
    A short
    A short
    Cheer Up and Smile
    Not so Dumb
    Torchy Turns the Trick
    Torchy's Nightcap
    What Price Taxi?
    Torchy's Vocation
31: Her Man
    A Woman of Experience
32: A Fool's Advice
    Mack Sennett Comedy
    shorts
33: International House
    Design for Living
    Professional Sweetheart
    Headline Shooters
    various shorts
    Important Witness
    Only Yesterday
    Flying Down to Rio
34: Manhattan Love Song
    Tomorrow's Children
    Young and Beautiful
    Strictly Dynamite

    a short
    Unknown Blonde
    Many Happy Returns
    Kelly of the U.S.A.
    That's Gratitude
    College Rhythm
35: Headline Woman
    A $1000 a Minute
    Tomorrow's Youth
    8 Bells
36: Don't Gamble with Love
    My Man Godfrey
    To Mary with Love
    The Mandarin Mystery
    Hats Off
    Tango
    Doughnuts and Society
37: Step Lively Jeeves!
    The Lady Escapes
    She Had to Eat
    Swing High, Swing Low
    Turn Off the Moon
    Easy Living
    Thrill of a Lifetime
    When Love Is Young
    A Star Is Born
    Dangerous Number
    She's Dangerous
    Hotel Haywire
    Dangerous Holiday
    All Over Town
    Life of the Party
    Stage Door
    Living on Love
38: Vivacious Lady
    She Married an Artist
    Rebecca of Sunnybrook
    Farm
    Three Blind Mice
    Always Goodbye
    Joy of Living
    Just Around the Corner
    Carefree
    Bluebeard's Eighth Wife
    Dr. Rhythm
    Love on Toast
    Mad About Music
    Meet the Mayor

39: Broadway Serenade
    The Girl Downstairs
    Four's a Crowd
    Topper Takes a Trip
    Fifth Avenue Girl
40: Turnabout
    The Villain Still Pursued
    Her
    Elsa Maxwell's Public
    Deb No. 1
    Christmas in July
    The Hit Parade of 1941
    The Bank Dick
    Spring Parade
41: Where Did You Get that
    Girl?
    A Girl, a Guy, and a Gob
    Flame of New Orleans
    Sullivan's Travels
    Bachelor Daddy
    Obliging Young Lady
    Tillie the Toiler
    Never Give a Sucker an
    Even Break
    Weekend for Three
    Mr. District Attorney
    in the Carter Case
42: George Washington Slept
    Here
    Moonlight Masquerade
    Palm Beach Story
    Now Voyager
    What's Cooking?
    Call Out the Marines
43: Two Weeks to Live
    Reveille with Beverly
    Holy Matrimony
    Crazy House
    Slick Chick
    Strictly in the Groove
    Honeymoon Lodge
    His Butler's Sister
44: Hail the Conquering Hero
    The Great Moment
    Reckless Age
45: The Horn Blows at Mid-
    night
    Hollywood and Vine
    See My Lawyer
    You Came Along

        Tell it to a Star
46: Lover Come Back
    Two Guys from Milwaukee
47: Calendar Girl
    I'll be Yours
    Mad Wednesday (or, The
    Sin of Harold Diddlebock)
48: Romance on the High Seas
49: My Dream Is Yours
    Down Memory Lane
57: The Story of Mankind

Irene Papas (1926-
1951: Necropolitia
53: The Man from Cairo
54: Theodora--Slave Empress
56: Tribute to a Bad Man
    The Power and the Prize
58: Attila the Hun
60: The Unfaithfuls
61: The Guns of Navarone
62: Antigone
63: Electra
64: Zorba the Greek
    The Moonspinners
68: The Desperate Ones
    We Still Kill the Old Way
    Beyond the Mountains
69: Z (Fr.)
    A Dream of Kings
    The Brotherhood
    Anne of the Thousand Days

Paul Panzer (1872-1958)
1928: Glorious Betsy   PT
29: Redskin   SSE
    Hawk of the Hills   S
31: First Aid
    The Montana Kid
    Cavalier of the West
33: A Bedtime Story
34: Bolero
39: Beasts of Berlin
45: Hotel Berlin
47: The Perils of Pauline

Jerry Paris
1950: Cyrano de Bergerac
53: The Glass Wall
    Sabre Jet

54: Drive a Crooked Road
Prisoner of War
55: Unchained
Marty
The Naked Street
The View from Pompey's
Head
Good Morning, Miss Dove
Hell's Horizon
56: D-Day, the 7th of June
I Lived Before
57: Zero Hour!
Man on the Prowl
58: Sing, Boy, Sing
The Female Animal
The Lady Takes a Flyer
The Naked and the Dead
59: No Name on the Bullet

Cecil Parker (1897-
1933: The Silver Spoon
A Cuckoo in the Nest
37: Storm in a Teacup
Dark Journey
38: The Lady Vanishes
The Citadel
46: Caesar and Cleopatra
Hungry Hill
47: Captain Boycott
The First Gentleman
49: Dear Mr. Prohack (or,
The Chiltern Hundreds)
The Weaker Sex
I Was Monty's Double (or,
Hell, Heaven, or
Hoboken)
Under Capricorn
Affairs of a Rogue
The Amazing Mr. Beecham
51: Tony Draws a Horse
52: The Man in the White
Suit
I Believe in You
The Magic Box
Quartet (The Colonel's
Lady seq.)
54: Isn't Life Wonderful?
The Detective (or, Father
Brown)
55: The Constant Husband

Cocktails in the Kitchen
(or, For Better, For
Worse)
56: The Court Jester
His Excellency
It's Great to be Young
The Lady Killers
23 Paces to Baker Street
57: True as a Turtle
Paradise Lagoon (or,
The Admirable Crichton)
58: Indiscreet
A Tale of Two Cities
59: Happy Is the Bride
The Wreck of the Mary
Deare
60: The Swiss Family Robinson
A French Mistress
Under Ten Flags
61: The Pure Hell of St.
Trinian's
On the Fiddle
Make Mine a Double (or,
The Night We Dropped a
Clanger)
62: Petticoat Pirates
Follow that Horse!
63: Heavens Above
64: The Comedy Man
Guns at Batasi
Carry on, Jack
The Brain
65: Study in Terror
The Amorous Adventures
of Moll Flanders
Operation Snafu
66: Lady L
A Man Could Get Killed
67: Psycho Circus
68: The Amorous Mr. Pawn
69: Oh, What a Lovely War!

Cecilia Parker (c1915-
1931: Young as You Feel
32: Honor of the West
The Trail Drive
Gun Justice
Unknown Valley
Open Road
Mystery Ranch

1079

33: Riders of Destiny
Rainbow Ranch
The Fugitive
Secret Sinners
34: The Man Trailer
The Painted Veil
I Hate Women
Here Is My Heart
Honor of the Range
The Lost Jungle
35: Enter Madame
Below the Deadline
Naughty Marietta
Ah, Wilderness!
High School Girl
36: Three Live Ghosts
Old Dutch
The Mine with the Iron
Door
In His Steps
37: A Family Affair
Hollywood Cowboy
Sweetheart of the Navy
Girl Loves Boy
38: You're Only Young Once
Judge Hardy's Children
Love Finds Andy Hardy
Out West with the Hardys
39: Burn 'em Up, O'Connor
Andy Hardy Gets Spring
Fever
The Hardys Ride High
Judge Hardy and Son
40: Andy Hardy Meets a
Debutante
41: Gambling Daughters
Andy Hardy's Private
Secretary
Life Begins for Andy
Hardy
42: The Courtship of Andy
Hardy
Grand Central Murder
Seven Sweethearts
Andy Hardy's Double Life
Suicide Squadron
44: Andy Hardy's Blonde
Trouble
46: Love Laughs at Andy
Hardy

58: Andy Hardy Comes Home

Eleanor Parker (1922-
1941: They Died with Their
Boots on
42: The Busses Roar
Men of the Sky (short)
43: Mission to Moscow
The Mysterious Doctor
By Hook and by Crook
44: Hollywood Canteen
Between Two Worlds
The Very Thought of You
Crime by Night
The Last Ride
45: Pride of the Marines
46: Never Say Goodbye
Of Human Bondage
Escape Me Never
47: Woman in White
48: Voice of the Turtle
49: Three Secrets
50: Chain Lightning
Caged
51: Valentino
Millionaire for Christy
Detective Story
52: Scaramouche
Above and Beyond
53: Escape from Fort Bravo
54: The Naked Jungle
Valley of the Kings
55: Many Rivers to Cross
Interrupted Melody
The Man With the Golden
Arm
56: The King and Four Queens
57: Lizzie
The Seventh Sin
59: A Hole in the Head
60: Home from the Hill
61: Return to Peyton Place
62: Madison Avenue
64: Panic Button
65: The Sound of Music
Harlow (Electro.)
66: The Oscar
The American Dream
67: Warning Shot
The Tiger and the Pussy-
cat

68: Eye of the Cat

Fess Parker (1921-
1952: Untamed Frontier
No Room for the Groom
Springfield Rifle
53: Thunder over the Plains
Island in the Sky
The Kid from Left Field
Take Me to Town
54: Them
55: Battle Cry
Davy Crockett--King of
the Wild Frontier
56: Davy Crockett and the
River Pirates
Daniel Boone, Trail-
blazer
The Great Locomotive
Chase
Westward Ho the Wagons!
57: Ol' Yeller
58: The Light in the Forest
59: The Hangman
Alias Jesse James
The Jayhawkers
62: Hell Is for Heroes
66: Smoky

Jean Parker (1915-
1932: Divorce in the Family
33: The Secret of Madame
Blanche
Made on Broadway
Storm at Daybreak
Gabriel over the White
House
Rasputin and the Empress
What Price Innocence?
Lady for a Day
Little Women
Wild Birds
34: Two Alone
You Can't Buy Everything
Have a Heart
Sequoia
Lazy River
Operator 13
Caravan
A Wicked Woman

Limehouse Blues
35: Princess O'Hara
Murder in the Fleet
36: The Ghost Goes West
Farmer in the Dell
Texas Rangers
37: Life Begins with Love
The Barrier
38: Penitentiary
Arkansas Traveler
Romance of the Limber-
lost
39: She Married a Cop (short)
Flight at Midnight
The Flying Deuces
Zenobia
Romance of the Redwoods
Parents on Trial
40: Knights of the Range
Beyond Tomorrow
Son of the Navy
a short
41: Power Dive
Flying Blind
The Pittsburgh Kid
The Roar of the Press
No Hands on the Clock
42: Torpedo Boat
The Girl from Alaska
Hi Neighbor!
The Traitor Within
I Live on Danger
Hello Annapolis
Tomorrow We Live
43: High Explosive
Alaska Highway
Minesweeper
Deerslayer
44: Detective Kitty O'Day
The Girl Next Door
Lady in the Death House
The Navy Way
Bluebeard
One Body too Many
Dead Man's Eyes
45: Adventures of Kitty O'Day
47: Rolling Home
50: The Gunfighter
52: Toughest Man in Arizona
53: Those Redheads from
Seattle

```
54:  Black Tuesday                        Apache Drums
55:  A Lawless Street              52:  Caribbean
57:  The Parson and the            53:  The Vanquished
       Outlaw                             Sangaree
66:  Apache Uprising                      Kiss Me Kate
                                   54:  The Great Jesse James
Seth Parker: see Phillip Lord           Raid
                                   56:  The Naked Gun
Suzy Parker (1935-                 57:  Lure of the Swamp
1957:  Funny Face                  59:  Lone Texan
       Kiss Them for Me            60:  Walk Tall
58:  10 North Frederick                   Young Jesse James
59:  The Best of Everything               The High-Powered Rifle
61:  Circle of Deception           62:  Air Patrol
62:  The Interns                   64:  The Earth Dies Screaming
64:  Flight from Ashiya            66:  Waco
66:  Chamber of Horrors
                                   Barbara Parkins (1944-
Warren Parker                      1967:  Valley of the Dolls
1960:  Too Soon to Love            69:  Beyond the Valley of the
61:  The Hoodlum Priest                   Dolls
                                          The Kremlin Letter
Willard Parker (1912-
1937:  That Certain Woman          Larry Parks (1914-
       Over the Goal               1941:  Mystery Ship
       China Bandit                       Harvard, Here I Come!
       The Devil's Saddle                 Harmon of Michigan
         Legion                           Three Girls about Town
       Love Is on the Air                 You Belong to Me
38:  Invisible Menace                     Sing for Your Supper
       A Slight Case of Murder    42:  Blondie Goes to College
39:  Zero Hour!                            Canal Zone
43:  What a Woman!                         Flight Lieutenant
45:  The Fighting Guardsman                Submarine Raider
46:  One Way to Love                       Atlantic Convoy
       Relentless                         Honolulu Lu
       Renegades                          Hello Annapolis
48:  The Wreck of the                     You Were Never Lovelier
       Hesperus                           The Boogie Man Will Get
       You Gotta Stay Happy                 You
       The Mating of Millie                A Man's World
49:  Calamity Jane and Sam                 North of the Rockies
       Bass                                Alias Boston Blackie
       Slightly French                     They All Kissed the Bride
50:  Bodyhold                              Power of the Press
       Hunt the Man Down          43:  Deerslayer
       Bandit Queen                       Calling All Stars
       David Harding--Counter-            Reveille with Beverly
         spy                              Redhead from Manhattan
51:  My True Story                        Is Everybody Happy?
```

1082

43: First Comes Courage
44: The Racket Man
    The Black Parachute
    Stars on Parade
    Hey Rookie!
    She's a Sweetheart
45: Sergeant Mike
    Counter-Attack
46: Renegades
    The Jolson Story
47: Down to Earth
    The Swordsman
48: The Gallant Blade
49: Jolson Sings Again
50: Emergency Wedding
52: Love Is Better than Ever
58: The Cross-Up
62: Freud (or, The Secret
    Passion

Michael Parks (1938-
1965: Bus Riley's Back in Town
     Wild Seed
66: The Bible
    The Idol
67: The Happening
    Stranger on the Run (TV)
68: The Specialist (TV)
69: Then Came Bronson (TV
    pilot)

Parkyakarkus [Harry Einstein]
(1904-1958)
1936: Strike Me Pink
37: New Faces of 1937
    Life of the Party
38: She's Got Everything
42: A Yank in Libya
    The Yanks Are Coming
44: Sweethearts of the U.S.A.
45: Earl Carroll's Vanities
    Out of this World

Emory Parnell (c1900-
1939: Pacific Liner
     King of Alcatraz
     The Star Maker
     One Hour to Live
40: Sued for Libel
    If I Had My Way

Out West with the Peppers
41: The Case of the Black
    Parrot
    So Ends Our Night
    The Lady from Cheyenne
    A Shot in the Dark
    Kiss the Boys Goodbye
    The Blonde from Singapore
    Unholy Partners
    Louisiana Purchase
42: Cadets on Parade
    Wings for the Eagle
    They All Kissed the Bride
    Over My Dead Body
    I Married a Witch
43: Mission to Moscow
    That Natzy Nuisance
    Young Ideas
    The Unknown Guest
    Two Senoritas from Chicago
44: Address Unknown
    Casanova Brown
    The Falcon in Hollywood
    The Falcon in Mexico
    Gildersleeve's Ghost
    The Miracle of Morgan's
    Creek
    A Night of Adventure
    Seven Days Ashore
    Tall in the Saddle
    Wilson
45: Col. Effingham's Raid
    The Crime Doctor's
    Courage
    It's in the Bag
    Mama Loves Papa
    Sing Your Way Home
    Two O'Clock Courage
    What a Blonde
46: Deadline for Murder
    The Falcon's Alibi
    Little Iodine
    Queen of Burlesque
    Strange Triangle
    Abie's Irish Rose
    The Show-Off
47: Calendar Girl
    The Guilt of Janet Ames
    Violence
    Gas House Kids Go West

1083

47: The Crime Doctor's
Gamble
Stork Bites Man
48: Song of Idaho
Assigned to Danger
Blonde Ice
Mr. Blanding Builds His
Dream House
Here Comes Trouble
Strike it Rich
You Gotta Stay Happy
Words and Music
49: The Beautiful Blonde
from Bashful Bend
A Woman's Secret
Ma and Pa Kettle
Hellfire
Hideout
Rose of the Yukon
Alaska Patrol
Massacre River
50: Key to the City
Rock Island Trail
Unmasked
Beware of Blondie
County Fair
Chain Gang
To Please a Lady
Trail of Robin Hood
51: My True Story
Ma and Pa Kettle on the
Farm
Footlight Varieties
All that I Have
Honeychile
Golden Girl
Let's Go, Navy!
52: Oklahoma Annie
When in Rome
Ma and Pa Kettle at the
Fair
The Fabulous Señorita
And Now Tomorrow
Gobs and Gals
Lost in Alaska
53: Call Me Madam
Sweethearts on Parade
Safari Drums
Fort Vengeance
Shadow of Tombstone

54: Ma and Pa Kettle at
Home
Battle of Rogue River
Pride of the Blue Grass
The Rocket Man
55: You're Never too Young
The Looters
How to be Very, Very
Popular
Artists and Models
58: The Notorious Mr. Monks
Man of the West
The Hot Angel
61: The Two Little Bears

Helen Parrish (1922-1959)
1928: When the Babe Comes
Home   S
29: Fox Movietone Follies
30: His First Command
Big Trail
31: Cimarron
Seed
32: When a Feller Needs a
Friend
34: There's Always Tomorrow
35: Straight from the Heart
A Dog of Flanders
36: Make Way for a Lady
Three Smart Girls
38: Mad about Music
Little Tough Guy
Little Tough Guys in
Society
39: Three Smart Girls Grow
Up
Winter Carnival
First Love
40: I'm Nobody's Sweetheart
Now
You'll Find Out
41: Where Did You Get that
Girl?
Six Lessons from Madame
La Zonga
Too Many Blondes
42: They All Kissed the Bride
In Old California
X Marks the Spot
Tough as They Come

1084

43: The Mystery of the 13th
Guest
Cinderella Swings it
44: They Live in Fear
Meet Miss Bobby-Socks
45: Let's Go Steady
A Thousand and One
Nights
48: Trouble Makers
49: The Wolf Hunters
Quick on the Trigger

Leslie Parrish
1959: Li'l Abner
61: Portrait of a Mobster
62: The Manchurian Candidate
63: For Love or Money
64: Sex and the Single Girl
66: Three on a Couch
68: The Money Jungle
69: Inferno Road
The Devil's 8

Estelle Parsons (1928-
1967: Bonnie and Clyde (OSCAR)
68: Rachel, Rachel
69: Don't Drink the Water
I Never Sang for My
Father
Stranger
The Night the Sun Came
Out on Happy
Hollow Lane

Michael Pate (1920-
1949: The Rugged O'Riordans
51: Thunder on the Hill
The Strange Door
52: Five Fingers
Bitter Springs
The Black Castle
Face to Face
Target Hong Kong
53: Houdini
Scandal at Scourie
Julius Caesar
The Maze
The Royal African Rifles
El Alamein
Hondo

Secret of the Incas
King Richard and the
Crusaders
54: The Silver Chalice
55: A Lawless Street
56: The Court Jester
The Killer Is Loose
The Revolt of Mamie
Stover
Congo Crossing
Reprisal!
The Seventh Cavalry
57: Something of Value
The Oklahoman
The Tall Stranger
58: Desert Hell
Hong Kong Confidential
59: Green Mansions
Westbound
Curse of the Undead
60: Walk Like a Dragon
62: Sergeants Three
Beauty and the Beast
Tower of London
63: PT-109
McLintock!
Drums of Africa
California
64: Advance to the Rear
65: Major Dundee
Brainstorm
The Great Sioux Massacre
66: The Singing Nun
67: Return of the Gunfighter

Dorothy Patrick
1946: Boys' Ranch
The Mighty McGurk
Till the Clouds Roll By
47: New Orleans
High Wall
48: Alias a Gentleman
49: Come to the Stable
Follow Me Quietly
50: Blonde Bandit
House on the River
Belle of Old Mexico
Federal Agent at Large
Tarnished
Destination Big House

50: 711 Ocean Drive
Lonely Hearts Bandits
Under Mexicali Skies
51: The Big Gusher
52: Road Agent
Retreat, Hell!
Desert Passage
53: Savage Frontier
Tangier Incident
Half a Hero
Man of Conflict
Torch Song
54: Outlaw Stallion
55: Violent Saturday
Las Vegas Shakedown
56: The Peacemaker

Gail Patrick (1912-
1933: Mysterious Rider
Murders in the Zoo
To the Last Man
If I Had a Million
Mama Loves Papa
The Cradle Song
Pick Up
Phantom Broadcast
34: Death Takes a Holiday
Take the Stand
Murder at the Vanities
Wagon Wheels
The Crime of Helen
Stanley
35: One Hour Late
Rumba
Mississippi
Big Broadcast of 1936
Smart Girl
Two-Fisted
Wanderer of the Waste-
land
Doubting Thomas
No More Ladies
36: Two in the Dark
Preview Murder Mystery
Early to Wed
Murder with Pictures
The Lone Wolf Returns
My Man Godfrey
White Hunter
37: John Meade's Woman

Her Husband Lies
Artists and Models
Stage Door
38: Mad about Music
Wives Under Suspicion
Dangerous to Know
King of Alcatraz
39: Disbarred
Grand Jury Secrets
Man of Conquest
Reno
40: The Doctor Takes a Wife
My Favorite Wife
Gallant Sons
41: Love Crazy
Kathleen
42: We Were Dancing
Tales of Manhattan
Quiet Please, Murder
43: Hit Parade of 1943
Cheyenne Roundup
Women in Bondage
44: Up in Mabel's Room
45: Brewster's Millions
Twice Blessed
46: The Madonna's Secret
Claudia and David
Rendezvous with Annie
The Plainsman and the
Lady
47: Calendar Girl
King of Wild Horses
48: Inside Story
64: Big Parade of Comedy
(doc.)

Lee Patrick (1911-
1937: Border Cafe
Music for Madame
Danger Patrol
38: Crashing Hollywood
Night Spot
Condemned Women
Law of the Underworld
The Sisters
39: Fisherman's Wharf
40: Invisible Stripes
Strange Cargo
Saturday's Children
City of Conquest

40: Ladies Must Live
Money and the Woman
South of Suez
Father Is a Prince
41: The Maltese Falcon
Footsteps in the Dark
Honeymoon for Three
Million Dollar Baby
The Nurse's Secret
The Smiling Ghost
Dangerously They Live
42: Now Voyager
George Washington Slept
Here
In This Our Life
Somewhere I'll Find You
43: A Night to Remember
Jitterbugs
Nobody's Darling
Larceny with Music
44: Mrs. Parkington
Faces in the Fog
Gambler's Choice
Moon over Las Vegas
45: Mildred Pierce
Over 21
Keep Your Powder Dry
See My Lawyer
46: Strange Journey
Wake Up and Dream
The Walls Came Tumbling
Down
47: Mother Wore Tights
48: Inner Sanctum
The Snake Pit
49: The Doolins of Oklahoma
50: Caged
The Lawless
The Fuller Brush Girl
51: Tomorrow Is Another
Day
53: Take Me to Town
54: There's no Business Like
Show Business
58: Vertigo
Auntie Mame
Any Way the Wind Blows
59: Pillow Talk
60: Visit to a Small Planet
61: Goodbye Again

Summer and Smoke
62: A Girl Named Tamiko
63: Wives and Lovers
64: The Seven Faces of Dr.
Lao
The New Interns

Nigel Patrick (1913-
1939: Mrs. Pym of Scotland
Yard
47: Spring in Park Lane
The Noose
49: The Perfect Woman
51: The Browning Version
Trio (Mr. Knowall seq.)
52: The Sound Barrier
Encore (The Ant and the
Grasshopper seq.)
Pickwick Papers
54: Young Wives' Tale
55: A Prize of Gold
The Sea Shall not Have
Them
Wicked Wife
56: Forbidden Cargo
57: Raintree County
How to Murder a Rich
Uncle
58: Count Five and Die
The Man Inside
59: Sapphire
60: The Green Carnation
65: Johnny Nobody
66: Underworld Informer
69: The Battle of Britain
The Executioner

Luana Patten
1946: Little Mr. Jim
Song of the South
47: Fun and Fancy Free
48: Melody Time
So Dear to My Heart
56: Rock, Pretty Baby
57: Johnny Tremain
Joe Dakota
58: The Restless Years
59: The Young Captives
60: Home from the Hill
The Music Box Kid

61: A Thunder of Drums
Go Naked in the World
Little Shepherd of King-
dom Come
66: Follow Me, Boys!

Elizabeth Patterson (1974-1966)
1929: Words and Music
South Sea Rose
30: Lone Star Ranger
Harmony at Home
The Big Party
The Cat Creeps
31: Tarnished Lady
The Smiling Lieutenant
Daddy Long Legs
Penrod and Sam
Heaven on Earth
32: Husband's Holiday
So Big
The Expert
Play Girl
Miss Pinkerton
Two Against the World
Love Me Tonight
New Morals for Old
Guilty as Hell
Breach of Promise
Bill of Divorcement
The Way of Life
No Man of Her Own
Dangerous Brunette
Life Begins
They Call it Sin
33: They Just Had to Get
Married
Golden Harvest
Dinner at Eight
The Story of Temple
Drake
The Infernal Machine
Hold Your Man
The Secrets of the Blue
Room
34: Hide-Out
35: Chasing Yesterday
Men Without Names
So Red the Rose
36: Timothy's Quest
Her Master's Voice
Return of Sophie Lang

Three Cheers for Love
Go West Young Man
Small Town Girl
Old Hutch
37: A Night of Mystery
Hide Wide and Handsome
Hold 'em, Navy!
Night Club Scandal
38: Scandal Street
Bulldog Drummong's Peril
Bluebeard's Eighth Wife
Sing, You Sinners!
Sons of the Legion
39: The Story of Alexander
Graham Bell
Bulldog Drummond's Bride
Our Leading Citizen
Remember the Night
Bulldog Drummond's Secret
Police
The Cat and the Canary
Bad Little Angel
40: Anne of Windy Poplars
Earthbound
Who Killed Aunt Maggie?
Michael Shayne, Private
Detective
Adventure in Diamonds
41: Kiss the Boys Goodbye
Tobacco Road
Belle Starr
42: Almost Married
Beyond the Blue Horizon
Her Cardboard Lover
My Sister Eileen
I Married a Witch
43: Lucky Legs
The Sky's the Limit
44: Follow the Boys
Hail the Conquering Hero
Together Again
45: Col. Effingham's Raid
Lady on a Train
46: The Secret Heart
I've Always Loved You
47: The Shocking Miss Pilgrim
Out of the Blue
Welcome Stranger
Pal Joey
48: Miss Tatlock's Millions
49: Little Women

49: Intruder in the Dust
Song of Surrender
50: Bright Leaf
51: Katie Did It
52: The Washington Story
55: Las Vegas Shakedown
57: Pal Joey
59: The Oregon Trail
60: Tall Story

Lee Patterson (1929-
1951: 36 Hours
55: Above the Waves
56: Soho Incident
Spin a Dark Web
57: The Counterfeit Plan
Reach for the Sky
The Story of Esther
Costello
58: In Between Age
Mailbag Robbery
59: Third Man on the
Mountain
60: Jack the Ripper
The Three Worlds of
Gulliver
Cat and Mouse
63: The Ceremony

Neva Patterson (1922-
1953: Taxi
56: The Solid Gold Cadillac
57: Desk Set
An Affair to Remember
58: Too Much Too Soon
62: The Spiral Road
David and Lisa
64: Dear Heart
The Out-Of-Towners
68: Counterpoint

Virginia Patton
1944: Janie
Hollywood Canteen
The Last Ride
46: It's a Wonderful Life
Canyon Passage
47: The Burning Cross
A Double Life
48: Black Eagle

49: The Lucky Stiff

Marisa Pavan (1932-
1952: What Price Glory?
54: Down Three Dark Streets
Drum Beat
55: The Rose Tattoo
Diane
56: The Man in the Gray
Flannel Suit
57: Midnight Story
59: John Paul Jones
Solomon and Sheba

Katina Paxinou (1900-
1943: For Whom the Bell Tolls
(OSCAR)
Hostages
45: Confidential Agent
46: California
47: Mourning Becomes Electra
Uncle Silas
49: Prince of Foxes
55: Confidential Report
59: The Miracle
61: Rocco and His Brothers
62: Mr. Arkadin
Death of a Bandit
68: Zita

John Payne (1912-
1936: Dodsworth
Hats Off
37: Fair Warning
38: College Swing
Garden of the Moon
Love on Toast
39: Wings of the Navy
Indianapolis Speedway
Kid Nightingale
40: Star Dust
Maryland
The Great Profile
Tin Pan Alley
King of the Lumberjacks
Tear Gas Squad
41: The Great American Broad-
cast
Sun Valley Serenade
Moon over Miami

1089

41: Weekend in Havana
    Remember the Day
42: To the Shores of Tripoli
    Footlight Serenade
    Iceland
    Springtime in the Rockies
    Katina
43: Hello, Frisco, Hello
45: The Dolly Sisters
46: Sentimental Journey
    The Razor's Edge
    Wake Up and Dream
47: Miracle on 34th Street
    It's Only Human
48: Larceny
    The Saxon Charm
49: Captain China
    El Paso
    The Crooked Way
50: Tripoli
    The Eagle and the Hawk
51: Passage West (or, High
    Venture)
    Crosswinds
52: Blazing Forest
    Caribbean
    Kansas City Confidential
53: Raiders of the Seven
    Seas
    99 River Street
    The Vanquished
54: Rails into Laramie
    The Silver Lode
55: Hell's Island
    Santa Fe Passage
    Road to Denver
    Tennessee's Partner
56: Slightly Scarlet
    Rebel in Town
    The Boss
    Hold Back the Night
57: Bail Out at 43,000 Feet
    Hidden Fear
    Hide, Wide, and Free
    (narr. doc.)

Barbara Payton (1928-1967)
1940's: various westerns
49: Once More, Darling
    Trapped

50: Dallas
    Kiss Tomorrow Goodbye
51: Only the Valiant
    Drums in the Deep South
    Bride of the Gorilla
53: Four-Sided Triangle
    Run for the Hills
    The Bad Blonde
54: The Great Jesse James
    Raid
    The Flanagan Boy
55: Murder Is My Beat

Mary Peach (1934-
1959: Follow that Horse!
    Room at the Top
62: A Pair of Briefs
63: A Gathering of Eagles
65: No Love for Johnnie
66: Blues for Lovers
67: The Projected Man

Alice Pearce (1919-1967)
1949: On the Town
52: The Belle of New York
55: How to be Very, Very
    Popular
56: The Opposite Sex
62: Lad, a Dog
63: My Six Loves
    Tammy and the Doctor
    Beach Party
    The Thrill of it All
64: The Disorderly Orderly
    Kiss Me, Stupid
    Dear Heart
65: Dear Brigitte
    Darn that Cat
    Bus Riley's Back in Town
66: The Glass Bottom Boat

Jesse Pearson (1936-
1963: Bye Bye, Birdie
64: Advance to the Rear

Virginia Pearson (1888-1958)
1930: Danger Man
31: Primrose Path
32: Back Street

1090

Harold Peary (1908-
1940: Comin' 'Round the Mountain
41: Country Fair
Look Who's Laughing
42: Here We Go Again
Seven Days' Leave
The Great Gildersleeve
43: Gildersleeve's Bad Day
Gildersleeve on Broadway
44: Gildersleeve's Ghost
67: Clambake

Gregory Peck (1916-
1944: Days of Glory
The Keys of the Kingdom
45: The Valley of Decision
Spellbound
46: Duel in the Sun
The Yearling
47: The Macomber Affair
Gentleman's Agreement
48: The Paradine Case
Yellow Sky
The Walls of Jericho
49: Twelve O'Clock High
The Great Sinner
50: The Gunfighter
51: Only the Valiant
David and Bathsheba
Captain Horatio Horn-
blower
52: The World in His Arms
The Snows of Kilimanjaro
53: Roman Holiday
54: Night People
The Man with a Million
55: The Purple Plain
56: The Man in the Gray
Flannel Suit
Moby Dick
57: Designing Woman
58: The Big Country
The Bravados
59: Pork Chop Hill
On the Beach
Beloved Infidel
61: The Guns of Navarone
62: To Kill a Mockingbird
(OSCAR)
Cape Fear

63: How the West Was Won
Captain Newman, MD.
64: Behold a Pale Horse
65: Mirage
66: Arabesque
John F. Kennedy: Years
of Lightning, Days of
Drums (doc.)
67: Across the River and
into the Trees
68: Mackenna's Gold
69: The Chairman
The Stalking Moon
Marooned
An Exile

Edward Peil (1888-1958)
1930: Cock o' the Walk
31: Clearing the Range
The Texas Ranger
Wild Horse
32: The Gay Buckaroo
Charlie Chan's Chance
Local Bad Man
33: Tombstone Canyon
34: Blue Steel
The Man from Utah
Texas Ranger
Pursuit of Happiness
35: Million Dollar Baby
Mysterious Mr. Wong
Ladies Crave Excitement
37: Come on, Cowboys!
Two-Fisted Sheriff
38: Colorado Trail
39: The Night Riders
Spoilers of the Range
40: One Man's Law
41: Billy the Kid's Fighting
Pals
The Lone Rider in Ghost
Town
Texas Marshal
42: Black Dragons
Foreign Agent
43: Robin Hood of the Range

Pilar Pellicer (1940-1964)
1961: One-Eyed Jacks
Macario

64: Autumn Days
Rogelia
67: Los Bandidos
68: Days of the Evil Gun

Nat Pendleton (1899-1967)
1929: Laughing Lady
30: The Big Pond
Last of the Duanes
The Sea Wolf
Fair Warning
31: Mr. Lemon of Orange
Star Witness
Blonde Crazy
Spirit of Notre Dame
Pottsville Palooka
Secret Witness
Cauliflower Alley
Larceny Lane
Vigor of Youth
The Seas Beneath
Terror by Night
32: Play Girl
Cardigan's Last Case
Taxi
Attorney for the Defense
Hell Fire Austin
Exposure
You Said a Mouthful
Beast of the City
A Fool's Advice
By Whose Hand?
Night Club Lady
Horse Feathers
Manhattan Parade
Sign of the Cross
33: Deception
Baby Face
Whistling in the Dark
College Coach
Goldie Gets Along
Lady for a Day
Penthouse
The Chief
I'm No Angel
34: Fugitive Lovers
Lazy River
Manhattan Melodrama
Death on the Diamond
The Thin Man

The Gay Bride
Sing and Like it
The Defense Rests
The Cat's Paw
Girl from Missouri
Straight Is the Way
35: Times Square Lady
Baby Face Harrington
Reckless
Murder in the Fleet
Calm Yourself
Here Comes the Band
It's in the Air
36: The Garden Murder Case
The Great Ziegfeld
Sworn Enemy
Trapped by Television
Two in a Crowd
The Luckiest Girl in the
World
Sing Me a Love Song
37: Under Cover of Night
Song of the City
Gangway
Life Begins in College
38: Swing Your Lady
Arsene Lupin Returns
Fast Company
Shopworn Angel
The Chaser
The Crowd Roars
Meet the Mayor
Young Dr. Kildare
39: Burn 'em Up, O'Connor
Calling Dr. Kildare
It's a Wonderful World
6000 Enemies
On Borrowed Time
At the Circus
Another Thin Man
The Secret of Dr. Kildare
40: Northwest Passage
The Ghost Comes Home
Dr. Kildare's Strange Case
Phantom Raiders
The Golden Fleecing
Dr. Kildare's Crisis
Dr. Kildare's Wedding Day
Dr. Kildare Goes Home

40: Flight Command
41: Buck Privates
Top Sgt. Mulligan
The Mad Doctor of
Market Street
Death Valley
42: Jail House Blues
Calling Dr. Gillespie
Dr. Gillespie's New
Assistant
43: Dr. Gillespie's Criminal
Case
Swing Fever
47: Buck Privates Come
Home
Scared to Death
49: Death Valley
64: Big Parade of Comedy
Comedy (doc.)

Lea Penman (d. 1962)
1950: Fancy Pants
55: We're No Angels
57: Portland Exposé

Leonard Penn
1937: Between Two Women
The Firefly
38: Judge Hardy's Children
Man Proof
Girl of the Golden West
Toy Wife
Ladies in Distress
Marie Antoinette
39: Bachelor Mother
46: High School Hero
Her Sister's Secret
47: Hoppy's Holiday
I Cover Big Town
Killer at Large
The Hat Box Mystery
48: Courtin' Trouble
49: Not Wanted
Under Cover Man
50: The Girl from San Lorenzo
Woman from Headquarters
Gunfire
Lonely Hearts Bandits
Law of the Badlands
51: Sirocco

South of Caliente
52: A Yank in Indo-China
Outlaw Women
Thief of Damascus
And Now Tomorrow
Barbed Wire
No Holds Barred
53: Savage Mutiny
Flame of Calcutta
Murder Without Tears
54: The Saracen Blade
58: In the Money
67: Adventures of Batman
& Robin (ser. re-rel.)

Larry Pennell
1955: Seven Angry Men
The Far Horizons
Hell's Horizon
56: The Vagabond King
57: The Devil's Hairpin
58: The Space Children
59: The F.B.I. Story

Joe Penner (1904-1941)
1935: College Rhythm
36: Collegiate
37: New Faces of 1937
Life of the Party
38: Go Chase Yourself
I'm from the City
Mr. Doodle Kicks Off
39: The Day the Bookies Wept
40: Millionaire Playboy
The Boys from Syracuse

Jack Pennick (1895-1964)
1928: Why Sailors Go Wrong S
Plastered in Paris   SSE
29: Strong Boy   SSE
The Virginian
30: The Mighty
Navy Blues
City Girl
Paramount on Parade
Way Out West
Min and Bill
31: Hell Divers
32: Strangers of the Evening
Phantom Express

1093

32: Air Mail
If I Had a Million
Sky Bride
33: Renegades of the West
Hello Everybody!
Strange People
Tugboat Annie
Skyway
Man of Sentiment
34: Come on Marines!
The World Moves On
35: West Point of the Air
Steamboat 'Round the Bend
Waterfront Lady
36: Prisoner of Shark Island
The Music Goes 'Round
Drift Fence
Under Two Flags
Private Number
37: Wee Willie Winkie
The Big City
Live, Love, and Learn
Navy, Blue, and Gold
Great Guy
The Devil's Playground
Submarine
38: King of the Newsboys
Cocoanut Grove
You and Me
Submarine Patrol
The Buccaneer
Banjo on My Knee
Alexander's Ragtime Band
39: Stagecoach
Union Pacific
Mountain Rhythm
Star Maker
Drums Along the Mohawk
Tail Spin
Young Mr. Lincoln
40: The Grapes of Wrath
The Westerner
The Long Voyage Home
Northwest Mounted Police
41: Tobacco Road
Men of Boys Town
Lady from Louisiana
Sergeant York
Wild Geese Calling
45: They Were Expendable
46: My Darling Clementine

47: Unconquered
The Fugitive
48: Fort Apache
Three Godfathers
49: She Wore a Yellow Ribbon
Mighty Joe Young
The Fighting Kentuckian
50: When Willie Comes Marching Home
Rio Grande
51: Operation Pacific
The Fighting Coast Guard
The Sea Hornet
52: What Price Glory?
53: The Sun Shines Bright
The Beast from 20,000
Fathoms
55: The Long Gray Line
Mr. Roberts
56: The Searchers
57: Wings of Eagles
58: The Last Hurrah
The Buccaneer
59: The Horse Soldiers
60: The Alamo
Sergeant Rutledge
61: Two Rode Together
62: The Man Who Shot Liberty
Valance

George Peppard (1929-
1957: The Strange One (or, End
as a Man)
59: Pork Chop Hill
60: Home from the Hill
The Subterraneans
61: Breakfast at Tiffany's
62: How the West Was Won
63: The Victors
64: The Carpetbaggers
65: Operation Crossbow (or,
The Great Spy Mission)
The Third Day
66: The Blue Max
Tobruk
67: P.J.
69: What's so Bad about Feeling
Good?
The Plot
Pendulum
Hark!

69: House of Cards
The Executioner
Cannon for Cordoba
Chisholm

Barbara Pepper (1916-1969)
1933: Roman Scandals
34: Our Daily Bread
35: Let 'em Have it!
Waterfront Lady
Forced Landing
Sagebrush Troubadour
The Singing Vagabond
36: Showboat
Rogues' Tavern
M'Liss
The Big Game
Wanted: Jane Turner
Winterset
37: Sea Devils
Too Many Wives
You Can't Beat Luck
The Big Shot
Forty Naughty Girls
Music for Madame
The Westland Case
Portia on Trial
38: Hollywood Stadium
Mystery
Wide Open Faces
Lady in the Morgue
Army Girl
Outside the Law
39: They Made Me a
Criminal
The Magnificent Fraud
Colorado Sunset
Flight at Midnight
Three Sons
40: Forgotten Girls
Castle on the Hudson
Women in War
Framed
The Return of Frank
James
Foreign Correspondent
41: Manpower
Birth of the Blues
Man at Large
Three Sons o' Guns

42: One Thrilling Night
43: Girls in Chains
So This Is Washington
44: Since You Went Away
Cover Girl
Henry Aldrich Plays Cupid
45: Brewster's Millions
The Hidden Eye
Murder He Says
46: Prison Ship
47: The Millerson Case
Terror Trail
50: Unmasked
53: Inferno
57: The D.I.
63: A Child Is Waiting
64: Kiss Me, Stupid

Cynthia Pepper
1963: Take Her, She's Mine
64: Kissin' Cousins

George Periolat
1929: When Dreams Come
True   S
One Splendid Hour   S

Anthony Perkins (1932-
1953: The Actress
56: Friendly Persuasion
57: The Lonely Man
Fear Strikes Out
The Tin Star
58: This Bitter Earth
Desire Under the Elms
The Matchmaker
This Angry Age
59: Green Mansions
On the Beach
60: Tall Story
Psycho
61: Goodbye Again
62: Phaedra
63: The Trial
Five Miles to Midnight
64: Two Are Guilty
65: The Fool Killer
66: Is Paris Burning?
Violent Journey
67: The Scandal

68: She Let Him Continue
Champagne Murders
Pretty Poison
69: Catch 22
Hall of Mirrors

Millie Perkins (1939-
1959: The Diary of Anne Frank
61: Wild in the Country
64: Ensign Pulver
68: Wild on the Streets

Osgood Perkins (1892-1937)
1931: Tarnished Lady
32: Scarface
34: Madame Du Barry
Kansas City Princess
The President Vanishes
35: Secret of the Chateau
I Dream Too Much
36: Gold Diggers of 1937

Voltaire Perkins
1955: A Man Called Peter
The Far Horizons
56: Over-Exposed
58: Massacre
59: Compulsion

Gigi Perreau (1941-
1943: Madame Curie
Dark Waters
Abigail
Dear Heart
Two Girls and a Sailor
44: Death in a Doll's House
Mr. Skeffington
San Diego, I Love You
The Master Race
45: Yolanda and the Thief
Voice of the Whistler
46: Alias Mr. Twilight
47: High Barbaree
Song of Love
Green Dolphin Street
48: Family Honeymoon
Enchantment
49: Roseanna McCoy
My Foolish Heart
50: For Heaven's Sake

Never a Dull Moment
Shadow on the Wall
51: Reunion in Reno
The Lady Pays Off
Weekend with Father
52: Has Anybody Seen My Gal?
Bonzo Goes to College
56: There's Always Tomorrow
The Man in the Gray
Flannel Suit
Dance with Me, Henry
58: Wild Heritage
The Cool and the Crazy
59: Girls Town
61: Tammy Tell Me True
Look in Any Window
67: Hell on Wheels

Jack Perrin (1896-1967)
1929: Wild Blood   S
Harvest of Hate   S
Plunging Hoofs   S
Hoofbeats of Vengeance S
30: Beyond the Rio Grande
Ridin' Law
Romance of the West
31: Wild West Whoopee
The Kid from Arizona
The Sheriff's Secret
Lariats and Six-Shooters
32: .45 Calibre Echo
Hell Fire Austin
Dynamite Ranch
34: Rawhide Mail
36: Hair Trigger Casey
Desert Justice
38: The Purple Vigilantes
40: West of Pinto Basin
42: Broadway Big Shot
50: Bandit Queen

Joan Perry
1939: Blind Alibi
Good Girls Go to Paris
40: The Lone Wolf Strikes
41: Maisie Was a Lady
Strange Alibi
Bullets for O'Hara
Nine Lives Are not Enough
International Squadron

Maria Perschy
1961: Wet Asphalt
  62: Freud (or, The Secret
       Passion)
       Melody of Hate
  63: No Survivors, Please!
       Secret of the Sphinx
       Password to Courage
       Ordered to Love
  64: 633 Squadron
       Man's Favorite Sport?
  65: The Mad Executioner
  66: Kiss Kiss, Kill Kill!
       The Tall Women
       Ride the High Wind
  67: A Witch Without a Broom
       Five Golden Dragons
  68: The Desperate Ones
  69: Assignment: Istanbul

Nehemiah Persoff (1920-
1948: The Naked City
       A Double Life
  54: On the Waterfront
  56: The Wild Party
       The Harder They Fall
  57: Men in War
       The Wrong Man
       Street of Sinners
  58: The Badlanders
       This Angry Age
  59: Al Capone
       Some Like it Hot
       Green Mansions
       Never Steal Anything
       Small
       Day of the Outlaw
  61: The Big Show
       The Comancheros
  63: The Hook
  64: Fate Is the Hunter
       A Global Affair
  65: The Greatest Story Ever
       Told
  68: The Power
       The Day of the Owl
       (Il Giorno Della Civetta)
       Escape to Mindenao
  69: The Girl Who Knew too
       Much

The Money Jungle
Panic in the City

Brock Peters (1927-
1954: Carmen Jones
  59: Porgy and Bess
  62: To Kill a Mockingbird
       Heavens Above
  63: The L-Shaped Room
  65: Major Dundee
       The Pawnbroker
  67: The Incident
  68: P.J.
       The Way the Wheel Turns
  69: Daring Game
       The Last Cowboy
       The McMasters

House Peters, Jr.
1937: Public Cowboy No. 1
  48: Oklahoma Badlands
       Under California Stars
       Courtin' Trouble
       Desperadoes of Dodge City
  49: Renegades of Sonora
       Sheriff of Wichita
       Gunning for Justice
       Son of Billy the Kid
  50: Twilight in the Sierras
       Cow Town
       Border Treasure
  51: Spoilers of the Plains
       Gene Autry and the
       Mounties
       The Man from Sonora
       Three Desperate Men
       Blazing Bullets
  52: The Lion and the Horse
       Oklahoma Annie
       The Old West
       Red Planet Mars
       And Now Tomorrow
       Kansas Territory
       Waco
       Wyoming Roundup
  53: Port Sinister
       Winning of the West
  54: Overland Pacific
  56: Women of Pitcairn Island
  57: Black Patch

1097

58: The Man from God's
Country
59: Inside the Mafia
60: The Big Night
64: Rio Conchos
65: The Great Sioux
Massacre
67: Adventures of Batman and
Robin

Jean Peters (1926-
1947: Captain from Castile
48: Deep Waters
49: It Happens Every Spring
50: Love that Brute
51: Anne of the Indies
Take Care of My Little
Girl
As Young as You Feel
52: Wait till the Sun Shines,
Nellie
Viva Zapata!
Lure of the Wilderness
O. Henry's Full House
(The Last Leaf seq.)
53: Niagara
Pickup on South Street
Blueprint for Murder
Vicki
54: Three Coins in the
Fountain
Apache
Broken Lance
55: A Man Called Peter
59: The Best of Everything

Scott Peters
1957: Invasion of the Saucer
Men
The Outlaw's Son
The Amazing Colossal
Man
Hell Bound
Motorcycle Gang
58: Suicide Battalion
61: The Canadians
63: The Girl Hunters

Susan Peters (1921-1952)
1940: Santa Fe Trail

41: Three Sons o' Guns
Scattergood Pulls the
Strings
42: Escape from Crime
The Big Shot
Tish
Random Harvest
Dr. Gillespie's New
Assistant
Andy Hardy's Double
Trouble
43: Assignment in Brittany
Young Ideas
Song of Russia
45: Keep Your Powder Dry
48: Sign of the Ram

Paul Petersen (1944-
1967: The Happiest Millionaire
A Time for Killing

Dorothy Peterson
1930: Mothers' Cry
31: Furies
Up for Murder
Party Husband
The Reckless Hour
Penrod and Sam
Skyline
Traveling Husbands
The Plutocrat
Bought
Rich Man's Folly
Fires of Youth
32: Way Back Home
So Big
Cabin in the Cotton
She Wanted a Millionaire
The Beast of the City
Forbidden
Business and Pleasure
Night World
Attorney for the Defense
When a Fellow Needs a
Friend
Life Begins
Thrill of Youth
Payment Deferred
Call Her Savage
33: The Mayor of Hell

33: Hold Me Tight
Big Executive
I'm No Angel
Billion Dollar Scandal
Reform Girl
34: Side Streets
Beloved
As the Earth Turns
Treasure Island
Peck's Bad Boy
Uncertain Lady
35: Sweepstakes Annie
Laddie
Freckles
Society Doctor
Pursuit
Man of Iron
Only Eight Hours
36: The Country Doctor
Reunion
37: Under Cover of Night
Her Husband Lies
Confession
52nd Street
Girl Loves Boy
38: Breaking the Ice
Hunted Men
Girls on Probation
39: Dark Victory
The Flying Irishman
Two Bright Boys
Sabotage
Five Little Peppers
40: Too Many Husbands
Five Little Peppers at
Home
Lillian Russell
Women in War
Out West with the Peppers
Five Little Peppers in
Trouble
41: Cheers for Miss Bishop
Ride, Kelly, Ride
Henry Aldrich for
President
42: Saboteur
The Man in the Trunk
43: The Moon Is Down
Air Force
This Is the Army

44: This Is the Life
Mr. Skeffington
When the Lights Go on
Again
Woman in the Window
Faces in the Fog
46: Canyon Passage
Sister Kenny
47: That Hagen Girl

Howard Petrie (d. 1968)
1950: Walk Softly, Stranger
Rocky Mountain
51: No Questions Asked
Cattle Drive
52: Bend of the River
The Wild North
Red Ball Express
Carbine Williams
Woman of the North
Country
Pony Soldier
53: Fort Ti
Fair Wind to Java
Veils of Bagdad
54: Border River
The Bounty Hunter
Seven Brides for Seven
Brothers
The Bob Mathias Story
Sign of the Pagan
55: Rage at Dawn
Timberjack
How to be Very, Very
Popular
Return of Jack Slade
56: The Maverick Queen
A Kiss Before Dying
Johnny Concho
57: The Tin Star

Joanne Pettet (1944-
1966: The Group
67: The Robbery
The Night of the Generals
Casino Royale
68: Victorian Comedy
Blue
69: The Best House in London
The Long Day's Dying

Joseph Pevney (c1916-
1946: Nocturne
  47: Body and Soul
  48: Street with no Name
  49: Thieves' Highway
  50: Shakedown
      Undercover Girl
  51: The Iron Man
      The Strange Door
      Meet Danny Wilson
  52: Just Across the Street
  54: Because of You
      Desert Legion
  55: The Female on the Beach
      Three-Ring Circus
  56: Away All Boats
      Congo Crossing
  57: Tammy
      Man of a Thousand Faces
  58: Twilight for the Gods
  60: Cash McCall
  66: Night of the Grizzly

Lee Phelps (d. 1953)
1936: Boss Rider of Gun Creek
  37: Sandflow
      Touch to Handle
      Under Suspicion
      A Nation Aflame
      Boss of Lonely Valley
  38: Female Fugitive
      Sudden Bill Dorn
      The Gladiator
      Long Shot
      Trade Winds
  39: Kid Nightingale
      Gone With the Wind
  40: Hidden Gold
  41: Andy Hardy's Private
      Secretary
      A Shot in the Dark
  42: Scattergood Rides High
      War Dogs
      Life Begins at 8:30
  45: Don Juan Quilligan
      The Hidden Eye
  48: Michael O'Halloran
  49: Sky Dragons
      Angels in Disguise
      The Lone Wolf and His
      Lady

  50: The Girl from San
      Lorenzo
      Western Pacific Agent
      Timber Fury
      The Hills of Oklahoma
      Square Dance Katy
  53: The Marshal's Daughter
      Man of Conflict

James Philbrook
1957: Peyton Place
  58: I Want to Live!
  59: Warlock
  62: The Wild Westerners
  64: The Thin Red Line
  65: Finger on the Trigger
  66: Son of a Gunfighter
      Drums of Tabu

Lee Philips (1927-
1958: The Hunters
  59: Middle of the Night
  60: Tess of the Storm Country
  61: Return to Peyton Place
  64: Psychomania

Dorothy Phillips (1892-
1930: Jazz Cinderella
  55: Violent Saturday
  62: The Man Who Shot
      Liberty Valance

Eddie Phillips
1934: Woman Unafraid
  35: One Hour Late
      Danger Ahead
      The Ivory-Handled Gun
      The Throwback
  36: Soak the Rich
      Born to Fight
      Wildcat Trooper
      Wedding Present
      Ambush Valley
  37: Federal Bullets
  42: Billy the Kid Trapped
  43: Death Valley Manhunt
  44: Cyclone Prairie Ranger
  52: Buffalo Bill in Tomahawk
      Territory

William "Bill" Phillips (d. 1957)
1954: The Law vs Billy the Kid
55: New York Confidential
Fort Yuma
Top Gun
Ghost Town
56: The Broken Star
The Man in the Gray
Flannel Suit
The Fastest Gun Alive
Stagecoach to Fury
57: Revolt at Fort Laramie
Hellcats of the Navy

William Phipps
1947: Crossfire
48: The Arizona Ranger
Train to Alcatraz
The Twisted Road
Belle Starr's Daughter
Desperadoes of Dodge
City
49: The Man on the Eiffel
Tower
Big Jack
Johnny Allegro
Easy Living
Prison Warden
50: Rider from Tucson
51: Five
No Questions Asked
52: Rose of Cimarron
Flat Top
Fort Osage
53: War of the Worlds
Julius Caesar
The Twonky
Fort Algiers
Savage Frontier
Northern Patrol
54: Riot in Cell Block 11
Jesse James vs the
Daltons
Executive Suite
Two Guns and a Badge
Red River Shore
The Snow Creature
55: The Violent Men
Smoke Signal
The Far Horizons

Lord of the Jungle
The Indian Fighter
56: The Boss
Lust for Life
57: Badlands of Montana
The Brothers Rico
58: Escape from Red Rock
63: Black Gold
66: Incident at Phantom Hill
67: Gunfight in Abilene

Paul Picerni (1922-
1950: Breakthrough
Saddle Tramp
51: I Was a Communist for
the FBI
Inside the Walls of Folsom
Prison
Operation Pacific
Force of Arms
The Tanks Are Coming
52: Mara Maru
Operation Secret
Cattle Town
53: The Desert Song
She's Back on Broadway
House of Wax
The System
54: Drive a Crooked Road
The Bounty Hunter
The Shanghai Story
55: To Hell and Back
Dial Red O
Hell's Island
Lord of the Jungle
Bobby Ware Is Missing
56: The Come On
Flight to Hong Kong
Miracle in the Rain
57: Shadow on the Window
The Big Caper
Operation Mad Ball
The Brothers Rico
Omar Khayyam
58: Return to Warbow
Marjorie Morningstar
The Man Who Died Twice
Torpedo Run
59: The Young Philadelphians
The Young Marrieds

1101

60: Strangers When We Meet
68: The Scalphunters
69: Che!
   Airport

Irving Pichel (1891-1954)
1930: The Right to Love
31: An American Tragedy
   Murder by the Clock
   Road to Reno
   The Cheat
32: The Miracle Man
   Madame Butterfly
   Two Kinds of Women
   Forgotten Commandments
   Westward Passage
   Painted Woman
   Strange Justice
   Wild Girl
33: Mysterious Rider
   Woman Accused
   King of the Jungle
   Oliver Twist
   The Story of Temple
    Drake
   I'm No Angel
   Right to Romance
34: Fog Over Frisco
   Such Women Are
    Dangerous
   British Agent
   Return of the Terror
   I Am a Thief
   Silver Streak
   She Was a Lady
   Cleopatra
35: Special Agent
   She
   Three Kids and a Queen
36: Don't Gamble with Love
   House of a Thousand
    Candles
   Hearts in Bondage
   Dracula's Daughter
   Down to the Sea
   General Spanky
37: Join the Marines
   Armored Car
   The Sheik Steps Out
   High, Wide, and Handsome

38: Jezebel
   There Goes My Heart
   Gambling Ship
39: Juarez
   Newsboys' Home
   Exile Express
   Topper Takes a Trip
   Torture Ship
   Reno
51: Santa Fe
53: Martin Luther

Slim Pickens (1919-
1950: Rocky Mountain
52: Old Oklahoma Plains
   South Pacific Trail
   The Last Musketeer
   Colorado Sundown
   Border Saddlemates
   The Will Rogers Story
   Thunderbirds
   Irom Mountain Trail
   Down Laredo Way
   Old Overland Trail
   Shadows of Tombstone
53: The Sun Shines Bright
54: The Boy from Oklahoma
   Red River Shore
   The Outcast (or, The
    Fortune Hunter)
55: Santa Fe Passage
   The Last Command
56: The Great Locomotive
    Chase
   Stranger at My Door
   When Gangland Strikes
   Gun Brothers
57: Gunsight Ridge
58: The Sheepman
   Tonka
59: Escort West
60: The Chartroose Caboose
61: One--Eyed Jacks
   A Thunder of Drums
63: Savage Sam
64: Dr. Strangelove
65: Major Dundee
   In Harm's Way
   Up from the Beach
   The Glory Guys

1102

66: Stagecoach
An Eye for an Eye
67: The Flim Flam Man
Rough Night in Jericho
68: Will Penny
Never a Dull Moment
69: Joaquin Murietta
The Battle of Cable Hogue
The Savage Season
80 Steps to Jonah

Walter Pidgeon (1898-
1928: Woman Wise   S
Turn Back the Hours   S
Clothes Make the
Woman   S
Melody of Love
29: The Voice Within   PT
A Most Immoral Lady
Her Private Life
30: Bride of the Regiment
Viennese Nights
Toast of the Legion
Going Wild
The Gorilla
Sweet Kitty Bellairs
31: Hot Heiress
Kiss Me Again
32: Rockabye
33: The Kiss Before the
Mirror
34: Journal of a Crime
36: Big Brown Eyes
Fatal Lady
37: Girl Overboard
As Good as Married
She's Dangerous
A Girl with Ideas
Saratoga
My Dear Miss Aldrich
38: Man Proof
Too Hot to Handle
Shopworn Angel
Girl of the Golden West
Listen Darling
39: Society Lawyer
6000 Enemies
Stronger than Desire
Nick Carter, Master
Detective

40: It's a Date
Flight Command
The House Across the Bay
Sky Murder
Phantom Raiders
The Dark Command
41: Man Hunt
How Green Was My Valley
Blossoms in the Dust
Design for Scandal
42: Mrs. Miniver
White Cargo
43: The Youngest Profession
Madame Curie
44: Mrs. Parkington
45: Weekend at the Waldorf
46: Holiday in Mexico
Secret Heart
47: If Winter Comes
48: Julia Misbehaves
Command Decision
49: Red Danube
That Forsythe Woman
50: The Miniver Story
51: Soldiers Three
Calling Bulldog Drummond
The Unknown Man
The Sellout
52: Million Dollar Mermaid
The Bad and the Beautiful
53: Scandal at Scourie
Dream Wife
54: Executive Suite
Men of the Fighting Lady
The Last Time I Saw
Paris
Deep in My Heart
55: Hit the Deck
56: Forbidden Planet
The Rack
Those Wilder Years
61: Voyage to the Bottom of
the Sea
62: Big Red
Advise and Consent
67: Warning Shot
How I Spent My Summer
Vacation (TV)
68: At Any Price
Funny Girl

1103

69: The Vatican Story
     The Red Kitchen Murder
     Rascal (narr.)

Francis Pierlot (1876-1953)
1931: Night Angel
  40: The Captain Is a Lady
       Strike Up the Band
       Escape to Glory
       Always a Bride
  41: The Trial of Mary Dugan
       International Lady
       Submarine Zone
       Rise and Shine
       Remember the Day
  42: Just Off Broadway
       My Heart Belongs to
         Daddy
       Henry Aldrich, Editor
       Night Monster
       A Gentleman at Heart
  43: Doughgirls
       Mission to Moscow
       Mystery Broadcast
  44: The Very Thought of You
       Uncertain Glory
       Adventures of Mark Twain
       Bathing Beauty
  45: Hit the Hay
       Affairs of Susan
       Bewitched
       Fear
       Grissly's Millions
       The Hidden Eye
       How Do You Do?
       Life with Blondie
       Our Vines Have Tender
         Grapes
       Roughly Speaking
       A Tree Grows in Brooklyn
  46: The Catman of Paris
       The Crime Doctor's
         Manhunt
       Dragonwyck
       G. I. War Brides
       Two Guys from Milwaukee
       The Walls Came Tumbling
         Down
  47: Cigarette Girl
       The Late George Apley

     Philo Vance's Gamble
     Second Chance
     The Trespasser
     The Senator Was Indiscreet
  48: The Dude Goes West
       Chicken Every Sunday
       That Wonderful Urge
       The Accused
       I, Jane Doe
  49: Take One False Step
       Bad Boy
  50: Flame and the Arrow
       Copper Canyon
  51: The Lemon Drop Kid
       That's My Boy
       Savage Drums
       Anne of the Indies
  52: The Prisoner of Zenda
       Hold that Line!
  53: The Robe

Tempe Pigott (1884-1962)
1929: Seven Days' Leave
  30: Night Work
  31: Devotion
  32: Dr. Jekyll and Mr. Hyde
  33: Cavalcade
       Oliver Twist
       Man of the Forest
       Dr. Bull
       If I Were Free
  34: Long Lost Father
       One More River
       The Lemon Drop Kid
       Limehouse Blues
  35: The Devil Is a Woman
       Bride of Frankenstein
       Calm Yourself
  36: The White Angel
  38: Fools for Scandal
  39: Boys Reformatory
  49: The Fan

Ezio Pinza (1892-1957)
1947: Carnegie Hall
  51: Mr. Emporium
       Strictly Dishonorable
  53: Tonight We Sing

Tom Pittman (1933-1959)
1957: The True Story of Jesse
James
The Young Stranger
The Way to the Gold
Bernadine
No Time to be Young
Black Patch
58: The Proud Rebel
Apache Territory
59: Verboten!

Zasu Pitts (1900-1963)
1928: 13 Washington Square   S
29: The Dummy
Sins of the Fathers   S
The Squall
Her Private Life
Twin Beds
This Thing Called Love
The Argyle Case
Sunny Side Up
The Locked Door
Oh Yeah!
Paris
30: Monte Carlo
Lottery Bride
Little Accident
The Devil's Holiday
Honey
Passion Flower
War Nurse
Sin Takes a Holiday
Free Love
No, No, Nanette
The Squealer
31: River's End
Their Mad Moment
Bad Sister
The Guardsman
various shorts with
Thelma Todd
Beyond Victory
Secret Witness
Big Gamble
Woman of Experience
Seed
Finn and Hattie
Penrod and Sam
Terror by Night

32: Shopworn
Strangers of the Evening
Eternally Yours
Nurse Edith Cavell
40: It All Came True
41: Broadway Limited
Niagara Falls
Miss Polly
Weekend for Three
The Mexican Spitfire's
Baby
42: The Mexican Spitfire at
Sea
The Bashful Bachelor
So's Your Aunt Emma
Tish
46: Breakfast in Hollywood
Perfect Marriage
47: Life with Father
49: Francis
52: The Denver and the Rio
Grande
54: Francis Joins the Wacs
57: This Could be the Night
61: Teenage Millionaire
63: The Thrill of it All
It's a Mad Mad Mad Mad
World
64: Big Parade of Comedy
(doc.)

Edward C. Platt (1926-
1955: The Shrike
Illegal
Rebel Without a Cause
Sincerely Yours
56: Backlash
The Lieutenant Wore Skirts
Serenade
The Proud Ones
Storm Center
The Unguarded Moment
Reprisal!
Rock, Pretty Baby
Written on the Wind
57: The Tattered Dress
Designing Woman
House of Numbers
Omar Khayyam
The Helen Morgan Story

57: Oregon Passage
58: Damn Citizen
The Gift of Love
Summer Love
The High Cost of Loving
Gunman's Walk
The Last of the Fast
Guns
59: The Rebel Set
North by Northwest
They Came to Cordura
Inside the Mafia
Cash McCall
60: Pollyanna
61: The Fiercest Heart
Atlantis--The Lost
Continent
The Explosive Generation
62: Cape Fear
63: A Ticklish Affair
Black Zoo
64: Bullet for a Badman
65: The Man from Button
Willow

Louise Platt (1915-
1938: I Met My Love Again
Spawn of the North
39: Stagecoach
Tell No Tales
40: Forgotten Girls
Captain Caution
42: Street of Chance

Marc Platt (1913-
1945: Tonight and Every Night
46: Tars and Spars
47: Down to Earth
The Swordsman
When a Girl's Beautiful
54: Seven Brides for Seven
Brothers
55: Oklahoma!

Donald Pleasence (1919-
1952: The Big Day
55: The Beachcomber
56: 1984
The Man in the Sky
57: Stowaway Girl

The Black Tents
Manuela
58: Heart of a Child
A Tale of Two Cities
The Man Inside
59: Look Back in Anger
The Two-Headed Spy
60: Circus of Horrors
Sons and Lovers
Hell Is a City
The Shakedown
Wind of Chance
The Horsemasters
Killers of Kilimanjaro
Battle of the Sexes
The Wind Cannot Read
61: No Love for Johnny
Spare the Rod
The Risk
No Place Like Homicide
62: Lisa
The Inspector
The Caretakers
63: The Great Escape
64: The House Guest
Dr. Crippen
65: The Greatest Story Ever
Told
The Hallelujah Trail
66: Fantastic Voyage
Cul-de-Sac
67: You Only Live Twice
Night of the Generals
Matchless
Eye of the Devil
68: Will Penny
69: I Love You, I Hate You
(dual role)
The Man Who Killed
Himself
The Madwoman of Chaillot
Arthur! Arthur!

Suzanne Pleshette (1937-
1958: The Geisha Boy
62: Rome Adventure
Forty Pounds of Trouble
63: The Birds
Wall of Noise
64: A Distant Trumpet

64: Fate Is the Hunter
65: A Rage to Live
Youngblood Hawke
66: The Ugly Dachshund
Nevada Smith
Mr. Buddwing
67: The Adventures of Bullwhip Griffin
68: Wings of Fire
Blackbeard's Ghost
69: The Power
If It's Tuesday, This
Must be Belgium
Suppose They Gave a War
and Nobody Came?

Christopher Plummer (1927-
1958: Stage Struck
Scross the Everglades
64: Fall of the Roman
Empire
65: The Sound of Music
66: Inside Daisy Clover
67: Night of the Generals
Triple Cross
Oedipus the King
68: Lock Up Your Daughters
High Commissioner
Nobody Runs Forever
69: The Battle of Britain
Royal Hunt of the Sun
Waterloo

Rossana Podesta (1934-
1953: Cops and Robbers
Goodbye My Son
Luxury Girls
54: Voice of Silence
55: Ulysses
Helen of Troy
56: Rosanna
Santiago (or, The Gun
Runner)
58: Raw Wind in Eden
62: Fury of the Pagans
Temptation
The Slave of Rome
63: Sodom and Gomorrah
64: The Golden Arrow
Alone Against Rome

65: Seven Dwarfs to the Rescue
Seven Golden Men

Eric Pohlmann (1913-
1954: Flame and the Flesh
55: A Prize of Gold
The Constant Husband
Gentlemen Marry Brunettes
Quentin Durward
56: Lust for Life
House of Secrets
High Terrace
57: The Counterfeit Plan
Break in the Circle
Fire Down Below
Pickup Alley
Mark of the Phoenix
58: I Accuse!
59: John Paul Jones
Elephant Gun
Expresso Bongo
The House of Seven Hawks
60: Surprise Package
61: Passport to China
63: Cairo
55 Days of Peking
64: The Man Who Couldn't
Walk
Night Train to Paris
65: Those Magnificent Men in
Their Flying Machines
Carry on Spying
66: Where the Spies Are
Agent 8 3/4
68: Oak Leaves and Fig Leaf
(Ger.)

Sidney Poitier (1924-
1949: From Whom Cometh My
Help (doc.)
50: No Way Out
52: Cry the Beloved Country
(African Fury)
Red Ball Express
54: Go, Man, Go!
55: The Blackboard Jungle
56: Goodbye, My Lady
57: A Band of Angels
Edge of the City
Something of Value

1107

58: The Defiant Ones
The Mark of the Hawk
59: Porgy and Bess
60: All the Young Men
Virgin Island
61: A Raisin in the Sun
Paris Blues
29 to Duel
62: Pressure Point
63: Lilies of the Field
(OSCAR)
64: The Long Ships
65: The Greatest Story Ever
Told
The Bedford Incident
Synanon
66: Patch of Blue
Cross My Heart
The Slender Thread
Duel at Diablo
67: Call Me Back
In the Heat of the Night
To Sir with Love
Guess Who's Coming to
Dinner
68: For the Love of Ivy
69: The Lost Man
Privilege
Dodo Birds Can't Fly
Tick, Tick, Tick
I Am Somebody
Caribbean Idyll

Daphne Pollard (1894-
1928: Sinners in Love   S
29: Big Time
South Sea Rose
Sky Hawk
30: Loose Ankles
Swing High
What a Widow!
31: Bright Lights
The Lady Refuses
35: Bonnie Scotland
Thicker than Water
36: Our Relations
41: Tillie the Toiler
43: Kid Dynamite
The Dancing Masters

Michael J. Pollard (1939-
1962: Hemingway's Adventures
of a Young Man
63: The Stripper
Summer Magic
66: The Russians Are Coming,
The Russians Are Coming!
The Wild Angels
67: Caprice
Bonnie and Clyde
Enter Laughing
68: Jigsaw
69: Hannibal Brooks
Little Fauss and Big
Halsey
The Smugglers (TV)

Snub Pollard (1886-1962)
1931: Ex-Flame
32: Midnight Patrol
Make Me a Star
Purchase Price
34: Stingaree
36: Just My Luck
The Crime Patrol
The Gentleman from
Louisiana
The White Legion
Headin' for the Rio
Grande
37: Arizona Days
Riders of the Rockies
Hittin' the Trail
Tex Rides with the Boy
Scouts
A Nation Aflame
38: Frontier Town
Where the Buffalo Roam
Starlight over Texas
39: Song of the Buckaroo
40: Murder on the Yukon
47: Perils of Pauline
48: Blackmail
57: A Man of a Thousand Faces
60: Who Was that Lady?
Studs Lonigan
61: The Errand Boy
Pocketful of Miracles
Days of Thrills and
Laughter (doc.)

1108

Lily Pons (1904-
1935: I Dream too Much
36: That Girl from Paris
37: Hitting a New High
47: Carnegie Hall

Don Porter (1912-
1942: Eagle Squadron
Top Sergeant
Night Monster
Who Done It?
43: Eyes of the Underworld
Keep 'em Slugging
46: Danger Woman
She-Wolf of London
Cuban Pete
Wild Beauty
47: Buck Privates Come
Home
50: 711 Ocean Drive
51: The Racket
52: The Savage
Because You're Mine
The Turning Point
Cripple Creek
56: Our Miss Brooks
61: Bachelor in Paradise
63: Gidget Goes to Rome
64: Youngblood Hawke
68: Live a Little, Love a
Little

Eric Porter (1928-
1964: Fall of the Roman
Empire
The Pumpkin Eater
65: The Heroes of Telemark
67: Kaleidoscope
68: The Lost Continent

Jean Porter
1932: The Gambling Set
33: The Penal Code
34: Inside Information
42: Heart of the Rio Grande
About Face!
43: Fall In!
The Youngest Profession
That Nazty Nuisance
Calaboose

44: San Fernando Valley
Andy Hardy's Blonde
Trouble
Thrill of a Romance
Bathing Beauty
45: Twice Blessed
Abbott & Costello in
Hollywood
What Next, Corporal Har-
grove?
46: Till the End of Time
Betty Co-Ed
47: That Hagen Girl
Sweet Genevieve
Two Blondes and a
Redhead
Little Miss Broadway
51: Cry Danger
Kentucky Jubilee
G.I. Jane
53: Racing Blood
55: The Left Hand of God

Eric Portman (1903-1969)
1935: Abdul the Damned
Old Roses
36: Murder in the Red Barn
37: The Prince and the Pauper
38: Crimes of Stephen Hawke
Moonlight Sonata
39: The Invaders (or, The
49th Parallel)
His Brother's Keeper
40: Hyde Park Corner
42: One of Our Aircraft Is
Missing
43: Squadron Leader X
We Dive at Dawn
Million Like Us
44: Uncensored
Escape to Danger
45: The Cardinal
46: Great Day
Men of Two Worlds
Wanted for Murder
48: Dear Murderer
The Mark of Cain
49: A Canterbury Tale
Blind Goddess
Corridor of Mirrors

49: Daybreak
My Brother's Keeper
50: Cairo Road
52: The Spider and the Fly
The Magic Box
54: The Golden Mask
55: The Deep Blue Sea
56: His Excellency
Child in the House
57: The Colditz Story
The Good Companions
61: The Naked Edge
Freud (or, The Secret
Passion)
65: The Bedford Incident
66: The Spy with a Cold Nose
67: Deadfall
The Whisperers
68: Assignment to Kill
69: The Man Who Finally
Died

Guy Bates Post (1876-1968)
1936: Fatal Lady
Camille
'Til We Meet Again
Trouble for Two
The Case Against Mrs.
Ames
37: Champagne Waltz
Maytime
Maid of Salem
Blazing Barriers
Daughter of Shanghai
39: Juarez and Maximilian
42: Crossroads
47: A Double Life

Tom Poston (1927-
1953: The City that Never
Sleeps
62: Zotz!
63: The Old Dark House
Soldier in the Rain
69: Cold Turkey

Victor Potel (1889-1947)
1928: What Price Beauty?   S
Melody of Love   S
Captain Swagger   SSE

Little Shepherd of King-
dom Come   S
Lingerie   S
29: Marianne
The Virginian
30: Border Romance
Dough Boys
The Bad One
Call of the West
The Big Shot
Paradise Island
Virtuous Sin
31: 10¢ a Dance
The Squaw Man
32: Partners
Make Me a Star
Purchase Price
33: Hallelujah, I'm a Bum!
34: Thunder over Texas
Inside Information
Frontier Days
35: Mississippi
The Girl Friend
The Trail's End
Last of the Clintons
Lady Tubbs
Hard Rock Harrigan
Waterfront Lady
Whispering Smith Speaks
36: Three Godfathers
O'Malley of the Mounted
Yellow Dust
Song of the Saddle
God's Country and the
Woman
Down to the Sea
37: The Captain's Kid
White Bondage
Western Gold
Small Town Boy
Two-Gun Law
38: Outside the Law
39: Rovin' Tumbleweeds
40: Girl from God's Country
Christmas in July
41: Birth of the Blues
Sullivan's Travels
44: Going to Town
The Miracle of Morgan's
Creek

44: Hail the Conquering Hero
The Great Moment
45: Captain Tugboat Annie
Rhythm Roundup
Strange Illusion
46: The Glass Alibi
47: The Egg and I
The Millerson Case
Ramrod
Mad Wednesday (or,
The Sin of Harold Diddle-
back)

Dick Powell (1904-1962)
1932: Blessed Event
42nd Street
Too Busy to Work
33: Gold Diggers of 1933
Footlight Parade
Convention City
College Coach
The King's Vacation
34: Dames
Flirtation Walk
Wonder Bar
Happiness Ahead
Twenty Million Sweet-
hearts
35: A Midsummer Night's
Dream
Page Miss Glory
Thanks a Million
Shipmates Forever
Broadway Gondolier
Gold Diggers of 1935
Ginger
Woman Wanted
If You Could Only Cook
36: Colleen
Hard to Please
Always Leave Them
Laughing
Hearts Divided
Stage Struck
Hollywood Boulevard
Yours for the Asking
37: Gold Diggers of 1937
Hollywood Hotel
Varsity Show
The Singing Marine

On the Avenue
The College Coed
38: For Auld Lang Syne (doc.)
Cowboy from Brooklyn
Hard to Get
Going Places
39: Naughty but Nice
40: I Want a Divorce
Christmas in July
41: Model Wife
In the Navy
42: Star-Spangled Rhythm
43: Happy-Go-Lucky
Riding High
True to Life
44: Meet the People
It Happened Tomorrow
Farewell My Lovely
45: Murder My Sweet
Cornered
47: Johnny O'Clock
48: To the Ends of the Earth
Pitfall
Station West
Rogues' Regiment
49: Mrs. Mike
50: The Reformer and the
Redhead
Right Cross
51: Cry Danger
Tall Target
You Never can Tell
Callaway Went Thataway
(cameo)
52: The Bad and the Beautiful
53: Split Second (dir.)
54: Susan Slept Here
56: The Conqueror (dir.)
You Can't Run Away from
It (dir.)
57: The Enemy Below (Dir.)
58: The Hunters (dir.)
61: Cargo and Capital (narr.)

Eleanor Powell (1912-
1935: George White's Scandals
of 1935
36: Broadway Melody of 1936
Born to Dance
37: Rosalie

1111

37: Broadway Melody of 1938
39: Honolulu
40: Broadway Melody of 1940
41: Lady be Good
42: Ship Ahoy!
43: I Dood It
    Thousands Cheer
44: Sensations of 1945
50: The Duchess of Idaho

Jane Powell (1929-
1944: Song of the Open Road
45: Delightfully Dangerous
46: Holiday in Mexico
47: The Birds and the Bees
48: Three Daring Daughters
    Luxury Liner
    A Date with Judy
50: Nancy Goes to Rio
    Two Weeks with Love
51: Royal Wedding
    Rich, Young, and Pretty
53: Small Town Girl
    Three Sailors and a Girl
54: Seven Brides for Seven
     Brothers
    Athena
    Deep in My Heart
55: Hit the Deck
57: The Girl Most Likely
58: The Female Animal
    Enchanted Island

William Powell (1892-
1929: Charming Sinners
    The Canary Murder Case
    The Feathers
    Pointed Heels
    The Greene Murder Case
30: Behind the Makeup
    The Benson Murder Case
    Paramount on Parade
    Shadow of the Law
    Street of Chance
    For the Defense
31: Dishonored
    Road to Singapore
    Heat Wave
    Man of the World
    Ladies' Man

32: High Pressure
    One Way Passage
    Jewel Robbery
    Lawyer Man
33: Private Detective 62
    The Kennel Murder Case
    Double Harness
34: Fashions of 1934
    Manhattan Melodrama
    Evelyn Prentice
    The Thin Man
    The Key
35: Star of Midnight
    Reckless
    Escapade
    Rendezvous
36: After the Thin Man
    Libeled Lady
    The Great Ziegfeld
    The Ex-Mrs. Bradford
    My Man Godfrey
37: The Last of Mrs. Cheyney
    The Emperor's Candlesticks
    Double Wedding
38: The Baroness and the
     Butler
39: Another Thin Man
40: I Love You Again
41: Love Crazy
    Shadow of the Thin Man
42: Crossroads
43: The Youngest Profession
    The Heavenly Body
44: The Thin Man Goes Home
46: The Hoodlum Saint
    Ziegfeld Follies
47: The Senator Was Indiscreet
    Song of the Thin Man
    Life with Father
48: Mr. Peabody and the Mer-
    maid
49: Take One False Step
    Dancing in the Dark
51: It's a Big Country
52: The Treasure of Lost
    Canyon
53: The Girl Who Had Every-
    thing
    How to Marry a Millionaire
55: Mr. Roberts

64: Big Parade of Comedy   Witness for the Prosecution
      (doc.)   The Sun Also Rises

Tyrone Power (1914-1958)   Mala Powers (1931-
1932: Tom Brown of Culver   1942: Tough as They Come
  36: Girls' Dormitory   50: Outrage
      Ladies in Love   Edge of Doom
      Lloyds of London   Cyrano de Bergerac
  37: Love Is News   52: Rose of Cimarron
      Cafe Metropole   53: City Beneath the Sea
      Thin Ice   City that Never Sleeps
      Second Honeymoon   Geraldine
  38: In Old Chicago   54: Yellow Mountain
      Alexander's Ragtime Band   55: Rage at Dawn
      Marie Antoinette   Bengazi
      Suez   57: Tammy and the Bachelor
  39: Rose of Washington Square   Storm Rider
      Second Fiddle   Death in Small Doses
      Jesse James   The Unknown Terror
      The Rains Came   Man on the Prowl
      Daytime Wife   58: Sierra Baron
  40: Johnny Apollo   The Colossus of New York
      Brigham Young--Frontiers-   61: Fear No More
      man   Flight of the Lost Balloon
      The Mark of Zorro   66: Lost Island of Kioga
  41: Blood and Sand   69: Rogue's Gallery
      A Yank in the R.A.F.   Daddy's Gone A-Hunting
  42: Son of Fury
      The Black Swan   Stefanie Powers (1942-
      This Above All   1962: Experiment in Terror
  43: Crash Dive   The Interns
  46: The Razor's Edge   If a Man Answers
  47: Nightmare Alley   63: Palm Springs Weekend
      Captain from Castile   McLintock!
  48: Luck of the Irish   64: The New Interns
      That Wonderful Urge   Tammy Tell Me True
  49: Prince of Foxes   65: Die! Die! My Darling
  50: Black Rose   The Young Sinner
      American Guerrilla in   66: Stagecoach
      the Philippines   Love Has Many Faces
  51: Rawhide   67: Warning Shot
      I'll Never Forget You   69: Man Without Mercy
  52: Diplomatic Courier   Crescendo
      Pony Soldier
  53: Mississippi Gambler   Tom Powers (1890-1955)
      King of the Khyber Rifles   1944: Double Indemnity
  55: Untamed   Practically Yours
      The Long Gray Line   46: The Blue Dahlia
  56: The Eddy Duchin Story   The Last Crooked Mile
  57: Abandon Ship!   Two Years Before the
                          Mast

Tyrone Power (and friends) in "The Mississippi Gambler"

46: Her Adventurous Night
47: Angel and the Badman
    The Farmer's Daughter
    They Won't Believe Me
    I Love Trouble
    Son of Rusty
48: The Time of Your Life
    Up in Central Park
    Mexican Hayride
    Angel in Exile
    Station West
49: Scene of the Crime
    Special Agent
    Chicago Deadline
    East Side, West Side
50: Chinatown at Midnight
    Destination Moon
51: Fighting Coast Guard
    The Tall Target
    The Strip
52: Phone Call from a
      Stranger
    The Fabulous Señorita
    The Denver and the
      Rio Grande
    Bal Tabarin
    We're not Married
    Jet Job
    The Steel Trap
    Horizons West
53: Scared Stiff
    Hannah Lee
    Julius Caesar
    Sea of Lost Ships
    The Marksman
    Donovan's Brain
    The Last Posse
55: The Americano
    Ten Wanted Men
    New York Confidential
56: UFO

Judson Pratt (1916-
1957: Man Afraid
58: Flood Tide
    Monster on the Campus
60: The Rise and Fall of
      Legs Diamond
    Sgt. Rutledge
62: Kid Galahad

63: The Ugly American
64: A Distant Trumpet
    Cheyenne Autumn

Purnell Pratt (1882-1951)
1929: Alibi
    Through Different Eyes
    On with the Show   PT
    Fast Life
    The Trespasser
    Is Everybody Happy?
    The Locked Door
30: Puttin' on the Ritz
    Common Clay
    Lawful Larceny
    Road to Paradise
    The Gorilla
    Silver Lode
    Sinner's Holiday
    Paid
31: Bachelor Apartment
    Fires of Youth
    Dance, Fools, Dance
    The Prodigal
    Traveling Husbands
    Woman Pursued
    Up for Murder
    Public Defender
    The Spider
    The Gay Diplomat
    Secret Witness
    Terror by Night
32: Hat Check Girl
    Red Haired Alibi
    False Faces
    Unwritten Law
    Emma
    Ladies of the Big House
    Grand Hotel
    The Famous Ferguson Case
    Roadhouse Murder
33: Billion Dollar Scandal
    Pick Up
    I Cover the Waterfront
    A Shriek in the Night
    Sweetheart of Sigma Chi
    Headline Shooter
    The Chief
    Love, Honor, and Oh Baby!
    Midshipman Jack

34: The Witching Hour
Hell Cat
Name the Woman
Midnight Alibi
The Crimson Romance
School for Girls
35: The Casino Murder Case
The Winning Ticket
Death Flies East
Behind Green Lights
Rendezvous at Midnight
Black Fury
Diamond Jim
Ladies Crave Excitement
Waterfront Lady
It's in the Air
Red Salute
$1000 a Minute
Frisco Waterfront
Magnificent Obsession
36: Dancing Feet
The Return of Sophie Lang
Wives Never Know
Hollywood Boulevard
Straight from the Shoulder
The Plainsman
Wedding Present
37: Let's Make a Million
Murder Goes to College
Join the Marines
King of Gamblers
High, Wide, and Handsome
Under Suspicion
38: Come on, Rangers!
39: My Wife's Relatives
Colorado Sunset
Grand Ole Opry
41: Ringside Maisie

June Preisser
1939: Babes in Arms
Dancing Coed
Judge Hardy and Son
40: Strike Up the Band
Gallant Sons
41: Henry Aldrich for
President
42: Sweater Girl
43: Merrily We Sing
44: Babes on Swing Street

Murder in the Blue Room
45: I'll Tell the World
Let's Go Steady
46: Freddie Steps Out
High School Hero
Junior Prom
Her Sister's Secret
47: Sarge Goes to College
Vacation Days
Two Blondes and a Red-
head
48: Campus Sleuth
Smart Politics
The Music Man

Otto Preminger (1906-
1942: The Pied Piper
43: They Got Me Covered
Margin for Error
44: Laura (prod., dir.)
In the Meantime, Darling
45: Fallen Angel
A Royal Scandal (dir.)
46: Centennial Summer (prod.,
dir.)
Forever Amber (dir.)

Paula Prentiss (1939-
1960: Where the Boys Are
61: Bachelor in Paradise
The Honeymoon Machine
62: The Horizontal Lieutenant
63: Follow the Boys
64: Man's Favorite Sport?
The World of Henry Orient
Looking for Love
65: In Harm's Way
What's New Pussycat?
69: Catch 22
M-O-V-E

Micheline (Prelle) Presle (1922-
1938: Je Chante
Jeunes Filles en Détresse
L'Histoire de Rire
41: La Nuit Fantastique
Felicie Nanteuil
Seul Amour
Falbalas
45: Boule de Suif

1116

46: Diable au Corps
    (The Devil in the Flesh)
47: Jeux Sont Faix
48: Foolish Husbands
50: Under My Skin
    American Guerrillas in
    the Philippines
51: Adventures of Captain
    Fabian
    Sins of Pompeii
52: La Dame aux Camelias
54: Villa Borghese
    Napoleon
56: House of Ricordi
57: She Wolves
    Royal Affairs in Versailles
    It Happened in the Park
59: Blind Date
    The French Way
    The Bride Is Much Too
    Beautiful
60: Christine
    Chance Meeting
    Human Cargo
61: Five-Day Lover
    Time Out for Love
62: If a Man Answers
    Seven Capital Sins (Lust
    seq.)
63: The Prize
64: A Mistress for the
    Summer
    Dark Purpose
65: La Chasse à L'Homme
    (Male Hunt)
66: Hail Mafia!
67: King of Hearts
68: To Be a Crook

Elvis Presley (1935-
1956: Love Me Tender
57: Jailhouse Rock
    Loving You
58: King Creole
60: G.I. Blues
    The Flaming Arrow
61: Wild in the Country
    Blue Hawaii
62: Girls! Girls! Girls!
    Follow that Dream

    Kid Galahad
63: It Happened at the World's
    Fair
    Fun in Acapulco
64: Viva Las Vegas!
    Kissin' Cousins
    Roustabout
65: Girl Happy
    Harum Scarum
    Tickle Me
66: Paradise Hawaiian Style
    Frankie and Johnny
    Spin-Out
67: Easy Come, Easy Go
    Double Trouble
    Clambake
68: Stay Away Joe!
    Live a Little, Love a
    Little
    Speedway
69: Kiss My Firm but Pliant
    Lips
    Charro!
    The Trouble with Girls (or,
    The Chautauqua)
    Change of Habit

Harve Presnell (1933-
1964: The Unsinkable Molly
    Brown
65: The Glory Guys
    When the Boys Meet the
    Girls
69: Paint Your Wagon

Robert Preston (1917-
1938: King of Alcatraz
    Illegal Traffic
39: Disbarred
    Union Pacific
    Beau Geste
40: Typhoon
    Moon over Burma
    Northwest Mounted Police
41: The Lady from Cheyenne
    Parachute Battalion
    New York Town
    The Night of January 16th
    Midnight Angel
42: Pacific Blackout

1117

42: Pacific Blackout
This Gun for Hire
Reap the Wild Wind
Wake Island
43: Night Plane from Chung-
king
47: Wild Harvest
Varsity Girl
The Macomber Affair
48: Whispering Smith
Blood on the Moon
49: The Big City
The Lady Gambles
Tulsa
50: The Sundowners
51: When I Grow Up
My Outlaw Brother
Best of the Bad Men
52: Cloudburst
Face to Face
The Bride Comes to
Yellow Sky
55: The Last Frontier
56: Savage Wilderness
60: The Dark at the Top of
the Stairs
62: The Music Man
63: How the West Was Won
Island of Love
All the Way Home

Wayde Preston
1963: The Man on the Spying
Trapeze
68: Anzio
69: Today it's Me...
Tomorrow, You!

Marie Prevost (1898-1937)
1929: The Godless Girl   PT
Flying Fool
Divorce Made Easy
30: Party Girl
Ladies at Leisure
Sweethearts on Parade
War Nurse
Sideshow
31: Paid
Sporting Blood
A Gentleman's Fate

It's a Wise Child
Good Bad Girl
Lovable and Sweet
The Runaround
Hell Divers
The Sin of Madelon
Claudet
Reckless Living
32: Three Wise Girls
Carnival Boat
Slightly Married
33: The 11th Commandment
Parole Girl
36: Tango

Dennis Price (1915-
1944: A Canterbury Tale
A Place of One's Own
46: The Magic Bow
Hungry Hill
47: Snowbound
Dear Murderer
Jassy
Holiday Camp
Master of Bankdam
The White Unicorn
48: Good Time Girl
The Bad Lord Byron
49: Kind Hearts and Coronets
The Dancing Years
50: The Adventurers
51: Lady Godiva Rides Again
52: The House in the Square
Song of Paris
53: The Intruder
54: That Lady
55: Oh, Rosalinda
56: Private's Progress
Port Afrique
Charley Moon
57: Time Is My Enemy
58: The Naked Truth
She Played with Fire
Your Past Is Showing
60: I'm All Right, Jack
Oscar Wilde
Tunes of Glory
61: The Millionairess
62: The Victim
No Place Like Homicide!

62: Kill or Cure
63: Play it Cool
64: Tamahine
The Horror of it All
The Earth Dies Screaming
65: Curse of the Voodoo
A High Wind in Jamaica
Ten Little Indians
The Amorous Mr. Prawn
67: The Blast-Off
69: Venus in Furs

Kate Price (1872-1942)
1929: The Cohens and the
Kellys in Atlantic City PT
The Godless Girl   PT
Two Weeks Off
30: The Rogue Song
The Cohens and the
Kellys in Scotland
Dancing Sweeties
Shadow Ranch
The Cohens and the
Kellys in Africa
31: Ladies of the Jury
34: Have a Heart

Vincent Price (1911-
1938: Service de Luxe
39: The Private Life of
Elizabeth and Essex
Tower of London
40: Green Hell
The Invisible Man Returns
The House of Seven
Gables
Brigham Young--Frontiers-
man
Hudson's Bay
43: The Song of Bernadette
44: Buffalo Bill
The Eve of St. Mark
Wilson
Keys of the Kingdom
Laura
45: A Royal Scandal
Leave Her to Heaven
Czarina
46: Dragonwyck
Shock

47: The Long Night
Moss Rose
Jeopardy
48: The Three Musketeers
Rogues' Regiment
Up in Central Park
49: The Bribe
Bagdad
50: The Baron of Arizona
Champagne for Caesar
Curtain Call at Cactus
Creek
51: His Kind of Woman
Adventures of Captain
Fabian
52: Las Vegas Story
53: House of Wax (3-D)
54: Dangerous Mission
Mad Magician
Casanova's Big Night
55: Son of Sinbad
56: Serenade
While the City Sleeps
The Ten Commandments
57: The Story of Mankind
58: The Fly
House on Haunted Hill
59: The Return of the Fly
The Bat
The Tingler
The Big Circus
60: The House of Usher
61: The Master of the World
The Pit and the Pendulum
The Naked Terror
62: Souls for Sale
Reprieve
Convicts Four
Confessions of an Opium
Eater
Poe's Tales of Terror
Rage of the Buccaneers
Tower of London
63: The Raven
The Haunted Palace
Diary of a Madman
Twice Told Tales
Comedy of Terrors
64: The Mask of the Red Death
The Last Man on Earth

65: War Gods of the Deep
Tomb of Ligeia
The Jackals
Taboos of the World
(narr. doc.)
66: Dr. Goldfoot and the
Bikini Machine
67: 2165 A.D.
When the Sleeper Awakes
House of a Thousand
Dolls
The Case of M. Valdemar
The Black Cat
Morella
68: The Conqueror Worm
More Dead than Alive
69: The Oblong Box
The Gold Bug
Scream and Scream Again
The Trouble with Girls (or,
The Chautauqua)

Maudie Prickett
1946: Two-Fisted Stranger
The Fighting Frontiers-
man
47: Lone Hand Texan
Time Out of Mind
48: Song of Idaho
50: Messenger of Peace
51: Her First Romance
The Model and the
Marriage Broker
Pecos River
52: Stars and Stripes Forever
55: A Man Called Peter
Man with a Gun
57: The Phantom Stagecoach
58: Thundering Jets
59: The Legend of Tom
Dooley
North by Northwest
65: I'll Take Sweden
67: The Gnome-Mobile
69: Rascal
The Maltese Bippy

Oliver Prickett (1905-
1940: New York Town
41: Shadow of the Thin Man

H.M. Pulham, Esq.
Design for Scandal
42: I Married an Angel
Saboteur
The Postman Didn't Ring
Casablanca
Adventures of Mark Twain
Reunion in France
Get Hep to Love
43: Mission to Moscow
Sweet Rosie O'Grady
Greenwich Village
Up in Arms
National Barn Dance
Gypsy Wildcat
Corvette K-225
44: Destination: Tokyo
The Mask of Dimitrios
Doughgirls
Stranger in the Midst
The Thin Man
Col. Effingham's Raid
Jungle Queen
The Very Thought of You
Hollywood Canteen
45: Enchanted Voyage
Murder Mansion
Rhapsody in Blue
Conflict
A Medal for Benny
46: My Reputation
Inside Job
Blonde Alibi
Ginger
Live and Learn
The Mighty McGurk
47: Guilty
Out of the Past
Merton of the Movies
The Senator was Indiscreet
Nightmare Alley
The Road to Rome
Miracle of the Bells
48: Arch of Triumph
The Pirate
Good Sam
The Walls of Jericho
Summer Holiday
The Challenge
Moonrise

1120

48: Shed No Tears
Long Denial
49: The Girl from Jones
Beach
Colorado Territory
Ma and Pa Kettle
Ma and Pa Kettle Go to
Town
50: Father of the Bride
Ma and Pa Kettle on the
Farm
Let's Dance
51: The Lemon Drop Kid
Come Fill the Cup
Chain of Circumstances
52: Ma and Pa Kettle at the
Fair
The Stooge
The Greatest Show on
Earth
Room for One More
The Belle of New York
Son of Paleface
The Iron Mistress
Back to Broadway
Bowery Boys
53: So This Is Love
Ma and Pa Kettle on
Vacation
Julius Caesar
Houdini
Man of Wax
So Big
54: Casanova's Big Night
Ma and Pa Kettle at Home
The Long, Long Trailer
Susan Slept Here
Brigadoon
Drum Beat
55: Ma and Pa Kettle at
Waikiki
Moonfleet
The Cobweb
The Seven Little Foys
Bar Sinister (or, It's a
Dog's Life)
56: Lust for Life
57: Raintree County
The Beast of Budapest
58: Onionhead

Beau Geste
60: Bells Are Ringing

William Prince (1912-
1943: Destination: Tokyo
44: Hollywood Canteen
The Very Thought of You
45: Objective Burma!
Pillow to Post
46: Cinderella Jones
Shadow of a Woman
47: Carnegie Hall
Dead Reckoning
49: For Those Who Dare
Lust for Gold
50: Cyrano de Bergerac
56: Secret of Treasure
Mountain
The Vagabond King
58: Macabre

Andrew Prine (1935-
1958: Kiss Her Goodbye
62: The Miracle Worker
64: Advance to the Rear
66: Texas Across the River
68: Bandolero
The Devil's Brigade
69: Generation

Aileen Pringle (c1885-
1929: Dream of Love
The Single Man
Night Parade
30: Puttin' on the Ritz
Prince of Diamonds
Soldiers and Women
31: Subway Express
Murder at Midnight
Convicted
32: Police Court
Age of Consent
33: By Appointment Only
34: Love Past Thirty
Jane Eyre
Once to Every Bachelor
35: Sons of Steel
36: The Unguarded Hour
Piccadilly Jim
Wanted: Jane Turner

1121

37: The Last of Mrs. Cheyney
John Meade's Woman
Nothing Sacred
39: The Girl from Nowhere
The Hardys Ride High
Should a Girl Marry?
40: The Night of Nights
43: The Youngest Profession
Happy Land
44: A Wave, a Wac, and a
Marine
Since You Went Away

Lucien Prival (1900-
1929: Peacock Fan   S
30: Party Girl
In the Next Room
Hell's Angels   SSE
Last of the Lone Wolf
The Princess and the
Plumber
Lotus Lady
31: Young Sinners
32: Hollywood Speaks
Western Limited
Sherlock Holmes
Secrets of the French
Police
33: Grand Slam
The Sphinx
After Tonight
The Crime of Helen
Stanley
Return of Chandu
35: Pride of Frankenstein
Champagne for Breakfast
Born to Gamble
36: Darkest Africa
37: History Is Made at Night
River of Missing Men
High Flyers
Every Day's a Holiday
38: Mr. Wong, Detective
39: Confessions of a Nazy
Spy
Beasts of Berlin
Nurse Edith Cavell
Espionage Agent
40: Sky Murder
41: South of Panama

Man Hunt
42: Yukon Patrol
43: Submarine Base
46: The Falcon's Alibi

Jed Prouty (1879-1956)
1928: The Siren   S
Name the Woman   S
29: Danny Boy
Why Leave Home?
Fall of Eve
His Captive Woman   PT
Two Weeks Off
Broadway Melody
It's a Great Life
Imperfect Ladies
30: Girl in the Show
The Devil's Holiday
True to the Navy
The Fioradora Girl
31: Strangers May Kiss
Annabelle's Affairs
Secret Call
Age for Love
32: Business and Pleasure
Manhattan Tower
33: Skyway
No Questions Asked
Jimmy and Sally
The Big Bluff
34: Private Secretary
I Believed in You
Music in the Air
Private Scandal
35: One Hour Late
George White's Scandals
of 1935
Black Sheep
Navy Wife
36: Every Saturday Night
Little Miss Nobody
Educating Father
Back to Nature
Can this be Dixie?
Under Your Spell
Special Investigator
His Brother's Wife
The Texas Rangers
College Holiday
Happy-Go-Lucky

1122

37: The Jones Family Off to
the Races
Big Business with the
Joneses
The Jones Family in Hot
Water
The Jones Family Borrow-
ing Trouble
Life Begins in College
The Crime Nobody Saw
Sophie Land Goes West
Dangerous Holiday
One Hundred Men and a
Girl
Small Town Boy
You Can't Have Every-
thing
38: Love on a Budget
Walking Down Broadway
A Trip to Paris
Keep Smiling
Safety in Numbers
Everybody's Baby
Duke of West Point
Goodbye Broadway
Danger on the Air
Down on the Farm (or,
The Jones Family)
39: The Gracie Allen Murder
Case
The Jones Family in
Hollywood
Quick Millions
Hollywood Cavalcade
Too Busy to Work
Exile Express
40: Young as You Feel
Remedy for Riches
Barnyard Follies
41: The Lone Wolf Keeps a
Date
Pot o' Gold
Roar of the Press
Father Steps Out
Bachelor Daddy
Unexpected Uncle
City Limits
Look Who's Laughing
Go West Young Lady
42: The Affairs of Jimmy
Valentine

Scattergood Rides High
It Happened in Flatbush
Moonlight Masquerade
The Old Homestead
43: Mug Town
50: Guilty Bystander

Dorothy Provine (1937-
1958: The Bonnie Parker Story
Live Fast, Die Young
59: Riot in Juvenile Prison
The Thirty Foot Bride of
Candy Rock
63: It's a Mad Mad Mad Mad
World
Wall of Noise
64: Good Neighbor Sam
65: That Darn Cat
The Great Race
66: One Spy too Many
67: Kiss the Girls and Make
Them Die
Who's Minding the Mint?
68: Never a Dull Moment
69: The Sound of Anger (TV)

Jon Provost (1949-
1956: Back from Eternity
57: Escapade in Japan
63: Lassie's Great Adventure
66: This Property Is
Condemned

Juliet Prowse (1936-
1960: Can-Can
G.I. Blues
61: The Fiercest Heart
The Second Time Around
The Right Approach
65: Who Killed Teddy Bear?
Dingaka
66: Run for Your Wife
67: Spree

Cameron Prud'Homme (1892-1967)
1930: Abraham Lincoln
Doorway to Hell
Half Shot at Sunrise
31: Soldiers' Plaything
I Like Your Nerve
Honor of the Family

56: The Power and the Prize
Back from Eternity
The Rainmaker
63: The Cardinal

Ainslie Pryor
1955: The Girl in the Red
Velvet Swing
56: The Last Hunt
Ransom
Walk the Proud Land
Four Girls in Town
57: Shadow on the Window
Guns of Fort Petticoat
58: Cole Younger--Gun-
fighter
Kathy O'
The Left-Handed Gun
Onionhead

Roger Pryor (1903-1954)
1930: 2 shorts
33: The Collegiate Model
Moonlight and Pretzels
34: I Like It That Way
Romance in the Rain
I'll Tell the World
Wake Up and Dream
Gift of Gab
Belle of the Nineties
Lady by Choice
35: Strange Wives
Straight from the Heart
Headline Woman
Dinky
To Beat the Band
A $1000 a Minute
The Girl Friend
The Case of the Missing
Man
36: Return of Jimmy
Valentine
Ticket to Paradise
Sitting on the Moon
Missing Girls
39: The Man They Could not
Hang
40: Sued for Libel
Fugitive from Justice
The Man with Nine Lives

The Lone Wolf Meets a
Lady
Money and the Woman
Gambling on the High Seas
Glamour for Sale
41: She Couldn't Say No
Bowery Boy
South of Panama
Power Dive
Bullets for O'Hara
Richest Man in Town
Flying Blind
Gambling Daughters
The Officer and the Lady
42: Meet the Mob
Smart Alecks
I Live on Danger
So's Your Aunt Emma
43: Girls in Chains
Submarine Alert
Lady Bodyguard
44: Thoroughbreds
45: Scared Stiff
The Kid Sister
High Powered
Identity Unknown
The Cisco Kid Returns
The Man from Oklahoma

Frank Puglia (c1894-1962)
1934: Men in White
Viva Villa!
35: The Melody Lingers On
Bordertown
36: Fatal Lady
The Devil Is a Sissy
Bulldog Edition
The Gay Desperado
Garden of Allah
37: A Doctor's Diary
Bulldog Drummond's
Revenge
Mama Steps Out
Song of the City
The Bride Wore Red
When You're in Love
Maytime
You Can't Have Everything
38: Rascals
I'll Give a Million

38: Sharpshooters
Spawn of the North
Dramatic School
Barefoot Boy
39: Zaza
Forged Passport
In Old Caliente
Code of the Secret
  Service
Maisie
40: The Fatal Hour
Charlie Chan in Panama
Torrid Zone
Down Argentine Way
Arise My Love
Meet the Wildcat
The Mark of Zorro
41: That Night in Rio
Billy the Kid
The Parson of Panamint
Law of the Tropics
42: Who Is Hope Schuyler?
Secret Agent of Japan
Jungle Book
Always in My Heart
Flight Lieutenant
Escape from Hong Kong
Now Voyager
Casablanca
43: Action in the North
  Atlantic
Pilot No. 5
Mission to Moscow
Background to Danger
Princess O'Rourke
The Phantom of the Opera
Tarzan's Desert Mystery
For Whom the Bell Tolls
44: Ali Baba and the Forty
  Thieves
This Is the Life
Tall in the Saddle
Brazil
Together Again
45: A Song to Remember
Blood on the Sun
Roughly Speaking
Weekend at the Waldorf
46: Without Reservations
47: My Favorite Brunette

Station Road
Brute Force
Fiesta
The Lost Moment
Road to Rio
48: Dream Girl
Joan of Arc
49: Colorado Territory
Bride of Vengeance
Special Agent
Bagdad
50: Federal Agent at Large
Black Hand
Captain Carey, U.S.A.
The Desert Hawk
Walk Softly Stranger
53: The Bandits of Corsica
The Caddy
The Steel Lady
54: The Shanghai Story
56: Serenade
The First Texan
The Burning Hills
Accused of Murder
57: Duel at Apache Wells
Twenty Million Miles to
  Earth
59: Cry Tough
The Black Orchid
62: Girls! Girls! Girls!
65: The Sword of Ali Baba

William Pullen
1950: All About Eve
52: Caribbean
The Lawless Breed
53: The Farmer Takes a Wife
War Paint
The Redheads from Seattle
54: Ride Clear of Diablo
55: Strategic Air Command
Canyon Crossroads
57: Short Cut to Hell
Hell Canyon Outlaws

Lilo Pulver
1960: The Last Summer
61: One, Two, Three
62: Where the Truth Lies
63: Breakfast in Bed

64: A Global Affair
66: Le Jardinier D'Argenteuil

Liselotte Pulver (c1939-
1958: The Confessions of Felix
    Krull
    A Time to Love and a
    Time to Die
    Reaching for the Stars
61: The Spessart Inn
64: Buddenbrooks

Bernard Punsley
1939: Angels Wash Their Faces
    On Dress Parade
40: Give Us Wings
41: Hit the Road
    Mob Town
42: Tough as They Come
43: Mug Town

Dick Purcell (1908-1944)
1935: Ceiling Zero
36: Man Hunt
    Brides Are Like that
    Times Square Playboy
    The Law in Her Hands
    Bullets or Ballots
    Jail Break
    Men in Exile
    Broadway Playboy
    The Case of the Velvet
    Claws
    Public Enemy's Wife
    King of Hockey
37: The Captain's Kid
    Melody for Two
    Navy Blues
    Slim
    Wine, Women, and Horses
    Public Wedding
    Missing Witnesses
    Reported Missing
38: Alcatraz Island
    Accidents Will Happen
    Over the Wall
    Penrod's Double Trouble
    Garden of the Moon
    Valley of the Giants
    Flight Into Nowhere

    Air Devils
    Broadway Musketeers
    Mystery House
    Nancy Drew, Detective
    The Daredevil Drivers
39: Tough Kid
    Blackwell's Island
    Streets of New York
    Irish Luck
    Heroes in Blue
40: Private Affairs
    Outside the Three-Mile
    Limit
    New Moon
    Arise My Love
    The Bank Dick
    Flight Command
41: King of the Zombies
    Bullets for O'Hara
    The Pittsburgh Kid
    Flying Blind
    Two in a Taxi
    No Hands on the Clock
42: Torpedo Boat
    In Old California
    The Old Homestead
    The Phantom Killer
    I Live on Danger
    X Marks the Spot
43: Aerial Gunner
    High Explosives
    Idaho
    Reveille for Beverly
    Mystery of the 13th Guest
    No Place for a Lady
    Captain American (ser.)
44: Timber Queen
    Trocadero
    Leave it to the Irish
    Farewell My Lovely
53: Return of Captain America
    (re-rel. of Captain
    America)

Edmund Purdom (1925-
1953: Titanic
    Julius Caesar
54: The Student Prince
    The Egyptian
    Athena

55: The Prodigal
The King's Thief
Moment of Danger
56: Strange Intruder
60: The Cossacks
Nights of Rasputin
Trapped in Tangiers
Herod the Great
62: Loves of Salamambo
White Slave Ship
Last of the Vikings
Malaga
Fury of the Pagans
63: Suleiman the Conqueror
The Comedy Man
Lafayette
64: Last Ride to Santa Cruz
The Beauty Jungle
65: The Yellow Rolls-Royce
66: Contest Girl

Denver Pyle (1920-
1948: Where the North Begins
Train to Alcatraz
The Man from Colorado
Marshal of Amarillo
49: Red Canyon
Hellfire
Streets of San Francisco
Flame of Youth
50: Dynamite Pass
Federal Agent at Large
The Flying Saucers
Customs Agent
The Old Frontier
51: Rough Rider of Durango
Million Dollar Pursuit
Hills of Utah
52: Oklahoma Annie
Desert Passage
Canyon Ambush
Fargo
Man from the Black Hills
The Maverick
53: Goldtown Ghost Riders
Rebel City
Topeka
54: Ride Clear of Diablo
55: Run for Cover
Ten Wanted Men

To Hell and Back
Top Gun
56: Please Murder Me
The Naked Hills
The Seventh Cavalry
Yaqui Drums
57: The Lonely Man
Gun Duel in Durango
Destination: 60,000
The Domino Kid
Jet Pilot
58: The Left-Handed Gun
Fort Massacre
China Doll
The Party Crashers
A Good Day for Hanging
59: King of the Wild Stallions
Cast a Long Shadow
60: The Alamo
62: Geronimo
64: The Mail Order Bride
65: The Rounders
Shenandoah
The Great Race
Mara of the Wilderness
66: Gunpoint
Incident at Phantom Hill
67: Tammy and the Millionaire
Bonnie and Clyde
Welcome to Hard Times
68: Bandolero
Five Card Stud

John Qualen (1908-
1931: Street Scene
Arrowsmith
33: Counsellot-at-Law
34: Let's Fall in Love
Upperworld
Hi Nellie!
Sing and Like it
He Was Her Man
Our Daily Bread
Servants' Entrance
365 Nights in Hollywood
35: One More Spring
The Great Hotel Murder
Charlie Chan in Paris
Doubting Thomas
Orchids to You

1127

35: Thunder in the Night
The Farmer Takes a Wife
The Silk Hat Kid
Chasing Yesterday
The Three Musketeers
Black Fury
Man of Iron
Cheers of the Crowd
36: Whipsaw
The Country Doctor
Road to Glory
Girls' Dormitory
Reunion
Ring Around the Moon
Meet Nero Wolfe
37: Nothing Sacred
Seventh Heaven
Fifty Roads to Town
Angel's Holiday
She Had to Eat
Fit for a King
38: Bad Man of Brimstone
The Chaser
Joy of Living
Outside the Law
Five of a Kind
The Mad Miss Manton
39: Stand Up and Fight
Honeymoon in Bali
Mickey the Kid
Thunder Afloat
Four Wives
40: His Girl Friday
Blondie on a Budget
Angels over Broadway
The Grapes of Wrath
On Their Own
The Long Voyage Home
Youth Will be Served
Ski Patrol
Knute Rockne--All
American
41: Million Dollar Baby
Out of the Fog
The Shepherd of the Hills
Here Is a Man
Model Wife
All that Money can Buy
New Wine
42: Larceny, Inc.

Jungle Book
Tortilla Flat
Arabian Nights
Casablanca
43: Swing Shift Maisie
44: The Impostor
The American Romance
Dark Waters
45: Roughly Speaking
River Gang
Captain Kidd
46: Adventure
47: The Fugitive
Song of Scheherazade
High Conquest
48: My Girl Tisa
Alias a Gentleman
Sixteen Fathoms Deep
Hollow Triumph
49: The Big Steal
Captain China
50: The Buccaneer Girl
Jackpot
Woman on the Run
51: Flying Missile
Belle Le Grand
Goodbye My Fancy
52: Hans Christian Andersen
53: Ambush at Tomahawk Gap
I, the Jury
54: Student Prince
The High and the Mighty
Passion
The Other Woman
55: Unchained
The Sea Chase
At Gunpoint
56: The Searchers
Johnny Concho
Country Doctor
57: The Big Land
58: The Gun Runners
Terror in the Haunted
House
Revolt in the Big House
59: Anatomy of a Murder
60: Hell Bent for Leather
North to Alaska
61: Two Rode Together
The Comancheros

62: The Man Who Shot
Liberty Valance
63: The Prize
64: The Seven Faces of Dr.
Lao
Cheyenne Autumn
Those Calloways
65: Patch of Blue
I'll Take Sweden
The Sons of Katie Elder
66: A Big Hand for the Little
Lady
68: P.J.

Nena Quartaro (1911-
1929: The Red Mark   S
The Eternal Woman   S
Frozen River   PT
One Stolen Night   PT
30: Monsieur Le Fox
The Redeeming Sin   PT
The Virginian
Under a Texas Moon
Golden Dawn
31: The Hawk
Bachelor Father
Arizonian Terror
Men of the North
God's Gift to Women
The Squawk
His Last Hour
Trapped
Zeppelin
33: Man from Monterey
The Devil's Brother
43: A Lady Takes a Chance

Anthony Quayle (1913-
1948: Hamlet
55: Oh Rosalina!
Battle of the River Plate
(or, Pursuit of the Graf
Spee; or, Graf Spee)
56: No Time for Tears
57: The Wrong Man
Woman in a Dressing
Gown
58: Ice Cold Is Alex
Serious Charge
59: The Challenge

Tarzan's Greatest Adventure
60: The Man Who Wouldn't
Talk
Desert Attack
61: The Guns of Navarone
H.M.S. Defiant
62: Lawrence of Arabia
64: The Fall of the Roman
Empire
East of Sudan
A Touch of Hell
65: Operation Crossbow
A Study in Terror
66: The Poppy Is Also a
Flower (TV)
67: Mackenna's Gold
68: Misunderstood
Saraband for Dead Lovers
69: Before Winter Comes
Anne of the Thousand
Days
The Gaunt Woman

Eddie Quillan (1907-
1929: Godless Girl   PT
The Sophomore
Geraldine   PT
Noisy Neighbors   PT
Hot and Bothered
30: Up and at 'Em
Night Work
Big Money
A Little Bit of Everything
31: Sweepstakes
Looking for Trouble
a short
Tip Off
32: The Big Shot
The Optimist
Girl Crazy
Easy Money
33: Strictly Personal
Broadway to Hollywood
34: The Gridiron Flash
Hollywood Party
35: Mutiny on the Bounty
36: The Gentleman from
Louisiana
37: The Mandarin Mystery
London by Night

1129

37: Big City	Richard Quine (1920-
38: Swing, Sister, Swing!	1934: Jane Eyre
39: Made for Each Other	Little Men
The Flying Irish Man	35: Life Returns
Allegheny Uprising	Dinky
The Family Next Door	A Dog of Flanders
Young Mr. Lincoln	41: Babes on Broadway
40: The Grapes of Wrath	42: Tish
La Conga Nights	My Sister Eileen
Margie	For Me and My Gal
Dark Streets of Cairo	Dr. Gillespie's New
Hawaiian Nights	Assistant
41: Six Lessons from	Stand by for Action
Madame La Zonga	43: We've Never Been Licked
Where Did You Get that	46: Cockeyed Miracle
Girl?	48: Words and Music
Dancing on a Dime	Command Decision
Flame of New Orleans	50: No Sad Songs for Me
Too Many Blondes	Rookie Fireman
Flying Blind	
42: The Kid Glove Killer	Anthony Quinn (1915-
Priorities on Parade	1936: Parole!
43: Hi Ya, Sailor!	The Plainsman
It Ain't Hay	37: Swing High, Swing Low
Follow the Band	Waikiki Wedding
Melody Parade	The Last Train from
Here Comes Kelly	Madrid
44: Dark Mountain	Daughter of Shanghai
This Is the Life	Partners in Crime
Moonlight and Cactus	38: The Buccaneer
Mystery of the River	Dangerous to Know
Boat (ser.)	Tip-Off Girls
The Impostor	Hunted Men
Hi, Good Lookin'!	Bulldog Drummond in
Slightly Terrific	Africa
Dixie Jamboree	King of Alcatraz
Twilight on the Prairie	39: Union Pacific
45: Song of the Sarong	Island of Lost Men
Jungle Queen (ser.)	Television Spy
Jungle Raiders (ser.)	King of Chinatown
46: A Guy Could Change	40: Emergency Squad
Sensation Hunters	Parole Fixer
50: Sideshow	Road to Singapore
54: Brigadoon	The Ghost Breakers
63: Promises! Promises!	Texas Rangers Ride Again
Move Over Darling	City for Conquest
66: The Ghost and Mr.	41: The Wagons Roll at Night
Chicken	Blood and Sand
69: Angel in My Pocket	The Perfect Snob

41: Thieves Fall Out
Knockout
They Died with Their
Boots on
Bullets for O'Hara
42: Larceny, Inc.
Road to Morocco
Thunder Rock
The Black Swan
Roger Touhy--Gangster
43: The Ox-Bow Incident
Guadalcanal Diary
44: Buffalo Bill
Irish Eyes Are Smiling
Ladies of Washington
45: China Sky
Back to Bataan
Where Do We Go from
Here?
46: California
47: Black Gold
Tycoon
Sinbad the Sailor
The Imperfect Lady
51: The Long Dark Hall
The Brave Bulls
Mask of the Avenger
52: The Brigand
The World in His Arms
Against All Flags
Viva Zapata! (OSCAR)
53: Ride, Vaquero!
City Beneath the Sea
Seminole
Blowing Wild
Cavalleria Rusticana
East of Sumatra
54: The Long Wait
55: The Magnificent Matador
Ulysses
The Naked Street
Seven Cities of Gold
56: Lust for Life (OSCAR)
The Wild Party
La Strada
The Man from Del Rio
Angels of Darkness
57: The Ride Back
Wild Is the Wind
The Story of Esther
Costello

The Hunchback of Notre
Dame
The River's Edge
58: Hot Spell
Attila the Hun
The Buccaneer (dir.)
59: The Black Orchid
Last Train from Gun Hill
Warlock
60: Heller in Pink Tights
Portrait in Black
The Savage Innocents
61: Guns of Navarone
Circle of Deception
62: Barabbas
Lawrence of Arabia
Requiem for a Heavyweight
63: Fatal Desire
The Great Van Robbery
64: The Visit
Behold a Pale Horse
Zorba the Greek
East of Sudan
Hide and Seek
65: A High Wind in Jamaica
66: Marco the Magnificent
Lost Command
The Centurions
The Innocent
67: The Happening
The Rover
The 25th Hour
Guns for San Sebastian
68: The God Game
The Shoes of the Fisher-
man
The Magus
The Secret of Santa
Vittoria
Homo Fabian
The Boss
69: Dream of Kings
Nobody Loves Flapping
Eagle

Chips Rafferty (1909-
1938: Ants in His Pants
39: Dan Rudd M.P.
40: 40,000 Horsemen
42: Rats of Tobruk
46: The Overlanders

1131

46: The Loves of Joanna
Godden
47: Eureka Stockade
Bush Country Adventure
51: Bitter Spring
Fighting Rats of Tobruk
52: Kangaroo
53: The Desert Rats
54: King of the Coral Sea
56: Walk Into Paradise
57: Walk Into Hell
Smiley
59: Smiley Gets a Gun
60: The Sundowners
61: The Wackiest Ship in the
Army
62: Mutiny on the Bounty
66: They're a Weird Mob
67: Double Trouble
68: Kona Coast
69: Return of the Boomerang
Skullduggery

Frances Rafferty (1922-
1942: Seven Sweethearts
Private Miss Jones
The War Against Mrs.
Hadley
43: Dr. Gillespie's Criminal
Case
Young Ideas
Girl Crazy
Thousands Cheer
44: Dragon Seed
The Honest Thief
Mrs. Parkington
Barbary Coast Gent
45: The Hidden Eye
Abbott & Costello in
Hollywood
46: Bad Bascomb
47: Lost Honeymoon
Adventures of Don Coyotte
Curley
48: Lady at Midnight
Hal Roach Comedy
Carnival
An Old-Fashioned Girl
Money Madness
51: Rodeo

54: The Shanghai Story
61: Wings of Chance

George Raft (1903-
1931: Hush Money
Palmy Days
Quick Millions
32: Scarface
Dancers in the Dark
Madame Racketeer
Night After Night
Undercover Man
If I Had a Million
Night World
Love Is a Racket
Sporting Widow
33: The Eagle and the Hawk
Pick Up
Midnight Club
The Bowery
34: All of Me
Bolero
The Trumpet Blows
Limehouse Blues
35: Rumba
Stolen Harmony
The Glass Key
Every Night at Eight
She Couldn't Take It
36: It Had to Happen
Yours for the Asking
37: Souls at Sea
38: You and Me
Spawn of the North
39: The Lady's from Kentucky
Each Dawn I Die
I Stole a Million
40: The House Across the Bay
They Drive by Night
41: Manpower
42: Broadway
43: Hollywood Canteen
Background to Danger
44: Follow the Boys
45: Nob Hill
Johnny Angel
46: Mr. Ace
Nocturne
Whistle Stop
47: Intrigue

47: Christmas Eve
48: Race Street
Syndicate
Johnny Allegro (or,
Hounded)
Dangerous Profession
Outpost in Morocco
51: Lucky Nick Cain
52: Loan Shark
53: I'll Get You
The Man from Cairo
54: Rogue Cop
Black Widow
55: A Bullet for Joey
56: Around the World in 80
Days
59: Some Like it Hot
60: Jet over the Atlantic
Ocean's Eleven (cameo)
61: The Ladies' Man
64: For Those Who Think
Young
The Patsy
66: Five Golden Dragons
Rififi in Panama (Fr.)
67: The Upper Hand
Casino Royale
68: The Silent Treatment
Skidoo!

Rags Ragland (1906-1946)
1941: Ringside Maisie
Whistling in the Dark
42: Born to Sing
Sunday Punch
Maisie Gets Her Man
Panama Hattie
The War Against Mrs.
Hadley
Somewhere I'll Find You
Whistling in Dixie
43: Du Barry Was a Lady
Girl Crazy
Whistling in Brooklyn
44: Meet the People
Three Men in White
The Canterville Ghost
45: Her Highness and the
Bellboy
Anchors Aweigh

Abbott & Costello in
Hollywood
Ziegfeld Follies
46: The Hoodlum Saint

Luise Rainer (1910-
1935: Escapade
36: The Great Ziegfeld
(OSCAR)
37: The Good Earth (OSCAR)
The Emperor's Candle-
sticks
The Big City
38: Toy Wife
The Great Waltz
Dramatic School
43: Hostages
61: La Dolce Vita

Ella Raines (1921-
1943: Corvette K-225
Cry Havoc
44: Phantom Lady
Hail the Conquering Hero
Tall in the Saddle
Enter Arsene Lupin
The Suspect
45: The Strange Affair of
Uncle Harry
46: The Runaround
White Tie and Tails
47: Brute Force
Time Out of Mind
The Web
48: The Senator Was Indiscreet
49: Impact
The Bail Bond Story
The Walking Hills
A Dangerous Profession
50: The Second Face
The Singing Nuns
51: Fighting Coast Guard
52: Ride the Man Down
57: The Man in the Road

Ford Rainey (1908-
1949: White Heat
57: 3:10 to Yuma
58: The Badlanders
59: The Last Mile

59: John Paul Jones
60: Flaming Star
61: Two Rode Together
    Ada
    Claudelle Inglish
    Parrish
62: Forty Pounds of Trouble
    Dead to the World
63: Kings of the Sun
66: The Sand Pebbles
    Johnny Tiger
69: The Grove

Claude Rains (1889-1967)
1933: The Invisible Man
34: Crime Without Passion
35: The Man Who Reclaimed
    His Head
    The Mystery of Edwin
    Drood
    Clairvoyant
    The Last Outpost
36: Anthony Adverse
    Hearts Divided
    Stolen Holiday
37: The Prince and the
    Pauper
    They Won't Forget
38: Gold Is Where You Find
    It
    Adventures of Robin Hood
    White Banners
    Four Daughters
39: They Made Me a Criminal
    Sons of Liverty (short)
    Four Wives
    Mr. Smith Goes to
    Washington
    Daughters Courageous
40: Saturday's Children
    The Sea Hawk
    The Lady with Red Hair
41: Four Mothers
    Here Comes Mr. Jordan
    The Wolf Man
    Riot Squad
    King's Row
42: Moontide
    Now Voyager
    Casablanca

Eyes of the Underworld
43: Forever and a Day
    The Phantom of the Opera
44: Passage to Marseilles
    Mr. Skeffington
45: This Love of Ours
    Strange Holiday
46: Caesar and Cleopatra
    Deception
    Notorious
    Angel on My Shoulder
47: The Unsuspected
48: The Passionate Spring
49: One Woman's Story
    Song of Surrender
    Rope of Sand
50: The White Tower
    Where Danger Lives
51: Sealed Cargo
    The Man Who Watched
    Trains Go By
53: Paris Express
56: Lisbon
59: This Earth Is Mine
60: The Lost World
61: Battle of the Worlds
62: Lawrence of Arabia
63: Twilight of Honor
65: The Greatest Story Ever
    Told

Jessie Ralph (1876-1944)
1933: Elmer the Great
    Cocktail Hour
    Child of Manhattan
    Ann Carver's Profession
34: The Coming Out Party
    One Night of Love
    Evelyn Prentice
    Nana
    We Live Again
    Murder in the Vanities
    The Affairs of Cellini
35: David Copperfield
    Enchanted April
    Les Miserables
    Paris in Spring
    Vanessa--Her Love Story
    Mark of the Vampire
    I Live My Life

35: Glitter
Jalna
Bunker Bean
Metropolitan
I Found Stella Parrish
Captain Blood
36: The Garden Murder Case
The Unguarded Hour
San Francisco
After the Thin Man
Camille
Little Lord Fauntleroy
Yellow Dust
Walking on Air
37: The Good Earth
The Last of Mrs. Cheyney
Double Wedding
38: Love Is a Headache
Port of Seven Seas
Hold that Kiss
39: St. Louis Blues
Cafe Society
Four Girls in White
The Kid from Texas
Mickey the Kid
Drums Along the Mohawk
40: The Blue Bird
Star Dust
The Girl from Avenue A
I Can't Give You Anything
  But Love, Baby
The Bank Dick
I Want a Divorce
41: The Lady from Cheyenne
They Met in Bombay

Esther Ralston (1902-
1929: The Case of Lena
  Smith   S
The Betrayal   S
Wheel of Life
The Mighty
31: The Prodigal Lady
Lonely Wives
33: Black Beauty
To the Last Man
34: By Candlelight
Sadie McKee
Romance in the Rain
The Marines Are Coming

35: Strange Wives
Mr. Dynamite
Ladies Crave Excitement
Streamline Express
Forced Landing
36: Girl from Mandalay
Hollywood Boulevard
Reunion
37: As Good as Married
Shadows of the Orient
38: Slander House
40: Tin Pan Alley
41: San Francisco Docks

Vera Hruba Ralston (1919-
1942: Ice-Capades Revue
44: The Lady and the Monster
Storm over Lisbon
45: Lake Placid Serenade
Dakota
46: Murder in the Music Hall
The Plainsman and the
  Lady
47: The Flame
Wyoming
48: Angel on the Amazon
I, Jane Doe
49: The Fighting Kentuckian
The Wild Blue Yonder
50: Surrender
51: Belle Le Grande
52: Hoodlum Empire
53: Fair Wind to Java
Perilous Journey
54: Jubilee Trail
55: Timberjack
56: Accused of Murder
57: Spoilers of the Forest
58: Gunfire at Indian Gap
The Notorious Mr. Monks
The Man Who Died Twice

Marjorie Rambeau (1889-
1930: Her Man
Min and Bill
31: Dark Star
Leftover Ladies
Son of India
Inspiration
The Easiest Way

1135

31: Silence
A Tailor Made Man
Strangers May Kiss
The Secret Six
This Modern Age
Laughing Sinners
Hell Divers
33: Strictly Personal
The Warrior's Husband
A Man's Castle
34: Joe Palooka
A Modern Hero
Ready for Love
Grand Canary
35: Under Pressure
Dizzy Dames
37: First Lady
38: Merrily We Live
Woman Against Woman
39: Sudden Money
The Rains Came
Laugh it Off
40: Heaven with a Barbed
Wire Fence
Santa Fe Marshal
Primrose Path
Twenty-Mule Team
Tugboat Annie Sails Again
East of the River
41: Tobacco Road
Three Sons o' Guns
42: Broadway
43: In Old Oklahoma
44: Oh, What a Night!
Army Wives
45: Salome, Where She
Danced
48: The Walls of Jericho
49: Any Number can Play
The Lucky Stiff
Abandoned
53: Torch Song
Forever Female
Bad for Each Other
55: A Man Called Peter
The View from Pompey's
Head
56: Slander
57: The Man of a Thousand
Faces

Ward Ramsey
1960: Dinosaurus!
Seven Ways from Sundown
The Great Impostor
61: Posse from Hell
Tammy Tell Me True
62: Lover Come Back
Cape Fear

Sally Rand (1903-
1933: Hotel Variety
34: Bolero

Jack Randall
1937: Riders of the Dawn
Stars over Arizona
Blazing Barriers
38: Man's Country
The Mexicali Kid
Gun Packer
39: Wild Horse Canyon
Overland Mail
40: Pioneer Days
Covered Wagon Days
Land of Six-Guns
Wild Horse Range
The Kid from Santa Fe

Meg Randall
1949: The Life of Riley
Ma and Pa Kettle
Criss Cross
Abandoned
50: Ma and Pa Kettle Go to
Town
52: Without Warning

Rebel Randall
1943: Happy Go Lucky
44: Seven Doors to Death
Dead or Alive
46: Tangier
The Shadow Returns
51: Roaring City

Stuart Randall
1950: Bells of Coronado
Rider from Tucson
Rustlers on Horseback
Storm Warning

51: Tomahawk
Wells Fargo Gunmaster
Rough Riders of Durango
The Hoodlum
Tomorrow Is Another Day
Arizona Manhunt
52: Bugles in the Afternoon
This Woman Is Dangerous
Carbine Williams
Kid Monk Baroni
The Pride of St. Louis
The Bushwackers
Rancho Notorious
Hurricane Smith
Park Row
O. Henry's Full House
(The Clarion Call seq.)
Captive Women
Hiawatha
Pony Soldier
53: Sword of Venus
Pony Express
Arena
Vicky
Captain John Smith and
Pocahontas
54: This Is My Love
Southwest Passage
Naked Alibi
They Rode West
55: Chief Crazy Horse
Female on the Beach
Headline Hunters
56: Pardners
The Indestructible Man
57: Run of the Arrow
59: Verboten!
61: Frontier Uprising
Posse from Hell
64: Taggart!
65: Fluffy

Tony Randall (1920-
1957: Oh Men! Oh Women!
Will Success Spoil Rock
Hunter?
No Down Payment
59: The Mating Game
Pillow Talk
60: The Adventures of
Huckleberry Finn

Let's Make Love
61: Lover Come Back
62: Boys' Night Out
63: Island of Love
64: The Brass Bottle
The Seven Faces of Dr.
Lao
Send Me No Flowers
65: Fluffy
66: The Alphabet Murders
Amanda
Bang! Bang! You're Dead!
67: Where Were You When the
Lights Went Out?
Hello Down There!

Ron Randell (1918-
1935: Southern Cross
47: Pacific Adventure
It Had to be You
Bulldog Drummond at Bay
Bulldog Drummond Strikes
Back
48: Sign of the Ram
Mating of Millie
Loves of Carmen
49: Omoo-Omoo, the Shark
God
The Lone Wolf and His
Lady
Make-Believe Ballroom
50: Counterspy Meets Scotland
Yard
Tyrant of the Sea
51: China Corsair
Lorna Doone
52: The Brigand
Captive Women
53: Mississippi Gambler
Girl on the Pier
Kiss Me Kate
55: Desert Sands
I Am a Camera
56: Quincannon, Frontier Scout
57: Beyond Mombasa
The Gold Virgin
Davy
Morning Call
The Story of Esther Costello
The Girl in Black Stockings
Hostage

58: The Strange Case of Dr.
    Manning
61: Most Dangerous Man
    Alive
    King of Kings
62: The Longest Day
    The Phoney American
63: Follow the Boys
64: Gold for the Caesars
66: Legend of a Gunfighter

Anders Randolph (1876-1931)
1929: The Viking   S
      Noah's Ark   PT
      Sin Sisters   SSE
      Dangerous Curves
      Young Nowheres
      Shanghai Lady
      Show of Shows
      The Last Performance PT
30:   Sons of the Gods
      The Way of All Men
      Going Wild
      Maybe It's Love
      Night Owls

Donald Randolph
1950: Gambling House
      Under the Gun
      Rogues of Sherwood Forest
      The Desert Hawk
51:   Fourteen Hours
      Flame of Stamboul
      The Prince Who Was a
        Thief
      The Golden Horde
52:   Harem Girl
      The Brigand
      Assignment: Paris
      Night Without Sleep
53:   Gunsmoke
      Dream Wife
      The Caddy
54:   The Mad Magician
      The Adventures of Hajji
        Baba
      Khyber Patrol
      The Gambler from Natchez
      Phffft!
55:   Chief Crazy Horse

    The Purple Mask
    Son of Sinbad
56: Over-Exposed
    The Rawhide Years
57: The Deadly Mantis
    My Gun Is Quick
58: Cowboy

Isabel Randolph
1940: On Their Own
      Ride, Tenderfoot, Ride
      Barnyard Follies
      Sandy Gets Her Man
      Yesterday's Heroes
41:   Look Who's Laughing
      Small Town Deb
42:   Here We Go Again
43:   Follow the Band
      Hoosier Holiday
      O My Darling Clementine
44:   Standing Room Only
      Jamboree
      Wilson
45:   The Man Who Walked
        Alone
      The Missing Corpse
      Practically Yours
      Tell it to a Star
46:   Our Hearts Were Growing
        Up
48:   If You Knew Susie
49:   Feudin' Rhythm
50:   The Fuller Brush Girl
      Mary Ryan, Detective
51:   Secrets of Monte Carlo
      A Wonderful Life
      Two Dollar Bettor
52:   Thundering Caravans
53:   The Lady Wants Mink
54:   The Shanghai Story
55:   You're Never too Young
56:   Hot Shots

Lillian Randolph
1940: Little Men
41:   West Point Widow
      Gentleman from Dixie
      All American Coed
42:   The Mexican Spitfire Sees
        A Ghost

1138

42: Hi Neighbor!
    The Great Gildersleeve
43: Gildersleeve's Bad Day
    Hoosier Holiday
    Gildersleeve on Broadway
44: Adventures of Mark Twain
    Gildersleeve's Ghost
    Three Little Sisters
45: A Song for Miss Julie
46: Child of Divorce
    It's a Wonderful Life
47: The Bachelor and the
    Bobby-Soxer
48: Sleep My Love
49: Once More, My Darling
64: Hush, Hush, Sweet
    Charlotte!

    The Unseen
46: Anna and the King of Siam
    Heart Beat
    Holiday in Mexico
    Our Hearts Were Growing
    Up
47: Her Husband's Affairs
    Pirates of Monterey
    Song of My Heart
48: Saigon
    The Kissing Bandit
49: Free for All
    The Pirates of Capri
50: Hit Parade of 1951
52: Anything can Happen
53: Tonight We Sing
    The Stars Are Singing
56: Hot Blood

Lois Ranson
1940: Money to Burn
    Grandpa Goes to Town
    Earl of Puddlestone
    Under Texas Skies
    Grand Ole Spry
    Friendly Neighbors
    Meet the Missus
41: Petticoat Politics
    Cheers for Miss Bishop
    Angels with Broken Wings
42: Pierre of the Plains
43: The Renegade

Mikhail Rasumny (1893-1956)
1940: Comrade X
41: Hold Back the Dawn
    Shanghai Gesture
    Forced Landing
42: Wake Island
    This Gun for Hire
    Yokel Boy
    Road to Morocco
43: For Whom the Bell Tolls
    Her Heart in Her Throat
    Hostages
44: And the Angels Sing
    Practically Yours
    Henry Aldrich Plays Cupid
45: Masquerade in Mexico
    A Medal for Benny
    A Royal Scandal
    The Stork Club

E.J. Ratcliffe (1893-
1929: Jazz Age   S
    Four Feathers   SSE
    Show of Shows
    Sally
    Skinner Steps Out
30: Wide Open
    The Cohens and the Kellys
    in Scotland
33: I Loved a Woman

Basil Rathbone (1892-1967)
1929: This Mad World
    Barnum Was Right
    The Last of Mrs.
    Cheyney   PT
30: A Notorious Affair
    Sin Takes a Holiday
    The Bishop Murder Case
    The Lady of Scandal
    The Flirting Widow
    High Road
    A Lady Surrenders
31: Once a Lady
32: One Precious Year
    A Woman Commands
33: After the Ball
34: Loyalties
35: David Copperfield
    Anna Karenina
    A Tale of Two Cities
    The Last Days of Pompeii

35: Captain Blood
A Feather in Her Hat
Kind Lady
36: Romeo and Juliet
Garden of Allah
Private Number
37: Tovarich
House of Menace
Love from a Stranger
Confession
Make a Wish
38: Adventures of Marco Polo
Dawn Patrol
If I Were King
Adventures of Robin Hood
39: The Hound of the Basker-
villes
Tower of London
The Sun Never Sets
The Son of Frankenstein
The Adventures of
Sherlock Holmes
Rio
40: Rhythm of the River
The Mark of Zorro
The Mad Doctor
A Date with Destiny
41: The Black Cat
Paris Calling
International Lady
42: Crossroads
Fingers at the Window
Sherlock Holmes and the
Voice of Terror
Sherlock Holmes and the
Secret Weapon
43: Sherlock Holmes in
Washington
Above Suspicion
Sherlock Holmes Faces
Death
44: Sherlock Holmes and the
Spider Woman
The Scarlet Claw
The Pearl of Death
Frenchman's Creek
Bathing Beauty
45: The House of Fear
Pursuit to Algiers
The Woman in Green

46: Terror by Night
Dressed to Kill
Heartbeat
49: The Adventures of Ichabod
and Mr. Toad (voice)
54: Casanova's Big Night
55: We're No Angels
56: Court Jester
The Black Sleep
58: The Last Hurrah
62: The Magic Sword (voice)
Tales of Terror
63: Comedy of Terrors
65: Planet of Blood
Voyage to Prehistoric
Planet
66: The Ghost in the Invisible
Bikini
67: Hillbillies in the Haunted
House
69: Queen of Blood (re-rel.
of '65 Planet of Blood)

Gregory Ratoff (1897-1960)
1932: Symphony of Six Millions
What Price Hollywood?
a short
Melody of Life
Roar of the Dragon
Deported
Skyscraper Souls
Once in a Lifetime
Secrets of the French
Police
Undercover Man
33: Professional Sweetheart
Headline Shooters
I'm No Angel
Sitting Pretty
Girl Without a Room
Broadway Through a Key-
hole
Sweepings
34: Let's Fall in Love
George White's Scandals
of 1934
The Great Flirtation
35: Remember Last Night
This Woman Is Mine
(writ., act.)

35: King of Burlesque
36: Here Comes Trouble
    Sins of Man
    Under Two Flags
    Road to Glory
    Falling in Love
    Sing, Baby, Sing
    Under Your Spell
    Trouble Ahead
37: Top of the Town (writ.,
    act.)
    Cafe Metropole
    Seventh Heaven
    You Can't Have Every-
    thing (writ.)
    Lancer Spy (dir.)
38: Sally, Irene, and Mary
    Forbidden Territory
    Gateway
39: Wife, Husband, and
    Friend (dir.)
    Rose of Washington
    Square
    Barricade
    Elsa Maxwell's Hotel for
    Women
    Daytime Wife
    Intermezzo
40: I Was an Adventuress
    The Great Profile
    Elsa Maxwell's Public
    Deb No. 1
41: Adam Had Four Sons
    The Men in Her Life
    (prod., dir.)
42: Two Yanks in Trinidad
    Footlight Serenade
43: The Heat's On (prod.,dir.)
    Something to Shout About
    (dir.)
    Song of Russia (dir.)
44: Irish Eyes Are Smiling
45: Where Do We Go From
    Here?
    Paris Underground
46: Black Magic (prod., dir.)
    Do You Love Me?
47: Carnival in Costa Rica
50: If This be Sin
    All About Eve

51: Operation X
52: O. Henry's Full House
    (The Last Leaf seq.)
53: Taxi (dir.)
56: Abdullah's Harem (dir.,
    act.)
57: The Sun Also Rises
60: Exodus
    Once More with Feeling
    Oscar Wilde (dir.)
61: The Big Gamble

Herbert Rawlinson (1885-1953)
1928: Wages of Conscience   S
33: a short
    Moonlight and Pretzels
    Enlighten Thy Daughter
35: The People's Enemy
    Men Without Names
    Confidential
    Show Them No Mercy
    Convention Girl
36: Dancing Feet
    Bullets or Ballots
    A Son Comes Home
    Hollywood Boulevard
    Mad Holiday
    God's Country and the
    Woman
    Hitchhike to Heaven
    Ticket to Paradise
37: Don't Pull Your Punches
    The Go-Getter
    That Certain Woman
    Over the Goal
    Love Is on the Air
    Nobody's Baby
    Mysterious Crossing
    Back in Circulation
    Make a Wish
38: Hawaii Calls
    Orphans of the Street
    Women Are Like That
    Under the Big Top
    The Kid Comes Back
    Torchy Gets Her Man
    Secrets of an Actress
39: Dark Victory
    You Can't Get Away with
    Murder

40: Money to Burn
   The Five Little Peppers
      at Home
   Free, Blonde, and 21
   Framed
   Seven Sinners
41: Flying Wild
   I Wanted Wings
   Scattergood Meets Broad-
      way
   A Gentleman from Dixie
   Bad Man at Deadwood
   I Killed that Man
   Riot Squad
42: Arizone Cyclone
   The Panther's Claw
   Broadway Big Shot
   S.O.S. Coast Guard
   The Yukon Patrol
   Smart Alecks
   Stagecoach Buckaroo
   Hello Annapolis
   Foreign Agent
   War Dogs
   Lady Gangster
43: Lost Canyon
   Cosmo Jones in The Crime
      Smasher
   Colt Comrades
   Where Are Your Children?
   Two Weeks to Live
   The Woman of the Town
44: Riders of the Deadline
   Sailor's Holiday
   Lumberjack
   Shake Hands with Murder
   Forty Thieves
   Oklahoma Raiders
   Marshal of Reno
   Marshal of Gunsmoke
   Nabonga
   Goin' to Town
   Sheriff of Sundown
46: Accomplice
48: The Argyle Secrets
   The Gallant Legion
   The Counterfeiters
   Silent Conflict
   Sinister Journey
   The Strange Gamble

49: Brimstone
   Fighting Man of the Plains
51: Gene Autry and the
   Mounties

Aldo Ray (1926-
1951: Saturday's Hero
52: The Marrying Kind
   Pat and Mike
53: Let's Do it Again
   Miss Sadie Thompson
55: Battle Cry
   We're No Angels
   Three Stripes in the Sun
56: Nightfall
57: Men in War
58: The Naked and the Dead
   God's Little Acre
59: Four Desperate Men
60: The Day They Robbed the
   Bank of England
65: Sylvia
   Johnny Nobody
   Nightingale in the Sun
66: Dead Heat on a Merry-Go-
   Around
   What Did You Do in the
   War, Daddy?
67: Riot on Sunset Strip
   Welcome to Hard Times
   Kill a Dragon
   The Violent Ones
68: The Power
   Suicide Command
   Now Is the Moment
   The Green Berets
69: Man Without Mercy
   Deadlock

Charles Ray (1891-1943)
1932: The Bride's Bereavement
   (2 reels)
34: Ladies Should Listen
   School for Girls
   Ticket to a Crime
35: Welcome Home
36: Just My Luck
   Hollywood Boulevard
40: A Little Bit of Heaven

Harry Raybould
1957: The Amazing Colossal
        Man
  58: Girl in the Woods

Martha Raye (1916-
1936: Rhythm on the Range
        Big Broadcast of 1937
        College Holiday
  37: The Hideaway Girl
        Waikiki Wedding
        Mountain Music
        Artists and Models
        Double or Nothing
  38: Big Broadcast of 1938
        Give Me a Sailor
        College Swing
        Tropic Holiday
  39: Never Say Die
        $1000 a Touchdown
  40: The Farmer's Daughter
        Boys from Syracuse
  41: Navy Blues
        Keep 'em Flying
        Hellzapoppin'!
  44: Pinup Girl
        Four Jills and a Jeep
  47: Monsieur Verdoux
  62: Billy Rose's Jumbo
  69: The Phynx

Gary Raymond (1935-
1957: The Moonrakers
  59: Look Back in Anger
        Suddenly Last Summer
  61: El Cid
        The Millionairess
  63: Jason and the Argonauts
        The Playboy of the
        Western World
  65: The Greatest Story Ever
        Told
  66: Traitor's Gate

Gene Raymond (1908-
1931: Personal Maid
        Stolen Heaven
  32: If I Had a Million
        Ladies of the Big House
        Forgotten Commandments

        The Night of June 13th
        Red Dust
  33: Ex-Lady
        Zoo in Budapest
        Anne Carver's Profession
        Brief Moment
        The House on 56th Street
        Flying Down to Rio
  34: Coming Out Party
        I Am Suzanne
        Transatlantic Merry-Go-
          Round
        Sadie McKee
  35: Behold My Wife
        The Woman in Red
        Hooray for Love
        Seven Keys to Baldpate
  36: Transient Lady
        Love on a Bet
        The Bride Walks Out
        Walking on Air
        The Smartest Girl in Town
        That Girl from Paris
  37: There Goes My Girl
        Life of the Party
  38: She's Got Everything
        Stolen Heaven
  40: Cross-Country Romance
  41: Mr. and Mrs. Smith
        Smilin' Through
  46: The Locket
  48: Assigned to Danger
        Sofia
        Million Dollar Weekend
          (prod., dir., act.)
  55: Hit the Deck
  57: Plunder Road
  64: The Best Man
        I'd Rather be Rich
  65: The Hanged Man

Guy Raymond
1966: The Russians Are Coming,
        The Russians Are Coming!
  67: The Reluctant Astronaut
  68: The Ballad of Josie

Paula Raymond (c1928-
1948: Rusty Leads the Way
        Racing Luck

49: Challenge of the Range
50: The Devil's Doorway
    The Duchess of Idaho
    Crisis
    Grounds for Marriage
51: Inside Straight
    The Tall Target
    Texas Carnival
    The Sellout
53: The Bandits of Corsica
    The City that Never
    Sleeps
    The Beast from 20,000
    Fathoms
54: King Richard and the
    Crusaders
    The Human Jungle
55: The Gun that Won the
    West
61: The Flight that Disappear-
    ed
62: The Hand of Death
66: The Spy with My Face
69: The Blood of Dracula

Robin Raymond
1941: Johnny Eager
42: Moontide
43: Girls in Chains
    Secrets of the Under-
    ground
44: Are These Our Parents?
    Ladies in Washington
45: A Letter for Evie
    Men in Her Diary
    Rogues' Gallery
46: Talk about a Lady
47: A Likely Story
    The Web
48: Prince of Thieves
50: Wabash Avenue
53: The Glass Wall
54: There's No Business Like
    Show Business
56: Beyond a Reasonable
    Doubt
58: High School Confidential
61: Wild in the Country

Ronald Reagan (1912-
1937: Love Is on the Air

Submarine D-1
Hollywood Hotel
38: Sergeant Murphy
    Swing Your Lady
    Accidents Will Happen
    Cowboy from Brooklyn
    Boy Meets Girl
    Girls on Probation
    Going Places
    Brother Rat
39: Secret Service of the Air
    Dark Victory
    Naughty but Nice
    Hell's Kitchen
    Code of the Secret Service
    Smashing the Money Ring
    Angels Wash Their Faces
40: Brother Rat and a Baby
    An Angel from Texas
    Murder in the Air
    Knute Rockne--All American
    Tugboat Annie Sails Again
    Santa Fe Trail
41: The Bad Man
    Million Dollar Baby
    International Squadron
    Nine Lives Are Not Enough
    Kings Row
42: Juke Girl
    Desperate Journey
43: This Is the Army
47: Voice of the Turtle
    That Hagen Girl
    Stallion Road
49: Night Unto Night
    John Loves Mary
    The Girl from Jones Beach
    The Hasty Heart
50: Louisa
    Storm Warning
51: Bedtime for Bonzo
    The Last Outpost
    Hong Kong
52: Bonzo Goes to College
    She's Working Her Way
    Through College
    The Winning Team
53: Tropic Zone
    Law and Order
54: Prisoner of War
    Cattle Queen of Montana

1144

55: Tennessee's Partner	65: Morituri--The Saboteur
57: Hellcats of the Navy	Code Name
Bombs over China	66: Duel at Diablo
Cavalry Charge	Fantastic Voyage
64: The Killers	

Rex Reason (1928-
1952: Storm over Tibet
53: Salome
Mission over Korea
China Venture
55: This Island Earth
Smoke Signal
Kiss of Fire
Lady Godiva
56: The Creature Walks
Among Us
Rawhide Years
Raw Edge
The Desperadoes Are in
Town
57: Under Fire
Badlands of Montana
A Band of Angels
58: Rawhide Trail
Thundering Jets
59: The Sad Horse
Miracle of the Hills

Rhodes Reason (1930-
1956: Emergency Hospital
Crime Against Joe
Flight to Hong Kong
The Desperadoes Are in
Town
57: Voodoo Island
Jungle Heat
59: The Big Fisherman
Yellowstone Kelly
61: A Fever in the Blood
68: King Kong Escapes

William Redfield (1927-
1939: Back Door to Heaven
55: Conquest of Space
56: The Proud and Profane
58: I Married a Woman
62: The Connection
Instant Love
64: Hamlet

Robert Redford (1937-
1962: War Hunt
65: Inside Daisy Clover
66: The Chase
This Property Is Condemned
Situation Hopeless but not
Serious
67: Barefoot in the Park
68: Tell Them Willie Boy Is
Here
69: The Downhill Racers
Butch Cassidy and the
Sundace Kid

Colin Redgrave (1939-
1966: A Man for All Seasons
67: A Deadly Affair
68: The Charge of the Light
Brigade
69: Oh! What a Lovely War!
The Magus
The Girl with a Pistol
David Copperfield (TV)

Lynn Redgrave (1943-
1964: Girl with Green Eyes
66: Georgy Girl
67: The Deadly Affair
68: Smashing Time
69: The Virgin Soldiers
Angel, Angel, Down We
Go
Blood Kin

Sir Michael Redgrave (1908-
1938: The Lady Vanishes
39: Climbing High
Stolen Life
40: The Stars Look Down
A Window in London
41: The Remarkable Mr. Kipps
Atlantic Fury
Jeannie
42: Sons of the Sea
The Big Blockade

42: Lady in Distress
43: Thunder Rock
45: Johnny in the Clouds
The Way to the Stars
Dead of Night
46: The Captive Heart
The Years Between
47: The Man Within
Fame Is the Spur
Mourning Becomes
Electra
48: The Smuggler
The Secret Beyond the
Door
51: The Browning Version
52: The Importance of Being
Earnest
54: The Green Scarf
55: The Dam Busters
Confidential Report
Oh, Rosalinda!
The Night My Number
Came Up
The Sea Shall not Have
Them
56: 1984
57: Time Without Pity
The Happy Road
58: The Quiet American
Law and Disorder
59: Shake Hands with the
Devil
The Wreck of the Mary
Deare
60: Behind the Mask
61: The Innocents
62: Loneliness of the Long
Distance Runner
63: Mr. Arkadin
No, My Darling Daughter
65: Young Cassidy
66: The Hill
67: Heroes of Telemark
The 25th Hour
68: Assignment: K
Heidi (TV)
69: The Battle of Britain
Oh! What a Lovely War!
Goodbye, Mr. Chips
Connecting Rooms

David Copperfield (TV)

Vanessa Redgrave (1937-
1963: Tom Jones
65: Morgan!
The Pack
66: Blow-Up
Red and Blue (short)
A Man of All Seasons
67: Camelot
The Sailor from Gibraltar
68: The Charge of the Light
Brigade
The Loves of Isadora
69: A Quiet Place in the
Country
Oh! What a Lovely War
The Seagull
Cyril

Joyce Redman (1919-
1963: Tom Jones
65: Othello
67: Amorous Adventures of
Moll Flanders
68: Prudence and the Pill

Liam Redmond (1913-
1945: I See a Dark Stranger
48: Captain Boycott
52: The Gentle Gunman
High Treason
54: The Divided Heart
Tonight's the Night
56: Jacqueline
Safari
23 Paces to Baker Street
57: Night of the Demon
58: The Curse of the Demon
59: The Boy and the Bridge
60: Scent of Mystery
Under Ten Flags
62: Kid Galahad
64: The Luck of Ginger Coffey
65: The Amorous Adventures
of Moll Flanders
66: The Ghost and Mr. Chicken
Tobruk
67: The Last Safari
The 25th Hour

67: The Adventures of Bullwhip Griffin

Rodd Redwing
1930: The Squaw Man
39: Gunga Din!
Lives of a Bengal Lancer
45: Objective Burma!
46: Out of the Depths
49: Apache Chief
Song of India
51: Little Big Horn
52: Buffalo Bill in Tomahawk
Territory
Rancho Notorious
The Pathfinder
53: Winning of the West
Conquest of Cochise
Saginaw Trail
54: The Creature from the
Black Lagoon
Cattle Queen of Montana
56: Jaguar
The Mole People
57: Copper Sky
58: The Flame Barrier
60: Flaming Star
62: Sergeants Three
68: Shalako
69: Charro!
The McMasters

Alan Reed (1907-
1944: Days of Glory
45: Nob Hill
46: The Postman Always
Rings Twice
50: Perfect Strangers
Emergency Wedding
The Redhead and the
Cowboy
52: Viva Zapata!
Actors and Sin
53: I, the Jury
Geraldine
54: Woman's World
55: The Far Horizons
Kiss of Fire
The Desperate Hours
The Lady and the Tramp
(voice)

56: Rock, Pretty Baby
Timetable
Revolt of Mamie Stover
He Laughed Last
57: The Tarnished Angels
58: Marjorie Morningstar
59: A Thousand and One
Arabian Nights (voice)
61: Breakfast at Tiffany's
66: That Man Flintstone (voice)
69: A Dream of Kings
Archy and Mehitabel
(voice)

Alan Reed, Jr.
1956: Rock, Pretty Baby
57: Peyton Place
58: Going Steady
64: The New Interns

Donna Reed (1921-
1941: The Get-Away
Shadow of the Thin Man
The Bugle Sounds
42: The Courtship of Andy
Hardy
The Human Comedy
Apache Trail
Calling Dr. Gillespie
Mokey
Eyes in the Night
43: The Man from Down Under
Crazy to Kill
Thousands Cheer
Dr. Gillespie's Criminal
Case
44: See Here, Private Har-
grove!
Mrs. Parkington
45: The Picture of Dorian
Gray
Gentle Annie
They Were Expendable
46: Faithful in My Fashion
It's a Wonderful Life
47: Green Dolphin Street
48: Beyond Glory
49: Chicago Deadline
51: Saturday's Hero
52: Scandal Sheet
Hangman's Knot

53: Raiders of the Seven Seas
Trouble Along the Way
The Caddy
From Here to Eternity
(OSCAR)
Gun Fury
54: They Rode West
3 Hours to Kill
The Last Time I Saw
Paris
55: The Far Horizons
The Benny Goodman Story
56: Ransom!
Backlash
57: Beyond Mombasa
58: The Whole Truth
60: Pepe

Florence Reed (1883-1967)
1930: The Code of Honor
34: Great Expectations
35: Frankie and Johnnie
41: Shanghai Gesture

Marshall Reed
1944: Tucson Raiders
Range Law
Law Men
Mojave Firebrand
Partners of the Trail
Gangsters of the Frontier
45: Law of the Valley
46: Drifting Along
The Haunted Mine
Shadows on the Range
Gentleman from Texas
Raiders of the South
47: Angel and the Badman
West of Dodge City
Trailing Danger
Land of the Lawless
The Fighting Vigilantes
Song of the Wasteland
Prairie Express
Stage of Mesa City
Cheyenne Takes Over
48: Tornado Range
The Bold Frontiersman
The Gallant Legion
Triggerman

Hidden Danger
Song of the Drifter
Back Trail
The Fighting Ranger
The Rangers Ride
Renegades of Sonora
49: Stampede
Gun Runner
Law of the West
Frontier Investigator
Navajo Trail Raiders
Square Dance Jubilee
West of El Dorado
Western Renegades
Brand of Fear
Roaring Westward
Riders of the Dusk
50: The Cowboy and the Prize-
fighter
Rider from Tucson
The Savage Horde
Radar Secret Service
Over the Border
Six-Gun Mesa
Cherokee Uprising
Silver Raiders
Outlaw Gold
Law of the Panhandle
51: Oh, Susanna
Nevada Badmen
Abilene Trail
Montana Desperado
Canyon Raiders
Hurricane Island
Purple Heart Diary
Texas Lawmen
The Whistling Hills
Lawless Cowboys
52: Sound Off!
The Rough Tough West
Laramie Mountains
Kansas Territory
Canyon Ambush
Night Raiders
The Longhorn
Montana Incident
Texas City
53: Cow Country
57: The Night the World
Exploded

58: The Lineup
59: The Ghost of Zorro
62: The Wild Westerners
Third of a Man
69: A Time for Killing

Maxwell Reed (1920-
1946: The Years Between
47: Daybreak
48: The Brothers
Holiday Camp
49: The Dark Man
Night Beat
50: Blackout
51: Flame of Araby
There Is Another Sun
52: The Clouded Yellow
53: Sea Devils
55: The Square Ring
56: The Brain Machine
Shadow of Fear
Before I Wake
61: Pirates of Tortuga
62: The Notorious Landlady
67: Picture Mommy Dead

Oliver Reed (1938-
1960: The Rebel
61: No Love for Johnnie
62: Curse of the Werewolf
Pirates of Blood River
The Damned
63: Paranoiac
64: The System
The Crimson Blade
65: These Are the Damned
Brigand of Kandahar
66: The Trap
The Party's Over
The Shuttered Room
Girl Getters
67: The Jokers
68: Oliver
69: Hannibal Brooks
Women in Love
Take a Girl Like You
The Assassination Bureau
The McMasters
The Lady in the Car

Philip Reed (1900-
1933: Female
The House on 56th Street
College Coach
34: Big Hearted Herbert
A Lost Lady
Dr. Monica
Jimmy the Gent
Journal of a Crime
Registered Nurse
Gambling Lady
Bedside
Fashions of 1934
Affairs of a Gentleman
Glamour
35: Maybe It's Love
Woman in Red
The Case of the Curious
Bride
The Girl from Tenth
Avenue
Sweet Music
a short
Accent on Youth
36: The Murder of Dr. Harrigan
Klondike Annie
The Last of the Mohicans
The Luckiest Girl in the
World
37: Madame X
38: Merrily We Live
41: Aloma of the South Seas
Weekend for Three
42: A Gentleman After Dark
43: Old Acquaintance
46: People Are Funny
Once and for All
Her Sister's Secret
Rendezvous with Annie
Hot Cargo
47: Big Town After Dark (or,
Underworld After Dark)
Song of Scheherazade
Pirates of Monterey
I Cover Big Town
Song of the Thin Man
48: Guilty Assignment
Big Town Scandal
Bodyguard

48: Unknown Island
49: Manhandled
    Daughter of the West
50: Bandit Queen
    Tripoli
    Davy Crockett--Indian
    Scout
52: Target
53: Take Me to Town
55: The Girl in the Red
    Velvet Swing
57: The Tattered Dress
65: Harum Scarum

Robert Reed (1932-
1967: Hurry Sundown
68: Star!
69: The Maltese Bippy

Walter Reed
1942: The Mayor of 44th Street
    Seven Days' Leave
    The Mexican Spitfire's
    Elephant
    Army Surgeon
43: Bombardier
    Petticoat Larceny
    The Mexican Spitfire's
    Blessed Event
46: Child of Divorce
47: Banjo
    Night Song
48: Western Heritage
    Return of the Bad Men
    Mystery in Mexico
    Fighter Squadron
    Angel on the Amazon
50: The Lawless
    Young Man with a Horn
    The Eagle and the Hawk
    The Sun Sets at Dawn
51: Wells Fargo Gunmaster
52: Target
    Desert Passage
    The Blazing Forest
    Horizons West
53: The Clown
    War Paint
    Those Redheads from
    Seattle

54: Dangerous Mission
    The Yellow Tomahawk
    Return from the Sea
55: Hell's Island
    Far Horizons
    Bobby Ware Is Missing
56: Emergency Hospital
    Seven Men from Now
    Rock, Pretty Baby
    Dance with Me, Henry
57: The Lawless Eighties
    Slim Carter
58: The Deep Six
    Summer Love
    Missile Monsters
59: Arson for Hire
60: 13 Fighting Men
    Macumba Love
    Sgt. Rutledge
64: Where Love Has Gone
65: Convict Stage
    Fort Courageous
66: Moment to Moment
69: Tora! Tora! Tora!

George Reeves (1914-1959)
1939: Gone with the Wind
40: Till We Meet Again
    Torrid Zone
    Tear Gas Squad
    Ladies Must Live
    Calling All Husbands
    Always a Bride
    a short
    Argentine Nights
    Gambling on the High Seas
    Father Is a Prince
    Knute Rockne--All American
    The Fighting 69th
41: Blue, White, and Perfect
    a short
    Strawberry Blonde
    Dead Men Tell
    Lydia
    Blood and Sand
    Man at Large
42: The Mad Martindales
43: Buckskin Frontier
    So Proudly We Hail!
    Border Patrol

1150

43: Hoppy Serves a Writ
The Leather Burners
The Last Will and
Testament of Tom Smith
(doc.)
Colt Comrades
Bar-20
44: Winged Victory
47: Variety Girl
48: The Sainted Sisters
Jungle Goddess
Jungle Jim
Thunder in the Pines
49: The Great Lover
Samson and Delilah
Adventures of Sir
Galahad (ser.)
Pirate Ship
Special Agent
The Mutineers
50: The Good Humor Man
51: Superman and the Mole
Men (serial)
52: Bugles in the Afternoon
Rancho Notorious
53: The Blue Gardenia
From Here to Eternity
Forever Female
56: Westward Ho, the Wagons!

Steve Reeves (1926-
1954: Athena
59: Goliath and the Barbarian
The Sword of Sirac
Judos
Hercules
60: The Giant of Marathon
Last Days of Pompeii
Hercules Unchained
61: David and Goliath
The White Warrior
Morgan the Pirate
The Thief of Bagdad
62: The Trojan Horse
63: Duel of the Titans
The Slave
Last Glory of Troy
The Pirate Prince
65: The Avenger
Sandokan the Great

Phil Regan (1906-
1934: The Key
Housewife
Dames
Student Tour
35: Sweet Adeline
The Girl from Tenth
Avenue
We're in the Money
Stars over Broadway
Go into Your Dance
In Caliente
Broadway Hostess
a short
36: Laughing Irish Eyes
Happy Go Lucky
37: Hit Parade
Manhattan Merry-Go-
Round
38: Outside of Paradise
39: She Married a Cop
Flight at Midnight
40: Tugboat Annie Sails
Again
41: Las Vegas Nights
43: Sweet Rosie O'Grady
45: Sunbonnet Sue
46: Swing Parade of 1946
Sweetheart of Sigma Chi
50: Three Little Words

Frank Reicher (1876-1965)
1928: Someone to Love   S
Four Sons   SSE
29: Her Private Affair
Black Waters
The Changeling
Strange Cargo
Mr. Antonio
His Captive Woman
31: Gentleman's Fate
Beyond Victory
Suicide Fleet
32: A Woman Commands
The Crooked Circle
Mata Hari
Scarlet Dawn
33: Jennie Gerhardt
Captured
Ever in My Heart

33: Before the Dawn
Song of Kong
King Kong
Topaze
Employees' Entrance
34: Hi Nellie!
Journal of a Crime
Countess of Monte Cristo
I Am a Thief
Little Man, What Now?
Let's Talk it Over
No Greater Glory
Return of the Terror
The Case of the Howling
Dog
The Fountain
35: A Dog of Flanders
Mills of the Gods
The Florentine Dagger
Remember Last Night
Rendezvous
The Man Who Broke the
Bank at Monte Carlo
The Story of Louis
Pasteur
36: The Murder of Dr.
Harrington
Magnificent Obsession
The Invisible Ray
Sutter's Gold
The Country Doctor
Under Two Flags
Girls Dormitory
Along Came Love
Star for a Night
Till We Meet Again
Murder on a Bridle Path
The Ex-Mrs. Bradford
Second Wife
Anthony Adverse
37: The Great O'Malley
Stolen Holiday
Under Cover of Night
Espionage
Stage Door
The Emperor's Candle-
sticks
The Road Back
Prescription for Romance
Fit for a King

Lancer Spy
Laughing at Trouble
Night Key
On Such a Night
38: Rascals
Prison Nurse
City Streets
I'll Give a Million
Suez
Torchy Gets Her Man
39: Mystery of the White Room
Woman Doctor
Juarez
The Magnificent Fraud
Our Neighbors the Carters
The Escape
South of the Border
Everything Happens at
Night
40: Dr. Cyclops
Typhoon
The Man I Married
Devil's Island
South of Karanga
Sky Murder
Lady in Question
41: Flight from Destiny
They Dare not Love
Shining Victory
The Nurse's Secret
Underground
Dangerously They Live
42: Nazi Agent
To be or not to Be
Mystery of Marie Roget
Beyond the Blue Horizon
The Gay Sisters
Secret Enemies
The Mummy's Tomb
Scattergood Survives a
Murder
Night Monster
43: The Song of Bernadette
The Canterville Ghost
Mission to Moscow
Yanks Ahoy!
Tornado
44: Adventures of Mark Twain
Address Unknown
The Mummy's Ghost

44: Gildersleeve's Ghost
The Hitler Gang
The Conspirators
45: A Medal for Benny
The Jade Mask
House of Frankenstein
The Tiger Woman
Hotel Berlin
The Big Bonanza
Blonde Ransom
46: The Shadow Returns
The Strange Mr.Gregory
My Pal Trigger
Home in Oklahoma
47: Mr. District Attorney
Violence
Yankee Fakir
The Secret Life of Walter
Mitty
Escape Me Never
48: Carson City Raiders
Fighting Mad
49: Samson and Delilah
50: Cargo to Capetown
Kiss Tomorrow Goodbye
51: The Lady and the Bandit

Beryl Reid
1968: Star! (or, Those Were
the Happy Times)
The Killing of Sister
George
69: The Assassination Bureau

Carl Benton Reid (1895-
1941: The Little Foxes
42: Tennessee Johnson
43: The North Star
50: In a Lonely Place
Convicted
The Fuller Bush Girl
The Killer that Stalked
New York
The Flying Missile
Stage to Tucson
51: The Great Caruso
Smuggler's Gold
Lorna Doone
Criminal Lawyer
The Family Secret
52: Indian Uprising

Carbine Williams
The First Time
Boots Malone
The Brigand
The Will Rogers Story
53: Escape from Fort Bravo
54: The Command
Broken Lance
The Egyptian
Athena
55: Wichita
One Desire
The Left Hand of God
The Spoilers
56: A Day of Fury
The Last Wagon
Strange Intruder
Battle Hymn
57: Spoilers of the Forest
Time Limit
58: The Last of the Fast Guns
Tarzan's Fight for Life
59: The Trap
60: The Bramble Bush
The Gallant Hours
62: Pressure Point
The Underwater City
66: Madame X

Elliott Reid (1920-
1940: The Ramparts We Watch
43: Young Ideas
44: The Story of Dr.Wassell
47: A Double Life
50: Sierra
51: The Whip Hand
53: Gentlemen Prefer Blondes
Vicki
54: Woman's World
60: Inherit the Wind
61: The Absent-Minded
Professor
63: Son of Flubber
The Thrill of it All
Move Over, Darling
Who's Been Sleeping in
My Bed?
66: Follow Me, Boys!
67: Blackbeard's Ghost
69: The One with the Fuzz

Ed Reimers
1951: Hard, Fast, and
Beautiful
On the Loose

Carl Reiner (1920-
1959: Happy Anniversary
60: The Gazebo
61: Gidget Goes Hawaiian
63: It's a Mad Mad Mad Mad
World
The Thrill of it All
65: The Art of Love
66: The Russians Are Coming,
The Russians Are Coming!
Don't Worry, We'll Think
of a Title
67: A Guide for the Married
Man
69: Generation

Lee Remick (1935-
1957: A Face in the Crowd
58: The Long Hot Summer
59: Anatomy of a Murder
These Thousand Hills
60: Wild River
61: Sanctuary
62: The Days of Wine and
Roses
Experiment in Terror
63: The Wheeler Dealers
The Traveling Lady
The Running Man
65: Baby, the Rain Must Fall
The Hallelujah Trail
68: No Way to Treat a Lady
The Detective
Hard Contract
69: Airport
The Severed Head

Duncan Renaldo (1904-
1928: Gun Runner   S
Naughty Duchess   S
The Devil's Skipper S
Clothes Make the
Woman   S
Marcheta   S
Romany Love   S

29: Bridge of San Luis
Rey   PT
Pals of the Prairies   SSE
31: Trader Jprm
32: Trapped in Tia Juana
34: Public Stenographer
The Moth
36: Moonlight Murder
Lady Luck
Rebellion
37: Two Minutes to Play
Mile a Minute Love
38: Crime Afloat
Rose of the Rio Grande
Spawn of the North
39: Zaza
Rough Riders Round-Up
Juarez and Maximilian
The Kansas Terrors
Cowboys from Texas
South of the Border
40: Heroes of the Saddle
Pioneers of the West
Covered Wagon Days
Gaucho Serenade
Rocky Mountain Rangers
Oklahoma Renegades
41: South of Panama
Down Mexico Way
Outlaws of the Desert
Gauchos of Eldorado
42: A Yank in Libya
43: Secret Service in Darkest
Africa (ser.)
For Whom the Bell Tolls
Mission to Moscow
Border Patrol
Tiger Rangs
Hands Across the Border
The Desert Song
44: The Fighting Seabees
The San Antonio Kid
Call of the South Seas
Sheriff of Sundown
45: Adventure
The Cisco Kid Returns
In Old Mexico
South of the Rio Grande
47: Jungle Flight
48: Sword of the Avenger

48: Valiant Hombre
    Bells of San Fernando
49: Gay Amigo
    The Daring Caballero
    Satan's Craddle
    The Girl from San
      Lorenzo
    The Lady and the Bandit
    We Were Strangers
50: The Capture
59: Zorro Rides Again

Georges Renavent (1893-1969)
1935: Whipsaw
36: The Invisible Ray
    The Sky Parade
37: History Is Made at Night
    Seventh Heaven
    Cafe Metropole
    Wife, Doctor, and Nurse
    The Sheik Steps Out
    Love Under Fire
    Fight for Your Lady
    Charlie Chan at Monte
      Carlo
    Love and Hisses
38: Jezebel
    Gold Diggers in Paris
    I'll Give a Million
    Artists and Models
      Abroad
39: Topper Takes a Trip
    The Three Musketeers
    Pack Up Your Troubles
40: The House Across the
      Bay
    Turnabout
    Son of Monte Cristo
    Comrade X
41: Road to Zanzibar
    That Night in Rio
    Sullivan's Travels
43: Mission to Moscow
    Wintertime
    The Desert Song
44: Our Hearts Were Young
      and Gay
45: Captain Eddie
46: Catman of Paris
    Tarzan and the Leopard
      Woman

47: Ladies' Man
    The Foxes of Harrow
51: Secrets of Monte Carlo
52: Mara Maru

James Rennie (1889-1965)
1930: Girl of the Golden West
    Bad Man
31: Illicit
    The Lash
    Party Husband
41: Skylark
42: Tales of Manhattan
    Crossroads
    Now Voyager
44: Wilson
45: A Bell for Adano

Michael Rennie (1909-
1937: Gang Way
38: The Divorce of Lady X
    This Man in Paris
40: Dangerous Moonlight
41: Ships with Wings
45: I'll be Your Sweetheart
46: The Wicked Lady
    White Cradle Inn
    Caesar and Cleopatra
47: Root of All Evil
48: Idol of Paris
    Uneasy Terms
49: The Golden Madonna
50: Trio (Sanatorium seq.)
    The Black Rose
    The Body Said No
51: The 13th Letter
    The Day the Earth Stood
      Still
    I'll Never Forget You
52: Phone Call from a
      Stranger
    Five Fingers
    Les Miserables
53: Sailor of the King
    Dangerous Crossing
    The Robe
    King of the Khyber Rifles
54: Demetrius and the
      Gladiators
    Princess of the Nile
    Desiree

1155

55: Mambo
     Seven Cities of Gold
     Soldier of Fortune
     The Rains of Ranchipur
56: Teenage Rebel
57: Island in the Sun
     Omar Khayyam
59: Third Man on the
     Mountain
60: The Lost World
63: Mary, Mary
65: Night of the Tiger
66: Ride Beyond Vengeance
     Cybord 2087
67: Hotel
68: The Power
     The Devil's Brigade
     Death on the Run
     Subterfuge
     The Young, the Evil, and
     the Savage
69: Operation Terror
     Krakatoa--East of Java

Eva Renzi
1966: Funeral in Berlin
68: The Pink Jungle
     That Woman

Tommy Rettig (1941-
1950: Two Weeks with Love
     The Jackpot
     Panic in the Streets
     For Heaven's Sake
51: The Strip
     Elopement
     Weekend with Father
52: Gobs and Gals
     Paula
53: The Lady Wants Mink
     The 5000 Fingers of Dr. T
     So Big
54: River of No Return
     The Raid
     The Egyptian
55: The Cobweb
     At Gunpoint
56: The Last Wagon

Anne Revere (1903-
1934: Double Door

40: One Crowded Night
     The Howards of Virginia
41: Men of Boys Town
     Remember the Day
     The Devil Commands
     The Flame of New Orleans
42: The Gay Sisters
     Are Husbands Necessary?
     The Falcon Takes Over
     Meet the Stewarts
     Star-Spangled Rhythm
43: The Song of Bernadette
     Shantytown
     Old Acquaintance
     The Meanest Man in the
     World
44: Standing Room Only
     Rainbow Island
     Keys of the Kingdom
     Sunday Dinner for a
     Soldier
     The Thin Man Goes Home
45: National Velvet (OSCAR)
     Don Juan Quilligan
     Fallen Angel
46: Dragonwyck
47: The Shocking Miss Pilgrim
     Forever Amber
     Body and Soul
     A Gentleman's Agreement
     When the Devil Commands
     Carnival in Costa Rica
48: The Secret Beyond the
     Door
     Scudda Hoo! Scudda Hey!
     Deep Waters
49: You're My Everything
50: The Great Missouri Raid
51: A Place in the Sun
69: Tell Me that You Love
     Me, Junie Moon

Dorothy Revier (1909-
1928: The Warning   S
     The Siren   S
     Submarine   S
     Red Dance   SSE
     Beware of Blondes   S
     Sinners' Parade   S
29: The Quitter   S
     Light Fingers   PT

1156

29: Tanned Legs
   The Iron Mask
   Dance of Life
   Donovan' Affair
   Father and Son
30: The Bad Man
   Murder on the Roof
   Black Sheep
   The Mighty
   Light Thinkers
   Hold Everything
   Call of the West
   Vengeance
   Sin Flood
   Way of All Men
   The Squealer
31: Graft
   Anybody's Blonde
   Black Camel
   The Avenger
32: The Last Ride
   Sally of the Subway
   Sin's Pay Day
   No Living Witness
   Night World
   Arm of the Law
   The Beauty Parlor
   Widow in Scarlet
   Face on the Barroom
   Floor
   A Scarlet Week-End
   The King Murder
33: Secrets of Wu Sin
   Love Is Dangerous
   The Thrill Hunter
   Love Is Like that
   Above the Clouds
34: By Candlelight
   Fighting Rangers
   Unknown Blonde
   The Curtain Falls
   Green Eyes
   When a Man Sees Red
35: $20 a Week
   Circus Shadows
   Circumstantial Evidence
   The Eagle's Brood
   Lady in Scarlet
36: The Cowboy and the Kid

Clive Revill (1930-
PT 1957: Reach for the Sky
    59: The Headless Ghost
    65: Bunny Lake Is Missing
PT 66: A Fine Madness
       Kaleidoscope
       The Double Man
    67: Modesty Blaise
       Fathom
    68: The Shoes of the Fisher-
       man
       The Italian Secret Service
       High Commissioner
       Nobody Runs Forever
    69: Triple Cross
       The Assissination Bureau
       A Severed Head
       The Private Life of
       Sherlock Holmes

Alejandro Rey
1963: Fun in Acapulco
  65: Synanon
  66: Blindfold

Adeline De Walt Reynolds
(1863-1961)
1941: Come Live with Me
     Shadow of the Thin Man
  42: Tales of Manhattan
     The Tuttles of Tahiti
     Iceland
     Street of Chance
  43: The Human Comedy
     Behind the Rising Sun
     Happy Land
     Son of Dracula
  44: Going My Way
     Old Lady
     Since You Went Away
  45: The Corn Is Green
     A Tree Grows in Brooklyn
  48: The Girl from Manhattan
  49: The Sickle or the Cross
  51: Here Comes the Groom
  52: Lydia Bailey
     Pony Soldier
  54: Witness to Murder

Burt Reynolds (1936-
1961: Angel Baby
Armored Command
65: Operation C.I.A.
67: Fade In
Navajo Joe
68: Sam Whiskey
Golden Bullet
Shark
69: Impasse
100 Rifles
Skullduggery

Craig Reynolds (1907-1949)
1930: Coquette
34: Cross Country Cruise
I'll Tell the World
Love Birds
35: 4 Hours to Kill
Paris in Spring
The Case of the Lucky
Legs
Man of Iron
Ceiling Zero
36: Treachery Rides the
Range
The Golden Arrow
Sons o' Guns
Stage Struck
Broadway Playboy
Brides Are Like That
Times Square Playboy
Jailbreak
Smart Blonde
Here Comes Carter!
The Case of the Black Cat
37: Penrod and Sam
Melody of Two
Slim
The Great Garrick
Back in Circulation
Under Suspicion
The Case of the Stutter-
ing Bishop
Footloose Heiress
38: Making the Headlines
Female Fugitives
House of Mystery
I Am a Criminal
Slander House

Romance on the Run
Gold Mine in the Sky
39: The Mystery of Mr. Wong
Navy Secrets
Bad Little Angel
The Gentleman from
Arizona
Wall Street Cowboy
40: The Fatal Hour
Son of the Navy
I Take this Oath
44: Nevada
The Strange Affair of
Uncle Harry
45: Divorce
46: Just Before Dawn
Queen of Burlesque
48: My Dog Shep
The Man from Colorado

Debbie Reynolds (1932-
1948: June Bride
50: Daughter of Rosie O'Grady
Three Little Words
Two Weeks with Love
51: Mr. Imperium
52: Singing in the Rain
Skirts Ahoy!
53: I Love Melvin
Give a Girl a Break
Affairs of Dobie Gillis
54: Susan Slept Here
Athena
55: Hit the Deck
The Tender Trap
56: The Catered Affair
Bundle of Joy
57: Tammy and the Bachelor
58: This Happy Feeling
59: The Mating Game
Say One for Me
It Started with a Kiss
The Gazebo
60: Pepe
The Rat Race
61: The Pleasure of His
Company
Night Without End
The Second Time Around
62: How the West Was Won

63: Mary, Mary
     My Six Loves
64: The Unsinkable Molly
     Brown
65: Goodbye Charlie
66: The Singing Nun
67: Divorce American Style
68: How Sweet It Is!

Gene Reynolds
1936: Thank You Jeeves
     Sins of Man
     Too Many Parents
     Let's Sing Again
     Turmoil
37: The Californian
     Madame X
     Thunder Trail
     Heidi
38: In Old Chicago
     The Crowd Roars
     Of Human Hearts
     Love Finds Andy Hardy
     Boys Town
39: The Spirit of Culver
     They Shall Have Music
     Bad Little Angel
     The Flying Irishman
40: The Blue Bird
     Edison the Man
     The Mortal Storm
     Gallant Sons
     Santa Fe Trail
41: Andy Hardy's Private
     Secretary
     The Penalty
     The Senate Page Boys
     Adventure in Washington
42: The Tuttles of Tahiti
     Eagle Squadron
48: Jungle Patrol
     Man's Heritage
     Melody of Youth
53: 99 River Street
54: Down Three Dark Streets
     Country Girl
     The Bridges at Toko-Ri
55: Diane

Joyce Reynolds (1924-
1942: Yankee Doodle Dandy
     George Washington Slept
       Here
43: The Constant Nymph
     Thank Your Lucky Stars
44: Adventures of Mark Twain
     Hollywood Canteen
     Janie
47: Always Together
48: Wallflower
49: Girls School
50: Dangerous Inheritance
58: Terror from Year 5000

Marjorie Reynolds (1921-
1933: College Humor
     Wine, Women, and Song
35: Big Broadcast of 1936
37: Murder in Greenwich
       Village
     Tex Rides with the Boy
       Scouts
     Champagne Waltz
     College Holiday
     Tailspin Tommy (ser.)
38: Mr. Wong
     Six-Shootin' Sheriff
     Man's Country
     Black Bandit
     Rebellious Daughters
     Overland Express
39: Streets of New York
     Stunt Pilot
     Mr. Wong in Chinatown
     Sky Patrol
     Danger Flight
     Racketeers of the Range
     Timber Stampede
     Mystery Plane
40: The Fatal Hour
     Midnight Limited
     Doomed to Die
     Chasing Trouble
41: Up in the Air
     Enemy Agent
     Robin Hood of the Pecos
     Secret Evidence

41: Law of the Timber
Dude Cowboy
The Great Swindle
Tillie the Toiler
Cyclone on Horseback
Top Sgt. Mulligan
42: Holiday Inn
Star-Spangled Rhythm
43: Dixie
44: Ministry of Fear
Up in Mabel's Room
Three Is a Family
45: Duffy's Tavern
Bring on the Girls
46: Meet Me on Broadway
Monsieur Beaucaire
The Time of Their Lives
The Ghost Steps Out
47: Heaven Only Knows
48: Bad Men of Tombstone
49: That Midnight Kiss
50: Customs Agent
The Great Jewel Robbery
Rookie Fireman
51: Home Town Story
His Kind of Woman
52: No Holds Barred
Models, Inc.
55: Mobs, Inc.
59: Juke Box Rhythm
64: The Silent Witness

Vera Reynolds (1900-1962)
1929: Tonight at Twelve
30: The Last Dance
Lone Rider
Back from Shanghai   S
Borrowed Wives
31: Lawless Woman
Hell Bent for Frisco
Neck and Neck
32: Dragnet Patrol
The Monster Walks
Gorilla Ship
Tangled Destinies

William Reynolds (1931-
1951: The Desert Fox
The Cimarron Kid
52: Has Anybody Seen My Gal?

Francis Goes to West
Point
Carrie
Son of Ali Baba
The Raiders
53: Gunsmoke
The Mississippi Gambler
55: Cult of the Cobra
All that Heaven Allows
56: There's Always Tomorrow
Away All Boats
57: The Land Unknown
Mister Cory
58: The Big Beat
The Thing that Couldn't
Die
64: FBI Code 98
Distant Trumpet
66: Follow Me, Boys!

Barbara Rhodes
1968: Don't Just Stand There!
The Shakiest Gun in the
West

Betty Jane Rhodes (1921-
1936: Forgotten Faces
Arizona Raiders
Jungle Jim
37: Life of the Party
Stage Door
38: a short
40: Oh Johnny, How You can
Love!
41: Mountain Moonlight
Along the Rio Grande
42: Sweater Girl
Priorities on Parade
Star-Spangled Rhythm
43: Salute for Three
44: You Can't Ration Love
Practically Yours

Erik Rhodes (1906-
1934: The Gay Divorcee
35: A Night at the Ritz
Charlie Chan in Paris
The Nitwits
Old Man Rhythm
Top Hat

1160

35: Another Face
36: Two in the Dark
     Chatterbox
     One Rainy Afternoon
     Special Investigator
     Second Wife
     The Smart Girl in Town
37: Criminal Lawyer
     Woman Chases Man
     Music for Madame
     Fight for Your Lady
     Beg, Borrow, or Steal
38: Dramatic School
     Say it in French
     Meet the Girls
     The Mysterious Mr. Moto
        of Devil's Island
39: On Your Toes

Grandon Rhodes
1944: Follow the Boys
       The Impostor
       Sensations of 1945
45:    Hollywood and Vine
46:    The Magnificent Doll
47:    Born to Kill
       Too Many Winners
       Ride the Pink Horse
       Song of My Heart
48:    Gentleman from Nowhere
       Blondie's Reward
       Road House
       Walk a Crooked Mile
49:    Canadian Pacific
       It Happens Every Spring
       The Clay Pigeon
       Streets of Laredo
       All the King's Men
       Tell it to the Judge
       Blondie's Secret
       Miss Mink of 1949
       Dancing in the Dark
       Tucson
50:    And Baby Makes Three
       Woman from Headquarters
       The Lost Volcano
       Born Yesterday
51:    Detective Story
52:    Cripple Creek
53:    A Blueprint for Murder

     On Top of Old Smoky
54: Human Desire
55: Revenge of the Creature
     A Man Alone
56: The Earth vs the Flying
     Saucers
     These Wilder Years
57: The 27th Day
     The Wayward Girl
58: The Notorious Mr. Monks
60: The Bramble Bush
     Oklahoma Territory

Madlyn Rhue (1938-
1959: Operation Petticoat
61:    The Ladies' Man
       A Majority of One
62:    Escape from Zahrain
63:    It's a Mad Mad Mad Mad
          World
64:    He Rides Tall
67:    Stranger on the Run
69:    Kenner

Renie Riano
1937: Tovarich
       You're a Sweetheart
38:    Outside of Paradise
       Spring Madness
       Thanks for Everything
       Men Are Such Fools
       Four's a Crowd
       Nancy Drew, Detective
39:    Wife, Husband, and Friend
       The Honeymoon's Over
       Disputed Passage
       Nancy Drew and the Hidden
          Staircase
       Day-Time Wife
       Nancy Drew, Trouble
          Shooter
40:    The Man Who Wouldn't
          Talk
       The Ghost Comes Home
       Kit Carson
       Remedy for Riches
41:    You're the One
       Adam Had Four Sons
       Affectionately Yours
       Ice-Capades Revue

1161

41: You Belong to Me
42: Whispering Ghosts
    Blondie for Victory
43: The Man from Music
    Mountain
    None but the Lonely
    Heart
44: Jam Session
    Take It or Leave It
    Three Is a Family
45: Club Havana
    A Song for Miss Julie
46: Bringing Up Father
    So Goes My Love
    Bad Bascomb
47: Winter Wonderland
48: Maggie and Jiggs in
    Society
    Maggie and Jiggs in Court
    The Time of Your Life
49: Maggie and Jiggs in Jack-
    pot Jitters
50: Maggie and Jiggs Out
    West
51: As Young as You Feel
    The Barefoot Milkman
64: Pajama Party
65: The Family Jewels
66: Three on a Couch
    Fireball 500

Florence Rice (1911-
1934: Fugitive Lady
  35: Carnival
    The Best Man Wins
    Under Pressure
    The Awakening of Jim
    Burke
    Escape from Devil's
    Island
    Death Flies East
  36: Panic on the Air
    The Blackmailer
    Guard that Girl!
    Sworn Enemy
    Jim Burke's Boy
    Superspeed
    The Rare Book Murder
    Pride of the Marines
    Women Are Trouble

    The Longest Night
37: Man of the People
    Married Before Breakfast
    Navy, Blue, and Gold
    Double Wedding
    Under Cover of Night
    Beg, Borrow, or Steal
    All Is Confusion
    Riding on Air
38: Paradise for Three
    Fast Company
    Sweethearts
    Vacation from Love
39: Stand Up and Fight
    Four Girls in White
    Miracles for Sale
    The Kid from Texas
    At the Circus
    Little Accident
40: Cherokee Strip
    Broadway Melody of 1940
    Phantom Raiders
    The Secret Seven
    Girl in 313
41: Mr. District Attorney
    The Blonde from Singapore
    Father Takes a Wife
    Doctors Don't Tell
    Borrowed Hero
42: Tramp, Tramp, Tramp
    Let's Get Tough
    Boss of Big Town
43: The Ghost and the Guest
    Stand By, All Networks

Joan Rice (1930-
1952: The Story of Robin Hood
    The Crowded Day
    One Good Turn
  53: Curtain Up
    His Majesty O'Keefe
    Glory at Sea
  55: Women in Prison
    A Day to Remember
    Police Dog
  56: Blonde Bait
    The Long Knife
  62: Payroll

Irene Rich (1897-
1928: Craig's Wife   S
      Ned McCobb's
        Daughter   SSE
      Women They Talk
        About   PT
      Perfect Crime   PT
      Powder My Back   SSE
  29: The Exalted Flapper   SSE
      Shanghai Rose   S
      Daughters of Desire   S
  30: They Had to See Paris
      Father's Son
      So This Is London
      On Your Back
      Check and Double Check
      a short
  31: Mad Parade
      The Champ
      Beau Ideal
      Strangers May Kiss
      Five and Ten
  32: Down to Earth
      Her Mad Night
      Manhattan Tower
      Daughters of Luxury
  38: That Certain Age
  39: Everybody's Hobby
  40: The Mortal Storm
      Queen of the Yukon
      Lady in Question
  41: Keeping Company
      Three Sons o' Guns
  42: This Time for Keeps
  47: Angel and the Badman
      The Calendar Girl
      New Orleans
  48: Fort Apache
      Joan of Arc

Lillian Rich (1905-1954)
1931: Once a Lady
      Grief Street
      The Devil Plays
  32: Mark of the Spur

Addison Richards (1887-1964)
1934: Lone Cowboy
      Let's be Ritzy
      Love Captive
      Beyond the Law
      Our Daily Bread
      The Case of the Howling
        Dog
      Gentlemen Are Born
      St. Louis Kid
      Babbitt
  35: The Riot Squad
      Only Eight Hours
      The White Cockatoo
      Home on the Range
      Sweet Music
      Dinky
      The G Men
      Alias Mary Dow
      A Dog of Flanders
      Front Page Woman
      Here Comes the Band
      Little Big Shot
      Freckles
      The Eagle's Brood
      The Frisco Kid
      Ceiling Zero
  36: Colleen
      China Clipper
      Man Hunt
      Road Gang
      Song of the Saddle
      The Walking Dead
      Sutter's Gold
      The Law in Her Hands
      Jailbreak
      Anthony Adverse
      Public Enemy's Wife
      The Case of the Velvet
        Claws
      Hot Money
      Trailin' West
  37: Black Legion
      Smart Blonde
      Ready, Willing, and Able
      Her Husband's Secretary
      Draegerman Courage
      Dance, Charlie, Dance
      White Bondage
      The Singing Marine
      Love Is on the Air
      The Barrier
  38: Prison Nurse
      The Black Doll

38: Alcatraz Island
Accidents Will Happen
Valley of the Giants
Boys Town
The Last Express
Flight to Fame
39: They Made Her a Spy
Twelve Crowded Hours
Whispering Enemies
Off the Record
Burn 'em Up, O'Connor
Inside Information
Andy Hardy Gets Spring
  Fever
They All Come Out
Thunder Afloat
Espionage Agent
Geronimo
Bad Lands
Nick Carter, Master
  Detective
40: Boom Town
Northwest Passage
The Man from Montreal
The Man from Dakota
Charlie Chan in Panama
The Lone Wolf Strikes
Slightly Honorable
Edison the Man
Gangs of Chicago
Andy Hardy Meets a
  Debutante
South to Karanga
Girls from Havana
Wyoming
Black Diamonds
Cherokee Strip
Moon over Burma
Arizona
Flight Command
My Little Chickadee
41: Western Pacific
Tall, Dark, and Handsome
Andy Hardy's Private
  Secretary
Back in the Saddle
I Wanted Wings
The Great Lie
Men of Boys Town
Sheriff of Tombstone

Mutiny in the Arctic
Her First Beau
Badlands of Dakota
International Squadron
Texas
42: My Favorite Blonde
Secret Agent of Japan
The Lady Has Plans
The Man with Two Lives
Cowboy Serenade
Pacific Rendezvous
Friendly Enemies
A-Haunting We Will Go
Top Sergeant
War Dogs
Seven Days' Leave
Men of Texas
The Pride of the Yankees
Secret Enemies
The Flying Tigers
Secrets of a Coed
43: Air Force
Underground Agent
Headin' for God's Country
Corvette K-225
A Guy Named Joe
Where Are Your Children?
The Mystery of the 13th
  Guest
Mystery Broadcast
The Deerslayer
44: The Sullivans
The Fighting Seabees
Smart Guy
Follow the Boys
Three Men in White
Moon over Las Vegas
A Night of Adventure
Roger Touhy-Gangster
Are These Our Parents?
Marriage Is a Private
  Affair
Since You Went Away
Three Little Sisters
Barbary Coast Gent
Bordertown Trail
The Mummy's Curse
45: God Is My Co-Pilot
The Chicago Kid
Bells of Rosarita

45: Bewitched
The Adventures of Rusty
Spellbound
Strange Confession
Leave Her to Heaven
Betrayal from the East
Come Out Fighting
Danger Signal
Grissly's Millions
I'll Remember April
Men in Her Diary
Rough, Tough, and Ready
The Shanghai Cobra
46: Anna and the King of
Siam
Love Laughs at Andy
Hardy
Secrets of a Sorority Girl
Angel on My Shoulder
The Criminal Court
The Hoodlum Saint
Renegades
Step by Step
Don't Gamble with
Strangers
47: The Millerson Case
48: Call Northside 777
Lulu Belle
49: The Rustlers
Henry the Rainmaker
50: Davy Crockett--Indian
Scout
55: High Society
Illegal
Fort Yuma
56: The Broken Star
Fury at Gunsight Pass
Walk the Proud Land
When Gangland Strikes
Reprisal!
Everything but the Truth
57: Last of the Badmen
Gunsight Ridge
58: The Saga of Hemp Brown
59: The Oregon Trail
61: Frontier Uprising
The Gambler Wore a Gun
The Flight that Dis-
appeared
62: Saintly Sinners

63: The Raiders
64: For Those Who Think
Young

Ann Richards (1918-
1937: It Isn't Done
Tall Timber
Lovers
The Rudd Family
Come Up Smiling
100,000 Cobbers
The Woman in the House
42: Dr. Gillespie's New
Assistant
Random Harvest
44: An American Romance
45: Love Letters
46: Badman's Territory
The Searching Wind
A Scandal in Paris
47: Lost Honeymoon
Love from a Stranger
48: Sorry, Wrong Number
52: Breakdown

Gordon Richards (1894-1964)
1945: White Pongo
Kitty
46: Larceny in Her Heart
47: The Imperfect Lady
Flight to Nowhere
Linda be Good
48: Women in the Night
Thirteen Lead Soldiers
50: The Big Hangover
The Man Who Cheated
Himself
56: High Society

Grant Richards
1939: Risky Business
Inside Information
42: Just Off Broadway
60: Oklahoma Territory
12 Hours to Kill
The Music Box Kid
61: You Have to Run Fast
Secret of Deep Harbor

Jeff Richards
1950: Kill the Umpire
  51: Tall Target
     The Strip
     Angels in the Outfield
     The Sellout
  52: Above and Beyond
     Desperate Search
  53: Code #3
     The Big Leaguer
     Battle Circus
  54: Crest of the Waves
     Seven Brides for Seven
       Brothers
  55: Many Rivers to Cross
     The Marauders
     It's a Dog's Life (or,
       Bar Sinister)
  56: The Opposite Sex
  57: Don't Go Near the Water
  59: Island of Lost Women
     Born Reckless
  60: Secret of the Purple Reef
  66: Waco

Keith Richards
1942: Reap the Wild Wind
     The Forest Rangers
  43: Alaska Highway
     So Proudly We Hail!
  47: Seven Were Saved
     Queen of the Amazons
     The Case of the Baby-
       Sitter
     Road to the Big House
  48: The Gay Ranchero
     Where the North Begins
     Sons of Adventure
     Walk a Crooked Mile
  49: Duke of Chicago
     Captain China
     The Blonde Bandit
     Shadows of the West
  50: West of the Great Divide
     North of the Great Divide
  51: Spoilers of the Plains
     Tales of Robin Hood
  53: Rebel City
  56: Yaqui Drums
  57: Untamed Youth

     The Buster Keaton Story
  58: Ambush at Cimarron Pass
  61: The Gambler Wore a Gun
  62: Incident in an Alley

Paul Richards (1924-
1954: Phantom of the Rue Morgue
     Pushover
     Playgirl
  55: Tall Man Riding
  56: The Houston Story
     Scandal Incorporated
  57: Hot Summer Night
     The Black Whip
     The Strange One
     Monkey on My Back
     The Unknown Terror
  58: Blood Arrow
  59: Four Fast Guns
  60: All the Young Men
  67: The St. Valentine's Day
       Massacre
  69: The Fire Within
     Beneath the Planet of the
       Apes

Stephen Richards: see Mark
Stevens

Jack Richardson (1883-
1931: Unfaithful
     Gun Smoke
     Playthings of Hollywood
     Lightnin' Smith's Return
     Mystery Train
  32: Land of Wanted Men
     Without Honor
     Scandal for Sale
     They Never Come Back
     The Man from New Mexico
  34: Gun Justice
  35: The Perfect Clue
  40: Gun Code
  41: Mr. Celebrity
  46: Romance of the West
  56: The Proud and the Profane
  59: A Summer Place
  68: Beyond the Law

John Richardson (1936-
1958: Bachelor of Hearts
65: She
66: One Million B.C.
68: The Vengeance of She
A Nun at the Crossroads
69: Stand-In for a Killing

Sir Ralph Richardson (1902-
1933: The Ghoul
34: Friday the 13th
The Return of Bulldog
Drummond
Bulldog Jack
35: Java Head
King of Paris
36: Things to Come
37: Thunder in the City
The Man Who Could Work
Miracles
38: Divorce of Lady X
South Riding
The Citadel
Q Planes
39: Four Feathers
40: The Lion Has Wings
On the Night of the Fire
42: The Avengers (or, The
Day Will Dawn)
43: The Silver Fleet
46: School for Secrets
47: Anna Karenina
48: The Lost Illusion
49: The Fallen Idol
The Heiress
51: An Outcast of the Islands
52: Breaking the Sound
Barrier
Home at Seven (dir.)
53: The Holly and the Ivy
Murder on Monday
56: Richard III
The Passionate Stranger
57: Smiley
60: Oscar Wilde
Our Man in Havana
The Exodus
61: Lion of Sparta
62: 300 Spartans
Long Day's Journey into
the Night

64: Woman of Straw
65: Doctor Zhivago
66: Khartoum (or, The Battle
for Khartoum)
The Wrong Box
67: Falstaff (narr.)
68: The Midas Run
The Bed-Sitting Room
69: The Battle of Britain
Oh! What a Lovely War!
The Looking Glass War
David Copperfield (TV)

Charles Richman (1870-1940)
1934: His Double Life
The President Vanishes
35: After Office Hours
George White's Scandals
of 1935
Biography of a Bachelor
Girl
The Case of the Curious
Bride
Becky Sharp
The Glass Key
In Old Kentucky
My Marriage
Thanks a Million
36: The Ex-Mrs. Bradford
Parole!
In His Steps
I'd Give My Life
Under Your Spell
Sing Me a Love Song
37: Make a Wish
The Life of Emile Zola
Lady Behave
38: Adventures of Tom Sawyer
Blondes at Work
The Cowboy and the Lady
39: Dark Victory
Exile Express
40: Devil's Island

Mark Richman (1927-
1956: Friendly Persuasion
57: The Strange One
58: Girls on the Loose
59: The Black Orchid
61: Crime Busters
65: Dark Intruder

1167

66: Agent for H. A. R. M.
67: A Dandy in Aspic
68: For Singles Only
69: The Girl Who Knew too
    Much

Kane Richmond (1906-
1930: Twelve Leather Pushers
    (ser.)
31: Stepping Out
    Politics
    Cavalier of the West
    Campus Champs
    Open House
32: Huddle
    West of Broadway
    Strangers May Kiss
34: Devil Tiger
    Let's Fall in Love
    Voice in the Night
    The Crime of Helen
    Stanley
    I Can't Escape
35: The Lost City
    Circus Shadows
    Confidential
    Forced Landing
36: Private Number
    Born to Fight
    Raging Blood
    With Love and Kisses
37: The Reckless Way
    Devil Diamond
    Nancy Steele Is Missing
    Headline Crasher
    Tough to Handle
    Anything for a Thrill
    Young Dynamite
38: Mars Attacks the World
39: Tail Spin
    Winner Take All
    Return of the Cisco Kid
    Charlie Chan in Reno
    Chicken Wagon Family
    20,000 Men in a Year
    The Escape
40: Charlie Chan in Panama
    Sailor's Lady
    Murder over New York
    Knute Rockne--All
    American

41: Play Girl
    Mountain Moonlight
    Riders of the Purple Sage
    Great Guns
    Hard Guy
    Double Cross
42: A Gentleman at Heart
    Spy Smasher (ser; feature
    Spy Smasher Returns)
43: Action in the North
    Atlantic
    Three Russian Girls
    There's Something about
    a Soldier
44: Ladies Courageous
    Bermuda Mystery
    Roger Touhy--Gangster
    Haunted Harbor (ser.)
45: Jungle Raiders (ser.)
    Black Market Babies
    The Tiger Woman
    Brenda Starr-Reporter
    (ser.)
46: The Mighty McGurk
    The Shadow Returns
    Passkey to Danger
    Don't Gamble with
    Strangers
    Behind the Mask
    The Missing Lady
    Traffic in Crime
47: Brick Bradford (ser.)
    Black Gold
48: Stage Struck
51: Pirates Harbor (ser.)

Warner Richmond (1895-1948)
1929: Strange Cargo
    Redeeming Sin   PT
    Stark Mad
    Voice of the Storm   S
    Big News
30: Men Without Women
    Strictly Modern
    Billy the Kid
31: Quick Millions
    Huckleberry Finn
32: The Woman from Monte
    Carlo
    Beast of the City
    Strangers of the Evening

1168

32: Hell's Highway
33: King of the Jungle
     Fast Workers
     Corruption
     Mama Loves Papa
     This Day and Age
     Police Call
     Life in the Raw
34: Lost Jungle
     Happy Landing
35: Under Pressure
     Mississippi
     Headline Woman
     Rainbow's End
     Smoky Smith
     New Frontier
     The Courageous Avenger
     Singing Vagabond
36: Hearts in Bondage
     Below the Deadline
     Heart of the West
     The White Legion
     Song of the Gringo
     Headin' for Rio Grande
37: The Gold Racket
     A Lawman Is Born
     Riders of the Dawn
     Wallaby Jim of the
       Islands
     Stars over Arizona
     Federal Bullets
     Where Trails Divide
38: Wolves of the Sea
     Six-Shootin' Sheriff
     Prairie Moon
39: Wild Horse Canyon
40: Rhythm of the Rio Grande
     Men with Steel Faces
     The Golden Trail
     Rainbow over the Range
46: Colorado Serenade

Tom Ricketts (d. 1938)
1930: The Vagabond King
     Prince of Diamonds
     Broken Dishes
     Sea Legs
31: Man of the World
     Side Show
     Ambassador Bill

     Surrender
32: Farewell to Arms
     Forbidden
     Thrill of Youth
33: He Learned about Women
     Women Won't Tell
     Forgotten
     Mama Loves Papa
34: In Love with Life
     Little Man, What Now?
     Stolen Sweets
     The Curtain Falls
35: Forsaking All Others
     Sons of Steel
     Now or Never
     A Tale of Two Cities
36: Hi Gaucho!
     He Went to College
37: Maid of Salem
38: Bluebeard's Eighth Wife
     Young Fugitives
     The Young in Heart

Don Rickles (1926-
1958: Run Silent, Run Deep
59: The Rabbit Trap
60: The Rat Race
63: X, the Man with X-Ray
       Eyes
64: Muscle Beach Party
     Bikini Beach
65: Beach Blanket Bingo
67: Enter Laughing
68: The Money Jungle
69: Where It's At
     The Warriors

John Ridgely (1909-1968)
1937: Submarine D-1
38: The Patient in Room 18
     Blondes at Work
     Forbidden Valley
     Torchy Blane in Panama
     White Banners
     Cowboy from Brooklyn
     My Bill
     The Invisible Menace
     Little Miss Thoroughbred
     Hard to Get
     Going Places

38: Torchy Gets Her Man
39: The Cowboy Quarterback
King of the Underworld
You Can't Get Away with
  Murder
The Return of Dr. X
Nancy Drew and the
  Hidden Staircase
Kid Nightingale
Dark Victory
Secret Service of the Air
Wings of the Navy
They Made Me a Criminal
Everybody's Hobby
Indianapolis Speedway
Torchy Plays with
  Dynamite
40: Brother Orchid
Torrid Zone
River's End
Flight Angels
They Drive by Night
Father Is a Prince
The Man Who Talked too
  Much
41: The Wagons Roll at Night
Strange Alibi
Here Comes Happiness
Million Dollar Baby
Navy Blues
International Squadron
The Great Mr. Nobody
The Man Who Came to
  Dinner
42: The Big Shot
Bullet Scars
Wings for the Eagle
Secret Enemies
43: Air Force
Northern Pursuit
Destination Tokyo
44: Hollywood Canteen
Arsenic and Old Lace
Doughgirls
45: Danger Signal
God Is My Co-Pilot
Pride of the Marines
46: The Big Sleep
My Reputation
Two Guys from Milwaukee

47: Cheyenne
The Man I Love
Nora Prentiss
Possessed
That Way with Women
That's My Man
Cry Wolf
High Wall
48: The Iron
Night Winds
Luxury Liner
Sealed Verdict
Trouble Makers
Command Decision
49: Once More My Darling
Border Incident
Tucson
Task Force
50: Beauty on Parade
Saddle Tramp
The Lost Volcano
Rookie Fireman
South Sea Sinners
The Petty Girl
51: A Place in the Sun
Half Angel
The Last Outpost
When the Redskins Rode
Thunder in God's Country
The Blue Veil
As You Were
52: The Greatest Show on
  Earth
Room for One More
Outcasts of Poker Flat
Fort Osage

Stanley Ridges (1892-1951)
1938: Yellow Jack
The Mad Miss Manton
If I Were King
There's that Woman Again
39: Let Us Live
Silver on the Sage
Union Pacific
Each Dawn I Die
Espionage Agent
Dust be My Destiny
Nick Carter, Master
  Detective

40: Black Friday
41: The Sea Wolf
    Mr. District Attorney
    Sergeant York
    They Died with Their
      Boots on
42: To Be or Not to Be
    The Lady Is Willing
    The Big Shot
    Eagle Squadron
    Eyes in the Night
43: Tarzan Triumphs
    Air Force
    This Is the Army
44: The Master Race
    The Story of Dr. Wassell
    Wilson
45: The Suspect
    Captain Eddie
    God Is My Co-Pilot
    The Phantom Speaks
46: Because of Him
    Mr. Ace
    Canyon Passage
48: An Act of Murder
49: You're My Everything
    Streets of Laredo
    Thelma Jordan
    Task Force
50: Paid in Full
    No Way Out
51: The Groom Wore Spurs

Fritzi Ridgeway (1898-1960)
1929: Red Hot Speed   PT
      This Is Heaven   PT
30:   Hell's Heroes
      Price of Diamonds
35:   No Ransom

Diana Rigg
1968: A Midsummer Night's
        Dream (TV)
69:   The Assassination Bureau
      On Her Majesty's Secret
        Service
      The Assassination of
        Julius Caesar

Cyril Ring (d. 1967)
1933: Emergency Call

        Too Much Harmony
        Neighbors' Wives
34:     Hollywood Hoodlums
36:     Border Patrolman
        Wedding Present
41:     Hot Spot
42:     The Navy Comes Through
        Army Surgeon
        Over My Dead Body
43:     Dixie
        Melody Parade
44:     Hot Rhythm
        Follow the Boys
        Secret Command
45:     Hollywood and Vine
47:     Hollywood Barn Dance
        Body and Soul

Rin-Tin-Tin (1916-1932)
1929:   Million Dollar Collar   PT
        The Frozen River   PT
        Show of Shows
        Tiger Rose
30:     On the Border
        Dog of the Regiment
        The Man Hunter
        Rough Waters
35:     Skull and Crown (R-T-T,
        Jr.)

Elizabeth Risdon (1888-1958)
1935:   Guard that Girl!
        Crime and Punishment
36:     Don't Gamble with Love
        Lady of Secrets
        The King Steps Out
        The Final Hour
        Craig's Wife
        Theodora Goes Wild
37:     The Woman I Love
        Make Way for Tomorrow
        Mountain Justice
        They Won't Forget
        Dead End
38:     Mannequin
        Mad About Music
        Tom Sawyer, Detective
        Cowboy from Brooklyn
        My Bill
        Girls on Probation
        The Affairs of Annabel

1171

39: The Great Man Votes
Sorority House
The Girl from Mexico
Five Came Back
Full Confession
The Man Who Dared
The Mexican Spitfire
Huckleberry Finn
I Am not Afraid
The Roaring Twenties
Forgotten Woman
Disputed Passage
40: The Man Who Wouldn't
Talk
Abe Lincoln in Illinois
Honeymoon Deferred
Ma, He's Making Eyes
at Me
Saturday's Children
Sing, Dance, Plenty Hot
The Howards of Virginia
The Mexican Spitfire Out
West
Slightly Tempted
Let's Make Music
41: High Sierra
Footlight Fever
Mr. Dynamite
Nice Girl?
The Mexican Spitfire's
Baby
42: Jail House Blues
The Mexican Spitfire at
Sea
The Man Who Returned
to Life
The Lady Is Willing
Reap the Wild Wind
The Mexican Spitfire Sees
a Ghost
Are Husbands Necessary?
I Live on Danger
Journey for Margaret
The Mexican Spitfire's
Elephant
Random Harvest
43: The Amazing Mrs.
Holliday
Higher and Higher
Lost Angel
Cobra Woman

Never a Dull Moment
44: The Canterville Ghost
Weird Woman
In the Meantime Darling
Tall in the Saddle
Blonde Fever
45: The Fighting Guardsman
Grissly's Millions
Mama Loves Papa
A Song for Miss Julie
The Unseen
46: Lover Come Back
Roll on Texas Moon
They Made Me a Killer
The Walls Came Tumbling
Down
47: The Egg and I
The Shocking Miss Pilgrim
High Wall
Life with Father
Mourning Becomes Electra
48: The Bride Goes Wild
Every Girl Should be
Married
Sealed Verdict
Bodyguard
49: Down Dakota Way
Guilty of Treason
50: Sierra
The Secret Fury
Bunco Squad
Hills of Oklahoma
The Milkman
51: In Old Amarillo
My True Story
Bannerline
52: Scaramouche

Tex Ritter (1907-
1936: Song of the Gringo
Heading for the Rio
Grande
37: Arizona Days
Trouble in Texas
Hittin' the Trail
Swing, Cowboy, Swing
Riders of the Rockies
Tex Rides with the Boy
Scouts
Rollin' Plains
Mystery of the Hooded
Horsemen

38: Frontier Town
    The Utah Trail
    Starlight over Texas
    Where the Buffalo Roam
39: Song of the Buckaroo
    Rollin' Westward
    Down the Wyoming Trail
    Riders of the Frontier
    Roll, Wagons, Roll
    Sundown on the Prairie
    The Man from Texas
40: Westbound Stage
    Rhythm of the Rio Grande
    Pals of the Silver Sage
    The Golden Trail
    Rainbow over the Range
    Take Me back to
      Oklahoma
    Arizona Frontier
    Riding with Buffalo Bill
    A-Headin' for Cheyenne
    Round-Up Time in the
      Rockies
41: Rolling Home to Texas
    Ridin' the Cherokee Trail
    The Pioneers
    The Lone Star Vigilantes
42: Deep in the Heart of
      Texas
    Little Joe the Wrangler
43: Cheyenne Roundup
    Tenting Tonight on the
      Old Camp Ground
    The Old Chisholm Trail
    Lone Star Trail
    Frontier Badmen
44: Arizona Trail
    Cowboy Canteen
    Marshal of Gunsmoke
    Oklahoma Raiders
    The Whispering Skull
    Gangsters of the Frontier
    Dead or Alive
45: Enemy of the Law
    Flaming Bullets
    Three in the Saddle
    Marked for Murder
46: Frontier Fugitive
50: Holiday Rhythm
52: High Noon (sang title)

55: Apache Ambush
66: Nashville Rebel
67: What Am I Bid?

Thelma Ritter (1905-1969)
1947: Miracle on 34th Street
48: A Letter to Three Wives
    Northside 777
49: Father Was a Fullback
    City Across the River
50: All About Eve
    I'll Get by
    Perfect Strangers
51: The Mating Season
    Will You Love Me in
      December?
    As Young as You Feel
    The Model and the
      Marriage Broker
52: With a Song in My Heart
53: The Farmer Takes a
      Wife
    Pickup on South Street
    Titanic
54: Rear Window
55: Lucy Gallant
    Daddy Long Legs
56: The Proud and Profane
59: A Hole in the Head
    Pillow Talk
61: The Misfits
    The Second Time Around
62: Birdman of Alcatraz
    How the West Was Won
63: For Love or Money
    A New Kind of Love
    Move Over Darling
65: Boeing! Boeing!
67: The Incident
68: What's so Bad about
      Feeling Good?

The Ritz Brothers (Al, 1903-
1965; Jim, 1905-; & Harry, 1908-)
1933: shorts
36: Sing, Baby, Sing
37: One in a Million
    On the Avenue
    Life Begins in College
    You Can't Have Everything

38: Kentucky Moonshine
Straight Place and Show
Goldwyn Follies
39: The Three Musketeers
The Gorilla
Pack Up Your Troubles
40: Argentine Nights
42: Behind the Eight Ball
43: Never a Dull Moment
Hi Ya, Chum!
45: Everything Happens to Us
64: The Sound of Laughter
(doc.)

Carlos Rivas
1955: A Bullet for Joey
Hell's Island
56: The King and I
The Beast of Hollow
Mountain
57: The Big Boodle
The Deerslayer
The Black Scorpion
Panama Sal
58: Machete
59: The Miracle
60: The Unforgiven
Pepe
64: Madmen of Mandoras
69: True Grit
King Gun

Bert Roach (1891-
1929: Last Warning   PT
Honeymoon   S
Desert Rider   S
The Argyle Case
The Time, the Place, and
the Girl
Twin Beds
Young Nowheres
Show of Shows
The Aviator
So Long Letty
30: No, No, Nanette
Hold Everything
Song of the Flame
Lawful Larceny
Viennese Nights
Liliom

Captain Thunder
The Princess and the
Plumber
31: Bad Sister
Three Girls Lost
Six-Cylinder Love
Arrowsmith
Compromised
32: Murder in the Rue Morgue
Hotel Continental
Night World
Bird of Paradise
Evenings for Sale
33: Hallelujah, I'm a Bum!
Daring Daughters
Easy Millions
Secret Sinners
34: Marrying Widows
Paris Interlude
Half a Sinner
35: Traveling Saleslady
Here Comes the Band
Guard that Girl!
36: Love Before Breakfast
Sons o' Guns
San Francisco
God's Country and the
Woman
37: Sing While You're Able
The Girl Said No
The Emperor's Candle-
sticks
Double Wedding
Prescription for Romance
38: Mad about Music
Stolen Heaven
Romance on the Run
Algiers
Mannequin
Inside Story
The Great Waltz
39: Rose of Washington Square
The Man in the Iron Mask
Nurse Edith Cavell
40: Yesterday's Heroes
41: You're the One
Bachelor Daddy
42: Fingers at the Window
Dr. Renault's Secret
Quiet Please, Murder

43:	Hi Diddle Diddle	34:	Burn 'em Up, Barnes
44:	Sensations of 1945		(ser.; same title feature)
45:	Bedside Manner		All of Me
46:	Decoy		Woman Unafraid
	Little Giant		Woman Condemned
	The Man from Rainbow		Take the Stand
	Valley		The Crimson Romance
	The Missing Lady		The President Vanishes
	Rendezvous 24		One Exciting Adventure
	Sing While You Dance	35:	Ladies Crave Excitement
47:	The Perils of Pauline		The Crusaders
		36:	The White Legion

Jason Robards, Sr. (1893-1963)

1928:	On Trial	S	37: Sweetheart of the Navy
	Casey Jones	S	38: Cipher Bureau
29:	Trial Marriage	S	Clipped Wings
	Some Mother's Boy	S	Flight to Fame
	The Gamblers		Mystery Plane
	Flying Marines	PT	39: Sky Pirate
	Paris	S	Stunt Pilot
	The Isle of Lost Ships		Sky Patrol
30:	Crazy that Way		Danger Flight
	Peacock Alley		I Stole a Million
	Abraham Lincoln		Juarez and Maximilian
	Last Dance		Range War
	Sisters		40: The Fatal Hour
	Jazz Cinderella		44: Bermuda Mystery
	Lightnin'		Mlle Fifi
31:	Charlie Chan Carries On		The Master Race
	Subway Express		45: Betrayal from the East
	Ex-Bad Boy		A Game of Death
	Salvation Nell		Isle of the Dead
	Full of Notions		Man Alive
	Caught Plastered		Wanderer of the Wasteland
	Law of the Tongs		What a Blonde!
32:	Discarded Lovers		46: Bedlam
	Unholy Love		Ding Dong Williams
	Klondike		The Falcon's Adventure
	White Eagle		The Falcon's Alibi
	Pride of the Legion		Step by Step
	Slightly Married		Vacation in Reno
	The Docks of San		47: Desperate
	Francisco		Thunder Mountain
33:	Corruption		Trail Street
	The Devil's Mate		Riffraff
	Dance Hall Hostess		Seven Keys to Baldpate
	Ship of Wanted Men		Under the Tonto Rim
	Public Stenographer		Wild Horse Mesa
	Carnival Lady		48: Fighting Father Dunne
	Strange Alibi		Guns of Hate
			Mr. Blanding Builds His
			Dream House

48: Return of the Bad Men
Western Heritage
Son of God's Country
49: Rimfire
Post Office Investigator
Alaska Patrol
Impact
Feudin' Rhythm
Horsemen of the Sierras
South of Death Valley
Riders of the Whispering
Pines
51: The Second Woman
61: Wild in the Country

Jason Robards, Jr. (1920-
1959: The Journey
61: By Love Possessed
62: Tender Is the Night
Long Day's Journey into
Night
63: Act One
65: A Thousand Clowns
66: Big Hand for the Little
Lady
Any Wednesday
67: Divorce American Style
The St. Valentine's Day
Massacre
Hour of the Gun
68: The Night They Raided
Minsky's
Once Upon a Time in the
West
The Loves of Isadora
69: The Ballad of Cable Hogue
Tora! Tora! Tora!
The Assassination of
Julius Caesar

Gale Robbins (1924-
1944: In the Meantime, Darling
46: Mr. Hex
48: My Girl Tisa
Race Street
My Dear Secretary
49: Oh, You Beautiful Doll!
50: Three Little Words
The Fuller Brush Girl
Between Midnight and
Dawn

51: Strictly Dishonorable
52: Belle of New York
The Brigand
53: Calamity Jane
55: Double Jeopardy
The Girl in the Red Velvet
Swing
58: Quantrill's Raiders
Gunsmoke in Tucson

Richard Rober (1906-1952)
1948: Smart Girls
49: Port of New York
50: Sierra
Backfire
Deported
Watch the Birdie
51: Passage West
The Tall Target
The Well
Man in the Saddle
52: Kid Monk Baroni
Outlaw Women
The Devil Makes Three
O. Henry's Full House
(Clarion Call seq.)
The Savage
52: Jet Pilot

Lyda Roberti (1910-1938)
1932: Million Dollar Legs
The Kid from Spain
33: Three-Cornered Moon
Torch Singer
34: College Rhythm
35: George White's 1935
Scandals
Big Broadcast of 1936
37: Nobody's Baby
Pick a Star
38: Wide Open Faces

Allene Roberts (1928-
1950: Bomba on Panther Island
Union Station
51: Santa Fe
The Hoodlum
A Wonderful Life
52: Kid Monk Baroni

Beverly Roberts (1914-
1936: The Singing Kid
Sons o' Guns
Two Against the World
Hot Money
China Clipper
God's Country and the
Woman
37: Her Husband's Secretary
War Lord
Expensive Husbands
The Perfect Specimen
West of Shanghai
38: Making the Headlines
Outside the Law
House of Mystery
Flirting with Fate
Call of the Yukon
The Tenth Avenue Kid
The Daredevil
39: The Strange Case of Dr.
Meade
I Was a Convict
Main Street Lawyer
Tropic Fury
40: Buried Alive

Desmond Roberts (1894-
1933: The King's Vacation
Christopher Strong
Tarzan and His Mate
Blind Adventure
34: Grand Canary
Jane Eyre
Of Human Bondage
The Fountain
House of Danger
Limehouse Blues
The Menace
35: Clive of India
54: Beau Brummel

Florence Roberts (1861-1940)
1930: Eyes of the World
31: Bachelor Apartment
Kept Husbands
Everything's Rosie
Too Many Crooks
Fanny Foley Herself
32: Westward Passage

Make Me a Star
All American
33: Officer 13
Dangerously Yours
Daring Daughters
Melody Cruise
Torch Singer
Hoopla
34: Miss Fane's Baby Is
Stolen
Babes in Toyland
35: The Nut Farm
Rocky Mountain Mystery
Les Miserables
Sons of Steel
Accent on Youth
Harmony Lane
Public Opinion
Your Uncle Dudley
36: Every Saturday Night
The Next Time We Love
Educating Father
Nobody's Fool
Back to Nature
37: Off to the Races
Nobody's Baby
Big Business
The Life of Emile Zola
Borrowing Trouble
Hot Water
38: Love on a Budget
A Trip to Paris
Safety in Numbers
Down on the Farm
The Storm
Personal Secretary
39: Quick Millions
Too Busy to Work
40: Abe Lincoln in Illinois
Young As You Feel
On Their Own

Leona Roberts
1937: Border Cafe
There Goes the Groom
38: Of Human Hearts
Bringing Up Baby
Condemned Women
This Marriage Business
Crime Ring

1177

38: Having a Wonderful Time
The Affairs of Annabel
I Stand Accused
Kentucky
39: Persons in Hiding
Bachelor Mother
The Escape
Gone with the Wind
Swanee River
40: The Blue Bird
Thou Shalt Not Kill
Abe Lincoln in Illinois
Sued for Libel
Gangs of Chicago
Queen of the Mob
Golden Gloves
Comin' Round the Mountain
Blondie Plays Cupid
Wildcat Bus
46: The Madonna's Secret

Lynn Roberts (1919-
1937: Dangerous Holiday
Stella Dallas
Love Is on the Air
Mama Runs Wild
38: Heart of the Rockies
Call the Mesquiteers
Hollywood Stadium
Mystery
The Higgins Family
Billy the Kid Returns
The Lone Ranger
Dick Tracy Returns (ser.)
39: Everything's on Ice
The Mysterious Miss X
My Wife's Relations
Rough Riders' Round-Up
40: High School
Hi-Yo, Silver!
Street of Memories
41: Romance of the Rio
Grande
The Bride Wore Crutches
Moon over Miami
The Last of the Duanes
Riders of the Purple Sage
42: Young America
The Man in the Trunk
Dr. Renault's Secret

Quiet Please, Murder
44: The Port of Forty Thieves
The Ghost that Walks Alone
My Buddy
45: Big Bonanza
Behind City Lights
The Phantom Speaks
Girls of the Big House
The Chicago Kid
46: The Magnificent Rogue
Sioux City Sue
47: Winter Wonderland
The Pilgrim Lady
That's My Gal
Saddle Pals
Robin Hood in Texas
48: Eyes of Texas
Sons of Adventure
Timber Trail
Madonna of the Desert
Secret Service Investigator
Lightnin' in the Forest
49: Trouble Preferred
50: Call of the Klondike
The Blazing Sun
The Great Plane Robbery
Dynamite Pass
Hunt the Man Down
52: Because of You
The Blazing Forest
53: Port Sinister

Pernell Roberts (1928-
1958: Desire Under the Elms
The Sheepman
59: Ride Lonesome
61: The Errand Boy
69: Four Rode Out

Rachel Roberts (c1931-
1952: Valley of Song
54: The Weak and the Wicked
57: The Good Companions
59: Our Man in Havana
60: Saturday Night and Sunday
Morning
61: Girl on Approval
63: This Sporting Life
68: A Flea in Her Ear

1178

Roy Roberts (1900-
1943: Guadalcanal Diary
  44: Roger Touhy--Gangster
      The Sullivans
      Tampico
      Wilson
  45: A Bell for Adano
      Caribbean Mystery
      Circumstantial Evidence
      Within These Walls
      Col. Effingham's Raid
  46: Behind Green Lights
      It Shouldn't Happen to a
        Dog
      Johnny Comes Marching
        Home
      My Darling Clementine
      Smoky
      Strange Triangle
  47: The Brasher Doubloon
      The Shocking Miss
        Pilgrim
      Captain from Castile
      Daisy Kenyon
      The Foxes of Harrow
      A Gentleman's Agreement
      Nightmare Alley
  48: Fury at Furnace Creek
      The Gay Intruders
      Joan of Arc
      No Minor Vices
      Chicken Every Sunday
      He Walked by Night
      Forces of Evil
  49: Calamity Jane and Sam
        Bass
      Flaming Fury
      A Kiss for Corliss
      Bodyhold
      Miss Grant Takes Rich-
        mond
      The Reckless Moment
  50: Chain Lightning
      The Palomino
      Borderline
      Wyoming Mail
      The Second Face
      The Killer that Stalked
        New York
      Stage to Tucson

  51: The Enforcer
      I Was a Communist for
        the F.B.I.
      Santa Fe
      The Man with a Cloak
      The Cimarron Kid
  52: Hoodlum Empire
      The Big Trees
      Cripple Creek
      Stars and Stripes Forever
      The Man Behind the Gun
  53: House of Wax
      Second Chance
      Lone Hand
      The Glory Brigade
      Sea of Lost Ships
      Tumbleweed
  54: Dawn at Socorro
      They Rode West
      The Outlaw Stallion
  55: I Cover the Underworld
      Wyoming Renegades
      Big House, U.S.A.
      The Last Command
  56: The First Texan
      The Boss
      The White Squaw
      The King and Four Queens
  57: Yaqui Drums
  62: The Chapman Report
      The Underwater City
  64: Those Calloways
  65: I'll Take Sweden
  66: Hotel
  67: Tammy and the Millionaire
  68: Now You See it, Now You
        Don't (TV)

Tracey Roberts
1955: The Prodigal
      Murder Is My Beat
  56: Edge of Hell
      Hollywood or Bust
  57: The Wayward Girl
  61: Go Naked in the World

Cliff Robertson (1925-
1955: Picnic
  56: Autumn Leaves
  57: The Girl Most Likely

1179

58: The Naked and the Dead
59: Battle of the Coral Sea
    Gidget
60: As the Sea Rages
61: Underworld, U.S.A.
    The Big Show
    All in a Night's Work
62: The Interns
63: My Six Loves
    PT-109
    Sunday in New York
64: The Best Man
    633 Squadron
65: Love Has Many Faces
    Up from the Beach
    Masquerade
67: The Honey Pot
68: The Devil's Brigade
    Charly (OSCAR)
69: Too Late the Hero
    The Sunshine Patriot
    (dual role; TV)
    Between Hello and Good-
    bye
    The Mechanic
    Land Redeemed

Dale Robertson (1920-
1949: Fighting Man of the Plains
  50: Caribou Trail
      Two Flags West
  51: Call Me Mister
      Take Care of My Little
      Girl
      Golden Girl
  52: Lydia Bailey
      Return of the Texan
      The Outcasts of Poker
      Flat
      O. Henry's Full House
      (The Clarion Call seq.)
  53: Devil's Canyon
      The Silver Whip
      The Farmer Takes a
      Wife
      City of Bad Men
  54: Gambler from Natchez
      Sitting Bull
  55: Top of the World
      Son of Sinbad

56: A Day of Fury
    High Terrace
    Dakota Incident
57: Hell Canyon Outlaws
60: Fast and Sexy
64: Law of the Lawless
    Blood on the Arrow
65: Coast of Skeletons
    The Man from Button
    Hollow (cartoon voice)

Guy Robertson
1934: King Kelly of the U.S.A.

Willard Robertson (1886-1948)
1932: Sky Devils
  33: Central Airport
  34: Heat Lightning
      Dark Hazard
      The Gambling Lady
      One Is Guilty
      Two Alone
      The Whirlpool
      I'll Tell the World
      Upper World
      Murder in the Private Car
      Death on the Diamond
      Housewife
      Here Comes the Navy
      Have a Heart
  35: Biography of a Bachelor
      Girl
      Secret Bride
      Million Dollar Baby
      Mills of the Gods
      Laddie
      Straight from the Heart
      Black Fury
      Oil for the Lamps of
      China
      The Old Homestead
      O'Shaughnessy's Boy
      Dante's Inferno
      The Virginia Judge
      His Night Out
      Forced Landing
  36: The Three Godfathers
      Dangerous Waters
      I Married a Doctor
      The First Baby

1180

36: The Gorgeous Hussy
 The Last of the Mohicans
 The Man Who Lived Twice
 Wanted: Jane Turner
 Winterset
 That Girl from Paris
37: John Meade's Woman
 Larceny on the Air
 Park Avenue Logger
 The Go-Getter
 This Is My Affair
 Roaring Timber
 Exclusive
 Hot Water
38: Gangs of New York
 Island in the Sky
 You and Me
 Men with Wings
 Kentucky
 Torchy Gets Her Man
39: Jesse James
 Heritage of the Desert
 My Son Is a Criminal
 Each Dawn I Die
 Range War
 Two Bright Boys
40: My Little Chickadee
 Remember the Night
 Castle on the Hudson
 The Lucky Cisco Kid
 Brigham Young--Frontiers-
   man
 Northwest Mounted Police
41: The Monster and the Girl
 Men of the Timberland
 The Night of January 16th
 Texas
42: Juke Girl
43: Air Force
 Background to Danger
 No Time for Love
44: Nine Girls
45: Along Came Jones
46: Perilous Holiday
 Renegades
 To Each His Own
47: My Favorite Brunette
 Deep Valley
48: Fury at Furnace Creek
 Sitting Pretty

Paul Robeson (1898-
1930: Borderline
33: The Emperor Jones
35: Sanders of the River
36: Show Boat
37: King Solomon's Mines
38: The Song of Freedom
 Dark Sands
 Jericho
41: The Proud Valley
42: Native Land
 Tales of Manhattan

Bartlett Robinson
1956: The Birds and the Bees
 Toward the Unknown
 Battle Hymn
57: The Spirit of St. Louis
58: Girl in the Woods
 No Time for Sergeants
 I Want to Live!
59: The Stranger in My Arms
 Warlock
64: Where Love Has Gone
 A Distant Trumpet
 Ready for the People
65: Joy in the Morning
66: The Fortune Cookie
68: Live a Little, Love a
 Little
 The Bamboo Saucer

Bill "Bojangles" Robinson
(1878-1949)
1935: The Little Colonel
 In Old Kentucky
37: One Mile from Heaven
38: The Littlest Rebel
 Rebecca of Sunnybrook
   Farm
 Road Demon
 Up the River
 Just Around the Corner
43: Stormy Weather

Charles Robinson
1965: Dear Brigitte
66: The Sand Pebbles
 The Singing Nun
 Shenandoah

67: The Flim Flam Man
68: For Singles Only
A Time to Sing
69: The Fire Within
Crossroads
The Pendulum of Gates
A.W.O.L.--A Way of
Life
Todd
Come in, Children

Chris Robinson (1940-
1959: The Diary of a High
School Bride
60: Because They're Young
61: The Long Rope
The Young Savages
62: 13 West Street
Bird Man of Alcatraz
68: Portrait of Violence

Dewey Robinson (1898-1950)
1931: Enemies of the Law
32: When Paris Sleeps
The Captain's Wife
Woman from Monte Carlo
Cheaters at Play
Law and Order
Painted Woman
The Big Broadcast
Hat Check Girl
Blonde Venus
Six Hours to Live
Scarlet Dawn
Women Won't Tell
33: Diplomaniacs
Soldiers of the Storm
Laughing at Life
Notorious but Nice
She Done Him Wrong
A Lady's Profession
Her Forgotten Past
Murder on the Campus
34: Shadows of Sing Sing
Big Shakedown
The Countess of Monte
Carlo
Behold My Wife
35: a short
Goin' to Town

Pursuit
A Midsummer Night's
Dream
His Night Out
Too Young to Kill
36: Dangerous Waters
The Return of Jimmy
Valentine
All-American Chump
Missing Girls
Florida Special
37: On the Avenue
The Slave Ship
The Toast of New York
New Faces of 1937
Super Sleuth
Marry the Girl
Mama Runs Wild
38: Broadway Musketeers
Ride a Crooked Mile
Army Girl
39: Navy Secrets
Forged Passport
40: The Blue Bird
I Can't Give You Anything
but Love, Baby
Diamond Frontier
The Great McGinty
Tin Pan Alley
41: Two Yanks in Trinidad
You're the One
42: Jail House Blues
Rubber Racketeers
Isle of Missing Men
'Neath Brooklyn Bridge
Palm Beach Story
43: Casablanca
The Ghost Ship
Woman of the Town
44: Mrs. Parkington
Timber Queen
The Chinese Cat
Trocadero
When Strangers Marry
Wilson
Alaska
45: Black Market Babies
Fashion Model
Hollywood and Vine
The Lady Confesses

45: Pardon My Past
There Goes Kelly
46: Behind the Mask
The Missing Lady
Mr. Hex
47: I Wonder Who's Kissing
Her Now
The Wistful Widow of
Wagon Gap
48: Angels' Alley
Fighting Mad
Let's Live Again
The Checkered Coat
49: The Beautiful Blonde
of Bashful Bend
Hellfire
Tough Assignment
50: Buccaneer's Girl
At War with the Army

Edward G. Robinson (1893-
1929: The Hole in the Wall
30: Widow from Chicago
Little Caesar
Night Ride
Outside the Law
East Is West
A Lady to Love
The Idol
31: Five Star Final
The Honorable Mr. Wong
Smart Money
32: Tiger Shark
Two Seconds
The Hatchet Man
Silver Dollar
33: Little Giant
I Loved a Woman
34: Dark Hazard
The Man with Two Faces
35: The Whole Town's Talking
Barbary Coast
36: Bullets or Ballots
37: Thunder in the City
Kid Galahad
The Last Gangster
38: A Slight Case of Murder
The Amazing Dr. Clitter-
house
I Am the Law

39: Confessions of a Nazi Spy
Blackmail
40: Dr. Ehrlich's Magic Bullet
Brother Orchid
A Dispatch from Reuter's
41: The Sea Wolf
Manpower
Unholy Partners
42: Larceny, Inc.
Tales of Manhattan
Moscow Strikes Back
43: Flesh and Fantasy
Destroyer
44: Tampico
Double Indemnity
Mr. Winkle Goes to War
Woman in the Window
45: Our Vines Have Tender
Grapes
Scarlet Street
Journey Together
46: The Stranger
47: The Red House
48: Night Has a Thousand
Eyes
All My Sons
Key Largo
49: House of Strangers
It's a Great Feeling
51: Operation X
52: Actors and Sin
53: Vice Squad
The Big Leaguer
The Glass Key
54: Black Tuesday
55: Violent Men
Tight Spot
A Bullet for Joey
Hell on Frisco Bay
Illegal
56: Nightmare
The Ten Commandments
59: Hole in the Head
60: Pepe
Seven Thieves
Israel (narr.)
62: My Geisha
Two Weeks in Another
Town
63: The Prize

1183

1184

28: Turkish Delight   S
31: Mother's Millions
32: Letty Lynton
    Strange Interlude
    Two Against the World
    The Engineer's Daughter
    Red Headed Woman
    Little Orphan Annie
    If I Had a Million
33: Reunion in Vienna
    Dinner at Eight
    Beauty for Sale
    Broadway to Hollywood
    Solitaire Man
    Dancing Lady
    Lady for a Day
    One Man's Journey
    Alice in Wonderland
    The White Sister
    Men Must Fight
34: You Can't Buy Everything
    Straight Is the Way
    Lady by Choice
35: Vanessa--Her Love Story
    Reckless
    Age of Indiscretion
    Anna Karenina
    Grand Old Girl
    Strangers All
    Mills of the Gods
    Three Kids and a Queen
36: Wife Versus Secretary
    The Captain's Kid
    Rainbow on the River
37: Woman in Distress
    A Star Is Born
    The Perfect Specimen
38: The Adventures of Tom
    Sawyer
    Bringing Up Baby
    The Texans
    Four Daughters
39: They Made Me a Criminal
    Yes, My Darling Daughter
    Daughters Courageous
    Four Wives
    The Kid from Kokomo
    Nurse Edith Cavell
    That's Right, You're
     Wrong

40: Irene
    The Texas Rangers Ride
     Again
    Granny Get Your Gun
41: Four Mothers
    Million Dollar Baby
    Playmates
42: Joan of Paris

John Roche (1896-1952)
1929: Dream Melody   S
    The Donovan Affair
    The Awful Truth
    Unholy Night
    This Thing Called Love
30: Monte Carlo
    Sin Takes a Holiday
32: Winner Take All
    Prosperity
33: Beauty for Sale
35: Just My Luck

Claire Rochelle
1939: Code of the Fearless
    Missing Daughters
    El Diablo Rides
40: The Kid from Santa Fe
41: North from the Lone Star
42: Secrets of a Coed
    Prison Girls
43: Harvest Melody
44: Men on Her Mind
    Waterfront
    Shake Hands with Murder
    Swing Hostess
45: Double Exposure
46: Blonde for a Day

"Rochester": see Eddie Anderson

Blossom Rock: see Marie Blake

Jack Rockwell (d. 1946)
1934: Trail Drive
    Gun Justice
    Wheels of Destiny
    Smoking Guns
    When a Man Sees Red
    'Neath Arizona Skies
    Brand of Hate

35: Lawless Frontier
Justice of the Range
Tumbling Tumbleweeds
Outlawed Guns°
Valley of Wanted Men
The Man from Guntown
36: The Lawless '90s
Heroes of the Range
The Singing Cowboy
Rogue of the Range
The Traitor
Roarin' Guns
Guns and Guitars
37: Bar-Z Bad Men
Riders of the Rockies
The Red Rope
Texas Trail
38: Under Western Stars
West of Cheyenne
Prairie Moon
Law of the Plains
Shine on Harvest Moon
Black Bandit
39: Rough Riders' Round-Up
Silver on the Sage
The Man from Sundown
Days of Jesse James
40: Bullets for Rustlers
Santa Fe Marshal
Hidden Gold
Stagecoach War
Cherokee Strip
Pony Post
41: The Pinto Kid
Border Vigilantes
Wide Open Town
Thunder Over the Prairie
Twilight on the Trail
Secrets of the Wasteland
42: Undercover Man
Tombstone, the Town Too
  Tough to Die
43: Fighting Frontier
Dead Man's Gulch
The Black Hills Express
The Renegade
Wagon Tracks West
44: Forty Thieves
Mystery Man
Trigger Trail

Gunsmoke Mesa
Lumberjack
The Vigilantes Ride
West of the Rio Grande
45: Both Barrels Blazing
Flame of the West
Frontier Feud
Lawless Empire
Outlaws of the Rockies
Phantom of the Plains
Rough Riders of Cheyenne
Rough Ridin' Justice
46: Canyon Passage
Cowboy Blues
Drifting Along
Frontier Gun Law
The Gentleman from Texas
Roaring Rangers
Two-Fisted Stranger
Under Arizona Skies

Robert Rockwell
1948: You Gotta Stay Happy
49: Alias the Champ
The Red Menace
50: Blonde Bandit
Federal Agent at Large
Belle of Old Mexico
Unmasked
Destination Big House
Woman from Headquarters
Trial Without Jury
Lonely Hearts Bandits
Prisoners in Petticoats
51: The Frogmen
56: Our Miss Brooks
68: Sol Madrid

Ziva Rodann
1957: Pharaoh's Curse
Courage of Black Beauty
Forty Guns
The Story of Mankind
Teenage Doll
59: Last Train from Gun Hill
The Big Operator
Blood and Steel
60: Macumba Love
The Private Lives of Adam
  and Eve

60: College Confidential
    The Story of Ruth
61: Giants of Thessaly
62: Samar
64: Three Nuts in Search of
    a Bolt

Estelita Rodriguez (1915-1966)
1945: Along the Navajo Trail
    Mexicana
47: On the Spanish Trail
48: The Gay Ranchero
    Old Los Angeles
49: Susanna Pass
    The Golden Stallion
50: Belle of Old Mexico
    Federal Agent at Large
    Sunset in the West
    Hit Parade of 1951
    California Passage
51: Cuban Fireball
    In Old Amarillo
    Pals of the Golden West
    Havana Rose
52: The Fabulous Señorita
    Tropical Heat Wave
    South Pacific Trail
53: Sweethearts on Parade
    Tropic Zone
59: Rio Bravo
66: Jesse James Meets
    Frankenstein's Daughter

Charles "Buddy" Rogers (1904-
1927-29: Wings   SSE
28: Someone to Love   S
    Varsity   PT
    Close Harmony
    Here Comes the Band-
    wagon
    Illusion
    Abie's Irish Rose
    River of Romance
    Men Must Fight
    Halfway to Heaven
30: Heads Up!
    Paramount on Parade
    Safety in Numbers
    Young Eagles
    Follow Through

31: Along Came Youth
    The Movie Man
    The Ice Man
    The Lawyer's Secret
    Road to Reno
    Working Girls
32: This Reckless Age
33: Best of Enemies
    Take a Chance
35: Dance Band
    Old Man Rhythm
36: Once in a Million
37: This Way, Please
    Week-End Millionaire
38: Let's Make a Night of It
As producer only, 1939 on:
39: The Mexican Spitfire
40: The Mexican Spitfire Out
    West
41: The Golden Hoofs
    Double Trouble
    The Mexican Spitfire's
    Baby
    Sing for Your Supper
42: They Raid by Night
    The Mexican Spitfire at
    Sea
    The Mexican Spitfire Sees
    a Ghost
43: The Mexican Spitfire's
    Blessed Event
    That Nazty Nuisance
    The Dancing Masters
48: An Innocent Affair (or,
    Don't Trust Your Husband)
57: The Parson and the Outlaw

Ginger Rogers (1911-
1930: Young Man of Manhattan
    Campus Sweethearts (short)
    Queen High
    Checker comedies
    Follow the Leader
31: Manhattan Mary
    The Sap from Syracuse
    A Night in a Dormitory
    Honor Among Lovers
    Suicide Fleet
    Big Timber
    Looking for Trouble

31: Tip-Off
32: Carnival Boat
The Tenderfoot
The 13th Guest
Hat Check Girl
You Said a Mouthful
33: Professional Sweetheart
Gold Diggers of 1933
42nd Street
Flying Down to Rio
Broadway Bad
A Shriek in the Night
Don't Bet on Love
Sitting Pretty
Chance at Heaven
34: Gay Divorcee
Rafter Romance
Finishing School
Twenty Million Sweet-
hearts
Change of Heart
Upper World
Romance in Manhattan
35: Roberta
Top Hat
Star of Midnight
In Person
36: Follow the Fleet
Stepping Toes
Swing Time
37: Shall We Dance?
Stage Door
38: Having a Wonderful Time
Vivacious Lady
Carefree
39: Bachelor Mother
Fifth Avenue Girl
The Story of Vernon and
Irene Castle
40: Kitty Foyle (OSCAR)
Primrose Path
Lucky Partners
41: Tom, Dick, and Harry
42: Roxie Hart
Tales of Manhattan
The Major and the Minor
Once Upon a Honeymoon
43: Tender Comrade
Safeguarding Military
Information (short)

44: Lady in the Dark
I'll be Seeing You
Battle Station (short)
Ginger Rogers Finds a
Bargain (war bonds short)
45: Weekend at the Waldorf
46: Heartbeat
The Magnificent Doll
47: It Had to be You
49: The Barkleys of Broadway
50: Perfect Strangers
Storm Warning
51: The Groom Wore Spurs
52: We're Not Married
Dreamboat
Monkey Business
53: Forever Female
54: Black Widow
Twist of Fate
55: Tight Spot
56: First Traveling Saleslady
Teenage Rebel
57: Oh Men! Oh Women!
65: Harlow (Magna.)
66: Confession

Jean Rogers (1916-
1934: Eight Girls in a Boat
35: The Great Air Mystery
(ser.)
Manhattan Moon
Stormy
Fighting Youth
36: Two in a Crowd
Don't Get Personal
Conflict
Flash Gordon
Spaceship to the Unknown
(ser.)
Ace Drummond (ser.)
The Adventures of Frank
Merriwell (ser.)
37: Mysterious Crossing
My Man Godfrey
When Love Is Young
The Wildcatter
Night Key
Reported Missing
38: Out for Murder
Always in Trouble

38: While New York Sleeps
Inside Story
Mars Attacks the World
Flash Gordon's Trip to
Mars (ser.)
Perils from the Planet
Mongo (ser.)
Meridian 7-1212
The Mysterious Mr. Moto
of Devil's Island
Time Out for Murder
39: Elsa Maxwell's Hotel for
Women
Stop, Look, and Love
40: Heaven with a Barbed
Wire Fence
The Man Who Wouldn't
Talk
Viva Cisco Kid!
Charlie Chan in Panama
Brigham Young--Frontiers-
man
Yesterday's Heroes
Let's Make Music
41: Dr. Kildare's Victory
Design for Scandal
42: Sunday Punch
Pacific Rendezvous
The War Against Mrs.
Hadley
43: A Stranger in Town
Swing Shift Maisie
Whistling in Brooklyn
45: Rough, Tough, and Ready
The Great Mystic
46: The Strange Mr. Gregory
Gay Blades
Hot Cargo
47: Undercover Maisie
Backlash
48: Speed to Spare
Fighting Back
51: The Second Woman

Roy Rogers (1912- ; w/"Trigger"
1932-1965)
1935: 2 reels with Joan Davis
Tumbling Tumbleweeds
(bit)
36: The Big Show with Gene
Autry

37: Old Barn Dance
The Old Corral
38: Under Western Stars
Billy the Kid Returns
Come on Rangers!
Shine on Harvest Moon
39: Rough Riders' Roundup
Frontier Pony Express
Southward Ho!
In Old Caliente
Wall Street Cowboy
Saga of Death Valley
Days of Jesse James
Jeepers Creepers
The Arizona Kid
40: The Dark Command
Young Buffalo Bill
The Carson City Kid
The Ranger and the Lady
Colorado
Young Bill Hickok
The Border Legion
41: Robin Hood of the Pecos
Arkansas Judge
In Old Cheyenne
Sheriff of Tombstone
Nevada City
Bad Man of Deadwood
Red River Valley
42: Jesse James at Bay
Man from Cheyenne
South of Santa Fe
Sunset on the Desert
Romance on the Range
Sons of the Pioneers
Heart of the Golden West
Ridin' Down the Canyon
Sunset Serenade
43: Idaho
Hoosier Holiday
In Old Oklahoma
King of the Cowboys
Song of Texas
Silver Spurs
The Man from Music
Mountain
Hands Across the Border
44: Lights of Old Santa Fe
Song of Nevada
The Cowboy and the
Senorita

44: Yellow Rose of Texas
San Fernando Valley
Brazil
Hollywood Canteen
Casanova in Burlesque
45: Lake Placid Serenade
Utah
Bells of Rosarita
Don't Fence Me In!
Along the Navajo Trail
Hitchhike to Happiness
The Man from Oklahoma
46: The Show-Off
Under Nevada Skies
Home in Oklahoma
Song of Arizona
Rainbow over Texas
My Pal Trigger
Roll on Texas Moon
Out California Way
47: Helldorado
Hit Parade of 1947
Bells of San Angelo
Springtime in the Sierras
On the Old Spanish Trail
Apache Rose
48: Under California Stars
The Gay Ranchero
Melody Time
Grand Canyon Trail
Night-Time in Nevada
Eyes of Texas
49: The Far Frontier
Susanna Pass
Down Dakota Way
The Golden Stallion
50: Twilight in the Sierras
Bells of Coronado
Trigger, Jr.
Sunset in the West
North of the Great Divide
51: Trail of Robin Hood
Heart of the Rockies
Spoilers of the Plains
In Old Amarillo
South of Caliente
Pals of the Golden West
52: Son of Paleface
59: Alias Jesse James

Will Rogers (1874-1935)
1929: They Had to See Paris
30: Happy Days
So This Is London
Lightnin'
31: The Plutocrat
Young as You Feel
Ambassador Bill
A Connecticut Yankee
32: Business and Pleasure
Down to Earth
Too Busy to Work
33: State Fair
Dr. Bull
Mr. Skitch
34: David Harum
Handy Andy
Judge Priest
35: County Chairman
Life Begins at Forty
In Old Kentucky
Doubting Thomas
Steamboat 'Round the Bend
57: Golden Age of Comedy
(doc.)

Will Rogers, Jr. (1912-
1952: The Will Rogers Story
53: The Eddie Cantor Story
54: The Boy from Oklahoma
58: Wild Heritage

Gustavo Rojo
1956: Alexander the Great
58: Buchanan Rides Alone
The Buccaneer
59: It Started with a Kiss
The Miracle
62: Revolt of the Mercenaries
65: Ghengis Khan
66: The Tall Women
67: The Fickle Finger of Fate
A Witch Without a Broom
68: The Christmas Kid
69: The Valley of Gwangi

Gilbert Roland (1905-
1929: New York Nights
30: Monsieur Le Fox

1190

30: Resurrection (Span.)
    The Cardboard Lover
    Men of the North
31: Men in Her Life
32: The Passionate Plumber
    Woman in Room 13
    A Parisian Romance
    Gigolette
    No Living Witness
    Call Her Savage
    Life Begins
33: Tarnished Youth
    World Wide
    Our Betters
    Gigolettes of Paris
    After Tonight
    She Done Him Wrong
34: Elinor Norton
35: Mystery Woman
    Ladies Love Danger
37: Midnight Taxi
    Last Train from Madrid
    Thunder Trail
38: Gateway
39: Juarez
40: Rangers of Fortune
    Isle of Destiny
    The Sea Hawk
    Gambling on the High
    Seas
41: Angels with Broken Wings
    My Life with Caroline
42: Enemy Agents Meet
    Ellery Queen
    Isle of Missing Men
45: Captain Kidd
    The Gay Cavalier
46: Beauty and the Bandit
    Cisco and the Angel
    Romance of the Rancho
    South of Monterey
47: High Conquest
    Pirates of Monterey
    The Tenderfoot
    The Other Love
    Riding the California
    Trail
    Robin Hood of Monterey
    King of the Bandits
48: The Dude Goes West

49: Malaya
    We Were Strangers
50: The Crisis
    The Furies
    The Torch
51: Mark of the Renegade
    The Bullfighter and the
    Lady
    The Tall Men
52: My Six Convicts
    Glory Alley
    The Miracle of Our Lady
    of Fatima
    Apache War Smoke
    The Bad and the Beautiful
53: Thunder Bay
    Diamond Queen
    Beneath the Twelve-Mile
    Reef
54: The French Line
55: Underwater!
    The Racers
    That Lady
    The Treasure of Pancho
    Villa
56: Around the World in 80
    Days
    Bandido
    Three Violent People
57: The Midnight Story
58: The Last of the Fast Guns
    Mr. Pharaoh and Cleopatra
    (Cuban)
59: The Big Circus
    The Wild and the Innocent
60: Guns of the Timberland
62: Samar
64: Cheyenne Autumn
65: The Reward
66: The Poppy Is Also a
    Flower (TV)
68: Sonora
    Any Gun can Play (Ital.-
    Span.)

Guy Rolfe (1915-
1945: Hungry Hill
47: Nicholas Nickleby
    Uncle Silas
    Broken Journey

1191

49:	Portrait from Life	53:	Blowing Wild
50:	The Spider and the Fly	54:	The Shanghai Story
51:	Prelude to Fame		Tanganyika
52:	Ivanhoe		Down Three Dark Streets
54:	King of the Khyber Rifles	55:	The Far Country
58:	It's Never Too Late	56:	Joe Macbeth
59:	Yesterday's Enemy		The Bottom of the Bottle
60:	The Strangler of Bombay		Great Day in the Morning
61:	Snow White and the		Rebel in Town
	Three Stooges	57:	Five Steps to Danger
	King of Kings	58:	Bitter Victory
	Mr. Sardonicus	59:	Desert Desperadoes
62:	Taras Bulba	61:	Look in Any Window
64:	Fall of the Roman		Miracle of the Cowards
	Empire	65:	Love Has Many Faces
66:	The Alphabet Murders		

Lina Romay
1942:	You Were Never Lovelier

Yvonne Romain
1962:	Frightened City	43:	The Heat's On
64:	Devil Doll		Stage Door Canteen
66:	The Swinger		Tropicana
67:	Double Trouble	44:	Two Girls and a Sailor
			Bathing Beauty

Ruth Roman (1924-
1944:	Ladies Courageous	45:	Weekend at the Waldorf
	Since You Went Away	46:	Adventure
45:	You Came Along		Love Laughs at Andy Hardy
47:	Queen of the Jungle (ser.)	47:	Honeymoon
48:	Good Sam	48:	Embraceable You
	Belle Starr's Daughter	49:	Cheyenne Cowboy
	The Whip Son		Joe Palooka in The Big
	The House of Seven		Fight
	Gables		The Big Wheel
49:	The Window		The Lady Takes a Sailor
	Champion	52:	Man Behind the Gun
	Beyond the Forest		
	Always Leave Them		
	Laughing	Carlos Romero
50:	Three Secrets	1958:	The World Was His Jury
	Colt .45		The Gun Runners
	Barricade	59:	They Came to Cordura
	Dallas	62:	The Deadly Duo
	Thundercloud	64:	Island of the Blue Dolphins
51:	Lightning Strikes Twice	66:	The Professionals
	Strangers on a Train		
	Tomorrow Is Another Day	Cesar Romero (1907-
	Starlift	1934:	The Thin Man
52:	Invitation		British Agent
	Mara Maru		Cheating Cheaters
	Young Man with Ideas	35:	Strange Wives
			Clive of India
			Cardinal Richelieu

35: The Devil Is a Woman
Hold 'em, Yale!
The Good Fairy
Diamond Jim
Metropolitan
Show Them No Mercy
Rendezvous
36: Love Before Breakfast
Nobody's Fool
Public Enemy's Wife
15 Maiden Lane
37: Wee Willie Winkle
Dangerously Yours
Armored Car
She's Dangerous
38: Happy Landing
Always Goodbye
My Lucky Star
Five of a Kind
39: The Little Princess
Return of the Cisco Kid
Wife, Husband, and
Friend
Charlie Chan at Treasure
Island
Frontier Marshal
40: Cisco Kid and the Lady
He Married His Wife
The Gay Caballero
Viva Cisco Kid
41: Romance of the Rio
Grande
Tall, Dark, and Hand-
some
The Great American
Broadcast
Dance Hall
Weekend in Havana
Ride on, Vaquero!
42: A Gentleman at Heart
Tales of Manhattan
Orchestra Wives
Springtime in the Rockies
43: Wintertime
Coney Island
47: Carnival in Costa Rica
Captain from Castile
48: Deep Waters
That Lady in Ermine
Julia Misbehaves

49: The Beautiful Blonde
from Bashful Bend
50: Once a Thief
Love that Brute
51: Lost Continent
F.B.I. Girl
Happy Go Lovely
52: The Jungle
Scotland Yard Inspector
53: Prisoners of the Casbah
Shadow Man
54: Vera Cruz
55: The Americano
The Racers
56: Leather Saint
Around the World in 80
Days
57: The Story of Mankind
58: Villa!
60: Pepe
Ocean's Eleven
61: Seven Women from Hell
62: If a Man Answers
63: Donovan's Reef
We Shall Return
The Castilian
64: A House Is Not a Home
65: Two on a Guillotine
Marriage on the Rocks
Sgt. Deadhead, the Astro-
naut
67: Batman
68: Hot Millions
Skidoo!
The House of Girls
69: The Rebels
What's in it for Harry?
The Midas Run
Crooks and Coronets
A Talent for Loving
Latitude Zero
Something's Happened to
Dexter
Proud, Damned, and
Dead

Mickey Rooney (1922-
1932: The Information Kid
Fast Companions
My Pal, the King

33: The Big Cage
Life of Jimmy Dolan
Broadway to Hollywood
The Big Chance
The Chief
34: Love Birds
I Like it that Way
Lost Jungle
Upper World
Half a Sinner
Death on a Diamond
Beloved
Manhattan Melodrama
Chained
Blind Date
The Hideout
35: A Midsummer Night's
Dream
The Healer
Ah, Wilderness!
County Chairman
36: Riffraff
The Devil Is a Sissy
Little Lord Fauntleroy
Down the Stretch
37: A Family Affair
Captains Courageous
Live, Love, and Learn
Thoroughbreds Don't Cry
You'll Only be Young
Once
Slave Ship
Hoosier Schoolboy
38: Love Is a Headache
Judge Hardy's Children
Hold that Kiss
Lord Jeff
Love Finds Andy Hardy
Boys Town
Stablemates
Outwest with the Hardys
(SPECIAL AWARD)
39: Huckleberry Finn
Andy Hardy Gets Spring
Fever
Babes in Arms
Judge Hardy and Son
The Hardys Ride High
40: Young Tom Edison
Andy Hardy Meets a
Debutante

Strike Up the Band
41: Life Begins for Andy
Hardy
Babes on Broadway
Andy Hardy's Private
Secretary
Men of Boys Town
42: A Yank at Eton
The Courtship of Andy
Hardy
Andy Hardy's Double Life
Andy Hardy Steps Out
43: The Human Comedy
Girl Crazy
Thousands Cheer
44: National Velvet
Andy Hardy's Blonde
Trouble
46: Ziegfeld Follies
Love Laughs at Andy
Hardy
47: Killer McCoy
48: Summer Holiday
Words and Music
49: The Big Wheel
50: He's a Cockeyed Wonder
Quicksand
Fireball
51: My Outlaw Brother (or,
My Brother, the Outlaw)
The Strip
52: Sound Off!
53: Off Limits
All Ashore
Slight Case of Larceny
54: Drive a Crooked Road
The Bridges at Toko-Ri
The Atomic Kid
55: The Twinkle in God's Eye
56: The Bold and the Brave
The Magnificent Roughnecks
Jaguar
Francis in The Haunted
House
57: Operation Madball
Baby Face Nelson
58: Andy Hardy Comes Home
A Nice Little Bank that
Should be Robbed
59: The Last Mile
Big Operator

60: Private Lives of Adam
and Eve
Platinum High School
61: King of the Roaring
Twenties
Breakfast at Tiffany's
Everything's Ducky
62: Requiem for a Heavy-
weight
63: It's a Mad Mad Mad Mad
World
64: The Secret Invasion
65: 24 Hours to Kill
How to Stuff a Wild Bikini
66: Ambush Bay
The Devil Takes the
Count
68: Skidoo!
The Extraordinary Seaman
The Devil in Love
69: Billy Bright
A Woman for Charley (TV)
80 Steps to Jonah

Teddy Rooney (1950-
1958: Andy Hardy Comes Home
59: It Happened to Jane
60: Seven Ways from Sundown

Timmy Rooney (1947-
1965: Village of the Giants
67: Riot on Sunset Strip

Buddy Roosevelt (1898-
1930: Way Out West
31: Westward Bound
Lightnin' Smith's Return
32: Wild Horse Mesa
33: The Fourth Horseman
35: Powdersmoke Range
37: The Old Corral
38: The Buccaneer
46: Boss Cowboy
47: Buck Privates Come
Home
52: The Belle of New York
56: Around the World in 80
Days

Hayden Rorke
1949: For Those Who Dare

Sword in the Desert
50: Double Crossbones
51: Father's Little Dividend
Inside Straight
Francis Goes to the Races
The Prince Who Was a
Thief
The Law and the Lady
When World Collide
Starlift
52: Room for One More
Skirts Ahoy!
Above and Beyond
Wild Stallion
Rogue's March
53: Confidentially Connie
The Girl Next Door
South Sea Woman
54: Lucky Me
Drum Beat
55: The Eternal Sea
All that Heaven Allows
58: This Happy Feeling
The Restless Years
59: The Stranger in My Arms
Pillow Talk
60: I Aim at the Stars
61: Parrish
Tammy Tell Me True
Back Street
A Pocketful of Miracles
63: Spencer's Mountain
The Thrill of it All
64: The Unsinkable Molly
Brown
I'd Rather be Rich
A House Is not a Home
Youngblood Hawke
65: The Night Walker

Rosanna Rory
1956: The River Changes
57: Hell Canyon Outlaws
The Big Boodle
60: Robin Hood and the Pirates
The Angel Wore Red
The Big Deal on Madonna
Street
61: Come September
62: Jessica
64: Captain Falcon

Françoise Rosay (1891-
1929: One Woman Idea   SSE
      Spite Marriage (Fr.)   S
  31: Le Petit Café
      Magnificent Lie
  32: Casanova Wider Willen
      (Parlor, Bedroom, and
      Bath)
  33: Le Grand Jeu
  35: La Kernesse Heroique
  36: Kenny
      Pension Mimosas
  37: Un Carnet de Bal
      Maternité
  38: Les Gens du Voyage
      (Traveling People)
  39: Bizarre, Bizarre
      The Devil Is an Empress
  41: Une Femme Disparue
  45: Johnny Frenchman
      The Half Way House
  46: Macadam
  48: Quartet (The Alien Corn
      seq.)
  49: Sarabande for Dead Lovers
  50: September Affair
  51: The 13th Letter
  53: Woman of Evil
  54: The Red Inn
  55: That Lady
      The Naked Heart
      Maria Chapdelaine
  57: Interlude
      The Seventh Sin
  58: Me and the Colonel
      Le Joueur
  59: Du Rififi Chez les
      Femmes
      The Sound and the Fury
  61: Stop Me Before I Kill!
  62: Back Streets of Paris
  65: Up from the Beach
  66: Cloportes
  67: The 25th Hour
  68: It Won't Do to Take God's
      Children for Wild Geese

Rose Marie
1954: Top Banana
  66: Don't Worry, We'll Think
      of a Title

Dead Heat on a Merry-
Go-Round

Maxie Rosenbloom (1903-
1933: Mr. Broadway
      King for a Night
  36: Muss 'em Up!
      Kelly the Second
  37: Don't Pull Your Punches
      Two Wise Maids
      Big City
      Nothing Sacred
  38: Mr. Moto's Gamble
      Kid Comes Back
      Submarine Patrol
      His Exciting Night
      Gangs of New York
      The Amazing Dr. Clitter-
      house
  39: Women in the Wind
      Naughty but Nice
      Private Detective
      The Kid from Kokomo
      20,000 Men a Year
      Each Dawn I Die
  40: Grandpa Goes to Town
      Passport to Alcatraz
      Elsa Maxwell's Public
      Deb No. 1
  41: Ringside Maisie
      The Stork Pays Off
      Louisiana Purchase
  42: To the Shores of Tripoli
      Harvard, Here I Come!
      Smart Alecks
      The Yanks Are Coming
      The Boogie Man Will Get
      You
  43: My Son the Hero
      Here Comes Kelly
      Swing Fever
  44: Three of a Kind
      Ghost Crazy
      Slick Chick
      Irish Eyes Are Smiling
      Follow the Boys
      Night Club Girl
      Crazy Knights
      Allergic to Love
  45: Penthouse Rhythm
      Men in Her Diary

45: Trouble Chasers
48: Hazard
51: Skipalong Rosenbloom
Mr. Universe
55: Abbott & Costello Meet
the Keystone Kops
56: Hollywood or Bust
58: I Married a Monster
from Outer Space
59: The Beat Generation
66: Don't Worry, We'll Think
of a Title

Bodil Rosing (d. 1942)
1929: Why be Good?   S
The Betrayal   S
Broadway Daddies   S
Eternal Love   SSE
30: The Bishop Murder Case
Hello Sister
All Quiet on the Western
Front
A Lady's Morals
Oh What a Man!
Soul Kiss
Part-Time Wife
31: An American Tragedy
Three Who Loved
Surrender
32: Downstairs
The Match King
33: Crime of the Century
Reunion in Vienna
Ex-Lady
34: Mandalay
Little Man, What Now?
Such Women Are Danger-
ous
King Kelly of the U.S.A.
The Crimson Romance
The Painted Veil
35: Roberta
A Night at the Ritz
4 Hours to Kill
Let 'em Have It!
Thunder in the Night
36: Hearts in Bondage
37: Michael O'Halloran
38: The First Hundred Years
You Can't Take it With
You

39: Confessions of a Nazi Spy
Beasts of Berlin
The Star Maker
41: Reaching for the Sun
No Greater Sin
Man at Large
Marry the Boss's Daughter

Anthony Ross (1906-
1950: Perfect Strangers
The Gunfighter
The Vicious Years
The Skipper Who Surprised
His Wife
Between Midnight and Dawn
The Flying Missile
51: On Dangerous Ground
53: Taxi
Girls in the Night
54: Rogue Cop
The Country Girl

Katharine Ross (1943-
1965: Shenandoah
66: The Longest Hundred Miles
67: The Singing Nun
Mr. Buddwing
The Graduate
Games
68: The Ski Bums
A Nice Girl Like Me
Bullitt
69: A Man Named Gannon
The Hellfighters
Tell Them Willie Boy Is
Here
Butch Cassidy and the
Sundance Kid
The Public Eye

Lanny Ross (1906-
1934: Melody in Spring
College Rhythm
38: The Lady Objects
43: Stage Door Canteen
46: Home in Oklahoma

Michael Ross
1950: Blonde Dynamite
51: The Well
Golden Girl

52: Lost in Alaska
Don't Bother to Knock
Against All Flags
53: Those Redheads from
Seattle
Tarzan and the She-Devil
Tangier Incident
54: Captain Kidd and the
Slave Girl
55: Night Freight
The Return of Jack Slade
Artists and Models
Jail Busters
56: The Lieutenant Wore
Skirts
Hollywood or Bust!
57: The Buster Keaton Story
Short Cut to Hell
Kiss Them for Me
58: Attack of the Fifty Foot
Woman
64: The Disorderly Orderly

Shirley Ross (1909-
1934: Manhattan Melodrama
Girl from Missouri
Blonde Bombshell
Merry Widow
Jail Birds of Paradise
35: Age of Indiscretion
Calm Yourself
36: The Devil's Squadron
San Francisco
The Big Broadcast of
1937
37: Hideaway Girl
Waikiki Wedding
Blossoms of Broadway
38: Big Broadcast of 1938
Prison Farm
Thanks for the Memory
39: Paris Honeymoon
Cafe Society
Some Like it Hot
Unexpected Father
41: Sailor on Leave
Kissed for Breakfast
45: A Song for Miss Julie

Lillian Roth (1910-
1929: Illusion

The Love Parade
30: The Vagabond King
Animal Crackers
Sea Legs
Paramount on Parade
Madame Satan
Honey
33: Take a Chance
Ladies They Talk About
64: The Sound of Laughter
(doc.)

Jean Rouverol
1934: It's a Gift
Private Worlds
Bar-20 Rides Again
Mississippi
36: The Leavenworth Case
Fatal Lady
37: The Road Back
Stage Door
38: Annabel Takes a Tour
Western Jamboree
The Law West of Tomb-
stone

Dan Rowan & Dick Martin
1969: The Maltese Bippy
The Money Game
The Servant Game
See also: Dick Martin

Henry Rowland
1940: Safari
42: The Pied Piper
Berlin Correspondent
The Phantom Plainsmen
43: The Moon Is Down
Paris After Dark
44: Winged Victory
46: Rendezvous 24
Gallant Journey
48: To the Victor
Rogue's Regiment
50: The Showdown
51: Sealed Cargo
52: Wagon Team
Wyoming Roundup
53: Prince of Pirates
Rebel City
Topeka

53: El Alamein
Captain John Smith and
Pocahontas
54: Return to Treasure Island
55: Wyoming Renegades
Kiss of Fire
56: Uranium Boom
Women of Pitcairn Island
Hot Shots
57: Gun Duel in Durango
Hell on Devil's Island
Chicago Confidential
Looking for Danger
58: Street of Darkness
Wolf Larsen

Gena Rowlands (1936-
1958: The High Cost of Living
62: The Spiral Road
Lonely Are the Brave
63: A Child Is Waiting
67: Tony Rome
68: Faces
69: McCaine
Opening Night
At Any Price

Selena Royle (1904-
1943: Stage Door Canteen
44: Main Street after Dark
The Sullivans
30 Seconds over Tokyo
Mrs. Parkington
45: This Man's Army
46: Gallant Journey
The Green Years
The Harvey Girls
Night and Day
No Leave, No Love
Till the End of Time
Courage of Lassie
47: Romance of Rosy Ridge
Cass Timberlane
48: Smart Woman
Summer Holiday
You Were Meant for Me
Joan of Arc
A Date with Judy
Moonrise
49: You're My Everything

My Dream Is Yours
Bad Boy
The Heiress
50: The Big Hangover
The Damned Don't Cry
51: He Ran All the Way
Come Fill the Cup
55: Murder Is My Beat

Benny Rubin (1899-
1929: Naughty Baby   SSE
Marianne
Imperfect Ladies
30: They Learned About Women
Lord Byron of Broadway
Montana Moon
Children of Pleasure
Hot Curves
Sunny Skies
Love in the Rough
Leathernecking
35: George White's Scandals
of 1935
Go Into Your Dance
38: The Headleys at Home
40: Let's Make Music
41: Double Trouble
Sunny
Here Comes Mr. Jordan
Zis Boom Bah!
42: The Bashful Bachelor
Mr. Wise Guy
52: Just This Once
53: Tangier Incident
El Alamein
54: Yankee Pasha
The Law vs Billy the Kid
Masterson of Kansas
56: Meet Me in Las Vegas
57: 18 and Anxious
Up in Smoke
59: A Hole in the Head
61: The Errand Boy
A Pocketful of Miracles
64: A House Is Not a Home
The Disorderly Orderly
The Patsy
65: That Funny Feeling
66: The Ghost in the Invisible
Bikini

67: Thoroughly Modern Millie
69: Airport

Evelyn Rudie
1955: The View from Pompey's
Head
57: The Wings of Eagles
The Restless Breed
58: The Gift of Love

Herbert Rudley (1911-
1940: Abe Lincoln in Illinois
44: Marriage Is a Private
Affair
The Big Noise
The Master Race
The Seventh Cross
45: A Walk in the Sun
Brewster's Millions
Rhapsody in Blue
46: Decoy
48: Hollow Triumph
Casbah
Joan of Arc
54: The Silver Chalice
55: Artists and Models
56: The Court Jester
That Certain Feeling
Raw Edge
The Black Sleep
58: The Young Lions
The Bravados
Tonka
59: The Jayhawkers
Beloved Infidel
60: Hell Bent for Leather
Who Was that Lady?

Charles Ruggles (1891-
1929: Battle of Paris
Gentlemen of the Press
The Lady Lies
30: Roadhouse Nights
Young Man of Manhattan
Queen High
Her Wedding Night
Charley's Aunt
31: Girl Habit
Beloved Bachelor
Honor Among Lovers

The Smiling Lieutenant
Honest Finder
The Lawyer's Secret
32: Husband's Holiday
Madame Butterfly
Trouble in Paradise
Evenings for Sale
Love Me Tonight
70,000 Witnesses
This Reckless Age
One Hour with You
This Is the Night
The Night of June 13th
If I Had a Million
33: Murders in the Zoo
Terror Abroad
Mama Loves Papa
Girl Without a Room
Alice in Wonderland
Melody Cruise
34: Melody in Spring
Murder in the Private Car
Friends of Mr. Sweeney
Six of a Kind
Pursuit of Happiness
Goodbye Love
35: Ruggles of Red Gap
People Will Talk
Big Broadcast of 1936
No More Ladies
36: Anything Goes
Early to Bed
Wives Never Know
Mind Your Own Business
Hearts Divided
Tops Is the Limit
37: Turn Off the Moon
Exclusive
38: Bringing Up Baby
Breaking the Ice
Service Deluxe
His Exciting Night
39: Yes, My Darling Daughter
Boy Trouble
Sudden Money
Invitation to Happiness
Night Work
Balalaika
40: The Farmer's Daughter
Opened by Mistake

40: Maryland
    Elsa Maxwell's Public
       Deb No. 1
    No Time for Comedy
41: The Invisible Woman
    Honeymoon for Three
    Model Wife
    The Perfect Snob
    Go West Young Lady
    The Parson of Panamint
42: Friendly Enemies
43: Dixie Dugan
44: The Doughgirls
    Our Hearts Were Young
       and Gay
    Three Is a Family
45: Incendiary Blonde
    Bedside Manner
46: Gallant Journey
    A Stolen Life
47: It Happened on 5th Avenue
    My Brother Talks to
       Horses
    The Perfect Marriage
    Ramrod
48: Give My Regards to
       Broadway
49: Look for the Silver Lining
    The Lovable Cheat
61: The Pleasure of His
       Company
    All in a Night's Work
    The Parent Trap
63: Papa's Delicate Condition
    Son of Flubber
64: I'd Rather be Rich
66: The Ugly Dachshund
    Follow Me, Boys!

Barbara Ruick
1952: Invitation
    Fearless Fagan
    You for Me
    Apache War Smoke
    Above and Beyond
53: I Love Melvin
    Confidentially Connie
    Affairs of Dobie Gillis
56: Carousel

Janice Rule (1928-
1951: Goodbye My Fancy
    Starlift
52: Holiday for Sinners
    Gun for a Coward
53: Rogues' March
56: A Woman's Devotion
    Battle Shock
58: Bell, Book, and Candle
60: The Subterraneans
64: Invitation to a Gunfighter
66: The Chase
    Alvarez Kelly
67: The Ambushers
    Welcome to Hard Times
68: The Swimmer
    Shadow on the Land (TV)
69: Trial Run (TV)

Sig Rumann (1885-1967)
1929: Royal Box
34: The World Moves On
    Servants' Entrance
    Marie Galante
35: The Wedding Night
    East of Java
    Under Pressure
    Spring Tonic
    The Farmer Takes a Wife
    A Night at the Opera
36: The Princess Comes
       Across
    Bold Caballero
    I Loved a Soldier
37: On the Avenue
    Dead Yesterday
    Seventh Heaven
    Midnight Taxi
    Think Fast, Mr. Moto
    This Is My Affair
    Love Under Fire
    Thin Ice
    Lancer Spy
    Heidi
    Thank You, Mr. Moto
    Maytime
    The Great Hospital Mystery
    A Day at the Races
    Nothing Sacred

38: Paradise for Three
The Great Waltz
The Saint in New York
I'll Give a Million
Suez
Girls on Probation
39: Never Say Die
Honolulu
Ninotchka
Remember?
Confessions of a Nazi Spy
Only Angels Have Wings
40: The Story of Dr. Ehrlich's
Magic Bullet
Outside the Three-Mile
Limit
I Was an Adventuress
Four Sons
Bitter Sweet
Victory
41: So Ends the Night
That Uncertain Feeling
The Man Who Lost Him-
self
Shining Victory
Love Crazy
World Premiere
The Wagons Roll at Night
42: Remember Pearl Harbor
Crossroads
Enemy Agents Meet
Ellery Queen
Berlin Correspondent
China Girls
To Be or Not to Be
Desperate Journey
43: They Came to Blow Up
America
Sweet Rosie O'Grady
The Song of Bernadette
Tarzan Triumphs
Government Girl
44: The Hitler Gang
The Devil's Brood
Goodbye, My Love
It Happened Tomorrow
Summer Storm
45: A Royal Scandal
House of Frankenstein
The Dolly Sisters

Men in Her Diary
She Went to the Races
46: A Night in Casablanca
Faithful in My Fashion
Night and Day
47: Mother Wore Tights
48: The Emperor Waltz
If You Knew Susie
Give My Regards to
Broadway
49: Border Incident
51: On the Riviera
52: The World in His Arms
O. Henry's Full House
(Gift of the Magi seq.)
53: Houdini
Stalag 17
Ma and Pa Kettle on
Vacation
54: The Glenn Miller Story
White Christmas
Three-Ring Circus
Living It Up
55: Many Rivers to Cross
The Spy Chasers
57: The Wings of Eagles
62: The Errand Boy
64: Robin and the 7 Hoods
65: 36 Hours
66: The Fortune Cookie
The Last of the Secret
Agents

Barbara Rush (1927-
1950: Molly (or, The Goldbergs)
51: The First Legion
When Worlds Collide
The Flaming Feather
Quebec
53: Prince of Pirates
It Came from Outer Space
54: Taza, Son of Cochise
Magnificent Obsession
The Black Shield of Fal-
worth
55: Captain Lightfoot
Kiss of Fire
56: The World in My Corner
Bigger than Life
Flight to Hong Kong

57: Oh Men! Oh Women!
No Down Payment
58: Harry Black and the Tiger
The Young Lions
59: The Young Philadelphians
60: The Bramble Bush
Strangers When They
Meet
63: Come Blow Your Horn
64: Robin and the 7 Hoods
67: Hombre
68: Strategy of Terror (TV)

Andy Russell
1945: The Stork Club
46: Breakfast in Hollywood
Make Mine Music
47: Copacabana

Gail Russell (1924-1961)
1943: Henry Aldrich Gets
Glamour
44: The Uninvited
Lady in the Dark
Our Hearts Were Young
and Gay
45: Salty O'Rourke
The Unseen
Her Heart in Her Throat
46: Our Hearts Were Growing
Up
The Virginian
The Bachelor's Daughters
47: The Angel and the Bad-
man
Variety Girl
Calcutta
48: Moonrise
Night Has a Thousand
Eyes
Song of Adventure
The Wake of the Red
Witch
49: El Paso
Captain China
The Great Dan Patch
Song of India
50: The Lawless
51: Air Cadet
53: Devil's Canyon

56: 7 Men from Now
57: The Tattered Dress
58: No Place to Land
61: The Silent Call

Jane Russell (1921-
1943: The Outlaw
46: The Young Widow
48: Paleface
Yellow Sky
51: His Kind of Woman
Double Dynamite
52: Montana Belle
Macao
Son of Paleface
Las Vegas Story
53: Gentlemen Prefer Blondes
54: The French Line
55: Underwater!
Gentlemen Marry Brunettes
Foxfire
Tall Men
56: Hot Blood
Revolt of Mamie Stover
57: The Fuzzy Pink Night-
gown
62: It's Only Money
64: Fate Is the Hunter
66: Johnny Reno
Waco
67: Born Losers (bit)

John Russell (1921-
1937: The Duke Comes Back
The Frame Up
38: Always Goodbye
Prison Break
Five of a Kind
I Am Not Afraid
Mr. Smith Goes to
Washington
The Man Who Dared
Sabotage
40: The Blue Bird
The Man I Married
The Lady with Red Hair
45: Don Juan Quilligan
A Bell for Adano
Within These Walls
46: Somewhere in the Night

1203

47: Forever Amber
48: Yellow Sky
    Sitting Pretty
49: The Story of Molly X
    The Gal Who Took the
    West
    Slattery's Hurricane
50: Undertow
    Saddle Tramp
51: Fighting Coast Guard
    The Fat Man
    The Barefoot Mailman
    Man in the Saddle
52: Hoodlum Empire
    Oklahoma Annie
53: Fair Wind to Java
    The Sun Shines Bright
54: Jubilee Trail
55: Hell's Outpost
    The Last Command
57: Untamed Youth
    Hell Bound
    The Dalton Girls
58: Fort Massacre
59: Rio Bravo
    Yellowstone Kelly
66: Apache Uprising
67: Fort Utah
    Hostile Guns
68: Buckskin
    If He Hollers, Let Him
    Go
    Night Hunt
69: Hangmen from Hell
    Jungle Terror
    Cannon for Cordoba

Kurt Russell (1942-
1966: Follow Me, Boys!
68: The One and Only
    Original Family Band
69: The Horse in the Gray
    Flannel Suit

Rosalind Russell (1912-
1934: The President Vanishes
    Evelyn Prentice
35: The Night Is Young
    Forsaking All Others
    West Point of the Air

    Reckless
    The Casino Murder Case
    China Seas
    Rendezvous
36: It Had to Happen
    Under Two Flags
    Trouble for Two
    Craig's Wife
37: Night Must Fall
    Live, Love, and Learn
38: Man Proof
    Four's a Crowd
    The Citadel
39: Fast and Loose
    The Women
40: His Girl Friday
    Hired Wife
    No Time for Comedy
41: This Thing Called Love
    They Met in Bombay
    The Feminine Touch
    Design for Scandal
42: Take a Letter, Darling
    My Sister Eileen
43: Flight for Freedom
    What a Woman!
45: Roughly Speaking
    She Wouldn't Say Yes
46: Sister Kenny
47: The Guilt of Janet Ames
    Mourning Becomes Electra
48: The Velvet Touch
49: Tell it to the Judge
50: A Woman of Distinction
52: Never Wave at a Wac
55: Girl Rush
    Picnic
58: Auntie Mame
61: A Majority of One
62: Five Finger Exercise
64: Gypsy
66: Trouble with Angels
67: Oh Dad, Poor Dad, Mama's
    Hung You in the Closet
    and I'm Feeling So Sad
68: Rosie
69: Where Angels Go Trouble
    Follows
    The Unexpected Mrs.
    Pollifax

Rosalind Russell and Robert Montgomery,
amateur detectives in "Fast and Loose"

Ann Rutherford (1920-
1935: Waterfront Lady
The Singing Vagabond
Melody Trail
36: The Lawless Nineties
Down to the Sea
Doughnuts and Society
The Harvester
Comin' 'Round the
Mountain
The Oregon Trail
The Lonely Trail
37: The Devil Is Driving
Public Cowboy No. 1
38: Of Human Hearts
Judge Hardy's Children
Dramatic School
A Christmas Carol
You're Only Young Once
Love Finds Andy Hardy
Out West with the Hardys
39: Four Girls in White
The Hardys Ride High
These Glamour Girls
Gone With the Wind
Andy Hardy Gets Spring
Fever
Dancing Coed
Judge Hardy and Son
40: The Ghost Comes Home
Pride and Prejudice
Wyoming
Andy Hardy Meets a
Debutante
41: Washington Melodrama
Whistling in the Dark
Badlands of Dakota
Andy Hardy's Private
Secretary
Life Begins for Andy
Hardy
42: This Time for Keeps
The Courtship of Andy
Hardy
Orchestra Wives
Whistling in Dixie
Andy Hardy's Double Life
43: Happy Land
Whistling in Brooklyn
44: Laramie Trail

Bermuda Mystery
45: 2 O'Clock Courage
Bedside Manner
46: Inside Job
The Madonna's Secret
Murder in the Music Hall
47: Secret Life of Walter Mitty
48: Adventures of Don Juan
50: Operation Haylift

Dame Margaret Rutherford (1892-
1937: Talk of the Devil
Dusty Ermine
Hideout in the Alps
Beauty and the Barge
43: The Demi-Paradise
44: Yellow Canary
English Without Tears
45: Blithe Spirit
46: Miranda
48: Meet Me at Dawn
49: Passport to Pimlico
While the Sun Shines
50: The Happiest Days of Your
Life
Her Favorite Husband
52: The Magic Box
Castles in the Air
Miss Robin Hood
The Importance of Being
Earnest
53: Curtain Up
Aunt Clara
The Runaway Bus
54: Mad about Men
55: An Alligator Named Daisy
Innocents in Paris
Trouble in Store
57: The Smallest Show on
Earth
Dick and the Duchess
60: I'm All Right, Jack
Just My Luck
61: On the Double
Meet Miss Marple
62: Murder She Said
63: Murder at the Gallop
The Mouse on the Moon
The V.I.P.'s (OSCAR)
64: Murder Most Foul

64: Murder Ahoy!
65: Big Town Operators
66: The Alphabet Murders
   (cameo)
67: Falstaff
   The Countess from Hong
   Kong
68: The Wacky World of
   Mother Goose
   Song of Norway
69: Arabella

Basil Ruysdael (d. 1959)
1929: The Cocoanuts
49: File on Thelma Jordan
   Pinky
   The Girl and the Doctor
   Come to the Stable
   Colorado Territory
50: One Way Street
   Broken Arrow
   High Lonesome
   Gambling House
51: Raton Pass
   Half Angel
   My Forbidden Past
   The Scarf
   People Will Talk
52: Carrie
   Boots Malone
54: The Shanghai Story
55: The Blackboard Jungle
   The Violent Men
   Davy Crockett--King of
   the Wild Frontier
   Pearl of the South Pacific
   Diane
56: Jubal
   These Wilder Years
58: The Last Hurrah
59: The Horse Soldiers
   The Story of Ruth

Irene Ryan (1903-
1941: Melody for Three
44: Hot Rhythm
   San Diego, I Love You
45: That's the Spirit
   The Beautiful Cheat
   That Night with You

46: Diary of a Chambermaid
   Little Iodine
47: Woman on the Beach
   Heading for Heaven
48: Texas, Brooklyn, and
   Heaven
   My Dear Secretary
   An Old-Fashioned Girl
49: There's a Girl in My
   Heart
51: Meet Me After the Show
   Half Angel
52: Blackbeard the Pirate
   Bonzo Goes to College
   The Wac from Walla Walla
54: Ricochet Romance
57: Spring Reunion
   Rockabilly Baby
60: Desire in the Dust
66: Don't Worry We'll Think
   of a Title

Peggy Ryan (1924-
1937: Women Men Marry
   Top of the Town
   What's Cookin'?
39: She Married a Cop
   The Flying Irishman
42: Get Hep to Love
   Girls Town
   Miss Annie Rooney
   Private Buckaroo
   Give Out, Sisters!
   When Johnny Comes
   Marching Home
43: Top Man
   Mr. Big
44: The Merry Monahans
   Chip Off the Old Block
   Bowery to Broadway
   Follow the Boys
   Babes on Swing Street
   Merrily We Sing
   This Is the Life
45: Patrick the Great
   That's the Spirit
   Here Come the Coeds
   On Stage, Everybody!
   Men in Her Diary
49: Shamrock Hill

1207

49: There's a Girl in My
    Heart
53: All Ashore

Robert Ryan (1913-
1940: Golden Gloves
    Queen of the Mob
    Name, Age, and
      Occupation
    Northwest Mounted Police
42: Bombardier
43: The Sky's the Limit
    Behind the Rising Sun
    The Iron Major
44: Marine Raiders
    Gangway for Tomorrow
    Hitler's Gang
    Tender Comrade
45: Paris Underground
47: Woman on the Beach
    Trail Street
    Crossfire
48: Return of the Bad Men
    Berlin Express
    The Boy with Green Hair
    Act of Violence
49: The Set-Up
    Caught
    I Married a Communist
50: Born To Be Bad
    The Woman on Pier 13
    Secret Fury
51: Best of the Bad Men
    Flying Leathernecks
    The Racket
    On Dangerous Ground
52: Beware My Lovely
    Clash by Night
    Horizons West
53: The Naked Spur
    The City Beneath the Sea
    Inferno
54: Alaska Seas
    About Mrs. Leslie
    Her 12 Men
    Bad Day at Black Rock
55: Escape to Burma
    House of Bamboo
    The Tall Men
56: The Proud Ones

    The Best Things in Life
      Are Free
    Back from Eternity
57: Men in War
58: God's Little Acre
    Lonelyhearts
59: Day of the Outlaw
    Odds Against Tomorrow
60: Ice Palace
61: The Canadians
    The King of Kings
62: The Longest Day
    Billy Budd
63: The Battle of the Bulge
64: The Inheritance (narr.doc.)
65: The Crooked Road
    The Secret Agents
66: The Professionals
    The Dirty Game
67: The Busy Body
    The Law and Tombstone
    The Dirty Dozen
    The Prodigal Gun
    Hour of the Gun
68: Anzio!
    The Wild Bunch
    Krakatoa--East of Java
69: Custer of the West (cameo)
    Amnesty for a Gun
    A Minute to Pray, a
      Second to Die
    Captain Nemo and the
      Floating City

Sheila Ryan (1921-
1940: The Gay Caballero
41: Great Guns
    Golden Hoofs
    Dead Men Tell
    Dressed to Kill
    We Go Fast
42: Who Is Hope Schuyler?
    The Lone Star Ranger
    Pardon My Stripes
    A-Haunting We Will Go
    Careful, Soft Shoulders
43: The Cobra Strikes
    The Gang's All Here
44: Song of Texas
    Ladies of Washington

Robert Ryan

44: Something for the Boys
45: Caribbean Mystery
    Getting Gertie's Garter
46: Deadline for Murder
    Slightly Scandalous
47: The Big Fix
    The Lone Wolf in Mexico
    Heartaches
    Philo Vance's Secret
     Mission
    Railroaded
48: Caged Fury
49: Hideout
    Ringside
    Joe Palooka in The
     Counterpunch
50: Western Pacific Agent
    Mule Train
    Square Dance Katy
51: Fingerprints Don't Lie
    Gold Raiders
    Jungle Manhunt
    Mask of the Dragon
53: On Top of Old Smoky
    Pack Train
58: Street of Darkness

Tim Ryan (d. 1956)
1940: I'm Nobody's Sweetheart
    Now
41: Where Did You Get that
    Girl?
    Lucky Devils
    A Man Betrayed
    Ice-Capades Revue
    Public Enemies
    Harmon of Michigan
    Bedtime Story
42: Sweetheart of the Fleet
    The Man in the Trunk
    Get Hep to Love
    Stand by for Action
43: Mystery of the 13th Guest
    Riding High
    The Sultan's Daughter
    Hit Parade of 1943
    Two Weeks to Live
    Sarong Girl
    True to Life
    Melody Parade

44: Detective Kitty O'Day
    Hi Beautiful
    Hot Rhythm
    Kansas City Kitty
    Shadow of Suspicion
    Crazy Knights
    Swingtime Johnny
45: Swingin' on a Rainbow
    Adventures of Kitty O'Day
    Fashion Model
    Rockin' in the Rockies
46: Bringing Up Father
    Dark Alibi
    Wife Wanted
47: News Hounds
    Blondie's Holiday
    Body and Soul
48: Jiggs and Maggie in
     Society
    The Shanghai Chest
    Jiggs and Maggie in Court
    Luck of the Irish
    The Golden Eye
49: Sky Dragons
    Ringside
    Joe Palooka in The
     Counterpunch
50: Military Academy with
     that 10th Avenue Gang
    The Petty Girl
    Maggie and Jiggs Out
     West
    Joe Palooka in Humphrey
     Takes a Chance
51: The Cuban Fireball
    All that I Have
52: Fargo
    No Holds Barred
    Here Come the Marines
53: The Marksman
56: Fighting Trouble
57: The Buster Keaton Story

Sabu (1927-1963)
1937: Elephant Boy
38: Drums
40: The Thief of Bagdad
42: Jungle Book
    Arabian Nights
43: White Savage

44: Cobra Woman
46: Tangier
47: Black Narcissus
48: Man-Eater of Kumoan
    End of the River
49: Song of India
51: Savage Drums
54: Hell, Elephant!
56: Jaguar
57: Sabu and the Magic Ring
63: Rampage
64: A Tiger Walks

Eva Marie Saint (1924-
1954: On the Waterfront
      (OSCAR)
56: That Certain Feeling
57: Raintree Country
    A Hatful of Rain
59: North by Northwest
60: Exodus
62: All Fall Down
64: 36 Hours
65: The Sandpiper
66: The Russians Are Coming,
    The Russians Are Coming!
    Grand Prix
68: The Stalking Moon
69: Loving

Lili St. Cyr (1920-
1958: The Naked and the Dead
      I, Mobster

Raymond St.Jacques (1930-
1965: The Pawnbroker
      Mr. Moses
66: Mr. Buddwing
67: The Comedians
68: Madigan
    The Green Berets
    Betrayal
69: Night Hunt
    If He Hollers, Let Him
    Go
    Up Tight
    Simon Bolivar
    Change of Mind
    "A" Is for "Assassin"
    Cotton Comes to Harlem

Susan St. James (1946-
1967: Where Angels Go, Trouble
      Follows
68: New Faces in Hell
69: What's so Bad About
    Feeling Good?
    Jigsaw
    It Takes a Thief (TV pilot)
    The Name of the Game
    (TV pilot)

Al "Fuzzy" St. John (1893-1963)
1929: Dance of Life
      She Goes to War   PT
30: Hell Harbor
    Western Knights
    Two Fresh Eggs
    The Oklahoma Cyclone
    Land of Missing Men
31: Aloha
    Son of the Plains
32: Police Court
    Riders of the Desert
    Law of the North
33: His Private Secretary
    Riders of Destiny
34: Public Stenographer
35: Wanderer of the Wasteland
    Bar-20 Rides Again
36: Hopalong Cassidy Returns
    Trail Dust
    The Millionaire Kid
    West of Nevada
37: Outcasts of Poker Flat
    A Lawman Is Born
    Saturday's Heroes
    Melody of the Plains
    Sing, Cowboy, Sing
38: Rangers' Roundup
    Knight of the Plains
    Call of the Yukon
    Frontier Scout
    The Song and Bullets
39: Trigger Pals
    She Goes to War
40: Friendly Neighbors
    Texas Terrors
    Murder on the Yukon
    Marked Men
41: Billy the Kid's Fighting
    Pals

41: The Lone Rider in Ghost
      Town
    The Apache Kid
    The Lone Rider Ambushed
    A Missouri Outlaw
    Billy the Kid: Wanted
    Billy the Kid's Roundup
    The Lone Rider Fights
      Back
42: Jesse James Jr.
    Arizona Terrors
    Stagecoach Express
    Billy the Kid Trapped
    Billy the Kid's Smoking
      Guns
    Law and Order
43: My Son the Hero
    The Mysterious Rider
    Fugitive of the Plains
    The Renegade
44: The Drifter
    Wolves of the Range
    Law of the Saddle
    Frontier Outlaws
    Valley of Vengeance
    I'm from Arkansas
    Thundering Gunslingers
    Fuzzy Settles Down
    Rustlers' Hideout
    Oath of Vengeance
    Wild Horse Phantom
45: Border Badmen
    Lightnin' Raiders
    Fighting Bill Carson
    Stagecoach Outlaws
    Prairie Rustlers
    Devil Riders
    Gangsters' Den
46: His Brother's Ghost
    Gentlemen with Guns
    Terrors on Horseback
    Ghosts of Hidden Valley
    Overland Riders
    Prairie Badmen
    Outlaws of the Plains
    Shadows of Death
    Blazing Frontiers
47: Law of the Lash
    Pioneer Justice
    Ghost Town Renegades

    Return of the Lash
    Border Feud
48: Fighting Vigilantes
    Cheyenne Takes Over
    Panhandle Trail
    Raiders of Red Rock
    Stage to Mesa City
    Frontier Fighters
    Code of the Plains
    My Dog Shep
    Mark of the Lash
49: Outlaw Country
    Son of Billy the Kid
    Son of a Badman
    Frontier Revenge
    Dead Man's Gold

Betta St. John (1929-
1953: Dream Wife
    All the Brothers Were
      Valiant
    The Robe
54: Dangerous Mission
    The Saracen Blade
    The Student Prince
    The Law vs Billy the Kid
55: Alias John Preston
    The Naked Dawn
57: Tarzan and the Lost Safari
    High Tide at Noon
58: The Snorkel
    Corridors of Blood
60: Tarzan the Magnificent
61: City of the Dead
63: Horror Hotel

Howard St. John (1905-
1949: Shockproof
    The Undercover Man
50: Customs Agent
    The Men
    David Harding, Counterspy
    711 Ocean Drive
    Mister 880
    Born Yesterday
    Counterspy Meets Scotland
      Yard
    The Sun Sets at Dawn
51: Goodbye My Fancy
    Strangers on a Train

51: Saturday's Heroes
Close to My Heart
Starlift
The Big Night
52: Stop, You're Killing Me!
54: 3 Coins in the Fountain
55: Illegal
The Tender Trap
56: The World in My Corner
58: Summer Love
The Snorkel
59: Li'l Abner
60: Cry for Happy
61: Sanctuary
Lover Come Back
One, Two, Three
62: Madison Avenue
63: Lafayette
64: Strait-Jacket
Fate Is the Hunter
Sex and the Single Girl
Strange Bedfellows
Quick Before It Melts
67: Banning
Matchless
69: Don't Drink the Water

Jill St. John (1940-
1958: Summer Love
59: The Remarkable Mr.
Pennypacker
Holiday for Lovers
60: The Lost World
61: The Roman Spring of
Mrs. Stone
62: Tender Is the Night
63: Come Blow Your Horn
Who's Sleeping in My
Bed?
Who's Minding the Store?
64: Honeymoon Hotel
66: The Oscar
The Liquidator
Fame Is the Name of
the Game
67: How I Spent My Summer
Vacation
8 on the Lam
Banning
The King's Pirate

68: Tony Rome

John St. Polis (1887-c1942)
1929: Coquette
Why be Good?
The Fast Life
30: Party Girl
Melody Man
In the Next Room
Guilty?
Kismet
The Bad One
On the Make
Captain Thunder
31: Doctors' Wives
Transgression
Men of the Sky
Their Mad Moment
Heartbreak
32: Alias the Doctor
Lena Rivers
Symphony of 6 Million
Forbidden Company
The Crusader
Gambling Sex
33: Terror Trail
The World Gone Mad
Sing, Sinner, Sing
Notorious but Nice
King of the Arena
34: Guilty Parents
35: Death from a Distance
Lady in Scarlet
36: 3 on the Trail
Below the Deadline
The Dark Hour
The Border Patrolman
37: Paradise Isle
38: Saleslady
International Crime
Phantom Ranger
Mr. Wong-Detective
39: Boys' Reformatory
They Shall Have Music
40: Rocky Mountain Rangers
On the Spot
The Haunted House

Marin Sais (1888-
1938: Pioneer Trail

1213

38: Phantom Gold
39: Juarez and Maximilian
40: Wild Horse Range
44: Enemy of Women
    Frontier Outlaws
    Oath of Vengeance
45: Border Badmen
    Lightning Raiders
46: Rendezvous 24
    Terrors on Horseback
49: Ride, Ryder, Ride!
    Roll, Thunder, Roll!
50: Cowboy and the Prize-
    fighter
    The Fighting Redhead

S. Z. Sakall (1884-1955)
1927-1939: European films
30: Why Cry at Parting?
40: It's a Date
    Florian
    My Love Came Back
    Spring Parade
41: That Night in Rio
    The Devil and Miss Jones
    The Man Who Lost Him-
    self
    Ball of Fire
42: 7 Sweethearts
    Broadway
    Yankee Doodle Dandy
    Casablanca
43: Wintertime
    Thank Your Lucky Stars
44: Hollywood Canteen
    Shine on Harvest Moon
45: Wonder Man
    Christmas in Connecticut
    The Dolly Sisters
    San Antonio
46: Cinderella Jones
    2 Guys from Milwaukee
    Never Say Goodbye
    The Time, the Place,
    and the Girl
47: Cynthia
48: Whiplash
    April Showers
    Romance on the High Seas
    Embraceable You

49: Look for the Silver Lining
    My Dream Is Yours
    In the Good Old Summer-
    time
    Oh, You Beautiful Doll!
50: Montana
    A Swirl of Glory
    Daughter of Rosie O'Grady
    Tea for Two
51: Sugarfoot
    Lullabye of Broadway
    Painting the Clouds with
    Sunshine
    It's a Big Country
53: Small Town Girl
54: The Student Prince

Charles "Chick" Sale (1885-1936)
1931: Star Witness
32: The Hurry Call
    The Expert
    When a Feller Needs a
    Friend
    Stranger in Town
33: Men of America
    Lucky Day
    The Chief
34: Treasure Island
35: Rocky Mountain Mystery
36: It's a Great Life
    Man Hunt
    The Gentleman from
    Louisiana
    The Man I Marry
37: You Only Live Once

Virginia Sale
1929: Fancy Baggage   PT
      The Kid's Clever   S
      Below the Deadline   S
30:   Embarrassing Moment
      Lovin' the Ladies
      Show Girl in Hollywood
      Back Pay
      Dude Wrangler
      Bright Lights
      Broken Dishes
      Moby Dick
31:   Big Business Girl
      My Past

1214

31: Many a Slip
Gold Dust Gertie
Too Young to Marry
Her Majesty Love
32: Fireman, Save My Child!
Man Wanted
Those We Love
Bachelor Mother
33: Iron Master
Smoke Lightning
Oliver Twist
34: Love Past 30
Smarty
Registered Nurse
The Man with 2 Faces
Madame Du Barry
Embarrassing Moments
35: It's a Small World
After the Dance
37: Outcast
Meet the Missus
Dangerous Holiday
Topper
38: The Jury's Secret
40: I Can't Give You Anything
But Love, Baby
Gold Rush Maisie
Flowing Gold
Calling All Husbands
41: Miss Polly
42: Harvard, Here I Come
Miss Annie Rooney
The Big Shot
44: Dark Mountain
Hi Beautiful!
The Thin Man Goes Home
When Strangers Marry
45: Blazing the Western Trail
Danger Signal
She Gets Her Man
46: Badman's Territory
47: The Case of the Baby-
sitter
The Hat Box Mystery
67: How to Succeed Without
Really Trying

Albert Salmi (1928-
1958: The Brothers Karamazov
The Bravados

60: The Unforgiven
Wild River
64: The Outrage
67: The Flim Flam Man
Hour of the Gun
The Ambushers
68: 3 Guns for Texas

Walter Sande
1941: Parachute Battalion
Confessions of Boston
Blackie
42: Sweetheart of the Fleet
43: The Purple V
Corvette K-225
After Midnight with Boston
Blackie
Reveille with Beverly
The Chance of a Lifetime
44: The Singing Sheriff
I Love a Soldier
To Have and Have Not
45: Along Came Jones
The Daltons Ride Again
The Spider
What Next, Corporal
Hargrove?
46: The Blue Dahlia
Nocturne
No Leave, No Love
47: The Red House
Woman on the Beach
Wild Harvest
Christmas Eve
In Self Defense
Killer McCoy
48: Prince of Thieves
Blonde Ice
Half Past Midnight
Wallflower
49: Bad Boy
Canadian Pacific
Joe Palooka in The Counter-
punch
Miss Mink of 1949
Rim of the Canyon
Tucson
Strange Bargain
50: The Kid from Texas
Dark City

51: Payment on Demand
Warpath
A Place in the Sun
Tomorrow Is Another Day
The Basketball Fix
The Racket
I Want You
Red Mountain
52: Mutiny
Red Planet Mars
The Duel at Silver Creek
Bomba and the Jungle
Girl
The Steel Trap
53: The Great Sioux Uprising
The Kid from Left Field
A Blueprint for Murder
54: Overland Pacific
Apache
Bad Day at Black Rock
55: Wichita
Texas Lady
56: Anything Goes
The Maverick Queen
Canyon River
Gun Brothers
57: Drango
The Iron Sheriff
Johnny Tremain
59: Last Train from Gun Hill
60: Oklahoma Territory
The Gallant Hours
Noose for a Gunman
Sunrise at Campobello
64: The Quick Gun
65: Young Dillinger
I'll Take Sweden
66: The Navy vs the Night
Monsters
69: Death of a Gunfighter

George Sanders (1906-
1929: Strange Cargo
The Shape of Things to
Come
Find the Lady
Dishonour Bright
36: My Second Wife
Lloyds of London
37: The Outsider

The Man Who Could Work
Miracles
Love Is News
Slave Ship
The Lady Escapes
Lancer Spy
38: International Settlement
4 Men and a Prayer
39: The Saint Strikes Back
The Saint in London
Nurse Edith Cavell
Allegheny Uprising
Confessions of a Nazi Spy
Mr. Moto's Last Warning
40: Green Hell
The Saint's Double Trouble
House of the 7 Gables
Rebecca
Foreign Correspondent
Bitter Sweet
The Son of Monte Cristo
The Saint Takes Over
41: Rage in Heaven
The Gay Falcon
Man Hunt
Sundown
The Saint in Palm Springs
42: Her Cardboard Lover
Tales of Manhattan
The Moon and Sixpence
Son of Fury
The Falcon's Brother
The Falcon Takes Over
Quiet Please-Murder!
Black Swan
43: This Land Is Mine
Paris After Dark
They Came to Blow Up
America
Appointment in Berlin
44: The Lodger
Action in Arabia
Summer Storm
45: The Picture of Dorian
Gray
Hangover Square
The Strange Affairs of
Uncle Harry
46: A Scandal in Paris
The Strange Woman

46: Never Say Goodbye
    While the City Sleeps
    Death of a Scoundrel
47: Forever Amber
    The Ghost and Mrs. Muir
    Private Affairs of Bel
    Ami
    Lured
48: Personal Column
49: The Fan
    Samson and Delilah
50: All About Eve (OSCAR)
51: I Can Get it for You
    Wholesale
    (or, Only the Best)
    The Light Touch
52: Ivanhoe
    Captain Black Jack
    Assignment: Paris
53: Call Me Madame
54: Witness to Murder
    King Richard and the
    Crusaders
55: Jupiter's Darling
    Moonfleet
    The Scarlet Coat
    The King's Thief
    Night Flight
56: Never Say Goodbye
    While The City Sleeps
    That Certain Feeling
    Death of a Scoundrel
57: The 7th Sin
58: The Whole Truth
    From the Earth to the
    Moon
    Outcasts of the City
59: That Kind of Woman
    Solomon and Sheba
60: The Last Voyage
    Village of the Damned
    Touch of Larceny
    Bluebeard's 10 Honey-
    moons
61: Call Me Genius
    5 Golden Hours
    Trouble in the Sky
62: In Search of the Castaways
    Operation Snatch
63: Cairo

    The Cracksman
64: Dark Purpose
    A Shot in the Dark
65: The Amorous Adventures
    of Moll Flanders
    Ecco (narr.)
66: The Quiller Memorandum
67: Trunk to Cairo
    Warning Shot
    Good Times
    King of Africa
68: The Jungle Book
    The Long Day's Dying
    The Best House in London
69: Thin Air
    The Candy Man
    The Kremlin Letter

Johnny Sands (1927-
1947: Blaze of Noon
    Born to Speed
50: The Lawless
    The Admiral Was a Lady
    2 Flags West
51: Target Unknown
    The Basketball Fix
52: Aladdin and His Lamp

Tommy Sands (1936-
1958: Sing, Boy, Sing (or, The
    Singing Idol)
    The Mardi Gras
61: The Parent Trap
    Babes in Toyland
    Love in a Goldfish Bowl
62: The Longest Day
64: Ensign Pulver
65: None But the Brave
67: The Violent Ones

Olga San Juan (1927-
1944: Caribbean Romance (short)
    Rainbow Island
45: Out of this World
    Duffy's Tavern
    Bambolera
    Little Witch
46: Blue Skies
47: Variety Girl
    Catalina

1217

48: Are You with it?
Countess of Monte Carlo
One Touch of Venus
49: The Beautiful Blonde
from Bashful Bend
60: The Third Voice

Tom Santschi (1879-1931)
1929: In Old Arizona
The Yellowback   S
Wagon Master   PT
The Shannons of Broad-
way
30: The Utah Kid
Paradise Island
The 4th Alarm
31: The River's End
10 Nights in a Barroom
32: The Last Ride

Michael Sarrazin (1941-
1967: Gunfight in Abilene
The Flim Flam Man
68: The Sweet Ride
Journey to Shiloh
Wylie
69: In Search of Gregory
They Shoot Horses, Don't
They?
Eye of the Cat
Run, Shadow, Run
A Man Called Gannon

Ann Savage (1921-
1943: What a Woman!
2 Senoritas from Chicago
Dangerous Blondes
Footlight Glamour
Saddles and Sagebrush
Passport to Suez
After Midnight with Boston
Blackie
Klondike Kate
One Dangerous Night
44: Ever Since Venus
2-Man Submarine
Dancing in Manhattan
The Last Horseman
The Unwritten Code
45: Lady Chaser

Apology for Murder
One Exciting Night
Scared Stiff
The Spider
46: The Dark Horse
The Last Crooked Mile
47: Jungle Flight
Renegade Girl
49: Satan's Cradle
50: Pygmy Island
51: Pier No. 23
53: The Woman They Almost
Lynched

Telly Savalas (1924-
1960: The Interns
61: Mad Dog Coll
The Young Savages
The Young Doctors
62: Cape Fear
Bird Man of Alcatraz
63: Love Is a Ball
The Man from the Diner's
Club
Johnny Cool
64: The New Interns
65: Genghis Khan
The Battle of the Bulge
The Greatest Story Ever
Told
John Goldfarb, Please
Come Home
66: Beau Geste
The Slender Thread
67: The Dirty Dozen
68: Sol Madrid
Buona Sera, Mrs. Campbell
The Scalphunters
Mackenna's Gold
Day of the Landgrabber
69: The Assassination Bureau
A Man and a Half
To Hell with the Gringos
Viva Max!
Crooks and Coronets
The Warriors
6 Days at Dongs
Trog

Joe Sawyer (c1908-

1933: College Humor
34: Jimmy the Gent
35: Special Agent
Little Big Shot
Moonlight on the Prairie
I Found Stella Parish
The Frisco Kid
Man of Iron
36: The Petrified Forest
Freshman Love
The Walking Dead
Big Brown Eyes
And Sudden Death
Murder With Pictures
Special Investigator
Crash Donovan
Great Guy
The Leathernecks Have
   Landed
Pride of the Marines
Two in a Crowd
37: Black Legion
San Quentin
Slim
Navy Blues
Midnight Madonna
Reported Missing
The Lady Fights Back
Motor Madness
They Gave Him a Gun
38: Tarzan's Revenge
Passport Husband
Always in Trouble
Heart of the North
Stolen Heaven
The Storm
Gambling Ship
39: The Lady and the Mob
You Can't Get Away with
   Murder
Confessions of a Nazi
   Spy
Inside Information
I Stole a Million
Frontier Marshal
Sabotage
The Roaring Twenties
40: The Grapes of Wrath
The House Across the Bay
The Man from Montreal

The Dark Command
King of the Lumberjacks
Lucky Cisco Kid
The Long Voyage Home
Melody Ranch
The Border Legion
Santa Fe Trail
Wildcat Bus
41: The Lady from Cheyenne
Sergeant York
Tanks a Million
Belle Starr
Last of the Duanes
Down Mexico Way
Swamp Water
They Died with Their
   Boots On
You're in the Navy Now
42: Sundown Jim
Hay Foot!
Brooklyn Orchid
Wrecking Crew
43: Taxi, Mister!
Buckskin Frontier
McGuerins from Brooklyn
The Outlaw
Fall In
Hit the Ice
Prairie Chickens
Tornado
Yanks Ahoy!
Alaska Highway
Let's Face it
Sleepy Lagoon
Tarzan's Desert Mystery
44: Moon over Las Vegas
South of Dixie
Hey Rookie!
The Singing Sheriff
45: High Powered
Brewster's Millions
The Naughty Nineties
46: Deadline at Dawn
Gilda
Joe Palooka--Champ
Inside Job
G.I. War Brides
The Runaround
47: Roses Are Red
Christmas Eve
Big Town After Dark
A Double Life

47: A Double Life
48: If You Knew Susie
     Fighting Father Dunne
     Half Past Midnight
     Here Comes Trouble
     Coroner Creek
     Fighting Back
     The Untamed Breed
49: Deputy Marshal
     Stagecoach Kid
     The Gay Amigo
     Kazan
     And Baby Makes Three
     Lucky Stiff
     Tucson
50: Curtain Call at Cactus
       Creek
     Traveling Saleswoman
     Blondie's Hero
     Operation Haylift
     The Flying Missile
51: Pride of Maryland
     Comin' 'Round the
       Mountain
     As You Were
52: Indian Uprising
     Red Skies of Montana
53: It Came from Outer Space
54: Taza, Son of Cochise
     Riding Shotgun
     Johnny Dark
55: The Kettles in the Ozarks
56: The Killing
60: North to Alaska

John Saxon (1935-
1955: Running Wild
56: The Unguarded Moment
     Rock Pretty Baby
58: Summer Love
     The Restless Years
     The Reluctant Debutante
     This Happy Feeling
59: Cry Tough
     The Big Fisherman
60: Portrait in Black
     The Unforgiven
     The Plunderers
61: Posse from Hell
62: War Hunt

     Nightmare
     Mr. Hobbs Takes a
       Vacation
63: The Cardinal
64: The Evil Eye
65: The Ravagers
     The Cavern
66: Queen of Blood (re-rel.
       in '69 as Planet of Blood)
     The Appaloosa
67: Winchester 73
     The Night Caller
     Blood Beast from Outer
       Space
68: For Singles Only
     A Dandy in Aspic
     Istanbul Express (TV)
69: Death of a Gunfighter

Syd Saylor (1895-
1930: Light of the Western Skies
     Border Legion
     Men Without Law
31: Unfaithful
     Fighting Caravans
     Playthings of Hollywood
     A Lawyer's Secret
     I Take This Woman
     Caught
     Sidewalks of New York
32: Law of the Seas
     Million Dollar Legs
     Lady and Gent
     The Crusader
     Tangled Destinies
33: Justice Takes a Holiday
     The Nuisance
     Gambling Ship
     Man of Sentiment
34: Lost Jungle
     Young and Beautiful
     Dude Ranger
     When a Man Sees Red
35: The Wilderness Mail
     Headline Woman
     Code of the Mounted
     Ladies Crave Excitement
     Men of Action
36: Hitchhike to Heaven
     Kelly the Second

1220

36: The Sky Parade
Nevada
The Last Assignment
Kelly of the Secret
  Service
Prison Shadows
Headin' for Rio Grande
Secret Valley
37: Arizona Days
Guns in the Dark
Meet the Boy Friend
Wild and Woolly
Sea Racketeers
The Wrong Road
Wallaby Jim of the Islands
Exiled to Shanghai
38: The Black Doll
Born to the West
Little Miss Broadway
There Goes My Heart
Crashin' Through Danger
39: Union Pacific
$1000 a Touchdown
40: Abe Lincoln in Illinois
Arizona
41: Wyoming Wildcat
The Great American
  Broadcast
Miss Polly
Borrowed Hero
42: A Gentleman at Heart
The Man in the Trunk
That Other Woman
Time to Kill
43: He Hired the Boss
Harvest Melody
44: Hey Rookie!
Swingtime Johnny
3 of a Kind
45: Bedside Manner
The Navajo Kid
46: Deadline for Murder
6 Guns for Hire
Thunder Town
47: Fun on a Weekend
48: Prince of Thieves
Sitting Pretty
Racing Luck
Triple Threat
49: Big Jack

Dancing in the Dark
50: Mule Train
52: The Hawk of Wild River
Belles on Their Toes
55: The Toughest Man Alive
59: Escort West

Gia Scala (1933-
1956: All that Heaven Allows
Never Say Goodbye
Price of Fear
4 Girls in Town
57: The Big Boodle
The Garment Jungle
Don't Go Near the Water
A Tip on a Dead Jockey
58: The Tunnel of Love
Ride a Crooked Trail
59: The Two-Headed Spy
The Angry Hills
Battle of the Coral Sea
60: I Aim at the Stars
61: The Guns of Navarone
62: Triumph of Robin Hood

Frank Scannell
1944: Shadow of Suspicion
45: An Angel Comes to
  Brooklyn
47: Hit Parade of 1947
I Wonder Who's Kissing
  Her Now
Kilroy Was Here
Linda by Good
48: French Leave
When My Baby Smiles at
  Me
Apartment for Peggy
Ladies of the Chorus
49: Alias the Champ
54: The Country Girl
57: The Tattered Dress
The Incredible Shrinking
  Man
The Night the World
  Exploded
58: The Screaming Mimi
59: Arson for Hire
60: High Time
64: The Disorderly Orderly

Paul Scardon (1875-1954)
1941: Lady from Louisiana
The Son of Davy Crockett
42: Today I Hang
44: The Adventures of Mark
Twain
46: Down Missouri Way
47: Magic Town
48: Sign of the Ram
Fighting Mad
The Shanghai Chest

Natalie Schafer
1944: Marriage Is a Private
Affair
45: Molly and Me
Keep Your Powder Dry
Masquerade in Mexico
Wonder Man
47: Dishonored Lady
The Other Love
Repeat Performance
The Secret Beyond the
Door
48: The Snake Pit
49: Caught
51: Payment on Demand
Take Care of My Little
Girl
The Law and the Lady
Callaway Went Thataway
52: Has Anyone Seen My Gal?
Just Across the Street
53: The Girl Next Door
55: Female on the Beach
56: Forever Darling
Anastasia
57: Oh Men! Oh Women!
Bernadine
61: Susan Slade
Back Street

William Schallert (1925-
1950: Lonely Hearts Bandits
51: The Man from Planet X
52: Storm over Thibet
Captive Women
Flat Top
53: Sword of Venus
Port Sinister

54: Riot in Cell Block 11
Shield for Murder
Black Tuesday
Gog
55: Smoke Signal
Hell's Horizon
Top of the World
56: Bigger than Life
Written on the Wind
57: The Incredible Shrinking
Man
The Tattered Dress
The Girl in the Kremlin
Man in the Shadow
The Tarnished Angels
58: Cry Terror
59: Day of the Outlaw
Blue Denim
Pillow Talk
60: The Gallant Hours
62: Lonely Are the Brave
67: In the Heat of the Night
Hour of the Gun
68: Speedway
Will Penny
Sam Whiskey
69: Colossus
Tora! Tora! Tora!
The Computer Wore Tennis
Shoes

Carl Schell
1962: Escape from East Berlin
63: Werewolf in a Girls'
Dormitory
66: The Blue Max

Maria Schell (1926-
1942: Steinbruch
47: Der Engel Mit der Posaune
(The Angel with the
Trumpet)
48: Maresi
49: Nach Dem Sturm
50: Es Kommt Ein Tag
51: Dr. Holl
The Magic Box
52: Bis Wir Uns Wiedersehen
53: So Little Time
The Heart of the Matter
Der Traumende Mund
(Dreaming Lips)

1222

53: So Lange du da Bist (As
Long as You're Near Me)
Tagebuch Einter Verlieb-
ten (Diary of a Lover)
54: Die Letzte Brucke (The
Last Bridge)
Angelika
Napoleon
55: Her Uber Leben Und Tod
Die Ratten
56: Gervaise
Liebe
57: Rose Bernd
Le Notti Bianche
58: The Brothers Karamazov
Une Vie
59: The Hanging Tree
Schinderhannes
Raubfischer in Hellas
60: Cimarron
As the Sea Rages
61: Das Riesenrad
The Mark
62: Ich Bin Auch Eine Nur
Frau
End of Desire
63: L'Assassin Connait la
Musique
Duel in the Forest
68: 99 Women
69: The Tiger by the Tail

Maximilian Schell (1930-
1954: Kinder, Mutter, un Ein
General
58: The Young Lions
61: Judgment at Nuremberg
(OSCAR)
62: 5 Finger Exercise
The Reluctant Saint
63: The Condemned of Altona
Girl from Flanders
64: Topkapi!
Hamlet
65: Return from the Ashes
67: The Battle Horns
The Deadly Affair
Beyond the Mountains
Counterpoint
68: The Castle

The Russian Garden (dir.)
Krakatoa--East of Java
Heidi (TV)
69: The Venetian Twins (dual
role)
Simon Bolivar

Rosanna Schiaffino (1939-
1960: The Minotaur
61: La Notte Brava
62: 2 Weeks in Another Town
Crime Does Not Pay
63: Girl from Flanders
Blood on His Sword
The Victors
Lafayette
64: The Long Ships
65: The Cavern
66: El Greco
Arrivederci, Baby!
Mandragola
67: Red Dragon
68: A Nun at the Crossroads
69: Simon Bolivar
Check to the Queen (Ital.)

Joseph Schildkraut (1896-1964)
1929: Show Boat   PT
Shipwrecked   S
Mississippi Gambler
Carnival
30: Cock o' the Walk
Night Ride
Blue Danube
34: Viva Villa!
Sisters Under the Skin
Cleopatra
The Tell-Tale Heart
35: The Crusades
36: Garden of Allah
37: Slave Ship
Lancer Spy
The Life of Emile Zola
(OSCAR)
A Star Is Born
Souls at Sea
Lady Behave
38: The Baroness and the
Butler
Suez

38: Marie Antoinette
39: Mr. Moto Takes a
    Vacation
    Idiot's Delight
    Lady of the Tropics
    Man in the Iron Mask
    The Rains Came
    Pack Up Your Troubles
    The 3 Musketeers
40: Shop Around the Corner
    Phantom Raiders
    Rangers of Fortune
    Meet the Wildcat
41: The Tell-Tale Heart
    Parson of Panamint
45: The Cheaters
    Flame of Barbary Coast
46: Monsieur Beaucaire
    The Plainsman and the
    Lady
47: Northwest Outpost
48: Gallant Legion
    Old Los Angeles
59: Diary of Anne Frank
61: King of the Roaring
    Twenties
64: Dust of Desire
    Song of Love
65: The Greatest Story Ever
    Told

Gus Schilling (1908-1957)
1941: Citizen Kane
    Lucky Devils
    Ice-Capades Revue
    It Started with Eve
    Appointment for Love
    Dr. Kildare's Victory
42: Broadway
    You Were Never Lovelier
    Moonlight in Havana
    The Magnificent Ambersons
43: Hers to Hold
    Hi, Buddy!
    Lady Bodyguard
    The Amazing Mrs. Holliday
    Chatterbox
    Larceny with Music
44: Sing a Jingle
45: A Thousand and One Nights

It's a Pleasure!
River Gang
See My Lawyer
46: Dangerous Business
47: Calendar Girl
    Stork Bites Man
48: Return of October
    Macbeth
    Lady from Shanghai
    Angel on the Amazon
49: Bride for Sale
50: Hit Parade of 1951
    Our Very Own
51: Honeychile
    Gasoline Alley
    On Dangerous Ground
52: One Big Affair
54: She Couldn't Say No
55: Run for Cover
56: Glory
    Bigger than Life

Stefan Schnabel (1912-
1942: Journey into Fear
56: Crowded Paradise
57: The 27th Day
58: The Muggers
61: The Secret Ways
    The Big Show
    Ça Va Etre ta Fetes
62: The Counterfeit Traitor
    2 Weeks in Another Town
63: The Ugly American
    Rampage

Romy Schneider (1938-
1958: The Story of Vickie
    The Pursuits and Loves
    of Queen Victoria
59: Mon Petit (or, Monpti)
60: Christine
62: Boccaccio '70 (The Job
    seq.)
    Forever My Love
63: The Cardinal
    The Victors
    The Trial
    Magnificent Sinner
64: Good Neighbor Sam
65: What's New Pussy Cat?

1224

66: 10:30 P.M.--Summer
Maedchen in Uniform
67: Triple Cross
68: Otley
69: The Pool
Don't You Cry

Ernestine Schumann-Heink
(1861-1936)
1935: Here's to Romance

Ferdinand Schumann-Heink
(1893-1955)
1930: Worldly Goods
Hell's Angels
31: The Seas Beneath
My Pal, the King
33: Gigolettes of Paris
34: The World Moves On
Fugitive Road
35: Symphony of Living
43: Mission to Moscow

Paul Scofield (1922-
1955: That Lady
58: Carve Her Name with
Pride
65: The Train
66: A Man for All Seasons
(OSCAR)
69: King Lear

George C. Scott (1927-
1959: The Hanging Tree
Anatomy of a Murder
61: The Hustler
The Power and the Glory
63: The List of Adrian
Messenger
64: Dr. Strangelove
65: The Yellow Rolls-Royce
66: The Flim Flam Man
68: Petulia
69: Patton--Blood and Guts
5 S.O.B.'s

Gordon Scott (1927-
1955: Tarzan's Hidden Jungle
57: Tarzan and the Lost Safari
58: Tarzan and the Trappers

Tarzan's Fight for Life
59: Tarzan's Greatest
Adventure
60: Tarzan the Magnificent
62: Coriolanus, Hero Without
a Country
The Lion of St. Mark
63: Beast of Babylon vs the
Son of Hercules
64: Goliath and the Vampires
Hero of Rome
65: Samson and the 7 Miracles
of the World
66: The Tramplers

Janette Scott (1938-
1949: No Place for Jennifer
50: No Highway
51: Prehistoric Women
The Magic Box
55: Now and Forever
57: As Long as They're Happy
The Good Companions
59: Happy Is the Bride
The Devil's Disciple
60: School for Scoundrels
61: Double Bunk
62: 2 and 2 Make 6
63: Paranoiac
The Day of the Triffids
Siege of the Saxons
The Old Dark House
64: The Beauty Jungle
65: Crack in the World
66: Contest Girl
67: Bikini Paradise
68: His and Hers

Ken Scott
1955: Desire in the Dust
57: 3 Faces of Eve
Stopover Tokyo
58: From Hell to Texas
The Bravados
The Fiend Who Walked
the West
59: This Earth Is Mine
Woman Obsessed
5 Gates to Hell
Beloved Infidel

61: The Fiercest Heart
    Pirates of Tortuga
    The Second Time Around
63: Police Nurse
65: Raiders from Beneath the
    Sea
    The Naked Brigade
66: Fantastic Voyage
    The Murder Game

Lizabeth Scott (1924-
1945: You Came Along
46: The Strange Love of
    Martha Ivers
47: Dead Reckoning
    Desert Fury
    I Walk Alone
    Variety Girl
48: Pitfall
    Interference
49: Easy Living
    Too Late for Tears
50: Paid in Full
    Dark City
    The Company She Keeps
51: Two of a Kind
    The Racket
52: A Stolen Face
53: Scared Stiff
    Bad for Each Other
54: Silver Lode
57: The Weapon
    Loving You
58: Quantrill's Raiders

Martha Scott (1914-
1940: Our Town
    The Howards of Virginia
41: Cheers for Miss Bishop
    They Dare Not Love
    One Foot in Heaven
43: Stage Door Canteen
    In Old Oklahoma
    War of the Wildcats
    Hi Diddle Diddle
47: So Well Remembered
49: Strange Bargain
51: When I Grow Up
55: The Desperate Hours
56: The Ten Commandments

57: Sayonara
    18 and Anxious
59: Ben-Hur

Pippa Scott (1935-
1956: The Searchers
58: Auntie Mame
    As Young as You Are
63: My Six Loves
68: Petulia
69: The One with the Fuzz
    Cold Turkey

Randolph Scott (1903-
1929: Far Call   SSE
31: Women Men Marry
32: Sky Bride
    Island of Lost Souls
    Lusitania Secret
    A Successful Calamity
    Hot Saturday
33: Heritage of the Desert
    Wild Horse Mesa
    Hello, Everybody!
    Murders in the Zoo
    Supernatural
    Sunset Pass
    To the Last Man
    The Cocktail Hour
    Broken Dreams
    Man of the Forest
34: Last Roundup
    Wagon Wheels
    Thundering Herd
35: Home on the Range
    Rocky Mountain Mystery
    Roberta
    Village Tale
    She
    So Red the Rose
36: Follow the Fleet
    And Sudden Death
    Go West, Young Man
    The Last of the Mohicans
37: Hide, Wide, and Handsome
38: The Road to Reno
    Rebecca of Sunnybrook
    Farm
    The Texans
39: Jesse James

1226

39: Susannah of the Mounties
Frontier Marshal
20,000 Men a Year
Coast Guard
40: Virginia City
My Favorite Wife
When the Daltons Rode
41: Western Union
Belle Starr
Paris Calling
42: To the Shores of Tripoli
The Spoilers
Pittsburgh
43: Desperadoes
Bombardier
Corvette K-225
Gung Ho!
44: Belle of the Yukon
45: China Spy
Captain Kidd
46: Home Sweet Suicide
Abilene Town
Badman's Territory
The Assassin
47: Trail Street
Gunfighters
Christmas Eve
48: Albuquerque
Coroner Creek
Return of the Badmen
49: Canadian Pacific
The Walking Hills
The Doolins of Oklahoma
Fighting Man of the Plains
50: Caribou Trail
The Nevadan
Colt .45
Thundercloud
51: A Swirl of Glory
Santa Fe
Sugarfoot
Fort Worth
Man in the Saddle
Starlift
52: Carson City
The Man Behind the Gun
Hangman's Knot
53: The Stranger Wore a
Gun
Thunder over the Plains

54: Riding Shotgun
The Bounty Hunter
55: 10 Wanted Men
Rage at Dawn
Tall Man Riding
A Lawless Street
56: 7 Men from Now
The 7th Cavalry
57: The Tall T
Decision at Sundown
Shootout at Medicine Bend
58: Buchanan Rides Alone (or,
The Name's Buchanan)
59: Westbound
Ride Lonesome
60: Comanche Station
62: Ride the High Country

Zachary Scott (1914-1965)
1944: Mask of Dimitrios
Hollywood Canteen
45: San Antonio
Danger Signal
Mildred Pierce
The Southerner
46: Her Kind of Man
47: Stallion Road
The Unfaithful
Cass Timberlane
48: Ruthless
Whiplash
49: Flaxy Martin
South of St. Louis
Death in a Doll's House
Bed of Roses
Flamingo Road
One Last Fling
50: Born to be Bad
Pretty Baby
Guilty Bystander
Colt .45
Shadow on the Wall
Thundercloud
51: Lightning Strikes Twice
The Secret of Convict Lake
Let's Make It Legal
52: Stronghold
Wings of Danger
53: Appointment in Honduras
55: Shot Gun

55: Flame of the Islands
Treasure of Ruby Hills
56: Bandido
57: The Counterfeit Plan
Man in the Shadows
Flight into Danger
60: Natchez Trail
61: The Young One
62: It's Only Money

Vito Scotti
1960: Pay or Die
Where the Boys Are
61: Master of the World
The Explosive Generation
63: Dime on a Halo
Captain Newman, M.D.
64: Wild and Wonderful
Rio Conchos
The Pleasure Seekers
65: Von Ryan's Express
66: Blindfold
What Did You Do in the
War, Daddy?
67: The Perils of Pauline
The Caper of the Golden
Bulls
Warning Shot
68: The Secret War of Harry
Frigg
Head
How Sweet It is
69: Cactus Flower

Alexander Scourby (1913-
1952: Affair in Trinidad
Because of You
The Redhead from
Wyoming
53: The Big Heat
The Glory Brigade
54: The Silver Chalice
55: Sign of the Pagan
56: Giant
Ransom
58: Me and the Colonel
59: The Big Fisherman
The Shaggy Dog
60: 7 Thieves
The Man on the String

61: The Devil at 4 O'Clock
65: China (narr. doc.)

Frank Scully
1945: Along Came Jones
Boston Blackie Booked on
Suspicion
Boston Blackie's Rendez-
vous
I Love a Bandleader
Love Letters
46: Blackie and the Law
A Close Call for Boston
Blackie
Crime Doctor's Man Hunt
Dangerous Business
The Gentleman Misbehaves
It's Great to be Young
One Way to Love
The Phantom Thief
Renegades
Talk about a Lady
Throw a Saddle on a Star
Out of the Depths
47: South of the Chisholm
Trail
Wild Harvest
48: Trapped by Boston Blackie
Blondie's Reward
49: Boston Blackie's Chinese
Venture
Bodyhold
Joe Palooka in The Counter-
punch

Jackie Searle (1920-
1929: Daughters of Desire   S
30: Tom Sawyer
31: Skippy
Finn and Hattie
Forbidden Adventure
Sooky
Huckleberry Finn
32: The Miracle Man
Lovers Courageous
Hearts of Humanity
33: Oliver Twist
One Year Later
The World Changes
Alice in Wonderland

1228

33: High Gear
Dangerous Crossroads
Topaze
Officer No. 13
Return of Casey Jones
34: She Was a Lady
No Greater Glory
Murder on the Blackboard
Strictly Dynamite
Peck's Bad Boy
A Wicked Woman
Great Expectations
35: Unwelcome Stranger
Ginger
36: Little Lord Fauntleroy
Gentle Julia
37: Two Wise Maids
Wild and Woolly
38: Little Tough Guy
That Certain Age
Little Tough Guys in
Society
39: Angels Wash Their Faces
40: Military Academy
My Little Chickadee
41: Glamour Boy
Small Town Deb
47: The Fabulous Dorseys
48: The Paleface

Fred Sears
1947: The Locket
West of Dodge City
The Corpse Came C.O.D.
Down to Earth
For the Love of Rusty
Law of the Canyon
Blondie's Anniversary
48: Adventures in Silverado
Blondie in the Dough
Phantom Valley
Rusty Leads the Way
Whirlwind Raiders
The Gallant Blade
49: The Blazing Trail
Boston Blackie's Chinese
Venture
Laramie
South of Death Valley
The Lone Wolf and His
Lady

50: David Harding--Counterspy
Texas Dynamo
Hoedown
Counterspy Meets Scotland
Yard
51: My True Story
Fort Savage Raider
The Big Gusher
Bonanza Town
Cyclone Fury
The Kid from Amarillo
52: The Rough Tough West
Laramie Mountains

Heather Sears (1935-
1956: Dry Rot
57: The Story of Esther
Costello (or, The Golden
Virgin)
59: Room at the Top
4 Desperate Men
60: Sons and Lovers
62: Phantom of the Opera
64: Saturday Night Out
65: Black Torment

James Seay
1940: Women Without Names
Emergency Squad
Those Were the Days
The Way of All Flesh
Queen of the Mob
Oklahoma Renegades
Golden Gloves
Northwest Mounted Police
The Son of Monte Cristo
41: The Face Behind the Mask
Mr. Celebrity
Two in a Taxi
The Kid from Texas
42: The Man from Cheyenne
Enemy Agents Meet Ellery
Queen
Time to Kill
Tramp Tramp Tramp
Home in Wyoming
Highways by Night
47: Miracle on 34th Street
Heartaches
The Secret Beyond the
Door

1229

48: The Cobra Strikes
Slippy McGee
An Innocent Affair
The Checkered Coat
The Strange Mrs. Crane
49: Red Canyon
I Cheated the Law
Prejudice
50: Military Academy with
    that 10th Avenue Gang
Union Station
Hunt the Man Down
51: Close to My Heart
The Day the Earth Stood
    Still
When the Redskins Rode
52: Brave Warrior
Models, Inc.
Voodoo Tiger
53: Problem Girls
Fort Ti
Phantom from Space
The Homesteaders
Jack McCall--Desperado
Captain John Smith and
    Pocahontas
54: Killers from Space
Captain Kidd and the
    Slave Girl
The Steel Cage
Return to Treasure Island
Vera Cruz
55: Kiss Me Deadly
56: Gun Brothers
Man in the Vault
57: Beginning of the End
The Amazing Colossal
    Man
58: Street of Darkness
The Buccaneer
60: The Threat
61: Secret of Deep Harbor
64: Whatever Happened to
    baby Jane?
69: There Was a Crooked
    Man

Dorothy Sebastian (1904-1957)
1928: Our Dancing Daughters   S
Their Hour   S

Wyoming   S
House of Scandal   S
29: The Rainbow   S
Woman of Affairs   S
Spirit of Youth   S
The Devil's Appletree   S
Unholy Night
His First Command
Spite Marriage   S
Morgan's Last Raid   S
The Single Standard   S
30: Free and Easy
Hell's Island
Ladies Must Play
Brothers
The Utah Kid
Montana Moon
Our Blushing Brides
Officer O'Brien
31: The Deceiver
Lightning Flyer
Ships of Hate
Big Gamble
32: They Never Come Back
33: Contraband
Ship of Wanted Men
37: The Mysterious Pilot (ser.)
39: Rough Riders' Round-Up
The Arizona Kid
41: Kansas Cyclone
Among the Living

Jean Seberg (1938-
1957: Saint Joan
58: Bonjour Tristesse
59: The Little Mouse that
    Roared
60: Let No Man Write My
    Epitaph
Congo Vivo
61: Breathless
The 5 Day Lover
Playtime
62: Time Out for Love
63: In the French Style
64: Lilith
65: Backfire
66: Moment to Moment
A Fine Madness
67: Road to Corinth

68: Birds of Peru
Pendulum
69: Paint Your Wagon
Total Danger
Airport
Heat Wave

Rolfe Sedan (1896-
1929: The Iron Mask   PT
Making the Grade   PT
One Hysterical Night
30: Sweethearts and Wives
32: The Devil on Deck
35: All the King's Horses
Paris in Spring
$1000 a Minute
36: Anything Goes
The Smartest Girl in Town
37: Rhythm in the Clouds
38: Bluebeard's 8th Wife
Stolen Heaven
I'll Give a Million
A Desperate Adventure
Under the Big Top
39: The Story of Vernon and
Irene Castle
Ninotchka
Juarez and Maximilian
Everything Happens at
Night
40: Laughing at Danger
41: Law of the Tropics
54: Phantom of the Rue
Morgue

George Segal (1939-
1961: The Young Doctors
62: The Longest Day
63: Act One
64: The New Interns
Invitation to a Gunfighter
65: King Rat
The Centurions
Ship of Fools
66: Who's Afraid of Virginia
Woolf?
The Last Command
The Quiller Memorandum
67: St. Valentine's Day
Massacre

68: No Way to Treat a Lady
Bye Bye, Braverman
The Runaround
69: Southern Star
Tenderly (Ital.)
The Bridge at Remagen
Loving
The Owl and the Pussycat

Vivienne Segal (1897-
1930: Viennese Nights
Song of the West
Golden Dawn
Bride of the Regiment
34: Cat and the Fiddle

Sarah Selby
1944: San Diego, I Love You
45: The Beautiful Cheat
46: Little Iodine
47: Stork Bites Man
48: Trapped by Boston Blackie
49: Beyond the Forest
53: Battle Circus
55: The McConnell Story
Battle Cry
57: An Affair to Remember
No Time to be Young
Short Cut to Hell
Stopover Tokyo
62: Moon Pilot
Tower of London
64: Taggart!
67: Don't Make Waves

Marian Seldes (1928-
1951: The Lonely Night
52: Mr. Lincoln
57: The True Story of Jesse
James
The Young Stranger
58: The Light in the Forest
59: The Big Fisherman
Crime and Punishment,
U.S.A.
65: The Greatest Story Ever
Told

William Self (1921-
1946: Decoy

47: Marshal of Cripple Creek
48: Red River
49: Father Was a Fullback
Sands of Iwo Jima
50: Breakthrough
51: The Thing
52: Pat and Mike

Elizabeth Sellars (1923-
1948: Floodtide
49: Jet Storm
50: Madeleine
52: Cloudburst
The Hunted
The Stranger in Between
53: The Gentle Gunman
54: Recoil
The Barefoot Contessa
Desiree
55: 3 Cases of Murder
Prince of Players
56: Forbidden Cargo
The Last Man to Hang
57: Decision Against Time
58: Law and Disorder
60: The Day They Robbed
the Bank of England
63: 55 Days at Peking
Never Let Go
64: The Chalk Garden
67: The Mummy's Shroud

Peter Sellers (1924-
1954: Orders Are Orders
Our Girl Friday (voice of
parrot)
55: The Man Who Never Was
(voice of Churchill)
56: The Lady Killers
57: John and Julie
The Naked Truth
58: The Smallest Show on
Earth
Tom Thumb
Up the Creek
Your Past Is Showing
Carlton Browne of the
F.O.
59: The Mouse that Roared
Big Time Operators

A Carol for Another
Christmas
60: Man in a Cocked Hat
The Catbird Seat
I'm All Right, Jack
Battle of the Sexes
61: The Millionairess
Two-Way Stretch
The Road to Hong Kong
(cameo)
62: Waltz of the Toreadors
Lolita
Trial and Error
Never Let Go
Only Two can Play
I Love Money (or, Mr.
Topaze)
63: Wrong Arm of the Law
Dock Brief
Heavens Above
64: Dr. Strangelove
The Pink Panther
The World of Henry Orient
A Shot in the Dark
65: What's New Pussycat?
66: The Wrong Box
After the Fox
67: Casino Royale
The Bobo
Woman Times 7 (Funeral
Procession seq.)
68: The Party
I Love You, Alice B.
Toklas
69: The Magic Christian

Charles Sellon (1878-
1929: Hot Stuff
Bulldog Drummond
The Gamblers
Girl in the Glass Cage
Man and the Moment
Big News
The Saturday Night Kid
The Vagabond Lover
Sweetie
Men Are Like That
30: Burning Up
Honey
Under a Texas Moon

1232

30: Social Lion
Let's Go Native
Love Among the
Millionaires
Borrowed Wives
Big Money
For the Love o' Lil
Sea Legs
Tom Sawyer
31: Man to Man
Painted Desert
Behind Office Doors
Laugh and Get Rich
Dude Ranch
Age for Love
Penrod and Sam
Tip-Off
32: The Drifter
Carnival Boat
Dark Horse
Make Me a Star
Speed Madness
Ride Him, Cowboy!
Central Park
33: Employees' Entrance
Strictly Personal
Central Airport
As the Devil Commands
34: Private Scandal
Elmer and Elsie
It's a Gift
Ready for Love
Bright Eyes
35: One Hour Late
The Casino Murder Case
Life Begins at 40
It's a Small World
Diamond Jim
Alias Mary Dow
Welcome Home
In Old Kentucky
The Devil Is a Woman

Harry Semels
1933: Drum Taps
Young Blood
King of the Wild Horses
The Thrill Hunter
34: Down to Their Last Yacht
35: Revenge Rider

Les Miserables
Sons of Steel
36: Under Two Flags
The Gay Desperado
37: Hotel Haywire
Swing it, Professor!
38: Blockade
39: King of the Turf
Overland Mail
43: Chance of a Lifetime

Jacques Sernas (1925-
1950: Barrier of the Law
The Golden Salamander
53: L'Envers du Paradis
The Lure of Sila
Luxury Girls
55: Jump into Hell
Helen of Troy
Maddalena
59: Sign of the Gladiator
60: Nights of Lucretia Borgia
The Goddess of Love
61: La Dolce Vita
62: The Loves of Salamambo
Son of Spartacus
63: The Huns
The Centurions
Duel of the Titans
55 Days at Peking
The Slave
64: Goliath and the Vampires
66: The Balearic Caper

Jean Servais (1910-
1931: Criminal
36: La Valse Eternelle
47: La Danse de Mort
48: Une si Jolie Petite Place
51: Le Plaisir
55: Rififi
58: Les Jeux Dangereux
He Who Must Die
59: Heroes and Sinners
Tamango
61: Dangerous Hideaway
62: The World in My Pocket
The Gentle Art of Murder
(The Spider's Web seq.)
64: That Man from Rio

1233

66: Lost Command
67: Every Man Is My Enemy
68: Seated at His Right
Better a Widow (Ital.)
69: They Came to Rob Las
Vegas

Almira Sessions
1937: A Family Affair
40: Little Nellie Kelly
Chad Hanna
41: She Knew All the Answers
Sun Valley Serenade
3 Girls About Town
Sullivan's Travels
43: The Ox-Bow Incident
My Kingdom for a Cook
The Heat's On
44: The Miracle of Morgan's
Creek
Henry Aldrich's Little
Secret
Dixie Jamboree
45: Fear
She Wouldn't Say Yes
The Southerner
The Woman Who Came
Back
46: Diary of a Chambermaid
Do You Love Me?
The Missing Lady
47: Monsieur Verdoux
For the Love of Rusty
48: Arthur Takes Over
Apartment for Peggy
The Bishop's Wife
49: Night Unto Night
Roseanna McCoy
The Fountainhead
50: The Old Frontier
52: Oklahoma Annie
56: The Scarlet Hour
Calling Homicide
68: Rosemary's Baby
69: The Boston Strangler
Do Not Go Gentle Into
the Night
Tick, Tick, Tick

Pilar Seurat
1961: The Young Savages
7 Women from Hell
Battle at Bloody Beach

Johnny Seven
1958: Cop Hater
59: The Last Mile
60: Guns of the Timberland
The Apartment
The Music Box Kid
61: The Boy Who Caught a
Crook
65: The Greatest Story Ever
Told
66: What Did You Do in the
War, Daddy?
Navajo Run
67: Gunfight at Abilene
The Destructors
69: Hangmen from Hell
The Love God

Anne Seymour (1909-
1949: All the King's Men
51: The Whistle at Eaton Falls
57: 4 Boys and a Gun
Man on Fire
58: Handle with Care
The Gift of Love
Desire Under the Elms
60: Home from the Hill
Pollyanna
The Subterraneans
All the Fine Young
Cannibals
61: Misty
64: Good Neighbor Sam
Stage to Thunder Rock
Where Love Has Gone
65: Mirage
66: Blindfold
Waco
67: How to Succeed in Business
Without Even Trying
Fitzwilly
68: Stay Away, Joe!

Dan Seymour (1915-
1942: Bombs over Burma
Road to Morocco
Casablanca
43: Tahiti Honey
Tiger Fangs
44: To Have and Have Not
45: Confidential Agent
46: Cloak and Dagger
A Night in Casablanca
47: Hard Boiled Mahoney
Philo Vance's Gamble
Slave Girl
Intrigue
48: Key Largo
Johnny Belinda
Highway 13
49: Trail of the Yukon
51: The Blue Veil
52: Mara Maru
Rancho Notorious
Glory Alley
Face to Face
53: The System
Second Chance
Tangier Incident
54: Human Desire
55: Abbott & Costello Meet
the Mummy
Moonfleet
56: Beyond a Reasonable
Doubt
57: The Buster Keaton Story
The Sad Sack
Undersea Girl
59: Watusi
The Return of the Fly

Sara Shane
1954: Magnificent Obsession
Sign of the Pagan
55: Daddy Long Legs
56: 3 Bad Sisters
The King and 4 Queens
57: Affair in Havana
59: Tarzan's Greatest
Adventure

Harry Shannon (1890-1964)
1930: Heads Up

40: Young As You Feel
City of Chance
Young Tom Edison
Parole Fixer
Tear Gas Squad
The Sailor's Lady
One Crowded Night
Too Many Girls
Tugboat Annie Sails Again
Gambling on the High
Seas
Girl from Avenue A
41: Citizen Kane
The Saint in Palm Springs
42: The Lady Is Willing
This Gun for Hire
The Falcon Takes Over
In Old California
The Big Street
Mrs. Wiggs of the
Cabbage Patch
Once Upon a Honeymoon
43: Idaho
Someone to Remember
Song of Texas
Gold Town
Alaska Highway
Headin' for God's Country
True to Life
44: The Sullivans
The Eve of St. Mark
The Yellow Rose of Texas
Ladies of Washington
The Mummy's Ghost
When the Lights Go On
Again
45: Captain Eddie
Crime, Inc.
Within These Walls
46: I Ring Doorbells
The Last Crooked Mile
Night Editor
San Quentin
47: The Devil Thumbs a Ride
The Farmer's Daughter
Nora Prentiss
The Red House
Time Out of Mind
Dangerous Years
Exposed

47: The Invisible Wall
48: Lady from Shanghai
    Fighting Father Dunne
    Mr. Blanding Builds His
    Dream House
    Feudin', A-Fussin', an'
    A-Fightin'
49: Rustlers
    Champion
    The Devil's Henchmen
    Mary Ryan, Detective
    Tulsa
    Mr. Soft Touch
50: Tarnished
    The Whipped
    Singing Nuns
    Cow Town
    Curtain Call at Cactus
    Creek
    Where Danger Lives
    3 Little Words
    The Killer that Stalked
    New York
    The Flying Missile
    Hunt the Man Down
51: Pride of Maryland
    Al Jennings of Oklahoma
    The Scarf
52: Boots Malone
    Flesh and Fury
    High Noon
    The Outcasts of Poker
    Flat
    Lure of the Wilderness
53: Cry of the Hunted
    Kansas Pacific
    Jack Slade
54: Witness to Murder
55: The Violent Men
    The Marauders
    The Tall Men
    At Gunpoint
56: Come Next Spring
    The Peacemaker
    Written on the Wind
57: The Lonely Man
    Duel at Apache Wells
    Hell's Crossroads
58: Man or Gun
    The Buccaneer

61: Wild in the Country
62: Gypsy

Peggy Shannon (1911-1941)
1931: The Secret Call
    Silence
    Road to Reno
    Touchdown
32: Hotel Continental
    This Reckless Age
    Society Girl
    Painted Woman
    False Faces
33: The Deluge
34: Fury of the Jungle
    Back Page
35: Night Life of the Gods
    The Fighting Lady
    The Case of the Lucky
    Legs
36: The Man I Marry
37: Youth on Parole
38: Girls on Probation
39: Blackwell's Island
    Fixer Dugan
40: Cafe Hostess
    The House Across the Bay
    Triple Justice

Omar Sharif (1924-
1959: Goha
62: Lawrence of Arabia
64: Behold a Pale Horse
    The Fall of the Roman
    Empire
65: The Yellow Rolls-Royce
    Dr. Zhivago
    Genghis Khan
66: The Poppy Is Also a
    Flower (TV)
    Marco the Magnificent
67: Night of the Generals
68: Once Upon a Time (or,
    Happy Ever After)
    Funny Girl
    More than a Miracle
69: Mackenna's Gold
    Mayerling
    The Italian Genius
    The Last Valley

69: The Horseman
The Appointment
Che!
Out of This World

Karen Sharpe
1952: Strange Fascination
Bomba and the Jungle
Girl
Army Bound
53: Mad at the World
54: The High and the Mighty
55: Man with the Gun
56: The Man in the Vault
58: Tarawa Beachhead
64: The Disorderly Orderly

William Shatner (1931-
1958: The Brothers Karamazov
61: Judgment at Nuremberg
The Explosive Generation
The Intruder
62: I Hate Your Guts!
64: The Outrage
69: Shame
Sole Survivor (TV)

Mickey Shaughnessy (1920-
1952: The Marrying Kind
Last of the Comanches
53: From Here to Eternity
55: Conquest to Space
57: Designing Woman
Slaughter on 10th Avenue
Until They Sail
Jailhouse Rock
Don't Go Near the Water
The Burglar
58: The Sheepman
Gunman's Walk
A Nice Little Bank that
Should be Robbed
59: Dont Give Up the Ship
Edge of Eternity
The Hangman
60: The Adventures of Huckle-
berry Finn
North to Alaska
Sex Kittens Go to College
College Confidential

61: Dondi
A Pocketful of Miracles
King of the Roaring
Twenties
62: How the West Was Won
64: A Global Affair
A House Is Not a Home
67: A Boy Called Nuthin' (TV)
68: Never a Dull Moment

C. Montague Shaw (1884-1968)
1932: Silent Witness
Pack Up Your Troubles
Sherlock Holmes
33: The Masquerader
The Big Brain
34: Sisters Under the Skin
Shock
35: Two Sinners
36: The Leathernecks Have
Landed
My American Wife
37: Riders of the Whistling
Skull
Parole Racket
The Frame Up
The Sheik Steps Out
A Nation Aflame
38: 4 Men and a Prayer
Little Miss Broadway
Mars Attacks the World
39: The 3 Musketeers
The Rains Came
Stanley and Livingstone
40: My Son My Son
Charlie Chan's Murder
Cruise
The Gay Caballero
41: Burma Convoy
Hard Guy
Charley's Aunt
42: Thunder Birds
45: An Angel Comes to
Brooklyn
46: Road to the Big House
47: Thunder in the Valley

Reta Shaw (1912-
1955: Picnic
57: Man Afraid

57: The Pajama Game
    All Mine to Give
58: The Lady Takes a Flyer
60: Pollyanna
61: Sanctuary
    Bachelor in Paradise
64: Mary Poppins
66: Made in Paris
    The Ghost and Mr. Chicken

    Critic's Choice
66: The Wild Angels
67: Tony Rome
    St. Valentine's Day
    Massacre
68: Live a Little, Love a
    Little
    Something for a Lonely
    Man (TV)

Robert Shaw (1927-
1951: The Lavender Hill Mob
54: Dam Busters
59: Sea Fury
62: The Valiant
64: Tomorrow at 10
    The Guest
    From Russia with Love
    The Caretakers
    The Luck of Ginger Coffey
65: Battle of the Bulge
66: A Man for All Seasons
    (OSCAR)
68: The Royal Hunt of the
    Sun
    The Birthday Party
69: Custer of the West
    Luther (TV)
    The Battle of Britain
    Figures in a Landscape

Dick Shawn (c1929-
1956: The Opposite Sex
60: Wake Me When It's Over
    The Wizard of Baghdad
63: It's a Mad Mad Mad Mad
    World
65: A Very Special Favor
66: What Did You Do in the
    War, Daddy?
    Penelope
67: Way Way Out
    The Producers
69: The Happy Ending

Victoria Shaw (1935-
1955: Cattle Station
56: The Eddy Duchin Story
59: Edge of Eternity
    The Crimson Kimono
66: To Trap a Spy
    Alvarez Kelly

Konstantin Shayne
1939: Paris Honeymoon
43: 5 Graves to Cairo
    Mission to Moscow
    For Whom the Bell Tolls
44: Passage to Marseille
    The Falcon in Hollywood
    The Man in Half Moon
    Street
    None but the Lonely Heart
    The 7th Cross
    Till We Meet Again
45: Escape in the Fog
    Her Highness and the Bell-
    boy
46: Dangerous Millions
    The Stranger
47: The Secret Life of Walter
    Mitty
    Song of Love
    Christmas Eve
48: To the Victor
    Night Wind
    Cry of the City
    Angel on the Amazon
49: The Red Danube

Joan Shawlee (1929-
1952: The Marrying Kind
53: All Ashore
54: A Star Is Born
    Pride of the Blue Grass
55: Conquest of Space
    Bowery to Bagdad
57: A Farewell to Arms
59: Some Like it Hot
60: The Apartment
63: Irma la Douce

1238

36: San Francisco
37: The Road Back
The Prisoner of Zenda
It Could Happen to You
52nd Street
Live, Love, and Learn
38: Too Hot to Handle
The Great Waltz
39: Broadway Serenade
Joe and Ethel Turp Call
on the President
40: The Blue Bird
Friendly Neighbors
41: Ziegfeld Girl
42: Tish
43: Hitler's Hangman
Crime Doctor
44: Atlantic City

Moira Shearer (1926-
1948: Red Shoes
52: Tales of Hoffman
53: The Story of 3 Loves
55: The Man Who Loved
Redheads
59: Peeping Tom
62: Black Tights

Norma Shearer (1904-
1929: The Trial of Mary Dugan
The Last of Mrs. Cheyney
Hollywood Revue of 1929
30: Let Us be Gay
The Divorcee (OSCAR)
Their Own Desire
31: A Free Soul
Strangers May Kiss
Private Lives
32: Smilin' Through
Strange Interlude
34: Rip Tide
The Barretts of Wimpole
Street
36: Romeo and Juliet
37: Marie Antoinette
39: Idiot's Delight
The Women
40: Escape
42: Her Cardboard Lover
We Were Dancing

Johnny Sheffield (1932-
1939: Tarzan Finds a Son
Babes in Arms
40: Little Orvie
Lucky Cisco Kid
Knute Rockne--All
American
41: Million Dollar Baby
Tarzan's Secret Treasure
42: Tarzan's New York
Adventure
43: Tarzan Triumphs
Tarzan's Desert Mystery
44: The Great Moment
Our Hearts Were Young
and Gay
Wilson
The Man in Half Moon
Street
45: Roughly Speaking
Tarzan and the Amazons
46: Tarzan and the Leopard
Woman
47: Tarzan and the Huntress
49: Bomba, the Jungle Boy
50: Bomba on Panther Island
The Lost Volcano
Bomba and the Hidden City
51: The Lion Hunters
Bomba and the Elephant
Stampede
52: African Treasure
Bomba and the Jungle Girl
53: Safari Drums
54: The Golden Idol
The Killer Leopard
55: Lord of the Jungle
56: The Black Sheep

Reginald Shefield (1901-1957)
1928: Adorable Cheat
Sweet 16
30: The Green Goddess
Old English
31: Partners of the Trail
34: The House of Rothschild
Of Human Bondage
35: Cardinal Richelieu
Black Sheep
Society Fever

35:	Splendour		Notorious Sophie Land
37:	Another Dawn		Shoot the Works
38:	Female Fugitive		Limehouse Blues
	The Buccaneer		Kiss and Make Up
40:	Earthbound		Mrs. Wiggs of the
41:	Suspicion		Cabbage Patch
42:	Eyes of the Night		Wagon Wheels
43:	Tonight We Raid Calais	35:	Enter Madame
	Bomber's Moon		Ladies Should Listen
44:	The Great Moment		Home on the Range
	The Man in Half Moon		Behold My Wife
	Street		Car No. 99
45:	Captain Kidd		Rocky Mountain Mystery
46:	3 Strangers		The Glass Key
	Centennial Summer		The Crusades
48:	Kiss the Blood Off My		Fighting Youth
	Hands		Blood of Courage
49:	Mr. Belvedere Goes to		Mississippi
	College	36:	Sing Me a Love Song
	Prison Warden	37:	The Great O'Malley
53:	Second Chance		Black Legion
56:	23 Paces to Baker Street		Footloose Heiress
	The Secret of Treasure		San Quentin
	Mountain		Wine, Women, and Horses
57:	The Story of Mankind	38:	Alcatraz Island
58:	The Buccaneer		Little Miss Thoroughbred
			The Patient in Room 18

Gene Sheldon

1945:	Where Do We Go From		She Loved a Fireman
	Here?		Mystery House
	The Dolly Sisters		The Cowboy from Brooklyn
51:	Golden Girl		Angels with Dirty Faces
54:	3 Ring Circus		A Letter of Introduction
60:	Toby Tyler		Broadway Musketeers
	The Sign of Zorro	39:	They Made Me a Criminal
61:	Babes in Toyland		Dodge City
			Naughty but Nice
			Indianapolis Speedway

Jon Shepodd

1955:	The Return of Jack Slade		Winter Carnival
56:	Attack!		Angels Wash Their Faces
57:	Dragon Wells Massacre	40:	It All Came True
	Oregon Passage		Castle on the Hudson
			Torrid Zone
			They Drive by Night

John Sheppard: see Shepperd Strudwick

		City for Conquest
	41:	Honeymoon for Three

Ann Sheridan (1916-1967)

1933:	Bolero		Navy Blues
34:	Come on, Marines!		The Man Came to Dinner
	Murder at the Vanities		Kings Row
		42:	Juke Girl
			George Washington Slept
			Here

42: The Animal Kingdom
    Wings for the Eagle
43: Edge of Darkness
    Thank Your Lucky Stars
44: Shine on Harvest Moon
    The Doughgirls
46: One More Tomorrow
47: Nora Prentiss
    The Unfaithful
48: Good Sam
49: Silver River
    I Was a Male War Bride
50: Woman on the Run
    Stella
52: Steel Town
    Just Across the Street
53: Take Me to Town
    Appointment in Honduras
56: Come Next Spring
    The Opposite Sex
57: Woman and the Hunter

Lowell Sherman (1885-1934)
1929: Evidence
    General Crack
30: Mammy
    Ladies of Leisure
    He Knew Women
    Midnight Mystery
    Lawful Larceny
    Oh Sailor, Behave!
    Pay Off
31: Bachelor Apartment
    Royal Bed
    High Stakes
32: The Greeks Had a Word
    for Them
    What Price Hollywood?
    False Faces

Ransom Sherman
1943: Swing Your Partner
47: Yankee Fakir
    The Bachelor and the
    Bobby-Soxer
    Always Together
    A Gentleman's Agreement
48: Are You With It?
    Winter Meeting
    Countess of Monte Cristo

    Whiplash
49: One Last Fling
    Flaming Fury
    Always Leave Them
    Laughing
50: Pretty Baby

Vincent Sherman (1906-
1934: Speed Wings
    One Is Guilty
    Hell Bent for Love
    Girl in Danger
    The Crime of Helen
    Stanley
    Midnight Alibi

Gale Sherwood
1947: Song of My Heart
48: Rocky

Roberta Sherwood (1912-
1963: The Courtship of Eddie's
    Father

George Shibata
1959: Pork Chop Hill
60: Hell to Eternity
    The Wackiest Ship in the
    Army
63: The Ugly American
66: Around the World Under
    the Sea

Arthur Shields (1900-
1932: Sign of the Cross
36: The Plough and the Stars
39: Drums Along the Mohawk
40: The Long Voyage Home
    Little Nellie Kelly
41: Lady Scarface
    The Gay Falcon
    How Green Was My Valley
    Confirm or Deny
42: Broadway
    This Above All
    Pacific Rendezvous
    Gentleman Jim
    The Black Swan
    Nightmare
43: Lassie Come Home

43: The Man from Down
    Under
44: Keys of the Kingdom
    National Velvet
    Youth Runs Wild
45: Roughly Speaking
    The Corn Is Green
    Too Young to Know
    The Valley of Decision
46: Three Strangers
    Gallant Journey
    The Verdict
47: The Shocking Miss
    Pilgrim
    Easy Come, Easy Go
    The Fabulous Dorseys
    7 Keys to Baldpate
48: Fighting Father Dunne
    Tap Roots
    My Own True Love
49: The Fighting O'Flynn
    Challenge to Lassie
    Red Light
    She Wore a Yellow Ribbon
50: Tarzan and the Slave Girl
51: The People Against
    O'Hara
    Apache Drums
    Sealed Cargo
    Blue Blood
    A Wonderful Life
    The Barefoot Mailman
52: The Quiet Man
53: Scandal at Scourie
    South Sea Woman
54: Pride of the Blue Grass
    The World for Ransom
56: The King and 4 Queens
57: The Daughter of Dr.Jekyll
58: Enchanted Island
59: Night of the Quarter Moon
60: For the Love of Mike
62: The Pigeon that Took
    Rome

James Shigeta (1933-
1959: The Crimson Kimono
60: Walk Like a Dragon
61: Cry for Happy
    Bridge to the Sun
    Flower Drum Song

66: Paradise--Hawaiian Style
67: Nobody's Perfect
68: Escape to Mindinao

Teru Shimada
1932: Night Club Lady
33: Midnight Club
34: 4 Frightened People
36: Revolt of the Zombies
    The White Legion
49: Tokyo Joe
50: Emergency Wedding
54: The Bridges at Toko-Ri
    The Snow Creature
55: House of Bamboo
56: Navy Wife
    Battle Hymn
59: Battle of the Coral Sea
    Tokyo After Dark
60: The Wackiest Ship in the
    Army
65: King Rat
66: Walk, Don't Run!
    One Spy Too Many
67: You Only Live Twice
69: Maharlika

Joanna Shimkus (1943-
1967: Paris Vu Par The Guest
68: Boom!
    Zita
    Ho!
    Six in Paris (Montpartnasse
    et Lavallois seq.)
69: The Lost Man
    The Virgin and the Gypsy
    Privilege

Nina Shipman
1959: Say One for Me
    Blue Denim
    The Oregon Trail
60: High Time

Anne Shirley (1918-
1928: Mother Knows Best   PT
29: Sins of the Fathers   S
30: City Girl
31: Rich Man's Folly
32: Three on a Match

1243

32: Young America   Bill Shirley
So Big   1941: Rookies on Parade
Purchase Price   Doctors Don't Tell
33: The Life of Jimmy Dolan   Sailors on Leave
a short   Ice-Capades Revue
34: Private Lessons   42: Hi, Neighbor!
Picture Palace   Flying Tigers
a short   44: 3 Little Sisters
The Key   52: I Dream of Jeanie
Anne of Green Gables   Abbott & Costello Meet
35: School for Girls   Captain Kidd
Chasing Yesterday   53: Sweethearts on Parade
Steamboat 'Round the Bend
36: Chatterbox   Ann Shoemaker (1891-
M'Liss   1934: Dr. Monica
Make Way for a Lady 35: The Woman in Red
37: Too Many Wives   Stranded
Meet the Missus   A Dog of Flanders
Stella Dallas   Alice Adams
38: Condemned Women 36: Sins of Man
Mother Carey's Chickens 37: Shall We Dance?
Law of the Underworld   Life of the Party
A Man to Remember   Stella Dallas
Girls' School   39: Romance of the Redwoods
39: Boy Slaves   They All Come Out
Sorority House   Babes in Arms
Career   40: My Favorite Wife
40: Vigil in the Night   The Farmer's Daughter
Anne of Windy Poplars   The Marines Fly High
Saturday's Children   Seventeen
41: West Point Widow   Curtain Call
All that Money can Buy An Angel from Texas
Unexpected Uncle   Strike Up the Band
4 Jacks and a Jill   Ellery Queen, Master
Here Is a Man   Detective
42: Mayor of 44th Street   The Girl from Avenue A
The Powers Girl   41: Scattergood Pulls the
43: Lady Bodyguard   Strings
Bombardier   You'll Never Get Rich
The Man from Brooklyn 43: Above Suspicion
Here Comes the Bride 44: Man from Frisco
Government Girl   Mr. Winkle Goes to War
Cocktails for Two   30 Seconds over Tokyo
44: Man from Frisco   45: What a Blonde!
Music in Manhattan   Conflict
45: Pan-Americana   47: Magic Town
Murder My Sweet (or, 48: The Return of the Whistler
Farewell My Lovely)   Sitting Pretty
49: Make Mine Laughs   Wallflower

49: A Woman's Secret
Shockproof
50: The House by the River
60: Sunrise at Campobello
66: The Fortune Cookie

Dinah Shore (1917-
1943: Thank Your Lucky Stars
44: Belle of the Yukon
Follow the Boys
Up in Arms
46: Make Mine Music
Till the Clouds Roll By
47: Fun and Fancy Free
52: Aaron Slick from Pun'kin
Crick

Roberta Shore (1942-
1959: The Shaggy Dog
Blue Denim
60: Because They're Young
Strangers When we Meet
61: The Young Savages
62: Lolita

Antrim Short
1937: The Big Show
Artists and Models

Gertrude Short (1902-1968)
1934: Love Birds
The Key
St. Louis Kid
35: Helldorado
Woman Wanted
Affairs of Susan
37: Park Avenue Logger
Stella Dallas
38: Tip-Off Girls

Max Showalter [Casey Adams]
(1917-
1949: Always Leave Them
Laughing
52: With a Song in My Heart
What Price Glory?
My Wife's Best Friend
53: Miagara
Destination Gobi
Dangerous Crossing

Vicki
54: Night People
Naked Alibi
Down Three Dark Streets
55: Return of Jack Slade
56: The Indestructible Man
Never Say Goodbye
Bus Stop
57: Dragoon Wells Massacre
The Monster that Challenged
the World
Designing Woman
58: Female Animal
Voice in the Mirror
The Naked and the Dead
59: It Happened to Jane
60: Elmer Gantry
61: Return to Peyton Place
Summer and Smoke
62: The Music Man
Bon Voyage!
63: My Six Loves
Move Over, Darling!
64: Fate Is the Hunter
Sex and the Single Girl
65: How to Murder Your Wife
66: Lord Love a Duck
69: A Talent in Loving

Lee Shumway (1884-
1928: Hit of the Show   PT
29: The Leatherneck   PT
Evangeline   PT
So This Is College?
Night Parade
30: Lone Star Ranger
Show Girl in Hollywood
Sweet Mamas
Sante Fe Trail
Widow from Chicago
32: Partners
34: The Lemon Drop Kid
Girl o' My Dreams
35: The Mysterious Mr. Wong
Million Dollar Baby
Hard Rock Harrigan
Outlawed Guns
The Ivory-Handled Gun
Frisco Waterfront
36: The Preview Murder
Mystery

36: Song of the Trail
Go Get 'em Haines
37: Hollywood Cowboy
Windjammer
Hollywood Round-Up
A Nation Aflame
Night Club Scandal
38: Outlaws of the Prairie
Rawhide
Spawn of the North
Painted Desert
Buffalo Bill Rides Again
41: 2-Gun Sheriff
Prairie Schooners
Murder by Invitation
42: Arizona Terrors
Jesse James, Jr.
Priorities on Parade
43: Dead Man's Gulch
45: Oregon Trail
46: Angel on My Shoulder
Roll on Texas Moon
47: Buffalo Bill Rides Again

George Sidney (1878-1945)
1928: The Cohens and the Kellys
in Paris   S
The Flying Romeos   S
Give and Take   SSE
29: The Cohens and the Kellys
in Atlantic City   PT
30: The Cohens and the Kellys
in Scotland
Around the Corner
31: Caught Cheating
32: High Pressure
The Cohens and the Kellys
in Hollywood
33: The Cohens and the Kellys
in Trouble
34: Rafter Romance
Manhattan Melodrama
35: Diamond Jim
37: Good Old Soak

Sylvia Sidney (1910-
1929: Through Different Eyes
31: Nice Women
That Old-Fashioned Girl
Crossroads

Many a Slip
Bad Girl
Street Scene
Her Dilemma
Confessions of a Coed
An American Tragedy
32: Ladies of the Big House
5 Minutes from the
Station
The Miracle Man
Merrily We Go to Hell
Madame Butterfly
If I Had a Million
Make Me a Star
33: Pick Up
Jennie Gerhardt
34: Good Dame
30 Day Princess
35: Behold My Wife!
Accent on Youth
Mary Burns--Fugitive
36: Trail of the Lonesome
Pine
Fury
37: Sabotage (or, A Woman
Alone)
You Only Live Once
Dead End
38: City Streets
You and Me
39: One Third of a Nation
41: The Wagons Roll at Night
45: Blood on the Sun
46: Mr. Ace
The Searching Wind
47: Love from a Stranger
The Stray Lamb
52: Les Miserables
55: Violent Saturday
56: Behind the High Wall

Simone Signoret (1921-
1942: Bolero
45: Le Couple Ideal
Les Demons de L'Aube
46: Macadam
47: Fantomas
Dedee D'Anvers
48: Guerriers dans L'Ombre
L'Impasse Les Deux Anges

48: Maneges
49: Swiss Tour
    La Ronde
    Against the Wind
50: Ombre and Lumiere
52: Casque D'Or
53: Therese Raquin
55: Les Diaboliques
56: Witches of Salem
57: The Adulteress
58: The Day and the Hour
    The Crucible
59: Room at the Top (OSCAR)
    Time Running Out
60: Dedee
62: Back Streets of Paris
    Term of Trial
63: The Naked Autumn
64: Sweet and Sour
    Today We Live
65: Ship of Fools
    Love a La Carte
66: The Sleeping Car Murder
    Is Paris Burning?
67: The Deadly Affair
68: Games
    Le Joli Mai
69: The Seagull
    Dragees au Poivre
    L'Americain
    The World, My Wilderness

Milton Sills (1882-1930)
1929: His Captive Woman   PT
    Love and the Devil   SSE
30: Man Trouble
    The Sea Wolf

Henry Silva (1928-
1952: Viva Zapata!
56: Crowded Paradise
57: The Tall T
    A Hatful of Rain
58: The Bravados
    The Law and Jake Wade
    Ride a Crooked Trail
59: Green Mansions
    The Jayhawkers
60: Ocean's 11
    Cinderfella

62: The Manchurian Candidate
    Sergeants 3
63: Johnny Cool
    A Gathering of Eagles
64: The Secret Invasion
65: The Return of Mr. Moto
66: The Reward
    The Plainsman
67: Matchless
    Hail, Mafia!
    A River of Dollars
    The Hills Run Red
68: Never a Dull Moment

Frank Silvera (1914-
1951: Fear and Desire
    The Cimarron Kid
52: Viva Zapata!
    The Fighter
    The Miracle of Our Lady
        of Fatima
55: Killer's Kiss
56: Crowded Paradise
58: The Bravados
59: Crime and Punishment,
        U. S. A.
60: The Mountain Road
    Key Witness
62: Mutiny on the Bounty
63: Toys in the Attic
65: The Greatest Story Ever
        Told
66: The Appaloosa
67: Hombre
    St. Valentine's Day Massacre
68: Guns of the Magnificent 7
    Betrayal
    The Stalking Moon
    Up Tight!
69: Che!

Jay Silverheels (c1920-
1947: Captain From Castile
48: Fury at Furnace Creek
    The Prairie
    Singing Spurs
    Yellow Sky
    Key Largo
49: Sand
    Lust for Gold

49: The Feathered Serpent
    For Those Who Dare
    Laramie
    Trail of the Yukon
    The Cowboy and the
      Indians
50: Broken Arrow
51: Red Mountain
52: Brave Warrior
    Battle of Apache Pass
    The Will Rogers Story
    Yankee Buccaneer
    The Pathfinder
53: Jack McCall--Desperado
    The Nebraskan
    War Arrow
54: Saskatchewan (or,
      O'Rourke of the Royal
      Mounted)
    4 Guns to the Border
    The Black Dakotas
    Drums Across the River
    Masterson of Kansas
55: The Vanishing American
56: The Lone Ranger
    Walk the Proud Land
58: Return to Warbow
    The Lone Ranger and the
      Lost City of Gold
59: Alias Jesse James
66: Indian Paint
69: Smith!
    True Grit
    The Phynx

Phil Silvers (1911-
1940: Hit Parade of 1941
41: The Penalty
    Tom, Dick, and Harry
    You're in the Army Now
    Wild Man of Borneo
    Lady be Good
    Ice-Capades Revue
42: Roxie Hart
    My Gal Sal
    Footlight Serenade
    Just Off Broadway
    All Through the Night
43: Coney Island
    A Lady Takes a Chance

44: Cover Girl
    4 Jills in a Jeep
    Something for the Boys
    Take It or Leave It
45: Diamond Horseshoe
    Don Juan Quilligan
    Where Do We Go from
      Here?
    A 1000 and One Nights
46: If I'm Lucky
50: Summer Stock
54: Top Banana
    Lucky Me
62: 40 lbs of Trouble
63: It's a Mad Mad Mad Mad
      World
66: The Oscar
    A Funny Thing Happened
      on the Way to the Forum
67: A Guide for the Married
      Man
68: Follow that Camel!
69: Buona Sera, Mrs. Campbell

Sid Silvers (1908-
Collaborated on writing plus
acting*
1929: Show of Shows
30: Oh Sailor, Behave!
      (co-writ.)
    Follow the Leader
    Dancing Sweeties
33: My Weakness
34: Bottoms Up*
    Transatlantic Merry-Go-
      Round
    Kentucky Kernels*
35: Broadway Melody of '36*
36: Walking on Air*
    Born to Dance*
37: Broadway Melody of '38*
    52nd Street (co-writ.)
39: The Gorilla
42: The Fleet's In
    For Me and My Gal
46: Mr. Ace

Alastair Sim (1900-
1934: The Riverside Murder
35: The Private Secretary

1248

35: A Fire Has Been
    Arranged
    Wedding Group
    Troubled Waters
36: Keep Your Sets, Please!
    The Man in the Mirror
    She Got What She Wanted
    Strange Experiment
    Widow's Island
    My Partner, Mr. Davis
37: Melody and Romance
    The Squealer
    Gangway
38: Sailing Along
    The Terror
    Alf's Button Afloat
    Climbing High
    This Man Is News
    Inspector Hornleigh
39: This Man in Paris
    Inspector Hornleigh on a
    Holiday
40: Lost on the Western
    Front
    Husband-in-Law
    Waterloo Bridge
41: Inspector Hornleigh Goes
    to It
    Cottage to Let
42: Let the People Sing
43: Bombsight Stolen
47: Green for Danger
    Captain Boycott
    London Belongs to Me
48: Dulcimer Street
50: Hue and Cry
    Happiest Days of Your
    Life
    Stage Fright
51: Laughter in Paradise
    Folly to be Wise
54: An Inspector Calls
55: Innocents of Paris
    Belles of St. Trinian's
56: Wee Geordie
57: Escapade
    The Green Man
58: The Doctor's Dilemma
    Blue Murder at St.
    Trinian's

60: School for Scoundrels
61: The Millionairess
    Left, Right, and Center
    The Anatomist

Jean Simmons (1929-
1944: Give Us the Moon
45: Mr. Emmanuel
    The Way to the Stars
    Sports Day
    Sexton Blake
    Kiss the Bride Goodbye
46: Caesar and Cleopatra
47: Great Expectations
    Hungry Hill
    Black Narcissus
    Uncle Silas
    Blue Lagoon
48: Hamlet
49: Woman in the Hall
    Adam and Evalyn
    (Sanatorium seq.)
51: So Long at the Fair
    Cage of Gold
    The Inheritance
52: Clouded Yellow
    Androcles and the Lion
    Angel Face
53: Young Bess
    Affair with a Stranger
    The Actress
    The Robe
54: She Couldn't Say No
    A Bullet Is Waiting
    The Egyptian
    Desiree
55: Footsteps in the Fog
    Guys and Dolls
56: Hilda Crane
57: This Could be the Night
    Until They Sail
58: Home Before Dark
    The Big Country
59: This Earth Is Mine
60: Spartacus
    Elmer Gantry
    The Grass Is Greener
61: Wild in the Country
63: All the Way Home
64: Life at the Top

66: Mr. Buddwing
67: Divorce--American Style
Rough Night at Jericho
68: Heidi (TV)
69: The Happy Ending

Richard Simmons
1942: Stand by for Action
43: The Youngest Profession
Pilot No. 5
Thousands Cheer
46: Love Laughs at Andy
Hardy
47: Lady in the Lake
Undercover Maisie
This Time for Keeps
48: On an Island with You
49: Look for the Silver
Lining
50: Duchess of Idaho
Dial 1119
51: The Well
52: I Dream of Jeanie
Glory Alley
Above and Beyond
Desperate Search
53: Battle Circus
Flight Nurse
54: Men of the Fighting Lady
55: You're Never Too Young
62: Sergeants 3
64: Robin and the 7 Hoods

Ginny Simms (1918-
1939: That's Right, You're
Wrong
40: You'll Find Out
41: Playmates
42: Here We Go Again
7 Days' Leave
43: Hit the Ice
44: Broadway Rhythm
45: Shady Lady
46: Night and Day
51: Disc Jockey

Larry Simms (1934-
1937: The Last Gangster Goes
to Washington
38: Blondie

39: Blondie Meets the Boss
Mr. Smith
Blondie Takes a Vacation
Blondie Brings Up Baby
40: Blondie on a Budget
Blondie Has Servant
Problems
Blondie Plays Cupid
41: Blondie Goes Latin
Blondie in Society
42: Blondie Goes to College
Blondie's Blessed Event
The Gay Sisters
43: Footlight Glamour
It's a Great Life
45: Leave it to Blondie
Life with Blondie
46: Blondie Knows Best
Blondie's Lucky Day
47: Blondie's Big Moment
Blondie's Anniversary
Blondie's Holiday
48: Blondie in the Dough
Blondie's Reward
49: Blondie Hits the Jackpot
Blondie's Big Deal
Madame Bovary
50: Blondie's Hero
Beward of Blondie

Robert F. Simon
1950: Where the Sidewalks End
54: The Black Dakotas
Rogue Cop
Roogie's Bump
55: 7 Angry Men
Chief Crazy Horse
The Girl in the Red
Velvet Swing
The Court-Martial of
Billy Mitchell
The Benny Goodman Story
56: The Rack
The Catered Affair
Bigger than Life
The First Traveling Sales-
lady
57: Edge of the City
Spring Reunion
58: Gunman's Walk

1250

58: The Buccaneer
59: Face of Fire
Compulsion
Operation Petticoat
The Last Angry Man
60: Pay or Die
The Facts of Life
Wizard of Baghdad
Tess of the Storm
Country
61: Ada
62: The Spiral Road
Alcatraz Express
63: Wall of Noise
A New Kind of Love
Captain Newman, M.D.
64: Fate Is the Hunter
66: Blindfold
67: The Reluctant Astronaut

Simone Simon (1914-
1931: Le Chanteur Inconnu
La Petite Chocolatière
Le Roi des Palaces
L'Etoile de Valence
Les Yeux Noires
Les Beaux Jours
34: Lac aux Dames
36: Girls' Dormitory
Ladies in Love
37: Seventh Heaven
Love and Hisses
38: Josette
Dark Eyes
39: La Bête Humaine
41: All that Money can Buy
Here Is a Man
42: The Cat People
43: Tahiti Honey
44: Johnny Doesn't Live Here
Anymore
The Silent Bell
Mademoiselle Fifi
And So They Were Married
Curse of the Cat People
49: Temptation Harbour
Lost Women
Donna Senza Nome
50: La Ronde
Pit of Loneliness

Olivia
51: Le Plaisir
54: Double Destiny
56: The Extra Day

Ivan Simpson (1875-
1934: Mystery of Mr. X
Man of Two Worlds
House of Rothschild
The World Moves On
British Agent
Among the Missing
35: Shadow of Doubt
Mark of the Vampire
David Copperfield
The Bishop Misbehaves
The Perfect Gentleman
Mutiny on the Bounty
East of Java
Splendour
Captain Blood
36: Little Lord Fauntleroy
Mary of Scotland
37: Maid of Salem
The Prince and the Pauper
London by Night
38: Invisible Enemy
The Baroness and the
Butler
Adventures of Robin Hood
39: The Hound of the Basker-
villes
Made for Each Other
Never Say Die
Rulers of the Sea
40: The Invisible Man Returns
New Moon
42: Nazi Agent
The Male Animal
They All Kissed the Bride
Youth on Parade
Random Harvest
43: This Land of Mine
2 Weeks to Live
Forever and a Day
My Kingdom for a Cook
44: The Hour Before the Dawn
Jane Eyre

1251

Russell Simpson (1880-1959)

1929: Innocents of Paris
Noisy Neighbors — PT
My Lady's Past — PT
The Kid's Clever — S
The Sap — PT
30: Lone Star Ranger
Abraham Lincoln
Barber John's Baby
Billy the Kid
Man to Man
31: The Great Meadow
Susan Lennox
32: Law and Order
Ridin' for Justice
Lena Rivers
Honor of the Press
Riding Tornado
Flames
Cabin in the Cotton
Hello Trouble!
Silver Dollar
Call Her Savage
33: Face in the Sky
Hello Everybody!
34: 3 on a Honeymoon
Carolina
The Frontier Marshal
Ever Since Eve
16 Fathoms Deep
The World Moves On
35: West of the Pecos
Motive for Revenge
The Hoosier School-
master
Way Down East
Paddy O'Day
County Chairman
36: Man Hunt
The Harvester
Girl of the Ozarks
The Crime of Dr. Forbes
Ramona
San Francisco
37: Green Light
That I May Live
Mountain Justice
Maid of Salem
Yodelin' Kid from Pine
Ridge

Wild West Days (ser.)
Paradise Isle
38: Gold Is Where You Find It
Valley of the Giants
Heart of the North
39: Dodge City
Western Caravans
Desperate Trails
Drums Along the Mohawk
40: The Grapes of Wrath
Girl of the Golden West
The Virginian
46: California Gold Rush
Virginia City
The Refugee
Brigham Young--Frontiers-
man
Santa Fe Trail
41: Tobacco Road
Citadel of Crime
Wild Geese Calling
The Last of the Duanes
Bad Men of Missouri
Swamp Water
Wild Bill Hickok Rides
42: The Lone Star Ranger
Shut My Big Mouth
The Spoilers
Tennessee Johnson
43: Border Patrol
Moonlight in Vermont
Woman of the Town
44: Texas Masquerade
Man from Frisco
45: The Big Bonanza
Along Came Jones
They Were Expendable
46: Bad Bascomb
My Darling Clementine
47: The Romance of Rosie
Ridge
The Millerson Case
Bowery Buckaroos
The Fabulous Texan
Death Valley
48: Albuquerque
My Dog Shep
Tap Roots
Coroner Creek
Sundown in Santa Fe

49: Tuna Clipper
The Gal Who Took the
West
Free for All
The Beautiful Blonde
from Bashful Bend
50: Wagonmaster
Saddle Tramp
Call of the Klondike
51: Comin' 'Round the
Mountain
Across the Wide Missouri
52: Ma and Pa Kettle at the
Fair
Lone Star
Meet Me at the Fair
Feudin' Fools
53: The Sun Shines Bright
54: Broken Lance
7 Brides for 7 Brothers
55: The Last Command
The Tall Men
56: The Brass Legend
Friendly Persuasion
57: The Tin Star
The Lonely Man
59: The Horse Soldiers

Frank Sinatra (1915-
1941: Las Vegas Nights
42: Ship Ahoy!
43: Reveille with Beverly
Higher and Higher
44: Step Lively
45: Anchors Aweigh
The House I Live In
(short)
46: Till the Clouds Roll By
47: Words and Music
It Happened in Brooklyn
48: Miracle of the Bells
The Kissing Bandit
49: Take Me to the Ball
Game
On the Town
51: Double Dynamite
52: Meet Danny Wilson
53: From Here to Eternity
(OSCAR)
54: Suddenly (or, A Town
Called Suddenly)

Young at Heart
55: Not As a Stranger
Guys and Dolls
The Tender Trap
Man with the Golden Arm
56: Johnny Concho
High Society
G.I. Woman Chasers
Around the World in 80
Days
57: The Joker Is Wild
Pride and the Passion
The Jester
Pal Joey
58: Kings Go Forth
Some Came Running
59: A Hole in the Head
Never So Few
60: Ocean's 11
Can-Can
Pepe
61: The Devil at 4 O'Clock
The Road to Hong Kong
(cameo)
62: Sergeants 3
The Manchurian Candidate
63: Come Blow Your Horn
The List of Adrian
Messenger (cameo)
A New Kind of Love (sang
title)
4 For Texas
64: Robin and the 7 Hoods
65: None but the Brave
Von Ryan's Express
66: The Oscar (cameo)
Marriage on the Rocks
Assault of a Queen
Cast a Giant Shadow
67: Tony Rome
The Naked Runner
68: The Detective
69: The Chairman
Lady in Cement
The Amigos

Frank Sinatra, Jr. (1943-
1968: A Man Called Adam

Nancy Sinatra (1940-
1964: For Those Who Think
Young

1253

64: Get Yourself a College
Girl
66: Last of the Secret Agents
65: Marriage on the Rocks
66: The Oscar
The Wild Angels
The Ghost in the
Invisible Bikini
67: You Only Live Twice
(sang Title)
Tony Rome (sang title)
68: Speedway

Ronald Sinclair (1924-
1938: A Christmas Carol
39: Tower of London
The 5 Little Peppers
The Light that Failed
40: Earl of Chicago
5 Little Peppers at Home
Out West with the Peppers
5 Little Peppers in
Trouble
41: That Hamilton Woman
42: Desperate Journey

Doris Singleton
1957: Affair in Reno
58: Voice in the Mirror

Penny Singleton (1912-
1936: After the Thin Man
37: Vogues of 1938
Sea Racketeers
38: Swing Your Lady
Men Are Such Fools
Boy Meets Girl
Garden of the Moon
Racket Busters
Hard to Get
Outside of Paradise
Secrets of an Actress
Mr. Chump
The Mad Miss Manton
Blondie
39: Blondie Meets the Boss
Blondie Takes a Vacation
Blondie Brings Up Baby
40: Blondie on a Budget
Blondie Has Servant
Problems

Blondie Plays Cupid
41: Blondie Goes Latin
Blondie in Society
Go West with Blondie
42: Blondie Goes to College
Blondie's Blessed Event
Blondie for Victory
43: Footlight Glamour
It's a Great Life
45: Leave it to Blondie
Life with Blondie
46: Young Widow
Blondie Knows Best
Blondie's Lucky Day
47: Blondie's Big Moment
Blondie's Anniversary
Blondie's Holiday
48: Blondie's in the Dough
Blondie's Reward
49: Blondie Hits the Jackpot
Blondie's Big Deal
50: Beware of Blondie
Blondie's Hero
64: The Best Man

Lilia Skala
1953: Call Me Madam
63: Lilies of the Field
65: Ship of Fools
67: Caprice
Ironside (TV)
68: Charly
The Sunshine Patriot (TV)

Hal Skelly (1891-1934)
1929: Dance of Life
Woman Trap
30: Behind the Makeup
Men Are Like That
31: The Struggle
33: Hotel Variety
Shadow Laughs

Red Skelton (1914-
1938: Having a Wonderful Time
40: Flight Command
41: Lady be Good
The People vs Dr.Kildare
Dr. Kildare's Wedding Day
Whistling in the Dark
42: Whistling in Dixie

1254

42: Ship Ahoy
    Maisie Gets Her Man
    Panama Hattie
43: Du Barry Was a Lady
    Thousands Cheer
    I Dood It!
    Whistling in Brooklyn
44: Bathing Beauty
46: Ziegfeld Follies
    The Show-Off
47: Merton of the Movies
    My Life Is Yours
    Mary Names the Day
48: The Fuller Brush Man
    A Southern Yankee
    The Red Mill
49: Neptune's Daughter
50: Yellow Can Man
    Three Little Words
    Watch the Birdie
51: Excuse My Dust
    Texas Carnival
52: Lovely To Look At
53: The Clown
    Half a Hero
    The Great Diamond
    Mystery
56: Around the World in 80
    Days
57: Public Pigeon No. 1
60: Ocean's 11 (cameo)
64: Big Parade of Comedy
    (doc.)
65: Those Magnificent Men in
    Their Flying Machines

Alison Skipworth (1875-1952)
1929: Strictly Unconventional
    The Circle
30: Oh, What a Man!
    Sporting Widow
    Raffles
    Du Barry--Woman of
    Passion
    Outward Bound
31: Devotion
    Virtuous Husbands
    Tonight or Never
    Night Angel
    Road to Singapore

32: High Pressure
    Sinners in the Sun
    Madame Racketeer
    Night After Night
    Unexpected Father
    If I Had a Million
33: He Learned About Women
    A Lady's Profession
    Tonight Is Ours
    Song of Songs
    Midnight Club
    Tillie and Gus
    Alice in Wonderland
34: Six of a Kind
    Wharf Angel
    Notorious Sophie Lang
    Here Is My Heart
    Shoot the Works
    The Captain Hates the Sea
    Coming Out Party
35: The Casino Murder Case
    The Devil Is a Woman
    Shanghai
    Becky Sharp
    Doubting Thomas
    The Girl from 10th Avenue
    Dangerous
    Hitch Hike Lady
36: The Princess Comes Across
    Satan Met a Lady
    The Gorgeous Hussy
    Two in a Crowd
    White Hunter
    Stolen Holiday
37: Two Wise Maids
38: King of the Newsboys
    Ladies in Distress
    Wide Open Faces

Cornelia Otis Skinner (1901-
1946: The Uninvited
68: The Swimmer

Jeremy Slate
1962: Girls! Girls! Girls!
63: Wives and Lovers
65: I'll Take Sweden
    The Sons of Katie Elder
67: Born Losers
    Wings of Fire

1255

68: The Mini-Skirt Mon
The Devil's Brigade
69: True Grit
Hell's Angels
Girl in the Leather Skirt
The Hooked Generation

Tod Slaughter (1885-1956)
1935: Maria Marten
36: Sweeney Todd
38: The Crimes of Stephen
Hawke
40: Crimes at the Dark House
41: The Face at the Window
43: The Curse of the Wray-
dons
48: The Greed of William
Hart
51: Never Too Late to Mend
53: The Hooded Terror

Martha Sleeper (1910-
1928: Danger Street   S
29: Taxi No. 13
Voice of the Storm
30: Our Blushing Brides
Madam Satan
War Nurse
31: 10¢ a Dance
Girls Demand Excitement
A Tailor Made Man
Confessions of a Co-Ed
32: Huddle
Rasputin and the Empress
33: Lady of the Night
Midnight Mary
Penthouse
Broken Dreams
34: Spitfire
West of the Pecos
35: Tomorrow's Youth
The Great God Gold
The Scoundrel
2 Sinners
36: Rhythm on the Range
37: 4 Days' Wonder
45: The Bells of St. Mary's

Walter Slezak (1902-
1942: Once Upon a Honeymoon

43: This Land Is Mine
The Fallen Sparrow
44: Lifeboat
And Now Tomorrow
Step Lively
Sylvester the Great
Till We Meet Again
The Princess and the
Pirate
45: Salome, Where She Danced
The Spanish Main
46: Cornered
47: Sinbad the Sailor
Born to Kill
Riffraff
48: The Pirate
49: The Inspector General
50: Yellow Cab Man
Abbott & Costello in the
Foreign Legion
Spy Hunt
51: Bedtime for Bonzo
People Will Talk
53: Confidentially Connie
Call Me Madam
White Witch Doctor
54: The Steel Cage
57: 10,000 Bedrooms
Deadlier than the Male
59: The Miracle
60: The Gazebo
61: Come September
62: The Wonderful World of
the Brothers Grimm
63: Wonderful Life
64: Emil and the Detectives
Swinger's Paradise
65: A Very Special Favor
24 Hours to Kill
67: Caper of the Golden Bulls
68: Heidi (TV)

Everett Sloane (1910-1965)
1941: Citizen Kane
42: Journey Into Fear
48: Lady from Shanghai
49: Prince of Foxes
50: The Men
51: Bird of Paradise
The Enforcer

51: Sirocco
The Blue Veil
Murder, Inc.
The Prince Who Was a
Thief
52: The Sellout
53: Way of a Gaucho
55: The Big Knife
56: Patterns
Somebody Up There Likes
Me
Lust for Life
Massacre at Sand Creek
58: Marjorie Morningstar
The Gun Runners
60: Home from the Hill
61: By Love Possessed
62: Brushfire!
63: The Man from the
Diner's Club
64: The Patsy
The Disorderly Orderly
Ready for the People

Phillips Smalley (1875-19?)
1929: True Heaven
High Voltage
30: Peacock Alley
Midnight Special
Charley's Aunt
31: Lawless Woman
High Stakes
Lady from Nowhere
32: The Greeks Had a Word
for Them
Murder at Dawn
Hell's Headquarters
Escapade
Sinister Hands
Widow in Scarlet
Face on the Barroom
Floor
33: Midnight Warning
Cocktail Hour
34: The Big Race
Bolero
Stolen Sweets
Madame Du Barry
35: Night Life of the Gods
All the King's Horses

Hold 'em, Yale!
It's in the Air
37: Hotel Haywire

Alexis Smith (1921-
1940: Lady with Red Hair
41: The Smiling Ghost
Dive Bomber
Passage from Hong Kong
Flight from Destiny
Steel Against the Sky
42: Gentleman Jim
43: Thank Your Lucky Stars
The Constant Nymph
The Animal Kingdom
44: Hollywood Canteen
The Adventures of Mark
Twain
The Doughgirls
45: The Horn Blows at Mid-
night
Rhapsody in Blue
Conflict
San Antonio
46: One More Tomorrow
Night and Day
Of Human Bondage
47: Stallion Road
The Two Mrs. Carrolls
48: Woman in White
Decision of Christopher
Blake
Whiplash
49: South of St. Louis
Any Number can Play
One Last Fling
50: Undercover Girl
Wyoming Mail
Montana
51: Here Comes the Groom
Cave of the Outlaws
52: The Turning Point
53: Split Second
54: The Sleeping Tiger
55: The Eternal Sea
57: Beau James
58: This Happy Feeling
59: The Young Philadelphians

C. Aubrey Smith (1863-1948)
1931: Bachelor Father
Dancing Partner
Never the Twain Shall
Meet
Just a Gigolo
Man in Possession
Guilty Hands
Daybreak
Son of India
Surrender
Polly of the Circus
Phantom of Paris
32: Tarzan the Ape Man
But the Flesh Is Weak
Love Me Tonight
No More Orchids
33: They Just Had to Get
Married
The Barbarian
Adorable
Luxury Liner
Secrets
Morning Glory
Bombshell
Queen Christina
The Monkey's Paw
34: House of Rothschild
Bulldog Drummond
Strikes Back
One More River
Cleopatra
Caravan
Curtain at 8
Madame Du Barry
The Firebird
Gambling Lady
35: The Gilded Lily
Right to Live
Clive of India
The Scarlet Empress
Lives of a Bengal Lancer
The Crusades
The Florentine Dagger
China Seas
Jalna
Transatlantic Tunnel
36: Little Lord Fauntleroy
Garden of Allah
Romeo and Juliet

Lloyds of London
37: Wee Willie Winkie
The Prisoner of Zenda
The Hurricane
Thoroughbreds Don't Cry
38: 4 Men and a Prayer
Kidnapped
60 Glorious Years
39: East Side of Heaven
The Sun Never Sets
The Under-Pup
4 Feathers
5 Came Back
Eternally Yours
Another Thin Man
Balalaika
40: A Bill of Divorcement
City of Chance
Beyond Tomorrow
Queen of Destiny
Rebecca
Waterloo Bridge
A Little Bit of Heaven
41: Maisie Was a Lady
Free and Easy
Dr. Jekyll and Mr. Hyde
43: Forever and a Day
2 Tickets to London
Madame Curie
Flesh and Fantasy
44: The White Cliffs of Dover
Secrets of Scotland Yard
Sensations of 1945
The Adventures of Mark
Twain
45: Forever Yours (or, They
Shall Have Faith)
Scotland Yard Investigator
And Then There Were
None
46: Rendezvous with Annie
Cluny Brown
47: High Conquest
Unconquered
48: An Ideal Husband
49: Little Women

Charles Smith
1938: Boys Town
40: The Shop Around the
Corner

1258

40: Tom Brown's School Days
41: Cheers for Miss Bishop
Adventure in Washington
Henry Aldrich for
President
42: Henry and Dizzy
The Major and the Minor
Youth on Parade
Henry Aldrich, Editor
43: Henry Aldrich Gets
Glamour
Henry Aldrich Swings It
A Guy Named Joe
Henry Aldrich Haunts a
House
44: Henry Aldrich, Boy Scout
Henry Aldrich's Little
Secret
Henry Aldrich Plays Cupid
Wing and a Prayer
San Fernando Valley
Lady in the Dark
45: God Is My Co-Pilot
Out of this World
46: Three Little Girls in
Blue
Wake Up and Dream
47: The Trouble with Women
Joe Palooka in The
Knockout
Out of the Blue
2 Blondes and a Redhead
48: Campus Honeymoon
49: Adventure in Baltimore
50: 2 Weeks with Love
A Modern Marriage
51: Rhythm Inn
67: The Gnome-Mobile

Constance Smith (1930-
1947: Brighton Rock
The Gay Lady (or,
Trottie True)
Now Barabbas
Murder at the Window
49: Blackmail
50: The Mudlark
Room to Let
The Perfect Woman

51: The 13th Letter
I'll Never Forget You
Lucky Nick Cain
52: Red Skies on Montana
Lure of the Wilderness
53: Taxi!
Treasure of the Golden
Condor
54: The Man in the Attic
55: The Big Tip-Off
58: Cross Up

Ethel Smith (1921-
1944: Bathing Beauty
45: George White's Scandals
Twice Blessed
46: Cuban Pete
Easy to Web
48: Melody Time
67: C'mon, Let's Live a
Little

Hal Smith
1952: O. Henry's Full House
(The Last Leaf seq.)
58: Hot Car Girl
60: The Apartment
62: The 3 Stooges Meet
Hercules
64: Hey There, It's Yogi Bear!
(cartoon voice)
Dear Heart
65: The Great Race
66: The Ghost and Mr.
Chicken
69: Archy and Mehitable
(voice)
A Yellowstone Christmas
(voice)

John Smith (1931-
1952: No Holds Barred
54: The High and the Mighty
55: 7 Angry Men
We're No Angels
Wichita
Desert Sands
Ghost Town
56: The Bold and the Brave

1259

56: Quincannon, Frontier
    Scout
    Rebel in Town
    Friendly Persuasion
    Women of Pitcairn Island
57: Tomahawk Trail
    Fury at Sundown
    The Kettles on Old Mac-
    Donald's Farm
    The Lawless '80s
    The Crooked Circle
58: Handle with Care
59: Island of Lost Women
64: Circus World
66: Waco

Keely Smith (1932-
1958: Thunder Road
    Senior Prom
59: Hey Boy! Hey Girl!

Kent Smith (1907-
1936: The Garden Murder Case
39: Back Door to Heaven
42: The Cat People
43: Forever and a Day
    Hitler's Children
    This Land Is Mine
    3 Russian Girls
44: Youth Runs Wild
    The Curse of the Cat
    People
46: The Spiral Staircase
47: Nora Prentiss
    Magic Town
48: Voice of the Turtle
    Design for Death (narr.)
49: The Fountainhead
    My Foolish Heart
50: The Damned Don't Cry
    This Side of the Law
52: Paula
56: Comanche
57: Sayonara
58: The Badlanders
    Imitation General
    Party Girl
    The Muggers
59: This Earth Is Mine
60: Strangers When We Meet

61: Susan Slade
62: Moon Pilot
63: The Balcony
64: Youngblood Hawke
    A Distant Trumpet
    The Young Lovers
66: The Trouble with Angels
67: A Covenant with Death
    The Games
68: Kona Coast
    The Money Jungle
69: Death of a Gunfighter
    Assignment to Kill

Maggie Smith (1934-
1959: Nowhere to Go
63: The V.I.P's
64: The Pumpkin-Eater
65: Othello
    Young Cassidy
67: It Comes Up Murder (or,
    Honey Pot)
68: Hot Millions
    The Prime of Miss Jean
    Brodie
69: Oh! What a Lovely War

Queenie Smith (1898-
1935: Mississippi
36: Showboat
39: On Your Toes
46: From this Day Forward
    The Killers
    Nocturne
47: The Long Night
48: Sleep My Love
    The Snake Pit
50: The Great Rupert
    Prisoners in Petticoats
51: The First Legion
55: My Sister Eileen
56: Hot Shots
    You Can't Run Away with
    It
    Fighting Trouble
57: Sweet Smell of Success
68: The Legend of Lylah Clare

Roger Smith (1932-
1957: No Time to be Young

58: Auntie Mame
64: Those Who Think Young
68: Up the Junction
69: Beginners 3
    Operation Cross Eagles

Eric Snowden
1934: Shock
36: Forbidden Heaven
54: Jungle Gents

Leigh Snowden (1932-
1955: Kiss Me Deadly
    Francis in the Navy
    All that Heaven Allows
    The Square Jungle
56: Outside the Law
    The Creature Walks
      Among Us
    I've Lived Before
57: Hot Rod Rumble

Snowflake [Fred Toones]
1934: Murder in the Private Car
    Lady by Chance
35: Stolen Property
    Ladies Love Danger
    Valley of Wanted Men
    Riddle Ranch
36: Frontier Justice
    Hair-Trigger Casey
    Hell-Ship Morgan
    The Lawless '90s
    Desert Justice
    Born to Fight
    The Singing Cowboy
    The Gorgeous Hussy
    College Holiday
    The Lonely Trail
37: Range Defenders
    The Duke Comes Back
38: Wild Horse Rodeo
    Hawaiian Buckaroo
    Under the Big Top
40: Seventeen
    Remember the Night
    The Biscuit Eater
    One Man's Law
    The Tulsa Kid
    Texas Terrors

    Frontier Vengeance
41: 2-Gun Sheriff
    The Apache Kid
    Death Valley Outlaws
    A Missouri Outlaw
42: Queen of Broadway
44: Yellow Rose of Texas
    Firebrands of Arizona
    Hidden Valley Outlaws
46: Fool's Gold
47: Bells of San Angelo

Abraham Sofaer (1896-
1931: Dreyfus
36: Rembrandt
40: Crook's Tour
46: A Matter of Life and Death
51: Quo Vadis?
53: His Majesty O'Keefe
54: The Naked Jungle
    Elephant Walk
56: Bhowani Junction
    King of Kings
    The First Texan
57: Omar Khayyam
    The Story of Mankind
    The Sad Sack
62: Taras Bulba
63: Captain Sinbad
    Twice Told Tales
65: The Greatest Story Ever
      Told
68: Head
69: Che!

Sojin (1891-1954)
1929: 7 Footsteps to Satan   SSE
    China Slaver   S
    Careers   PT
    Unholy Night
    Show of Shows
30: Back from Shanghai
    Golden Dawn
    Dude Wrangler

Vladimir Sokoloff (1890-1962)
1930: West Front 1918
32: L'Atlantide
35: Mayerling
37: The Life of Emile Zola

37: Expensive Husbands
    The Prisoner of Zenda
    West of Shanghai
    Conquest
    Beg, Borrow, or Steal
38: The Amazing Dr. Clitter-
    house
    Arsene Lupin Returns
    Alcatraz Island
    Blockade
    Spawn of the North
    Ride a Crooked Mile
39: Juarez
    The Real Glory
40: Comrade X
41: Love Crazy
42: Crossroads
    Road to Morocco
43: Mission to Moscow
    For Whom the Bell Tolls
    Song of Russia
44: Passage to Marseilles
    Till We Meet Again
    The Conspirators
45: Back to Bataan
    The Blonde from Brooklyn
    Paris Underground
    A Royal Scandal
    Scarlet Street
46: Cloak and Dagger
    A Scandal in Paris
    Two Smart People
48: To the Ends of the Earth
50: The Baron of Arizona
52: Macao
57: Istanbul
    I Was a Teenage Werewolf
    Sabu and the Magic Ring
60: Confessions of a Counter-
    spy
    Man on a String
    Beyond the Time Barrier
    The Magnificent 7
    Cimarron
61: Mr. Sardonicus
    The 3 Penny Opera
62: Taras Bulba

Julie Sommars
1965: The Great Sioux Massacre
  66: The Pad and How to Use It

Elke Sommer (1941-
1959: The Day It Rained
  63: The Victors
      The Prize
  64: Love Italian Style
      A Shot in the Dark
      Why Bother to Knock?
  65: The Art of Love
      Most Dangerous Game
      The Dolls (Treatise on
      Eugenics seq.)
      Bambole!
  66: Friend of the Jaguar
      The Oscar
      Traveling Luxury
      Heaven and Cupid
      Ship of Dead
      Boy, Did I Get a Wrong
      Number!
      Frontier Hellcat
  67: Deadlier than the Male
      The Corrupt Ones
      The Venetian Affair
  68: The Wicked Dreams of
      Paula Schultz
      The Wrecking Crew
  69: The House of 7 Joys
      The Heroes
      They Came to Rob Las
      Vegas

Joanie Sommers
1961: Everything's Ducky
  64: The Lively Set

Gale Sondergaard (1900-
1936: Anthony Adverse (OSCAR)
  37: Maid of Salem
      7th Heaven
      The Life of Emile Zola
  38: Lord Jeff
      Dramatic School
      Sons of Liberty (short)
  39: Juarez
      The Life of Hjam Solomon
      Never Say Die
      The Cat and the Canary
  40: The Llano Kid
      The Blue Bird
      The Mark of Zorro
      The Letter

1262

41: The Black Cat
     Paris Calling
42: My Favorite Blonde
     Enemy Agents Meet
     Ellery Queen
43: Appointment in Berlin
     A Night to Remember
     Isle of Forgotten Sins
     The Strange Death of
       Adolph Hitler
44: Sherlock Holmes and the
       Spider Woman
     The Prisoner of Japan
     The Climax
     Follow the Boys
     The Invisible Man's
       Revenge
     Gypsy Wildcat
     Christmas Holiday
     Enter Arsene Lupin
45: A Night in Paradise
46: Anna and the King of Siam
     The Spider Woman
       Strikes Back
     The Time of Their Lives
     The Ghost Steps Out
47: The Road to Rio
     The Pirates of Monterey
49: East Side, West Side
69: The Slaves

Sons of the Pioneers and
Bob Nolan
1939: Western Caravans
     Riders of the Black River
     Outposts of the Mounties
     The Stranger from Texas
40: 2-Fisted Ranger
     Blazing 6 Shooters
     Bullets from Rustlers
     West of Abilene
41: The Pinto Kid
     Outlaws of the Panhandle
     Red River Valley
42: South of Santa Fe
     The Man from Cheyenne
     Romance of the Range
     Sons of the Pioneers
     Call of the Canyon
     Sunset Serenade

       Heart of the Golden West
43: King of the Cowboys
     Idaho
     Song of Texas
     Silver Spurs
     The Man from Music
       Mountain
     Hands Across the Border
44: Light of Old Santa Fe
     The Cowboy and the
       Senorita
     Hollywood Canteen
     San Fernando Valley
     Song of Nevada
     Yellow Rose of Texas
45: Along the Navajo Trail
     Bells of Rosarita
     Don't Fence Me In
     Home on the Range
     The Man from Oklahoma
     Sunset in Eldorado
46: Ding Dong Williams
     Home in Oklahoma
     My Pal Trigger
     Texas Moon
     Rainbow over Texas
     Roll on Texas Moon
     Song of Arizona
     Under Nevada Skies
47: Helldorado
     Bells of San Angelo
     Hit Parade of 1947
     Springtime in the Sierras
     On the Old Spanish Trail
48: Melody Time
     The Gay Ranchero
     Under California Stars
     Eyes of Texas
     Night Time in Nevada
50: Rio Grande
62: Legend of Lobo (voices)

Jack Soo (1934-
1961: The Flower Drum Song
63: Who's Been Sleeping in My
       Bed?
66: The Oscar
67: Thoroughly Modern Millie
68: The Green Berets

Ann Sothern (1911-
1934: Let's Fall in Love
       Melody in Spring
       Hell Cat
       Blind Date
       The Party's Over
       Kid Millions
35:    Folies Bergère
       8 Bells
       Hooray for Love
       Grand Exit
       The Girl Friend
       Her Sacrifice
       The Ghost Walks
36:    Panic in the Air
       Don't Gamble with Love
       Hell-Ship Morgan
       You May be Next
       My American Wife
       Walking on Air
       Smartest Girl in Town
37:    Dangerous Number
       50 Roads to Town
       There Goes My Gal
       Super Sleuth
       There Goes the Groom
       Danger! Love at Work
38:    She's Got Everything
       Trade Winds
39:    Maisie
       Fast and Furious
       Joe and Ethel Turp Call
         on the President
       Elsa Maxwell's Hotel for
         Women
40:    Congo Maisie
       Gold Rush Maisie
       Dulcy
       Brother Orchid
41:    Maisie Was a Lady
       Lady be Good
       Ringside Maisie
42:    Maisie Gets Her Man
       Panama Hattie
43:    3 Hearts for Julia
       Swing Shift Maisie
       Cry Havoc
       Thousands Cheer
44:    Maisie Goes to Reno
46:    Up Goes Maisie

47:    Undercover Maisie
       Indian Summer
48:    April Showers
       A Letter to 3 Wives
       Words and Music
       Death in the Doll's House
49:    The Judge Steps Out
50:    Nancy Goes to Rio
       Shadow on the Wall
53:    Blue Gardenia
64:    Lady in a Cage
       The Best Man
65:    Sylvia
67:    The Outsider (TV pilot)
68:    Chubasco

Olan Soulé
1951: Cuban Fireball
53:    Destination Big House
       Call Me Madam
54:    Dragnet
       Human Desire
55:    Prince of Players
       Daddy Long Legs
       Queen Bee
65:    Girl Happy
67:    The Bubble
68:    The Destructors

Catherine Spaak (1945-
1963: The Easy Life
       18 in the Sun
64:    Of Wayward Love
       The Empty Canvas
       Crazy Desire
65:    The Little Nuns
       Circle of Love
       Malamondo
66:    Weekend at Dunkirk
67:    The Hotel
       The Liar
       I Don't Make Love--I Make
         War
       Made in Italy
68:    Drop Dead, My Love!
       The Matriarch
       The Libertine
       The Man with the Balloons
69:    The Matriarch (Ital.)
       A Rather Complicated Girl
         (Ital.)

69: Switchboard Girls

Arthur Space
1941: Riot Squad
  42: Quiet Please, Murder
    Tortilla Flat
  43: Whistling in Brooklyn
    The Dancing Masters
  44: The Big Noise
    The Ghost Walks Alone
    Wilson
  45: Abbott & Costello in
    Hollywood
    Leave Her to Heaven
    Our Vines Have Tender
    Grapes
  46: Black Beauty
    Boys Ranch
    The Cockeyed Miracle
    Home in Oklahoma
    Mysterious Mr. Valentine
  47: The Guilt of Janet Ames
    Millie's Daughter
    The Red House
    Secret of the Whistler
    The Crimson Key
    Her Husband's Affairs
    Rustlers of Devil's
    Canyon
    Big Town After Dark
    I Love Trouble
    The Invisible Wall
  48: The Fuller Brush Man
    Silver River
    Fighter Squadron
    A Southern Yankee
  49: Mr. Belvedere Goes to
    College
    The Lone Wolf and His
    Lady
    Miss Grant Takes Rich-
    mond
  50: Mary Ryan, Detective
    Father Is a Bachelor
    The Vanishing Westerner
    The Fuller Brush Girl
    The Good Humor Man
  51: Night Riders of Montana
    Her First Romance
    Tomahawk

    The Barefoot Mailman
    Utah Wagon Train
  52: Sound Off!
    Rainbow 'Round My
    Shoulder
    African Treasure
    Fargo
    Here Come the Marines
    Feudin' Fools
  53: Confidentially Connie
    Back to God's Country
    Last of the Pony Riders
    Missile Base at Taniak
  54: Yankee Pasha
    Target: Earth
  55: Foxfire
    The Claw Monsters
    A Man Alone
  57: The Spirit of St. Louis
    20 Million Miles to Earth
  58: Twilight for the Gods
  59: Day of the Outlaw
  60: Gunfighters of Abilene
  64: Taggart!
  68: The Shakiest Gun in the
    West

Fay Spain
1957: The Crooked Circle
    The Abductors
    Teenage Doll
  58: God's Little Acre
  59: Al Capone
    The Beat Generation
  60: The Private Lives of
    Adam and Eve
  63: Black Gold
    Thunder Island
    Hercules and the Captive
    Women
  64: Flight to Fury
  66: The Gentle Rain
  67: Welcome to Hard Times
  69: The Grove

Ned Sparks (1884-1957)
1928: The Big Noise   S
  29: Nothing but the Truth
    The Canary Murder Case
    Strange Cargo

29: Street Girl
30: Love Comes Along
Double Cross Roads
The Devil's Holiday
Fall Guy
Conspiracy
Leathernecking
31: The Iron Man
Secret Call
Corsair
Kept Husbands
32: The Miracle Man
Big City Blues
Blessed Event
The Crusader
33: Gold Diggers of 1933
Lady for a Day
Too Much Harmony
Alice in Wonderland
Going Hollywood
42nd Street
Secrets
34: Hi Nellie!
35: Private Scandal
Marie Galante
Imitation of Life
Sing and Like It
Down to Their Last Yacht
Operator 13
Servants' Entrance
Sweet Adeline
Sweet Music
George White's Scandals
of 1935
36: Collegiate
The Bride Walks Out
One in a Million
37: Wake Up and Live
This Way, Please
38: Hawaii Calls
39: The Star Maker
Two's Company
41: For Beauty's Sake
43: Stage Door Canteen
47: Magic Town

Randy Sparks
1958: Thunder Road
60: The Big Night
College Confidential

Camilla Sparv (1943-
1964: 18 in the Sun
66: Trouble with Angels
Dead Heat on a Merry-Go-
Round
67: Murderers' Row
Assignment K
68: High Commissioner
Nobody Runs Forever
69: Mackenna's Gold
The Downhill Racers

G.D. Spradlin (c1925-
1968: Will Penny
69: Number One
Colossus
Zabriskie Point
Tora! Tora! Tora!
Hell's Angels
Monte Walsh

Ronald Squire (1886-1958)
1944: Don't Take it to Heart
46: While the Sun Shines
48: Woman Hater
50: The Rocking Horse Winner
52: Encore
53: My Cousin Rachel
54: Always a Bride
The Man with a Million
Scotch on the Rocks
55: Now and Forever
Footsteps in the Fog
56: Around the World in 80
Days
57: Raising a Riot
Island in the Sun
Sea Wife
The Silent Affair
58: Law and Disorder
Inn of the 6th Happiness
59: Count Your Blessings

Robert Stack (1919-
1939: First Love
40: When the Daltons Rode
The Mortal Storm
A Little Bit of Heaven
41: Nice Girl?
Badlands of Dakota

42: To Be or Not to Be
Eagle Squadron
A Date with Judy
Miss Tatlock's Millions
49: John Paul Jones
50: Mr. Music
51: The Bullfighter and the
Lady
My Brother, the Outlaw
52: Bwana Devil (3-D)
53: War Paint
Conquest of Cochise
Sabre Jet
54: The Iron Glove
The High and the Mighty
55: House of Bamboo
Good Morning, Miss Dove
56: Great Day in the Morning
Written on the Wind
57: The Tarnished Angels
Pylon
58: The Gift of Love
59: Guns of Zangara
60: The Last Voyage
62: The Alcatraz Express
The Scarface Mob
63: The Caretakers
66: Is Paris Burning?
67: The Corrupt Ones
68: The Story of a Woman
69: Angel, Angel, Down We
Go

Hanley Stafford (1899-1968)
1951: Lullaby of Broadway
52: Here Come the Marines
Just This Once
A Girl in Every Port
53: The Affairs of Dobie
Gillis
55: The Go-Getter

Joan Staley
1961: The Ladies' Man
Dondi
Gun Fight
Valley of the Dragons
62: Cape Fear
Belle Sommers
63: A New Kind of Love

Johnny Cool
64: Roustabout
66: Gunpoint
67: The Ghost and Mr.
Chicken

Terence Stamp (1939-
1962: Billy Budd
63: Term of Trial
65: The Collector
66: Modesty Blaise
67: Far from the Madding
Crowd
68: Blue
Poor Cow
Theorem
69: Spirits of the Dead
For the First Time
Toby Dammit
The Mind of Mr. Soames

Lionel Stander (c1908-
1935: The Scoundrel
Page Miss Glory
The Gay Deception
We're in the Money
Hooray for Love
I Live My Life
If You Could Only Cook
36: The Music Goes Round
Mr. Deeds Goes to Town
Meet Nero Wolfe
I Loved a Soldier
More than a Secretary
The Milky Way
Soak the Rich
They Met in a Taxi
37: League of Frightened Men
A Star Is Born
The Last Gangster
38: No Time to Marry
Professor Beware
The Crowd Roars
39: The Ice Follies of 1939
What a Life!
41: The Bride Wore Crutches
43: Guadalcanal Diary
Tahiti Honey
Hangmen Also Die
45: The Big Show-Off

46: A Boy, a Girl, and a Dog
Spectrer of the Rose
In Old Sacramento
The Kid from Brooklyn
Gentleman Joe Palooka
47: Mad Wednesday (or, The
Sin of Harold Diddlebock)
48: Texas, Brooklyn, and
Heaven
Call Northside 777
Unfaithfully Yours
Trouble Makers
51: 2 Gals and a Guy
St. Benny the Dip
63: The Moving Finger
65: The Loved One
66: Promise Her Anything
Cul de Sac
67: Gates to Paradise
A Dandy in Aspic
The Outrider
68: Once Upon a Time in
the West
7 Times 7
The Right Girls
69: Once Upon a Time in
America
They Shoot Horses, Don't
They?

Sir Guy Standing (1873-1937)
1933: The Story of Temple
Drake
Midnight Club
Hell and High Water
The Cradle Song
A Bedtime Story
The Eagle and the Hawk
34: Death Takes a Holiday
Now and Forever
The Witching Hour
Imitation of Life
Double Door
35: Lives of a Bengal Lancer
Car 99
Annapolis Farewell
The Big Broadcast of
1936
36: Return of Sophie Lang

Palm Springs
I'd Give My Life
37: Lloyds of London
Bulldog Drummond
Escapes

Wyndham Standing (1880-
1929: Widscomb Fair   S
30: Billy the Kid
Hell's Angels
32: Silent Witness
33: A Study in Scarlet
Design for Living
34: Limehouse Blues
35: Clive of India
36: Mary of Scotland
Beloved Enemy
39: Rulers of the Sea
Bulldog Drummond's
Secret Police
Man in the Iron Mask
47: The Private Affairs of
Bel Ami

Arnold Stang (1925-
1945: Let's Go Steady
48: So This Is New York
51: 2 Gals and a Guy
55: The Man with the Golden
Arm
61: Dondi
Alakazam the Great!
(cartoon voice)
62: The Wonderful World
of the Brothers Grimm
63: It's a Mad Mad Mad Mad
World
65: Pinocchio in Outer Space
(voice)
68: Skidoo!
69: Hello, Down There!

Kim Stanley (1925-
1958: The Goddess
64: Seance on a Wet Afternoon
66: 3 Sisters
69: UMC

Paul Stanton
1934: The Most Precious Thing
in Life

34: Wednesday's Child
35: Strangers All
    Whipsaw
    Let 'em Have It!
    Red Salute
    Another Face
36: It Had to Happen
    Every Saturday Night
    Charlie Chan at the Circus
    Sins of Man
    Half Angel
    The Crime of Dr. Forbes
    Road to Glory
    Poor Little Rich Girl
    Private Number
    Sing, Baby, Sing
    The Longest Night
    Dimples
    Career Woman
    Crack-Up
    Night Waitress
37: Midnight Taxi
    A Star Is Born
    It Could Happen to You
    Youth on Parole
    Danger! Love at Work
    Portia on Trial
    Paid to Dance
    City Girl
38: Rascals
    Law of the Underworld
    Kentucky Moonshine
    My Lucky Star
    Army Girl
39: The Story of Alexander
      Graham Bell
    Rose of Washington
      Square
    Bachelor Mother
    Stronger than Desire
    20,000 Men a Year
    The Star Maker
    Hollywood Cavalcade
    Stanley and Livingstone
40: The Man Who Wouldn't
      Talk
    And One Was Beautiful
    Queen of the Mob
    I Love You Again
41: The People vs Dr.
      Kildare

The Big Store
Whistling in the Dark
Night of January 16th
Midnight Angel
42: The Magnificent Dope
    Across the Pacific
43: Slightly Dangerous
    Air Raid Wardens
    So's Your Uncle
44: Allergic to Love
    Mr. Winkle Goes to War
    Once Upon a Time
45: She Gets Her Man
46: Crime of the Century
    Hit the Hay
    Holiday in Mexico
    Shadow of a Woman
47: That's My Gal
    Welcome Stranger
    Cry Wolf
    Her Husband's Affairs
    My Wild Irish Rose
48: Here Comes Trouble
49: The Fountainhead
52: Jet Job

Barbara Stanwyck (1907-
1929: The Locked Door
      Mexicali Rose
30: Ladies of Leisure
    Voice of Hollywood (short)
31: 10¢ a Dance
    Illicit
    Forbidden
    Night Nurse
32: So Big
    Purchase Price
    Jewel Robbery
    Shopworn
33: The Bitter Tea of General
      Yen
    Brief Moment
    Ladies They Talk About
    Baby Face
    Ever In My Heart
34: Lost Lady
    Gambling Lady
35: Secret Bride
    Woman in Red
    Annie Oakley
36: A Message to Garcia

Barbara Stanwyck and Ray Milland

36: Banjo on My Knee
The Bride Walks Out
His Brother's Wife
37: The Plough and the Stars
Breakfast for Two
Interns Can't Take Money
This Is My Affair
Stella Dallas
38: Always Goodbye
The Mad Miss Manton
39: Union Pacific
Golden Boy
40: Remember the Night
41: Meet John Doe
The Lady Eve
Ball of Fire
You Belong to Me
42: The Great Man's Lady
The Gay Sisters
43: Lady of Burlesque
Flesh and Fantasy
44: Hollywood Canteen
Double Indemnity
45: Hollywood Victory
Caravan
Christmas in Connecticut
46: The Bride Wore Boots
My Reputation
The Strange Love of
Martha Ivers
California
47: The Other Love
The Two Mrs. Carrolls
Variety Girl
Cry Wolf
48: B. F.'s Daughter
Sorry, Wrong Number!
49: The Lady Gambles
East Side, West Side
Thelma Jordan
Eyes of Hollywood (short)
50: The Furies
No Man of Her Own
To Please a Lady
51: The Man with a Cloak
52: Clash by Night
53: Jeopardy
All I Desire
Titanic
Blowing Wild

The Moonlighter
54: Executive Suite
Witness to Murder
Cattle Queen of Montana
55: The Violent Men
Escape to Burma
56: There's Always Tomorrow
The Maverick Queen
These Wilder Years
57: Crime of Passion
Trooper Hook
40 Guns
61: Sanctuary
62: Walk on the Wild Side
64: The Night Walker
Roustabout
The Molly Kincaid Story

Jean Stapleton
1960: Bells Are Ringing
61: Something Wild
67: Up the Down Staircase

Maureen Stapleton (1925-
1959: Lonelyhearts
60: The Fugitive Kind
62: A View from the Bridge
63: Bye Bye, Birdie
69: Airport
Cold Turkey

Pauline Starke (1900-
1929: Man, Woman, and Wife
The Viking
30: Royal Romance
What Men Want
35: $20 a Week

Ringo Starr (1940-
1968: Candy
69: The Magic Christian
The Impotent
See also: The Beatles

Charles Starrett (1904-
1930: Fast and Loose
The Royal Family of
Broadway
31: Damaged Love
Start Cheering

1271

31: The Viking
Silence
Age of Love
Touchdown
32: Sky Bride
The Mask of Fu Manchu
Lady and Gent
33: Mr. Skitch
Jungle Bride
Our Betters
Return of Casey Jones
Sweetheart of Sigma Chi
34: Silver Streak
Gentlemen Are Born
One in a Million
Call it Luck
Transient Love
This Man Is Mine
Stolen Sweets
Three on a Honeymoon
Green Eyes
A Girl Must Live
Desirable
Gun Law
35: So Red the Rose
Sons of Steel
A Shot in the Dark
Make a Million
One New York Night
What Price Crime?
36: Along Came Love
Secret Patrol
The Gallant Avenger
Mysterious Defender
Stampede
37: Shooting Showdown
2-Gun Law
38: Swingtime in the Saddle
Law of the Plains
Call of the Rockies
Cattle Raiders
West of Cheyenne
Colorado Trail
South of Arizona
Outlaws of the Prairie
Start Cheering
39: West of Santa Fe
Spoilers of the Range
Western Caravans
The Man from Sundown

Riders of Black River
Outpost of the Mounties
Stranger from Texas
40: Bullets for Rustlers
Blazing Six-Shooters
2-Fisted Rangers
Texas Stagecoach
West of Abilene
The Durango Kid
Thundering Frontier
41: Outlaws of the Panhandle
The Pinto Kid
The Medico of Painted
  Springs
Thunder over the Prairie
Prairie Stranger
42: West of Tombstone
Lawless Plainsmen
Down Rio Grande Way
Riders of the Northland
Bad Men of the Hills
Overland to Deadwood
43: Riding Through Nevada
Fighting Buckaroo
Heroes of the Sagebrush
Texas Rifles
Cowboy in the Clouds
Pardon My Gun
Law of the Northwest
Robin Hood of the Range
Hail to the Rangers!
44: Sundown Valley
Cowboy Canteen
Riding West
Sagebrush Heroes
Cyclone Prairie Rangers
Cowboy from Lonesome
  River
Saddle Leather Law
45: Blazing the Western Trail
Both Barrels Blazing
Lawless Empire
Outlaws of the Rockies
Return of the Durango Kid
Rough Ridin' Justice
Rustlers of the Badlands
46: The Desert Horseman
Fighting Frontiersman
Frontier Gun Law
Galloping Thunder

46: Gunning for Vengeance
Land Rush
Roaring Rangers
2-Fisted Stranger
Heading West
Texas Panhandle
47: Lone Hand Texan
Terror Trail
West of Dodge City
Law of the Canyon
Prairie Raiders
South of the Chisholm Trail
Riders of the Lone Star
The Stranger from Ponca
City
48: Buckaroos from Powder
River
Last Days of Boot Hill
Phantom Valley
6-Gun Law
West of Sonora
Whirlwind Raiders
Trail to Laredo
Blazing Across the Pecos
49: Blazing Trail
Challenge of the Range
Desert Vigilante
El Dorado Pass
Horsemen of the Sierras
Laramie
South of Death Valley
Quick on the Trigger
50: Outcast of Black Mesa
Texas Dynamo
Trail of the Rustler
Streets of Ghost Town
Across the Badlands
Raiders of Tomahawk
Lightning Guns
51: Riding the Outlaw Trail
Prairie Roundup
Snake River Desperadoes
Fort Savage Raiders
Bonanza Town
Cyclone Fury
The Kid from Amarillo
Pecos River
52: Smoky Canyon
The Hawk of Wild River
The Kid from Broken
Gun

The Rough Tough West
Junction City
Laramie Mountains

Myrtle Stedman (1888-1938)
1930: The Lummox
The Love Racket
Truth about Youth
32: Widow in Scarlet
Alias Mary Smith
Forbidden Company
33: One Year Later
34: Beggars in Ermine
School for Girls
36: Song of the Saddle
Gambling with Souls
37: Green Light

Anthony Steel (1920-
1948: Saraband for Dead Lovers
50: The Wooden Horse
The Mudlark
51: Laughter in Paradise
The Ivory Hunters
52: Outpost in Malaya
Encore
53: Master of Ballantrae
Something Money Can't
Buy
Albert, RN
54: 100 Hour Hunt
The Malta Story
55: West of Zanzibar
The Sea Shall Not Have
Them
Break for Freedom
56: Storm over the Nile
Passage Home
57: Checkpoint
The Black Tent
Out of the Clouds
Valerie
58: Harry Black and the Tiger
62: The Tiger of the 7 Seas
63: The Switch
66: Honeymoon
Hell Is Empty
68: Rabbit in the Pit (Ger.)
Anzio

Barbara Steel (1938-

1958: Bachelor of Hearts
59: Sapphire
60: The Devil's Mask
61: The Pit and the Pendulum
62: The Horrible Mr.
     Hitchcock
63: 8 1/2
    The Castle of Terror
64: The Spectre
65: The Revenge of the Blood
    Beast (or, Sister of
    Satan)
    The Hours of Love
66: Nightmare Castle
68: Terror Creatures from
    the Grave
    The Crimson Altar

Bob Steele (1907-

1928: Man in the Rough   S
      Spirit of Youth   S
      Driftin' Sands   S
      Crooks Can't Win   S
      Riding Renegade   S
      Breed of the Sunsets   S
      Captain Careless   S
      Lightning Speed   S
      Headin' for Danger   S
      Trail of Courage   S
  29: Laughing at Death   S
      The Invaders   SSE
      Come and Get It   S
      The Amazing Vagabond   S
  30: Breezy Hill   S
      Land of Missing Men
      Oklahoma Cyclone
      Near the Rainbow's End
      Headin' North
      The Cowboy and the
        Outlaw
      Hunted Men
      Texas Cowboy
      Western Honor
      The Man from Nowhere
  31: Ridin' Fool
      Sunrise Trail
      Nevada Buckaroo
  32: Law of the West
      South of Santa Fe

Near the Trail's End
Riders of the Desert
The Man from Hell's Edges
Son of Oklahoma
Texas Buddies
Hidden Valley
The Fighting Champ
33: Young Blood
    Breed of the Border
    California Trail
    Trailin' North
    The Gallant Fool
    Rangers' Code
    Galloping Romeo
34: Demon for Trouble
    Mystery Squadron (ser.)
    Brand of Fate
35: Powdersmoke Range
    Kid Courageous
    No Man's Range
    Big Calibre
    Rider of the Law
    The Ridin' Fool
    Alias John Law
36: Cavalry
    The Kid Ranger
    Sundown Saunders
    Trail of Terror
    Brand of Outlaws
    Last of the Warrens
    Arizona Gunfighter
37: Border Phantom
    Doomed at Sundown
    Gun Lords of Stirrup
      Basin
    The Red Rope
    Ridin' the Lone Trail
    The Trusted Outlaw
    The Gun Ranger
    The Colorado Kid
    Lightnin' Crandall
38: Desert Patrol
    Thunder in the Desert
    Paroled to Die
39: Of Mice and Men
    Smoky Trail
    El Diablo Rides
40: The Carson City Kid
    Under Texas Skies
    The Trail Blazers

1274

40:	Lone Star Raiders
41:	The Great Train Robbery
	Billy the Kid's Fighting Pals
	Prairie Schooners
	Pals of the Pecos
	Saddlemates
	Gangs of Sonora
	Outlaws of Cherokee Trail
	Gauchos of Eldorado
	West of Cimmaron
42:	Prairie Pioneers
	Code of the Outlaws
	Raiders of the Range
	Westward Ho!
	The Phantom Plainsmen
	Valley of Haunted Men
43:	Shadows on the Sage
	Blocked Trail
	Riders of the Rio Grande
	Santa Fe Scouts
	Revenge of the Zombies
44:	Sonora Stagecoach
	Westward Bound
	The Utah Kid
	Outlaw Trail
	Marked Trails
	Arizona Whirlwind
	Trigger Law
45:	Navajo Kid
	Northwest Trail
46:	Thunder Town
	Gun Man
	Sheriff of Redwood Valley
	The Big Sleep
	Rio Grande Raiders
	Ambush Trail
47:	6 Guns for Hire
	Twilight on the Rio Grande
	Exposed
	Killer McCoy
	Bandits of Dark Canyon
	Cheyenne
49:	South of St. Louis
50:	The Savage Horde
51:	Silver Canyon
	Cattle Drive
	The Enforcer

52:	Rose of Cimarron
	The Lion and the Horse
53:	Savage Frontier
	San Antone
	Column South
	Island in the Sky
54:	Drums Across the River
	The Outcast
55:	Fighting Chance
56:	Steel Jungle
	Pardners
57:	Gun for a Coward
	Duel at Apache Wells
	The Parson and the Outlaw
58:	Once Upon a Horse
	Giant from the Unknown
59:	Rio Bravo
	Pork Chop Hill
	The Atomic Submarine
60:	Hell Bent for Leather
61:	The Comancheros
62:	The Wild Westerners
	6 Black Horses
64:	Bullet for a Badman
	Taggart!
65:	The Bounty Killer
	Requiem for a Gunfighter
	Outlaw Trail
	Town Tamer
68:	Hang 'em High
69:	The Great Bank Robbery

Karen Steele (1934-
1954:	Man Crazy
55:	Marty
56:	Toward the Unknown
	The Sharkfighters
57:	Bailout at 43,000
	Decision at Sundown
59:	Ride Lonesome
	Westbound
60:	The Rise and Fall of Legs Diamond
63:	40 lbs of Trouble
66:	Cyborg 2087
69:	The Happy Ending
	A Boy, A Girl

Tommy Steele (1936-
1957:	Rock Around the World

58: Kill Me Tomorrow
    Satan's Satellites
    Missile Monsters
59: The Ghost of Zorro
    The Duke Wore Jeans
60: Tommy the Toreador
62: It's All Happening
64: The Dream Maker
67: The Happiest Millionaire
68: Finian's Rainbow
    Half a Sixpence
    Run, Rebel, Run
69: Where's Jack?

Larry Steers (1881-1951)
1928: Phantom Flyer   S
29: Just Off Broadway   S
    Redskin   SSE
    Wheel of Life
    In Old California
    Dark Skies
30: Let's Go Places
    The Thoroughbreds
31: Secret Call
    Grief Street
32: Two Kinds of Women
33: Cocktail Hour
36: Navy Born
38: a short
41: Riding the Wind
43: Hands Across the Border
44: Atlantic City
    The Mojave Firebrand
45: White Pongo
47: The Gangster
48: Fighting Mad

Rod Steiger (1925-
1951: Teresa
54: On the Waterfront
55: The Big Knife
    Oklahoma!
    The Court-Martial of
      Billy Mitchell
56: Jubal
    The Harder They Fall
    Back from Eternity
57: Run of the Arrow
    The Unholy Wife
    Across the Bridge

58: Cry Terror
59: Al Capone
60: 7 Thieves
61: The Mark
62: 13 West Street
    The Movie Maker (or,
      Slow Fade to Black, TV)
    Reprieve
    Hands Upon the City
    The Longest Day
63: Convicts 4
    The World in My Pocket
65: The Pawnbroker
    Dr. Zhivago
    The Loved One
    Time of Indifference
66: The Lady and the Prawler
67: The Girl and the General
    In the Heat of the Night
      (OSCAR)
68: No Way to Treat a Lady
    The Sergeant
    And There Came a Man
      (semi-doc. of Pope John
      XXIII)
69: The Illustrated Man
    Waterloo
    The Hunting Party
    The Warriors
    Galileo
    The Guilt Merchants

Anna Sten (1907-
1934: Nana
    We Live Again
35: The Wedding Night
37: Two Who Dared
38: Woman Alone
39: Exile Express
40: The Man I Married
41: So Ends Our Night
43: Chetniks
    3 Russian Girls
    They Came to Blow Up
      America
48: Let's Live a Little
55: Soldier of Fortune
56: Runaway Daughters
57: Heaven Knows, Mr. Allison
62: The Nun and the Sergeant

1276

Karel Stepanek (1899-
1943: They Met in the Dark
46: The Captive Heart
48: The Fallen Idol
50: State Secret
55: Cockleshell Heroes
64: Devil Doll
65: Operation Crossbow
66: The Second Best Agent
in the Whole Wide World
67: The Frozen Dead

Henry Stephenson (1874-1956)
1932: Cynara
Red-Headed Woman
Guilty as Hell
Bill of Divorcement
The Animal Kingdom
33: Little Women
Queen Christina
Tomorrow at 7
Double Harness
My Lips Betray
If I Were Free
Blind Adventure
34: Man of Two Worlds
The Richest Girl in the
World
30 Day Princess
Stingaree
The Mystery of Mr. X
What Every Woman Knows
One More River
Outcast Lady
She Loves Me Not
All Men Are Enemies
35: Mutiny on the Bounty
Vanessa--Her Love Story
Reckless
The Flame Within
O'Shaughnessy's Boy
The Night Is Young
Rendezvous
The Perfect Gentleman
Captain Blood
36: Beloved Enemy
Half Angel
Hearts Divided
Give Me Your Heart
Walking on Air

Little Lord Fauntleroy
Charge of the Light
Brigade
37: When You're in Love
The Prince and the Pauper
The Emperor's Candle-
sticks
Conquest
Wise Girl
38: The Young in Heart
The Baroness and the
Butler
Suez
Marie Antoinette
Dramatic School
39: Tarzan Finds a Son
The Private Lives of
Elizabeth and Essex
The Adventures of
Sherlock Holmes
40: It's a Date
Little Old New York
Spring Parade
Down Argentine Way
41: The Man Who Lost Him-
self
The Lady from Louisiana
42: This Above All
Rings on Her Fingers
43: Mr. Lucky
The Man Trap
Half Way to Shanghai
44: The Hour Before Dawn
Secrets of Scotland Yard
The Reckless Age
2 Girls and a Sailor
45: Tarzan and the Amazons
46: The Green Years
Heartbeat
Night and Day
Of Human Bondage
The Return of Monte Cristo
47: Dark Delusion
The Homestretch
The Locket
Time Out of Mind
Ivy
Song of Love
48: Julia Misbehaves
Enchantment

1277

49: Challenge to Lassie
51: Oliver Twist

James Stephenson (1903-1941)
1937: The Perfect Crime
The Man Who Made
  Diamonds
Dark Stairway
It's in the Blood
Mr. Satan
38: The Cowboy from
  Brooklyn
White Banners
Nancy Drew, Detective
Boy Meets Girl
Heart of the North
When Were You Born?
39: Confessions of a Nazi Spy
King of the Underworld
Beau Geste
Devil's Island
On Trial
Secret Service of the Air
Adventures of Jane Arden
Torchy Blane in China-
  town
The Old Maid
Private Lives of
  Elizabeth and Essex
Espionage Agent
We Are Not Alone
a short
40: Murder in the Air
Calling Philo Vance
The Sea Hawk
The Letter
Wolf of New York
River's End
A Dispatch from Reuter's
South of Suez
41: International Squadron
Shining Victory
Flight from Destiny

Step'n'fetchit (1896-
1929: Show Boat   PT
Big Time
Fox Movietome Follies
Hearts in Dixie
Salute

In Old Kentucky
The Kid's Clever
Through Different Eyes
The Galloping Ghost
Ghost Talks
30: Cameo Kirby
Swing High
Big Fight
31: The Prodigal
Neck and Neck
33: Wild Horse Mesa
34: Stand Up and Cheer
Carolina
David Harum
Judge Priest
The World Moves On
Marie Galante
Bachelor of Arts
35: County Chairman
Helldorado
One More Spring
Charlie Chan in Egypt
Steamboat 'Round the Bend
The Virginia Judge
36: 36 Hours to Kill
Dimples
37: On the Avenue
Love Is News
50 Roads to Town
39: Elephants Never Forget
Zenobia
48: Miracle in Harlem
52: Bend in the River
53: The Sun Shines Bright

Ford Sterling (1883-1939)
1929: Fall of Eve
30: Girl in the Snow
Sally
Show Girl in Hollywood
Bride of the Regiment
Kismet
31: Her Majesty Love
33: Alice in Wonderland
35: Behind the Green Lights
Headline Woman
Black Sheep

Jane Sterling (1923-
1948: Johnny Belinda

50: Union Station
The Skipper Surprised
His Wife
Caged
Mystery Street
51: Appointment with Danger
The Mating Season
The Big Carnival (or,
The Ace in the Hole)
Rhybarb
52: Flesh and Fury
A Sky Full of Moon
53: Pony Express
The Vanquished
Split Second
54: Alaska Seas
The High and the Mighty
Return from the Sea
The Human Jungle
55: Women's Prison
Female on the Beach
Man with a Gun
56: 1984
Screaming Eagles
The Harder They Fall
57: Slaughter on 10th Avenue
58: The Female Animal
High School Confidential
Kathy O'
61: Love in a Goldfish Bowl
67: The Incident
68: The Squeeze Play
The Put-On
69: The Angry Breed

Robert Sterling (1917-
1938: Blondie Meets the Boss
Only Angels Have Wings
40: Manhattan Heartbeat
Yesterday's Heroes
The Gay Caballero
41: The Penalty
I'll Wait for You
The Get-Away
Ringside Maisie
2-Faced Woman
Dr. Kildare's Victory
Johnny Eager
42: This Time for Keeps
Somewhere I'll Find You

46: Secret Heart
49: Roughshod
50: Bunco Squad
The Sundowners
51: Show Boat
53: Column South
61: Voyage to the Bottom of
the Sea
Return to Peyton Place
64: A Global Affair

Tisha Sterling (1945-
1965: Village of the Giants
68: The Name of the Game Is
K-I-L-L
69: Coogan's Bluff
Big Daddy
Norwood
Hark!

Angela Stevens
1952: Without Warning
The Kid from Broken Gun
53: Savage Mutiny
Jack McCall--Desperado
55: Creature with the Atom
Brain
The Naked Street
Devil Goddess
56: Blackjack Ketchum--
Desperado
57: Utah Blaine
Shadow on the Window

Charles Stevens (1893-1964)
1929: The Mysterious Dr. Fu
Manchu
The Iron Mask
The Virginian
30: The Big Trail
Tom Sawyer
31: The Conquering Horde
32: South of the Rio Grande
The Stoker
Mystery Ranch
33: When Strangers Marry
California Trail
Police Call
Drum Taps
34: Fury of the Jungle

35: Lives of a Bengal Lancer
    Call of the Wild
36: Here Comes Trouble
    The Bold Caballero
37: Wild West Days (ser.)
    Ebb Tide
38: The Crime of Dr. Hallett
    Forbidden Valley
    Flaming Frontiers (ser.)
39: The Renegade Ranger
    Frontier Marshal
    Desperate Trails
40: Wagons Westward
    Kit Carson
41: The Bad Man
    Blood and Sand
42: Beyond the Blue Horizon
    Pierre of the Plains
    Tombstone, the Town Too
     Tough to Die
44: Marked Trails
45: The Mummy's Curse
    San Antonio
    South of the Rio Grande
46: Border Bandits
47: Buffalo Bill Rides Again
48: Fury at Furnace Creek
    Belle Starr's Daughter
49: The Feathered Serpent
    Ambush
    The Walking Hills
50: The Savage Horde
    The Showdown
    Indian Territory
    California Passage
51: Oh Susanna!
    Warpath
52: Smoky Canyon
53: Savage Mutiny
    Ride, Vaquero!
54: Jubilee Trail
    Killer Leopard
55: The Vanishing American

Connie Stevens (1938-
1957: 18 and Anxious
    Young and Dangerous
58: Rock-A-Bye Baby
    Dragstrip Riot
    The Party Crashers

61: Susan Slade
    Parrish
63: Palm Springs Weekend
64: Two on a Guillotine
65: Summer Tour
    Never Too Late
67: Way Way Out
69: Mr. Jericho

Craig Stevens (1918-
1941: Melody Lane (or,
    Memories of...; short)
    Affectionately Yours
    Dive Bomber
    Law of the Tropics
    Steel Against the Sky
42: The Hidden Hand
    Spy Ship
    Secret Enemies
44: Since You Went Away
    The Doughgirls
    Hollywood Canteen
45: Roughly Speaking
    God Is My Co-Pilot
    Too Young to Know
46: Humoresque
    The Man I Love
47: That Way with Women
    Love and Learn
49: Night Unto Night
    The Lady Takes a Sailor
50: Where the Sidewalk Ends
    The Blues Busters
    The Name's Buchanan
51: Katie Did It
    The Lady from Texas
    Drums in the Deep South
52: Phone Call from a
    Stranger
53: Abbott & Costello Meet
    Dr. Jekyll and Mr. Hyde
    Murder Without Tears
54: The French Line
55: Duel on the Mississippi
57: The Deadly Mantis
58: Buchanan Rides Alone
61: Dangerous Hideaway
    Flashpoint
62: Double Exposure
    The Fanatics

```
62:  Trouble Zone              49:  Port of New York
63:  Love Me, Love Me Not?     50:  Harriet Craig
67:  Gunn                      53:  Vice Squad
68:  The Limbo Line                 Tumbleweed
                               56:  Jungle Hell
Harvey Stevens                 59:  Missile to the Moon
1939:  The Oklahoma Kid
       You Can't Get Away with  Mark Stevens [through '45 as
       Murder                   Stephen Richards] (1915-
       The House of Fear       1941:  2 Faced Woman
       Grand Jury Secrets       44:  Passage to Marseille
       Beau Geste                    Hollywood Canteen
40:    Abe Lincoln in Illinois   45:  Objective Burma
       The Fighting 69th             God Is My Co-Pilot
       Parole Fixer                  Pride of the Marines
       Stagecoach War                Roarin' Guns
41:    Sergeant York                 Rhapsody in Blue
       Our Wife                      Within these Walls
42:    The Courtship of Andy     46:  From This Day Forward
       Hardy                         The Dark Corner
       Joe Smith, American       47:  I Wonder Who's Kissing
       The Lady Is Willing            Her Now
       George Washington Slept   48:  The Street with No Name
       Here                          The Snake Pit
                                 49:  Sand
                                      Dancing in the Dark
Inger Stevens (1934-                  Oh, You Beautiful Doll!
1957:  Man on Fire              50:  Between Midnight and
58:    Cry Terror                    Dawn
       The Buchaneer                 Please Believe Me
59:    The World, the Flesh,    51:  Katie Did It
       and the Devil                 Target Unknown
64:    The New Interns               Little Egypt
67:    The Borgia Stick (TV)         Reunion in Reno
       A Guide for the Married  52:  Mutiny
       Man                      53:  Jack Slade
       Fury at Fire Creek            The Big Frame
68:    Madigan                       Torpedo Alley
       Hang 'em High            54:  Ketchikan
       House of Cards                Cry Vengeance (act., dir.)
       5 Card Stud              56:  Timetable (act., dir.)
       A Time for Killing (or,  57:  Gunsight Ridge
       The Long Ride Home)      58:  Gun Fever
69:    A Dream of Kings              Gunsmoke in Tucson
                                 59:  The Return of Jack Slade
Katherine "K.T." Stevens (1919-  60:  September Storm
1934:  Peck's Bad Boy           64:  Fate Is the Hunter
40:    Kitty Foyle                   Frozen Alive
42:    The Great Man's Lady     65:  Escape from Hell Island
43:    9 Girls                  66:  Sunscorched
44:    Address Unknown
```

Onslow Stevens (1902-

1932: Heroes of the West (ser.)
Radio Patrol (ser.)
Jungle Mystery (ser.)
Okay America!
Once in a Lifetime
The Golden West
Born to Fight
33: Nagana
Peg O' My Heart
Secret of the Blue Room
Only Yesterday
Counsellor-at-Law
Grand Exit
Yellow Dust
34: Bombay Mail
House of Danger
This Side of Heaven
The Vanishing Shadow
(ser.)
The Crosby Case
Life Returns
I'll Tell the World
I Can't Escape
Affairs of a Gentleman
In Love with Life
35: A Notorious Gentleman
The 3 Musketeers
Born to Gamble
F Man
3 on a Trail
Bridge of Sighs
Under Two Flags
Forced Landing
36: Straight from the Shoulder
Murder with Pictures
Easy Money
37: You Can't Buy Luck
Flight from Glory
There Goes the Groom
39: When Tomorrow Comes
Those High Grey Walls
40: Mystery Sea Raiders
Who Killed Aunt Maggie?
The Man Who Wouldn't
Talk
41: The Monster and the Girl
42: Sunset Serenade
43: Idaho
Appointment in Berlin

Hands Across the Border
45: House of Dracula
46: Angel on My Shoulder
Canyon Passage
O.S.S.
48: Night Has a 1000 Eyes
The Gallant Blade
The Creeper
Walk a Crooked Mile
49: Red Hot and Blue
Bomba the Jungle Boy
50: State Penitentiary
One Too Many
Revenue Agent
Mark of the Gorilla
Motor Patrol
The Lonely Heart Bandit
51: Lorna Doone
All that I Have
The Hills of Utah
The Family Secret
Sirocco
The Sealed Cargo
52: The San Francisco Story
53: Charge at Feather River
A Lion Is in the Streets
54: Fangs of the Wild
Them
They Rode West
Follow the Hunter
55: New York Confidential
56: Tribute to a Bad Man
Outside the Law
57: Kelly and Me
58: The Party Crashers
The Buccaneer
Tarawa Beachhead
Lonelyhearts
60: All the Fine Young Cannibals
62: The Couch
63: Geronimo's Revenge

Risé Stevens (1913-
1941: The Chocolate Soldier
44: Going My Way
47: Carnegie Hall

Stella Stevens (1936-
1959: Say One for Me
Li'l Abner

1282

61: Man-Trap
62: Too Late Blues
Girls! Girls! Girls!
63: The Nutty Professor
The Courtship of Eddie's
Father
64: Advance to the Rear
65: Synanon
The Secret of My Success
66: The Silencers
67: Where Angels Go Trouble
Follows
Bend of Gold
68: Luv
69: How to Save a Marriage
and Ruin Your Life
Sol Madrid
The Mad Room
The Ballad of Cable
Hogue

Warren Stevens
1951: The Frogmen
Mr. Belvedere Rings the
Bell
52: Deadline U.S.A.
Red Skies of Montana
Phone Call from a
Stranger
53: The "I Don't Care" Girl
54: The Barefoot Contessa
Gorilla at Large
Black Tuesday
55: The Man from Bitter
Ridge
Robber's Roost
Women's Prison
Duel on the Mississippi
56: Forbidden Planet
On the Threshold of Space
The Price of Fear
Accused of Murder
58: Hot Spell
The Case Against
Brooklyn
Man or Gun
Intent to Kill
59: No Name on the Bullet
62: Belle Sommers
Stagecoach to Dancers'
Rock

40 lbs. of Trouble
66: Madame X
Gunpoint
An American Dream
68: Madigan
The Sweet Ride

Houseley Stevenson (1879-
1936: Isle of Fury
37: Once a Doctor
43: Happy Land
46: Somewhere in the Night
Little Miss Big
47: Dark Passage
The Brasher Doubloon
Time Out of Mind
Ramrod
Thunder in the Valley
48: Joan of Arc
4 Faces West
The Challenge
Casbah
Kidnapped
You Gotta Stay Happy
49: Take One False Step
The Lady Gambles
Calamity Jane and Sam
Bass
Colorado Territory
Sorrowful Jones
Leave it to Henry
The Gal Who Took the
West
All the King's Men
Knock on Any Door
Masked Raiders
The Walking Hills
50: Sierra
Edge of Doom
The Sun Sets at Dawn
51: The Hollywood Story
The Secret of Convict
Lake
Cave of Outlaws
All that I Have
52: The Wild North
Oklahoma Annie

Venetia Stevenson
1958: Darby's Rangers
59: Island of Lost Women

59: Day of the Outlaw
60: 7 Ways to Sundown
The Big Night
Jet over the Atlantic
Studs Lonigan
61: The Sergeant Was a Lady
63: Horror Hotel

Elaine Stewart (1929-
1951: Sailor Beware
52: Sky Full of Moon
The Bad and the Beautiful
Desperate Search
You for Me
Everything I Have Is
Yours
53: Code 2
Slight Case of Larceny
Young Bess
Take the High Ground
54: Brigadoon
Adventures of Hajji Baba
57: The Tattered Dress
Night Passage
58: High Hell
59: Escort West
60: The Rise and Fall of
Legs Diamond
61: The Most Dangerous Man
Alive
63: The 7 Revenges

James Stewart (1908-
1935: The Murder Man
36: Important News (Chick
Sale short)
Rose Marie
Wife versus Secretary
Small Town Girl
Speed
The Gorgeous Hussy
Born to Dance
After the Thin Man
The Next Time We Love
37: Seventh Heaven
The Last Gangster
Navy Blue and Gold
38: Of Human Hearts
Shopworn Angel
You Can't Take it With
You

Vivacious Lady
39: Ice Follies of 1939
It's a Wonderful World
Made for Each Other
Mr. Smith Goes to
Washington
Destry Rides Again
40: Shop Around the Corner
The Mortal Storm
The Philadelphia Story
(OSCAR)
No Time for Comedy
41: Come Live with Me
Ziegfeld Girl
Pot o' Gold
42: Fellow Americans (short)
Winning Your Wings (short)
46: It's a Wonderful Life
47: Magic Town
48: On Our Merry Way (or, A
Miracle can Happen)
Call Northside 777
The Rope
You Gotta Stay Happy
10,000 Kids and a Cop
(doc.)
49: The Stratton Story
Malaya
How Much do You Owe?
50: Winchester 73
Broken Arrow
Harvey
The Jackpot
51: No Highway in the Sky
52: The Greatest Show on
Earth
Carbine Williams
Bend of the River
53: Thunder Bay
Naked Spur
54: The Glenn Miller Story
Rear Window
55: Far Country
Strategic Air Command
The Man from Laramie
56: The Man Who Knew Too
Much
57: Spirit of St. Louis
Night Passage
58: Vertigo
Bell, Book, and Candle

59: An Anatomy of a Murder
The F.B.I. Story
60: The Mountain Road
61: 2 Rode Together
X-15 (narr.)
62: The Man Who Shot
Liberty Valance
Mr. Hobbs Takes a
Vacation
How the West Was Won
63: Take Her She's Mine
64: Cheyenne Autumn
65: Dear Brigitte
Shenandoah
66: Flight of the Phoenix
67: The Rare Breed
68: Bandolero
69: Firecreek
The Cheyenne Social Club

Paul Stewart (1908-
1941: Johnny Eager
Citizen Kane
43: Government Girl
Mr. Lucky
49: The Window
Easy Living
Illegal Entry
Champion
12 O'Clock High
50: Walk Softly, Stranger
Edge of Doom
51: Appointment with Danger
52: Deadline U.S.A.
The Bad and the Beautiful
We're Not Married
Carbine Williams
53: The Juggler
The Joe Louis Story
54: Prisoner of War
Deep in My Heart
55: The Cobweb
Chicago Syndicate
Hell on Frisco Bay
Kiss Me Deadly
56: The Wild Party
57: Top Secret Affair
58: King Creole
59: Beyond All Limits
63: A Child Is Waiting

65: The Greatest Story Ever
Told
67: In Cold Blood
68: The Scalphunters
69: How to Commit Marriage
Jigsaw
Suppose They Gave a War
and Nobody Came?

Peggy Stewart
1937: Wells Fargo
38: Little Tough Guy
That Certain Age
39: Everybody's Hobby
40: All This and Heaven Too
41: Back Street
43: Girls in Chains
44: Tucson Raiders
Code of the Prairie
Stagecoach to Monterey
Sheriff of Las Vegas
Silver City Kid
Firebrands of Arizona
Cheyenne Wildcat
45: Bandits of the Badlands
Marshal of Laredo
Oregon Trail
Rough Riders of Cheyenne
The Tiger Woman
Utah
The Vampire's Ghost
46: Alias Billy the Kid
California Gold Rush
Conquest of Cheyenne
Days of Buffalo Bill
The Invisible Informer
Red River Renegades
Sheriff of Redwood Valley
47: Stagecoach to Denver
Vigilantes of Boomtown
Rustlers of Devil's Canyon
Trail to San Antone
49: Dead Man's Gold
Frontier Revenge
Desert Vigilante
Ride, Ryder, Ride!
50: Hollywood Varieties
51: Pride of Maryland
52: Montana Incident
Kansas Territory

1285

61: When the Clock Strikes
    Gun Street
68: The Way West

Roy Stewart (1889-1933)
1929: In Old Arizona
    Probation
    The Viking
30: The Great Divide
    Men Without Women
    Lone Star Ranger
    Rough Romance
    Born Reckless
31: Fighting Caravans
32: Mystery Ranch
    Exposed
33: Fargo Express
    Come on, Tarzan!
    Zoo in Budapest
    Rustlers' Roundup

Dorothy Stickney (1900-
1931: Working Girls
34: The Little Minister
    Murder at the Vanities
38: I Met My Love Again
39: What a Life!
44: The Uninvited
48: Miss Tatlock's Millions
53: The Great Diamond
    Mystery
56: The Catered Affair
59: The Remarkable Mr.
    Pennypacker
69: Strangers

Linda Stirling
1944: San Antonio Kid
    Sheriff of Sundown
    Vigilantes of Dodge City
45: The Cherokee Flash
    Santa Fe Saddlemates
    Sheriff of Cimarron
    The Topeka Terror
    Wagon Wheels Westward
    D-Day on Mars
46: The Invisible Informer
    Cyclostrode-X
    The Madonna's Secret
    The Mysterious Mr.
    Valentine

    Rio Grande Raiders
47: The Pretender

Carl Stockdale (1874-1942?)
1928: The Terror   S
    Shepherd of the Hills   S
    My Home Town   S
    Jazzland   S
29: China Bound   S
    The Love Parade
    The Black Pearl
    Broken Barriers   S
    The Carnation Kid   PT
30: The Furies
    Hideout
    The Sisters
    Hell's Island
32: Get that Girl
33: Vampire Bat
34: Monte Carlo Nights
    Rocky Rhodes
35: The Crimson Trail
    Mary Jane's Pa
    Circumstantial Evidence
    Dr. Socrates
    Outlawed Guns
    The Ivory-Handled Gun
36: The Leavenworth Case
    Ring Around the Moon
    Revolt of the Zombies
37: Battle of Greed
    The Lost Horizon
    A Nation Aflame
    Courage of the West
38: Rawhide Blockade
    Hawaiian Buckaroo
39: Boy Slaves
    Marshal of Mesa City
40: Pioneers of the Frontier
    Kronga-The Wild Stallion
    Stage to Chino
    Thundering Frontier
    Wagon Train
41: Scattergood Pulls the
    Strings
    Along the Rio Grande
    The Return of Daniel Boone
    Scattergood Meets Broadway
    Dangerous Lady

Dean Stockwell (1936-
1945: Anchors Aweigh
       Valley of Decision
       Abbott & Costello in
         Hollywood
46: The Green Years
       Home Sweet Homicide
       The Mighty McGurk
47: The Arnelo Affair
       The Romance of Rosy
         Ridge
       Song of the Thin Man
       A Gentleman's Agreement
48: The Boy with the Green
         Hair
       Deep Waters
49: Down to the Sea in Ships
       The Secret Garden
50: Stars in My Crown
       The Happy Years
       Kim
51: Cattle Drive
57: Gun for a Coward
       The Careless Years
59: Compulsion
60: Sons and Lovers
62: Long Day's Journey Into
       the Night
65: Rapture
68: Psych-Out
69: Dunwich Horrors

Guy Stockwell (1938-
1960: 3 Swords of Zorro
65: The War Lord
66: Beau Geste
       And Now Miguel
       Blindfold
       The Plainsman
       The Million Dollar Collar
67: Tobruk
       Banning
68: The King's Pirate
       In Enemy Country
       The Monitors
       The Adversaries (TV)
       The Sound of Anger (TV)
69: King Gun

Arthur Stone (1897-
1929: Captain Lash   SSE

Fugitives   SSE
New Year's Eve   SSE
Through Different Eyes
Red Wine   SSE
Fox Movietone Follies of
  1929
The Far Call   SSE
Frozen Justice
30: The Vagabond King
       Mamba
       On the Level
       Girl of the Golden West
       The Bad Man
31: The Lash
       Conquering Horde
       Bad Company
       The Secret Menace
32: The Big Shot
       Broken Wing
       So Big
       Roar of the Dragon
       That's My Baby
34: I'll Tell the World
       Love Birds
       She Had to Choose
35: Bordertown
       Charlie Chan in Egypt
       Hot Tip
36: Fury
38: Go Chase Yourself
48: Ruthless
49: The Sickle or the Cross

Ezra Stone (1917-
1940: Those Were the Days
43: This Is the Army

Fred Stone (1874-1959)
1935: Alice Adams
36: Trail of the Lonesome
       Pine
       The Farmer in the Dell
       My American Wife
       Grand Jury
37: Hideaway
       Life Begins in College
38: Quick Money
39: No Place to Go
40: Konga-The Wild Stallion
       The Westerner

1287

George E. Stone (1904-1966)

1929: Redeeming Sin   PT
      Naughty Baby   SSE
      Weary River   PT
      The Girl in the Glass
        Cage   PT
      2 Men and a Maid
      Skin Deep
      Melody Lane
30:   Under a Texas Moon
      The Medicine Man
      Little Caesar
31:   The Front Page
      Cimarron
      Five-Star Final
      The Spider
      Sob Sister
32:   Taxi!
      File No. 113
      The Woman from Monte
        Carlo
      The World and the Flesh
      The Last Mile
      The Phantom of Crestwood
33:   Vampire Bat
      42nd Street
      Sailor be Good!
      Song of the Eagle
      Emergency Call
      The Wrecker
      The Big Brain
      Sing, Sinner, Sing
      Penthouse
      Ladies Must Love
      He Couldn't Take It
      King for a Night
34:   Frontier Marshal
      Viva Villa!
      Return of the Terror
      The Dragon Murder Case
      Embarrassing Moments
35:   One Hour Late
      Secret of the Chateau
      Million Dollar Baby
      Public Hero No. 1
      Hold 'em, Yale!
      Make a Million
      Moonlight on the Prairie
      The Frisco Kid
36:   Bullets or Ballots

      Freshman Love
      Man Hunt
      Anthony Adverse
      King of Hockey
      Jailbreak
      Rhythm on the Range
      Polo Joe
      The Captain's Kid
      Here Comes Carter!
37:   Back in Circulation
      The Adventurous Blonde
38:   Mr. Moto's Gamble
      A Slight Case of Murder
      Over the Wall
      Alcatraz Island
      You and Me
      The Long Shot
      Submarine Patrol
39:   You Can't Get Away with
        Murder
      The Housekeeper's
        Daughter
40:   The Night of Nights
      I Take this Woman
      Island of Doomed Men
      Northwest Mounted Police
      Slightly Tempted
      Cherokee Strip
41:   Road Show
      The Face Behind the Mask
      Broadway Limited
      Last of the Duanes
      Confessions of Boston
        Blackie
      His Girl Friday
42:   The Affairs of Jimmy
        Valentine
      The Lone Star Rangers
      Little Tokyo, U.S.A.
      The Devil with Hitler
43:   After Midnight with Boston
        Blackie
      The Chance of a Lifetime
44:   Strangers in the Night
      Timber Queen
      My Buddy
      One Mysterious Night
      Roger Touhy--Gangster
45:   Scared Stiff
      Boston Blackie Booked on
        Suspicion

45: Boston Blackie's Rendez-
vous
One Exciting Night
Doll Face
46: Blackie and the Law
Close Call for Boston
Blackie
The Phantom Thief
Sentimental Journey
Suspense
Abie's Irish Rose
48: Trapped by Boston
Blackie
Untamed Breed
49: Dancing in the Dark
52: A Girl in Every Port
Bloodhounds of Broadway
53: Pickup on South Street
The Robe
Combat Squad
54: The Miami Story
Steel Cage
Broken Lance
3 Ring Circus
55: Guys and Dolls
The Man with a Golden
Arm
56: Slightly Scarlet
57: Sierra Stranger
The Story of Mankind
59: Some Like it Hot
The Tijuana Story
Baby Face Nelson
Calypso Heat Wave
61: A Pocketful of Miracles

Harold J. Stone
1956: The Harder They Fall
Somebody Up There Likes
Me
Slander
57: The Wrong Man
Man Afraid
The Garment Jungle
House of Numbers
The Invisible Boy
59: These 1000 Hills
60: Spartacus
62: The Chapman Report
63: Showdown

X-The Man with the
X-Ray Eyes
65: The Greatest Story Ever
Told
Girl Happy
67: The Big Mouth
St. Valentine's Day
Massacre

Lewis Stone (1879-1953)
1929: Trial of Mary Dugan
Madame X
Wonder of Women
Woman of Affairs
Wild Orchids
30: Their Own Desire
The Big House
Strictly Unconventional
Romance
Office Wife
Passion Flower
Father's Son
Wet Parade
31: Strictly Dishonorable
Phantom of Paris
My Past
The Sin of Madelon Claudet
Always Goodbye
The Secret Six
Inspiration
The Lullaby
32: Justice for Sale
Mata Hari
Letty Lynton
Grand Hotel
New Morals for Old
Unashamed
Red-Headed Woman
Strange Interlude
After Divorce
Night Court
Divorce in the Family
Mask of Fu Manchu
The Son-Daughter
33: Looking Forward
Men Must Fight
Queen Christina
Bureau of Missing Persons
The White Sister
34: You Can't Buy Everything

34: The Girl from Missouri
Treasure Island
Mystery of Mr. X
35: David Copperfield
Vanessa-Her Love Story
West Point of the Air
Public Hero No. 1
Woman Wanted
China Seas
Shipmates Forever
36: 3 Godfathers
The Unguarded Hour
Small Town Girl
Sworn Enemy
Suzy
Don't Turn 'em Loose
Miracle in the Sand
37: Outcast
The 13th Chair
The Man Who Cried Wolf
38: You're Only Young Once
Bad Man of Brimstone
Judge Hardy's Children
Love Finds Andy Hardy
Yellow Jack
The Chaser
Out West with the Hardys
Stolen Heaven
39: Ice Follies of 1939
The Hardys Ride High
Andy Hardy Has Spring
Fever
Joe and Ethel Turp Call
on the President
Judge Hardy and Son
40: Sporting Blood
Andy Hardy Meets a
Debutante
41: Andy Hardy's Private
Secretary
Life Begins for Andy
Hardy
The Bugle Sounds
42: The Courtship of Andy
Hardy
Andy Hardy's Double Life
44: Andy Hardy's Blonde
Trouble
45: The Hoodlum Saint
46: Love Laughs at Andy
Hardy

Three Wise Fools
48: State of the Union
On Account of Anthony
49: The Sun Comes Up
Any Number can Play
50: Stars in My Crown
Key to the City
Grounds for Marriage
51: Night Unto Morning
Angels in the Outfield
Bannerline
The Unknown Man
It's a Big Country
52: Just This Once
Talk about a Stranger
Scaramouche
The Prisoner of Zenda
53: All the Brothers Were
Valiant

Milburn Stone (1904-
1936: The Milky Way
China Clipper
The Princess Comes
Across
The 3 Musketeers
Two in a Crowd
37: A Doctor's Diary
Atlantic Flight
Federal Bullets
Blazing Barriers
Swing it, Professor
Youth on Parole
The 13th Man
The Man in Blue
38: Port of Missing Girls
Mr. Boggs Steps Out
Wives Under Suspicion
Sinners in Paradise
Crime School
Paroled from the Big
House
California Frontier
39: Mystery Plane
King of the Turf
Society Smugglers
Blind Alibi
Young Mr. Lincoln
Stunt Pilot
Tropic Fury
Sky Patrol

39: Danger Flight
Nick Carter , Master
 Detective
Charlie McCarthy,
 Detective
Crashing Through
40: Chasing Trouble
Enemy Agent
An Angel from Texas
Framed
Colorado
The Great Plane Robbery
Give Us Wings
41: The Phantom Cowboy
The Great Train Robbery
Death Valley Outlaws
42: Reap the Wild Wind
Rubber Racketeers
Frisco Lil
Police Bullets
43: Keep 'em Slugging
You Can't Beat the Law
Sherlock Holmes Faces
 Death
Captive Wild Woman
Get Going
Corvette K-225
Gung Ho!
The Mad Ghoul
44: The Impostor
Hi Good Lookin'!
Hat Check Honey
Moon over Las Vegas
Jungle Woman
Phantom Lady
Twilight on the Prairie
The Great Alaskan
 Mystery (ser.)
45: The Master Key (ser.)
The Beautiful Cheat
The Dalton Ride Again
The Frozen Ghost
I'll Remember April
On Stage, Everybody!
She Gets Her Man
Strange Confession
Swing out, Sister!
46: Danger Woman
Inside Job
Little Miss Big

The Spider Woman
 Strikes Back
Strange Conquest
Her Adventuruous Night
47: Killer Dill
The Michigan Kid
Heading for Heaven
48: Train to Alcatraz
49: The Green Promise
Calamity Jane and Sam
 Bass
Sky Dragons
The Judge
50: No Man of Her Own
The Fireball
Snow Dog
Branded
51: Road Block
52: The Atomic City
The Savage
53: The Sun Shines Bright
Arrowhead
Pickup on South Street
54: The Siege of Red River
Black Tuesday
55: The Long Gray Line
White Feather
Smoke Signal
The Private War of Major
 Benson
57: Drango

Paula Stone (1916-
1935: Hop A Long Cassidy
36: Treachery Rides the Range
Two Against the World
The Case of the Velvet
 Claws
Colleen
The Singing Kid
Trailin' West
37: The Girl Said No
Red Lights Ahead
Atlantic Flight
Swing it, Professor
38: In Old Chicago
Island in the Sky
Down in Arkansas
Convicts at Large
39: Laugh it Off

39: Idiot's Delight   Trouble Preferred

Arthur Storch (1925-
1957: The Strange One
58: The Mugger
60: Girl of the Night

Larry Storch (1923-
1951: The Prince Who Was a
Thief
58: Gun Fever
The Last Blitzkrieg
60: Who Was that Lady?
62: 40 lbs. of Trouble
64: Wild and Wonderful
Captain Newman, M.D.
Sex and the Single Girl
65: The Great Race
A Very Special Favor
That Funny Feeling
Bus Riley's Back in
Town
68: The Monitors
69: The Great Bank Robbery

June Storey
1940: Rancho Grande
In Old Missouri
Gaucho Serenade
Caroline Moon
Ride, Tenderfoot, Ride
Barnyard Follies
41: The Lone Wolf Takes a
Chance
Dance Hall
Hello Sucker!
Dangerous Lady
42: Girls' Town
44: End of the Road
45: Road to Alcatraz
Song of the Prairie
46: The Strange Woman
47: Killer McCoy
48: Secret Service
Investigator
Train to Alcatraz
Miraculous Journey
The Snake Pit
Cry of the City
49: Miss Mink of 1949

Gale Storm (1922-
1940: Tom Brown's School Days
One Crowded Hour
41: Saddlemates
Gambling Daughters
Jesse James at Bay
Let's Go Collegiate
Red River Valley
City of Missing Girls
42: Smart Alecks
Foreign Agent
Rhythm Parade
The Man from Cheyenne
Lure of the Islands
43: Cosmo Jones in the Crime
Smashers
Campus Rhythm
Where Are Your Children?
Revenge of the Zombies
Nearly 18
44: The Right to Love
45: Forever Yours
G.I. Honeymoon
Sunbonnet Sue
46: Swing Parade of 1946
47: It Happened on 5th Avenue
The Tenderfoot
48: The Dude Goes West
49: Stampede
Abandoned
50: The Kid from Texas
Between Midnight and
Dawn
The Underworld Story
The Whipped
Curtain Call at Cactus
Creek
51: Al Jennings of Oklahoma
Texas Rangers
52: Woman of the North
Country

Ludwig Stossel (1883-
1940: Jennie
4 Sons
The Man I Married
Dance, Girl, Dance
41: Man Hunt

41: Underground
    Great Guns
    Marry the Boss's
      Daughter
42: The Pride of the Yankees
    Woman of the Year
    Icebound
    Who Done It?
    Casablanca
    Pittsburgh
    The Great Impersonation
    All Through the Night
43: Hitler's Hangman
    Action in the North
      Atlantic
    They Came to Blow Up
      America
    Above Suspicion
    Hers to Hold
44: The Climax
    Bluebeard
    Lake Placid Serenade
45: Dillinger
    Her Highness and the
      Bellboy
    House of Dracula
    Yolanda and the Thief
    Miss Susie Slagle's
46: Cloak and Dagger
    Temptation
    Girl on the Spot
47: The Beginning or the
      End?
    Song of Love
    This Time for Keeps
48: A Song Is Born
49: The Great Sinner
51: As Young As You Feel
    Corky of Gasoline Alley
52: The Merry Widow
    No Time for Flowers
53: Call Me Madam
    The Sun Shines Bright
    Geraldine
58: Me and the Colonel
    From the Earth to the
      Moon
59: The Blue Angel

Rose Stradner (1916-1958)
1937: The Last Gangster

39: Blonde Alibi
44: Keys of the Kingdom

Glenn Strange (1911-
1935: New Frontier
    House of Frankenstein
37: Adventure's End
    Arizona Days
38: The Painted Trail
    Pride of the West
    In Old Mexico
    Mysterious Rider
    Sunset Trail
    Border Wolves
    The Last Stand
    Gun Packer
    Black Bandit
    Call of the Rockies
39: Rough Riders' Round-Up
    Blue Montana Skies
    Law of the Pampas
    Range War
    Overland Mail
    The Llano Kid
    The Fighting Gringo
    Days of Jesse James
40: Pioneer Days
    Rhythm of the Rio Grande
    Pals of the Silver Sage
    Covered Wagon Trails
    Land of 6 Guns
    Stage to Chino
    3 Men from Texas
    Triple Justice
    Wagon Train
41: San Francisco Docks
    Saddlemates
    Wide Open Town
    The Kid's Last Ride
    Dude Cowboy
    The Bandit Trail
    Badlands of Dakota
    Fugitive Valley
    The Driftin' Kid
    Come on, Danger!
    Billy the Kid Wanted
    Billy the Kid's Roundup
42: Sunset on the Desert
    Arizona Cyclone
    Billy the Kid Trapped
    Romance on the Range

42: Down Texas Way
    The Mad Monster
    Stagecoach Buckaroo
    Little Joe--The Wrangler
43: The Desperadoes
    The Kid Rides Again
    Wild Horse Stampede
    Mission to Moscow
    Black Market Rustlers
    False Colors
    The Woman of the Town
44: The Monster Maker
    Silver City Kid
    Arizona Trail
    The Contender
    40 Thieves
    Sonora Stagecoach
    Return of the Rangers
    Valley of Vengeance
    Trail to Gunsight
    The San Antonio Kid
45: House of Frankenstein
    House of Dracula
46: Renegades of the Rio
    Grande
47: Beauty and the Bandit
    The Wistful Widow of
    Wagon Gap
    Frontier Fighters
48: Abbott & Costello Meet
    Frankenstein
    The Far Frontier
    Silver Trails
49: Master Minds
    Rimfire
    Roll, Thunder, Roll
50: Comanche Territory
    Double Crossbones
51: Texas Carnival
    Comin' 'Round the
    Mountain
52: The Lawless Breed
53: The Great Sioux Uprising
    Veils of Bagdad
55: The Road to Denver
    The Vanishing American
57: Last Stagecoach West
    Gunfire at Indian Gap
58: Quantrill's Raiders

Susan Strasberg (1938-
1955: Picnic
    The Cobweb
58: Stage Struck
50: Kapo
61: The Scream of Fear
62: Hemingway's Adventures
    of a Young Man
64: The Disorder
    The High Bright Sun
66: McGuire, Go Home!
67: The Trip
68: The Candy Man
    Psych-Out
    Chubasco
    The Name of the Game
    Is K-I-L-L
69: The Brotherhood
    Fall Out
    The Flight
    Marcus Welby, M.D.(TV)
    The Sisters
    The Prisoner
    The Bait

Gil Stratton, Jr.
1943: Girl Crazy
47: Dangerous Years
48: Half Past Midnight
49: Mr. Belvedere Goes to
    College
    Tucson
50: Hot Rod
52: Here Come the Marines!
    Hold that Line!
    Battle Zone
    Army Bound
56: Bundle of Joy

Robert Strauss (1913-
1951: Sailor Beware
52: Jumping Jacks
    The Redhead from
    Wyoming
53: Stalag 17
    Here Come the Girls
    Money from Home
    Act of Love
54: The Atomic Kid

54: The Bridges at Toko-Ri
55: 7 Year Itch
The Man with a Golden
Arm
56: Attack!
58: Frontier Gun
I, Mobster
59: The 4-D Man
Li'l Abner
Inside the Mafia
60: September Storm
Wake Me When It's Over
61: Dondi
The Last Time I Saw
Archie
The George Raft Story
20 Plus 2
62: Girls! Girls! Girls!
63: The Thrill of it All
64: Stage to Thunder Rock
65: Family Jewels
Harlow (Magna.)
That Funny Feeling
66: Frankie and Johnnie
67: Fort Utah

Barbra Streisand (1942-
1968: Funny Girl (OSCAR)
69: Hello, Dolly!
On a Clear Day You Can
See Forever (3 roles)
The Owl and the Pussycat

Ray Stricklyn (1930-
1956: Crime in the Streets
The Catered Affair
The Proud and Profane
Somebody Up There Likes
Me
The Last Wagon
58: 10 North Frederick
Return of Dracula
59: The Remarkable Mr.
Pennypacker
The Big Fisherman
60: The Lost World
The Plunderers
Young Jesse James
65: Arizona Raiders

Elaine Stritch (1925-
1956: The Scarlet Hour
3 Violent People
57: A Farewell to Arms
58: The Perfect Furlough
59: Kiss Her Goodbye
65: Who Killed Teddy Bear?

Woody Strode (1923-
1941: Sundown
51: The Lion Hunters
52: Caribbean
53: The City Beneath the Sea
54: The Gambler from Natchez
56: The Ten Commandments
58: Tarzan's Fight for Life
The Buccaneer
59: Pork Chop Hill
60: Spartacus
Sergeant Rutledge
The Last Voyage
61: Sins of Rachel Cade
2 Rode Together
62: The Man Who Shot
Liberty Valance
63: Tarzan's 3 Challenges
65: Genghis Khan
66: The Professionals
7 Women
68: Shalako
69: Once Upon a Time in the
West
Seated at His Right
Che!
King Gun

Edson Stroll
1959: The Wild and the Innocent
61: Snow White and the 3
Stooges
62: 3 Stooges in Orbit
64: McHale's Navy
65: McHale's Navy Joins the
Air Force

Nipo Strongheart (1891-1967)
1951: Across the Wild Missouri
Westward the Women
52: Lone Star

52:   Pony Soldiers

Claude Stroud
1950: Gunfire
     Border Rangers
     All About Eve
55:   Love Me or Leave Me
58:   The Cry Baby Killer
59:   The Rookie
61:   Breakfast at Tiffany's
63:   My 6 Loves
     Promises, Promises
64:   The Man from Galveston
68:   The Ballad of Josie
     Coogan's Bluff
     How to Save a Marriage
     and Ruin Your Life
     Something for a Lonely
     Man (TV)
69:   Explosion
     Tick, Tick, Tick

Don Stroud (1942-
1967: Banning
     Games
     The Ballad of Josie
68:   Madigan
69:   What's so Bad About
     Feeling Good?
     Tick, Tick, Tick
     Bloody Mama

Shepperd Strudwick [John
Sheppard] (1907-
1938: That Mothers May Live
     Fast Company
     Marie Antoinette
40:   Congo Maisie
     Dr. Kildare's Strange
     Case
     Flight Command
41:   Remember the Day
     Belle Starr
     Cadet Girl
     The Men in Her Life
42:   The Loves of Edgar Allan
     Poe
     Rings on Her Fingers
     10 Gentlemen from West
     Point
     Dr. Renault's Secret

43:   Chetniks
45:   Roughly Speaking
     Objective Burma!
     Pride of the Marines
     Too Young to Know
46:   Home Sweet Homicide
     Strange Triangle
48:   Joan of Arc
     Enchantment
     Fighter Squadron
49:   The Red Pony
     Chicago Deadline
     Reckless Moment
50:   The Kid from Texas
     All the King's Men
     Let's Dance
     3 Husbands
51:   A Place in the Sun
56:   The Eddie Duchin Story
     Beyond a Reasonable Doubt
     Autumn Leaves
57:   That Night!
     Sad Sack
59:   Girl on the Run
64:   Psychomania
68:   Daring Game
69:   Slaves

Gloria Stuart (1911-
1932: The All-American
     The Old Dark House
     Airmail
     Street of Women
     Back Street
     Laughter in Hell
33:   Kiss Before the Mirror
     Private Jones
     The Girl in 419
     It's Great to be Alive
     Secret of the Blue Room
     The Invisible Man
     Roman Scandals
     Sweepings
34:   Beloved
     I Like it that Way
     Gift of Gab
     Love Captive
     Here Comes the Navy
     I'll Tell the World
35:   Maybe It's Love
     Gold Diggers of 1935

35:	Laddie
36:	My Second Wife
	Professional Soldier
	Prisoner of Shark Island
	Poor Little Rich Girl
	The Crime of Dr. Forbes
	36 Hours to Kill
	The Girl on the Front
	Page
	Wanted: Jane Turner
37:	Girl Overboard
	The Lady Escapes
	Life Begins in College
38:	Change of Heart
	Rebecca of Sunnybrook
	Farm
	Island in the Sky
	Keep Smiling
	Meridian 7-1212
	The Lady Objects
	Time Out for Murder
39:	The 3 Musketeers
	It Could Happen to You
	Winner Take All
	The Life of Dr. Paul
	Joseph Goebbels
43:	Here Comes Elmer
44:	The Whistler
	Enemy of Women
46:	She Wrote the Book

Nick Stuart (1906-

1929:	Gold Diggers of Broadway	
	Girls Gone Wild	SSE
	Joy Street	SSE
	Chasing Through	
	Europe	SSE
	Why Leave Home?	
30:	Swing High	
	The 4th Alarm	
31:	Sheer Luck	
	Mystery Train	
	Sundown Trail	
33:	Police Call	
	Secret Sinners	
34:	Demon for Trouble	
35:	Secrets of Chinatown	
36:	Rio Grande Romance	
	Underworld Terror	
	Put on the Spot	

Randy Stuart

1948:	Sitting Pretty
	Street with No Name
	Apartment for Peggy
49:	I Was a Male War Bride
	The Fan
	Whirlpool
	Dancing in the Dark
50:	All About Eve
	Stella
51:	I Can Get it for You
	Wholesale
52:	Room for One More
56:	Star in the Dust
57:	The Incredible Shrinking
	Man
58:	The Man from God's
	Country

Margaret Sullavan (1911-1960)

1933:	Only Yesterday
34:	Little Man, What Now?
35:	The Good Fairy
	So Red the Rose
36:	Next Time We Love
	The Moon's Our Home
38:	Three Comrades
	The Shopworn Angel
	The Shining Hour
39:	When Tomorrow Comes
40:	The Shop Around the
	Corner
	The Mortal Storm
41:	So Ends Our Night
	Back Street
	Appointment for Love
43:	Cry Havoc
50:	No Sad Songs for Me

Barry Sullivan (1912-

1942:	We Refuse to Die
43:	High Explosives
	The Woman of the Town
44:	Lady in the Dark
	Rainbow Island
	And Now Tomorrow
45:	Duffy's Tavern
	Getting Gertie's Garter
46:	2 Years Before the Mast
	Suspense

1297

46: The Gangster
    Framed
47: Ain't No Time for Glory
48: Smart Woman
    Badmen of Tombstone
49: Any Number can Play
    The Great Gatsby
    Tension
50: The Outriders
    Grounds for Marriage
    A Life of Her Own
    Nancy Goes to Rio
51: 3 Guys Named Mike
    Cause for Alarm
    Inside Straight
    Payment on Demand
    Mr. Imperium
    No Questions Asked
    The Unknown Man
52: Skirts Ahoy!
    The Bad and the Beautiful
53: Jeopardy
    Cry of the Hunted
    China Venture
54: Loophole
    Her 12 Men
    The Miami Story
    Playgirl
55: The Queen Bee
    Texas Lady
    Strategic Air Command
56: The Maverick Queen
    Julie
57: 40 Guns
    The Way to the Gold
    Dragoon Wells Massacre
58: Wolf Larsen
    Another Time, Another
     Place
60: The Purple Gang
    The Demon Planet
    7 Ways from Sundown
62: Light in the Piazza
63: A Gathering of Eagles
64: Pyro
    Man in the Middle
    Stage to Thunder Rock
    War Lords of Outer Space
65: My Blood Runs Cold
    Harlow (Magna.)

    Planet of the Vampires
66: The American Dream
    The Poppy Is Also a
     Flower (TV)
    Intimacy
67: Buckskin
68: Willie Boy
    It Takes All Kinds
69: The Red Kitchen Murder
    The Immortal (TV)

Francis L. Sullivan (1903-1956)
1931: Missing Rembrandt
32: F.P. No. 1
33: Red Wagon
34: Jew Suss
    Chu Chin Chow
    Return of Bulldog
     Drummond
    What Happened Then?
    Great Expectations
    Cheating Cheaters
35: Strange Wives
    The Mystery of Edwin
     Drood
    Her Last Affair
36: Interrupted Honeymoon
    Fine Feathers
    A Woman Alone (or,
     Sabotage)
    Spy of Napoleon
    The Limping Man
37: Non-Stop New York
    Action for Slander
    Dinner at the Ritz
    First and the Last
    The Drum
    The Gables Mystery
    Kate Plus 10
38: The Citadel
    The Vanishing Train
    Climbing High
    The Ware Case
39: 4 Just Men
    Young Man's Fancy
40: 21 Days Together
41: Pimpernel Smith
    The Foreman Went to
     France
    The Day Will Dawn

42:	The Avengers		All Through the Night
43:	The Butler's Dilemma		2 Yanks in Trinidad
44:	Difflers 3		Parachute Nurse
45:	The Lady from Lisbon		Inside the Law
46:	Caesar and Cleopatra		My Sister Eileen
47:	Great Expectations	43:	The More the Merrier
	The Man Within		They Got Me Covered
	Laughing Lady		Thousands Cheer
48:	Joan of Arc		2 Senoritas from Chicago
49:	Red Danube	44:	The Ghost that Walks
	Broken Journey		Alone
50:	Night and the City		Secret Command
51:	Oliver Twist		2 Girls and a Sailor
	My Favorite Spy	45:	Along Came Jones
	Behave Yourself		Boston Blackie Booked
52:	Caribbean		on Suspicion
53:	Plunder of the Sun		Boston Blackie's Rendez-
	Sangaree		vous
54:	Drums of Tahiti		I Love a Bandleader
55:	Hell's Island		Love Letters
	The Prodigal	46:	Blackie and the Law
			A Close Call for Boston

Jean Sullivan

1944:	Hollywood Canteen		Blackie
	Uncertain Glory		The Crime Doctor's Man
45:	Escape in the Desert		Hunt
			Dangerous Business

Liam Sullivan

1962:	The Magic Sword		The Gentleman Misbehaves
64:	One Man's Way		It's Great to be Young
			One Way to Love
			The Phantom Thief

Frank Sully (1910-

1939:	Some Like it Hot		Renegades
40:	The Grapes of Wrath		Talk about a Lady
	The Night of Nights		Throw a Saddle on a Star
	Lillian Russell		Out of the Depths
	The Doctor Takes a Wife	47:	South of Chisholm Trail
	Cross-Country Romance		Wild Harvest
	Young People	48:	Trapped by Boston
	The Return of Frank		Blackie
	James		Blondie's Reward
	Yesterday's Heroes	49:	Boston Blackie's Chinese
41:	Submarine Zone		Venture
	A Girl, a Guy, and a		Bodyhold
	Gob		Joe Palooka in The
	Private Nurse		Counterpunch
	Mountain Moonlight	50:	Joe Palooka Meets Humphrey
	Let's Go Collegiate		Blondie's Hero
42:	Rings on Her Fingers		Beauty on Parade
	Sleepytime Gal		Square Dance Katy
			Killer Shark
			Joe Palooka in Humphrey
			Takes a Chance

50: Rookie Fireman
51: Prairie Roundup
    Man in the Saddle
52: With a Song in My Heart
    No Room for the Groom
53: Take Me to Town
    Northern Patrol
54: Battle of Rogue River
    Silver Lode
55: Jungle Moon
    The Naked Street
56: You Can't Run Away
    From It
57: The Buckskin Lady
    Rockabilly Baby
59: The Last Hurrah
63: Bye Bye, Birdie

Yma Sumac (1922-
1954: Secret of the Incas
57: Omar Khayyam

George "Slim" Summerville
(1892-1946)
1929: Goodbye, Broadway (or,
    The Shannons of Broad-
    way)
    Strong Boy   SSE
    King of the Rodeo   S
    Tiger Rose
    Last Warning   PT
30: One Hysterical Night
    Troopers 3
    Under Montana Skies
    All Quiet on the Western
    Front
    King of Jazz
    Little Accident
    Her Man
    The Spoilers
    See American Thirst
    Free Love
31: Heaven on Earth
    The Front Page
    Reckless Living
    The Bad Sister
    Many a Slip
    Lasca of the Rio Grande
32: Unexpected Father
    Racing Youth

Tom Brown of Culver
Airmail
They Just Had to Get
    Married
33: Her First Mate
    Out All Night
    Love, Honor, and Oh Baby!
34: The Love Birds
    Their Big Moment
35: Love Begins at 40
    The Farmer Takes a Wife
    Way Down East
36: Captain January
    The Country Doctor
    Pepper
    White Fang
    Can This be Dixie?
    Reunion
37: Off to the Races
    Love Is News
    The Road Back
    50 Roads to Town
38: Kentucky Moonshine
    Submarine Patrol
    Up the River
    Rebecca of Sunnybrook
    Farm
    Five of a Kind
39: Jesse James
    Winner Take All
    Charlie Chan in Reno
40: Henry Goes to Arizona
    Anne of Windy Poplars
    Gold Rush Maisie
41: Western Union
    Tobacco Road
    Puddin'head
    Highway West
    Niagara Falls
    Miss Polly
42: The Vanishing Shadow
    (ser.)
44: Bride by Mistake
    Swing in the Saddle
    I'm From Arkansas
45: Sing Me a Song of Texas
46: The Hoodlum Saint

Clinton Sundberg (1906-
1946: Love Laughs at Andy
    Hardy

1300

46: The Mighty McGurk
    Undercurrent
47: Living in a Big Way
    Undercover Maisie
    Song of Love
    The Hucksters
    Good News
48: Easter Parade
    Good Sam
    Mr. Peabody and the
      Mermaid
    A Date with Judy
    Words and Music
    The Kissing Bandit
    Command Decision
49: In the Good Old Summer-
      time
    Big Jack
    The Barkleys of Broad-
      way
50: Father Is a Bachelor
    Key to the City
    Annie Get Your Gun
    Duchess of Idaho
    The Toast of New
      Orleans
    2 Weeks with Love
    Mrs. O'Malley and Mr.
      Malone
51: On the Riviera
    The Fat Man
    As Young as You Feel
52: The Belle of New York
53: The Girl Next Door
    Main Street to Broadway
    Sweethearts on Parade
    The Caddy
56: The Birds and the Bees
61: Bachelor in Paradise
62: The Wonderful World of
      the Brothers Grimm
    How the West Was Won
67: Hotel
68: Shadow over Elveron
      (TV)

Grady Sutton (1908-
1928: The Sophomore
    Tanned Legs
    Hit the Deck

      Boy Friend
32: This Reckless Age
    Pack Up Your Troubles
    Hot Saturday
33: The Story of Temple
      Drake
    College Humor
    Sweetheart of Sigma Chi
    The Pharmacist (short)
    Only Yesterday
34: Bachelor Bait
    shorts
    Gridiron Flash
35: Laddie
    Stone of Silver Creek
    Alice Adams
    The Man on the Flying
      Trapeze
    Dr. Socrates
36: Palm Springs
    Valiant Is the Word for
      Carrie
    My Man Godfrey
    King of the Royal Mounted
    Pigskin Parade
37: We Have Our Moments
    Stage Door
    Dangerous Holiday
    Love Takes Flight
    Waikiki Wedding
    Turn Off the Moon
    2 Minutes to Play
    Behind the Mike
38: Vivacious Lady
    Having a Wonderful Time
    Alexander's Ragtime
      Band
    Hard to Get
    3 Loves Has Nancy
    The Mad Miss Manton
39: You Can't Cheat an
      Honest Man
    The Flying Irishman
    3 Sons
    It's a Wonderful World
    Angels Wash Their Faces
40: Torrid Zone
    The Bank Dick
41: She Knew All the Answers
    Father Takes a Wife

1301

41: Flying Blind
Doctors Don't Tell
42: The Bashful Bachelor
Dudes Are Pretty People
Whispering Ghosts
43: Lady Takes a Chance
What a Woman!
44: Johnny Doesn't Live
Here Anymore
Allergic to Love
The Great Moment
Since You Went Away
Goin' to Town
45: Hi Beautiful!
A Royal Scandal
Three's a Crowd
Her Lucky Night
Captain Eddie
A Bell for Adano
Anchors Aweigh
Song of the Prairie
46: The Fabulous Suzanne
Hit the Hay
It's Great to be Young
The Magnificent Rogue
Nobody Lives Forever
Partners in Time
Susie Steps Out
47: Beat the Band
Philo Vance's Gamble
My Wild Irish Rose
48: My Dog Shep
My Dear Secretary
Jiggs and Maggie in Court
Last of the Wild Horses
49: Grand Canyon
Air Hostess
54: A Star Is Born
62: Billy Rose's Jumbo
65: Tickle Me
66: Paradise Hawaiian Style
The Chase
68: I Love You, Alice B.
Toklas
Something for a Lonely
Man (TV)
69: The Great Bank Robbery
Suppose They Gave a War
and Nobody Came?

John Sutton (1908-1963)
1937: Bulldog Drummond Comes
Back
Bulldog Drummond's
Revenge
38: The Blonde Cheat
4 Men and a Prayer
Adventures of Robin Hood
39: The Private Lives of
Elizabeth and Essex
Tower of London
Zaza
Arrest Bulldog Drummond!
Susannah and the Mounties
Bulldog Drummond's Bride
Charlie McCarthy--
Detective
40: Hudson's Bay
The Invisible Man Returns
Christable Caine
Sandy Is a Lady
I Can't Give You Anything
but Love, Baby
South of Karanga
Murder over New York
41: A Very Young Lady
Moon over Her Shoulder
A Yank in R.A.F.
42: My Gal Sal
Thunder Birds
10 Gentlemen from West
Point
43: Tonight We Raid Calais
44: Jane Eyre
The Hour Before Dawn
46: Claudia and David
47: The Captain from Castile
48: The 3 Musketeers
Mickey
Adventures of Casanova
49: Bagdad
The Fan
The Bride of Vengeance
50: Second Face
51: Payment on Demand
David and Bathsheba
The Second Woman
52: The Thief of Damascus
Captain Pirate

1302

52: The Golden Hawk
My Cousin Rachel
The Lady in the Iron
Mask
53: Sangaree
East of Sumatra
56: The Amazon Trader
Death of a Scoundrel
59: The Bat
Return of the Fly
Beloved Infidel
The Story of Divorce
61: The Canadians
64: Of Human Bondage
67: The Last Safari

Kay Sutton
1938: The Saint in New York
This Marriage Business
Carefree
Smashing the Rackets
I'm from the City
39: S.O.S. Tidal Wave
40: The Man from Montreal
The Man Who Talked
too Much
Laughing at Danger
The Bank Dick
41: Flying Blind
You're Out of Luck
62: State Fair

Mack Swain (1876-1935)
1928: Caught in the Fog   PT
29: The Cohens and the Kellys
in Atlantic City   PT
Last Warning   PT
Marianne
30: Redemption
The Sea Bat
31: Finn and Hattie
32: Midnight Patrol

Gloria Swanson (1898-
1928: Queen Kelly   NT
Sadie Thompson   NT
29: The Trespasser
30: What a Widow!
31: Tonight or Never
Indiscreet

33: Perfect Understanding
34: Music in the Air
41: Father Takes a Wife
50: Sunset Boulevard
52: 3 for Bedroom C
56: Nero's Big Weekend (or,
My Son Nero)
68: Black Point

Gladys Swarthout (1904-1969)
1936: Rose of the Rancho
Give Us This Night
37: The Champagne Waltz
38: Romance in the Dark
39: Ambush

Bob Sweeney
1958: The Last Hurrah
60: Toby Tyler
62: Moon Pilot
63: Son of Flubber
64: Marnie

Blanche Sweet (1896-
1929: The Woman in White   S
30: Woman Racket
Show Girl in Hollywood
The Silver Horde
34: The Battle
59: The 5 Little Pennies

Inga Swenson (1935-
1961: The Miracle Worker
62: Advise and Consent

Karl Swenson
1957: 4 Boys and a Gun
58: Kings Go Forth
59: The Hanging Tree
No Name on the Bullet
60: The Gallant Hours
The Ice Palace
One Foot in Hell
North to Alaska
Flaming Star
61: Judgment at Nuremberg
62: Walk on the Wild Side
Lonely Are the Brave
The Spiral Road
Sword in the Stone (voice)

```
63:  The Birds                           Mrs. Wiggs of the
64:  The Man from Galveston                 Cabbage Patch
65:  Major Dundee                         Johnny Doughboy
     The Sons of Katie Elder   43:  Shantytown
66:  The Cincinnati Kid          44:  Going My Way
67:  Hour of the Gun                    Rosie the Riveter
68:  Seconds                             The Great Mike
69:  Brighty of the Grand        46:  The Gas House Kids
     Canyon                             Courage of Lassie
     Tick, Tick, Tick            47:  The Gas House Kids Go
                                        West
Joseph Swickard (1867-1940)          The Gas House Kids in
1929:  Eternal Woman          S         Hollywood
       The Devil's Chaplain   S    48:  State of the Union
       Bachelor's Club        SSE       Big Town Scandal
       The Veiled Woman       S         On Our Merry Way
       Frozen River           PT        A Letter to 3 Wives
       Phantoms of the North  S    50:  Redwood Forest Trail
       Dark Skies                  51:  Two Dollar Bettor
30:    Mamba                       52:  Pat and Mike
       Spng of the Caballero       53:  Island in the Sky
34:    Cross Streets               54:  The High and the Mighty
35:    The Lost City                    This Is My Love
       A Dog of Flanders                Track of the Cat
36:    The Millionaire Kid         56:  Dig that Uranium
       Caryl of the Mountains           Between Heaven and Hell
       Boss Rider of Gun Creek     57:  Motorcycle Gang
37:    Sandflow                    58:  The Defiant Ones
       Last of the Penitentes
       The Girl Said No      Basil Sydney (1894-1967)
38:    You Can't Take it With  1933:  The Midshipmaid
       You                     35:  Transatlantic Tunnel
                               36:  Rhodes, the Diamond
Carl "Alfalfa" Switzer (1926-1959)    Master
1930's:"Our Gang" Kid Comedies  37:  Talk of the Devil
36:    Too Many Parents          46:  Caesar and Cleopatra
       General Spanky            48:  Hamlet
       Easy to Take                   Jassy
       Right in Your Lap         50:  Treasure Island
       Kelly the Second               The Angel with the Trumpet
       Pick a Star               51:  The Magic Box
37:    Wild and Woolly           54:  Hell Below Zero
38:    Scandal Street            55:  Simba
39:    a short                        The Dam Busters
40:    I Love You Again          56:  Around the World in 80
       Barnyard Follies               Days
41:    Reg'lar Fellers           57:  Island in the Sun
42:    Henry and Dizzy                Sea Wife
       The War Against Mrs.      59:  A Question of Adultery
       Hadley                         John Paul Jones
```

The Devil's Disciple
60: The 3 Worlds of
Gulliver

T

Ralph Taeger (1935-
1964: The Carpetbaggers
Stage to Thunder Rock
A House Is Not a Home
69: The Delta Factor

Miiko Taka
1957: Sayonara
60: Cry for Happy
Hell to Eternity
61: A Girl Named Tamiko
Operation Bottleneck
64: A Global Affair
65: The Art of Love
66: Walk, Don't Run!

Lyle Talbot (1904-
1932: Three on a Match
The Nightingale
Love Is a Racket
Big City Blues
Without Consent
No More Orchids
The Purchase Price
Unholy Love
Stranger in Town
The 13th Guest
Klondike
33: Ladies They Talk About
The Life of Jimmy Dolan
A Shriek in the Night
20,000 Years in Sing Sing
Girl Missing
Mary Stevens, M.D.
College Coach
She Had to Say Yes
Havana Widows
Parachute Jumper
34: Mandalay
Registered Nurse
The Dragon Murder Case
Return of the Terror
A Lost Lady
Murder in the Clouds
Fog over Frisco

Heat Lightning
One Night of Love
35: Party Wire
Red Hot Tires
While the Patient Slept
Oil for the Lamps of
China
Page Miss Glory
It Happened in New York
Chinatown Squad
Out Little Girl
The Case of the Lucky
Legs
Broadway Hostess
36: Trapped by Television
The Singing Kid
Murder by an Aristocrat
Boulder Dam
The Law in Her Hands
Go West Young Man
Mind Your Own Business
37: 3 Legionnaires
Affairs of Cappy Ricks
Second Honeymoon
What Price Vengeance?
38: Change of Heart
One Wild Night
Gateway
Call of the Yukon
I Stand Accused
The Arkansas Traveler
39: Forged Passport
Second Fiddle
They Asked for It
Torture Ship
40: He Married His Wife
Parole Fixer
A Miracle on Main Street
42: The Mexican Spitfire's
Elephant
She's in the Army
A Night for Crime
They Raid by Night
43: Man of Courage
44: Up in Arms
Sensations of 1945
One Body too Many
Dixie Jamboree
The Falcon Out West
Are These Our Parents?
Mystery of the River Boat
(ser.)

44: Gambler's Choice
46: Strange Impersonation
Song of Arizona
Murder Is My Business
Nick Carter, Detective
(ser.)
47: Gun Town
Danger Street
The Vicious Circle
Vigilante (ser.)
48: Appointment with Murder
The Devil's Cargo
Winner Take All
Parole, Inc.
Highway 13
Shep Comes Home
49: Fighting Fools
Mutineers
Sky Dragons
Renegade
Ringside
Mississippi Rhythm
Joe Palooka in The Big
Fight
Thunder in the Pines
Quick on the Trigger
50: Atom Man vs Superman
Jackpot
Champagne for Caesar
Border Rangers
Revenue Agent
Cherokee Uprising
Tall Timber
51: Blue Blood
The Man from Sonora
Abilene Trail
Mask of the Dragon
Fingerprints Don't Lie
Hurricane Island
Jungle Manhunt
Gold Raiders
Purple Heart Diary
Varieties on Parade
Fury of the Congo
52: Sea Tiger
Untamed Woman
The Old West
Outlaw Women
With a Song in My Heart
Desperadoes Outpost

Feudin' Fools
Kansas Territory
Montana Incident
African Treasure
Texas City
53: Trail Blazers
Down Among the Shelter-
ing Palms
Star of Texas
White Lightning
54: Captain Kidd and the
Slave Girl
Tobor the Great
The Steel Cage
There's No Business Like
Show Business
Trader Tom of the China
Seas (ser.)
55: Jail Busters
Sudden Danger
56: The Great Man
Calling Homicide
58: Mr. Notorious Mr. Monks
High School Confidential
The Hot Angel
59: City of Fear
Plan 9 from Outer Space
60: Sunrise at Campobello
66: Target: Sea of China
67: Adventures of Batman and
Robin

Nita Talbot (1930-
1956: Bundle of Joy
58: I Married a Woman
Once Upon a Horse
62: Who's Got the Action?
65: A Very Special Favor
That Funny Feeling
Girl Happy
67: The Cool Ones

Gloria Talbott
1953: Northern Patrol
55: We're No Angels
Lucy Gallant
Crashout
All that Heaven Allows
56: The Young Guns
The Strange Intruder

1306

57: The Oklahoman
The Kettles on Old Mac-
   Donald's Farm
Daughter of Dr. Jekyll
Taming Sutton's Girl
Cyclops
58: Cattle Empire
I Married a Monster
   from Outer Space
59: Alias Jesse James
Girls' Town
The Oregon Trail
60: Oklahoma Territory
The Leech Woman
65: Arizona Raiders
66: An Eye for an Eye

Hal Taliaferro
1939: Western Caravans
Daughter of the Tong
Saga of Death Valley
Outpost of the Mounties
40: Bullets for Rustlers
Pioneers of the West
2-Fisted Rangers
Hi-Yo, Silver!
The Man with 9 Lives
The Carson City Kid
Colorado
Young Bill Hickok
Cherokee Strip
The Border Legion
41: In Old Cheyenne
Sheriff of Tombstone
The Great Train Robbery
Border Vigilantes
Law of the Range
Along the Rio Grande
Bad Man of Deadwood
Jesse James at Bay
Red River Valley
Riders of the Timberline
42: Romance on the Range
Tombstone, the Town too
   Tough to Die
Sons of the Pioneers
American Empire
Little Joe--The Wrangler
43: The Man from Music
   Mountain

The Woman of the Town
Hoppy Serves a Writ
Idaho
Song of Texas
Silver Spurs
The Leather Burners
44: The Cowboy and the
   Senorita
Lumberjack
Vigilantes of Dodge City
40 Thieves
Yellow Rose of Texas
Utah
46: Heading West
The Plainsman and the
   Lady
47: Ramrod
48: The Gallant Legion
Red River
West of Sonora
49: Brimstone
50: The Savage Horde
51: The Sea Hornet
52: Junction City

Marion Talley (1907-
1936: Follow Your Heart

Norma Talmadge (1897-1957)
1930: New York Nights
Du Barry-Woman of
   Passion

Richard Talmadge (1898-
1929: Bachelor's Club
Poor Millionaire
31: Yankee Don
Dancing Dynamite
32: Scareheads
Get that Girl
Speed Madness
35: The Fighting Pilot
Now or Never
36: The Speed Reporter
48: Black Eagle
62: How the West Was Won
   (stuntman)
65: Never Too Late
What's New, Pussycat?
66: Hawaii

66:   Casino Royale

William Talman (1915-1968)
1949:   I Married a Communist
        Red Hot and Blue
50:   The Kid from Texas
        Armed Car Robbery
51:   The Racket
52:   One Minute to Zero
53:   The Hitch Hiker
        The City that Never
        Sleeps
55:   Smoke Signal
        Big House U.S.A.
        Crashout
56:   The Uranium Boom
        The Man Is Armed
57:   The Persuader
        Hell on Devil's Island
59:   2-Gun Lady
67:   The Ballad of Josie

Russ Tamblyn (1935-
1948:   The Boy with Green Hair
49:   Reign of Terror (or,
        The Black Book)
        Samson and Delilah
        Deadly Is the Female
        The Kid from Cleveland
50:   Captain Carey, U.S.A.
        Father of the Bride
51:   As Young As You Feel
        Father's Little Dividend
52:   The Winning Team
        Retreat, Hell!
53:   Take the High Ground
54:   7 Brides for 7 Brothers
55:   Many Rivers to Cross
        Hit the Deck
56:   The Last Hunt
        The Fastest Gun Alive
        Young Guns
57:   Don't Go Near the Water
        Peyton Place
58:   High School Confidential
        Tom Thumb
60:   Cimarron
61:   The West Side Story
62:   The Wonderful World of
        the Brothers Grimm

        How the West Was Won
63:   The Haunting
        Follow the Boys
64:   The Long Ships
66:   Son of a Gunfighter
68:   Free Grass
69:   The Blood Seekers

Akim Tamiroff (1899-
1932:   Okay, America!
33:   Queen Christina
34:   Chained
        Here Is My Heart
        The Captain Hates the Sea
        Sadie McKee
        The Great Flirtation
        Whom the Gods Destroy
35:   Lives of a Bengal Lancer
        Naughty Marietta
        The Winning Ticket
        China Seas
        Rumba
        The Last Outpost
        Black Sheep
        Big Broadcast of 1936
        Paris in Spring
        Two Fisted
        Go into Your Dance
        Black Fury
        Gay Deception
        The Story of Louis Pasteur
36:   Desire
        Woman Trap
        The General Died at Dawn
        The Jungle Princess
        Anthony Adverse
37:   The Soldier and the Lady
        (or, Michael Strogoff)
        Her Husband Lies
        King of Gamblers
        High, Wide, and Handsome
        The Great Gambini
38:   The Buccaneer
        Spawn of the North
        Dangerous to Know
        Ride a Crooked Mile
39:   Paris Honeymoon
        Union Pacific
        The Magnificent Fraud
        King of Chinatown

39: Honeymoon in Bali
    Disputed Passage
40: Geronimo
    The Way of All Flesh
    Untamed
    The Great McGinty
    Northwest Mounted Police
41: Texas Rangers Ride
        Again
    New York Town
    The Corsican Brothers
42: Tortilla Flat
    Are Husbands Necessary?
43: 5 Graves to Cairo
    For Whom the Bell Tolls
    His Butler's Sister
44: The Bridge of San Luis
        Rey
    Dragon Seed
    Miracle of Morgan's
        Creek
    Can't Help Singing
46: Pardon My Past
    A Scandal in Paris
47: Fiesta
    The Gangster
48: My Girl Tisa
    10th Avenue Angel
    Relentless
49: Black Magic (or,
        Cagliastro)
53: Desert Legion
54: You Know What Sailors
        Are
55: They Who Dare
56: Black Sleep
    Anastasia
57: Battle Hell
    The Yangtse Incident
58: Touch of Evil
    Me and the Colonel
59: Desert Desperadoes
60: The Tartar Invasion
    Ocean's 11
61: Romanoff and Juliet
    Daggers of Blood
62: The Reluctant Saint
    Mr. Arkadin
    Don Quixote
63: With Fire and Sword

The Trial
Light and Day
Cartouche
64: Topkapi!
    Panic Button
65: The Dolls--Bambole!
        (Monsignor Cupid seq.)
    The Alphaville
66: Lt. Robin Crusoe, USN.
    Marco the Magnificent
    The Liquidator
    Hotel Paradiso
    After the Fox
67: Every Man's Woman
    The Great Catherine
    The Vulture
    A Rose for Everyone
68: The Runaround
    Tenderly (Ital.)
69: Venus in Furs
    100 Rifles
    The Great Bank Robbery
    Then Came Bronson (TV)

Jessica Tandy (1909-
1932: This Is the Night
38: Murder in the Family
44: The 7th Cross
45: The Valley of Decision
46: Dragonwyck
    The Green Years
47: Forever Amber
48: A Woman's Vengeance
50: September Affair
51: The Desert Fox
58: The Light in the Forest
59: Moon and Sixpence (TV)
62: Hemingway's Adventures
        of a Young Man
63: The Birds

Yoko Tani (c1933-
1957: The Wind Cannot Read
58: The Quiet American
59: The Savage Innocents
60: Piccadilly Third Stop
61: Samson and the 7 Miracles
        of the World
62: My Geisha
    Marco Polo the Magnificent

63: Who's Been Sleeping in My Bed?
66: Invasion
68: The Power

56: Blackjack Ketchum-Desperado
57: The Tijuana Story
60: Noose for a Gunman

William Tannen

1940: New Moon
Sky Murder
Flight Command
41: The Big Store
Whistling in the Dark
Dr. Jekyll and Mr. Hyde
42: Joe Smith, American
Fingers at the Window
Nazi Agent
Woman of the Year
Pacific Rendezvous
Stand by for Action
43: Air Raid Wardens
Pilot No. 5
44: The Canterville Ghost
48: An Innocent Affair
49: Alaska Patrol
The Mysterious Desperado
Riders of the Range
50: Chain Gang
Sunset in the West
Pygmy Island
51: A Yank in Korea
New Mexico
Insurance Investigator
The Roaring City
Blue Blood
52: Without Warning
Jungle Jim and the
Forbidden Land
Jet Job
53: Dangerous Crossing
Raiders of the 7 Seas
Jack McCall-Desperado
99 River Street
El Paso Stampede
54: Jesse James vs the
Daltons
Sitting Bull
Captain Kidd and the
Slave Girl
The Law vs Billy the Kid
55: Dial Red O
Devil Goddess

Lilyan Tashman (1900-1934)

1929: Trial of Mary Dugan
New York Nights
Bulldog Drummond
Manhandled
Gold Diggers of Broadway
The Lone Wolf's Daughter
Marriage Playground
30: No, No, Nanette
On the Level
Puttin' on the Ritz
Matrimonial Bed
Leathernecking
One Heavenly Night
The Cat Creeps
Queen of Scandal
31: Girls about Town
Up Pops the Devil
Finn and Hattie
Millie
Mad Parade
Road to Reno
Murder by the Clock
32: Those We Love
The Wiser Sex
Revolt
The Scarlet Dawn
33: Style
Mama Loves Papa
Too Much Harmony
Wine, Women, and Song
34: Riptide

Sharon Tate (1943-1969)

1965: Vampire Killers
"13"
67: Don't Make Waves
Eye of the Devil
Valley of the Dolls
68: Fearless Vampire Killers
(or, Pardon Me but
Your Teeth Are in My
Neck)
69: 13 Chairs
The Wrecking Crew

69: House of 7 Joys

Richard Tauber (1892-1948)
1930: Die Grosse Attraktion
      Ich Glaut Nie Mehran
      Eine Frau
31: Melodie Der Liebe
32: Blossom Time
35: Land Without Music
37: Heart's Desire
      Pagliacci
38: Forbidden Music
45: The Lisbon Story

Brad Taylor
1944: Sing, Neighbor, Sing
      Atlantic City
45: Swingin' on a Rainbow

Don Taylor (1920-
1943: Girl Crazy
      Swing Shift Maisie
      Salute to the Marines
44: Winged Victory
46: Red Dragon
47: Song of the Thin Man
48: The Naked City
      Washington Girl
      For the Love of Mary
      Ridin' Down the Trail
49: Battleground
50: Father of the Bride
      Ambush
51: Target Unknown
      Father's Little Dividend
      Submarine Command
      Flying Leathernecks
      The Blue Veil
52: Japanese War Bride
53: Stalag 17
      Girls of Pleasure Island
      Destination Gobi
54: Johnny Dark
55: I'll Cry Tomorrow
56: The Bold and the Brave
      Men of Sherwood Forest
      Ride the High Iron
57: Love Slaves of the
      Amazon
62: The Savage Guns

64: Ride the Wild Surf (dir.)

Elizabeth Taylor (1930-
1940: Man or Mouse
43: Lassie Come Home
44: National Velvet
      White Cliffs of Dover
      Jane Eyre
46: Courage of Lassie
47: Life with Father
      Cynthia
      Killer McCoy
      Rich Full Lips
48: A Date with Judy
      Julia Misbehaves
49: Little Women
50: Conspirator
      The Big Hangover
      Father of the Bride
51: Father's Little Dividend
      A Place in the Sun
      Quo Vadis (bit)
      Callaway Went Thataway
      (cameo)
52: Love Is Better than Ever
      Ivanhoe
53: The Girl Who Had Every-
      thing
54: Rhapsody
      Elephant Walk
      Beau Brummel
      The Last Time I Saw
      Paris
56: Giant
57: Raintree County
60: Suddenly Last Summer
      Butterfield 8 (OSCAR)
63: Cleopatra
64: The V.I.P.'s
      Becket (bit)
65: The Sandpiper
66: Who's Afraid of Virginia
      Woolf? (OSCAR)
67: Taming of the Shrew
68: The Comedians
      Reflections in a Golden
      Eye
69: Dr. Faustus (bit)
      Boom!
      Secret Ceremony

69: The Only Game in Town

Estelle Taylor (1899-1958)
1928: Singapore Mutiny   S
      Lady Raffles   S
      Honor Bound   S
      While New York Sleeps
      Monte Cristo
      Bayou
      The Whip Woman   S
      Pusher in the Face
29:   Where East Is East   S
30:   Liliom
31:   Street Scene
      Unholy Garden
      Cimarron
32:   Western Limited
      Call Her Savage
38:   various shorts
45:   The Southerner

Ferris Taylor (1893-1961)
1937: Mr. Todd Takes the Air
38:   He Couldn't Say No
      Santa Fe Stampede
      The Daredevil Drivers
39:   You Can't Cheat an
        Honest Man
      Man of Conquest
      The Zero Hour
      S.O.S. Tidal Wave
      Mountain Rhythm
      Main Street Lawyer
40:   Chip of the Flying U.
      Rancho Grande
      Flight Angel s
      One Crowded Night
      Ladies Must Live
      Grand Ole Opry
      Diamond Frontier
      Always a Bride
41:   She Couldn't Say No
      Ridin' on a Rainbow
      The Saint in Palm Springs
      A Man Betrayed
      County Fair
42:   Hello, Annapolis!
43:   Gold Town
      Hoosier Holiday
      Henry Aldrich Haunts a
        House

      Happy Land
44:   Beautiful But Broke
      Wilson
      The Town Went Wild
      End of the Road
45:   Col. Effingham's Raid
46:   Centennial Summer
      Decoy
      The Man from Rainbow
        Valley
      Bringing Up Father
      Rendezvous 24
48:   My Dog Rusty
50:   2 Flags West
54:   The Siege of Red River

Forrest Taylor (1883-1965)
1934: Riders of Destiny
35:   Mississippi
      Rider of the Law
      Courageous Avenger
      Between Men
36:   Rio Grande Romance
      Too Much Beef
      Kelly of the Secret Service
      West of Nevada
      Prison Shadows
      Men of the Plains
      Put on the Spot
      Headin' for the Rio Grande
37:   Arizona Days
      The Mystery of the Hooded
        Horsemen
      The Red Rope
      Riders of the Dawn
      2 Minutes to Play
38:   The Painted Trail
      Heroes of the Hills
      The Last Stand
      Desert Patrol
      Outlaw Express
      Gun Packer
      Black Bandit
      Law of the Texan
      Lightning Carson Rides
        Again
39:   Riders of Black River
40:   Chip of the Flying U.
      Straight Shooters
      Rhythm of the Rio Grande
      Wild Horse Range

40: Frontier Crusader
West of Abilene
The Durango Kid
The Kid from Santa Fe
Trailing Double Trouble
41: Billy the Kid's Fighting
Pals
Flying Wild
Ridin' on a Rainbow
Kansas Cyclone
Wranglers' Roost
Ridin' on the Cherokee
Trail
The Lone Star Vigilantes
42: Sunset on the Desert
Home in Wyomin'
A Night for Crime
Sons of the Pioneers
King of the Stallions
The Yanks are Coming
The Living Ghost
Outlaws of Pine Ridge
The Pay-Off
The Spoilers
43: The Rangers Take Over
Song of Nevada
Man of Courage
Sleepy Lagoon
Corregidor
Fighting Buckaroo
Silver Spurs
44: Lady in the Death House
Shake Hands with Murder
3 Little Sisters
Sundown Valley
The Last Horseman
Sonora Stagecoach
Mystery Man
Mojave Firebrand
Cyclone Prairie Rangers
Outlaws of Santa Fe
Sagebrush Heroes
45: Identity Unknown
Dangerous Intruder
Strange Voyage
Bandits of the Badlands
Rough Ridin' Justice
46: The Caravan Trail
The Glass Alibi
Romance of the West

Colorado Serenade
Texas Pnahandle
Driftin' River
Santa Fe Uprising
47: Stagecoach to Denver
Yankee Fakir
The Pretender
Rustlers of Devil's Canyon
Along the Oregon Trail
The Stranger from Ponca
City
48: Buckaroo from Powder
River
4 Faces West
Coroner Creek
The Mysterious Golden
Eye
49: The Lawton Story
Death Valley Gunfighter
Stallion Canyon
Navajo Trail Raiders
Deputy Marshal
The Fighting Redhead
50: The Cowboy and the Prize-
fighter
Forbidden Jungle
The Fighting Stallion
Code of the Silver Sage
Cherokee Uprising
Rustlers on Horseback
51: Prairie Roundup
Blazing Bullets
52: Border Saddlemates
Park Row
South Pacific Trail
Smoky Canyon
Night Riders
53: The Marshal's Daughter
Iron Mountain Trail
54: Bitter Creek

Joan Taylor
1949: Fighting Man of the Plains
52: The Savage
53: War Paint
54: Rose Marie
55: Fort Yuma
Apache Woman
56: Earth vs the Flying Saucers

1313

57: Omar Khayyam
War Drums
20,000 Miles to Earth

Kent Taylor (1907-
1931: Road to Reno
32: Merrily We Go to Hell
The Devil and the Deep
Make Me a Star
Sign of the Cross
If I Had a Million
2 Kinds of Women
Husband's Holiday
Forgotten Commandments
33: Sunset Pass
Sinners in the Sun
Blonde Venus
Mysterious Rider
Under the Tonto Rim
The Story of Temple
Drake
A Lady's Profession
I'm No Angel
White Woman
The Cradle Song
34: Death Takes a Holiday
Double Door
Mrs. Wiggs of the
Cabbage Patch
Limehouse Blues
David Harum
35: County Chairman
College Scandal
Smart Girl
Without Regret
2-Fisted
36: My Marriage
Florida Special
Sky Parade
The Accusing Finger
Ramona
37: When Love Is Young
Wings over Honolulu
Love in a Bungalow
The Lady Fights Back
A Girl with Ideas
Prescription for Romance
38: The Jury's Secret
The Last Express
39: The Gracie Allen Murder
Case

5 Came Back
3 Sons
Escape to Paradise
40: I Take this Woman
2 Girls on Broadway
Sued for Libel
Girl in 313
The Girl from Avenue A
Men Against the Sky
I'm Still Alive
41: Washington Melodrama
Repent at Leisure
42: Frisco Lil
Mississippi Gambler
Tombstone, the Town
Too Tough to Die
Army Surgeon
Gang Busters (ser.)
43: Halfway to Shanghai
Bomber's Moon
44: Alaska
Roger Touhy--Gangster
45: The Daltons Ride Again
46: Notorious Gentlemen
Dangerous Millions
Deadline for Murder
Smooth as Silk
Tangier
Young Widow
47: Second Chance
The Crimson Key
48: Half Past Midnight
49: The Sickle or the Cross
50: Western Pacific Agent
Federal Agent at Large
Trial Without Jury
51: Payment on Demand
54: Playgirl
55: Secret Venture
Ghost Town
56: Slightly Scarlet
Track the Man Down
Frontier Gambler
57: The Iron Sheriff
58: Fort Bowie
Gang War
60: Walk Tall
61: The Purple Hills
62: The Broken Land
The Firebrand
63: The Day Mars Invaded the
Earth

1314

```
63:  Harbor Lights              49:  The Bribe
64:  Land of the Lawless             Ambush
65:  The Crawling Hand         50:  Devil's Doorway
68:  Brides of Blood                The Big Apple
                                     The Conspirator
Robert Taylor (1911-1969)      51:  Quo Vadis?
1934:  Handy Andy                    Westward the Women
       Only 8 Hours            52:  Ivanhoe
       There's Always Tomorrow       Above and Beyond
       A Wicked Woman          53:  Ride, Vaquero!
       Too Late to Love             All the Brothers Were
35:    Buried Loot (short)           Valiant
       Society Doctor               Knights of the Round Table
       Jackpot                 54:  Valley of the Kings
       Times Square Lady            Rogue Cop
       West Point of the Air   55:  Many Rivers to Cross
       Murder in the Fleet          Quentin Durward
       Broadway Melody of 1936 56:  The Last Hunt
36:    Magnificent Obsession        D-Day, the 6th of June
       Small Town Girl              The Power and the Prize
       The Gorgeous Hussy      57:  The Tip on a Dead Jockey
       Camille                 58:  Saddle the Wind
       His Brother's Wife           The Law and Jake Wade
       Private Number               Party Girl
37:    Personal Property       59:  The Hangman
       Broadway Melody of 1938      The House of the 7 Hawks
       This Is My Affair       60:  Killers of Kilimanjaro
       Lest We Forget          63:  Cattle King (or, Guns of
38:    A Yank at Oxford             Wyoming)
       Three Comrades               Miracle of the White
       The Crowd Roars              Stallions
39:    Stand Up and Fight      64:  A House Is not a Home
       Lucky Night                  The Big Parade of Comedy
       Lady of the Tropics          (doc.)
       Remember?               65:  The Night Walker
40:    Waterloo Bridge              Cry of the Laughing Owls
       Escape                  66:  Return of the Gunfighter
       Flight Command               Johnny Tiger
41:    Billy the Kid           67:  Savage Pampas
       When Ladies Meet             Hondo
       Johnny Eager            68:  Where Angels Go Trouble
42:    Her Cardboard Lover          Follows
       Stand by for Action          The Hot Line (or, The
43:    The Youngest Profession      Day the Hot Line Got
       Bataan                       Hot)
       Song of Russia               The Glass Sphinx
44:    The Fighting Lady (doc.)     The Last of the Comancheros
46:    Undercurrent
47:    High Wall               Rod Taylor (1929-
48:    The Secret Land         1955:  The Virgin Queen
```

55: Long John Silver
Top Gun
Hell on Frisco Bay
56: King of the Corral Sea
Giant
The Catered Affair
World Without End
57: Raintree County
58: Separate Tables
Step Down to Terror
59: Ask Any Girl
60: The Time Machine
61: 101 Dalmatians (cartoon
voice)
63: The Birds
The V.I.P.'s
A Gathering of Eagles
7 Seas to Calais
Sunday in New York
64: Fate Is the Hunter
36 Hours
65: Young Cassidy
66: The Glass Bottom Boat
The Liquidator
Do Not Disturb
67: Hotel
Chuka
Last Bus to Banjo Creek
Dark of the Sun
68: Hell for Heroes
High Commissioner
69: The Mercenary
Nobody Runs Forever
The Man Who Had Power
over Women
Zabriskie Point
Darker than Amber
The Hawks at Noon

Vaughn Taylor (1911-
1951: Francis Goes to the Races
Up Front
52: Meet Danny Wilson
Back at the Front
54: It Should Happen to You
57: This Could be the Night
Jailhouse Rock
Decision at Sundown
58: Cowboy
Party Girl

The Screaming Mimi
The Lineup
Andy Hardy Comes Home
Cat on a Hot Tin Roof
Gunsmoke in Tucson
59: Warlock
Blue Denim
60: The Gallant Hours
Psycho
The Plunderers
The Wizard of Baghdad
62: Diamond Head
63: Twilight Hour
64: The Carpetbaggers
The Unsinkable Molly
Brown
FBI Code 98
65: Zebra in the Kitchen
Dark Intruder
66: The Russians Are Coming,
The Russians Are Coming!
The Professionals
67: In Cold Blood
68: The Power
69: The Shakiest Gun in the
West
Fever Heat
The Ballad of Cable Hogue

Leigh Taylor-Young (1944-
1969: I Love You, Alice B.
Toklas
The Big Bounce
The Adventurers
The Games
The Buttercup Chain

Ray Teal (1902-
1938: Western Jamboree
40: Cherokee Strip
Prairie Schooner (or,
Through the Storm)
Pony Post
Adventures of Red Ryder
(ser.)
Northwest Passage
41: They Died with Their
Boots on
Outlaws of the Panhandle
(or, Faro Jack)

41: Wild Bill Hickok Rides
42: Apache Trail
44: Wing and a Prayer
Strange Affair
None Shall Escape
45: Captain Kidd
Along Cames Jones
The Fighting Guardsman
Strange Voyage
46: The Best Years of Our
Lives
Bandit of Sherwood Forest
Blondie Knows Best
Canyon Passage
Deadline for Murder
The Missing Lady
Till the Clouds Roll by
47: Road to Rio
Unconquered
The Michigan Kid
Brute Force
Ramrod
Driftwood
The Man from Colorado
48: Countess of Monte Cristo
Whispering Smith
Joan of Arc
49: Once More, My Darling
It Happens Every Spring
Ambush
Streets of Laredo
Blondie Hits the Jackpot
Rusty's Birthday
50: No Way Out
Our Very Own
The Men
The Redhead and the
Cowboy
Davy Crockett--Indian
Scout
Harbor of Missing Men
The Kid from Texas
Edge of Doom
When You're Smiling
Winchester 73
51: Forth Worth
Tomorrow Is Another Day
The Big Carnival (or,
Ace in the Hole)
Along the Great Divide
The Secret of Convict
Lake

Distant Drums
The Flaming Feather
52: The Lion and the Horse
Captive City
Montana Belle
The Turning Point
Jumping Jacks
Carrie
Hangman's Knot
The Wild North
Cattle Town
54: Ambush at Tomahawk Gap
The Wild One
The Command
About Mrs. Leslie
Rogue Cop
55: Rage at Dawn
The Indian Fighter
Run for Cover
Desperate Hours
The Man from Bitter
Ridge
Apache Ambush
56: The Young Guns
The Burning Hills
57: A Band of Angels
Utah Blaine
The Phantom Stagecoach
The Oklahoman
The Wayward Girl
The Tall Stranger
Decision at Sundown
The Guns of Fort Petticoat
58: Saddle the Wind
Gunman's Walk
Girl on the Run
60: Inherit the Wind
Home from the Hill
61: One-Eyed Jacks
Posse from Hell
Judgment at Nuremberg
63: Cattle King (or, Guns of
Wyoming)
64: Bullet for a Badman
Taggart!
69: The Liberation of Lord
Byron Jones

Conway Tearle (1878-1938)
1929: Smoke Bellew   S
Gold Diggers of Broadway
Evidence

30: Lost Zeppelin
The Lady Who Dared
Truth about Youth
31: Captivation
Morals for Women
32: False Madonna
Pleasure
Vanity Fair
Man About Town
The King Murder
33: Day of Reckoning
Should Ladies Behave?
34: Stingaree
15 Wives
Sing Sing Nights
35: Headline Woman
The Trail's End
Judgment Book
36: Klondike Annie
Desert Guns
The Preview Murder
Mystery
Romeo and Juliet

Veree Teasdale (c1897-
1929: Syncopation
30: Vitaphone #1028--The
Duel (short)
Vitaphone #1074--The
Intruder (short)
The Sap from Syracuse
32: Skycraper Souls
Payment Deferred
Luxury Liner
Her New Chauffeur
33: They Just Had to Get
Married
Terror Abroad
Love, Honor, and Oh
Baby!
Roman Scandals
34: Fashions of 1934
Goodbye Love
A Modern Hero
Madame Du Barry
Desirable
The Firebrand
Doctor Monica
35: A Midsummer Night's
Dream
36: The Milky Way
37: First Lady

39: Topper Takes a Trip
Fifth Avenue Girl
40: Turnabout
I Take this Woman
Love Thy Neighbor
41: Come Live with Me

Irene Tedrow (1907-
1937: They Won't Forget
40: We Who Are Young
41: Cheers for Miss Bishop
42: Journey into Fear
Eagle Squadron
The Moon and Sixpence
43: Dr. Gillespie
44: Song of the Open Road
45: The Strange Affair of
Uncle Harry
The Crime Doctor's
Warning
46: Just Before Dawn
They Won't Believe Me
48: The Mating of Millie
49: Air Hostess
Thieves' Highway
50: The Company She Keeps
53: A Lion Is in the Streets
54: Not as a Stranger
55: Santa Fe Passage
56: Capital Offense
The Ten Commandments
57: Slander
Lovin' You
58: Hot Spell
59: Never so Few
60: Please Don't Eat the
Daisies
61: The Parent Trap
62: The Deadly Duo
64: Joy in the Morning
65: The Greatest Story Ever
Told
66: The Cincinnati Kid
For Pete's Sake
69: The Comic
Getting Straight

Olive Tell (1896-1951)
1929: Trial of Mary Dugan
The Very Idea
Hearts in Exile
30: Cock O' the Walk

1318

30: Lawful Larceny
    Love Comes Along
31: Ladies' Man
    10¢ a Dance
    The Right of Way
    Woman Hungry
    Devotion
    Delicious
33: Strictly Personal
34: Private Scandal
    The Witching Hour
    Scarlet Empress
35: 4 Hours to Kill
    Shanghai
36: Yours for the Asking
    Polo Joe
    In His Steps
    Brilliant Marriage

Shirley Temple (1927-
1932: Baby Burlesk
    The Incomparable Miss
      Legs Sweetrick
    The Pie Covered Wagon
    Polly-Tax in Washington
    Frolicks of Youth
    Red-Haired Alibi
    Out All Night
    Fox Follies
    Glad Rags to Riches
33: To the Last Man
34: Baby Take a Bow
    Bright Eyes
    (SPECIAL AWARD)
    Carolina
    Girl in Pawn
    When New York Sleeps
    Now I'll Tell
    Stand Up and Cheer
    Little Miss Marker
    Change of Heart
    Now and Forever
35: Curly Top
    Our Little Girl
    The Littlest Rebel
    The Little Colonel
36: Captain January
    Poor Little Rich Girl
    Dimples
    Stowaway
37: Heidi
    Wee Willie Winkie

38: Rebecca of Sunnybrook
      Farm
    Little Miss Broadway
    Just Around the Corner
39: The Little Princess
    Susannah of the Mounties
40: The Blue Bird
    Young People
41: Kathleen
42: Miss Annie Rooney
43: (a citation)
44: Since You Went Away
    I'll be Seeing You
45: Kiss and Tell
47: The Bachelor and the
      Bobby-Soxer
    That Hagen Girl
    Honeymoon
48: Fort Apache
49: Mr. Belvedere Goes to
      College
    Adventure in Baltimore
    The Story of Seabiscuit
    A Kiss for Corliss
64: The Sound of Laughter
      (doc.)

Max Terhune (1891-
1936: The 3 Mesquiteers
37: The Hit Parade
    Ghost Town Gold
    Roarin' Lead
    Come on, Cowboys!
    Riders of the Whistling
      Skull
    The Big Show
    Range Defenders
    Gunsmoke Ranch
    Mama Runs Wild
    Manhattan Merry-Go-
      Round
    The Trigger Trio
38: Wild Horse Rodeo
    Call of the Mesquiteers
    The Purple Vigilantes
    Outlaws of Sonora
    Riders of the Black Hills
    Ladies in Distress
    Heroes of the Hills
    Santa Fe Stampede
    Pals of the Saddle
    Overland Stage Raiders

39: The Night Riders
     Man of Conquest
     3 Texas Steers
40: The Range Busters
     Trailing Double Trouble
     West of Pinto Basin
41: Trail of the Silver Spurs
     Tumbledown Ranch in
       Arizona
     Wranglers' Roost
     The Kid's Last Ride
     Fugitive Valley
42: Rock River Renegades
     Texas to Bataan
     Trail Riders
     Boot Hill Bandits
     Texas Trouble Shooters
43: 2-Fisted Justice
     Cowboy Commandos
     Black Market Rustlers
44: Cowboy Canteen
     Sheriff of Sundown
47: Along the Oregon Trail
49: Gunning for Justice
     Sheriff of Medicine Bow
     Square Dance Jubilee

Steven Terrell
1957: Invasion of the Saucer
         Men
       Motorcycle Gang

Don Terry
1941: Mutiny in the Arctic
  42: Unseen Enemy
       Escape from Hong Kong
       Drums of the Congo
       Danger in the Pacific
       Moonlight in Havana
       Top Sergeant
  43: Sherlock Holmes in
         Washington
       White Savage

Philip Terry (c1912-
1937: Navy Blue and Gold
  38: Yellow Jack
       Hold that Kiss
       Mannequin
  39: 4 Girls in White
       a short
       Calling Dr. Kildare

     On Borrowed Time
     Balalaika
40: Those Were the Days
     Fugitive from a Prison
       Camp
41: The Monster and the Girl
     Dancing on a Dime
     The Parson of Panamint
     Public Enemies
42: Torpedo Boat
     Sweater Girl
     Are Husbands Necessary?
     Wake Island
43: Bataan
     Here Comes the Bride
44: Ladies Courageous
     Music in Manhattan
     Double Exposure
45: George White's Scandals
     The Lost Weekend
     Pan-Americana
46: The Dark Horse
     To Each His Own
47: Beat the Band
     Born to Kill
     7 Keys To Baldpate
52: Deadline, U.S.A.
58: Man from God's Country
60: The Leech Woman
61: The Explosive Generation
66: The Navy vs the Night
       Monsters

Ruth Terry
1939: Wife, Husband, and Friend
  40: Slightly Honorable
       An Angel from Texas
       Sing Dance Plenty Hot
  41: Blondie Goes Latin
       Rookies on Parade
       Appointment for Love
  42: Sleepytime Gal
       The Affairs of Jimmy
         Valentine
       Call of the Canyon
       Youth on Parade
       Heart of the Golden West
  43: The Man from Music
         Mountain
       Mystery Broadcast
       Hands Across the Border
       Pistol Packin' Mama

44: Jamboree
Goodnight Sweetheart
3 Little Sisters
Strangers in the Night
3 Is a Family
45: Lake Placid Serenade
Steppin' in Society
The Cheaters
Tell it to a Star
47: Smoky River Serenade
62: Hand on Death

Sheila Terry
1932: Week-End Marriage
The Crooner
Big City Blues
I Am a Fugitive of a
Chain Gang
Three on a Match
Scarlet Dawn
You Said a Mouthful
Madame Butterfly
Lawyer Man
33: Parachute Jumper
20,000 Years in Sing Sing
Haunted Gold
Mayor of Hell
Silk Express
The Sphinx
Private Detective 62
House on 56th Street
Son of a Sailor
Convention City
34: Take the Stand
When Strangers Meet
Rocky Rhodes
'Neath Arizona Skies
35: Lawless Frontier
Rescue Squad
Society Fever
36: Murder on a Bridle Path
Special Investigator
Go Get 'em Haines

Terry-Thomas (1911-
1956: Private's Progress
The Green Man
57: Brothers-in-Law
Happy Is the Bride
58: The Lucky Jinx
Blue Murder at St.
Trinian's

The Naked Truth
Carleton Browne of F.O.
Your Past Is Showing
tom thumb
59: Too Many Crooks
60: I'm All Right, Jack
School for Scoundrels
Make Mine Mink
The Man in the Cockeyed
Hat
61: His and Hers
Bachelor Flat
62: The Wonderful World
of the Brothers Grimm
A Matter of Who
Operation Snatch
Kill or Cure
63: It's a Mad Mad Mad Mad
World
The Mouse on the Moon
64: Strange Bedfellows
65: Wild Affair
How to Murder Your Wife
Our Man in Marrakesh
Those Magnificent Men
in Their Flying Machines
You Must be Joking!
66: Munster, Go Home!
Bang! Bang! You're Dead!
The Daydreamer
67: Perils of Pauline
Kiss the Girls and Make
Them Die
Rocket to the Moon
A Guide for the Married
Man
Those Fantastic Flying
Fools
68: Dangerous Diabolik
Arabella
His and Hers
Le Grand Vaudeville
Where Were You When
the Lights Went Out?
How Sweet It Is!
Don't Raise the Bridge,
Lower the Water
69: The Big Blast
2000 Years Later
13 Chairs
Those Daring Young Men
in Their Jaunty Jalopies

1321

Walter Tetley
1938: Lord Jeff
Prairie Moon
39: Spirit of Culver
Boy Slaves
They Shall Have Music
Tower of London
40: Military Academy
Under Texas Skies
Let's Make Music
42: Thunder Birds
Who Done It?
The Gorilla Man
44: Pin-Up Girl
45: Molly and Me

Joan Tetzel (1921-
1946: Duel in the Sun
47: The Paradine Case
49: The File of Thelma
Jordan
54: Hell Below Zero
65: Joy in the Morning

Heather Thatcher
1937: The 13th Chair
Mama Steps Out
Tovarich
38: Fools for Scandal
Girls' School
If I Were King
39: Beau Geste
41: Scotland Yard
Man Hunt
42: Son of Fury
The Moon and Sixpence
Journey for Margaret
The Undying Monster
44: Gaslight
52: The Hour of 13
54: Duel in the Jungle

Torin Thatcher (1905-
1932: But the Flesh Is Weak
The Prisoner of Zenda
34: General John Regan
35: Drake of England
School for Stars
The Red Wagon
37: The Man Who Could Work
Miracles
39: Young and Innocent

Climbing High
40: Let George Do It
41: Last Train to Munich
Law and Disorder
The Case of the Frightened
Lady
Barabbas
The Command Round and
the Proconsul
Old Mother Riley, M.P.
Major Barbara
42: Next to Kin
Saboteur
47: The Captive Heart
I See a Dark Stranger
Great Expectations
48: When the Bough Breaks
Jassy
The End of the River
Bonnie Prince Charlie
Lost Illusion
49: The Fallen Idol
50: The Black Rose
52: The Crimson Pirate
Affair in Trinidad
The Snows of Kilimanjaro
Blackbeard the Pirate
53: The Desert Rats
Houdini
The Robe
54: Knock on Wood
The Black Shield of Fal-
worth
Bengal Brigade
55: Helen of Troy
Lady Godiva of Coventry
Diane
Love Is a Many-Splendored
Thing
56: Istanbul
57: A Band of Angels
Witness for the Prosecution
58: 7th Voyage of Sinbad
Darby's Rangers
59: The Miracle
61: The Canadians
62: Jack, the Giant Killer
Mutiny on the Bounty
63: Drums of Africa
The Sweet and the Bitter
Music at Midnight
64: From Hell to Borneo

1322

65: The Sandpiper
66: Hawaii
67: The King's Pirate
68: The Strange Case of Dr.
Jekyll and Mr. Hyde
(TV)

Phyllis Thaxter (1921-
1944: 30 Seconds over Tokyo
45: Weekend at the Waldorf
Bewitched
47: Living in a Big Way
Sea of Grass
48: Act of Violence
10th Avenue Angel
Sign of the Ram
Blood on the Moon
50: The Breaking Point
No Man of Her Own
51: Fort Worth
Jim Thorpe--All-
American
Come Fill the Cup
52: She's Working Her Way
Through College
Operation Secret
Springfield Rifle
55: Women's Prison
57: Man Afraid
64: The World of Henry
Orient

Tina Thayer
1942: A Yank at Eton
Secrets of a Coed
Pay-Off
43: Jive Junction
44: Henry Aldrich's Little
Secret

Ernest Thesiger (1879-1961)
1929: West End Wives   S
32: The Old Dark House
The Ghoul
33: Only Girl
Night of the Party
34: My Heart Is Calling
35: The Bride of Frankenstein
36: The Man Who Could
Perform Miracles
38: They Drive by Night

44: Henry V
46: Caesar and Cleopatra
47: Beware of Pity
48: Jassy
49: A Place of One's Own
A Man Within
50: The Winslow Boy
Last Holiday
51: Laughter in Paradise
The Man in White
52: Bad Lord Byron
The Colonel's Lady
Portrait of Hildegarde
53: The Robe
54: The Detective
55: Quentin Durward
60: The Battle of the Sexes
Sons and Lovers
61: The Roman Spring of Mrs.
Stone

Ursula Thiess (1920-
1953: Monsoon
54: The Iron Glove
Bengal Brigade
55: The Americano
56: Bandido

Helen Thimig
1942: The Gay Sisters
43: The Moon Is Down
Edge of Darkness
44: The Hitler Gang
Strangers in the Night
None but the Lonely Heart
45: Roughly Speaking
Hotel Berlin
Isle of the Dead
This Love of Ours
46: Cloak and Dagger
The Locket
47: High Conquest
Cry Wolf
Escape Me Never
51: Decision Before Dawn

Roy Thinnes
1969: Doppelganger
The Other Man

1323

Danny Thomas (1914-
1947: Unfinished Dance
  48: Big City
  51: Call Me Mister
      I'll See You in My Dreams
  53: The Jazz Singer
  64: Looking for Love
  66: Don't Worry, We'll Think
      of a Title

Frank Thomas, Jr.
1941: Flying Cadets
      One Foot in Heaven
  42: Always in My Heart
      The Major and the Minor
  43: Hello, Frisco, Hello!

Frank M. Thomas (1922-
1936: The Ex-Mrs. Bradford
      The Last Outlaw
      Grand Jury
      We Who Are about to Die
      M'Liss
      The Big Game
      Without Orders
      Don't Turn 'em Loose
      Wanted: Jane Turner
      Mummy's Boys
  37: Don't Tell the Wife
      Criminal Lawyer
      We're on the Jury
      The Man Who Found
        Himself
      Outcasts of Poker Flat
      Racing Lady
      They Wanted to Marry
      Girl Loves Boy
      China Passage
      You Can't Buy Luck
      Meet the Missus
      You Can't Beat Love
      Behind the Headlines
      40 Naughty Girls
      The Toast of New York
      The Big Shot
      Breakfast for Two
      Danger Patrol
  38: Night Spot
      Crashing Hollywood
      Quick Money
      Everybody's Doing It
      Go Chase Yourself

This Marriage Business
Crime Ring
Blind Alibi
Maid's Night Out
Boys Town
Mr. Doodle Kicks Off
A Man to Remember
Little Tough Guys in
  Society
Nancy Drew, Detective
  39: Society Lawyer
      The Mysterious Miss X
      They Made Her a Spy
      Grand Jury Secrets
      Bachelor Mother
      They All Come Out
      Sage of Death Valley
      Death of a Champion
      Nancy Drew and the
        Hidden Staircase
      On Dress Parade
      Angels Wash Their Faces
      Nancy Drew, Trouble
        Shooter
  40: Shooting High
      Scandal Sheet
      Lillian Russell
      Invisible Stripes
      Chad Hanna
      Queen of the Mob
      Maryland
      Brigham Young--Frontiers-
        man
  41: Arkansas Judge
      Wyoming Wildcat
      A Shot in the Dark
      Among the Living
      3 Sons O' Guns
      Sierra Sue
  42: Reap the Wild Wind
      Sunset on the Desert
      The Great Man's Lady
      The Postman Didn't Ring
      Apache Trail
      The Talk of the Town
      Sunset Serenade
      Mountain Rhythm
  43: No Place for a Lady

Jameson Thomas (1892-1939)
1928: Roses of Picardy   S
  29: Piccadilly

1324

30: Elstree Calling
High Treason
Extravagance
The Hate Ship
The Farmer's Daughter
31: Lover Come Back
Night Life in Reno
Convicted
The Devil Plays
32: 3 Wise Girls
Trial of Vivienne Ware
Escapade
Phantom President
No More Orchids
33: Self Defense
Brief Moment
34: Bombay Mail
Beggars in Ermine
It Happened One Night
A Woman's Man
Stolen Sweets
Now and Forever
Scarlet Empress
Jane Eyre
The Moonstone
A Successful Failure
Lost Lady
The Curtain Falls
Sing Sing Nights
35: Lives of a Bengal Lancer
The World Accuses
Mister Dynamite
Charlie Chan in Egypt
The Last Outpost
Coronado
The Lady in Scarlet
36: Mr. Deeds Goes to Town
Lady Luck
37: The Man Who Cried Wolf
100 Men and a Girl
The League of Frightened
Men
38: Death Goes North

Carlos Thompson (c1920-
1953: Fort Algiers
54: The Flame and the Flesh
Valley of the Kings
56: Magic Fire
58: Raw Wind in Eden
59: Stefanie
60: Between Time and
Eternity

61: The Spessart Inn
62: Our Man in the Caribbean

Marshall Thompson (1926-
1944: The Reckless Age
The Purple Heart
Blonde Fever
45: They Were Expendable
The Clock
The Valley of Decision
46: Bad Bascomb
Gallant Bess
The Cockeyed Miracle
The Show-Off
The Secret Heart
47: Romance of Rosy Ridge
48: Homecoming
B.F.'s Daughter
Words and Music
Command Decision
49: Rosanna McCoy
Battleground
50: Stars in My Crown
Dial 1119
The House of Usher
The Devil's Doorway
Mystery Street
51: Tall Target
The Basketball Fix
52: My 6 Convicts
The Rose Bowl Story
53: The Caddy
54: Port of Hell
55: Battle Taxi
The Cult of the Cobra
The Crashout
To Hell and Back
Good Morning, Miss Dove
56: The Fiend Without a Face
57: Lure of the Swamp
58: It! The Terror from
Beyond Space
59: The First Man into Space
61: Flight of the Lost Balloon
62: No Man Is an Island
64: A Yank in Vietnam
65: Clarence, the Cross-Eyed
Lion
66: Around the World Under
the Sea
69: The Private World of
Dr. Blake

1325

Kenneth Thomson (1899-1967)
1929: Broadway Melody
Say it with Songs
The Girl from Havana
The Song Writer
The Careless Age
The Veiled Woman
The Bellamy Trial
The Letter
30: The Other Tomorrow
Sweet Mama
Wild Company
Reno
A Notorious Affair
Faithful
Children of Pleasure
Lawful Larceny
Sweethearts on Parade
Doorway to Hell
Just Imagine
31: Woman Hungry
Murder at Midnight
Bad Company
32: By Whose Hands?
Man Wanted
The Famous Ferguson
Case
Movie Crazy
70,000 Witnesses
13 Women
Her Mad Night
Lawyer Man
33: Jungle Bride
The Little Giant
Female
Son of a Sailor
Daring Daughters
Hold Me Tight
Sitting Pretty
From Headquarters
34: Cross Streets
In Old Santa Fe
Change of Heart
Many Happy Returns
35: Behold My Wife
Behind Green Lights
Whispering Smith Speaks
Hopalong Cassidy
Manhattan Butterfly
36: The Blackmailer
With Love and Kisses
37: Jim Harvey, Detective

Jerome Thor (1915-
1959: Riot in a Juvenile Prison
63: 55 Days at Peking

Larry Thor
1955: 5 Guns West
57: Portland Exposé
The Amazing Colossal Man
Hell Bound
Zero Hour!
58: Tarawa Beachhead
The Littlest Hobo
59: The Battle of the Coral
Sea

Jim Thorpe (1889-1953)
1932: White Eagle
My Pal, the King
Airmail
33: Wild Horse Mesa
35: Behold My Wife
Code of the Mounted
She
Wanderer of the Waste-
land
36: Sutter's Gold
Treachery Rides the
Range
Wildcat Trooper
37: Big City
40: Henry Goes to Arizona
Arizona Frontier
Prairie Schooners
44: Outlaw Trail
50: Wagonmaster

The Three Stooges (Moe Howard,
c1897 [which see also], joined
1923 -) (Larry Fine, joined
1923 -) (Shemp Howard, c1890-
1955 [which see also], joined
1923-32, & 1946-55) (Curly
[Jerome] Howard, 1906-1952,
joined 1932-46) (Joe De Rita
[which see also], joined 1958-)
1930's-40's: numerous 2 reelers
1933: Dancing Lady
The Little Pigskins (short)
34: Hollywood Party
37: Termites of 1938
We Wee Monsieur
38: Start Cheering

1326

41:	Time Out for Rhythm		Murder on the Yukon
44:	Ghost Crazy		Young Buffalo Bill
46:	Swing Parade of 1946		Northwest Mounted Police
51:	Gold Raiders		Hudson's Bay
53:	The Three Stooges in	41:	Western Union
	Spooks	42:	Shut My Big Mouth
59:	Have Rocket, Will Travel		King of the Stallions
60:	Stop, Look, and Laugh!	44:	Buffalo Bill
61:	Snow White and the Three		The Falcon Out West
	Stooges		Outlaw Trail
62:	The 3 Stooges Meet		Sonora Stagecoach
	Hercules	46:	Badman's Territory
63:	The 3 Stooges in Orbit		Romance of the West
	The 3 Stooges Go Around	47:	Renegade Girl
	the World in a Daze		The Senator Was Indiscreet
	It's a Mad Mad Mad Mad	48:	Blazing Across the Pecos
	World	49:	Ambush
	4 for Texas	50:	Colt .45
64:	Big Parade of Comedy		Davy Crockett--Indian
	(doc.)		Scout
65:	The Outlaws Is Coming!		Ticket to Tomahawk
			The Traveling Saleswoman

Frank Thring
1958: The Vikings
59: Ben-Hur
61: King of Kings
El Cid
68: Age of Consent

Ingrid Thulin (1929-
1957: Wild Strawberries
58: So Close to Life
59: The Magician
The Light
60: Brink of Life
62: The Four Horsemen of
the Apocalypse
63: Winter Light
64: The Silence
65: Return from the Ashes
66: Night Games
67: La Guerre Est Finie
68: The Hour of the Wolf
The Bathers
Adelaide
69: The Damned
The Ritual

Chief Thundercloud (1899-1955)
1939: Geronimo
40: Hi-Yo, Silver!
Typhoon

I Killed Geronimo
51: Santa Fe
52: Buffalo Bill in Tomahawk
Territory

Carol Thurston
1944: The Conspirators
The Story of Dr. Wassell
45: China Spy
46: Swamp Fire
47: Jewels of Brandenburg
The Last Round-Up
48: Rogue's Regiment
49: Arctic Manhunt
Apache Chief
51: Flaming Feather
52: Arctic Flight
53: Conquest of Cochise
Killer Ape
54: Yukon Vengeance
56: The Women of Pitcairn
Island
60: The Hypnotic Eye
63: Showdown

Greta Thyssen
1956: Accused of Murder
Bus Stop
58: The Beast of Budapest
59: Terror Is a Man

60: 3 Blondes in His Life
61: Journey to the 7th Planet
   Shadows

Lawrence Tibbett (1896-1960)
1930: The Rogue Song
   New Moon
   Parisian Belle
31: The Prodigal
   Cuban Love Song
35: Metropolitan
36: Under Your Spell

Gene Tierney (1920-
1940: The Return of Frank
   James
   Hudson's Bay
41: Tobacco Road
   Belle Starr
   Sundown
   The Shanghai Gesture
42: Song of Fury
   Rings on Her Fingers
   China Girls
   Thunder Birds
43: Heaven can Wait
44: Laura
45: A Bell for Adano
   Leave Her to Heaven
46: Dragonwyck
   The Razor's Edge
47: The Ghost and Mrs. Muir
48: The Iron Curtain
   That Wonderful Urge
49: Whirlpool
50: Night and the City
   Where the Sidewalk Ends
51: The Mating Season
   On the Riviera
   Secret of Convict Lake
   Close to My Heart
52: The Way of a Gaucho
   Plymouth Adventure
53: Never Let Me Go
54: Personal Affair
   The Egyptian
   Black Widow
55: The Left Hand of God
62: Advise and Consent
63: Toys in the Attic
64: The Pleasure Seekers
69: Daughter of the Mind (TV)

Lawrence Tierney (1919-
1943: The Ghost Ship
   The Falcon Out West
44: Youth Runs Wild
45: Dillinger
   Mama Loves Papa
   Back to Bataan
   Those Endearing Young
   Charms
46: Badman's Territory
   Step by Step
   San Quentin
47: The Devil Thumbs a Ride
   Born to Kill
48: Bodyguard
50: Shakedown
   Killed or be Killed
51: Best of the Bad Men
   The Hoodlum
52: The Bushwackers
   The Greatest Show on
   Earth
54: Steel Cage
56: Female Jungle
62: A Child Is Waiting
68: Custer of the West

Pamela Tiffin (1942-
1961: Summer and Smoke
   One, Two, Three
62: State Fair
63: Come Fly With Me
64: For Those Who Think
   Young
   The Lively Set
   The Pleasure Seekers
65: The Hallelujah Trail
66: Harper
67: The Protagonists
68: The Imperfect Murder
   Torture Me but Kill Me
   with Kisses (Ital.)
   Kiss the Other Sheik
69: Viva Max!
   Archangel

Zeffie Tilbury (1863-1945)
1929: Single Standard   S
30: Ship from Shanghai
31: Charlie Chan Carries On
34: Mystery Liner
35: Women Must Dress

35: The Mystery of Edwin
    Drood
    Werewolf of London
    Alice Adams
    Last Days of Pompeii
36: Desire
    The Bohemian Girl
    Give Me Your Heart
37: Maid of Salem
    Under Cover of Night
    Rhythm in the Clouds
    Bulldog Drummond Comes
    Back
    It Happened in Hollywood
38: Bulldog Drummond's Peril
    Josette
    Woman Against Woman
39: The Story of Alexander
    Graham Bell
    Arrest Bulldog Drummond!
    Tell No Tales
    Balalaika
40: The Grapes of Wrath
    Comin' 'Round the
    Mountain
41: Robacco Road
    She Couldn't Say No
    Sheriff of Tombstone

Ken Tobey (1919-
1947: Dangerous Venture
49: I Was a Male War Bride
    Free for All
    12 O'Clock High
50: Right Cross
    My Friend Irma Goes
    West
    Kiss Tomorrow Goodbye
    The Flying Missile
51: The Thing
52: Angel Face
53: Beast from 20,000 Fathoms
    Fighter Attack
54: Down Three Dark Streets
    The Steel Cage
55: Rage at Dawn
    Davy Crockett--King of
    the Wild Frontier
    It Came from Beneath
    the Sea
56: The Steel Jungle
    The Man in the Gray
    Flannel Suit

The Great Locomotive
    Chase
Davy Crockett and the
    River Pirates
The Search for Bridey
    Murphy
57: Gunfight at the O.K.
    Corral
    40 Guns to Apache Pass
    The Vampire
    The Wings of Eagles
58: Cry Terror
60: 7 Ways from Sundown
61: X-15
68: A Time for Killing
69: The Little Sister

George Tobias (1901-
1939: Maisie
    Ninotchka
    They All Come Out
    The Hunchback of Notre
    Dame
    Balalaika
40: Music in My Heart
    East of the River
    The Man Who Talked Too
    Much
    River's End
    Saturday's Children
    Torrid Zone
    City for Conquest
    They Drive by Night
    Calling All Husbands
    South of Suez
41: The Bride Came C.O.D.
    You're in the Army Now
    Strawberry Blonde
    Sergeant York
    Affectionately Yours
    Out of the Fog
42: My Sister Eileen
    Juke Girl
    Wings of the Eagle
    Captains of the Clouds
    Yankee Doodle Dandy
43: Thank Your Lucky Stars
    This Is the Army
    Mission to Moscow
    Air Force
44: The Mask of Dimitrios
    Between Two Worlds
    Make Your Own Bed

37: Murder on Diamond Bow
38: Action for Slander
South Riding
Poison Pen
41: Danny Boy
42: Ships With Wings
46: The 7th Veil
Daybreak
47: The Paradine Case
48: So Evil My Love
Passionate Friends
49: One Woman's Story
Gaiety George
50: Madeleine
51: The Lion Hunters
52: The Breaking of the
Sound Barrier
55: The Green Scarf
57: Time Without Pity
61: The Taste of Fear (or,
Scream of Fear)
64: Son of Captain Blood
65: Men of Yesterday
66: 90 Degrees in the Shade

Ann Todd (1932-
1939: Zero Hour
Zaza
Stronger than Desire
Intermezzo--A Love Story
Destry Rides Again
40: All This and Heaven Too
Little Orvie
Granny Get Your Gun
The Blue Bird
41: Blood and Sand
Private Nurse
Bad Man of Missouri
How Green Was My Valley
Remember the Day
42: On the Sunny Side
Beyond the Blue Horizon
43: Dixie Dugan
45: Pride of the Marines
Roughly Speaking
46: The Jolson Story
Margie
My Reputation
47: Homesteaders of Paradise
Valley
Dangerous Years
48: 3 Daring Daughters

Arthur Takes Over
49: Cover Up
50: Perfect Strangers

Richard Todd (1919-
1949: The Hasty Heart
50: For Them that Trespass
Stage Fright
51: Portrait of Clare
Lightning Strikes Twice
Flesh and Blood
52: The Story of Robin Hood
The Venetian Bird
53: The Sword and the Rose
Rob Roy, the Highland
Rogue
The Assassin
55: A Man Called Peter
The Virgin Queen
The Bed
Dam Busters
56: D-Day, the 6th of June
The Yangtse Incident
57: St. Joan
Battle Hell
58: Chase a Crooked Shadow
The Naked Earth
Danger Within
Intent to Kill
59: Breakout
60: Marie Antoinette
61: The Long, the Short, and
the Tall
The Boys
Jungle Fighters
62: The Longest Day
Crime Does Not Pay
(Man on the Avenue seq.)
The Gentle Art of Murder
The Hellions
63: Never Let Go
Sanders of the River
64: Why Bother to Knock?
65: Operation Crossbow (or,
The Great Spy Mission)
Coast of Skeletons
The Battle of Villa Fiorita
67: The Love-Ins
68: Subterfuge

Thelma Todd (1905-1935)
1928: Vamping Venus   S

1331

28: The Crash   S
    The Haunted House   SSE
    Heart to Heart   S
    Naughty Baby   SSE
29: Unaccustomed As We
    Are (short)
    Bachelor Girl   PT
    Trial Marriage   S
    Careers   PT
    Her Private Life
    House of Horrors   PT
    7 Footprints to Satan SSE
    Look Out Below
30: Hell's Angels
    Follow Through
    The Fighting Parson
    Another Fine Mess (short)
    Her Man
31: The Maltese Falcon
    Command Performance
    Broadminded
    Hot Heiress
    No Limit
    Monkey Business
    Beyond Victory
    Aloha
    Swanee River
    Corsair
32: Horsefeathers
    Call Her Savage
    Klondike
    Big Timer
    This Is the Night
    Speak Easily
    No Greater Love
    Cauliflower Alley
33: Deception
    Air Hostess
    Fra Diablo (The Devil's
    Brother)
    Sitting Pretty
    Mary Stevens, M.D.
    Son of a Sailor
    Cheating Blondes
    You Made Me Love You
    Counselor-at-Law
34: Hips, Hips, Hooray!
    Maid in Hollywood
    Joe Palooka
    Bottoms Up
    The Poor Rich
    The Cockeyed Vacaliers

    Take the Stand
35: Lightning Strikes Twice
    After the Dance
    Two for Tonight
36: The Bohemian Girl

Sidney Toler (1874-1947)
1929: Madame X
31: Vitaphone # 992--The
    Devil's Parade (short)
    White Shoulders
    Strictly Dishonorable
32: Strangers in Love
    The Phantom President
    Speak Easily
    Blonde Venus
    Is My Face Red?
    Radio Patrol
    Blondie of the Follies
    Tom Brown of Culver
33: He Learned about Women
    King of the Jungle
    The Way to Love
    The World Changes
    Billion Dollar Scandal
    Narrow Corner
34: Dark Hazard
    Massacre
    Registered Nurse
    Spitfire
    The Trumpet Blows
    Here Comes the Groom
    Upperworld
    Operator 13
35: Call of the Wild
    Daring Young Man
    Orchids to You
    Champagne for Breakfast
    This Is the Life
36: 3 Godfathers
    The Gorgeous Hussy
    The Longest Night
    Our Relations
    Give Me This Night
37: That Certain Woman
    Quality Street
    Double Wedding
38: Gold Is Where You Find
    It
    One Wild Night
    Up the River
    Charlie Chan in Honolulu

38: If I Were King
The Mysterious Rider
3 Comrades
Wide Open Faces
39: Disbarred
Law of the Pampas
The Kid from Kokomo
Charlie Chan in Reno
Charlie Chan at Treasure
Island
Charlie Chan in the City
in Darkness
King of Chinatown
Heritage of the Desert
Broadway Cavalier
40: Charlie Chan in Panama
Charlie Chan's Murder
Cruise
Charlie Chan at the Wax
Museum
Murder over New York
41: Charlie Chan in Rio
Dead Men Tell
42: Castle in the Desert
43: A Night to Remember
White Savage
Isle of Forgotten Sins
44: Charlie Chan in the
Secret Service
Charlie Chan in the
Chinese Cat
Black Magic
The Secret Clue
45: The Jade Mask
It's in the Bag
The Shanghai Cobra
46: The Red Dragon
Dark Alibi
47: The Trap

Tom and Jerry Cartoons
(1940-1952) (Oscar Winners)
1940: The Milky Way*
43: Yankee Doodle Mouse*
44: Mouse Trouble *
45: Quiet Please *
46: Cat Concerto*
48: The Little Orphan *
51: The 2 Musketeers *
52: Johann Mouse*

Sid Tomack (d. 1962)
1944: A Wave, a Wac, and
a Marine
46: The Thrill of Brazil
47: Blind Spot
For the Love of Rusty
Blondie's Holiday
A Double Life
48: My Girl Tisa
Homicide for Three
Hollow Triumph
49: House of Strangers
Boston Blackie's Chinese
Venture
The Crime Doctor's
Diary
Abandoned
Make-Believe Ballroom
50: Love that Brute
The Fuller Brush Girl
51: Never Trust a Gambler
Joe Palooka in Triple
Cross
52: Hans Christian Andersen
Somebody Loves Me
54: Living it Up
56: The Kettles in the Ozarks
57: Spring Reunion
61: Sail a Crooked Ship

Andrew Tombes (c1891-
1933: Moulin Rouge
37: Meet the Boy Friend
Charlie Chan at the
Olympics
Big City
39: What a Life!
Too Busy to Work
40: Wolf of New York
Money to Burn
Village Barn Dance
In Old Missouri
Captain Caution
Charter Pilot
41: Meet the Chump
Melody for Three
Wild Man of Borneo
Lady Scarface
Last of the Duanes
World Premiere

41:   A Dangerous Game
     Meet John Doe
     Mountain Moonlight
     Down Mexico Way
     Texas
     Louisiana Purchase
     Bedtime Story
42:   Blondie Goes to College
     Larceny, Inc.
     My Gal Sal
     They All Kissed the
      Bride
     Between Us Girls
43:   The Meanest Man in the
      World
     Coney Island
     Let's Face It
     Hi Diddle Diddle
     I Dood It!
     His Butler's Sister
     A Stranger in Town
     Swing Fever
     Crazy House
     Riding High
     My Kingdom for a Cook
44:   Can't Help Singing
     Goin' to Town
     Lake Placid Serenade
     Murder in the Blue Room
     Night Club Gal
     Phantom Lady
     The Reckless Age
     San Fernando Valley
     The Singing Sheriff
     Weekend Pass
45:   Bring on the Girls
     Don't Fence Me In
     Frontier Gal
     G. I. Honeymoon
     Patrick the Great
     Rhapsody in Blue
     You Came Along
46:   Badman's Territory
     Sing While You Dance
47:   Beat the Band
     The Devil Thumbs a Ride
     The Fabulous Dorseys
     Hoppy's Holiday
     Christmas Eve
48:   2 Guys from Texas
49:   Oh, You Beautiful Doll!
50:   Joe Palooka in Humphrey
     Takes a Chance

51:   A Wonderful Life
55:   How to be Very, Very
     Popular

Franchot Tone (1905-1968)
1932: The Wiser Sex
33:   Gabriel over the White
     House
     Today We Live
     Midnight Mary
     The Stranger's Return
     Stage Mother
     Bombshell
     Dancing Lady
     Lady of the Night
34:   Moulin Rouge
     The World Moves On
     Sadie McKee
     Four Walls
     Gentlemen Are Born
     Straight Is the Way
     The Girl from Missouri
35:   Lives of a Bengal Lancer
     Reckless
     One New York Night
     No More Ladies
     Mutiny on the Bounty
     Dangerous
36:   Exclusive Story
     Suzy
     The Gorgeous Hussy
     Love on the Run
     The King Steps Out
     Girls' Dormitory
37:   Quality Street
     They Gave Him a Gun
     Between Two Women
     The Bride Wore Red
38:   Man Proof
     Love Is a Headache
     3 Comrades
     3 Loves Has Nancy
39:   Fast and Furious
     The Girl Downstairs
     Thunder Afloat
40:   Trail of the Vigilantes
41:   Nice Girl?
     This Woman Is Mine
     She Knew All the Answers
     Highly Irregular
     Virginia
42:   The Wife Takes a Flyer
     Star-Spangled Rhythm

43: His Butler's Sister
True to Life
Test Pilot 5
5 Graves to Cairo
44: Phantom Lady
The Hour Before Dawn
Dark Waters
45: That Night With You
46: Because of Him
47: I Love Trouble
2 Men and a Girl
Amy Comes Across
Honeymoon
Lost Honeymoon
Her Husband's Affair
48: Every Girl Should be
Married
49: Jigsaw
Without Honor
50: The Man on the Eiffel
Tower
Gun Moll
51: Here Comes the Groom
58: Uncle Vanya
62: Advise and Consent
64: La Bonne Soupe
Big Parade of Comedy
(doc.)
65: In Harm's Way
See How They Run
Mickey One
68: Shadow over Elveron (TV)
69: Nobody Runs Forever

Sammee Tong (1905-1966)
1957: Hell Bound
58: Suicide Battalion
63: It's a Mad Mad Mad Mad
World
64: For Those Who Think
Young

Philip Tonge (1897-1961)
1952: Hans Christian Andersen
53: Small Town Girl
House of Wax
Scandal at Scourie
54: Elephant Walk
Khyber Patrol
Track of the Cat
The Silver Chalice
Ricochet Romance

55: The Prodigal
Desert Sands
56: Pardners
The Peacemaker
57: Les Girls
Witness for the
Prosecution
58: Darby's Rangers
Macabre
59: Invisible Invaders

Regis Toomey (1902-
1929: Wheel of Life
Illusion
Rich People
Alibi
30: Crazy that Way
Good Intentions
Light of the Western
Skies
Street of Chance
Framed
Steel Highway
Shadow of the Law
A Man from Wyoming
31: Perfect Alibi
Murder by the Clock
Playing the Game
Hours Between
Finn and Hattie
The Finger Points
Graft
Kick In
Scandal Sheet
Other Men's Women
24 Hours
Touchdown
32: Under 18
Sky Bride
Shopworn
Midnight Patrol
They Never Come Back
33: The Penal Code
Strange Adventure
State Trooper
Soldiers of the Storm
Laughing at Life
She Had to Say Yes
Picture Brides
34: What's Your Racket?
Big Time or Bust
Murder on the Blackboard

34: Redhead
She Had to Choose
35: Shadow of Doubt
Red Morning
G-Men
Skull and Crown
One Frightened Night
Manhattan Moon
Reckless Roads
The Great God Gold
36: Empire
Bulldog Edition
37: Shadows of the Orient
Midnight Taxi
Back in Circulation
Big City
Without Warning
Submarine D-1
38: Hunted Men
Illegal Traffic
His Exciting Night
The Invisible Menace
39: Street of Missing Men
Society Smugglers
Smashing the Spy Ring
The Mysterious Miss K
Wings of the Navy
Confessions of a Nazi Spy
Indianapolis Speedway
Trapped in the Sky
Hidden Power
Union Pacific
The Phantom Creeps (ser.)
Thunder Afloat
40: His Girl Friday
Arizona
Northwest Passage
Till We Meet Again
Northwest Mounted Police
41: Meet John Doe
Reaching for the Sun
A Shot in the Dark
The Nurse's Secret
Law of the Tropics
Dive Bomber
They Died with Their
Boots on
You're in the Army Now
42: Bullet Scars
I Was Framed
Forest Rangers
Tennessee Johnson

43: Jack London
Destroyer
44: Follow the Boys
Phantom Lady
Song of the Open Road
Dark Mountain
Murder in the Blue Room
The Doughgirls
When the Lights Go on
Again
45: Spellbound
Betrayal from the East
Follow that Woman!
Strange Illusion
46: The Big Sleep
Her Sister's Secret
Child of Divorce
Mysterious Intruder
47: The 13th Hour
The Guilty
The Big Fix
High Tide
Magic Town
48: I Wouldn't be in Your
Shoes
Station West
The Bishop's Wife
The Boy with Green Hair
49: Mighty Joe Young
Come to the Stable
Beyond the Forest
The Devil's Henchmen
50: Dynamite Pass
Undercover Girl
Frenchie
51: Navy Bound
Cry Danger
Tall Target
The People Against O'Hara
Show Boat
52: My 6 Convicts
Battle at Apache Pass
Just for You
My Pal Gus
Never Wave at a Wac
53: It Happens Every Thursday
Island in the Sky
The Nebraskan
The Man Between
54: The High and the Mighty
Human Jungle
Drums Across the River

34: What Every Woman Knows
Charlie Chan in London
35: Black Sheep
Bonnie Scotland
Harmony Lane
The Dark Angel
Captain Blood
36: The Country Doctor
Mary of Scotland
Beloved Enemy
37: Ebb Tide
38: Five of a Kind
39: Rulers of the Sea
Stanley and Livingstone

Ernest Torrence (1878-1933)
1929: Desert Nights
Silks and Saddles
Bridge of San Luis Rey
Speedway
Unholy Night
Untamed
30: Officer O'Brien
Strictly Unconventional
Call of the Flesh
Sweet Kitty Bellaire
31: Shipmates
Fighting Caravans
The Great Lover
Sporting Blood
Cuban Love Song
New Adventures of Get-
Rich-Quick Wallingford
32: Sherlock Holmes
Hypnotized
33: The Masquerader
I Cover the Waterfront

Raquel Torres (1908-
1928: White Shadows of the
South Seas   S
29: Bridge of San Luis Rey PT
Desert Rider   S
30: Sea Bat
Under the Texas Moon
Free and Easy
31: Aloha
33: So This Is Africa
Tampico
The Woman I Stole
Duck Soup
Red Wagon

Audrey Totter (1918-
1944: Main Street After Dark
45: Her Highness and the
Bellboy
Dangerous Partners
The Sailor Takes a Wife
The Hidden Eye
46: The Cockeyed Miralce
Lady in the Lake
The Postman Rings Twice
47: Beginning or the End?
The Unsuspected
48: High Wall
The Saxon Charm
10th Avenue Angel
49: Alias Nick Beal
Any Number can Play
Tension
The Set-Up
50: Under the Gun
51: The Blue Veil
The Sellout
F.B.I. Girl
52: Assignment: Paris
My Pal Gus
53: The Woman They Almost
Lynched
Cruisin' Down the River
Man in the Dark
Mission over Korea
Champ for a Day
54: Massacre Canyon
55: Women's Prison
A Bullet for Joey
The Vanishing American
57: Ghost Diver
58: Jet Attack
Man or Gun
64: The Carpetbaggers
65: Harlow (Magna.)
67: The Outsider (TV pilot)
68: Chubasco

Tamara Toumonova (1918-
1944: Days of Glory
53: Tonight We Sing
54: Deep in My Heart
56: Invitation to the Dance
66: Torn Curtain
69: The Private Life of
Sherlock Holmes

1338

Lupita Tovar (1911-
1929: Veiled Woman   S
  30: The Cat Creeps
      Desire of Death
  31: East of Borneo
      Border Love
      Yankee Don
  32: Santa
  35: An Old Spanish Custom
  38: Blockade
  39: Tropic Fury
      South of the Border
      The Fighting Gringo
  40: The Westerner
  41: 2-Gun Sheriff
  45: The Crime Doctor's
      Courage

Constance Towers
1955: Bring Your Smile Along
  59: The Horse Soldiers
  60: Sergeant Rutledge
  63: Shock Corridor
  64: The Naked Kiss
      Fate Is the Hunter

Aline Towne
1950: Harbor of Missing Men
      The Vanishing Westerner
      Highway 301
  51: Rough Riders of Durango
      Purple Heart Diary
  52: Confidence Girl
  53: A Blueprint for Murder
  54: Target: Sea of China
  56: Julie
  58: Satan's Satellites
  64: Send Me No Flowers

Rosella Towne (1919-
1928: Sergeant Murphy
      Patient in Room 18
      Blondes at Work
      Gold Diggers in Paris
      The Cowboy from
        Brooklyn
      Blockade
  39: Secret Service of the Air
      Women in the Wind
      Code of the Secret Service
  40: Rocky Mountain Rangers

Harry Townes (1918-
1954: The Sleeping Tiger
      Operation Manhunt
  55: A Prize of Gold
  56: The Mountain
  58: The Brothers Karamazov
      The Screaming Mimi
  59: Cry Tough
  61: Sanctuary
  65: The Bedford Incident
  67: Fitzwilly
  69: Heaven with a Gun

Colleen Townsend (1928-
1944: Janie
      Hollywood Canteen
  48: Walls of Jericho
      Chicken Every Sunday
  50: When Willie Comes
        Marching Home

Arthur Tracy (1903-
1932: The Big Broadcast
  35: Flirtation
  36: Limelight
  37: The Street Singer
      Command Performance
  38: Follow Your Star

Lee Tracy (1898-1968)
1930: Big Time
      On the Level
      Born Reckless
      Liliom
      She Got What She Wanted
  32: Half-Naked Truth
      Blessed Event
      The Night Mayor
      Washington Merry-Go-
        Round
      The Strange Love of
        Molly Louvain
      Love Is a Racket
      Dr. X
  33: Clear All Wires
      Phantom Fame
      Private Jones
      The Nuisance
      Dinner at 8
      Turn Back the Clock
      Bombshell

33: Advice to the Lovelorn
34: I'll Tell the World
    You Belong to Me
    Lemon Drop Kid
35: Carnival
    Two-Fisted
36: Sutter's Gold
    Wanted: Jane Turner
37: Criminal Lawyer
    Behind the Headlines
38: Crashing Hollywood
39: Fixer Dugan
    Spellbinder
40: Millionaires in Prison
42: The Pay-Off
43: Power of the Press
45: Betrayal from the East
47: High Tide
62: Advise and Consent
64: The Best Man
    Big Parade of Comedy
    (doc.)

Spencer Tracy (1900-1967)
1930: Taxi Talks
    The Hard Guy
    Up the River
31: Quick Millions
    6 Cylinder Love
    Goldie
32: She Wanted a Millionaire
    Sky Devils
    Disorderly Conduct
    Young America
    Society Girl
    The Painted Woman
    Me and My Gal
    We Humans
    After the Rain
33: 20,000 Years in Sing Sing
    The Face in the Sky
    Power and the Glory
    Shanghai Madness
    The Mad Game
    Man's Castle
    State Fair
    Pier No. 113
34: Looking for Trouble
    Show-Off
    Bottoms Up!
    Now I'll Tell
    Marie Galante

35: It's a Small World
    The Murder Man
    Dante's Inferno
    Riffraff
36: Whipsaw
    Fury
    San Francisco
    Libeled Lady
37: Captains Courageous
    (OSCAR)
    They Gave Him a Gun
    The Big City
    Mannequin
38: Test Pilot
    Boys Town (OSCAR)
39: Stanley and Livingstone
40: I Take This Woman
    Northwest Passage
    Edison the Man
    Boom Town
41: Men of Boys Town
    Dr. Jekyll and Mr. Hyde
42: Woman of the Year
    Tortilla Flat
    Ring of Steel (narr. short)
    Keeper of the Flame
43: A Guy Named Joe
44: Battle Stations (short)
    The 7th Cross
    30 Seconds over Tokyo
45: Without Love
47: Sea of Grass
    Cass Timberlane
48: State of the Union
49: Edward My Son
    Adam's Rib
50: Malaya
    Father of the Bride
51: Father's Little Dividend
    The People Against O'Hara
52: Pat and Mike
    Plymouth Adventure
53: The Actress
54: Broken Lance
    Bad Day at Black Rock
56: The Mountain
57: Desk Set
58: The Old Man and the Sea
    The Last Hurrah
60: Inherit the Wind
61: The Devil at 4 O'Clock
    Judgment at Nuremberg

1340

62: How the West Was Won
   (narr.)
63: It's a Mad Mad Mad Mad
   World
67: Guess Who's Coming to
   Dinner

William Tracy (1917-1967)
1938: Brother Rat
   Angels with Dirty Faces
39: The Jones Family in
   Hollywood
   Million Dollar Legs
40: The Amazing Mr.
   Williams
   Terry and the Pirates
   (ser.)
   Strike Up the Band
   Gallant Sons
   The Shop Around the
   Corner
41: Mr. and Mrs. Smith
   Tobacco Road
   Tillie the Toiler
   She Knew All the Answers
   Her First Beau
   Tanks a Million
   Cadet Girl
42: Young America
   Hayfoot
   To the Shores of Tripoli
   About Face
   George Washington Slept
   Here
   Fall In
43: Yanks Ahoy
48: Here Comes Trouble
   Walls of Jericho
49: Henry the Rainmaker
50: One Too Many
51: On the Sunny Side of the
   Street
   As You Were
52: Mr. Walkie-Talkie
57: The Wings of Eagles

Helen Traubel (1903-
1954: Deep in My Heart
61: The Ladies' Man
67: Peter Gunn

Henry Travers (1874-
1933: Reunion in Vienna
   Another Language
   My Weakness
   The Invisible Man
34: The Party's Over
   Death Takes a Holiday
   Ready for Love
   Born to be Bad
35: Maybe It's Love
   After Office Hours
   Escape
   Pursuit
   Captain Hurricane
   7 Keys to Baldpate
   4 Hours to Kill
36: Too Many Parents
38: The Sisters
39: Dark Victory
   You Can't Get Away with
   Murder
   Dodge City
   On Borrowed Time
   Remember?
   Stanley and Livingstone
   The Rains Came
40: The Primrose Path
   Anne of Windy Poplars
   Edison the Man
   Wyoming
41: Fall of Fire
   High Sierra
   A Girl, a Guy, and a Gob
   The Bad Man
   I'll Wait for You
42: Mrs. Miniver
   Pierre of the Plains
   Random Harvest
43: Shadow of a Doubt
   The Moon Is Down
   Madame Curie
44: Dragon Seed
   None Shall Escape
   The Very Thought of You
45: Thrill of Romance
   The Naughty '90s
   Bells of St. Mary's
46: Gallant Journey
   It's a Wonderful Life
   The Yearling

47: The Flame
48: Beyond Glory
49: The Girl from Jones
    Beach

William "Bill" Travers (1922-
1954: Romeo and Juliet
55: The Square Ring
    Footsteps in the Fog
56: Wee Geordie
    Bhowani Junction
57: The Barretts of Wimpole
    Street
    The Smallest Show on
    Earth
    The 7th Sin
58: The Bridal Path
59: The Passionate Summer
61: Gorgo
    The Green Helmet
    The Invasion Quartet
62: 2 Living, 1 Dead
66: Born Free
    Duel at Diablo
68: The Lions Are Free
    Ring of Bright Water
69: A Midsummer Night's
    Dream (TV)

June Travis (1914-
1935: Stranded
    Ceiling Zero
36: Times Square Playboy
    Jailbreak
    Earthworm Tractors
    Bengal Tiger
    The Big Game
    The Case of the Black
    Cat
37: Circus Girl
    Join the Marines
    Men in Exile
    Love Is on the Air
    Over the Goal
    Exiled to Shanghai
38: Over the Wall
    Go Chase Yourself
    The Marines Are Here
    The Gladiator
    Little Orphan Annie
    Night Hawk
    Mr. Doodle Kicks Off

39: Federal Man-Hunt

Richard Travis (1913-
1941: The Man Who Came to
    Dinner
42: The Postman Didn't Ring
    The Big Shot
    Escape from Crime
    Busses Roar
43: Truck Busters
    Mission to Moscow
44: The Last Ride
    Undercover Maisie
47: Big Town After Dark
    Jewels of Brandenburg
    Backlash
48: Waterfront at Midnight
    Out of the Storm
    Speed to Spare
49: Alaska Patrol
    Sky Liner
50: Operation Haylift
    Motor Patrol
    Lonely Hearts Bandits
    One Too Many
51: Passage West
    Danger Zone
    Roaring City
    Mask of the Dragon
    Lost Women
    Pier 23
    Fingerprints Don't Lie
55: The Annapolis Story
    City of Shadows
56: Blonde Bait
59: Missile to the Moon

Arthur Treacher (1894-
1930: Battle of Paris
33: short with Ruth Etting
    Alice in Wonderland
34: Gambling Lady
    The Captain Hates the Sea
    Viva Villa!
    Hollywood Party
    Student Tour
    The Key
    Madame Du Barry
    Bordertown
    Here Comes the Groom
    Forsaking All Others
    Fashions of 1934

35: David Copperfield
The Winning Ticket
Vanessa-Her Love Story
I Live My Life
Woman in Red
Go Into Your Dance
A Midsummer Night's
Dream
Bright Lights
Personal Maid's Secret
I Live for Love
The Daring Young Man
Orchids to You
The Nitwits
Curly Top
Magnificent Obsession
Splendor
Let's Live Tonight
No More Ladies
Remember Last Night
36: Anything Goes
Hitchhike Lady
Hard Luck Dame
Hearts Divided
Thank You, Jeeves!
Satan Met a Lady
Under Your Spell
Stowaway
The Case Against Mrs.
Ames
Mr. Cinderella
37: Step Lively, Jeeves!
She Had to Eat
You Can't Have Every-
thing
Thin Ice
Heidi
38: Mad about Music
Always in Trouble
My Lucky Star
Up the River
39: The Little Princess
Barricade
Bridal Suite
40: Brother Rat and a Baby
Irene
42: Star-Spangled Rhythm
43: The Amazing Mrs.
Holliday
Forever and a Day
44: Chip Off the Old Block
In Society

45: Delightfully Dangerous
That's the Spirit
Swing Out, Sister
47: Fun on a Weekend
Slave Girl
48: The Countess of Monte
Cristo
49: That Midnight Kiss
50: Love that Brute
64: Mary Poppins

Chief Big Tree
1939: Stagecoach
Susannah of the Mounties
Drums Along the Mohawk
40: Brigham Young-Frontiers-
man
Hudson's Bay
41: Western Union

Dorothy Tree (1909-
1939: The Mysterious Miss X
The Mystery of Mr. Wong
Confessions of a Nazi Spy
Television Spy
Charlie Chan in the City
in Darkness
40: Little Orvie
Abe Lincoln in Illinois
Knute Rockne-All-
American
Sky Murder
41: The Man Who Lost Him-
self
Singapore Woman
Highway West
42: Nazi Agent
43: Hitler, Dead or Alive
Edge of Darkness
Crime Doctor

Mary Lou Treen (1907-
1934: Happiness Ahead
Red Hot Tires
Babbitt
A Night at the Ritz
a short
Get Rich Quick
35: Traveling Saleslady
The Case of the Lucky
Legs
Shipmates Forever

1343

35: Page Miss Glory
Don't Bet on Blondes
The G Men
I Live for Love
The Girl on 10th Avenue
The Golden Arrow
36: Freshman Love
Murder by an Aristocrat
Love Begins at 20
Jailbreak
Brides Are Like That
God's Country and the
Woman
Colleen
The Murder of Dr.
Harrigan
Down the Stretch
37: The Captain's Kid
Fugitive in the Sky
Maid of Salem
Second Honeymoon
Dance, Charlie, Dance
Talent Scout
The Go Getter
The Missing Witness
Ever Since Eve
They Gave Him a Gun
Swing it, Sailor!
38: Sally, Irene, and Mary
Kentucky Moonshine
Young Fugitives
Strange Faces
39: First Love
40: Double Alibi
Danger on Wheels
The Girl in 313
Queen of the Mob
Black Diamonds
Kitty Foyle
41: Tall, Dark, and Hand-
some
Father Takes a Wife
You Belong to Me
Midnight Angel
42: The Great Man's Lady
The Night Before the
Divorce
Rings on Her Fingers
They All Kissed the
Bride
Between Us Girls
The Powers Girl

43: They Got Me Covered
Hit Parade of 1943
Lady Bodyguard
Proudly We Hail!
Mystery Broadcast
Hands Across the Border
44: The Navy Way
I Love a Soldier
Swing in the Saddle
Casanova Brown
In the Meantime Darling
45: The Blonde from Brooklyn
She Wouldn't Say Yes
Don Juan Quilligan
High Powered
Tahiti Nights
46: A Guy Could Change
It's a Wonderful Life
Strange Impersonation
Swing Parade of 1946
From This Day Forward
One Exciting Week
48: Let's Live a Little
The Stooge
50: Young Daniel Boone
52: Room for One More
53: Sailor Beware
The Caddy
Let's Do it Again
56: Bundle of Joy
The Birds and the Bees
When Gangland Strikes
57: Gun Duel in Durango
The Sad Sack
58: I Married a Monster
from Outer Space
61: All in a Night's Work
63: Who's Minding the Store?
66: Paradise, Hawaiian Style

Les Tremayne (1913-
1951: The Racket
The Blue Veil
52: Francis Goes to West
Point
It Grows on Trees
53: I Love Melvin
Under the Red Sea
Dream Wife
The Slime People
War of the Worlds
54: Susan Slept Here

55: A Man Called Peter
56: The Lieutenant Wore
    Skirts
    The Unguarded Moment
    Everything but the Truth
57: The Monolith Monsters
58: The Perfect Furlough
59: North by Northwest
    Say One for Me
60: The Gallant Hours
    The Angry Red Planet
    The Story of Ruth
64: Big Parade of Comedy
    (doc.)
66: The Fortune Cookie

Claire Trevor (1909-
1932: various shorts
33: Life in the Raw
    The Last Trail
    The Mad Game
    Jimmy and Sally
34: Hold that Girl
    Baby Take a Bow
    Wild Gold
35: Beauty's Daughter
    Elinor Norton
    Dante's Inferno
    Spring Tonic
    Black Sheep
    My Marriage
    Navy Wife
36: The Song and Dance Man
    Human Cargo
    To Mary with Love
    Star for a Night
    15 Maiden Lane
    Career Woman
37: Big Town Girl
    Time Out for Romance
    One Mile from Heaven
    Second Honeymoon
    King of Gamblers
    Dead End
38: Walking Down Broadway
    The Amazing Dr. Clitter-
    house
    5 of a Kind
    Valley of the Giants
39: Stagecoach
    I Stole a Million
    Allegheny Uprising

40: The Dark Command
41: Honky Tonk
    Texas
42: The Adventures of Martin
    Eden
    Crossroads
    Street of Chance
43: Desperadoes
    The Woman of the Town
44: Murder My Sweet (or,
    Farewell My Lovely)
45: Johnny Angel
46: Crack-Up
    The Bachelor's Daughters
47: Born to Kill
    Bachelor Girls
48: Raw Deal
    The Babe Ruth Story
    The Velvet Touch
    Key Largo (OSCAR)
49: Lucky Stiff
50: Border Line
51: Best of the Badmen
    Hard Fast and Beautiful
52: Hoodlum Empire
    My Man and I
    Stop! You're Killing Me!
53: The Stranger Wore a Gun
54: The High and the Mighty
55: Man Without a Star
    Lucy Gallant
56: The Mountain
58: Marjorie Morningstar
62: 2 Weeks in Another Town
63: The Stripper
65: How to Murder Your Wife

Hugh Trevor (1903-1933)
1929: Dry Martini   SSE
    Taxi No. 13   PT
    Hey, Rube!   S
    Love in the Desert   PT
    The Very Idea
    Night Parade
30: The Cuckoos
    Midnight Mystery
    Pay-Off
    Half Shot at Sunrise
    Conspiracy

Norman Trevor (1877-1929)
1929: Restless Youth   S

29: The Love Trap   PT
    Tonight at 12

Bobby Troup
1957: Bop Girl
  58: The High Cost of Living
  59: The 5 Pennies
      The Gene Krupa Story
  67: First to Fight
  69: Dragnet ('66 TV rel.)
      M-A-S-H
      Number One

Charles Trowbridge (1882-1967)
1931: Damaged Love
      I Take This Woman
      Silence
      Secret Call
  35: Calm Yourself
      Mad Love
      Rendezvous
      It's in the Air
  36: Exclusive Story
      The Garden Murder Case
      We Went to College
      Mother Steps Out
      Born to Dance
      Man of the People
      The Gorgeous Hussy
      Libeled Lady
      The Devil Is a Sissy
      Robin Hood of El Dorado
      Moonlight Murder
      Love on the Run
  37: Dangerous Number
      Espionage
      A Day at the Races
      Captains Courageous
      They Gave Him a Gun
      A Servant of the People
      Sea Racketeers
      Exiled to Shanghai
      That Certain Woman
      Without Warning
      Fit for a King
      Saturday's Heroes
      The 13th Chair
  38: Alcatraz Island
      The Buccaneer
      Submarine Patrol
      Thanks for Everything
      Kentucky

      Crime School
      Gang Bullets
      The Last Express
      Gangs of New York
      Crime Ring
      The Invisible Menace
      The Patient in Room 18
      College Swing
      Nancy Drew, Detective
  39: Risky Business
      King of Chinatown
      Tropic Fury
      King of the Underworld
      Pride of the Navy
      Boy Trouble
      On Trial
      The Story of Alexander
        Graham Bell
      Elsa Maxwell's Hotel for
        Women
      Swanee River
      Each Dawn I Die
      Confessions of a Nazi Spy
      Lady of the Tropics
      Joe and Ethel Turp Call
        on the President
      Mutiny on the Blackhawk
      The Man They Could Not
        Hang
  40: Johnny Apollo
      The Man with 9 Lives
      Knute Rockne-All American
      The Mummy's Hand
      Cherokee Strip
      Trail of the Vigilantes
      The Fighting 69th
      The Fatal Hour
      House of 7 Gables
      My Love Came Back
  41: The Great Lie
      The Tell-Tale Heart
      Strange Alibi
      The Nurse's Secret
      Dressed to Kill
      Rags to Riches
      Hurricane Smith
      Sergeant York
      Great Guns
      We Go Fast
      The Great Mr. Nobody
      Belle Starr
      Blue, White, and Perfect

42: Who Is Hope Schuyler?
10 Gentlemen from West
   Point
Sweetheart of the Fleet
That Other Woman
Over My Dead Body
43: Action in the North
   Atlantic
Mission to Moscow
The Story of Dr. Wassell
Wintertime
Sweet Rosie O'Grady
Salute to the Marines
44: Faces in the Fog
Summer Storm
Wing and a Prayer
Heavenly Days
Hey Rookie!
45: Col. Effingham's Raid
The Red Wagon
Mildred Pierce
They Were Expendable
46: The Hoodlum Saint
Shock
Smooth as Silk
Undercurrent
Valley of the Zombies
Don't Gamble with
   Strangers
Secret of the Whistler
47: The Beginning or the End?
Mr. District Attorney
The Private Affairs of Bel
   Ami
Sea Grass
Tarzan and the Huntress
Black Gold
Her Husband's Affairs
Key Witness
Song of My Heart
Tycoon
48: Stage Struck
Paleface
Hollow Triumph
49: Bad Boy
Mr. Soft Touch
50: Unmasked
Peggy
52: The Bushwackers
57: The Wings of Eagles

Ernest Truex (1889-
1933: Whistling in the Dark
The Warrior's Husband
34: a short
36: Everybody Dance
37: Mama Runs Wild
38: Freshman Year
Swing that Cheer
Swing, Sister, Swing
Start Cheering
The Adventures of Marco
   Polo
39: Ambush
Island of Lost Men
It's a Wonderful World
These Glamour Girls
Bachelor Mother
Little Accident
40: His Girl Friday
Slightly Honorable
Little Orvie
Lillian Russell
Dance, Girl, Dance
Calling All Husbands
Christmas in July
41: The Gay Vagabond
Tillie the Toiler
We Go Fast
Unexpected Uncle
42: Twin Beds
Private Buckaroo
Star-Spangled Rhythm
43: This Is the Army
Rhythm of the Islands
Fired Wife
The Crystal Ball
44: Chip Off the Old Block
Her Primitive Man
45: Club Havana
Men in Her Diary
Pan-Americana
46: Life with Blondie
A Night in Paradise
47: Always Together
48: The Girl from Manhattan
56: The Leather Saint
The Man Who Knew Too
   Much
The Ship that Died of
   Shame

57: Wicked as They Come
The Black Tent
All Mine to Give
58: Twilight for the Gods
65: Fluffy

Natalie Trundy
1957: The Monte Carlo Story
The Careless Years
60: Walk Like a Dragon
62: Mr. Hobbs Takes a
Vacation
69: Beneath the Planet of the
Apes

Glenn Tryon (1894-
1929: It Can be Done   PT
Broadway
The Kid's Clever   S
Barnum Was Right
Skinner Steps Out
30: Dames Ahoy!
Midnight Special
King of Jazz
Lonesome
31: Daybreak
Dragnet Patrol
The Sky Spider
Neck and Neck
The Secret Menace
32: The Widow in Scarlet
Tangled Destinies
The Pride of the Legion
33: Rafter Romance (screen
adapt.)
34: Bachelor Bail (writ.,
dir.)
Gridiron Flash (writ.,
dir.)
The Richest Girl in the
World (writ., dir.)
35: Roberta (add. dial.)
7 Keys to Baldpate (add.
dial.)
Daring Young Man (add.
dial.)
Orchids to You
36: Easy to Take
Small Town Boy (writ.)
38: The Law West of Tomb-
stone (dir.)
39: Carefree (writ.)

Beauty for the Asking
(dir.)
45: George White's Scandals
51: Hometown Story
65: Laurel & Hardy's
Laughing '20s (doc.)

Tom Tryon (1926-
1950: Fall of the House of
Usher
56: The Scarlet Hour
Screaming Eagles
3 Violent People
57: The Unholy Wife
58: I Married a Monster
from Outer Space
60: The Story of Ruth
61: Marines, Let's Go!
62: The Longest Day
Moon Pilot
63: The Cardinal
65: The Glory Guys
In Harm's Way
66: Winchester 73 (TV)
69: Color Me Dead

Forrest Tucker (1919-
1940: The Westerner
The Howards of Virginia
41: New Wine
Honolulu Lu
Camp Nuts
Emergency Landing
Canal Zone
42: Shut My Big Mouth
Tramp, Tramp, Tramp
Submarine Raider
Parachute Nurse
Counter Espionage
Spirit of Stanford
Keeper of the Flame
46: Never Say Goodbye
Dangerous Business
The Man Who Dared
Renegades
Talk about a Lady
The Yearling
47: Gunfighters
48: Adventures in Silverado
Coroner Creek
The Plunderers
Two Guys from Texas

49: Brimstone
Hellfire
The Big Cat
Sands of Iwo Jima
The Last Bandit
50: Rock Island Trail
California Passage
The Nevadan (or, The
Man from Nevada)
Forbidden Jungle
51; Warpath
The Fighting Coast Guard
Oh Susannah!
Crosswinds
Wild Blue Yonder
Flaming Feather
52: Bugles in the Afternoon
The Hoodlum Empire
Montana Belle
Hurricane Smith
Ride the Man Down
53: Devil's Canyon
San Antone
Flight Nurse
Pony Express
54: Jubilee Trail
Laughing Anne
Trouble in the Glen
55: Rage at Dawn
The Vanishing American
Finger Man
Night Freight
Paris Follies of 1956
Fresh from Paris
56: Stagecoach to Fury
3 Violent People
The Quiet Gun
57: The Deerslayer
Break in the Circle
Girl in the Woods
The Abominable Snowman
Pickup Alley
58: Auntie Mame
The Crawling Terror
Fort Massacre
Gunsmoke in Tucson
59: Counterplot
Cosmic Monsters
Creatures from Another
World
66: Don't Worry, We'll Think
of a Title

67: A Boy Called Nuthin' (TV)
68: The Night They Raided
Minskey's
69: Barquero

Richard Tucker (1869-1942)
1928: Captain Swagger   SSE
29: Lucky Boy   PT
My Man   PT
The Dummy
This Is Heaven   PT
Daughter of Desire
The Squall
Half Marriage
Unholy Night
30: Madonna of the Streets
Brothers
Peacock Alley
The Benson Murder Case
Puttin' on the Ritz
Shadow of the Law
Courage
Broken Dishes
Manslaughter
Recaptured Love
Safety in Number
College Lovers
The Bat Whispers
31: Hell Bound
Inspiration
The Deceiver
Stepping Out
Seed
Too Young to Marry
Holy Terror
Graft
Convicted
X Marks the Spot
Devil Plays
Maker of Men
32: Careless Lady
Successful Calamity
The Stoker
Guilty as Hell
Flames
The Crash
Pack Up Your Troubles
33: Iron Master
Daring Daughters
Her Resale Value
The World Gone Mad
Saturday's Millions

34: Show-Off
Public Stenographer
Road to Ruin
Countess of Monte Cristo
Money Means Nothing
Back Page
Handy Andy
Paris Interlude
Take the Stand
Successful Failure
Sing Sing Nights
35: Shadow of Doubt
Diamond Jim
Murder in the Fleet
Calm Yourself
Here Comes the Band
Symphony of Living
36: Ring Around the Moon
In Paris A.W.O.L.
The Plot Thickens
Flying Fortress
37: She's Dangerous
Headline Crasher
The Girl Said No
Armored Car
I Cover the War
River of Missing Men
Something to Sing About
Make a Wish
38: She's Got Everything
The Higgins Family
The Texans
Sons of the Legion
39: Risky Business
The Girl from Rio
The Covered Trailer
The Great Victor Herbert

Sophie Tucker (1884-1966)
1929: Honky Tonk
36: Gay Love
37: Broadway Melody of 1938
38: Thoroughbreds Don't Cry
44: Atlantic City
Follow the Boys
Sensations of 1945

Sonny Tufts (1912-
1943: So Proudly We Hail!
Government Girl
44: In the Meantime Darling
Here Come the Waves

I Love a Soldier
45: Bring on the Girls
Duffy's Tavern
46: Miss Susie Slagle's
The Virginian
Swell Guy
The Well-Groomed Bride
47: Easy Come, Easy Go
Blaze of Noon
Variety Girl
Cross My Heart
48: Untamed Breed
49: The Crooked Way
Easy Living
53: No Escape
Cat Women of the Moon
Run for the Hills
City on the Hunt
Glory at Sea
54: Serpent Island
55: 7 Year Itch
56: Come Next Spring
57: The Parson and the
Outlaw
65: Town Tamer

Tom Tully (c1902-
1943: Mission to Moscow
Northern Pursuit
Destination Tokyo
44: I'll be Seeing You
Secret Command
The Town Went Wild
45: The Unseen
46: Adventure
Till the End of Time
The Virginian
47: Intrigue
Killer McCoy
Lady in the Lake
48: Scudda Hoo! Scudda Hay!
Blood on the Moon
June Bride
Rachel and the Stranger
49: A Kiss for Corless
The Lady Takes a Sailor
Illegal Entry
50: Branded
Where the Sidewalk Ends
51: Tomahawk
The Lady and the Bandit
Texas Carnival

1350

52: Love Is Better than Ever
    Return of the Texan
    Lure of the Wilderness
    The Turning Point
    Ruby Gentry
53: The Jazz Singer
    The Moon Is Blue
    Sea of Lost Ships
54: The Caine Mutiny
    Arrow in the Dust
55: Love Me or Leave Me
    Soldier of Fortune
56: Behind the High Wall
58: 10 North Frederick
60: The Wackiest Ship in the
    Army
64: The Carpetbaggers
65: McHale's Navy Joins the
    Air Force
68: Coogan's Bluff
69: Any Second Now (TV)

51: Mr. Imperium
52: The Merry Widow
    The Bad and the Beautiful
53: Latin Lovers
54: Flame and the Flesh
    Betrayed
55: The Prodigal
    The Sea Chase
    The Rains of Ranchipur
56: Diane
57: Peyton Place
58: The Lady and the Flyer
    Another Time, Another
    Place
59: Imitation of Life
60: Portrait in Black
61: By Love Possessed
    Bachelor in Paradise
62: Who's Got the Action?
65: Love Has Many Faces
66: Madame X
69: The Big Cube

Lana Turner (1920-
1937: They Won't Forget
    The Great Garrick
38: Adventures of Marco Polo
    Love Finds Andy Hardy
    Rich Man Poor Girl
    Dramatic School
39: Calling Dr. Kildare
    These Glamour Girls
    Dancing Coed
40: Two Girls on Broadway
    We Who Are Young
41: Ziegfeld Girl
    Dr. Jekyll and Mr. Hyde
    Honky Tonk
    Johnny Eager
42: Somewhere I'll Find You
43: Slightly Dangerous
    The Youngest Profession
44: Marriage Is a Private
    Affair
45: Keep Your Powder Dry
    Weekend at the Waldorf
46: The Postman Always
    Rings Twice
47: Green Dolphin Street
    Cass Timberlane
48: Homecoming
    The 3 Musketeers
50: A Life of Her Own

Ben Turpin (1874-1940)
1929: Show of Shows
    The Love Parade
30: Swing High
31: Cracked Nuts
    Our Wife
32: Million Dollar Legs
    Make Me a Star
39: Hollywood Cavalcade
40: Saps at Sea

Rita Tishingham (1940-
1962: A Taste of Honey
63: The Leather Boys
    A Place to Go
64: Girl with Green Eyes
65: The Knack...and How to
    Get It
66: Dr. Zhivago
    The Trap
67: Smashing Time
68: Diamonds for Breakfast
69: The Guru

Lurene Tuttle
1947: Heaven Only Knows
48: Homecoming
    Mr. Blanding Builds His
    Dream House

48: Macbeth
51: Goodbye My Fancy
Tomorrow Is Another Day
The Whip Hand
52: Don't Bother to Knock
Room for One More
Never Wave at a Wac
53: Niagara
Affairs of Dobie Gillis
Give a Girl a Break
55: The Glass Slipper
Sincerely Yours
56: Slander
57: Untamed Youth
Sweet Smell of Success
60: Ma Barker's Killer Brood
Psycho
63: Critic's Choice
65: Nightmare in the Sun
66: The Fortune Cookie
67: The Ghost and Mr.
Chicken
68: The Horse in the Gray
Flannel Suit

Helen Twelvetrees (1908-1958)
1929: The Ghost Talks
True Heart
Blue Skies   SSE
Paris to Bagdad
Words and Music
30: Grand Parade
Her Man
The Cat Creeps
Swing High
31: Beyond Victory
Painted Desert
Millie
A Woman of Experience
Bad Company
Cardigan's Last Case
32: State's Attorney
Panama Flo
Young Bride
Unashamed
Is My Face Red?
33: A Bedtime Story
Disgraced!
My Woman
King for a Night
34: All Men Are Enemies
Now I'll Tell

She Was a Lady
35: One Hour Late
Times Square Lady
She Gets Her Man
Spanish Cape Mystery
Frisco Waterfront
37: Hollywood Round-Up
39: Persons in Hiding
Unmarried

Archie Twitchell (1907-1957)
1937: Partners in Crime
Hold 'em, Navy!
38: Her Jungle Love
Tip-Off Girls
Cocoanut Grove
Spawn of the North
The Texans
Illegal Traffic
39: King of Chinatown
Mickey the Kid
40: Granny Get Your Gun
Charlie Chan at the Wax
Museum
Young Bill Hickok
Behind the News
41: I Wanted Wings
West Point Widow
Among the Living
Prairie Stranger
Thundering Hoofs
42: Tragedy at Midnight
45: The Missing Corpse
46: Affairs of Geraldine
The French Key
Accomplice
47: The Arnelo Affair
Second Chance
Web of Danger
49: Follow Me Quietly
50: Revenue Agent
51: Kentucky Jubilee
Yes Sir, Mr. Bones
54: The Bounty Hunter

Conway Twitty (1933-
1960: Platinum High School
College Confidential
Sex Kittens Go to College

Beverly Tyler (1928-
1943: Best Foot Forward

1352

46: The Green Years
47: My Brother Talks to
   Horses
   The Beginning or the End?
50: The Palomino
   The Fireball
52: The Cimarron Kid
   Battle at Apache Pass
57: Voodoo Island
   Chicago Confidential
58: Toughest Gun in Tomb-
   stone
   Hong Kong Confidential

Harry Tyler (1888-1961)
1936: 3 Wise Guys
   2-Fisted Gentlemen
   The Man I Marry
37: Don't Tell the Wife
   Jim Hanvey, Detective
   The Girl Said No
   Midnight Madonna
   Love Takes Flight
   Youth on Parole
38: Mr. Boggs Steps Out
39: The Story of Alexander
   Graham Bell
   Jesse James
   The Lady's from Kentucky
   20,000 Men a Year
40: The Grapes of Wrath
   Little Old New York
   Johnny Apollo
   Young People
   Meet the Missus
   Behind the News
41: Tobacco Road
   The Bride Wore Crutches
   The Richest Man in Town
   Tillie the Toiler
   Remember the Day
42: The Mexican Spitfire Sees
   a Ghost
43: True to Life
44: Casanova in Burlesque
   The Adventures of Mark
   Twain
   Atlantic City
   Wilson
45: Identity Unknown
   The Woman Who Came
   Back

46: Behind Green Lights
   The Fabulous Suzanne
   I Ring Doorbells
   Johnny Comes Flying Home
   Somewhere in the Night
47: Fun on a Weekend
   Sarge Goes to College
   Winter Wonderland
   Heading for Heaven
48: Smart Politics
   Deep Waters
   Strike it Rich
   The Untamed Breed
   That Wonderful Urge
49: The Beautiful Blonde
   from Bashful Bend
   Hellfire
   Traveling Saleswoman
   Air Hostess
50: A Woman of Distinction
   Rider from Tucson
51: Santa Fe
   Bedtime for Bonzo
   Corky of Gasoline Alley
52: This Woman Is Dangerous
53: The Glass Web
54: Witness to Murder
55: The Naked Street
   A Lawless Street
   Jail Busters
56: Glory
   Day of Fury
57: Plunder Road

Tom Tyler (1904-1954)
1929: Trail of the Horse
   Thieves   S
   The Sorcerers   S
   Gun Law   S
   Idaho Red   SSE
   Pride of the Pawnee S
   Lone Horseman   S
   The Man from Nevada   S
   The Phantom Rider   S
30: 'Neath Western Skies S
   Call of the Desert   S
   Canyon of Missing
   Men   S
   Pioneers of the West S
31: Galloping Through
   A Man from Death Valley
   Rider of the Plains

31: West of Cheyenne
Rose of the Rio Grande
God's Country and the
Man
Partners of the Trail
32: The Man from New
Mexico
Phantom of the West (ser.)
Jungle Mystery (ser.)
Single-Handed Sanders
2-Fisted Justice
The Forty-Niners
Honor of the Mounted
33: When a Man Rides Alone
Deadwood Pass
Clancy of the Mounted
(ser.)
War of the Range
34: Riding Through
Tracy Rides
Riding the Lonesome Trail
Mystery Ranch
Fighting Hero
Terror of the Plains
35: Powder Smoke Range
The Silent Code
Unconquered Bandit
36: The Last Outlaw
Fast Bullets
Roamin' Wild
The Last Outlaw
37: Lost Ranch
38: Orphan of the Pecos
King of Alcatraz
Pinto Rustlers
Phantom of the Air (ser.)
39: The Night Riders
Frontier Marshal
Gone with the Wind
Stagecoach
The Westerner
40: The Light of the Western
Stars
Brother Orchid
The Mummy's Hand
Cherokee Strip
41: Texas Rangers Ride Again
Border Vigilantes
Outlaws of Cherokee Trail
Riders of the Timberline
Gauchos of Eldorado
West of Cimarron

Adventures of Captain
Marvel (ser.)
42: Code of the Outlaw
Raiders of the Range
Westward Ho!
Valley of the Sun
The Talk of the Town
The Phantom Plainsmen
43: Shadows of the Sage
Thundering Trails
Valley of Hunted Men
Blocked Trail
Riders of the Rio Grande
Santa Fe Scouts
The Phantom (ser.)
Wagon Tracks West
44: Boss of Boomtown
45: San Antonio
Sing Me a Song of Texas
46: Badmen's Territory
47: Cheyenne
48: The Dude Goes West
Return of the Bad Men
Blood on the Moon
The Golden Eye
49: She Wore a Yellow Ribbon
The Younger Brothers
I Shot Jesse James
For Those Who Dare
Square Dance Jubilee
Masked Raiders
50: Hostile Country
West of the Bravos
Marshal of Heldorado
Colorado Ranger
Crooked River
Fast on the Draw
Rio Grande Patrol
The Great Missouri Raid
51: Best of the Bad Men
52: Road Agent
53: Cow Country

Brandon Tynan (1879-1967)
1937: Parnell
Wells Fargo
Sh! The Octopus
38: Girl of the Golden West
Youth Takes a Fling
Nancy Drew, Detective
39: The Great Man Votes
The Lone Wolf Spy Hunt

1354

39: Lady and the Mob
40: It All Came True
Lucky Partners
Rangers of Fortune
41: Marry the Boss's
Daughter

Lenore Ulric (1892-
1929: Frozen Justice
South Sea Rose
36: Camille
46: Temptation
Notorious
2 Smart People
47: Northwest Outpost

Miyoshi Umeki (1929-
1957: Sayonara (OSCAR)
61: Flower Drum Song
Cry for Happy
62: Horizontal Lieutenant
A Girl Named Tamiko

Mary Ure (1933-
1956: Storm over the Nile
None But the Brave
58: Windom's Way
59: Look Back in Anger
60: Sons and Lovers
63: The Mind Benders
64: The Luck of Ginger
Coffrey
68: Where Eagles Dare
Custer of the West

Minerva Urecal (1894-1966)
1937: Her Husband's Secretary
The Go Getter
Oh, Doctor!
Love in a Bungalow
Exiled to Shanghai
38: Start Cheering
Prison Nurse
Frontier Scout
Air Devils
40: You Can't Fool Your Wife
Boys of the City
41: Arkansas Judge
Murder by Invitation
The Cowboy and the
Blonde
Man at Large

Accent on Love
Never Give a Sucker an
Even Break
42: Henry and Dizzy
Sweater Girl
The Corpse Vanishes
Sons of the Pioneers
That Other Woman
Quiet Please, Murder!
The Living Ghost
43: Riding Through Nevada
The Ape Man
Kid Dynamite
Ghosts on the Loose
So This Is Washington
44: The Bridge of San Luis
Rey
Louisiana Hayride
Moonlight and Cactus
Block Busters
County Fair
Crazy Knights
45: Medal for Benny
Kid Sister
Wanderer of the Wasteland
The Men in Her Diary
Who's Guilty? (ser.)
46: Sensation Hunters
Wake Up and Dream
Rainbow over Texas
Dark Corner
48: Sitting Pretty
Secret Service Investigator
Variety Time
Good Sam
The Snake Pit
Marshal of Amarillo
Sundown at Santa Fe
49: The Lovable Cheat
Master Minds
Holiday in Havana
Outcasts of the Trail
50: Arizona Cowboy
Quicksand
Traveling Saleswoman
My Blue Heaven
51: Stop that Cab!
52: Harem Girl
Aaron Slick from Punkin
Crick
Oklahoma Annie
Gobs and Gals

52: Lost in Alaska
    Anything can Happen
53: The Woman They Almost
    Lynched
    Niagara
55: Sudden Danger
56: Miracle in the Rain
    Crashing Las Vegas
    Tugboat Annie
60: The Adventures of Huckle-
    berry Finn
62: Mr. Hobbs Takes a
    Vacation
64: 7 Faces of Dr. Lao

Peter Ustinov (1921-
1941: Mein Kampf
    The Goose Steps Out
42: One of Our Aircraft Is
    Missing
    Let the People Sing
45: The Way Ahead (act.,
    dir., prod.)
    The True Glory
46: School for Secrets (dir.)
    Vice Versa (dir., prod.)
    Private Angelo
51: Odette
    Quo Vadis?
    Hotel Sahara
54: The Egyptian
    Beau Brummel
55: We're No Angels
    Lola Montez
    The Spies
    An Angel Flew over
    Brooklyn
57: Les Espions
59: The Man Who Wagged His
    Tail
60: School for Scoundrels
    The Sundowners
    Spartacus (OSCAR)
61: Romanoff and Juliet
62: Billy Budd
64: Topkapi (OSCAR)
    John Goldfarb, Please
    Come Home
66: Lady L (prod., dir.)
67: The Comedians
68: Hot Millions
    Blackbeard's Ghost

69: Viva Max!
    A Field of Buttercups
    Sherlock Holmes

Vera Vague [Barbara Jo Allen]
(c1904-
1940: Village Barn Dance
    Sing, Dance, Plenty Hot
    Melody and Moonlight
    Melody Ranch
41: Design for Scandal
    The Mad Doctor
    Kiss the Boys Goodbye
    Buy Me that Town
    Ice-Capades Revue
    Larceny, Inc.
42: Hi Neighbor!
    Ice-Capades of 1942
    Priorities on Parade
    Mrs. Wiggs of the
    Cabbage Patch
43: Rosie the Riveter
    Moon over Las Vegas
    Get Going
44: Henry Aldrich Plays
    Cupid
    Swing Your Partner
    Lake Placid Serenade
    Cowboy Canteen
    Girl Rush
45: Snafu
46: Earl Carroll Sketchbook
50: Square Dance Katy
56: Mohawk
    The Opposite Sex
59: Born to be Loved
    Sleeping Beauty (cartoon
    voice)

Virginia Vale
1939: 3 Sons
40: Marshal of Mesa City
    Legion of the Lawless
    Bullet Code
    You Can't Fool Your Wife
    Millionaires in Prison
    Prairie Law
    Stage to Chino
    Triple Justice
41: South of Panama
    Robbers of the Range
42: Broadway Big Shot

Lili Valenty
1962: The Rome Adventure
It Happened in Athens
Girls! Girls! Girls!

Rudy Vallee (1901-
1929: Radio Rhythm (short)
Rudy Vallee and His
Connecticut Yankees
(short)
Vagabond Lover
Glorifying the American
Girl
30: Campus Sweethearts
(3 reels)
31: Musical Justice (short)
32: Rudy Vallee Melodies
(short)
33: International House
34: George White's Scandals
of 1934
35: Sweet Music
38: For Auld Lang Syne (doc.)
Gold Diggers in Paris
39: Second Fiddle
41: Time Out for Rhythm
Too Many Blondes
42: Palm Beach Story
43: Happy Go Lucky
45: Man Alive!
It's in the Bag
46: People Are Funny
The Fabulous Suzanne
47: The Bachelor and the
Bobby-Soxer
Mad Wednesday
48: I Remember Mama
So This Is New York
My Dear Secretary
Unfaithfully Yours
49: Father Was a Fullback
Mother Is a Freshman
The Beautiful Blonde
from Bashful Bend
50: The Admiral Was a Lady
54: Ricochet Romance
55: Gentlemen Marry
Brunettes
57: The Helen Morgan Story
67: How to Succeed in
Business Without Really
Trying

68: Live a Little, Love a
Little
69: The Silent Treatment
The Night They Raided
Minsky's (voice)
The Phynx

Alida Valli (1921-
1936: I Due Sergenti
39: Manon Lescaut
41: Little Old World
Vita Ricomincia, Giovanni
46: Eugenie Grandet
47: The Paradine Case
Laugh Pagliacci
School Girl Diary
48: Miracle of the Bells
Weep No More
50: The Third Man
Walk Softly, Stranger
The White Tower
52: Lovers of Toledo
53: Senso
55: The Stranger's Hand
58: This Angry Age
The Night Heaven Fell
59: Les Dialogues des
Carmelites
61: The Wide Blue Road
62: The Happy Thieves
Il Grido (The Outcry)
The Long Absence (Fr.)
Horror Chamber of Dr.
Faustus
63: The Castilian
64: Disorder
Ophelia

Virginia Valli (1895-1968)
1929: Behind Closed Doors
The Isle of Lost Ships
Mr. Antonio
30: Lost Zeppelin
Guilty?
31: Night Life in Reno

Rick Vallin
1942: King of the Stallions
Nearly 18
Corregidor
The Lady from Chungking
A Night for Crime

1357

42: The Panther's Claw
Secrets of a Co-Ed
43: The Clancy Street Boys
Ghosts on the Loose
Isle of Forgotten Men
Wagon Tracks West
Riders of the Rio Grande
44: Smart Guy
Army Wives
46: Dangerous Money
Secrets of a Sorority
Girl
47: Last of the Redmen
Northwest Outpost
2 Blondes and a Redhead
48: Bob and Sally
Social Guidance
49: Tuna Clipper
Jungle Jim
Shamrock Hill
50: Comanche Territory
Captive Girl
State Penitentiary
Killer Shark
Snow Dog
Counterspy Meets Scotland
Yard
Rio Grande Patrol
Revenue Agent
51: The Magic Carpet
Jungle Manhunt
King of the Congo (ser.)
When the Redskins Rode
Hurricane Island
52: Aladdin and His Lamp
Woman in the Dark
Strange Fascination
Voodoo Tiger
53: Star of Texas
Bowery to Bagdad
The Homesteaders
Trail Blazers
Topka
The Marksman
54: The Golden Idol
55: Treasure of Ruby Hills
Dial Red O
57: The Tijuana Story
58: Escape from Red Rock
Bull Whip
59: Pier #5 - Havana
67: Adventures of Batman and
Robin

Raf Vallone (1916-
1948: Bitter Rice
49: Vendetta
50: Path of Hope
51: Il Cristo Prohibito
Under the Olive Tree
White Line
52: Barbed Wire
53: Teresa Raquin
Riviera
Rome--11 O'Clock
Strange Deception
Anita Garibaldi
The Beach
54: Anna
Daughters of Destiny
55: The Sign of Venus
Don Juan's Night of Love
57: Passionate Summer
The Adulteress
58: Guendalina
59: Andrea Chenier
The Sins of Rose Bernd
61: El Cid
2 Women
62: Phaedra
A View from the Bridge
The Adventures of Mandrin
63: The Cardinal
64: The Secret Invasion
65: Harlow (Para.)
66: Nevada Smith
67: Kiss the Girls and Make
Them Die
68: The Desperate Ones
Beyond the Mountains
69: The Italian Job

Vampira
1959: The Big Operator
The Beat Generation
60: Sex Kittens Go to College

Bobby Van (1916-
1952: Because You're Mine
Small Town Girl
53: Affairs of Dobie Gillies
Kiss Me Kate
66: The Navy vs the Night
Monsters

Lee Van Cleef (1925-
1950: The Showdown

52: High Noon
     Untamed Frontier
     Kansas City Confidential
53: Beast from 20,000
     Fathoms
     Arena
     Vice Squad
     White Lightning
     The Nebraskan
     The Lawless Breed
     Tumbleweed
     Jack Slade
54: Man Without a Star
     Rails into Laramie
     Arrow in the Dust
     The Desperado
     Yellow Tomahawk
     Dawn at Socorro
     Princess of the Nile
55: The Kentuckian
     The Naked Street
     10 Wanted Men
     Big Combo
     Treasure of Ruby Hills
     I Cover the Underworld
     Road to Denver
     A Man Alone
     The Vanishing American
56: The Conqueror
     Tribute to a Bad Man
     Pardners
     Red Sundown
     Accused of Murder
     It Conquered the World
     Backlash
57: The Lonely Man
     China Gate
     Joe Dakota
     The Quiet Gun
     The Badge of Marshal
     Brennan
     Gun Battle of Monterey
     Raiders of Old California
     The Last Stagecoach West
     Gunfight at the O.K.
     Corral
     The Tin Star
58: Day of the Bad Man
     The Young Lions
     The Bravados
     Machete
     Guns, Girls, and
     Gangsters

59: Ride Lonesome
61: Posse from Hell
     The Falcon and His Prey
62: The Man Who Shot Liberty
     Valance
63: How the West Was Won
66: Call to Glory (TV rel. in
     2 pts.)
67: Death Rides a Horse
     Sundown
     2 Magnificent Rogues
     For a Few Dollars More
     A Fistful of Dollars
68: Credo of Violence
     Days of Anger
     Mercenary for Any War
     The Good the Bad and the
     Ugly
     The Big Gundown
69: 2 Enemies
     Barquero
     Sabata
     The Professional Gun
     Gaucho
     Above the Law
     Man to Man
     The Man from Far Away
     From Dunkirk to London
     Scalawag
     El Condor

Mamie Van Doren (1933-
1953: Forbidden
     All-American
54: Yankee Pasha
     Francis Joins the Wacs
55: Ain't Misbehavin'
     The Second Greatest Sex
     Running Wild
56: Star in the Dust
57: Untamed Youth
     The Girl in Black Stockings
58: Teacher's Pet
     High School Confidential
     Guns Girls and Gangsters
59: Born Reckless
     The Beat Generation
     Girls' Town
     The Big Operator
     Vice Raid
60: Beauty and the Robot
     College Confidential
     Sex Kittens Go to College

60: The Private Lives of
Adam and Eve
64: 4 Nuts in Search of a
Bolt
65: The Navy vs the Night
Monsters
66: Las Vegas Hillbillies
67: You've Got to be Smart

John Van Dreelan
1958: A Time to Love and a
Time to Die
59: The Flying Fontaines
60: The Leech Woman
13 Ghosts
The Enemy General
Beyond the Time Barrier
The Wizard of Baghdad
Beauty and the Robot
65: Von Ryan's Express
66: Madame X
I Deal in Danger
68: The Duck Rings at Half
Past 7 (Ger.)
69: Topaz

Dick Van Dyke (1925-
1963: Bye Bye Birdie
64: Mary Poppins
What a Way to Go!
65: The Art of Love
66: Lt. Robin Crusoe, U.S.N.
67: Divorce--American Style
Fitzwilly
68: Chitty Chitty Bang Bang!
69: Some Kind of Nut
The Comic
Cold Turkey
I Do I Do

Jerry Van Dyke (1931-
1963: Courtship of Eddie's
Father
Palm Springs Weekend
McLintock!
65: Love and Kisses
68: An Angel in My Pocket

Peter Van Eyck (1913-1969)
1943: The Moon Is Down
5 Graves to Cairo
44: The Impostor

The Hitler Gang
Address Unknown
50: The Devil's Agent
51: Rommel-Desert Fox
53: Sailor of the King
Alerte au Said
54: Night People
55: Tarzan's Hidden Jungle
Jump into Hell
The Brain
A Bullet for Joey
The Wages of Fear
56: The Rawhide Years
Run for the Sun
Attack!
57: Retour de Maivelle (Fr.)
The Girl on the Third
Floor
58: Rosemary
The Snorkel
There's Always a Price
Tag
Flesh and the Woman
Flesh and Desire
59: The Glass Tower
60: The Rest Is Silence
61: Foxhole in Cairo
Law of War
62: The World in My Pocket
The Black Chapel
The Longest Day
Mr. Arkadin
Rebel Flight to Cuba
63: The River Line
64: Station 6 Sahara
65: An Alibi for Death
And so to Bed
The Spy Who Came in
from the Cold
66: The Dirty Game
The 1000 Eyes of Dr.
Mabuse
The Mystery of Thug Island
67: The Assignment
68: Shalako
Toviw and His 7 Daughters
(ger.)

Jo Van Fleet (1919-
1955: East of Eden (OSCAR)
The Rose Tattoo
I'll Cry Tomorrow

56: The King and 4 Queens
57: Gunfight at the O.K.
    Corral
58: This Angry Age
60: Wild River
67: Cool Hand Luke
68: I Love You, Alice B.
    Toklas
69: 80 Steps to Jonah

Joyce Van Patten (1935-
1951: Fourteen Hours
58: The Goddess
68: I Love You, Alice B.
    Toklas
69: Assault
    A Dynasty of Western
    Outlaws
    The Divine Sarah
    Pussycat, Pussycat, I
    Love You
    You and I
    The Trouble with Girls
    (or, Chautauqua)

Luis Van Rooten (1906-
1944: The Hitler Gang
46: Two Years Before the
    Mast
48: To the Ends of the Earth
    The Big Clock
    To the Victor
    Beyond Glory
    The Night Has a 1000 Eyes
    The Gentleman from
    Nowhere
    Boston Blackie's Honor
49: City Across the River
    Champion
    Boston Blackie's Chinese
    Venture
    The Secret of St. Ives
50: Cinderella (cartoon voice)
51: Detective Story
    My Favorite Spy
52: Lydia Bailey
55: The Sea Chase
57: The Unholy Wife
58: The Curse of the Faceless
    Man
61: Operation Eichmann

Edward Van Sloan (1882-1964)
1931: Dracula
    Frankenstein
32: The Infernal Machine
    Manhattan Parade
    Play Girl
    Man Wanted
    Behind the Mask
    The Mummy
    Thunder Below
    Forgotten Commandments
    The Last Mile
    Honeymoon in Bali
33: Silk Express
    The Working Man
    Trick for Trick
    It's Great to be Alive
    The Deluge
    Murder on the Campus
    The Death Kiss
    Billian Dollar Scandal
34: Death Takes a Holiday
    The Crosby Case
    Scarlet Empress
    The Life of Vergie Winters
    Manhattan Melodrama
    I'll Fix It
35: Grand Old Girl
    Mills of the Gods
    Woman in Red
    A Shot in the Dark
    Last Days of Pompeii
    Air Hawks
    Mystery of the Black Room
    Grand Exit
    The Story of Louis Pasteur
36: Road Gang
    Dracula's Daughter
    Sins of Man
37: The Man Who Found Him-
    self
38: Penitentiary
    Storm over Bengal
    Danger on the Air
39: The Phantom Creeps (ser.)
40: Abe Lincoln in Illinois
    The Doctor Takes a Wife
    The Secret Seven
    Before I Hang
42: A Man's World
43: Valley of Hunted Men

43: Mission to Moscow
Riders of the Rio Grande
Submarine Alert
The Masked Marvel (ser.)
End of the Road
44: The Conspirators
Captain America (ser.)
46: The Mask of Dijon
47: Betty Coed

Monique Van Vooren (1933-
1952: Tomorrow Is Too Late
53: Tarzan and the She Devil
55: Serie Noire
Ça Va Barder
57: 10,000 Bedrooms
58: Gigi
59: Happy Anniversary

Philip Van Zandt (1904-1951)
1941: City of Missing Girls
Ride on, Vaquero!
Citizen Kane
So Ends Our Night
43: Air Wardens
Tarzan Triumphs
Murder on the Waterfront
Hostages
Deerslayer
Tarzan's Desert Mystery
44: Call of the Jungle
The Big Noise
Swing Hostess
The Unwritten Code
45: House of Frankenstein
Counter-Attack
I Love a Bandleader
Outlaws of the Rockies
Sudan
A 1000 and One Nights
46: The Avalanche
Below the Deadline
Decoy
Joe Palooka--Champ
Somewhere in the Night
Don't Gamble with
Strangers
47: Slave Girl
The Last Frontier Up-
rising
48: April Showers

The Big Clock
The Vicious Circle
Street with No Name
The Shanghai Chest
Embraceable You
Walk a Crooked Mile
The Loves of Carmen
49: The Lady Gambles
The Lone Wolf and His
Lady
Red Hot and Blue
50: Where Danger Lives
Copper Canyon
The Petty Girl
Indian Territory
Between Midnight and Dawn
Cyrano de Bergerac
51: The Ghost Chasers
His Kind of Woman
Submarine Command
Two Dollar Bettor
52: The Thief of Damascus
Son of Ali Baba
Yukon Gold
53: Prisoners of the Casbah
54: Yankee Pasha
Playgirl
55: Untamed
I Covered the Underworld
56: Around the World in 80
Days
Uranium Boom
Our Miss Brooks
57: The Lonely Man
The Pride and the Passion

Vivian Vance (1912-
1950: Secret Fury
51: The Blue Veil

Victor Varconi (1896-1958)
1928: Sinners Parade   S
29: Eternal Love   SSE
Divine Lady   SSE
31: Captain Thunder
Doctors' Wives
Black Camel
Men in Her Life
Safe in Hell
32; Doomed Battalion
33: The Rebel

1362

34: The Song You Game Me
35: Roberta
    Mr. Dynamite
    A Feather in Her Hat
36: Dancing Pirate
    The Plainsman
37: Trouble in Morocco
    Big City
    Men in Exile
38: King of the Newsboys
    Suez
    Submarine Patrol
39: Mr. Moto Takes a
      Vacation
    Disputed Passage
    The Story of Vernon and
      Irene Castle
    Everything Happens at
      Night
40: Strange Cargo
    The Sea Hawk
41: Federal Fugitives
    Forced Landing
42: My Favorite Girl
    They Raid by Night
43: For Whom the Bell Tolls
44: The Story of Dr. Wassell
    The Hitler Gang
45: Scotland Yard Investigator
47: The Unconquered
    Where There's Life
    Pirates of Monterey
49: Samson and Delilah
57: The Man Who Turned to
      Stone
59: The Atomic Submarine

Evelyn Varden (1895-1958)
1949: Pinky
50: Cheaper by the Dozen
    When Willie Comes
      Marching Home
    Stella
51: Elopement
    Finders Keepers
52: Phone Call
54: The Student Prince
    Desiree
    Athena
55: The Night of the Hunter
56: Hilda Crane
    The Bad Seed

57: 10,000 Bedrooms

Norma Varden (c1898-
1930: East Meets West
32: A Night Like That
34: Turkey Time
35: The Student's Romance
    The Iron Duke
    Music Hath Charm
36: Where There's a Will
37: Fire over England
    Boys Will Be Boys
    Windbag the Sailor
    Foreign Affairs
    Stormy Weather
    Get Off My Foot!
    Wanted
    Make Up
39: Home from Home
    Shipyard Sally
40: The Lilas Domino
    Rhythm Racketeer
    The Earl of Chicago
41: The Mad Doctor
    Glamour Boy
    Scotland Yard
42: The Major and the Minor
    Random Harvest
43: What a Woman!
    The Good Fellows
44: Mlle. Fifi
    The White Cliffs of Dover
    National Velvet
45: Those Endearing Young
      Charms
    Bring on the Girls
    Hold that Blonde!
    Girls of the Big House
46: The Green Years
    The Searching Wind
47: Millie's Daughter
    Trouble with Women
    Bob, Son of Battle (or,
      Thunder in the Valley)
    The Senator Was Indiscreet
48: Let's Live a Little
    The Spiritualist
49: Adventure in Baltimore
    The Secret Garden
50: Fancy Pants
51: Strangers on a Train
    Thunder on the Hill

53: Young Bess
    Gentlemen Prefer Blondes
    Loose in London
55: Jupiter's Darling
57: Witness for the
    Prosecution
58: The Buccaneer
63: 13 Frightened Girls
64: Kisses for My President
65: A Very Special Favor
    The Sound of Music
66: Door-to-Door Maniac
67: Dr. Dolittle
68: Istanbul Express (TV)

Diane Varsi (1938-
1957: Peyton Place
58: From Hell to Texas
    10 North Frederick
59: Compulsion
61: Return to Peyton Place
67: Sweet Love, Bitter
68: Wild in the Streets
    Killers 3

Alberta Vaughn (1906-
1931: Wild Horse
    Working Girls
32: Dancers in the Dark
    Love in High Gear
    Daring Danger
    Midnight Morals
34: Randy Rides Alone

Dorothy Vaughn (1889-1955)
1935: Annapolis Farewell
36: Love Begins at 20
    Times Square Playboy
37: Hoosier Schoolboy
    Here's Flash Casey
    That Man's Here Again
    The Black Legion
    Michael O'Halloran
38: Quick Money
    Slander House
    Little Orphan Annie
    Gambling Ship
    Little Miss Thoroughbred
    Telephone Operator
39: Unexpected Father
    The Man in the Iron Mask
    First Love

40: Diamond Frontier
    The Old Swimmin' Hole
    The Ape
41: Secret Evidence
    Bad Men of Missouri
    3 Girls about Town
42: Lady Gangster
    Gentleman Jim
43: The Iron Major
    Sweet Rosie O'Grady
    Doughboys in Ireland
44: The Adventures of Mark
    Twain
    Henry Aldrich's Little
    Secret
    Sweet and Lowdown
    The Town Went Wild
45: Dancing in Manhattan
    What a Blonde!
46: Riverboat Rhythm
    That Hagen Girl
47: Trail to San Antone
    The Bamboo Blonde
    The Egg and I
    Robin Hood in Texas
48: The Bishop's Wife
    I Wouldn't be in Your
    Shoes
    Song of Idaho
49: Fighting Fools
    Manhattan Angel
    Home in San Antone
50: Ride from Tucson
    Square Dance Katy
51: A Wonderful Life

Frankie Vaughn (1928-
1955: Ramsbottom Rides Again
57: These Dangerous Years
58: Dangerous Youth
    Wonderful Things
    The Lady Is a Square
59: The Heart of a Man
60: Let's Make Love
61: The Right Approach
64: It's All Over Town

Hilda Vaughn (1898-1957)
1929: 3 Live Ghosts
30: Manslaughter
31: It's a Wise Child
    Susan Lennox

1364

31: A Tailor Made Man
32: Ladies of the Big House
The Phantom of Crest-
wood
33: Today We Live
No Other Woman
Dinner at 8
No Marriage Ties
34: Anne of Green Gables
35: The Wedding Night
I Live My Life
Straight from the Heart
Chasing Yesterday
Men Without Names
36: Trail of the Lonesome
Pine
Everybody's Old Man
Half Angel
The Accusing Finger
Banjo on My Knee
The Witness Chair
37: Danger: Love at Work!
38: Maid's Night Out
40: Charlie Chan at the Wax
Museum

Robert Vaughn (1932-
1957: Hell's Crossroads
No Time to be Young
To Trap a Spy
58: A Good Day for Hanging
Unwed Mother
Teenage Caveman
59: The Young Philadelphians
60: The Magnificent 7
61: The Big Show
63: The Caretakers
66: The Spy with My Face
One of Our Spies Is
Missing
One Spy Too Many
67: The Venetian Affair
68: Bullitt
69: The Mind of Mr. Soames
The Bridge at Ramagen
If It's Tuesday, This Must
be Belgium
The Assassination of Julius
Caesar

Michael Vavitch
1928: Glorious Betsy   PT

29: Wolf Song   PT
Divine Lady   SSE
The Bridge of San Luis
Rey   PT
30: A Devil with Women
War Nurse

Conrad Veidt (1893-1943)
1927: Magic Flame   S
28: The Man Who Laughs   S
L'Homme qui Rie (The
Man Who Laughs)   S
Erik the Great   S
Hands of Orlac   S
Love Makes Us
Blind   S
Mystic Mirror   S
Unwelcome Children   S
Life's Mockey   S
2 Brothers   S
29: The Man Who Cheated
Life   S
The Last Performance   PT
The Black Huzzar
NJU
Lucretia Borgia   S
3 Wax Men   S
30: Bride 68   PT
Great Power
Rasputin
31: The Last Company
32: Congress Dances
Cape Forlorn
33: Rome Express
F. P. No. 1
I Was a Spy
34: The Wandering Jew
Bella Donna
Jew Süss
35: Passing of the Third Floor
Back
36: King of the Damned
37: Under the Red Robe
Dark Journey
38: Storm over Asia
The Chessplayer
The Spy in Black
39: Thief of Bagdad
40: Blackout
Escape
Contraband
41: A Woman's Face

41: Whistling in the Dark
Men in Her Life
42: Nazi Agent
All Through the Night
Casablanca
43: Above Suspicion

Lupe Velez (1908-1944)
1927: The Gaucho   S
28: Stand and Deliver   S
29: Masquerade
Wolf Song   PT
Lady of the Pavements PT
Where East Is East   S
Tiger Rose
30: Hell Harbor
The Storm
East Is West
31: Resurrection
The Squaw Man
Cuban Love Song
32: Broken Wing
Kongo
The Half Naked Truth
33: Hot Pepper
Mr. Broadway
34: Joe Palooka
Laughing Boy
Hollywood Party
Strictly Dynamite
36: Morals of Marcus
Gypsy Melody
Under Your Spell
37: High Flyers
38: He Loved an Actress
39: Girl from Mexico
The Mexican Spitfire
40: The Mexican Spitfire
Out West
41: The Mexican Spitfire's
Baby Playmates
6 Lessons from Madame
La Zonga
42: The Mexican Spitfire at
Sea
The Mexican Spitfire Sees
a Ghost
The Mexican Spitfire's
Elephant
Honolulu Lu
43: Ladies' Day
The Redhead from
Manhattan

The Mexican Spitfire's
Blessed Event
64: Big Parade of Comedy
(doc.)

Evelyn Venable (1913-
1933: Cradle Song
34: David Harum
Death Takes a Holiday
Double Door
Mrs. Wiggs of the
Cabbage Patch
35: County Chairman
Little Colonel
Vagabond Lady
Alice Adams
Harmony Lane
36: Streamline Express
Star for a Night
North of Nome
Happy Go Lucky
37: Racketeer in Exile
38: My Old Kentucky Home
Female Fugitive
The Frontiersman
Hollywood Stadium
Mystery
The Headleys at Home
39: Heritage of the Desert
40: Lucky Cisco Kid
43: He Hired the Boss

Benay Venuta (1912-
1928: Trail of '98   S
31: Kiki
47: Repeat Performance
48: I Jane Doe
50: Annie Get Your Gun
51: Call Me Mister
54: Ricochet Romance
57: The Fuzzy Pink Nightgown

Vera-Ellen (1920-
1945: The Wonder Man
46: The Kid from Brooklyn
3 Little Girls in Blue
47: Carnival in Costa Rica
48: Words and Music
49: Love Happy
On the Town
50: Three Little Words
51: Happy Go Lovely
52: Belle of New York

1366

52: The Big Leaguer
54: White Christmas
57: Let's be Happy
59: Web of Evidence

Gwen Verdon (1926-
1951: On the Riviera
       David and Bathsheba
       Meet Me After the Show
53: The Farmer Takes a
       Wife
58: Damn Yankees

Elena Verdugo
1942: The Moon and Sixpence
43: The Devil's Brood
44: Rainbow Island
45: House of Frankenstein
       The Frozen Ghost
       Strange Voyage
46: Little Giant
47: Song of Scheherazade
49: Tuna Clipper
       Sky Dragons
       The Big Sombrero
       El Dorado Pass
       The Lost Tribe
50: Snow Dog
       The Lost Volcano
       Cyrano de Bergerac
51: Gene Autry and the
       Mounties
52: Thief of Damascus
       Jet Job
       The Pathfinder
53: The Marksman
       Knights of the Round
       Table
57: Panama Sal
68: How Sweet It Is!
       An Angel in My Pocket

Harold Vermilyea
1946: O.S.S.
47: A Gentleman's Agreement
48: The Big Clock
       The Emperor Waltz
       The Sainted Sisters
       The Miracle of the Bells
       Beyond Glory
       Sorry, Wrong Number
       California's Golden
       Beginning

49: Manhandled
       Chicago Deadline
50: Born to be Bad
51: Finders Keepers

Kaaren Verne (1918-1967)
1939: 10 Days in Paris
40: Sky Murder
41: Underground
       Kings Row
42: All Through the Night
       The Great Impersonation
43: Sherlock Holmes and
       the Secret Weapon
44: The 7th Cross
55: A Bullet for Joey
65: Ship of Fools
66: The Torn Curtain
       Madame X

Wally Vernon
1937: Mountain Music
       You Can't Have Everything
       This Way Please
38: Happy Landing
       Kentucky Moonshine
       Alexander's Ragtime Band
       Sharpshooters
       Meet the Girls
39: Tail Spin
       Broadway Serenade
       The Gorilla
       Chasing Danger
       Charlie Chan at Treasure
       Island
40: The Sailor's Lady
       Margie
       Sandy Gets Her Man
43: Tahiti Honey
       Get Going
       Fugitive from Sonora
       The Black Hills Express
       Here Comes Elmer
       Pistol Packin' Mama
       Reveille with Beverly
44: Call of the South Seas
       Outlaws of Santa Fe
       Silent Partners
       Silver City Kid
       Stagecoach to Monterey
       California Joe
48: Fighting Mad
       King of Gamblers

48: Winner Take All
49: Always Leave Them
    Laughing
    Square Dance Jubilee
50: Beauty on Parade
    Border Rangers
    Holiday Rhythm
    Gunfire
    Train to Tombstone
    Everybody's Dancing
52: What Price Glory?
    Bloodhounds of Broadway
53: Affair with a Stranger
56: Fury at Gunsight Pass
    The White Squaw
64: What a Way to Go!

Martha Vickers (1925-
1944: The Falcon in Mexico
46: The Big Sleep
    The Time, the Place,
    and the Girl
47: Love and Learn
    The Man I Love
    That Way with Women
48: Rustlers
49: Alimony
    Bad Boy
    Daughter of the West
55: The Big Bluff
57: The Burglar
59: 4 Fast Guns

Henri Vidal (1919-1959)
1946: Les Maudits
50: Quai de Grenelle
51: Fabiola
54: Port du Desir
55: The Wicked Go to Hell
56: Port Les Lilas
58: Gates of Paris
    Attila
    La Parisienne
    What Price Murder!
60: Come Dance with Me!

June Vincent
1943: Honeymoon Lodge
44: Babes on Swing Street
    Second Honeymoon
    The Climax
    Ladies Courageous

    Can't Help Singing
45: Here Come The Co-Eds
    That's the Spirit!
46: Black Angel
47: Song of Idaho
    The Challenge
48: The Creeper
    Shed No Tears
    The Lone Wolf and His
    Lady
    Trapped by Boston Blackie
49: Zamba
50: Mary Ryan, Detective
    The Counterspy Meets
    Scotland Yard
    Secrets of Monte Carlo
52: Colorado Sundown
    Night Without Sleep
    The Wac from Walla Walla
    Clipped Wings
53: Marry Me Again
55: City of Shadows
59: Miracle of the Hills

Helen Vinson (1907-
1932: Jewel Robbery
    2 Against the World
    The Crash
    They Call it Sin
    I'm a Fugitive from a
    Chain Gang
    Lawyer Man
33: Midnight Club
    The Power and the Glory
    As Husbands Go
    The Kennel Murder Case
    Little Giant
    Grand Slam
34: The Life of Vergie Winters
    Let's Try Again
    Broadway Bill
    The Captain Hates the Sea
35: A Notorious Gentleman
    The Wedding Night
    Private Worlds
    Age of Indiscretion
    Transatlantic Tunnel
36: King of the Damned
    Love in Exile
    Reunion
37: Vogues of 1938
    Live, Love, and Learn

1368

39: In Name Only
40: Married and in Love
Curtain Call
Enemy Agent
Torrid Zone
Beyond Tomorrow
41: Bowery Boy
Nothing but the Truth
44: Chip Off the Old Block
The Lady and the
Monster
Are These Our Parents?
The Thin Man Goes Home

Arthur Vinton
1934: Gambling Lady
Cross Country Cruise
A Very Honorable Guy
Man Trailer
Dames
Personality Kid
Jealousy
35: Rendezvous at Midnight
Unknown Woman
Little Big Shot
Circumstantial Evidence
Red Salute
King Solomon of Broadway

Michael Visaroff (1890-1951)
1929: Disraeli
Hungarian Rhapsory   SSE
The Exalted Flapper   SSE
Marquis Preferred   S
House of Horror   PT
Illusion
30: Dracula
Morocco
31: Arizona Terror
Mata Hari
Freaks
Chinatown after Dark
32: The Man Who Played God
33: Strange People
The Barbarian
The King of the Arena
34: The Merry Frinks
The Cat's Paw
Wagon Wheels
Picture Brides
Fugitive Road
The Marines Are Coming!

35: One More Spring
Mark of the Vampire
Break of Hearts
Paddy O'Day
Anna Karenina
36: The Gay Desperado
37: Champagne Waltz
The Soldier and the Lady
(or, Michael Strogoff)
Angel
38: Air Devils
Tropic Holiday
I'll Give a Million
39: Paris Honeymoon
Everything Happens at
Night
Juarez and Maximilian
40: 4 Sons
Charlie Chan at the Wax
Museum
The Son of Monte Cristo
43: For Whom the Bell Tolls
Mission to Moscow
Hostages
Paris after Dark
45: Yolanda and the Thief
47: Flight to Nowhere

Milly Vitale (1938-
1951: Revenge of the Pirates
53: The Juggler
55: The 7 Little Foys
Nero and the Burning of
Rome
56: War and Peace
60: Hannibal
Breath of Scandal
62: The Lion of Amalfi

Monica Vitti (1933-
1961: L'Avventura
La Notte
63: Trois Fables au Poivre
64: Nutty Naught Chateau
Sweet and Sour
Bebo's Girl
65: The Flying Saucer
The Dolls--Bombole!
(The Soup Seq.)
High Infidelity
Red Desert
66: Modesty Blaisé

68: The Queens (Queen
     Sabina seq.)
     I Married You for Fun
     The Chastity
69: The Girl with the Pistol
     The Scarlet Woman

Marina Vlady (1938-
1949: Orage D'Ete
53: Avant le Deluge
55: The Wicked Go to Hell
56: Crime and Punishment
58: The Sentence
59: Toi le Venin
     The Hunt
60: The Sentinel
62: 7 Capital Sins
     Climats
63: Dragées au Poivre
     The Conjugal
     The Double Agents
     The Steppe
64: Queen Bee
66: Crimes at Midnight
     Enough Rope
     Run for Your Wife
67: Falstaff
69: Time to Live

Emmett Vogan
1939: The Man Who Dared
     The Great Victor Herbert
40: Thou Shalt Not Kill
     Margie
41: The Lady from Cheyenne
     Horror Island
     Petticoat Politics
     Emergency Landing
     Hurricane Smith
     Badlands of Dakota
     Never Give a Sucker an
       Even Break
     Dangerous Lady
     Blue, White, and Perfect
42: Stardust on the Sage
     Top Sergeant
     The Mummy's Tomb
     Whistling in Dixie
     The Traitor Within
43: Dixie Dugan
     The Crime Smasher
     Lady Bodyguard

He Hired His Boss
Chatterbox
Here Comes Helly
Mystery Broadcast
Oh, My Darling Clementine
44: Are These Our Parents?
     Bermuda Mystery
     End of the Road
     Faces in the Fog
     Lady, Let's Dance
     Hat Check Honey
     The Mummy's Ghost
     Murder in the Blue Room
     Night Club Girl
     Swingtime Johnny
     Trocadero
45: Along the Navajo Trail
     Behind City Lights
     The Bullfighters
     Colorado Pioneers
     Corpus Christi Bandits
     Don Juan Quilligan
     The Lady Confesses
     The Señorita from the
       West
     She Gets Her Man
     Utah
     The Vampire's Ghost
     The Woman Who Came
       Back
46: Bowery Bombshell
     A Close Call for Boston
       Blackie
     Dangerous Money
     Freddie Steps Out
     The French Key
     The Gay Blades
     Joe Palooka--Champ
     The Jolson Story
     The Magnificent Doll
     Rendezvous 24
     The Shadow Returns
     Secrets of a Sorority Girl
     Sweetheart of Sigma Chi
47: Cigarette Girl
     The Homesteaders of
       Paradise Valley
     Jewels of Brandenburg
     I Wonder Who's Kissing
       Her Now
     Last of the Redmen
     News Hounds
48:

1370

48: Mary Lou
Docks of New Orleans
The Denver Kid
Ladies of the Chorus
49: Brothers in the Saddle
South of Rio
Sorrowful Jones
Arson, Inc.
Sky Dragons
Hold that Baby!
Post Office Investigator
Down Dakota Way
Alias the Champ
Cover-Up
The Sickle or the Cross
51: Pride of Maryland
The Big Gusher
Street Bandits
Pals of the Golden West
54: Red River Shore

Karl M. Vogler
1963: The Experiences of a
Lodger (Ger.)
Whiskey with Soda
A Man in His Best Years
66: The Blue Max
67: How I Won the War
69: Patton

Joan Vohs (1931-
1949: My Dream Is Yours
The Girl from Jones
Beach
Inspector General
Yes Sir, that's My Baby
50: Girls' School
County Fair
As You Were
53: Vice Squad
Fort Ti
Crazy Legs--All-
American
54: Sabrina
Cry Vengeance
Ketchikan
55: Fort Yuma
56: Terror at Midnight
57: Lure of the Swamp

Jon Voight (1938-
1968: The Hour of the Gun

Out of It
69: Midnight Cowboy
Catch 22
The Revolutionary

Theodore Von Eltz (1894-1964)
1929: The Awful Truth
The Voice of the Storm S
4 Feathers   SSE
The Very Idea
The Rescue   SSE
30: The Furies
Nothing to Wear
The Arizona Kid
The Divorcee
Love Among Millionaires
Kismet
The Cat Creeps
31: The Prodigal
The Secret Fix
Up Pops the Devil
Beyond Victory
Wicked
Once a Lady
Susan Lennox
Private Scandal
Heartbreak
32: Ladies of the Big House
Hotel Continental
Midnight Lady
Strangers of the Evening
Drifting Souls
A Scarlet Week-End
Red-Haired Alibi
The Unwritten Law
Breach of Promise
33: The 11th Commandment
Pleasure Cruise
Arizona to Broadway
High Gear
Jennie Gerhardt
Her Splendid Folly
Dance, Girl, Dance
Master of Men
35: Private Worlds
Behind Green Lights
Headline Woman
Confidential
Her Night Out
Magnificent Obsession
Elinore Norton
Smart Girl

35: Streamline Express
    Trails of the Wild
36: Beloved Enemy
    Ticket to Glory
    High Tension
    Suzy
    Sinner Take All
    Below the Deadline
    I Cover Chinatown
    Mind Your Own Business
37: A Man Betrayed
    Under Cover of Night
    Jim Hanvey, Detective
    Youth on Parole
    California Straight Ahead
    The Westland Case
    Topper
    Clarence
38: Inside Story
    Blondes at Work
    Pardon Our Nerve
39: They Made Her a Spy
    5th Avenue Girl
    The Sun Never Sets
    Legion of Lost Flyers
40: The Story of Dr. Ehrlich's
    Magic Bullet
    Little Old New York
    The Old Swimmin' Hole
    The Great Plane Robbery
    The Son of Monte Cristo
41: Ellery Queen's Penthouse
    Mystery
    I'll Wait for You
    A Shot in the Dark
42: The Man in the Trunk
    Quiet Please, Murder!
44: Follow the Boys
    Bermuda Mystery
    Since You Went Away
    Hollywood Canteen
45: Rhapsody in Blue
46: The Big Sleep
48: The Devil's Cargo
50: Trial Without Jury

Vyola Vonn
1941: Burma Convoy
54: Phantom of the Rue
    Morgue
    Paris Playboys
55: Spy Chasers

58: Lafayette Escadrille
59: The 30 Foot Bride of
    Candy Rock

Gustave Von Seyffertitz
(1863-1943)
1929: The Canary Murder Case
    The Case of Lena Smith S
    Come Across   PT
    His Glorious Night
    Chasing Through
    Europe   SSE
    7 Faces
30: Dangerous Paradise
    The Case of Sgt. Grischa
    The Bat Whispers
    Are You There?
31: Dishonored
    Ambassador Bill
32: Shanghai Express
    Roadhouse Murder
    The Penguin Pool Murder
    Rasputin and the Empress
    Afraid to Talk
    Doomed Battalion
33: When Strangers Marry
    Queen Christina
34: Mystery Liner
    Change of Heart
    The Moonstone
    Little Men
    Remember Last Night?
36: Murder on a Bridle Path
    Mad Holiday
38: In Old Chicago
    Cipher Bureau
39: Juarez and Maximilian
    Nurse Edith Cavell

Erich Von Stroheim (1886-1957)
1929: The Great Gabbo
30: 3 Faces East
31: Friends and Lovers
32: Lost Squadron
    As You Desire Me
    Walking Down Broadway
    (rel. in '33 as Hello Sister)
34: Crimson Romance
    Fugitive Road
    House of Strangers
35: The Crime of Dr. Crespi
36: The Devil's Doll

1372

37: Marthe Richard au
    Service de la France
    Between Two Women
    Grand Illusion
    Mlle. Docteur
    The Alibi
    Les Pirates du Rail
38: Walking Down Broadway
    Les Disparus de St. Agil
    L'Affaire LaFarge
    Gibraltar
39: Behind the Facade
    Rappel Immediat
    Pièges
    La Revolte des Vivants
    Lemond Trembera
    Tempête
    Boys' School
    Macao, L'Enfer du Jeu
    Menaces
    Paris--New York
40: Ultimatum
    I Was an Adventuress
41: So Ends the Night
    Personal Column
43: 5 Graves to Cairo
    The North Star
    Armored Attack
44: Storm over Lisbon
    The Lady and the Monster
45: The Great Flamarion
    Scotland Yard Investigator
46: La Foire aux Chimères
    On Ne Meurt Pas Comme
    Ça
    The Mask of Dijon
47: La Danse de Mort
48: Le Signal Rouge
49: Portrait d'un Assassin
50: Sunset Boulevard
52: Alraune
    La Maison de Crime
    Calibre 6.5 (Ital.; never
    rel.)
53: Minuit--Quai de Bercy
    Alerte au Sud
    L'Envers du Paradis
54: Napoleon
    Serie Noire
55: La Madonna du Sleepings
56: The Man with a 1000
    Faces (dir.)

Max Von Sydow (1926-
1951: Miss Julie
56: The 7th Seal
57: Wild Strawberries
58: So Close to Life
59: The Face
    The Magician
60: The Virgin Spring
    Brink of Life
    The Communicants
62: Through a Glass Darkly
    The Mistress
63: Winter Light
65: The Greatest Story Ever
    Told
66: Hawaii
    The Reward
    The Quiller Memorandum
67: Hour of the Wolf
    Black Palm Trees
68: Shame
69: Passion
    The Kremlin Letter
    Made in Sweden

Harry Von Zell (1906-
1945: How Do You Do?
    The Strange Affair of
    Uncle Harry
46: Till the End of Time
47: The Guilt of Janet Ames
    Where There's Life
48: The Saxon Charm
49: Dear Wife
    Von Zell Comedies
50: Where the Sidewalk Ends
    2 Flags West
    For Heaven's Sake
51: I Can Get it for You
    Wholesale (or, The Best
    of Everything)
    You're in the Navy Now
    Call Me Mister
52: Son of Paleface
66: Boy, Did I Get a Wrong
    Number!

George Voskovec (1905-
1930: Powder and Gas
32: Your Money or Your Life
34: Rej-Rup
35: The Golem

36: The World Is Ours
52: Anything can Happen
Affair in Trinidad
The Iron Mistress
57: 12 Angry Men
The 27th Day
58: Uncle Vanya
The Bravados
Wind Across the Everglades
60: Butterfield 8
64: Hamlet
65: The Spy Who Came In from the Cold
66: Mr. Buddwing
67: Beyond the Mountains
68: The Desperate Ones
69: The Boston Strangler

Peter Votrian
1955: A Man Called Peter
Big House, U.S.A.
Hell on Frisco Bay
56: Crime in the Streets
57: Fear Strikes Out
The Oklahoman

Ralph Votrian
1956: The Bold and the Brave
Screaming Eagles
Pillars of the Sky
Tea and Sympathy
57: Until They Sail
The Invisible Boy
58: Imitation General

Murvyn Vye (1913-
1947: Golden Earrings
48: Whispering Smith
49: A Connecticut Yankee in King Arthur's Court
52: Road to Bali
53: Destination Gobi
Pickup on South Street
54: River of No Return
Green Fire
Black Horse Canyon
55: Escape to Burma
Pearl of the South Pacific
56: The Best Things in Life Are Free
57: This Could be the Night

Voodoo Island
Short Cut to Hell
58: Girl in the Woods
In Love and War
59: Al Capone
60: The Boy and the Pirates
Pay or Die
61: King of the Roaring '20s
65: Andy

Charles Wagenheim
1940: 2 Girls on Broadway
Charlie Chan at the Wax Museum
41: Meet Boston Blackie
The Get-Away
42: Fingers at the Window
Sin Town
43: Half Way to Shanghai
I Escaped from the Gestapo
44: Summer Storm
The Black Parachute
Sergeant Mike
45: Within These Walls
Jungle Captive
Col. Effingham's Raid
The House on 92nd Street
46: The Dark Corner
47: The Lighthouse
48: Man-Eater of Kumaon
Scudda Hoo! Scudda Hay!
49: I Cheated the Law
50: A Lady Without Passport
Motor Patrol
51: House on Telegraph Hill
Pier 23
Street Bandits
55: Canyon Crossroads
The Prodigal
56: Blackjack Ketchum--Desperado
58: The Tunnel of Love
Toughest Gun in Tombstone
60: The Police Dog Story
62: Beauty and the Beast

Robert Wagner (1930-
1950: Halls of Montezuma
51: The Frogmen
Let's Make it Legal
52: With a Song in My Heart
What Price Glory?

1374

52: Stars and Stripes Forever
53: The Silver Whip
    Titanic
    Beneath the 12 Mile Reef
54: Prince Valiant
    Broken Lance
55: White Feather
56: Between Heaven and Hell
    Kiss Before Dying
    The Mountain
57: The True Story of Jesse
    James
    Stopover Tokyo
58: The Hunters
    In Love and War
59: Say One For Me
60: All the Fine Cannibals
    The Gallant Hours
61: Sail a Crooked Ship
62: The Longest Day
    War Lover
63: The Condemned of Altona
    Heavens Above
64: The Pink Panther
65: The Moving Target
66: Harper
67: How I Spent My Summer
    Vacation (TV)
    Banning
68: The Biggest Bundle of
    Them All
69: Don't Just Stand There!
    Winning

Jimmy Wakely (1914-
1939: Saga of Death Valley
40: Trailing Double Trouble
    Texas Terrors
    The Tulsa Kid
41: Twilight on the Trail
    Heart of the Rio Grande
    Stick to Your Guns
    6 Lessons from Madame
    La Zonga
42: Trail Dreaming
    Silver Bullet
    Boss of Hang Town Mesa
    Strictly in the Groove
    Deep in the Heart of Texas
    Little Joe the Wrangler
43: I'm from Arkansas
    Tenting Tonight on the Old
    Camp Ground

    The Old Chisholm Trail
    Lone Star Trail
    Robin Hood of the Pampas
44: Song of the Range
    Saddle Leather Law
    Cowboy from Lonesome
    River
    Sundown Valley
    Swing in the Saddle
    Cowboy Canteen
45: Sagebrush Heroes
    Cyclone Prairie Rangers
    The Lonesome Trail
    Rough Ridin' Justice
    Springtime in Texas
46: West of the Alamo
    Moon over Montana
    Trail to Mexico
    Drifting Along
47: Song of the Sierras
    Rainbow over the Rockies
    6 Gun Serenade
    Ridin' Down the Trail
    Song of the Drifter
48: Oklahoma Blues
    Range Renegades
    Courtin' Trouble
    Outlaw Brands
    Silver Trails
    The Rangers Ride
    Cowboy Cavalier
49: Gunlaw Justice
    Gun Runner
    Roaring Westward
    Brand of Fear
    Across the Rio Grande
    Lawless Code
53: The Marshal's Daughter
54: Arrow in the Dust
55: The Silver Star

Anton Walbrook (1900-1967)
1931: Salto Mortale
33: Regine
    Mond Uber Marvokko
    The Waltz War
34: Masquerade
    Die Englishe Heirat
    Eine Frau die Weisse Was
    Sie Will
35: The Student of Prague
    Zigeunerbaron (Gypsy Baron)
36: Allitria

37: The Soldier and the Lady
(or, Michael Strogoff)
Victoria the Great
38: The Rat
60 Glorious Years
40: Gaslight (or, Murder in
Thornton Street)
Dangerous Moonlight
42: The Invaders (or, The
49th Parallel)
Port Arthur (or,
Orders from Tokyo)
43: The Life and Death of
Colonel Blimp
45: The Man from Morocco
48: Red Shoes
Queen of Spades
50: La Ronde
54: Vienna Waltzes
55: Oh, Rosalinda
Lola Montez
57: St. Joan
58: I Accuse!

Raymond Walburn (1887-1969)
1930; Laughing Lady
34: Great Flirtation
The Defense Rests
Lady by Choice
Jealousy
Broadway Bill
The Count of Monte Cristo
35: Thanks a Million
Only 8 Hours
Death Flies East
Mills of the Gods
I'll Love You Always
It's a Small World
Welcome Home
She Married Her Boss
Redheads on Parade
36: The Great Ziegfeld
Mr. Deeds Goes to Town
The Lone Wolf Returns
Absolute Quiet
They Met in a Taxi
3 Wise Guys
The King Steps Out
Mr. Cinderella
Craig's Wife
37: Born to Dance
Breezing Home

Let's Get Married
High, Wide, and Handsome
Broadway Melody of 1938
Thin Ice
Murder in Greenwich
Village
38: Professor, Beware!
Start Cheering
Battle of Broadway
Gateway
Sweethearts
39: Let Freedom Ring
It Could Happen to You
Eternally Yours
The Under-Pup
40: Heaven with a Barbed-
Wire Fence
The Dark Command
Millionaires in Prison
Flowing Gold
Third Finger, Left Hand
Christmas in July
41: San Francisco Docks
Kiss the Boys Goodbye
Puddin' Head
Bachelor Party
Confirm or Deny
Rise and Shine
Louisiana Purchase
42: The Man in the Trunk
Lady Bodyguard
43: Dixie Dugan
The Desperadoes
Let's Face It
Dixie
44: And the Angels Sing
Hail the Conquering Hero
Heavenly Days
Music in Manhattan
45: The Cheaters
Honeymoon Ahead
I'll Tell the World
46: Affairs of Geraldine
Breakfast in Hollywood
Lover Come Back
The Plainsman and the
Lady
Rendezvous with Annie
47: Mad Wednesday (or, The
Sin of Harold Diddlebock)
48: State of the Union
49: Red Hot and Blue

49: Riding High
Leave it to Henry
Henry the Rainmaker
51: Father Takes the Air
53: Beautiful but Dangerous
54: She Couldn't Say No

Jane Wald
1962: The 3 Stooges in Orbit
63: Under the Yum-Yum Tree
64: What a Way to Go!
65: Dear Brigitte

Janet Waldo
1939: Persons in Hiding
The Star Maker
What a Life!
Zaza
40: All Women Have Secrets
Waterloo Bridge
One Man's Law
41: The Bandit Trail
The Silver Stallion
Land of the Open Range
66: That Man Flintstone
(cartoon voice)

Charles Waldron (1877-1946)
1939: On Borrowed Time
The Real Glory
40: Thou Shalt Not Kill
Remember the Night
And One Was Beautiful
Dr. Kildare's Strange
 Case
The Refugee
Streets of Memories
Untamed
The Stranger on the
 Third Floor
41: The Case of the Black
 Parrot
The Devil and Miss Jones
The Nurse's Secret
3 Sons O' Guns
Rise and Shine
42: Through Different Eyes
The Gay Sisters
Random Harvest
43: The Song of Bernadette
44: The Adventures of Mark
 Twain

The Black Parachute
Mlle Fifi
45: The Fighting Guardsman
46: The Big Sleep
47: For You I Die

Ethel Wales
1929: The Doctor's Secret
The Donovan Affair
Blue Skies   SSE
30: The Girl in the Show
The Saturday Night Kid
Loose Ankles
Under Montana Skies
Dude Wrangler
Tom Sawyer
31: Subway Express
The Flood
Criminal Code
Honeymoon Lane
Maker of Men
32: The Fighting Fool
Love in High Gear
The 13th Guest
Love Me Tonight
Klondike
Tangled Destinies
The Racing Strain
A Man's Land
33: The 11th Commandment
The Fighting Parson
34: Crime Doctor
35: Bar 20 Rides Again
Two Faces
36: Collegiate
38: The Gladiator
39: In Old Caliente
Days of Jesse James
40: Knights of the Range
Hidden Gold
Young Bill Hickok
41: Border Vigilantes
44: The Lumberjack
50: Tarnished

Wally Wales
1934: Fighting Through
35: Vanishing Riders
Powdersmoke Range
Heir to Trouble
Gun Play
36: Hair-Trigger Casey

1377

36: Avenging Waters
    The Traitor

Charlotte Walker (1878-1958)
1929: Paris Bound
      South Sea Rose
  30: Double Cross Roads
      3 Faces East
      Scarlet Pages
      Lightnin'
  33: Hotel Variety
  41: Scattergood Meets Broad-
      way

Cheryl Walker (1920-
1940: Chasing Trouble
  43: Shadows on the Sage
      Stage Door Canteen
      A Song for Miss Julie
  44: 3 Is a Family
      3 Little Sisters
  45: How Do You Do?
      Identity Unknown
      It's a Pleasure
      Rhythm Roundup
  46: Larceny in Her Heart
      Murder Is My Business
      Blonde for a Day
  47: Three on a Ticket
  48: Waterfront at Midnight

Clint Walker (1927-
1958: Fort Dobbs
  59: Yellowstone Kelly
  61: Gold of the 7 Saints
  64: Send Me No Flowers
  65: None but the Brave
  66: Crack of the Whip
      The Night of the Grizzly
  67: The Dirty Dozen
      Maya
  68: The Great Bank Robbery
      Sam Whiskey
      More Dead than Alive
      The Specialist (TV)

Helen Walker (1921-1968)
1942: Lucky Jordan
  43: The Good Fellows
  44: The Man in Half Moon
      Street
      Abroad with Two Yanks

45: Murder He Says
    Duffy's Tavern
46: Brewster's Millions
    People Are Funny
    Murder in the Music Hall
    Cluny Brown
    Her Adventurous Night
47: Nightmare Alley
    The Homestretch
48: Call Northside 777
    My Dear Secretary
    Nancy Goes to Rio
49: Impact
51: My True Story
52: Heaven Only Knows
53: Problems of Girls
55: The Big Combo

Johnnie Walker (1894-1949)
1930: Melody Man
      Ladies of Leisure
      Swellheads
      Let Us be Gay
      Girl of the Golden West
      Up the River
  31: Enemies of the Law

June Walker (1900-1966)
1930: War Nurse
  42: Through Different Eyes
  60: The Unforgiven
  63: A Child Is Waiting

Nancy Walker (1922-
1943: Best Foot Forward
      Girl Crazy
  44: Broadway Rhythm
  54: Lucky Me

Nella Walker
1930: Extravagance
      What a Widow!
  31: Hot Heiress
      Indiscreet
      Hugh Money
      Their Mad Moment
      Public Defender
      The Bargain
  32: Lady with a Past
      They Call It Sin
  33: 20,000 Years in Sing Sing
      Dangerously Yours

1378

33: Second Hand Wife
    Humanity
    Reunion in Vienna
    This Day and Age
    Ever in My Heart
    The House on 56th Street
34: 4 Frightened People
    All of Me
    Sensation Hunters
    The 9th Guest
    Fashions of 1934
    Change of Heart
    Madame Du Barry
    Elmer and Elsie
    Big-Hearted Herbert
    Fugitive Lady
35: Behold My Wife
    Woman in Red
    McFadden's Flats
    Bordertown
    A Dog of Flanders
    Going Highbrow
    Red Salute
36: Small Town Girl
    Captain January
    Don't Turn 'em Loose
37: 3 Smart Girls
    Stella Dallas
    45 Fathers
38: The Crime of Dr. Hallet
    The Rage of Paris
    Young Dr. Kildare
39: 3 Smart Girls Grow Up
    When Tomorrow Comes
    In Name Only
    Swanee River
40: The Saint Takes Over
    I Love You Again
    Kitty Foyle
41: Buck Privates
    Back Street
    A Girl, a Guy, and a
     Gob
    Repent at Leisure
    Kathleen
    Hellzapoppin'!
42: The Kid Glove Killer
43: Air Raid Wardens
    Wintertime
    Hers to Hold
44: In Society
    Ladies of Washington

    Murder in the Blue Room
    Take It or Leave It
45: Follow that Woman
    A Guy, a Gal, and a Pal
46: 2 Sisters from Boston
47: The Beginning or the End?
    The Locket
    Undercover Maisie
    That Hagen Girl
50: Nancy Goes to Rio
54: Sabrina

Ray Walker
1942: House of Errors
    Almost Married
43: Dixie Dugan
    Mission to Moscow
    Princess O'Rourke
    The Unknown Guest
    Crazy House
    Henry Aldrich Haunts a
     House
    Is Everybody Happy?
44: Swingtime Johnny
    The Man from Frisco
    South of Dixie
    Jam Session
    Silent Partner
    Stars on Parade
    My Buddy
45: Rogues' Gallery
    Eve Knew Her Apples
46: Tars and Spars
    Life with Blondie
    Dark Alibi
    Gay Blades
    Step by Step
    Secrets of a Sorority Girl
    Secret of the Whistler
47: The Pilgrim Lady
    That's My Gal
    Robin Hood in Texas
    The Unsuspected
48: The Sainted Sisters
    Black Bart
    April Showers
    Apartment for Peggy
49: Blondie's Big Deal
    Song of Surrender
    Angels in Disguise
    Pioneer Marshal
    Holiday in Havana

50: Hoedown
Bodyhold
Sideshow
Square Dance Katy
Under Mexicali Skies
Revenue Agent
Chinatown at Midnight
51: A Wonderful Life
The Harlem Globetrotters
Let's Go, Navy!
52: No Holds Barred
53: The Blue Gardenia
The Homesteaders
Rebel City
Marry Me Again
54: Pride of the Blue Grass
57: Kiss Them for Me

Robert Walker (1919-1951)
1940: Pioneer Days
41: I'll Sell My Life
43: Bataan
Madame Curie
44: See Here, Private Hargrove!
Since You Went Away
30 Seconds over Tokyo
45: The Clock
What Next, Corporal Hargrove?
Her Highness and the Bellboy
The Sailor Takes a Wife
46: Till the Clouds Roll By
47: The Beginning or the End?
Sea of Grass
Song of Love
48: One Touch of Venus
50: Please Believe Me
The Skipper Who Surprised His Wife
51: Vengeance Valley
Strangers on a Train
52: My Son John

Robert Walker, Jr. (1940-
1963: The Hook
The Ceremony
64: Ensign Pulver
67: The Happening
The War Wagon
68: Eve

The Savage 7
Killers 3
69: Easy Rider
Young Billy Young
Man Without Mercy

Jean Wallace (c1927-
1941: Louisiana Purchase
44: You Can't Ration Love
46: It Shouldn't Happen to a Dog
47: Blaze of Noon
48: When My Baby Smiles at Me
49: Jigsaw
The Man on the Eiffel Tower
Gun Moll
50: The Good Humor Man
51: Native Son
55: The Big Combo
56: Storm Fear
Star of India
57: The Devil's Hairpin
58: Macaibo
63: Lancelot and Guinivere (or, The Sword of Lancelot)
67: Beach Red (cameo)

Morgan Wallace (1885-1953)
1930: Sisters
Big Money
Up the River
31: It Pays to Advertise
Alexander Hamilton
Women Go on Forever
32: Hell's House
The Final Edition
Grand Hotel
Lady and Gent
Blonde Venus
Wild Girl
Steady Company
Fast Companions
33: Smoke Lightning
Terror Abroad
Jennie Gerhardt
Song of Songs
Mama Loves Papa
Above the Clouds
34: I Believed in You

1380

34: Trumpet Blows
Many Happy Returns
It's a Gift
Cheating Cheaters
35: Murder on a Honeymoon
The Devil Is a Woman
Dante's Inferno
Thundermountain
Confidential
$1,000 a Minute
36: Love on a Bet
Sutter's Gold
Human Cargo
Fury
Mister Cinderella
37: Charlie Chan at the
Olympics
The Californians
Under Suspicion
38: Lady in the Morgue
Numbered Woman
Woman Against Woman
Billy the Kid Returns
Gang Bullets
39: The Mystery of Mr. Wong
The Star Maker
40: I Love You Again
3 Men from Texas
Ellery Queen, Master
Detective
41: Scattergood Meets Broad-
way
45: Song of the Sarong
I'll Remember April
Dick Tracy
46: The Falcon's Alibi

Eli Wallach (1915-
1956: Baby Doll
58: The Lineup
60: The Magnificent 7
7 Thieves
61: The Misfits
62: Hemingway's Adventures
of a Young Man
How the West Was Won
63: The Victors
Act One
64: Kisses for My President
The Moonspinners
65: Lord Jim

Genghis Khan
66: How to Steal a Million
The Poppy Is Also a
Flower (TV)
67: Two Magnificent Rogues
Band of Gold
The Tiger Makes Out
MacKenna's Gold
68: A Lovely Way to Die
The Way the Wheel Turns
New York City--The
Most (doc.)
The Good, the Bad, and
the Ugly
How to Save a Marriage
and Ruin Your Life
69: The Brain
The Angel Levine
The Adventurers

Eddie Waller
1937: Sweetheart of the Navy
Small Town Boy
38: Call the Mesquiteers
Legion of Lost Flyers
State Police
39: Jesse James
I'm from Missouri
Return of the Cisco Kid
Mutiny on the Blackhawk
Two Bright Boys
New Frontier
Allegheny Uprising
40: Legion of the Lawless
The Grapes of Wrath
The Man from Montreal
Konga--The Wild Stallion
You're Not So Tough
Stagecoach War
Carolina Moon
Gold Rush Maisie
Texas Terrors
41: Double Date
Hands Across the Rockies
The Bandit Trail
The Son of Davy Crockett
42: The Lone Star Ranger
Sundown Jim
Night Monster
Scattergood Survives a
Murder

1381

43: Cinderella Swings It
Headin' for God's Country
My Kingdom for a Cook
A Lady Takes a Chance
44: Home in Indiana
The Adventures of Mark
Twain
45: The Man Who Walked
Alone
Dakota
The Missing Corpse
Rough Riders of Cheyenne
46: The Avalanche
Renegades
Singing on the Trail
Sing While You Dance
Sun Valley Cyclone
47: The Michigan Kid
Rustler's Round-Up
Abilene Town
Louisiana
Bandits of Dark Canyon
The Wild Frontier
48: Adventures of Silverado
Wreck of the Hesperus
Return of the Whistler
The Strawberry Roan
The Bold Frontiersman
Oklahoma Badlands
Black Bart
Carson City Raiders
The Denver Kid
Whispering Smith
Sundown in Santa Fe
Marshal of Amarillo
Desperadoes of Dodge
City
49: Death Valley Gunfighter
Frontier Investigator
Renegades of Sonora
Sheriff of Wichita
The Wyoming Bandit
Bandit King of Texas
For Those Who Dare
Navajo Trail Raiders
50: Gunmen of Abilene
Code of the Silver Sage
Salt Lake Raiders
Covered Wagon Raiders
Vigilante Hideout
Traveling Saleswoman
Frisco Tornado

He's a Cockeyed Wonder
Rustlers on Horseback
California Passage
52: Indian Uprising
Leadville Gunslinger
Black Hills
Montana Territory
Thundering Caravans
Desperadoes Outpost
53: Marshal of Cedar Creek
It Happens Every Thursday
Bandits of the West
Savage Frontier
99 River Street
Champ for a Day
El Paso Stampede
54: Make Haste to Live
55: Man Without a Star
The Far Country
Fox Fire
57: The Night Runner
The Phantom Stagecoach
The Restless Breed
58: The Day of the Bad Man

Deborah Walley (1943-
1961: Gidget Goes Hawaiian
62: Bon Voyage!
63: Summer Magic
64: The Young Lovers
65: Ski Party
Sgt. Deadhead, The
Astronaut
Beach Blanket Bingo
66: Ghost in the Invisible
Bikini
67: Spin-Out
It's a Bikini World

George Walsh (1892-
1932: Out of Singapore
Me and My Gal
33: Black Beauty
Return of Casey Jones
The Bowery
34: Belle of the '90s
35: Under Pressure
36: Klondike Annie
Rio Grande Romance
Put on the Spot

Kay Walsh (1914-
1934: How's Chances?
38: I See Ice
42: In Which We Serve
44: This Happy Breed
47: The October Man
48: Vice Versa
Oliver Twist
50: Encore
Stage Fright
51: Last Holiday
55: Cast a Dark Shadow
59: The Horse's Mouth
60: Tunes of Glory
64: The Beauty Jungle
Circus World
65: A Study in Terror
67: The Devil's Own
68: Bikini Paradise
69: Connecting Rooms

Ray Walston (1918-
1957: Kiss Them for Me
58: South Pacific
Damn Yankees
59: Say One for Me
60: The Apartment
Tall Story
Portrait in Black
62: Convicts 4
63: Wives and Lovers
Who's Minding the Store?
64: Kiss Me, Stupid
67: Caprice
69: Paint Your Wagon
Viva Max!

Jessica Walter (c1940-
1964: Lilith
66: The Group
67: Grand Prix
69: Number One

Luana Walters
1939: Mexicali Rose
40: The Return of Wild Bill
Hickok
The Durango Kid
The Tulsa Kid
The Range Busters
Blondie Plays Cupid
Misbehaving Husbands

41: Law of the Wild
No Greater Sin
Arizona Bound
Across the Sierras
The Kid's Last Ride
The Lone Star Vigilantes
Thundering Hoofs
42: The Corpse Vanishes
Lawless Plainsmen
Down Texas Way
Inside the Law
Bad Men of the Hills
43: Drums of Fu Manchu

Henry B. Walthall (1870-1936)
1928: Freedom of the Press   S
Love Me and the World
Is Mine   S
29: Speakeasy   S
Jazz Age   S
Bridge of San Luis
Rey   PT
Stark Mad
Black Magic   SSE
Man from Headquarters S
River of Romance
The Trespasser
In Old California
Phantom in the House
Blaze O' Glory
30: Temple Tower
Abraham Lincoln
Love Trader
31: Is There Justice?
Anybody's Blonde
32: Hotel Continental
Police Court
Strange Interlude
Alias Mary Smith
Chandu the Magician
Klondike
Cabin in the Cotton
Ride Him, Cowboy!
Central Park
Me and My Gal
33: 42nd Street
Self Defense
Flaming Signal
Somewhere in Sonora
Laughing at Life
Headline Shooter
Her Forgotten Past

1383

33: The Sin of Nora Moran
34: Viva Villa!
   Men in White
   Dark Hazard
   Beggars in Ermine
   Operator 13
   Murder in the Museum
   City Park
   Judge Priest
   Girl of the Limberlost
   The Lemon Drop Kid
   The Scarlet Letter
   Love Time
   Bachelor of Arts
35: Helldorado
   Dante's Inferno
   A Tale of Two Cities
36: The Garden Murder Case
   The Mine with the Iron
    Door
   Hearts in Bondage
   The Last Outlaw
   The Devil-Doll
   China Clipper

Douglas Walton (1896-1961)
1934: The Lost Patrol
   Madame Spy
   Murder in Trinidad
   Shock
   The Count of Monte
    Cristo
   Charlie Chan in London
35: Captain Hurricane
   The Dark Angel
   Hitchhike Lady
   Bride of Frankenstein
36: The Garden Murder Case
   I Conquer the Sea
   Mary of Scotland
   Thank You, Jeeves
   Camille
37: Damaged Goods
   Wallaby Jim of the Islands
   Flight from Glory
   A Nation Aflame
38: Storm over Bengal
39: The Story of Vernon and
    Irene Castle
   The Sun Never Sets
40: Raffles

Northwest Passage
The Long Voyage Home
Too Many Girls
41: Singapore Woman
   Hurry, Charlie, Hurry!
46: Dick Tracy vs Cueball
47: High Conquest
   High Tide
49: Secret of St. Ives

Sam Wanamaker (1919-
1948: Cloak and Dagger
   My Girl Tisa
49: Give Us this Day
51: Mr. Denning Drives North
55: The Secret
60: The Criminal
62: Taras Bulba
64: Man in the Middle
65: Those Magnificent Men in
    Their Flying Machines
   The Spy Who Came in
    from the Cold
67: Warning Shot
68: Danger Route
69: The Executioner (dir.)
   The Day the Fish Came
    Out

John Warburton (1899-
1932: Silver Lining
   Secrets of the French
    Police
33: A Study in Scarlet
   Blind Adventure
   Charlie Chan's Greatest
    Case
   Cavalcade
   Love Is Dangerous
   Love Is Like That
34: Let's Talk it Over
35: Becky Sharp
   Dizzy Dames
37: a short
   Partners of the Plains
38: The Sisters
39: Captain Fury
43: Marriage Is a Private
    Affair
44: Nothing But Trouble
   The White Cliffs of Dover

1384

45: Confidential Agent
Dangerous Partners
Saratoga Trunk
The Valley of Decision
47: Living in a Big Way
Tarzan and the Huntress
53: City Beneath the Sea
East of Sumatra
55: Headline Hunters
65: King Rat
66: Assault on a Queen

Richard "Skip" Ward
1959: The Road Racers
61: Voyage to the Bottom of
the Sea
63: The Nutty Professor
64: Night of the Iguana
Kitten with a Whip
Kiss Me, Stupid
67: Easy Come, Easy Go
Hombre
69: The Mad Room
The Learning Tree

Jack Warden (1920-
1950: Asphalt Jungle
51: The Man with My Face
You're in the Navy Now
52: Red Ball Express
53: From Here to Eternity
57: 12 Angry Men
Edge of the City
Bachelor Party
58: Darby's Rangers
Run Silent, Run Deep
59: The Sound and the Fury
That Kind of Woman
60: Wake Me When It's Over
62: Escape from Zahrain
63: Donovan's Reef
64: The Thin Red Line
66: Blindfold
69: Bye Bye, Braverman

Helen Ware (1877-1939)
1932: Night of June 13th
33: Ladies They Talk About
Girl Missing
The Keyhole
She Had to Say Yes
34: Flaming Gold
Sadie McKee

That's Gratitude
Romance in Manhattan
35: Secret of the Chateau
The Raven

Irene Ware (1911-
1934: Orient Express
Let's Talk it Over
You Belong to Me
King Kelly of the U.S.A.
35: Night Life of the Gods
Rendezvous at Midnight
Cheers of the Crowd
False Pretenses
Happiness C.O.D.
Whispering Smith Speaks
36: Murder at Glen Athol
O'Malley of the Mounted
In Paris A.W.O.L.
Federal Agent
The Dark Hour
Gold Diggers of 1937
40: Outside the 3-Mile Limit

Chris Warfield
1962: Incident in an Alley
63: Diary of a Madman

David Warner (1941-
1963: Tom Jones
66: Morgan
67: Work Is a 4 Letter Word
69: A Midsummer Night's
Dream (TV)
The Fixer
Michael Kohlhaas

H.B. Warner (1876-1958)
1929: Divine Lady   SSE
Trial of Mary Dugan
Conquest
The Doctor's Secret
Stark Mad
The Gamblers
The Argyle Case
Show of Shows
Tiger Rose
30: Wedding Rings
Green Goddess
The Furies
2nd Floor Mystery
Wild Company
On Your Back

30: Liliom
    The Princess and the
    Plumber
31: 5 Star Final
    Woman of Experience
    The Reckless Hour
32: The Menace
    Tom Brown of Culver
    A Woman Commands
    Cross Examination
    Charlie Chan's Chance
    Unholy Love
    The Crusader
    The Phantom of Crest-
    wood
    The Son-Daughter
33: Jennie Gerhardt
    Justice Takes a Holiday
    Supernatural
    Christopher Bean--Her
    Sweetheart
34: Grand Canary
    In Old Santa Fe
    Night Alarm
35: Behold My Wife
    Born to Gamble
    A Tale of Two Cities
36: The Garden Murder Case
    Rose of the Rancho
    Moonlight Murder
    Mr. Deeds Goes to Town
    The Blackmailer
    Along Came Love
37: Lost Horizon
    Victoria the Great
38: The Adventures of Marco
    Polo
    Girl of the Golden West
    Toy Wife
    Kidnapped
    Bulldog Drummond in
    Africa
    Army Girl
    You Can't Take it with
    You
39: Arrest Bulldog Drummond!
    Let Freedom Ring
    Bulldog Drummond's
    Secret
    Bulldog Drummond's
    Bride
    The Gracie Allen Murder
    Case

Mr. Smith Goes to
    Washington
    Nurse Edith Cavell
    The Rains Came
    Torpedoed
40: New Moon
41: Topper Returns
    City of Missing Girls
    Here Is a Man
    Ellery Queen and the
    Perfect Crime
    South of Tahiti
    The Corsican Brothers
42: A Yank in Libya
    Boss of Big Town
    Crossroads
43: Hitler's Children
    Women in Bondage
44: Action in Arabia
    Enemy of Women
    Faces in the Fog
45: Rogues' Gallery
    Captain Tugboat Annie
46: Strange Impersonation
    It's a Wonderful Life
    Gentleman Joe Palooka
47: Driftwood
    High Wall
48: Prince of Thieves
49: Hellfire
    The Judge Steps Out
    El Paso
50: Sunset Boulevard
51: The First Legion
    Journey into Light
    Savage Drums
    Here Comes the Groom
56: The Ten Commandments
58: Darby's Rangers

James Warren
1945: Wanderer of the Wasteland
46: Badman's Territory
    Ding Dong Williams
    Sunset Pass
47: Code of the West
49: The Judge Steps Out
52: Three for Bedroom C
53: Port Sinister
55: Secret Venture

Katharine Warren
1949: All the King's Men

1386

50:   Mary Ryan, Detective
      3 Secrets
      Harriet Craig
      Submarine
      And Baby Makes Three
      The Story of Molly X
      Tell it to the Judge
51:   Night into Morning
      The Prowler
      The People Against
       O'Hara
      The Tall Target
      Force of Arms
52:   This Woman Is Dangerous
      The Washington Story
      Son of Ali Baba
      The Steel Trap
53:   The Star
54:   The Glenn Miller Story
      The Caine Mutiny
55:   The Violent Men
      Inside Detroit
56:   Fury at Gunsight Pass
57:   Drango
61:   I'll Give My Life

Lesley Ann Warren (1946-
1967:   The Happiest Millionaire
68:   The One and Only Genuine
      Original Family Band

Ruth Warrick (1915-
1941:   Citizen Kane
      Obliging Young Lady
      The Corsican Brothers
42:   Journey into Fear
43:   Forever and a Day
      The Iron Major
44:   Secret Command
      Mr. Winkle Goes to War
      Guest in the House
45:   The Adventure of Rusty
      China Sky
46:   Perilous Holiday
      Song of the South
      Swell Guy
47:   Drift Wood
      Daisy Kenyon
48:   Arch of Triumph
      A Letter to 3 Wives
49:   The Great Dan Patch
      Make-Believe Ballroom

50:   Beauty on Parade
      Let's Dance
      Second Chance
      One Too Many
      3 Husbands
54:   Roogie's Bump
66:   Ride Beyond Vengeance
69:   The Great Bank Robbery

Robert Warwick (1878-1964)
1930:   Unmasked
31:   A Holy Terror
      The Royal Bed
      Not Exactly Gentlemen
32:   So Big
      The Dark Horse
      Woman from Monte Carlo
      Unashamed
      Dr. X
      The Rich Are Always
       with Us
      I Am a Fugitive from a
       Chain Gang
      Silver Dollar
      The Girl from Calgary
      Afraid to Talk
      Secrets of Wu Sin
33:   Charlie Chan's Greatest
       Case
      Frisco Jenny
      Ladies They Talk About
      Pilgrimage
      Female
34:   The Dragon Murder Case
      Jimmy the Gent
      Cleopatra
      School for Girls
35:   Night Life of the Gods
      Shot in the Dark
      Murder Man
      A Tale of Two Cities
      Code of the Mounties
      Hopalong Cassidy
36:   Whipsaw
      Tough Guy
      Return of Jimmy Valentine
      Bulldog Edition
      Bold Caballero
      Sutter's Gold
      The Bride Walks Out
      Can This be Dixie?
      Timber War

36: Mary of Scotland
Romeo and Juliet
In His Steps
White Legion
Adventure in Manhattan
37: The Prince and the
Pauper
The Life of Emile Zola
Let Them Live!
The Road Back
The Awful Truth
Counsel for Crime
Trigger Trio
Conquest
38: Spy Ring
Going Places
Adventures of Robin Hood
The Gangster's Boy
Blockade
Army Girl
Law of the Plains
Come on Leathernecks!
Squadron of Honor
39: Devil's Island
The Private Lives of
Elizabeth and Essex
Almost a Gentleman
The Magnificent Fraud
Juarez and Maximilian
In Old Monterey
40: On the Spot
New Moon
Konga--The Wild Stallion
Murder in the Air
The Sea Hawk
41: A Woman's Face
I Was a Prisoner on
Devil's Island
Louisiana Purchase
Sullivan's Travels
Spare a Coffin
42: Palm Beach Story
Secret Enemies
Tennessee Johnson
Cadets on Parade
Eagle Squadron
I Married a Witch
43: 2 Tickets to London
Dixie
Petticoat Larceny
Deerslayer
44: The Princess and the
Pirate

Bowery to Broadway
Kismet
Secret Command
Man from Frisco
45: Sudan
46: Criminal Court
The Falcon's Adventure
47: A Gentleman's Agreement
Pirates of Monterey
48: Fury at Furnace Creek
Adventures of Don Juan
Million Dollar Weekend
Gun Smugglers
49: A Woman's Secret
Impact
Francis
50: In a Lonely Place
Vendetta
Tarzan and the Slave Girl
51: The Sword of Monte Cristo
Sugarfoot
Maker of the Renegade
53: Mississippi Gambler
Jamaica Run
Salome
54: Silver Lode
Passion
55: Chief Crazy Horse
Escape to Burma
Lady Godiva
56: Walk the Proud Land
57: Shoot-Out at Medicine
Bend
58: The Buccaneer
59: Night of the Quarter Moon
It Started with a Kiss

Mona Washbourne (1903-
1948: Wide Boy
53: Child's Play
54: Doctor in the House
56: Cash on Delivery
57: The Good Companions
58: It's Great to be Young
59: Count Your Blessings
60: Brides of Dracula
63: Billy Liar
64: One Way Pendulum
My Fair Lady
Night Must Fall
65: The Collector
The Third Day
Ferry Across the Mersey

68: Mr. Brown, You've Got
    a Lovely Daughter
69: If...
    Fragment of Fear

Beverly Washburn
1950: The Killer that Stalked
    New York
51: Here Comes the Groom
52: Hans Christian Andersen
53: The Juggler
56: The Lone Ranger
57: Old Yeller
58: Summer Love
68: Winner
69: Pit Stop

Bryant Washburn (1889-1963)
1930: Swing High
    Vitaphone # 3740--Xmas
    Night
    Vitaphone # 3778--
    Niagara Falls
31: Liberty
    Kept Husbands
    Mystery Train
32: The Reckoning
    Arm of the Law
    Drifting Souls
    Exposure
    Forbidden Company
    Parisian Romance
    Thrill of Youth
33: What Price Innocence?
    Night of Terror
    The Devil's Mate
34: Public Stenographer
    The Return of Chandu
    The Curtain Falls
    Back Page
    The Woman Who Dared
    When Strangers Meet
35: The World Accuses
    $ 20 a Week
    Swell Head
    Danger Ahead
    The Throwback
36: The Millionaire Kid
    Bridge of Sighs
    Gambling with Souls
    The Preview Murder
    Mystery

Hollywood Boulevard
Sutter's Gold
Conflict
3 of a Kind
It Couldn't Have Happened
We Who Are About to Die
Jungle Jim (ser.)
37: Sea Racketeers
    The Westland Case
    Million Dollar Racket
38: I Demand Payment
39: Stagecoach
    Ambush
    Sky Patrol
41: Paper Bullets
42: The Yukon Patrol
    War Dogs
    Sin Town
43: Carson City Cyclone
    The Girl from Monterey
    Shadows on the Sage
    You Can't Beat the Law
    The Law Rides Again
44: The Falcon in Mexico
    Nabonga
45: 2 O'Clock Courage
    West of the Pecos
47: Sweet Genevieve

Willard Waterman
1950: Mystery Street
    Louisa
    Mrs. O'Malley and Mr.
    Malone
51: Darling, How Could You?
    Rhubarb
    On the Sunnyside of the
    Street
    It Happens Every Thursday
    Half a Hero
55: How to be Very, Very
    Popular
56: Hollywood or Bust
58: Auntie Mame
60: The Apartment
64: Get Yourself a College
    Girl

Ethel Waters (1900-
1929: On with the Show   PT
30: The Cotton Club
    New York Night

34: Hot n' Bothered
42: Tales of Manhattan
Cairo
43: Stage Door Canteen
Cabin in the Sky
49: Pinky
52: Member of the Wedding
Carib Gold
56: The Heart Is a Rebel
59: The Sound and the Fury

Pierre Watkin (1889-1960)
1935: Dangerous
36: Forgotten Faces
It Had to Happen
The Gentleman from
Louisiana
Sitting on the Moon
The Country Gentlemen
Nobody's Fool
Bunker Bean
Love Letters of a Star
37: Green Light
The Go Getter
Ever Since Eve
The Singing Marine
The Devil's Playground
Larceny on the Air
Bill Cracks Down
The Hit Parade
Sea Devils
Stage Door
Breakfast for Two
Paradise Isle
Michael O'Halloren
Interns Can't Take Money
The Californian
38: Midnight Intruder
State Police
Mr. Moto's Gamble
Dangerous to Know
The Tip-Off Girls
Illegal Traffic
There's Always a Woman
Girls' School
There's that Woman
Again
The Chaser
Mr. Doodle Kicks Off
Young Dr. Kildare
The Lady Objects
39: Risky Business

The Spirit of Culver
King of the Underworld
Wings of the Navy
Off the Record
Adventures of Jane Arden
The Mysterious Miss X
Wall Street Cowboy
Covered Trailer
They Made Her a Spy
Society Lawyer
Mr. Smith Goes to
Washington
Geronimo
Death of a Champion
The Great Victor Herbert
40: The Road to Singapore
The Saint Takes Over
Street of Memories
Captain Caution
I Love You Again
Golden Gloves
Out West with the Peppers
5 Little Peppers in
Trouble
The Bank Dick
Yesterday's Heroes
Father Is a Prince
41: Cheers for Miss Bishop
Petticoat Politics
A Man Betrayed
Meet John Doe
She Knew All the Answers
Adventures in Washington
Naval Academy
Nevada City
Buy Me that Town
Ellery Queen and the
Murder Ring
Ice-Capades Revue
Jesse James at Bay
42: The Adventures of Martin
Eden
Heart of the Rio Grande
Yokel Boy
The Magnificent Dope
The Pride of the Yankees
Whistling in Dixie
43: Cinderella Swings It
Mission to Moscow
Old Acquaintance
Jack London
Riding High

1390

44: Weekend Pass
    Bermuda Mystery
    Ladies of Washington
    South of Dixie
    Jubilee Woman
    Oh, What a Night!
    Atlantic City
    The Great Mike
    Dead Man's Eyes
    Shadow of Suspicion
    End of the Road
    Song of the Range
    Meet Miss Bobby-Socks
45: Strange Illusion
    The Phantom Speaks
    Docks of New York
    I'll Remember April
    Mr. Muggs Rides Again
    Over 21
    Follow that Woman!
    Apology for Murder
    Keep Your Powder Dry
    Three's a Crowd
    Allotment Wives
    Dakota
    Captain Tugboat Annie
    I'll Tell the World
    I Love a Bandleader
46: I Ring Doorbells
    Little Giant
    The Madonna's Secret
    So Goes My Love
    The Shadow Returns
    Murder Is My Business
    Swamp Fire
    Behind the Mask
    High School Hero
    The Missing Lady
    Claudia and David
    Secrets of a Sorority Girl
    Sioux City Sue
    G.I. War Brides
    Shock
    Her Sister's Secret
47: Violence
    Hard-Boiled Mahoney
    The Red Stallion
    Her Husband's Affair
    The Wild Frontier
    The Shocking Miss
     Pilgrim
    Beyond Our Own

48: The Hunted
    The Gentleman from
     Nowhere
    Mary Lou
    Glamour Girl
    State of the Union
    Trapped by Boston Blackie
    An Innocent Affair
    Daredevils of the Clouds
    The Counterfeiters
    The Strange Mrs. Crane
    Incident
    Fighting Back
    The Shanghai Chest
49: Knock on Any Door
    The Story of Seabiscuit
    Frontier Outpost
    Hold that Baby
    Alaska Patrol
    Zamba
50: The Big Hangover
    Rock Island Trail
    Blue Grass of Kentucky
    Over the Border
    Radar Secret Service
    Sunset in the West
    Redwood Forest Trail
    Last of the Buccaneers
    The Second Face
51: In Old Amarillo
    Two Lost Worlds
52: A Yank in Indo-China
    Scandal Sheet
    Thundering Caravans
    Hold that Line
53: The Stranger Wore a Gun
54: Johnny Dark
55: The Creature with the
    Atom Brain
    The Big Bluff
    Sudden Danger
56: The Maverick Queen
    Don't Knock the Rock
57: Spook Chasers
    Beginning of the End
    Pal Joey
59: The Flying Fontaines

Linda Watkins (1909-
1931: Sob Sister
    Good Sport
32: Gay Caballero

1391

32: Charlie Chan's Chance
Cheaters at Play
57: From Hell it Came
58: Going Steady
10 North Frederick
As Young as We Are
59: Cash McCall
60: Because They're Young
61: The Parent Trap
64: Good Neighbor Sam

Bobbs Watson (c1930-
1935: The Murder Man
37: Adventurous Blonde
You're a Sweetheart
38: Boys Town
In Old Chicago
Kentucky
39: On Borrowed Time
Calling Dr. Kildare
Blackmail
Everything's on Ice
Dodge City
The Story of Alexander
Graham Bell
40: Secrets of a Model
Dreaming Out Loud
Wyoming
Dr. Kildare's Crisis
41: Men of Boys Town
Hit the Road
Scattergood Pulls the
Strings
42: The Devil with Hitler
43: Hi Buddy!
That Nazty Nuisance
Hitler--Dead or Alive!
46: Night and Day
56: The Bold and the Brave
57: The Story of Mankind
62: Saintly Sinners
67: First to Fight

Lucile Watson (1879-1962)
1934: What Every Woman Knows
35: The Bishop Misbehaves
36: A Woman Rebels
Garden of Allah
37: 3 Smart Girls
38: Young in Heart
Sweethearts
39: Made for Each Other

The Women
40: Florian
Waterloo Bridge
41: Mr. and Mrs. North
Rage in Heaven
Footsteps in the Dark
The Great Lie
Model Wife
43: Watch on the Rhine
44: Till We Meet Again
The Thin Man Goes Home
Uncertain Glory
46: My Reputation
Tomorrow Is Forever
Never Say Goodbye
The Razor's Edge
Song of the South
47: Ivy
48: The Emperor Waltz
Julia Misbehaves
That Wonderful Urge
49: Little Women
Everybody Does It
50: Harriet Craig
Let's Dance
51: My Forbidden Past

Minor Watson (1890-1965)
1931: 24 Hours
33: Out Betters
Another Language
Babbitt
34: Pursuit of Happiness
35: Charlie Chan in Paris
Mr. Dynamite
Lady Tubbs
Mary Jane's Pa
Age of Indiscretion
Pursuit
Annapolis Farewell
36: Rose of the Rancho
The Longest Night
37: When's Your Birthday?
The Woman I Love
Saturday's Heroes
Dead End
That Certain Woman
Navy Blue and Gold
Checkers
38: Of Human Hearts
Fast Company
Boys Town

1392

38: Stablemates
Touchdown Army
While New York Sleeps
Love, Honor, and Behave
39: Huckleberry Finn
The Hardys Ride High
Maisie
The Boy Friend
News Is Made at Night
Here I Am a Stranger
Angels Wash Their Faces
The Flying Irishman
Television Spy
40: The Llamo Kid
20-Mule Team
Hidden Gold
Young People
Rangers of Fortune
Viva, Cisco Kid!
Gallant Sons
41: The Monster and the Girl
Mr. District Attorney
Western Union
The Parson of Panamint
Moon over Miami
Kiss the Boys Goodbye
Birth of the Blues
They Died with Their
Boots On
42: To the Shores of Tripoli
The Remarkable Andrew
Woman of the Year
Yankee Doodle Dandy
The Big Shot
Flight Lieutenant
Enemy Agents Meet
Ellery Queen
Gentleman Jim
Frisco Lil
43: Action in the North
Atlantic
Guadalcanal Diary
Yanks Ahoy!
Secrets in the Dark
The Crime Doctor's
Rendezvous
Crash Dive
Mission to Moscow
Princess O'Rourke
Happy Land
44: The Falcon Out West
Shadows in the Night

Henry Aldrich, Boy Scout
That's My Baby
Here Come the Waves
The Story of Dr. Wassell
The Thin Man Goes Home
45: God Is My Co-Pilot
Bewitched
A Bell for Adano
You Came Along
46: Boys Ranch
Courage of Lassie
48: A Southern Yankee
49: Thelma Jordan
Beyond the Forest
50: Mr. 880
The Jackie Robinson Story
51: Bright Victory
As Young as You Feel
Little Egypt
52: Untamed Frontier
My Son John
Face to Face
53: The Star
Roar of the Crowd
55: 10 Wanted Men
56: Rawhide Years
Trapeze
The Ambassador's
Daughter

Robert Watson (1888-1965)
1933: Moonlight Melody
36: Mary of Scotland
42: The Devil with Hitler
43: The Nazty Nuisance
The Hitler Gang
48: The Big Clock
49: Red Hot and Blue
52: Singing in the Rain
57: The Story of Mankind

David Wayne (1914-
1948: Portrait of Jennie
49: Adam's Rib
50: The Reformer and the
Redhead
My Blue Heaven
Stella
51: M
Up Front
As Young as You Feel
52: With a Song in My Heart

52: Wait Till the Sun Shines,
    Nellie
    We're Not Married
    O. Henry's Full House
    (The Cop and the Anthem
    seq.)
    I Married a Millionaire
53: Down Among the Shelter-
    ing Palms
    The "I Don't Care" Girl
    Tonight We Sing
    How to Marry a Millionaire
54: Hell and High Water
55: The Tender Trap
56: The Naked Hills
57: 3 Faces of Eve
    The Sad Sack
59: The Last Angry Man
61: The Big Gamble

John Wayne (1906-
1928: Hangman's House   S
30: The Big Trail
    Rough Romance
31: Girls Demand Excitement
    3 Girls Lost
    Arizona
    Men Are Like That
    Range Feud
    Maker of Men
32: Lady and Gent
    2-Fisted Law
    Texas Cyclone
    Haunted Gold
    The Big Stampede
    Shadow of the Eagle (ser.)
    Hurricane Express (ser.)
    Ride Him, Cowboy!
    The Hawk
33: The Three Musketeers
    (ser.)
    The Life of Jimmy Dolan
    The Man from Monterey
    Somewhere in Sonora
    The Telegraph Trail
    Baby Face
    His Private Secretary
    Sagebrush Trail
34: West of the Divide
    Lucky Texan
    Riders of Destiny
    Blue Steel

    Man from Utah
    Randy Rides Alone
    The Star Packer
    The Trail Beyond
    'Neath Arizona Skies
35: Lawless Frontier
    Rainbow Valley
    Paradise Canyon
    Dawn Rider
    Westward Ho!
    Lawless Range
    Desert Trail
    New Frontier
36: The Lawless '90s
    King of the Pecos
    The Oregon Trail
    Winds of the Wasteland
    The Sea Spoilers
    The Lonely Trail
    Conflict
37: California Straight Ahead
    Idol of the Crowds
    Adventure's End
    I Cover the War
38: Born to the West
    Hell Town
    Overland Stage Raiders
    Pals of the Saddle
    Santa Fe Stampede
    Red River Range
39: Night Riders
    3 Texas Steers (or, Danger
    Rides the Range
    Wyoming Outlaw
    New Frontier
    Allegheny Uprising (or,
    The First Rebel)
    Stagecoach
40: The Dark Command
    3 Faces West (or, The
    Refugee)
    The Long Voyage Home
    7 Sinners
41: Shepherd of the Hills
    A Man Betrayed
    Lady from Louisiana
    Lady for a Night
42: Reap the Wild Wind
    The Spoilers
    In Old California
    Flying Tigers
    Pittsburgh

42: Mlle France
43: War of the Wildcats
    Reunion
    The Lady Takes a
      Chance
    In Old Oklahoma (or,
      War of the Wildcats)
44: The Fighting Seabees
    Tall in the Saddle
45: Flame of Barbary Coast
    Back to Bataan
    Dakota
    They Were Expendable
46: Without Reservations
47: The Angel and the Badman
    Tycoon
48: Red River
    3 Godfathers
    The Wake of the Red
      Witch
    Fort Apache
49: The Fighting Kentuckian
    Sands of Iwo Jima
    She Wore a Yellow Ribbon
50: Rio Grande
51: Operation Pacific
    Flying Leathernecks
52: The Quiet Man
    Big Jim McLain
53: Trouble Along the Way
    Island in the Sky
    Star of Texas
54: Hondo
    The High and the Mighty
55: The Sea Chase
    Blood Alley
56: The Searchers
    The Conqueror
57: Jet Pilot
    Wings of Eagles
    Legend of the Lost
59: The Horse Soldiers
    Rio Bravo
60: The Alamo (act., dir.)
    North to Alaska
61: The Comancheros
62: Hatari!
    The Man Who Shot
      Liberty Valance
    The Longest Day
    How the West Was Won

63: Donovan's Reef
    McLintock!
64: Circus World
65: The Greatest Story Ever
      Told
    In Harm's Way
    The Sons of Katie Elder
66: Cast a Giant Shadow
67: El Dorado
    The War Wagon
68: The Green Berets
    The Hellfighters
69: True Grit
    Rio Lobo
    Chisholm
    The Undefeated
    The Million Dollar
      Kidnapping
    Norwood (cameo)

Nina Wayne (1943-
1966: Dead Heat on a Merry-
      Go-Round
67: Luv
69: The Comic

Pat Wayne (1939-
1955: The Long Gray Line
      Mister Roberts
56: The Searchers
60: The Alamo
61: The Comancheros
63: McLintock!
64: Cheyenne Autumn
65: Shenandoah
66: An Eye for an Eye
68: The Green Berets
69: King Gun

The Weaver Brothers & Elviry
(Frank, Leon, & Jane)
1939: Jeepers Creepers
40: In Old Missouri
    Grand Old Opry
    Friendly Neighbors
41: Arkansas Judge
    Mountain Moonlight
    Tuxedo Junction
42: Shepherd of the Ozarks
    The Old Homestead
    Mountain Rhythm

Dennis Weaver (1924-
1952: Horizons West
The Raiders
The Lawless Breed
The Redhead from
Wyoming
53: Mississippi Gambler
Law and Order
Column South
The Nebraskan
War Arrow
54: Dangerous Mission
The Bridges at Toko-Ri
55: 7 Angry Men
Chief Crazy Horse
10 Wanted Men
56: Storm Fear
58: Touch of Evil
60: The Gallant Hours
66: Duel at Diablo
67: Gentle Ben
68: Way Way Out
69: Mission: Batangas
"A Western"
Sledge
The Great Man's
Whiskers (TV)

Doodles Weaver (1914-
1937: Behind the Headlines
Topper
41: A Girl, a Guy, and a
Gob
42: The Pied Piper
44: Carolina Blues
Hey, Rookie!
The Singing Sheriff
Since You Went Away
The Story of Dr. Wassell
45: San Antonio
Thoroughbreds
53: Gentlemen Prefer Blondes
58: The Tunnel of Love
59: Frontier Gun
60: The Great Impostor
61: Ring of Fire
The Ladies' Man
Pocketful of Miracles
62: The Errand Boy
63: The Birds
Tammy and the Doctor
64: A Tiger Walks

Quick Before it Melts!
65: The Rounders
Zebra in the Kitchen
That Darn Cat
67: Rosie
The Spirit Is Willing
68: Road to Nashville
69: Bigfoot

Fritz Weaver (1926-
1964: Fail Safe
65: Guns of August (doc.)
66: The Crimson Curtain
(narr.)
To Trap a Spy
67: The Borgia Stick (TV)
69: The Maltese Bippy
A Walk in the Spring
Rain

Marjorie Weaver (1913-
1936: China Clipper
37: Big Business
This Is My Affair
The Californian
Hot Water
Life Begins in College
Second Honeymoon
38: Sally Irene and Mary
Kentucky Moonshine
3 Blind Mice
I'll Give a Million
Hold that Coed!
39: Young Mr. Lincoln
Chicken Wagon Family
The Honeymoon's Over
40: The Cisco Kid and the
Lady
Shooting High
Charlie Chan's Murder
Cruise
Maryland
Murder over New York
Michael Shayne, Private
Detective
41: Murder Among Friends
For Beauty's Sake
Men at Large
We Go Fast
42: The Man Who Wouldn't
Die
Just Off Broadway

42: The Mad Martindales
43: Baby Shoes
    Let's Face It
44: Pardon My Rhythm
    You Can't Ration Love
    The Great Alaskan
      Mystery
    Shadow of Suspicion
45: Fashion Model
    Leave it to Blondie
52: We're Not Married

Clifton Webb (1890-1966)
1944: Laura
46: The Dark Corner
    The Razor's Edge
48: Sitting Pretty
    Julie
49: Mr. Belvedere Goes to
      College
50: Cheaper by the Dozen
    For Heaven's Sake
51: Mr. Belvedere Rings the
      Bell
    Elopement
52: Dreamboat
    Stars and Stripes Forever
53: Titanic
    Mr. Scoutmaster
54: 3 Coins in the Fountain
    Woman's World
56: The Man Who Never Was
57: Boy on a Dolphin
59: The Remarkable Mr.
      Pennypacker
    Holiday for Lovers
    China Story
62: Satan Never Sleeps

Jack Webb (1920-
1948: He Walked by Night
50: Dark City
    Sunset Boulevard
    The Men
    Halls of Montezuma
51: Appointment with Danger
    You're in the Navy Now
      (or, USS Tea Kettle)
54: Dragnet
55: Pete Kelly's Blues
57: The D.I. (prod., dir., act.)
59: "30"

61: The Last Time I Saw
      Archie

Richard Webb
1941: I Wanted Wings
    Sullivan's Travels
42: The Remarkable Andrew
    American Empire
46: O.S.S.
47: Variety Girl
    Out of the Past
48: The Big Clock
    Night Has 1000 Eyes
    Isn't it Romantic?
    My Own True Love
49: A Connecticut Yankee in
      King Arthur's Court
    Sands of Iwo Jima
50: The Invisible Monster
      (ser.)
51: I Was a Communist for
      the FBI
    Distant Drums
    Starlift
52: This Woman Is Dangerous
    Carson City
    Mara Maru
53: The Nebraskan
54: Jubilee Trail
    The Black Dakotas
    3 Hours to Kill
55: Count Three and Pray
    Artists and Models
57: The Phantom Stagecoach
59: On the Beach
60: 12 to the Moon
63: Attack of the Mayan
      Mummy
65: Git!
    Town Tamer
66: Slaves of the Invisible
      Monster
    The Cat
69: The Gay Deceivers

Robert Webber (c1925-
1951: Highway 301
57: 12 Angry Men
62: The Nun and the Sergeant
63: The Stripper
65: The Sandpiper
    The Third Day

1397

65: Hysteria
66: The Silencers
Harper (or, The Moving
Target)
Dead Heat on a Marry-
Go-Round
67: The Hired Killer
The Dirty Dozen
Don't Make Waves
69: The Big Bounce

Virginia Weidler (1927-1968)
1930: Moby Dick
33: After Tonight
34: Long Lost Father
Stamboul Quest
Mrs. Wiggs of the
Cabbage Patch
35: Laddie
Freckles
Big Broadcast of 1936
Peter Ibbetson
36: Timothy's Quest
Girl of the Ozarks
Big Broadcast of 1937
Trouble for Two
Suicide Club
37: Maid of Salem
Souls at Sea
Outcasts of Poker Flat
38: Love Is a Headache
Too Hot to Handle
Out West with the Hardys
Scandal Street
Men with Wings
Mother Carey's Chickens
39: The Great Man Votes
Fixer Dugan
The Rookie Cop
The Lone Wolf Spy Hunt
The Under-Pup
The Women
Bad Little Angel
40: Young Tom Edison
Gold Rush Maisie
Henry Aldrich Goes to
Arizona
The Philadelphia Story
All This and Heaven Too
41: Keeping Company
I'll Wait for You
Barnacle Bill
Babes on Broadway

42: Born to Sing
This Time for Keeps
Once Upon a Thursday
43: Best Foot Forward
The Youngest Profession

Johnny Weissmuller (1904-
1929: Glorifying the American
Girl
Grantland Rice (doc. short)
32: Tarzan the Ape Man
33: Tarzan and His Mate
34: Hollywood Party
36: Tarzan Escapes
39: Tarzan Finds a Son
41: Tarzan's Secret Treasure
42: Tarzan's New York
Adventure
43: Stage Door Canteen
Tarzan Triumphs
Tarzan's Desert Mystery
Combat Correspondent
Homesick Angel
45: Tarzan and the Amazons
46: Tarzan and the Leopard
Woman
Swamp Fire
47: Tarzan and the Huntress
48: Tarzan and the Mermaids
Jungle Jim
49: The Lost Tribe
50: Captive Girl
Mark of the Gorilla
Pygmy Island
51: Fury of the Congo
Jungle Manhunt
52: Jungle Jim and the
Forbidden Lane
Voodoo Tiger
53: Savage Mutiny
Valley of the Headhunters
Killer Ape
54: Jungle Man-Eaters
Cannibal Attack
55: Jungle Moon
Devil Goddess
69: The Phynx

Niles Welch
1932: Cross Examination
Rainbow Trail
Border Devils
McKenna of the Mounted

32: Night Club Lady
A Scarlet Week-End
33: Mysterious Rider
Cornered
Come on, Tarzan!
Lone Avenger
Sundown Rider
34: Let's Fall in Love
Fighting Code
Cross Streets
35: Tomorrow's Youth
Stone of Silver Creek
The Ivory-Handled Gun
The Singing Vagabond
36: Empty Saddles

Raquel Welch (1942-
1964: Roustabout
A House Is Not a Home
65: A Swingin' Summer
66: The Fantastic Voyage
Our Man Flint
67: One Million B.C.
Fathom
The Oldest Profession
in the World (The Good
Old Days seq.)
Shout Loud...Louder...
I Don't Understand
The Sorcerers
Bedazzled
68: The Biggest Bundle of
Them All
Bandolero
The Queens (Queen
Elena seq.)
The Lady in Cement
69: 100 Rifles
Tilda
Flareup
Myra Breckenridge

Tuesday Weld (1943-
1956: Rock Rock Rock
59: Rally 'Round the Flag,
Boys!
The Five Pennies
60: The Private Lives of
Adam and Eve
Sex Kittens Go to College
High Time
Because They're Young

Beauty and the Robot
61: Return to Peyton Place
Bachelor Flat
62: Wild in the Country
63: Soldier in the Rain
65: I'll Take Sweden
The Cincinnati Kid
66: Lord Love a Duck
Any Wednesday
68: Pretty Poison
69: She Let Him Continue

Ben Welden (1901-
1933: Their Night Out
The Medicine Man
This Is the Life
Aunt Sally
General John Regan
34: The Girl in Possession
35: The Triumph of Sherlock
Holmes
37: Silent Barriers
Marked Woman
Another Dawn
Kid Galahad
Phantom Ship
Confession
That Certain Woman
Variety Show
Love Is on the Air
The Missing Witnesses
Back in Circulation
The Duke Comes Back
38: Alcatraz Island
Happy Landing
Always Goodbye
Little Miss Broadway
Straight Place and Show
Prison Nurse
10th Avenue Kid
The Night Hawk
Little Orphan Annie
The Saint in New York
Mystery House
Crime Ring
Smashing the Rackets
39: Federal Manhunt
I Was a Convict
The Lone Wolf Spy Hunt
Fugitive at Large
Rose of Washington Square
Hollywood Cavalcade

1399

39: Boys Reformatory
Sergeant Madden
The Star Maker
The Roaring '20s
40: Wolf of New York
Outside the 3-Mile Limit
Passport to Alcatraz
City for Conquest
41: Men of Boys Town
Strange Alibi
I'll Wait for You
Knockout
9 Lives Are Not Enough
42: All Through the Night
Bullet Scars
Maisie Gets Her Man
Stand by for Action
43: The Crime Doctor's
Rendezvous
Secrets of the Underworld
Here Comes Elmer!
44: The Fighting Seabees
Shadows in the Night
45: It's in the Bag
Circumstantial Evidence
Follow that Woman!
The Missing Corpse
46: Angel on My Shoulder
The Big Sleep
The Last Crooked Mile
Dangerous Business
Mr. Hex
47: Killer Dill
Too Many Winners
Heading for Heaven
The Pretender
Appointment with Murder
48: The Vicious Circle
A Song Is Born
Trapped by Boston
Blackie
Jinx Money
Lady at Midnight
49: Tough Assignment
Riders in the Sky
Search for Danger
Fighting Fools
Sorrowful Jones
Smart Girls Don't Talk
Impact
50: Mary Ryan, Detective
The Buccaneer's Girl
On the Isle of Samoa

51: The Lemon Drop Kid
My True Story
Tales of Robin Hood
53: All Ashore
54: Killers from Outer Space
Steel Cage
55: Ma and Pa Kettle at
Waikiki
56: Hollywood or Bust
Hidden Guns
57: Spook Chasers

Joan Weldon (1933-
1953: The Command
The System
The Stranger Wore a Gun
So This Is Love
54: Riding Shot Gun
Them
Deep in My Heart
57: Gunsight Ridge
58: Day of the Bad Man
Home Before Dark

Orson Wells (1915-
1940: Swiss Family Robinson
(narr.)
41: Citizen Kane (writ., act.,
prod., dir.)
42: The Magnificent Ambersons
(prod., dir.)
Journey Into Fear (act.,
prod., co-dir.)
It's All True (unrel.)
44: Jane Eyre
Follow the Boys
46: Tomorrow Is Forever
The Stranger
48: The Lady from Shanghai
(act., dir.)
Macbeth (act., dir.)
49: Prince of Foxes
Black Magic (or, Cagliostro)
50: The Third Man
The Black Rose
53: Trent's Last Case
54: Napoleon
Trouble in the Glen
55: 3 Cases of Murder
Othello (act., prod., dir.)
Confidential Report (act.,
prod., dir.)
56: Moby Dick

56: Fountain of Youth (short)
57: Man in the Shadow
Royal Affairs in
Versailles
58: The Long Hot Summer
Touch of Evil (act., dir.)
The Roots of Heaven
59: Compulsion
Master of the Congo
Jungle (doc.)
60: Crack in the Mirror
61: David and Goliath
Ferry to Hong Kong
(act., prod., dir.)
62: The Tartars
Mr. Arkadin
63: The Trial (act., prod.,
dir.)
The V.I.P.'s
Lafayette
64: The Finest Hour (narr.)
65: Marco The Magnificent
66: A Man for All Seasons
Is Paris Burning?
67: Falstaff
Casino Royale
The Sailor from Gibraltar
68: Oedipus the King
The Southern Star
An Immortal Story
House of Cards
Simon of the Desert
Fight for Rome (Pt. I,
Ger.)
69: 13 Chairs
Viva La Revolution!
Catch 22
The Battle on the River
Neretra
Waterloo
The Assassination of
Julius Caesar

William Wellman, Jr.
1958: Lafayette Escadrille
Darby's Rangers
High School Confidential
59: Pork Chop Hill
Macumba Love
61: Dondi
64: Rebel in the Ring
65: Winter A-Go-Go

Young Fury
67: Born Losers
The Happiest Millionaire
68: Hook, Line, and Sinker
The Private Navy of
Sgt. O'Farrell

Jacqueline Wells [Julie Bishop
since 1941] (1914-
1932: Any Old Port (short)
33: Tarzan the Fearless
Tillie and Gus
Alice in Wonderland
34: The Black Cat
Loud Speaker
Kiss and Make Up
Happy Landing
35: Square Shooter
Coronado
36: The Bohemian Girl
Night Cargo
37: Girls Can Play
Hard to Hold
The Frame Up
Counsel for Crime
Paid to Dance
38: She Married an Artist
When G-Men Step In
Flight into Nowhere
Little Miss Roughneck
The Main Event
Highway Patrol
Spring Madness
Flight to Fame
The Little Adventuress
39: My Son Is a Criminal
Kansas Terrors
Behind Prison Gates
Torture Ship
40: My Son Is Guilty
The Girl in 313
The Ranger and the Lady
Young Bill Hickok
Her First Romance
41: Back in the Saddle
As Julie Bishop:
41: The Nurse's Secret
International Squadron
Steel Against the Sky
42: Lady Gangster
Busses Roar
I Was Framed

1401

42: Escape from Crime
    The Hidden Hand
    The Hard Way
43: Princess O'Rourke
    Action in the North
      Atlantic
    Northern Pursuit
44: Hollywood Canteen
45: Rhapsody in Blue
    You Came Along
46: Cinderella Jones
    Murder in the Music Hall
    Idea Girl
    Strange Conquest
47: The Last of the Redmen
    High Tide
49: Deputy Marshal
    Threat
    Sands of Iwo Jima
51: Westward the Women
53: Sabre Jet
54: The High and the Mighty
55: Headline Hunters
57: The Big Land

John Wengraf
1942: Lucky Jordan
43: Mission to Moscow
    Paris After Dark
    Sahara
44: The 7th Cross
    Till We Meet Again
    U-Boat Prisoner
    Strange Affair
46: Tomorrow Is Forever
47: T-Men
48: Sofia
49: The Lovable Cheat
52: 5 Fingers
54: The Gambler from
      Natchez
    Paris Playboys
    Gog
55: The Racers
57: Oh Men! Oh Women!
    The Pride and the Passion
    Valerie
    The Disembodied
58: The Return of Dracula
60: Portrait in Black
    12 to the Moon
61: Judgment at Nuremberg

62: Hitler
63: The Prize
65: Ship of Fools

Barbara Werle
1965: Harum Scarum
    Battle of the Bulge
66: Seconds
67: Gunfight in Abilene
68: Krakatoa--East of Java
69: Man Without Mercy
    Charro

Oskar Werner (1922-
1949: Erotica
    Wonder of Our Days
51: Decision Before Dawn
    Angel with a Trumpet
    Wonder Boy
55: Lola Montez
56: The Last Ten Days
59: The Life and Loves of
      Mozart
62: Jules and Jim
65: Ship of Fools
66: Fahrenheit 451
    The Spy Who Came in
      from the Cold
67: Interlude
68: The Shoes of the Fisherman
    A Certain Judas
69: So Love Returns (act.,
      prod., dir.)

Richard Wessel (1913-1965)
1935: In Spite of Danger
37: Roundup Time in Texas
    Slim
    The Game that Kills
    Borrowing Trouble
38: Arson Gang Busters
39: They Made Me a Criminal
    Missing Daughters
    Beasts of Berlin
40: Cafe Hostess
    Brother Orchid
    So You Won't Talk
    The Border Legion
41: The Great Train Robbery
    Desert Bandit
    Tanks a Million
42: X Marks the Spot

1402

42: Dudes Are Pretty People
    The Traitor Within
43: Silver Spurs
46: In Old Sacramento
    In Fast Company
    Dick Tracy vs Cueball
47: Merton of the Movies
48: Pitfall
    When My Baby Smiles at
      Me
    Unknown Island
    Badmen of Tombstone
49: Slattery's Hurricane
    Frontier Outpost
    Canadian Pacific
    Blondie Hits the Jackpot
    Thieves' Highway
50: Beware of Blondie
    Watch the Birdie
51: The Scarf
    Texas Carnival
    Reunion in Reno
    Corky of Gasoline Alley
    Honeychile
52: Love Is Better than Ever
    The Belle of New York
    The Wac from Walla Walla
    Young Man with Ideas
    Blackbeard the Pirate
53: Gentlemen Prefer Blondes
    Champ for a Day
55: Bowery to Bagdad
56: Around the World in 80
    Days
63: Wives and Lovers
    Pocketful of Miracles
    Who's Minding the Store?

Dick Wesson (1922-
1950: Destination Moon
    Breakthrough
51: Inside the Walls of
    Folsom Prison
    Jim Thorpe--All American
    Force of Arms
    On the Sunnyside of the
    Street
    Starlift
52: About Face
    The Man Behind the Gun
53: The Desert Song
    Charge at Feather River

    Calamity Jane
55: Paris Follies of 1956
62: The Errand Boy

Adam West (1929-
1959: The Young Philadelphians
62: Geronimo
63: Tammy and the Doctor
    Soldier in the Rain
64: Robinson Crusoe on Mars
65: Mara of the Wilderness
    That Darn Cat
    The Outlaws Is Coming!
66: Batman
68: The Ballad of Black Lace
    The Girl Who Knew Too
    Much
    John Cain

Mae West (1892-
1932: Night After Night
    She Done Him Wrong
    (act., prod.)
33: I'm No Angel (act., writ.)
34: Belle of the '90s (or,
    It Ain't No Sin)
35: Goin' to Town
    Klondike Annie (act., writ.)
36: Go West, Young Man
    (act., writ.)
37: Every Day's a Holiday
40: My Little Chickadee (co-
    writ.)
43: The Heat's On
69: Myra Breckenridge

Gordon Westcott (1903-1935)
1932: Guilty as Hell
33: Crime of the Century
    He Learned about Women
    Heritage of the Desert
    The Working Man
    Lilly Turner
    Private Detective # 62
    Heroes for Sale
    Voltaire
    Footlight Parade
    Convention City
34: Fashions of 1934
    Fog over Frisco
    I've Got Your Number
    Dark Hazard

34: Call it Luck
Circus Clown
Registered Nurse
6 Day Bike Rider
The Case of the Howling
Dog
Kansas City Princess
Murder in the Clouds
35: White Cuckatoo
A Night at the Ritz
Go Into Your Dance
Going Highbrow
Bright Lights
Front Page Woman
This Is the Life
Two Fisted

Helen Westcott (1928-
1935: A Midsummer Night's
Dream
48: 13 Lead Soldiers
Smart Girls Won't Talk
Adventures of Don Juan
49: Mr. Belvedere Goes to
College
Homicide
Flaxy Martin
The Girl from Jones
Beach
One Last Fling
Alaska Patrol
Whirlpool
Dancing in the Dark
50: The Gunfighter
3 Came Home
51: Take Care of My Little
Girl
The Secret of Convict
Lake
52: Return of the Texan
Battles of Chief Pontiac
Phone Call from a
Stranger
With a Song in My Heart
53: Charge at Feather River
Cow Country
Abbott & Costello Meet
Dr. Jekyll and Mr. Hyde
56: Hot Blood
I Killed Wild Bill Hickok
58: God's Little Acre
The Last Hurrah

Monster on the Campus
Invisible Avenger
59: Day of the Outlaw
60: Studs Lonigan

James Westerfield (1916-
1941: Highway West
46: Undercurrent
The Chase
51: The Whistle at Eaton Falls
3 Hours to Kill
On the Waterfront
55: Chief Crazy Horse
The Violent Men
The Cobweb
The Scarlet Coat
Lucy Gallant
Man with a Gun
57: 3 Brave Men
Jungle Heat
Decision at Sundown
58: Cowboy
The Proud Rebel
59: The Shaggy Dog
The Gunfight at Dodge City
60: Wild River
The Plunderers
61: The Absent-Minded
Professor
Homicidal
62: Birdman of Alcatraz
63: Son of Flubber
64: Man's Favorite Sport?
Bikini Beach
65: The Sons of Katie Elder
That Funny Feeling
66: Dead Heat on a Merry-Go-
Round
67: Blue
68: Hang 'em High
69: Smith!
A Man Called Gannon
The Love God
True Grit

Helen Westley (1879-1943)
1934: Moulin Rouge
House of Rothschild
Death Takes a Holiday
Age of Innocence
Anne of Green Gables
35: Captain Hurricane

35:	Chasing Yesterday		Captain Hurricane
	Roberta		Dressed to Thrill
	Splendour		3 Live Ghosts
	The Melody Lingers On		A Feather in Her Hat
36:	Showboat	36:	The Gorgeous Hussy
	Half Angel		Pennies from Heaven
	Dimples		Craig's Wife
	Banjo on My Knee		The Rose Bowl
	Stowaway		The Invisible Ray
37:	Cafe Metropole	37:	Bulldog Drummond's
	Heidi		Revenge
	Sing and be Happy		When Love Is Young
	I'll Take Romance	38:	Goldwyn Follies
38:	The Baroness and the		First 100 Years
	Butler		Bulldog Drummond's Peril
	Rebecca of Sunnybrook	39:	When Tomorrow Comes
	Farm		The Cat and the Canary
	Alexander's Ragtime Band	40:	40 Little Mothers
	Keep Smiling		Hullabaloo
	She Married an Artist	41:	The Bad Man
39:	Zaza		The Chocolate Soldier
	Wife, Husband, and Friend	42:	They All Kissed the Bride
40:	Lillian Russell		The Remarkable Andrew
	All This and Heaven Too	43:	Princess O'Rourke
	The Captain Is a Lady		Hers to Hold
	Lady with Red Hair	44:	Her Primitive Man
41:	Henry Aldrich for	47:	The Late George Apley
	President	48:	The Velvet Touch
	Adam Had 4 Sons	62:	For Love or Money
	Lady from Louisiana		Don't Knock the Twist
	Sunny	66:	The Swinger
	Million Dollar Baby		The Ghost and Mr.Chicken
	The Smiling Ghost		The Chase
	Bedtime Story	67:	The Reluctant Astronaut
42:	My Favorite Spy	69:	Nobody Loves Flapping
			Eagle

Nydia Westman (1902-

1932:	Strange Justice		Rabbit Run
	Manhattan Tower		
33:	King of the Jungle	Jack Weston	
	From Hell to Heaven	1964:	The Incredible Mr. Limpet
	Bondage	65:	Mirage
	Way to Love	66:	The Cincinnati Kid
	The Cradle Song	67:	Code Name: Heraclitus
	Little Women		Wait Until Dark
34:	Two Alone	68:	The Thomas Crown Affair
	Success at Any Price		The Counterfeit Killer
	Ladies Should Listen		Now You See it, Now You
	The Trumpet Blows		Don't (TV)
	One Night of Love	69:	The April Fools
	Manhattan Love Song		The Cactus Flower
35:	Sweet Adeline		A New Leaf

Winifred Westover (1890-
1930:   The Lummox

Paul Wexler
1958:   The Buccaneer
        Stakeout on Dope Street
59:     The 4 Skulls of Jonathan
        Drake
        Day of the Outlaw
        Timbuktu
        The Miracle of the Hills
67:     The Way West
        The Busy Body

Michael Whalen (1899-
1930:   Outside These Walls
35:     Professional Soldier
36:     Song and Dance Man
        The Country Doctor
        Poor Little Rich Girl
        My Second Wife
        White Fang
        Sing, Baby, Sing
        Career Woman
        The Man I Marry
37:     Woman-Wise
        Time Out for Romance
        Wee Willie Winkie
        The Lady Escapes
38:     Change of Heart
        Walking Down Broadway
        Island in the Sky
        Speed to Burn
        Time Out for Murder
        Meridian 7-1212
        While New York Sleeps
        Inside Story
39:     Pardon Our Nerve
        Mysterious Miss X
        They Asked for It
40:     Ellery Queen--Master
        Detective
41:     Sign of the Wolf
        I'll Sell My Life
42:     Nazi Spy Ring
        Dawn Express
43:     Tahiti Honey
47:     The Gas House Kids in
        Hollywood
48:     Blonde Ice
        Highway 13
        Shep Comes Home

        Parole, Inc.
49:     Omoo-Omoo, the Shark
        God
        Sky Liner
        Son of a Badman
        Thunder in the Pines
        Tough Assignment
        Treasure of Monte Cristo
50:     Sarumba
51:     Kentucky Jubilee
        Mask of the Dragon
        According to Mrs. Hoyle
        Fingerprints Don't Lie
        G.I. Jane
52:     Waco
56:     The Phantom from 10,000
        Leagues
59:     Missile to the Moon
60:     Elmer Gantry
67:     Adventures of Batman and
        Robin

Bert Wheeler (1895-1968) &
Robert Woolsey (1889-1944)
1929:   Rio Rita
30:     The Cuckoos
        Dixiana
        Half Shot at Sunrise
        Hook, Line, and Sinker
31:     Too Many Cooks
        Cracked Nuts
        Caught Plastered
        Full of Notions
        Peach O'Reno
        Everything's Rosie
32:     Girl Crazy
        Hold 'em, Jail!
33:     Diplomaniacs
        So This Is Africa
34:     Kentucky Kernels
        Hips, Hips, Hooray!
        The Cockeyed Cavaliers
35:     The Nitwits
        The Rainmakers
36:     Mummy's Boys
        Silly Billies
37:     On Again, Off Again
39:     High Flyers
        Cowboy Quarterback
41:     Las Vegas Nights (or,
        The Gay City)

1406

Arleen Whelan (c1916-
1938: Kidnapped
Thanks for Everything
Gateway
39: The Boy Friend
Young Mr. Lincoln
Sabotage
40: Young People
Charter Pilot
41: Charley's Aunt
42: Castle in the Desert
Sundown Jim
43: Stage Door Canteen
47: The Senator Was
Indiscreet
Suddenly It's Spring
Ramrod
48: That Wonderful Urge
49: Dear Wife
51: Passage West
Flaming Feather
52: Never Wave at a Wac
53: Devil's Canyon
San Antone
The Sun Shine Bright
56: The Women of Pitcairn
Island
57: Raiders of Old California
The Badge of Marshal
Brennan

Charles "Slim" Whitaker
1939: The Fighting Gringo
New Frontier
40: Legion of the Lawless
Marshal of Mesa City
Bullet Code
Prairie Law
41: Arizona Bound
Cyclone on Horseback
Along the Rio Grande
Hands Across the Rockies
Come on Danger!
Billy the Kid Wanted
Billy the Kid's Roundup
42: The Mad Monster
The Silver Bullet
Billy the Kid's Smoking
Guns
43: The Fighting Frontier
The Mysterious Rider
The Desperadoes

44: The Laramie Trail
The Drifter
Oklahoma Raiders
Marshal of Gunsmoke
46: Overland Riders
Outlaw of the Plains
Panhandle Trail
Law of the Lash
48: The Westward Trail

Alice White (1907-
1928: Gentlemen Prefer
Blondes   S
Three Ring Marriage   S
Show Girl   S
The Mad Hour   S
Big Noise   S
Harold Teen   S
Lingerie   S
Broadway Daddies   S
29: Hot Stuff   S
The Girl from Woolworth's
Naughty Baby   SSE
Show of Shows
The Widow from Chicago
30: Sweet Mama
Sweethearts on Parade
Show Girl in Hollywood
Playing Around
31: Naughty Flirt
Murder at Midnight
33: Employees' Entrance
Luxury Liner
Picture Snatcher
King for a Night
34: Cross Country Cruise
Jimmy the Gent
A Very Honorable Guy
Gift of Gab
35: Sweet Music
Secret of the Chateau
37: Big City
38: Telephone Operator
King of the Newsboys
Annabella Takes a Tour
41: The Night of January 16th
42: Girls' Town
49: Flamingo Road

Carol White (1944-
1960: Never Let Go
67: Prehistoric Women

1407

68: Poor Cow
   I'll Never Forget What's
      'Is Name
69: Daddy's Gone A-Hunting
   The Fixer
   The Man Who Had Power
      Over Women
   The Impotent

Jesse White (1919-
1950: Harvey
51: Death of a Salesman
   Callaway Went Thataway
   Katie Did It
   Bedtime for Bonzo
   Francis Goes to the Races
52: Million Dollar Mermaid
   The Girl in White
53: Forever Female
   Gunsmoke
   Champ for a Day
54: Witness to Murder
   Hell's Half Acre
55: Not As a Stranger
   The Girl Rush
56: The Bad Seed
   Back from Eternity
   The Come On
   He Laughed Last
57: Designing Woman
   God Is My Partner
   Johnny Trouble
58: Marjorie Morningstar
   Country Music Holiday
59: 211 Grand Canal
60: The Rise and Fall of
      Legs Diamond
   The Big Night
61: A Fever in the Blood
   The Right Approach
   The Tomboy and the
      Champ
   On the Double
   3 Blondes in His Life
   Sail a Crooked Ship
62: It's Only Money
63: It's a Mad Mad Mad Mad
      World
   The Yellow Canary
64: Looking for Love
   A House Is Not a Home
   Pajama Party

Erasmus with Freckles
66: Dear Brigitte
   The Ghost in the
      Invisible Bikini
67: The Spirit Is Willing
   The Reluctant Astronaut
69: Togetherness

Lee "Lasses" White (d. 1949)
1939: Rovin' Tumbleweeds
40: Grandpa Goes to Town
   Oklahoma Renegades
41: Scattergood Baines
   Scattergood Pulls the
      Strings
   Riding the Wind
   The Bandit Trail
   Dude Cowboy
   Cyclone on Horseback
   Thundering Hoofs
   Land of the Open Range
   Come On, Danger!
43: Cinderella Swings It!
   The Unknown Guest
44: Alaska
   The Minstrel Man
   Song of the Range
   When Strangers Marry
   The Adventures of Mark
      Twain
45: Red Rock Outlaws
   Dillinger
   In Old Mexico
   The Lonesome Trail
   Saddle Serenade
   Springtime in Texas
46: Moon over Montana
   Trail to Mexico
   West of the Alamo
47: Rainbow over the Rockies
   6 Gun Serenade
   Song of the Sierras
   Louisiana
48: The Dude Goes West
   Indian Agent
   The Golden Eye
   Valiant Hombre
49: Mississippi Rhythm
50: The Texan Meets Calamity
      Jane

Leo White
1929: Smilin' Guns   S
      Born to the Saddle   S
      Campus Knights   S
  30: Roaring Ranch
      Along Came Youth
  34: Madame Du Barry
  35: All the King's Horses
  37: Tovarich

Wilfrid Hyde-White (1903-
1937: Murder by Hope
  49: The Third Man
      The Man on the Eiffel
      Tower
  51: Trio (Mr. Knowall seq.)
  53: Mr. Dennis Drives North
  54: Betrayed
      Mr. Potts Goes to
      Moscow
      Duel in the Jungle
      The Story of Gilbert &
      Sullivan
  55: See How They Run
      Midnight Escapade
      Quentin Durward
  56: Cash on Delivery
  57: Tarzan and the Lost
      Safari
      John and Julie
      The Silken Affair
  58: Up the Creek
  59: Northwest Frontier
      Bad Girl
      The Circle
      Libel
      City After Midnight
  60: Let's Make Love
      Flame over India
  61: On the Double
      Two-Way Stretch
  62: Ada
      In Search of the Cast-
      aways
  64: Operation Snafu
      My Fair Lady
  65: John Goldfarb, Please
      Come Home
      You Must be Joking!
  66: Ten Little Indians
      Our Man in Marrakesh

  67: The Million Eyes of Su-
      Muru
      You Only Live Twice
  68: P.J.
      His and Hers
      The Sunshine Patriot (TV)
  69: Gaily, Gaily
      Skullduggery
      Fragment of Fear

O. Z. Whitehead
1935: The Scoundrel
  40: The Grapes of Wrath
  47: My Brother Talks to
      Horses
      Romance of Rosy Ridge
  48: A Song Is Born
      Road House
  49: Ma and Pa Kettle
  51: The Hoodlum
  52: The San Francisco Story
      For Men Only
      We're Not Married
      Beware My Lovely
      Feudin' Fools
  58: The Last Hurrah
      Rally 'Round the Flag,
      Boys!
  60: The Chartroose Caboose
  61: 2 Rode Together
  62: Panic in the Year Zero
  63: Summer Magic

Jordan Whitfield (1917-
1938: You Can't Take it with
      You
  46: 3 Little Girls in Blue
      Swamp Fire
  48: Another Part of the Forest
  50: Right Cross
  54: Carmen Jones

Paul Whiteman (1890-1967)
1930: King of Jazz
  35: Thanks a Million
  40: Strike Up the Band
  44: Atlantic City
  45: Rhapsody in Blue
  47: The Fabulous Dorseys

1409

Barbara Whiting
1945: Junior Miss
  46: Centennial Summer
      Home Sweet Homicide
  47: Carnival in Costa Rica
  49: City Across the River
  51: I Can Get it for You
      Wholesale (or, The
      Best of Everything)
  52: Beware My Lovely
      Rainbow "Round My
      Shoulder
  53: Dangerous When Wet
  55: Paris Follies of 1956

Leonard Whiting (1950-
1968: Romeo and Juliet
  69: The Royal Hunt of the
      Sun

Margaret Whiting
1955: Fresh from Paris

Lloyd Whitlock (1900-1962)
1932: Sin's Pay Day
      Widow in Scarlet
      Tangled Destinies
  33: Midnight Warning
      Revenge at Monte Carlo
      Diamond Trail
      Laughing at Life
      The Whirlwind
      Her Splendid Folly
      One Year Later
  34: West of the Divide
      Lost Jungle
      Green Eyes
  35: Behind Green Lights
  36: Night Cargo
      Navy Born
      The Dark Hour

Gayne Whitman
1940: Misbehaving Husbands
  41: Parachute Battalion
  42: Phantom Killer
  44: My Gal Loves Music
  49: The Sickle or the Cross
  52: Big Jim McLain
      Strange Fascination
  53: One Girl's Confession
      Dangerous Crossing

Stuart Whitman (1929-
1951: When Worlds Collide
      The Day the Earth Stood
      Still
  53: The All-American
      The Silver Lode
      Passion
  56: 7 Men from Now
      No Sleep Till Dawn
  57: Johnny Trouble
      Hell Bound
      Crime of Passion
      War Drums
      The Girl in the Black
      Stockings
  58: The Decks Ran Red
      China Doll
      Darby's Rangers
      10 North Frederick
  59: These Thousand Hills
      The Sound and the Fury
      Try and Get Me
      Round-Dog Man
  60: Murder, Inc.
      The Story of Ruth
  61: Francis of Assisi
      The Fiercest Heart
      The Mark
      The Comancheros
  62: Convicts 4
      The Longest Day
      Reprieve
  64: Shock Treatment
      Rio Conchos
      Today We Live (or, The
      Day and the Hour)
      Signpost to Murder
  65: Those Magnificent Men in
      Their Flying Machines
  66: An American Dream
      The Sands of Kalahari
  68: The Last Escape
  69: The Heroes
      The Bait
      The Prisoner

James Whitmore (1921-
1949: Undercover Man
  50: Battleground
      Asphalt Jungle
      The Next Voice You Hear
      Mrs. O'Malley and Mr.
      Malone

50: The Outriders
Please Believe Me
51: Across the Wide Missouri
It's a Big Country
52: Because You're Mine
Above and Beyond
Shadow in the Sky
53: The Girl Who Had
Everything
All the Brothers Were
Valiant
Kiss Me Kate
The Great Diamond
Robbery
54: The Command
Them
55: Battle Cry
The McConnell Story
The Last Frontier
Oklahoma!
56: The Eddie Duchin Story
Crime in the Streets
57: The Young Don't Cry
58: The Deep Six
The Restless Years
59: Face of Fire
60: Who Was that Lady?
64: Black Like Me
Nobody's Perfect
67: Chuka
68: Madigan
Planet of the Apes
69: Waterhole No. 3
The Guns of the
Magnificent 7
The Split
Tora! Tora! Tora!

Eleanor Whitney
1935: Millions in the Air
36: The Rose Bowl
Timothy's Quest
Three Cheers for Love
College Holiday
Big Broadcast of 1937
37: Clarence
Turn Off the Moon
Blonde Trouble
Thrill of a Lifetime
38: Campus Confessions

Peter Whitney (1916-
1941: Underground
9 Lives Are Not Enough
The Blues in the Night
42: Rio Rita
Valley of the Sun
Spy Ship
Whistling in Dixie
Reunion
43: The Busses Roar
Destination Tokyo
Action in the North
Atlantic
44: Mr. Skeffington
45: Bring on the Girls
Hotel Berlin
Murder He Says
46: Blonde Alibi
The Brute Man
The Notorious Lone Wolf
Three Strangers
47: Northwest Outpost
Violence
48: The Iron Curtain
53: The Great Sioux Uprising
The Big Heat
All the Brothers Were
Valiant
54: The Black Dakotas
Gorilla at Large
Day of Triumph
55: The Sea Chase
The Last Frontier
56: Great Day in the Morning
Man from Del Rio
The Cruel Tower
57: The Domino Kid
58: Buchanan Rides Alone (or,
The Name's Buchanan)
62: The Wonderful World of
the Brothers Grimm
65: The Sword of Ali Baba
67: In the Heat of the Night
68: Chubasco
69: The Great Bank Robbery
The Ballad of Cable Hogue

Dame May Whitty (1865-1948)
1937: Night Must Fall
Conquest

37: The 13th Chair
38: I Met My Love Again
    The Lady Vanishes
39: Raffles
40: A Bill of Divorcement
41: One Night in Lisbon
    Suspicion
42: Mrs. Miniver
    Thunder Birds
43: The Constant Nymph
    Flesh and Fantasy
    Lassie Come Home
    Madame Curie
    Forever and a Day
    Slightly Dangerous
    Crash Dive
44: The White Cliffs of Dover
    Gaslight
45: My Name Is Julia Ross
46: Devotion
47: This Time for Keeps
    Green Dolphin Street
    If Winter Comes
48: Sign of the Ram
    The Return of October

Richard Whorf (1906-1966)
1934: Midnight
41: Blues in the Night
42: Juke Girl
    Yankee Doodle Dandy
    Keeper of the Flame
43: Assignment in Brittany
    The Cross of Lorraine
44: The Impostor
    Christmas Holiday
    Blonde Fever (dir.)
    Strange Confession
45: The Hidden Eye
    The Sailor Takes a
    Wife (dir.)
    Champion of Champions
46: Till the Clouds Roll By
    (dir.)
47: It Happened in Brooklyn
    (dir.)
    Love from a Stranger
48: Luxury Liner
50: Champagne for Caesar
    Chain Lightning
51: The Groom Wore Spurs

54: Autumn Fever
56: The Burning Hills (prod.)
57: Shoot-Out at Medicine
    Bend (prod.)
    Bomber B-52 (prod.)

Mary Wickes (c1912-
1941: The Man Who Came to
    Dinner
42: The Mayor of 44th Street
    Private Buckaroo
    Now Voyager
    Who Done It?
43: Rhythm of the Islands
    Happy Land
    My Kingdom for a Cook
    Higher and Higher
48: The Decision of Christopher
    Blake
    June Bride
49: Anna Lucasta
50: The Petty Girl
51: On Moonlight Bay
    I'll See You in My Dreams
52: The Will Rogers Story
    Young Man with Ideas
53: By the Light of the
    Silvery Moon
    The Actress
    Half a Hero
54: Destry
    White Christmas
55: Good Morning, Miss Dove
56: Dance with Me, Henry
57: Don't Go Near the Water!
59: It Happened to Jane
60: Cimarron
61: 101 Dalmatians (cartoon
    voice)
    Sins of Rachel Cade
62: The Music Man
64: Fate Is the Hunter
    Dear Heart
65: How to Murder Your Wife
66: The Trouble with Angels
67: Where Angels Go Trouble
    Follows
    The Spirit Is Willing

Richard Widmark (1914-
1947: Kiss of Death

1412

48: Cry of the City
Road House
Street with No Name
Yellow Sky
49: Down to the Sea in Ships
Slattery's Hurricane
50: Night and the City
Panic in the Streets
No Way Out
Halls of Montezuma
51: The Frogmen
52: Don't Bother to Knock
Red Skies of Montana
O. Henry's Full House
(The Clarion Call seq.)
My Pal Gus
53: Destination Gobi
Pickup on South Street
Take the High Ground
54: Hell and High Water
Garden of Evil
Broken Lance
55: A Prize of Gold
The Cobweb
56: Run for the Sun
Backlash
The Last Wagon
57: St. Joan
Time Limit (act., co-prod.)
Stopover Tokyo
58: The Law and Jake Wade
The Tunnel of Love
59: Warlock
Kingdom of Man
The Trap
60: The Alamo
61: The Secret Ways
Two Rode Together
Judgment at Nuremberg
62: How the West Was Won
64: Cheyenne Autumn
The Long Ships
Flight from Ashiya
65: The Bedford Incident
66: Alvarez Kelly
67: The Way West
68: Madigan
A Talent for Loving
69: Death of a Gunfighter
Captain Apache
The Moonshine War

Dorothea Wieck (1908-
1932: Maedchen in Uniform
33: The Cradle Song
61: Brainwashed

Crane Wilbur (1889-
1934: Name the Woman
35: High School Girl
Unknown Woman
Public Opinion
36: Captain Calamity

Claire Wilcox (1956-
1962: 40 lbs. of Trouble
63: Wives and Lovers

Frank Wilcox (1907-
1940: The Fighting 69th
Virginia City
Till We Meet Again
Tear Gas Squad
Murder in the Air
River's End
Santa Fe Trail
41: The Wagons Roll at Night
Affectionately Yours
A Shot in theDark
Navy Blues
Highway West
They Died with Their
Boots On
Wild Bill Hickok Rides
42: Lady Gangster
Murder in the Big House
Bullet Scars
Wings for the Eagle
Escape from Crime
Across the Pacific
Secret Enemies
The Hidden Hand
43: The Busses Roar
Night Freight
The North Star
Truck Busters
44: The Impostor
Follow the Boys
Adventures of Mark Twain
In the Meantime Darling
45: Conflict
46: Strange Triangle
Night Editor

46: The Devil's Mask
47: I Cover Big Town
Philo Vance Returns
Something in the Wind
A Gentleman's Agreement
Cass Timberlane
Blondie's Anniversary
The Beginning or the End?
Born to Speed
48: Miracle of the Bells
Caged Fury
49: The Mysterious Desperado
The Masked Raiders
Samson and Delilah
All the King's Men
The East Side Story
Renegades of the Rancho
Mister 880
The Clay Pigeon
50: The Kid from Texas
Blondie's Hero
Chain Gang
52: The Half-Breed
Treasure of Lost Canyon
Trail Guide
The Greatest Show on
Earth
Ruby Gentry
The Kid from Texas
Rainbow 'Round My
Shoulder
53: China Venture
Those Redheads from
Seattle
54: Those Young Texans
The Black Dakotas
Naked Alibi
55: Abbott & Costello Meet
the Keystone Kops
Carolina Cannonball
56: Never Say Goodbye
Uranium Boom
The Man in the Gray
Flannel Suit
Earth vs the Flying
Saucers
First Traveling Saleslady
A Strange Adventure
The 7th Cavalry
Dance with Me, Henry
Hollywood or Bust

57: Kelly and Me
Hell's Crossroads
The Beginning of the End
Pal Joey
58: The Man from God's
Country
Johnny Rocco
59: Go, Johnny, Go!
61: A Majority of One
Double Trouble
62: Swingin' Along

Robert Wilcox (1910-1955)
1936: Let Them Live!
The Stones Cry Out
The Cop
37: Carnival Queen
Wild and Wooly
Armored Car
The Man in Blue
City Girl
38: Little Tough Guy
Gambling Ship
Reckless Living
Rascals
Young Fugitives
Swing that Cheer
39: Undercover Doctor
Blondie Takes a
Vacation
The Man They Could Not
Hang
The Kid from Texas
40: The Lone Wolf Strikes
Island of Doomed Men
Dreaming Out Loud
Buried Alive
Gambling on the High
Seas
Father Is a Prince
46: The Unknown
Mysterious Dr. Satan
Wild Beauty
47: The Vigilantes Return
54: Day of Triumph

Henry Wilcoxon (1905-
193?: Two Way Street
Self-Made Lady
31: Perfect Lady
Flying Squad

31:	Lovelorn Lady	Cornel Wilde (1915-
32:	A Taxi to Paradise	1940: Lady with Red Hair

31: Lovelorn Lady
32: A Taxi to Paradise
Lord of the Manor
34: Princess Charming
Cleopatra
35: The Crusades
36: A Woman Alone
Last of the Mohicans
The President's Mystery
37: Souls at Sea
Jericho
38: Prison Nurse
Mysterious Mr. Moto of
Devil's Island
Five of a Kind
Keep Smiling
Arizona Wildcat
Dark Sands
If I Were King
39: Chasing Danger
Woman Doctor
Tarzan Finds a Son
40: Free, Blonde, and 21
Earthbound
The Crooked Road
Mystery Sea Raider
41: That Hamilton Woman
The Corsican Brothers
Scotland Yard
The Lone Wolf Takes a
Chance
South of Tahiti
42: That Man Who Wouldn't
Die
Mrs. Miniver
Johnny Doughboy
47: Dragnet
Unconquered
49: Samson and Delilah
A Connecticut Yankee
in King Arthur's Court
50: The Miniver Story
52: The Greatest Show on
Earth (co-prod.)
Scaramouche
56: The Ten Commandments
(prod.)
59: The Buccaneer (prod.)
65: War Lord
67: Armegeddon 1975
68: The Private Navy of Sgt.
O'Farrell

Cornel Wilde (1915-
1940: Lady with Red Hair
41: High Sierra
Knockout
The Perfect Snob
42: Manila Calling
Life Begins at 8:30
43: Wintertime
44: Guest in the House
45: A Song to Remember
A 1000 and One Nights
Leave Her to Heaven
46: The Bandit of Sherwood
Forest
Centennial Summer
47: Forever Amber
The Homestretch
It Had to be You
48: The Walls of Jericho
Road House
49: Shockproof
50: 4 Days' Leave
Trumpet to the Morn
2 Flags West
52: The Greatest Show on
Earth
Operation Secret
At Sword's Point
California Conquest
53: The Treasure of the
Golden Condor
Main Street to Broadway
Saadia
54: Passion
Woman's World
55: The Big Combo
The Scarlet Coat
56: Hot Blood (act., dir.)
Storm Fear
Star of India
57: Beyond Mombasa
Omar Khayyam
The Devil's Hairpin (act.,
prod., dir.)
58: Maracaibo
59: The Edge of Eternity
62: Constantine and the Cross
63: Lancelot and Guinevere
(or, Sword of Lancelot;
act., prod., dir.)
66: The Naked Prey (act.,
prod., dir.)

67: Beach Red
    The Raging Sea
68: End of the Season
69: The Comic

Gene Wilder
1967: Bonnie and Clyde
    The Producers
69: Two by Two

Michael Wilding (1912-
1939: There Ain't No Justice
40: Convoy
    Tilly of Bloomsbury
    Sailors 3
    Kipps
    Ships with Wings
    Cottage to Let
42: Undercover
    Secret Mission
43: Chetniks
44: English Without Tears
45: Dear Octopus
46: Carnival
47: The Courtneys of Curzon
    Street
    An Ideal Husband
    Into the Blue
48: Piccadilly Incident (or,
    They Met at Midnight)
49: Spring in Park Lane
    Under Capricorn
    His Man Gilbey
50: Stage Fright
51: Law and the Lady
    Lady with a Lamp
    The Man in the Dinghy
52: Derby Day
    Maytime in Mayfair
53: Torch Song
    Trent's Last Case
54: The Egyptian
55: The Glass Slipper
    The Scarlet Coat
57: Zarak
    Danger Within
59: Breakout
60: The World of Suzie Wong
61: The Naked Edge
    2 Enemies
62: The Best of Enemies

    A Girl Named Tamiko
69: The Sweet Ride
    Waterloo

Robert J. Wilke
1944: The San Antonio Kid
    Call of the Rockies
    Vigilantes of Dodge City
    Sheriff of Las Vegas
45: The Topeka Terror
    Sheriff of Cimarron
    Santa Fe Saddlemates
    Rough Riders of Cheyenne
    Corpus Christi Bandits
    Sunset in Eldorado
    Trail of the Badlands
46: Roaring Rangers
    The Inner Circle
    Out California Way
    Traffic in Crime
    Haunted Harbor
    King of the Texas Rangers
    Dick Tracy vs Crime, Inc.
47: Buck Privates Come Home
    The Vigilantes Return
    West of Dodge City
    Law of the Canyon
48: Last Days of Boot Hill
    6 Gun Law
    Daredevils of the Clouds
    Carson City Raiders
    West of Sonora
    Trail of Laredo
49: The Wyoming Bandit
    Laramie
    Frontier Outpost
50: Kill the Umpire!
    Outcast of Black Mesa
    (or, The Clue)
    Mule Train
    Beyond the Purple Hills
    Across the Badlands (or,
    The Challenge)
51: Gunplay
    Saddle Legion
    Best of the Badmen
    Pistol Harvest
    Hot Lead
    Cyclone Fury
    Overland Telegraph
52: The Las Vegas Story

52: Hellgate
Fargo
High Noon
Road Agent
Laramie Mountains (or,
Frontiers Desperadoes)
The Maverick
Cattle Town
Wyoming Roundup
53: Powder River
War Paint
Arrowhead
Cow Country
54: 2 Guns and a Badge
The Black Widow
20,000 Leagues Under
the Sea
The Lone Gun
55: Shotgun
Strange Lady in Town
Smoke Signal
Wichita
The Far Country
56: The Lone Ranger
Backlash
The Magnificent 7
The Rawhide Years
Canyon River
Gun the Man Down
Written on the Wind
Raw Edge
57: Hot Summer Night
Night Passage
The Tarnished Angels
58: Return to Warbow
Man of the West
59: Never Steal Anything
Small
60: Spartacus
61: The Long Rope
Blueprint for Robbery
63: The Gun Hawk
64: Shock Treatment
Fate Is the Hunter
65: The Hallelujah Trail
66: Smoky
67: Tony Rome
69: Joaquin Murietta

Guy Wilkerson (1898-
1937: Paradise Express

Mountain Justice
The Yodelin' Kid from
Pine Ridge
41: Spooks Run Wild
42: Swamp Woman
43: The Rangers Take Over
Border Buckaroos
44: Boss or Rawhide
Brand of the Devil
Gangsters of the Frontier
Guns of the Law
Gunsmoke Mesa
The Pinto Bandit
Trail of Terror
Return of the Rangers
Spooktown
Outlaw Roundup
The Whispering Skull
Dead or Alive
45: Captain Tugboat Annie
Enemy of the Law
Three in the Saddle
46: Frontier Fugitives
47: The Michigan Kid
48: Fury at Furnace Creek
49: Texas, Brooklyn, and
Heaven
50: The Great Missouri Raid
51: Comin' 'Round the Mountain
52: The Big Sky
55: Foxfire
56: Jubal
57: The Buster Keaton Story
Decision at Sundown
58: Cowboy
Wild Heritage
Man of the West
60: The Walking Target
61: Susan Slade
63: The Haunted Palace
65: War Party
69: True Grit

Warren William (1895-1948)
1931: Expensive Women
Honor of the Family
32: Woman from Monte Carlo
The Match King
Beauty and the Boss
The Dark Horse
Under 18

32: Mouthpiece
Skyscraper Souls
Three on a Match
33: Employees' Entrance
Gold Diggers of 1933
Mind Reader
Goodbye Again
Lady for a Day
34: Smarty
Upper World
The Case of the Howling
Dog
Secret Bride
Bedside
Dr. Monica
The Dragon Murder Case
Imitation of Life
Cleopatra
35: Living on Velvet
The Case of the Curious
Bride
The Case of the Lucky
Legs
Don't Bet on Blondes
Widow from Monte Carlo
36: The Case of the Velvet
Claws
Stage Struck
Satan Met a Lady
Times Square Playboy
Go West Young Man
37: Outcast
Midnight Madonna
The Firefly
Madame X
38: Arsene Lupin Returns
First Hundred Years
Wives Under Suspicion
39: The Lone Wolf's Spy
Hunt
The Gracie Allen Murder
Case
Man in the Iron Mask
Day-Time Wife
40: Lillian Russell
The Lone Wolf Strikes
The Lone Wolf Meets a
Lady
Arizona
Trail of the Vigilantes
41: The Wolf Man
The Lone Wolf Keeps a
Date

The Lone Wolf Takes a
Chance
Wild Geese Calling
Wild Bill Hickok Rides
42: Counter Espionage
Eyes of the Underworld
43: One Dangerous Night
Passport to Suez
45: Fear
47: Private Affairs of Bel Ami

Bill Williams (1916-
1944: Murder in the Blue Room
30 Seconds over Tokyo
Those Endearing Young
Charms
45: West of the Pecos
46: Deadline at Dawn
Till the End of Time
47: A Likely Story
49: Clay Pigeon
A Woman's Secret
The Stratton Story
Fighting Man of the
Plains
A Dangerous Profession
50: The Great Missouri Raid
Operation Haylift
Cariboo Trail
Blue Grass of Kentucky
Rookie Fireman
51: Blue Blood
Havana Rose
52: Rose of Cimarron
Son of Paleface
Bronco Buster
The Pace that Thrills
53: Torpedo Alley
54: Racing Blood
The Outlaw's Daughter
55: Apache Ambush
Hell's Horizon
56: Wiretappers
Broken Star
57: The Halliday Brand
The Storm Rider
Slim Carter
58: Space Masters X-7
Legion of the Doomed
59: Alaska Passage
60: Hell to Eternity
Oklahoma Territory
A Dog's Best Friend

1418

61: The Sergeant Was a Lady
64: Law of the Lawless
65: Tickle Me
The Hallelujah Trail
Space Flight IC-I
68: Buckskin

Cara Williams (1925-
1943: Happy Land
44: Something for the Boys
Sweet and Low Down
In the Meantime Darling
45: Don Juan Quilligan
The Spider
46: It's a Wonderful Life
Saddle Pals
Passkey to Danger
A Boy, a Girl, and a
Dog
47: Heading for Heaven
Boomerang
48: The Dude Goes West
Sitting Pretty
The Strange Mrs. Crane
Parole, Inc.
The Saxon Charm
Marshal of Amarillo
49: Grand Canyon
The Judge
Knock on Any Door
53: The Girl Next Door
54: The Great Diamond
Robbery
Monte Carlo Baby
56: Meet Me in Las Vegas
57: The Helen Morgan Story
58: The Defiant Ones
59: Never Steal Anything
Small
63: The Man from the
Diner's Club

Chili Williams
1947: Copacabana
Gas House Kids Go West
Heartaches
48: Assigned to Danger
Raw Deal

Emlyn Williams (1905-
1932: The Case of the
Frightened Lady

35: Roadhouse
38: The Citadel
40: The Last Days of Dolwyn
(writ., act., dir.)
41: Major Barbara
50: 3 Husbands
51: The Scarf
The Magic Box
52: Another Man's Poison
Ivanhoe
55: The Deep Blue Sea
58: I Accuse!
59: Web of Evidence
The Wreck of the Mary
Deare
Beyond this Place
63: The L-Shaped Room
67: Eye of the Devil
69: The Walking Stick
David Copperfield (TV)

Esther Williams (1923-
1942: Andy Hardy's Double Life
Andy Hardy Steps Out
43: A Guy Named Joe
44: Bathing Beauty
45: Thrill of a Romance
46: Ziegfeld Follies
Hoodlum Saint
Easy to Wed
47: This Time for Keeps
Fiesta
48: On an Island with You
49: Take Me Out to the Ball
Game
Neptune's Daughter
50: Pagan Love Song
Duchess of Idaho
51: Texas Carnival
Callaway Went Thataway
(cameo)
52: Skirts Ahoy!
Million Dollar Mermaid
53: Dangerous When Wet
Easy to Love
55: Jupiter's Darling
56: The Unguarded Moment
58: Raw Wind in Eden
61: The Big Show

Grant Williams (1930-
1957: The Incredible Shrinking
Man

1419

57: The Monolith Monsters	Gun Play
59: Lone Texan	Powdersmoke Range
60: 13 Fighting Men	The Littlest Rebel
The Leech Woman	Miss Pacific Fleet
61: Susan Slade	36: Muss 'em Up!
62: The Couch	Grand Jury
63: PT-109	The Big Game

Guinn "Big Boy" Williams
(1899-1962)

1928: My Man PT	Kelly the 2nd
Lucky Star	End of the Trail
29: Noah's Ark PT	North of Nome
Forward Pass	Career Woman
From Headquarters PT	The Vigilantes Are
30: Big Fight	Coming (ser.)
The Bad Man	37: You Only Live Once
College Lovers	A Star Is Born
Liliom	Don't Tell the Wife
31: The Great Meadow	The Singing Marine
Bachelor Father	Dangerous Holiday
Catch As Catch Can	She's No Lady
War Mamas	Big City
32: Ladies of the Jury	My Dear Miss Aldrich
Polly of the Circus	Wise Girl
Drifting Souls	38: Everybody's Doing It
70,000 Witnesses	Bad Man of Brimstone
You Said a Mouthful	Army Girl
Ladies of the Jury	Down in Arkansas
The Devil Is Driving	You and Me
33: Heritage of the Desert	Professor, Beware!
Phantom Broadcast	Hold that Coed!
Man of the Forest	I Demand Payment
College Coach	Flying Fists
Laughing at Life	The Marines Are Here
34: Rafter Romance	Crashing Through
Joe Palooka	39: Pardon Our Nerve
Mystery Squadron (ser.)	Dodge City
Half a Sinner	6000 Enemies
Flirtation Walk	Blackmail
Romance in the Rain	Fugitive at Large
Thunder over Texas	Street of Missing Men
Here Comes the Navy	Mutiny on the Blackhawk
a short	Legion of Lost Flyers
The Cheaters	Badlands
Silver Streak	40: The Fighting 69th
35: One in a Million	Castle on the Hudson
Cowboy Holiday	Virginia City
Private Worlds	Money and the Woman
The Glass Key	Santa Fe Trail
Village Talk	Alias the Deacon
Society Fever	Dulcy
	Wagons Westward
	41: 6 Lessons from Madame
	La Zonga

41: Country Fair
    Billy the Kid
    You'll Never Get Rich
    Swamp Water
    The Bugle Sounds
42: Mr. Wise Guy
    Silver Queen
    American Empire
    Between Us Girls
    Lure of the Islands
43: The Desperadoes
    Minesweeper
    Buckskin Frontier
    30 Seconds over Tokyo
    Hands Across the Border
44: Belle of the Yukon
    Swing in the Saddle
    Song of the Prairie
    Nevada
    The Cowboy and the
      Señorita
    The Cowboy Canteen
45: The Man Who Walked
      Alone
    Rhythm Roundup
    Sing Me a Song of Texas
46: Cowboy Blues
    Singing on the Trail
    Throw a Saddle on a Star
    That Texas Jubilee
47: King of the Wild Horses
    Singin' in the Corn
    Road to the Big House
48: Station West
    Bad Men of Tombstone
49: Brimstone
50: Hoedown
    Rocky Mountain
51: Al Jennings of Oklahoma
    Man in the Saddle
52: Springfield Rifle
    Hangman's Knot
54: Southwest Passage
    Outlaw's Daughter
56: Hidden Guns
    The Man from Del Rio
57: The Hired Gun
60: The Alamo
62: The Comancheros

Guy Williams (1926-
1952: Bonzo Goes to College

53: The Mississippi Gambler
55: 7 Angry Men
    Sincerely Yours
    The Last Frontier
57: I Was a Teenage Werewolf
60: The Sign of Zorro
62: Damon and Pythias
    The Prince and the
      Pauper
63: Captain Sinbad

John Williams (1903-
1948: A Woman's Vengeance
51: Turpin's Ride
54: Sabrina
    The Student Prince
    Dial M for Murder
55: To Catch a Thief
56: Solid Gold Cadillac
    D-Day, the 6th of June
57: Island in the Sun
    Will Success Spoil Rock
      Hunter?
    Witness for the
      Prosecution
59: The Young Philadelphians
60: Midnight Lace
    Visit to a Small Planet
64: Erasmus with Freckles
65: Dear Brigitte
    None but the Brave
    John Goldfarb, Please
      Come Home
    Harlow (Magna.)
66: The Last of the Secret
      Agents
67: Double Trouble
68: The Secret War of Harry
      Frigg
69: A Flea in Her Ear

Kathlyn Williams (1888-1960)
1929: Single Man   S
      Single Standard   S
30: Wedding Rings
    Road to Paradise
32: Unholy Love
33: Blood Money
35: Rendezvous at Midnight

Rhys Williams (1892-1969)
1941: How Green Was My Valley

1421

42: Remember Pearl Harbor
Cairo
Random Harvest
Eagle Squadron
Gentleman Jim
43: No Time for Love
45: The Corn Is Green
You Came Along
Blood on the Sun
The Bells of St. Mary's
46: Voice of the Whistler
The Spiral Staircase
So Goes My Love
Strange Woman
47: If Winter Comes
Moss Rose
Cross My Heart
Easy Come, Easy Go
The Farmer's Daughter
Imperfect Lady
The Trouble with Women
48: 10th Avenue Angel
Hills of Home
Black Arrow
49: Fighting Man of the Plains
Inspector General
The Crooked Way
Bad Boy
Tokyo Joe
50: The Devil's Doorway
Kiss Tomorrow Goodbye
Tyrant of the Sea
The Showdown
One Too Many
California Passage
51: Sword of Monte Cristo
The Light Touch
The Law and the Lady
Son of Dr. Jekyll
Never Trust a Gambler
Lightning Strikes Twice
Million Dollar Pursuit
52: Okinawa
Mutiny
The World in His Arms
Carbine Williams
Les Miserables
Meet Me at the Fair
53: Scandal at Scourie
Julius Caesar
Bad for Each Other
54: Man in the Attic

The Black Shield of
Falworth
Johnny Guitar
There's No Business Like
Show Business
55: Battle Cry
Many Rivers to Cross
The King's Thief
The Scarlet Coat
The Kentuckian
How to be Very, Very
Popular
56: Mohawk
The Fastest Gun Alive
The Boss
The Desperadoes Are in
Town
57: Nightmare
The Restless Breed
Raintree County
58: Merry Andrews
60: Midnight Lace
65: The Sons of Katie Elder
66: Our Man Flint

Roger Williams
1935: Rustlers' Paradise
Fighting Pioneers
Texas Rambler
Wagon Trail
Code of the Mounted
Vanishing Riders
Toll of the Desert
Saddle Aces
Trails of the Wild
Gun Play
Social Error
Adventurous Knights
Wanted Men
Border Patrol
The Last of the Clintons
Ghost Town
Cheyenne Kincaid
Code of the Desert
The Pecos Kid
Timber War
Men of Action
Gun Smoke over Guadalupe
The Arizona Wrangler
6 Gun Justice
Riding On
Branded a Coward

1422

35: Alias John Law
No Man's Range
The Fighting Coward
36: Frontier Justice
Song of the Trail
The Millionaire Kid
Desert Justice
The Last Assignment
The Cattle Thief
Wildcat Trooper
The Riding Avenger
Men of the Plains
Ambush Valley
Stormy Trails
37: Aces Wild
Guns in the Dark
Come on, Cowboys!
Riders of the Whistling
Skull
Heroes of the Alamo
38: Code of the Rangers
Call of the Mesquiteers
Heroes of the Hills
39: Mountain Rhythm
59: Zorro Rides Again
62: Swingin' Along

Foy Willing
1950: Twilight in the Sierras
Bells of Coronado
Trigger, Jr.
Sunset in the West
North of the Great Divide
Trail of Robin Hood
51: Heart of the Rockies
Spoilers of the Plains
Disc Jockey

Dave Willock
1939: Legion of Lost Flyers
41: Never Give a Sucker an
Even Break
42: The Fleet's In
Priorities on Parade
Lucky Jordan
43: Let's Face It
Princess O'Rourke
The Gang's All Here
44: Pin-Up Girl
She's a Sweetheart
Wing and a Prayer

45: Pride of the Marines
Spellbound
This Love of Ours
46: Joe Palooka--Champ
The Runaround
47: The Fabulous Dorseys
Stork Bites Man
48: So This Is New York
49: Chicago Deadline
50: Belle of Old Mexico
Louisa
51: Call Me Mister
Rodeo
Let's Go, Navy!
52: Flat Top
Jet Job
Battle Zone
53: It Came from Outer Space
55: Revenge of the Creature
57: The Buster Keaton Story
58: Queen of Outer Space
59: 10 Seconds to Hell
62: Whatever Happened to
Baby Jane?
63: Wives and Lovers
Four for Texas
64: Send Me No Flowers
65: Hush, Hush, Sweet
Charlotte

Chill Wills (1903-
1935: Bar-20 Rides Again
36: The Call of the Prairie
37: Way Out West
38: Lawless Valley
39: Arizona Legion
Sorority House
Racketeers of the Range
Timber Stampede
Allegheny Uprising (or,
The First Rebel)
Trouble in Sundown
40: Boom Town
Sky Murder
The Westerner
Tugboat Annie Sails Again
41: Western Union
The Bad Man (or, Two-Gun
Cupid)
Billy the Kid
Belle Starr

41: Honky Tonk
The Bugle Sounds
42: Tarzan's New York
Adventure
Her Cardboard Lover
Apache Trail
The Omaha Trail
Stand By for Action
43: Best Foot Forward
A Stranger in Town
44: See Here, Private Har-
grove!
The Honest Thief
Barbary Coast Gent
Meet Me in St. Louis
Sunday Dinner for a
Soldier
I'll be Seeing You
45: Leave Her to Heaven
What Next, Corporal
Hargrove?
46: Gallant Bess
The Harvey Girls
The Yearling
47: Heartaches
48: That Wonderful Urge
The Sainted Sisters
Family Honeymoon
Loaded Pistols
The Saxon Charm
Northwest Stampede
49: Tulsa
Red Canyon
Francis Series (voice of
horse)
50: Rio Grande
Rock Island Trail (or,
Transcontinent Express)
High Lonesome
The Sundowners (or,
Thunder in the Dust)
51: Oh! Susannah
Cattle Drive
Sea Hornet
Francis Goes to the Races
52: Bronco Buster
Ride the Man Down
Francis Goes to West
Point
53: Small Town Girl
The City that Never
Sleeps

The Man from the Alamo
Francis Covers Big Town
54: Tumbleweed
Francis Joins the Wacs
Ricochet Romance
55: Hell's Outpost
Timberjack
Francis in the Navy
56: Kentucky Rifle
Giant
Santiago
Francis in the Haunted
House
57: Gun for a Coward
Gun Glory
58: From Hell to Texas
The Manhunt
59: The Sad Horse
60: The Alamo
61: Gold of the 7 Saints
Where the Boys Are
The Deadly Companions
The Little Shepherd of
Kingdom Come
62: Young Guns of Texas
63: The Wheeler Dealers
McLintock!
The Cardinal
65: The Rounders
66: Fireball 500
69: Big Daddy
The Liberation of Lord
Byron Jones

Charles C. Wilson
1934: Harold Teen
Miss Kane's Baby Is
Stolen
I've Got Your Number
Circus Clown
Fog over Frisco
The Human Side
The Lemon Drop Kid
St. Louis Kid
35: The Gilded Lily
Behold My Wife
Port of Lost Dreams
The Perfect Clue
4 Hours to Kill
Men of the Hour
The Nitwits
The Glass Key

35: Smart Girl
Fighting Youth
The Case of the Lucky
 Legs
Music Is Magic
Public Menace
Show Them No Mercy
Another Face
Hitchhike Lady
36: Strike Me Pink
The Return of Jimmy
 Valentine
We're Only Human
Panic on the Air
The Mine with the Iron
 Door
Showboat
Educating Father
Ticket to Paradise
Earthworm Tractors
Down the Stretch
I'd Give My Life
Satan Met a Lady
The Gentleman from
 Louisiana
Grand Jury
The Magnificent Brute
Legion of Terror
Mind Your Own Business
37: They Wanted to Marry
Woman in Distress
Murder Goes to College
Find the Witness
The Devil Is Driving
Roaring Timber
Partners in Crime
Life Begins in College
Merry-Go-Round of 1938
Charlie Chan on Broadway
The Adventurous Blonde
38: State Police
Sally, Irene, and Mary
When Were You Born?
The 10th Avenue Kid
Little Miss Thoroughbred
Night Hawk
Hold that Coed
39: Fighting Thoroughbreds
Rose of Washington
 Square
Desperate Trails

Hotel for Women
Smashing the Money Ring
Return of Dr. X
The Cowboy Quarterback
40: He Married His Wife
Sandy Is a Lady
The Girl in 313
Knute Rockne--All
 American
Public Deb No. 1
Charter Pilot
41: Face Behind the Mask
Meet John Doe
Federal Fugitives
Broadway Limited
Dressed to Kill
The Officer and the Lady
Blues in the Night
42: Lady Gangster
Rings on Her Fingers
Escape from Crime
43: Silver Spurs
2 Señoritas from Chicago
44: The Big Noise
Hey, Rookie!
Kansas City Kitty
Shadows in the Night
45: Weekend at the Waldorf
46: Blonde for a Day
Bringing Up Father
Crime of the Century
The Gas House Kids
If I'm Lucky
I Ring Doorbells
Larceny in Her Heart
Passkey to Danger
47: Her Husband's Affair
48: Blazing Across the Pecos

Clarence Wilson
1930: Dangerous Paradise
Love in the Rough
31: Front Page
Night Life in Reno
Her Majesty Love
Sea Ghost
32: Amateur Daddy
Winner Take All
Purchase Price
Jewel Robbery
Down to Earth

1425

32: The Phantom of Crest-
wood
The Penguin Pool Murder
The All-American
33: Mysterious Rider
Smoke Lightning
Terror Abroad
Pick-Up Girl
Girl in 419
Flaming Guns
A Shriek in the Night
Son of Kong
King for a Night
Tillie and Gus
34: I Like it that Way
Love Birds
Unknown Blonde
Now I'll Tell
The Old-Fashioned Way
Bachelor Bait
Count of Monte Cristo
Successful Failure
The Lemon Drop Kid
Wake Up and Dream
I'll Fix It
35: Ruggles of Red Gap
When a Man's a Man
The Great Hotel Murder
Let 'em Have It!
One Frightened Night
Champagne for Breakfast
Waterfront Lady
36: Little Miss Nobody
Love Begins at 20
Rainbow on the River
Hats Off
The Case of the Black
Cat
37: 2 Wise Maids
Damaged Goods
The Westland Case
Small Town Boy

Dooley Wilson (1895-
1942: Casablanca
Night in New Orleans
Take a Letter, Darling
Cairo
43: Stormy Weather
2 Tickets to London
Higher and Higher

44: 7 Days Ashore
48: Racing Luck
49: Free for All
Come to the Stable
51: Passage West

Lois Wilson (1898-
1929: Conquest
Object: Alimony
The Gamblers
Show of Shows
Miss Information
Kid Gloves
Wedding Rings
30: Lovin' the Ladies
The Furies
Temptation
Once a Gentleman
31: Seed
Age of Love
32: The Expert
Divorce in the Family
Law and Order
Drifting Souls
The Crash
The Devil Is Driving
Rider of Death Valley
Secrets of Wu Sin
33: Obey the Law
Laughing at Life
The Deluge
Female
34: In the Money
No Greater Glory
Show-Off
School of Girls
There's Always Tomorrow
Ticket to a Crime
Bright Eyes
35: Life Returns
Public Opinion
Cappy Ricks Returns
Born to Gamble
Society Fever
36: The Return of Jimmy
Valentine
Wedding Present
37: Laughing at Trouble
39: Bad Little Angel
For Love or Money
40: Nobody's Children

1426

41: For Beauty's Sake
49: The Girl from Jones
    Beach

Marie Wilson (1917-
1934: Babes in Toyland
      My Girl Sally
35: Broadway Hostess
    Slide, Kelly, Slide
    Miss Pacific Fleet
    Stars over Broadway
36: Colleen
    Satan Met a Lady
    The Great Ziegfeld
    The Big Noise
    China Clipper
    King of Hockey
37: Melody for Two
    The Great Garrick
    Without Warning
    Public Wedding
38: Boys Meets Girl
    Fools for Scandal
    Broadway Musketeers
    The Invisible Menace
39: Should Husbands Work?
    The Sweepstakes Winner
    The Cowboy Quarterback
    Waterfront
41: Virginia
    Rookie Parade
    Flying Blind
42: Harvard, Here I Come
    Broadway
    She's in the Army
44: Shine on Harvest Moon
    You Can't Ration Love
    Music for Millions
46: No Leave, No Love
    Young Widow
47: Linda be Good
    Fabulous Joe
    The Private Affairs of
    Bel Ami
49: My Friend Irma
50: My Friend Irma Goes
    West
52: A Girl in Every Port
53: Never Wave at a Wac
    Marry Me Again
57: The Story of Mankind

62: Mr. Hobbs Takes a
    Vacation

Terry Wilson (1923-
1966: The Plainsman
67: The War Wagon
69: A Man Called Gannon

Tom Wilson (1880-
1929: Strong Boy   SSE
30: Darkened Skies
    The Big House
    Big Boy
31: Vice Squad
    Sooky
33: Blondie Johnson
    Picture Snatcher
    Silk Express
    The Chief
36: Early to Bed
    Love Begins at 20
    Treachery Rides the Range
37: The Captain's Kid
40: Devil's Island
    Always a Bride
55: The Tall Men
    View from Pompey's
    Head
56: Edge of Hell

Marek Windheim (1895-1960)
1937: I'll Take Romance
39: Ninotchka
    On Your Toes
41: Marry the Boss's Daughter
42: Holiday Inn
43: Mission to Moscow
    Hi Diddle Diddle
44: In Our Time
    Allergic to Love
    Mrs. Parkington
    Kismet
    Our Hearts Were Young
    and Gay
46: Tarzan and the Leopard
    Woman

William Windom (1923-
1962: To Kill a Mockingbird
63: Cattle King
    For Love or Money

64: One Man's Way
     The Americanization
     of Emily
67: The Detective
     Hour of the Gun
68: Prescription: Murder
     The Angry Breed
     The Gypsy Moths
     The Red Kitchen Murder
69: UMC (TV pilot)

Claire Windsor (1897-
1929: Captain Lash   SSE
     Midstream   PT
33: Sister to Judas
     Self Defense
     Constant Woman
34: Cross Streets
38: Barefoot Boy
45: How Do You Do?

Marie Windsor (1922-
1947: Song of the Thin Man
48: Force of Evil
     All-American Co-Ed
49: Hellfire
     The Fighting Kentuckian
     Outpost in Morocco
50: Dakota Lil
     The Showdown
     Frenchie
     Double Deal
51: Hurricane Island
     Little Big Horn (or,
     The Fighting 7th)
     Two Dollar Bettor
52: The Narrow Margin
     The Jungle
     Outlaw Women
     The Sniper
     Japanese War Bride
53: The Eddie Cantor Story
     Trouble Along the Way
     The Tall Texan
     The City that Never
     Sleeps
54: Hell's Half Acre
     Bounty Hunter
55: Abbott & Costello Meet
     the Mummy
     The Silver Star

No Man's Woman
56: The Killing
     2 Gun Lady
     The Cruel Swamp (or,
     Swamp Woman)
57: The Story of Mankind
     Unholy Wife
     The Girl in the Black
     Stockings
     The Parson and the
     Outlaw
58: Day of the Bad Man
     Island Women
63: Critic's Choice
     The Day Mars Invaded
     Earth
64: Mail Order Bride (or,
     West of Montana)
     Bedtime Story
66: Chamber of Horrors
69: The Good Guys and the
     Bad Guys

Joan Winfield
1941: Bullets for O'Hara
42: The Gorilla Man
43: Mission to Moscow
     Murder on the Waterfront
44: Hollywood Canteen
     The Adventures of Mark
     Twain
46: A Stolen Life
47: Imperfect Lady
48: Johnny Belinda
54: The Egyptian

Toby Wing
1932: The Kid from Spain
33: 42nd Street
     The Gold Diggers of 1933
     Too Much Harmony
     College Humor
     This Day and Age
34: The Search for Beauty
     Murder at the Vanities
     Come on, Marines!
     Kiss and Make Up
     School for Girls
35: One Hour Late
     Forced Landing
36: Mr. Cinderella

36:	With Love and Kisses	43:	Coney Island
37:	The Women Men Marry		A Lady Takes a Chance
	Sing While You're Able		Flesh and Fantasy
	Sing, Sinner, Sing!		Hers to Hold
	True Confession	44:	Broadway Rhythm
38:	Mr. Boggs Steps Out		Belle of the Yukon
	Silk and Saddle		Sunday Dinner for a
			Soldier

Charles Winninger (1884-1969)
1930: Soup to Nuts
31: Bad Sister
Gambling Daughters
The Devil Was Sick
Night Nurse
Flying High
God's Gift to Women
Fighting Caravans
Gun Smoke
Children of Dreams
The Sin of Madelon
Claudet
32: Husband's Holiday
34: Social Register
36: Show Boat
White Fang
37: Dancing for Love
3 Smart Girls
You're a Sweetheart
Woman Chases Man
Nothing Sacred
Cafe Metropole
You Can't Have
Everything
The Go Getter
Every Day's a Holiday
38: Goodbye Broadway
Hard to Get
39: 3 Smart Girls Grow Up
Destry Rides Again
Babes in Arms
Barricade
40: If I Had My Way
My Love Came Back
Beyond Tomorrow
Little Nellie Kelly
When Lovers Meet
41: Ziegfeld Girl
The Get-Away
My Life with Caroline
Pot O' Gold
42: Friendly Enemies

45: She Wouldn't Say Yes
State Fair
46: Lover Come Back
47: Living in a Big Way
Something in the Wind
48: Inside Story
Give My Regards to
Broadway
50: Father Is a Bachelor
53: The Sun Shines Bright
Torpedo Alley
The Perilous Journey
Champ for a Day
55: Las Vegas Shakedown
60: Raymie

Dick Winslow (1915-
1931: Seed
32: So Big
Tom Brown of Culver
Laughter in Hell
34: There's Always Tomorrow
One Exciting Adventure
35: Mutiny on the Bounty
42: 10 Gentlemen from West
Point
43: Is Everybody Happy?
48: French Leave
55: The Benny Goodman Story
56: Francis in the Haunted
House
61: Everything's Ducky
62: Twist All Night
65: Do Not Disturb
67: Riot on Sunset Strip
69: The Wrecking Crew
Airport

George "Foghorn" Winslow (1946-
1952: Monkey Business
My Pal Gus
Room for One More
53: Mr. Scoutmaster

53: Gentlemen Prefer
      Blondes
54: The Rocket Man
55: Artists and Models
56: Rock, Pretty Baby
58: Summer Love
      Wild Heritage

Jonathan Winters (1925-
1961: Alakazam the Great
         (cartoon voice)
  63: It's a Mad Mad Mad Mad
         World
  65: The Loved One
  66: The Russians Are Coming,
         The Russians Are Coming!
         Penelope
  67: 8 on the Lam
         Oh Dad, Poor Dad,
         Mama's Hung You in the
         Closet and I'm Feeling
         So Sad
  68: Now You See it, Now
         You Don't (TV)
  69: Viva Max!

Roland Winters (1904-
1946: 13 Rue Madeleine
  47: The Chinese Ring
  48: Return of October
         Cry of the City
         The Golden Eye
         The Feathered Serpent
  49: Once More My Darling
         Abbott & Costello Meet
         the Killer, Boris Karloff
         Tuna Clipper
         Sky Dragons
         A Dangerous Profession
         Guilty of Treason
         Malaya
  50: The West Point Story
         Captain Carey, U.S.A.
         Convicted
         Killer Shark
         To Please a Lady
         Between Midnight and
         Dawn
  51: Follow the Sun
         Inside Straight
         Raton Pass

Sierra Passage
52: She's Working Her Way
      Through College
53: So Big
56: Bigger than Life
57: Jet Pilot
      Top Secret Affair
59: Never Steal Anything
      Small
60: Cash McCall
61: Alakazam the Great
      (cartoon voice)
      Everything's Ducky
      Blue Hawaii
62: Follow that Dream

Shelley Winters (1922-
1943: What a Woman!
  44: The Racket Man
      Cover Girl
      2-Man Submarine
      She's a Soldier Too
      9 Girls
      Sailor's Holiday
      Soldiers in Slacks
      Knickerbocker Holiday
  45: Tonight and Every Night
      A 1000 and One Nights
  47: The Gangster
      Red River
      Living in a Big Way
  48: A Double Life
      Cry of the City
      Larceny
  49: The Great Gatsby
      Take One False Step
      Johnny Stool Pigeon
  50: South Sea Sinner
      Winchester 73
      Frenchie
  51: A Place in the Sun
      He Ran All the Way
      Behave Yourself!
      The Raging Tide
  52: Meet Danny Wilson
      Phone Call from a
      Stranger
      Untamed Frontier
      My Man and I
  54: Tennessee Champ
      Executive Suite

1430

54: Saskatchewan
   Playgirl
55: Mambo
   Night of the Hunter
   I Am a Camera
   Jagged Edges
   The Big Knife
   The Treasure of Pancho
   Villa
   I Died a 1000 Times
56: Cash on Delivery
59: The Diary of Anne Frank
   (OSCAR)
   Odds Against Tomorrow
60: Let No Man Write My
   Epitaph
61: The Young Savages
62: Lolita
   The Chapman Report
63: The Balcony
   Wives and Lovers
64: A House Is Not a Home
65: The Greatest Story Ever
   Told
   A Patch of Blue (OSCAR)
   Time of Indifference
66: Alfie
   Harper
67: Enter Laughing
68: Wild in the Streets
   The Scalphunters
   Buona Sera, Mrs.
   Campbell
69: The Mad Room
   The Man Who Killed
   Himself
   Let Me Count the Ways
   Arthur! Arthur!
   Bloody Mama

Jane Winton (1908-1959)
1929: Captain Lash   SSE
   Bridge of San Luis
   Rey   PT
   Scandal   PT
30: In the Next Room
   The Furies
   Hell's Angels
34: Hired Wife

Estelle Winwood (1883-
1934: The House of Trent

37: Quality Street
55: The Glass Slipper
56: The Swan
   23 Paces to Baker Street
58: This Happy Feeling
59: Darby O'Gill and the
   Little People
61: The Misfits
62: The Magic Sword (voice)
   The Notorious Landlady
   The Cabinet of Dr. Caligari
   Alive and Kicking
64: Dead Ringer
67: Camelot
   Games
68: The Producers
69: And Jenny Makes 3

Norman Wisdom (1920-
1953: Trouble in Store
54: One Good Turn
56: Up in the World
58: Just My Luck
59: Follow a Star
   The Square Peg
60: There Was a Crooked Man
61: The Bulldog Breed
62: On the Beat
63: A Stitch in Time
65: The Early Bird
66: Press for Time
68: The Night They Raided
   Minsky's
69: What's Good for the Goose

Joseph Wiseman (1918-
1950: With These Hands
51: Detective Story
   Viva Zapata!
   Les Miserables
53: Champ for a Day
54: The Silver Chalice
55: The Prodigal
   Mella (doc. narr.)
57: 3 Brave Men
   The Garment Jungle
   Eliahu (doc. narr.)
60: The Unforgiven
62: The Happy Thieves
63: Dr. No
67: The Outsider (TV pilot)
68: Bye Bye, Braverman

68: The Night They Raided
    Minsky's
    The Counterfeit Killer
69: Stiletto

Grant Withers (1904-1959)
1929: Greyhound Limited   PT
    Tiger Rose
    Madonna of Avenue A PT
    Show of Shows
    Saturday's Children   PT
    The Time, the Place, and
      the Girl
    In the Headlines
    Hearts in Exile
30: So Long Letty
    Sinners' Holiday
    The Steel Highway
    Soldiers and Women
    Back Pay
    Broken Dishes
    Scarlet Pages
    The Other Tomorrow
    Dancing Sweeties
    The 2nd Floor Mystery
31: Other Men's Women
    Too Young to Marry
    Swanee River
    In Strange Company
    First Aid
32: Red Haired Alibi
    Gambling Sex
33: Secrets of Wu Sin
34: The Red Rider (ser.)
35: Waterfront Lady
    Storm over the Andes
    Rip Roaring Riley
    Hold 'em, Yale!
    Goin' to Town
    The Fighting Marines
     (ser.)
    Ship Cafe
    Valley of Wanted Men
    Society Fever
    Skybound
36: Sky Parade
    Border Flight
    Lady be Careful
    Arizona Raiders
    Let's Sing Again
    Jungle Jim (ser.)

37: Paradise Express
    Bill Cracks Down
    Radio Patrol (ser.)
    Hollywood Roundup
38: Secret of a Treasure
    Island (ser.)
    3 Loves Has Nancy
    Touchdown Army
    Mr. Wong, Detective
    Telephone Operator
    Held for Ransom
39: Irish Luck
    Navy Secrets
    Boys' Dormitory
    Mr. Wong in Chinatown
    Mutiny in the Big House
    Mystery of Mr. Wong
    Daughter of the Tong
40: The Fatal Hour
    Son of the Navy
    On the Spot
    Tomboy
    Doomed to Die
    Phantom of Chinatown
    Men Against the Sky
    The Mexican Spitfire Out
     West
41: Let's Make Music
    Country Fair
    Billy the Kid
    You'll Never Get Rich
    Swamp River
    The Bugle Sounds
    The Get-Away
    Parachute Battalion
    The Masked Rider
42: Northwest Rangers
    Apache Trail
    Between Us Girls
    Woman of the Year
    Lure of the Islands
    Butch Minds the Baby
    Tennessee Johnson
43: In Old Oklahoma
    Alaska Trail
    A Lady Takes a Chance
    Gildersleeve's Bad Day
    Petticoat Larceny
    No Time for Love
44: Silent Partner
    The Yellow Rose of Texas

44: The Girl Who Dared
Goodnight Sweetheart
The Cowboy and the
  Senorita
Cowboy Canteen
The Fighting Seabees
45: Road to Alcatraz
China's Little Devils
Dakota
Bells of Rosarita
The Vampire's Ghost
Utah
Bring on the Girls
Dangerous Partners
46: In Old Sacramento
My Darling Clementine
Affairs of Geraldine
Throw a Saddle on a
  Star
That Texas Jamboree
Singing on the Trail
Cowboy Blues
Singin' in the Corn
47: The Ghost Goes Wild
Gunfighters
The Trespasser
Wyoming
Blackmail
Tycoon
King of the Wild Horses
Over the Santa Fe Trail
48: Bad Men of Tombstone
Station West
Wake of the Red Witch
Fort Apache
Old Los Angeles
The Fighting Kentuckian
Gallant Legion
Daredevils of the Clouds
Sons of Adventure
Angel in Exile
Night Time in Nevada
The Plunderers
Homicide for Three
49: Brimstone
The Last Bandit
Duke of Chicago
Hellfire
50: Tripoli
Rocky Mountain
Rock Island Trail
Bells of Coronado

Trigger, Jr.
The Savage Horde
Rio Grande
Hit Parade of 1951
Hoedown
51: Spoilers of the Plains
The Sea Hornet
Million Dollar Pursuit
Utah Wagon Train
Man in the Saddle
Al Jennings of Oklahoma
52: Hoodlum Empire
Captive of Billy the Kid
Woman of the North
  Country
Oklahoma Annie
Leadville Gunslinger
Tropical Heatwave
Springfield Rifle
Hangman's Knot
53: Fair Wind to Java
Champ for a Day
The Sun Shines Bright
Iron Mountain Trail
54: Massacre Canyon
Southwest Passage
Outlaw's Daughter
55: Run for Cover
Lady Godiva
56: The White Squaw
Hidden Guns
The Man from Del Rio
57: Hell's Crossroads
The Last Stagecoach West
The Hired Gun
58: I, Mobster

Jane Withers (1927-
1933: Handle with Care
34: Bright Eyes
35: Ginger
This Is the Life
The Farmer Takes a Wife
Paddy O'Day
36: Gentle Julia
Little Miss Nobody
Pepper
Can This be Dixie?
37: The Holy Terror
Angel's Holiday
Wild and Woolly
45 Fathers

37: Checkers
38: Rascals
Keep Smiling
Always in Trouble
Arizona Wildcat
39: Chicken Wagon Family
The Boy Friend
Pack Up Your Troubles
High School
40: Shooting High
Girl from Avenue A
Youth Will be Served
41: Golden Hoofs
A Very Young Lady
Her First Beau
Small Town Deb
42: Johnny Doughboy
The Mad Martindales
43: The North Star
44: My Best Gal
Faces in the Fog
45: Dangerous Partners
46: Affairs of Geraldine
47: Danger Street
56: Giant
61: The Right Approach
63: Captain Newman, M.D.

Cora Witherspoon (1890-1957)
1931: Night Angel
Peach O'Reno
32: Ladies of the Jury
34: Gambling
Midnight
35: Frankie and Johnnie
36: Libeled Lady
Piccadilly Jim
37: Quality Street
Personal Property
On the Avenue
Dangerous Number
The Big Shot
Madame X
Beg Borrow or Steal
38: He Couldn't Say No
3 Loves Has Nancy
Port of 7 Seas
Professor, Beware!
Marie Antoinette
Just Around the Corner
39: Woman Doctor

Dark Victory
Dodge City
For Love or Money
The Women
40: Charlie Chan's Murder
Cruise
I Was an Adventuress
The Bank Dick
43: Follies Girl
45: Over 21
Col. Effingham's Raid
This Love of Ours
46: I've Always Loved You
Dangerous Business
Young Widow
51: The Mating Season
52: Just for You
The First Time

Bill Wolfe
1936: Poppy
40: The Bank Dick
44: Follow the Boys

Ian Wolfe (c1888-
1934: The Barretts of Wimpole
Street
The Fountain
35: Clive of India
The Raven
Mad Love
Mutiny on the Bounty
$1000 a Minute
36: The Leavenworth Case
The Bold Caballero
37: The Prince and the Pauper
The Devil Is Driving
The Emperor's Candle-
sticks
Conquest
38: Arsene Lupin Returns
Orphans of the Street
39: Fast and Loose
Society Lawyer
On Borrowed Time
Allegheny Uprising
The Great Commandment
40: Earthbound
We Who Are Young
Hudson's Bay
42: Secret Agent of Japan

1434

42: Bombs over Burma
Nightmare
Holy Matrimony
The Falcon and the Coeds
The Song of Bernadette
43: The Moon Is Down
44: The Impostor
7 Days Ashore
The Invisible Man's
Revenge
Are These Our Parents?
Her Primitive Man
The Pearl of Death
The Merry Monahans
The Scarlet Claw
Murder in the Blue Room
45: Zombies on Broadway
The Brighton Strangler
Counter-Attack
Blonde Ransom
Love Letters
Confidential Agent
The Fighting Guardsman
47: Three Strangers
Tomorrow Is Forever
Bedlam
The Notorious Lone Wolf
The Searching Wind
The Bandit of Sherwood
Forest
Gentleman Joe Palooka
The Falcon's Adventure
That Way with Women
The Marauders
48: Mr. Blanding Builds His
Dream House
The Twisted Road
Julia Misbehaves
Johnny Belinda
Angel in Exile
49: The Judge Steps Out
Colorado Territory
The Younger Brothers
Joe Palooka in The
Counterpunch
50: Please Believe Me
Copper Canyon
The Petty Girl
The Magnificent Yankee
51: Mask of the Avenger
On Dangerous Ground
52: The Captive City

53: Scandal at Scourie
Houdini
Julius Caesar
The Actress
99 River Street
54: About Mrs. Leslie
7 Brides for 7 Brothers
Her 12 Men
The Steel Cage
The Silver Chalice
55: Moonfleet
The King's Thief
Rebel Without a Cause
Sincerely Yours
The Court-Martial of
Billy Mitchell
Diane
56: Gaby
57: Witness for the Prosecution
60: Pollyanna
The Lost World
61: All in a Night's Work
62: The Wonderful World of
the Brothers Grimm
63: The Diary of a Madman
64: One Man's Way
67: Games

Sir Donald Wolfit (1902-
1932: Ringer
Isn't Life Wonderful?
34: Death at Broadcasting
House
40: Hyde Park Corner
47: Guilty
5?: The Black Judge
52: Pickwick Papers
54: Svengali
55: Prize of Gold
56: Satellites in the Sky
57: The Man in the Road
The Traitor (or, The
Accursed)
58: I Accuse!
Blood of the Vampire
The Accursed
59: Room at the Top
The Angry Hills
The House of the 7 Hawks
Portrait of a Sinner (or,
The Rough and the Smooth)
61: The Mark

1435

62: Lawrence of Arabia
64: Dr. Crippen
    Becket
65: Hands of Orlac
    Life at the Top
67: 90 in the Shade
68: The Sandwich Man
    Charge of the Light
      Brigade
    Decline and Fall

Louis Wolheim (1883-1931)
1929: Wolf Song   PT
      Shady Lady   PT
      Square Shoulders   PT
      Condemned
      Frozen Justice
  30: All Quiet on the Western
        Front
      Ship from Shanghai
      Danger Lights
      The Silver Horde
  31: Sin Ship
      Gentleman's Fate

Anna May Wong (1907-1961)
1929: Piccadilly   SSE
  30: Wasted Love
      The Flame of Love
  31: Daughter of the Dragon
  32: Shanghai Express
  33: A Study in Scarlet
      Tiger Bay
  34: Chu Chin Chow
      Limehouse Blues
  35: Java Head
  37: Daughter of Shanghai
  38: Dangerous to Know
      When Were You Born?
  39: Island of Lost Men
      King of Chinatown
  41: Ellery Queen's Penthouse
        Mystery
  42: Bombs over Burma
      Lady from Chungking
  49: Impact
  60: Portrait in Black
  61: The Savage Innocents

Lana Wood (1944-
1956: The Searchers

62: 5 Finger Exercise
65: The Girls on the Beach
68: A Dandy in Aspic
    For Singles Only
    Free Grass

Natalie Wood (1938-
1946: Tomorrow Is Forever
      The Bride Wore Boots
  47: Miracle on 34th Street
      The Ghost and Mrs. Muir
  48: Scudda Hoo! Scudda Hay!
      Chicken Every Sunday
  49: Father Was a Fullback
      The Green Promise
  50: Our Very Own
      With All My Love
      No Sad Songs for Me
      The Jackpot
      Never a Dull Moment
  51: The Blue Veil
      Dear Brat
  52: Just for You
      The Rose Bowl Story
  53: The Star
  54: The Silver Chalice
  55: Rebel Without a Cause
      One Desire
  56: Cry in the Night
      G.I. Woman Chasers
      The Searchers
      The Burning Hills
      The Girl He Left Behind
  57: Bombers B-52
  58: Marjorie Morningstar
      Kings Go Forth
  59: Cash McCall
  60: All the Fine Young Cannibals
  61: West Side Story
      Splendor in the Grass
  62: Gypsy
  64: Sex and the Single Girl
      Love with the Proper
        Stranger
  65: The Great Race
  66: Inside Daisy Clover
      Penelope
      This Property Is Condemned
  69: Bob and Carol and Ted and
        Alice

1436

Peggy Wood (1892-
1929: Wonder of Women
  34: Handy Andy
  35: The Right to Live
       Jalna
  37: Call it a Day
       A Star Is Born
  39: The Housekeeper's
       Daughter
  46: The Magnificent Doll
       The Bride Wore Boots
  48: Dream Girl
  60: The Story of Ruth
  65: The Sound of Music

Joan Woodbury (1915-
1935: The Eagle's Brood
       Without Children
       The Fighting Coward
  36: Rogues' Tavern
       Anthony Adverse
       Song of the Gringo
       Last Assignment
       The Lion's Den
  37: Midnight Court
       There Goes My Girl
       Super-Sleuth
       40 Naughty Girls
       Living on Love
       They Gave Him a Gun
       Charlie Chan on Broadway
  38: Night Spot
       Crashing Hollywood
       Algiers
       Cipher Bureau
       Passport Husband
       Always in Trouble
       While New York Sleeps
  39: Chasing Danger
       Mystery of the White Room
  40: Barnyard Follies
  41: In Old Cheyenne
       Ride on, Vaquero!
       King of the Zombies
       Paper Bullets
       I'll Sell My Life
       2 Latins from Manhattan
       I Killed that Man
       Confessions of Boston
         Blackie
       Gangs, Inc.

  42: Shut My Big Mouth
       The Man from Headquarters
       Dr. Broadway
       Sweetheart of the Fleet
       Phantom Killer
       Sunset Serenade
       The Hard Way
       The Living Ghost
       A Yank in Libya
  43: You Can't Beat the Law
       The Desperadoes
       Here Comes Kelly
  44: The Whistler
       The Chinese Cat
  45: Bring on the Girls
       Flame of the West
       10¢ a Dance
       Brenda Starr, Reporter
         (ser.)
       Northwest Trail
  47: The Arnelo Affair
       Yankee Fakir
  48: Here Comes Trouble
  49: Boston Blackie's Chinese
       Venture
  56: The Ten Commandments
  64: The Time Travelers

Donald Woods (1904-
1934: She Was a Lady
       Charlie Chan's Courage
       As the Earth Turns
       Merry Wives of Reno
       Fog over Frisco
  35: Sweet Adeline
       Anna Karenina
       The Florentine Dagger
       The Case of the Curious
         Bride
       Stranded
       The Frisco Kid
       A Tale of Two Cities
       The Story of Louis Pasteur
  36: Road Gang
       Anthony Adverse
       Isle of Fury
       The White Angel
       a short
       A Son Comes Home
  37: Sea Devils
       Once a Doctor

37: Talent Scout
The Case of the Stutter-
ing Bishop
Charlie Chan on Broadway
Big Town Girl
38: The Black Doll
Danger on the Air
Romance on the Run
I Am the Law
39: Beauty for the Asking
The Mexican Spitfire
Heritage of the Desert
The Girl from Mexico
40: City of Chance
Forgotten Girls
If I Had My Way
Love, Honor, and Oh
Baby!
a short
The Mexican Spitfire
Goes West
41: Sky Raiders (ser.)
I Was a Prisoner on
Devil's Island
Bachelor Daddy
42: Through Different Eyes
The Gay Sisters
43: Watch on the Rhine
Corregidor
Hi-Ya, Sailor!
So's Your Uncle
44: The Bridge of San Luis
Rey
The Life of Dr. Paul
Joseph Goebels
Hollywood Canteen
45: Roughly Speaking
God Is My Co-Pilot
Wonder Man
Voice of the Whistler
46: Never Say Goodbye
The Time, the Place, and
the Girl
Night and Day
The Jade Lady
47: Return of Rin-Tin-Tin
Bells of San Fernando
Step-Child
49: Daughter of the West
Scene of the Crime
Free for All
Barbary Pirate

50: Mr. Music
Johnny One-Eye
The Lost Volcano
51: All that I Have
53: The Beast from 20,000
Fathoms
54: Undercover Agent
60: 13 Ghosts
5 Minutes to Live
61: I'll Give My Life
64: Kissin' Cousins
65: Moment to Moment
66: The Satan Bug
Door-to-Door Maniac
67: Tammy and the Millionaire
68: A Time to Sing
Istanbul Express (TV)
69: The Train
True Grit

Harry Woods (1889-1968)

1929:	China Bound	S
	Gun Law	S
	Desert Rider	S
	Phantom Rider	S
	The Viking	S
	Western Skies	
30:	Pardon My Gun	
	Lone Rider	
	'Neath Western Skies	
	Men Without Law	
31:	West of Cheyenne	
	Texas Ranger	
	In Old Cheyenne	
	Monkey Business	
	Palmy Days	
	Range Feud	
32:	Texas Gunfighter	
	Radio Patrol	
	Haunted Gold	
	I Am a Fugitive from a Chain Gang	
	Law and Order	
34:	St. Louis Kid	
	Scarlet Empress	
	The President Vanishes	
	Belle of the '90s	
	School for Girls	
	Shadows of Sing Sing	
	Devil Tiger	
	Circus Clown	
35:	When a Man's a Man	

35: Let 'em Have It!
Robin Hood of El Dorado
Ship Cafe
Heir to Trouble
36: The Plainsman
Rose of the Rancho
The Lawless '90s
Heroes of the Range
Silly Billies
Human Cargo
Ticket to Paradise
The Unknown Ranger
Conflict
37: I Promise to Pay
Outcast
Range Defenders
Courage of the West
38: The Buccaneer
Hawaiian Buckaroo
The Arizona Wildcat
Come on, Rangers!
Panamint's Bad Man
Blockheads
39: Frontier Marshal
Beau Geste
Union Pacific
Days of Jesse James
Mr. Moto in Danger
Island
Blue Montana Skies
The Man in the Iron
Mask
In Old California
40: South of Pago Pago
Isle of Destiny
Bullet Code
West of Carson City
The Ranger and the Lady
Triple Justice
Meet the Missus
41: Petticoat Politics
Sheriff of Tombstone
Last of the Duanes
42: Today I Hang
Romance on the Range
Down Texas Way
Riders of the West
Deep in the Heart of Texas
West of the Law
Dawn on the Great Divide
Forest Rangers

Reap the Wild Wind
43: Beyond the Last Frontier
Bordertown Gunfighters
Cheyenne Roundup
The Ghost Rider
Outlaws of Stampede Pass
44: Call of the Rockies
Marshal of Gunsmoke
Nevada
Tall in the Saddle
Westward Bound
45: Wanderer of the Wasteland
West of the Pecos
46: My Darling Clementine
47: Wild Rose Mesa
Wyoming
Tycoon
Trail Street
48: Western Heritage
The Gallant Legion
Indian Agent
49: She Wore a Yellow Ribbon
Colorado Territory
The Fountainhead
Hellfire
Masked Raiders
50: Traveling Saleswoman
Short Grass
Law of the Badlands
52: Lone Star
Rancho Notorious

Joanne Woodward (1930-
1955: Count Three and Pray
56: Kiss Before Dying
57: 3 Faces of Eve (OSCAR)
No Down Payment
58: The Long Hot Summer
Rally 'Round the Flag, Boys!
59: The Sound and the Fury
The Fugitive Kind
60: From the Terrace
61: Paris Blues
63: The Stripper
A New Kind of Love
64: Signpost to Murder
66: A Fine Madness
67: Big Hand for the Little
Lady
68: Winning
Rachel, Rachel

69: Hall of Mirrors
40 Carats

Norman Wooland (1910-
1948: Hamlet
Escape
I Know You
49: All Over the Town
Background
51: Angel with a Trumpet
Quo Vadis?
54: Romeo and Juliet
55: The Master Plan
56: Richard III
Teenage Daughter
Guilty
No Road Back
The Bandit
59: Portrait of a Sinner (or,
The Rough and the
Smooth)
The Bandit of Zhobe
Night Train to Inverness
Bad Girl
61: The Guns of Navarone
62: Barabbas
64: Fall of the Roman Empire
65: Saul and David
66: The (Fighting) Prince
of Donegal
Walk in the Shadow
67: The Projected Man

Monty Woolley (1889-1963)
1937: Live Love and Learn
Nothing Sacred
38: Arsene Lupin Returns
Girl of the Golden West
3 Comrades
Lord Jeff
a short
Everybody Sing!
Artists and Models Abroad
Young Dr. Kildare
39: Never Say Die
Man about Town
Dancing Coed
41: The Man Who Came to
Dinner
42: The Pied Piper
Life Begins at 8:30

43: Holy Matrimony
44: Since You Went Away
Irish Eyes Are Smiling
45: Molly and Me
46: Night and Day
47: The Bishop's Wife
48: Miss Tatlock's Millions
Will You Love Me in
December?
51: As Young as You Feel
55: Kismet

Sheb Wooley
1952: High Noon
Bugles in the Afternoon
Cattle Town
A Sky Full of Moon
54: The Boy from Oklahoma
56: Giant
57: The Black Whip
Trooper Hook
Ride a Violent Mile
58: Terror in a Texas Town

Robert Woolsey: see Bert Wheeler

Frederick Worlock (c1887-
1939: Miracles for Sale
Lady of the Tropics
Balalaika
40: Strange Cargo
Moon over Burma
Murder over New York
South of Suez
Hudson's Bay
Northwest Passage
The Earl of Chicago
The Sea Hawk
41: Rage in Heaven
Man Hunt
Dr. Jekyll and Mr. Hyde
A Yank in the R.A.F.
How Green Was My Valley
International Lady
Free and Easy
42: Pacific Rendezvous
Pierre of the Plains
Eagle Squadron
The Black Swan
London Blackout Murders
Captains of the Clouds

42: Random Harvest
Madero (short)
Pier 29 (short)
43: Air Raid Wardens
Sherlock Holmes Faces
Death
Appointment in Berlin
Thumbs Up
Madame Curie
44: The Lodger
Secrets of Scotland Yard
Jane Eyre
National Velvet
45: Captain Kidd
Fatal Witness
Hangover Square
Pursuit ot Algiers
Scotland Yard Investigator
Woman in Green
The Picture of Dorian
Gray
46: Dressed to Kill
She Wolf of London
Terror by Night
47: The Imperfect Lady
Forever Amber
A Woman's Vengeance
Last of the Redmen
Singapore
The Lone Wolf in London
Love from a Stranger
48: A Double Life
Joan of Arc
Hills of Home
The Woman in White
Johnny Belinda
60: Spartacus
61: 101 Dalmatians (cartoon
voice)
62: The Notorious Landlady
66: Spin-Out

Barbara Worth
1929: Fury of the Wild   S
Plunging Hoofs   S
Bachelor's Club   SSE
Below the Deadline   S
34: Fighting Trooper
35: Men of Action
Racing Luck

Constance Worth (1913-1963)
1937: China Passage
Windjammer
39: Mystery of the White Room
40: The Invisible Killer
Angels over Broadway
The Llano Kid
41: Honky Tonk
Kansas Cyclone
Forced Landing
Cyclone on Horseback
Meet Boston Blackie
Borrowed Hero
43: She Has What it Takes
Klondike Kate
City Without Men
Crime Doctor
The Crime Doctor's
Strangest Case
44: Cyclone Prairie Rangers
Sagebrush Heroes
45: Dillinger
The Kid Sister
Why Girls Leave Home
46: Deadline at Dawn
Sensation Hunters

William Worlthington (d. 1941)
1934: One Exciting Adventure
35: $20 a Week
Keeper of the Bees
36: Can This be Dixie?

Fay Wray (1907-
1929: Thunderbolt
Pointed Heels
4 Feathers   SSE
30: Behind the Makeup
Paramount on Parade
Border Legion
The Texan
The Sea God
31: Captain Thunder
The Lawyer's Secret
Unholy Garden
Dirigible
The Finger Points
The Conquering Horde
Hounds of Zaroff
Not Exactly Gentlemen

32: The Stowaway
Dr. X
Most Dangerous Game
33: Mystery of the Wax
Museum
King Kong
Below the Sea
Tampico
Ann Carver's Profession
The Woman I Stole
Master of Men
Vampire Bat
The Big Brain
One Sunday Afternoon
Shanghai Express
The Bowery
34: Madame Spy
Countess of Monte Cristo
Cheating Cheaters
Affairs of Cellini
Viva Villa!
Black Moon
White Lies
Once to Every Woman
Woman in the Dark
The Captain Hates the Sea
The Richest Girl in the
World
35: Mills of the Gods
Bulldog Jack
The Clairvoyant
Come Out of the Pantry
36: When Nights Were Bold
They Met in a Taxi
Roaming Lady
37: Once a Hero
Murder in Greenwich
Village
It Happened in Hollywood
38: The Jury's Secret
39: Navy Secrets
Smashing the Spy Ring
40: Wildcat Bus
41: Adam Had Four Sons
Melody for Three
42: Not a Ladies' Man
53: Small Town Girl
Treasure of the Golden
Condor
55: Hell on Frisco Bay
Queen Bee
The Cobweb

56: Rock, Pretty Baby
57: Tammy and the Bachelor
Out of Time
Crime of Passion
58: Dragstrip Riot
Summer Love

John Wray
1930: New York Nights
All Quiet on the Western
Front
31: Quick Millions
Silence
Safe in Hell
32: High Pressure
Woman from Monte Carlo
The Miracle Man
The Mouthpiece
The Rich Are Always with
Us
Miss Pinkerton
Doctor X
Central Park
The Match King
33: The Death Kiss
34: Lone Cowboy
Bombay Mail
Big Shakedown
The Crosby Case
The Most Precious Thing
in Life
Love Captive
The Defense Rests
15 Wives
Embarrassing Moments
I'll Fix It
Green Eyes
I Am a Thief
35: The Great Hotel Murder
The Whole Town's Talking
Ladies Love Danger
Stranded
Men Without Names
Atlantic Adventure
Bad Boy
The Frisco Kid
36: Mr. Deeds Goes to Town
Poor Little Rich Girl
A Son Come Home
Sworn Enemy
We Who Are About to Die
The President's Mystery

1442

36: Valiant Is the Word for
Carrie
37: You Only Live Once
Circus Girl
A Man Betrayed
Outcast
The Devil Is Driving
On Such a Night
38: House of Mystery
Making the Headlines
The Black Doll
Gangs of New York
Crime Takes a Holiday
The 10th Avenue Kid
Spawn of the North
A Man to Remember
39: Risky Business
Pacific Liner
Each Dawn I Die
The Amazing Mr.Williams
The Cat and the Canary
Smuggled Cargo
Blackmail
40: The Man from Dakota
Remember the Night

Ben Wright
1955: Prince of Players
The Racers
A Man Called Peter
56: On the Threshold of Space
23 Paces to Baker Street
D-Day, the 6th of June
Johnny Concho
The Power and the Prize
57: Pharaoh's Curse
Kiss Them for Me
58: Desert Hell
Villa!
59: These 1000 Hills
The Wreck of the Mary
Deare
Journey to the Center of
the Earth
61: Operation Bottleneck
Judgment at Nuremberg
62: Mutiny on the Bounty
63: A Gathering of Eagles
65: My Blood Runs Cold
The Sound of Music
66: The Fortune Cookie
67: The Jungle Book (voice)

Teresa Wright (1918-
1941: The Little Foxes
42: The Pride of the Yankees
Mrs. Miniver (OSCAR)
43: Shadow of a Doubt
44: Casanova Brown
45: Those Endearing Young
Charms
46: The Best Years of Our
Lives
Mrs. Loring's Secret
47: Pursued
Trouble with Women
Imperfect Lady
48: Enchantment
50: The Capture
The Men
52: Something to Live for
California Conquest
The Steel Trap
53: Count the Hours
The Actress
54: Track of the Cat
56: The Search for Bridey
Murphy
57: Escapade in Japan
58: The Restless Years
69: The Happy Ending
Hail, Hero!

Will Wright (1891-1962)
1936: China Clipper
39: Silver on the Sage
40: Blondie Plays Cupid
41: The Richest Man in Town
42: The Postman Didn't Ring
Wildcat
Shut My Big Mouth
43: In Old Oklahoma (or, War
of the Wildcats)
Reveille with Beverly
Lucky Legs
Murder in Times Square
Cowboy in Manhattan
45: Salome Where She Danced
Eve Knew Her Apples
Road to Utopia
Gun Smoke
Rhapsody in Blue
Grissly's Millions
The Strange Affair of
Uncle Harry

45: Sleepy Lagoon
46: Bewitched
  Hot Cargo
  The Inner Circle
  Johnny Comes Flying Home
  The Madonna's Secret
  One Exciting Week
  Rendezvous with Annie
47: Blaze of Noon
  Cynthia
  Wild Harvest
  Along the Oregon Trail
  Keeper of the Bees
  Mother Wore Tights
48: Act of Violence
  Act of Murder
  Relentless
  The Inside Story
  Green Grass of Wyoming
  The Twisted Road
  The Walls of Jericho
  Disaster
  Whispering Smith
  California's Golden
    Beginning
  Black Eagle
49: Mrs. Mike
  Lust for Gold
  No Way Out
  Big Jack
  Brimstone
  For Those Who Dare
  Adam's Rib
  Miss Grant Takes Rich-
    mond
50: Ticket to Tomahawk (or,
    The Sheriff's Daughter)
  All the King's Men
  Dallas
  The Las Vegas Story
  Paula
  Lure of the Wilderness
  The House by the River
  The Savage Horde
  Sunset in the West
51: My Forbidden Past
  Vengeance Valley
  Excuse My Dust
  The Tall Target
  People Will Talk
52: O. Henry's Full House
    (The Clarion Call seq.)

53: Niagara
  The Last Posse
54: The Wild One
  Johnny Guitar
  River of No Return
  The Raid
55: The Man with the Golden
    Arm
  Tall Men
  The Court-Martial of Billy
    Mitchell
56: These Wilder Years
57: The Iron Sheriff
  Johnny Tremaine
  The Wayward Bus
58: The Missouri Traveler
  Quantrille's Raiders
  Gunman's Walk
59: Alias Jesse James
  The 30 Foot Bride of
    Candy Rock
61: The Deadly Companions
  20 Plus 2
62: Cape Fear
64: Fail Safe

William Wright (d. 1949)
1941: Rookies on Parade
  Nothing but the Truth
  Glamour Boy
  World Premiere
  The Devil Pays Off
42: True to the Army
  Night in New Orleans
  Sweetheart of the Fleet
  Parachute Nurse
43: A Night to Remember
  Cowboy in Manhattan
  Here Comes Elmer
44: Dancing in Manhattan
  One Mysterious Night
45: Eadie Was a Lady
  Escape in the Fog
  State Fair
46: Down Missouri Way
  Lover Come Back
  The Mask of Dijon
47: Philo Vance Returns
  The Gas House Kids Go
    West
48: King of Gamblers
49: Daughter of the Jungle

1444

49: Rose of the Yukon
Impact
All the King's Men
Air Hostess

Maris Wrixon
1938: Broadway Musketeers
39: Jeepers Creepers
The Private Lives of
Elizabeth and Essex
40: British Intelligence
Flight Angels
The Man Who Talked too
Much
The Ape
41: The Case of the Black
Parrott
Footsteps in the Dark
Million Dollar Baby
A Shot in the Dark
Bullets for O'Hara
Sunset in Wyoming
42: Spy Ship
Sons of the Pioneers
The Old Homestead
43: Woman in Bondage
44: Waterfront
Trail to Gunsight
45: White Pongo
This Love of Ours
The Master Key (ser.)
Black Market Babies
46: The Glass Alibi
Face of Marble
48: Highway 13
51: As You Were

Jane Wyatt (1913-
1934: One More River
Great Expectations
35: We're Only Human
36: The Luckiest Girl in
the World
37: Lost Horizon
40: Girl from God's Country
41: Hurricane Smith
Kisses for Breakfast
Weekend for Three
42: The Navy Comes Through
Army Surgeon
43: Buckskin Frontier

The Kansan
44: None but the Lonely Heart
46: The Bachelor's Daughters
Strange Conquest
47: Boomerang
A Gentleman's Agreement
48: No Minor Vices
Pitfall
49: Bad Boy
Task Force
Canadian Pacific
50: Our Very Own
My Blue Heaven
The Man Who Cheated
Himself
The House by the River
51: Criminal Lawyer
52: Hurricane Smith
57: The Interlude
61: The 2 Little Bears
65: See How They Run
66: Never Too Late

Margaret Wycherly (1881-1956)
1929: The 13th Chair
34: Midnight
38: Wanderlust (short)
40: Victory
41: Sergeant York
42: Crossroads
Random Harvest
Keeper of the Flame
43: The Moon Is Down
Assignment in Brittany
Hangmen Also Die
44: Experiment Perilous
45: Johnny Angel
46: The Yearling
Enchanted Cottage
47: Something in the Wind
Forever Amber
48: Loves of Carmen
49: White Heat
51: The Man with a Cloak
53: The President's Lady
That Man from Tangier

Than Wyenn
1955: Pete Kelly's Blues
Good Morning, Miss Dove
57: The Beginning of the End

Jane Wyatt with Chester Morris
"Girl from God's Country"

57: The Invisible Boy
59: Imitation of Life
60: The Boy and the Pirates
67: Sullivan's Empire
68: Now You See It, Now
    You Don't (TV)

Jane Wyman (1914-
1935: King of Burlesque
36: My Man Godfrey
    Cain and Mabel
    Smart Blonde
    Gold Diggers of 1937
37: Ready, Willing, and Able
    The King and the Chorus
        Girl
    Public Wedding
    The Singing Marine
    Slim
    Mr. Todd Takes the Air
    various shorts
38: He Couldn't Say No
    Spy Ring
    The Crowd Roars
    Brother Rat
    Wide Open Faces
    Fools for Scandal
39: Torchy Plays with
        Dynamite
    Tail Spin
    The Kid from Kokomo
    Kid Nightingale
    Private Detective
40: Brother Rat and a Baby
    Flight Angels
    An Angel from Texas
    My Love Came Back
    Tugboat Annie Sails Again
    Gambling on the High Seas
    Sunday Punch (2 reels)
41: Honeymoon for Three
    The Body Disappears
    Bad Men of Missouri
    You're in the Army Now
42: Larceny, Inc.
    My Favorite Spy
    Footlight Serenade
43: Princess O'Rourke
44: Hollywood Canteen
    The Doughgirls
    Make Your Own Bed

    Crime by Night
45: The Lost Weekend
46: One More Tomorrow
    Night and Day
    The Yearling
47: Cheyenne (or, The
        Wyoming Kid)
    Magic Town
48: Johnny Belinda (OSCAR)
49: Kiss in the Dark
    It's a Great Feeling
    The Lady Takes a Sailor
50: Stage Fright
    Glass Menagerie
51: Starlift
    3 Guys Named Mike
    The Blue Veil
    Here Comes the Groom
52: Just for You
    The Story of Will Rogers
53: Let's Do it Again
    So Big
54: Magnificent Obsession
55: Lucy Gallant (or, Oil
        Town)
    All that Heaven Allows
56: Miracle in the Rain
59: Holiday for Lovers
60: Pollyanna
62: Bon Voyage!
68: How to Commit Marriage

Patrice Wymore (1927-
1950: Tea for Two
    Rocky Mountain
51: I'll See You in My Dreams
    Starlift
52: The Big Trees
    Man Behind the Gun
    She's Working Her Way
        Through College
53: She's Back on Broadway
59: The Sad Horse
60: Ocean's 11
66: Chamber of Horrors

H.M. Wynant
1957: Run for the Arrow
    Decision at Sundown
    Oregon Passage
58: Run Silent, Run Deep

1447

63: It Happened at the World's
    Fair
    The Wheeler Dealers

Ed Wynn (1887-1966)
1930: Follow the Leader
33: The Chief
43: Stage Door Canteen
51: Alice in Wonderland
56: The Great Man
58: Marjorie Morningstar
59: The Diary of Anne Frank
60: Cinderfella
61: The Absent-Minded
    Professor
    Babes in Toyland
63: Son of Flubber
64: The Patsy
    The Sound of Laughter
    (doc. narr.)
    Mary Poppins
    Erasmus with Freckles
    Those Calloways
65: The Greatest Story Ever
    Told
    Dear Brigitte
    That Darn Cat
66: The Daydreamer
67: Warning Shot
    The Gnome-Mobile

Keenan Wynn (1916-
1942: Northwest Rangers
    For Me and My Gal
    Somewhere I'll Find You
43: Lost Angel
44: Gambler's Choice
    See Here, Private Har-
    grove!
    Since You Went Away
    Marriage Is a Private
    Affair
    Between Two Women
45: The Clock
    Without Love
    Weekend at the Waldorf
    What Next, Corporal Har-
    grove?
46: Easy to Web
    No Leave No Love
    The Thrill of Brazil
    Mr. Groggs Returns
    The Cockeyed Miracle
    Ziegfeld Follies

47: The Hucksters
    Song of the Thin Man
    My Dear Secretary
48: B.F.'s Daughter
    The Three Musketeers
    The Red Mill
49: Neptune's Daughter
    That Midnight Kiss
50: Annie Get Your Gun
    Three Little Words
    Love that Brute
51: Royal Wedding
    Kind Lady
    Angels in the Outfield
    It's a Big Country
    Texas Carnival
52: Phone Call from a
    Stranger
    Fearless Fagan
    Sky Full of Moon
    The Belle of New York
    Holiday for Sinners
    Desperate Search
53: Battle Circus
    Code Two
    All the Brothers Were
    Valiant
    Kiss Me Kate
54: The Long, Long Trailer
    Tennessee Champ
    Men of the Fighting Lady
55: The Glass Slipper
    The Marauders
    Running Wild
    Shack Out on 101
56: The Man in the Gray
    Flannel Suit
    The Naked Hills
    Johnny Concho
    The Great Man
    The Rack
57: Joe Butterfly
    The Fuzzy Pink Nightgown
    Don't Go Near the Water
58: Some Came Running
    A Time to Love and a
    Time to Die
    The Perfect Furlough
    The Deep Six
59: A Hole in the Head
    That Kind of Woman

1448

60: The Crowded Sky
Operation Mermaid
61: The Power and the Prize
(TV)
Absent-Minded Professor
King of the Roaring '20s
62: The Scarface Mob
Requiem for a Heavy-
Weight
63: Son of Flubber
64: Stage to Thunder Rock
The Patsy
Honeymoon Hotel
Man in the Middle
Dr. Strangelove
65: Bikini Beach
The Americanization of
Emily
The Great Race
Nightmare in the Sun
66: Promise Her Anything
Around the World Under
the Sea
Stagecoach
The Night of the Grizzly
67: Warning Shot
The War Wagon
Welcome to Hard Times
68: Mackenna's Gold
Point Blank
Run Like a Thief
Finian's Rainbow
The Monitors
Once Upon a Time in the
West
Red Kitchen Murder (TV)
The Last of the
Comancheros
Smith!
Viva Max!
Loving
God Bless You, Uncle
Sam!
80 Steps to Jonah
69: The Magic Pear Tree
(voice)

May Wynn (1930-
1954: The Caine Mutiny
They Rode West
55: The Violent Men

55: The Violent Men
56: This Man Is Armed
The White Squaw
57: Taming Sutton's Girl
The Unknown Terror
58: The Hong Kong Affair

Dana Wynter (1930-
1951: White Corridors
53: Col. March, Investigator
55: The View from Pompey's
Head
56: Invasion of the Body
Snatchers
D-Day, the 6th of June
57: Something of Value
58: Fraulein
In Love and War
59: Shake Hands with the Devil
60: Sink the Bismarck!
61: On the Double
63: The List of Adrian
Messenger
66: Danger Has Two Faces
68: Night Hunt
69: Any Second Now (TV)
If He Hollers, Let Him Go
The Fire Within
Crossroads
Airport

Diana Wynyard (1906-1964)
1932: Rasputin and the Empress
33: Cavalcade
Men Must Fight
Reunion in Vienna
34: Where Sinners Meet
Let's Try Again
Over the River (or,
One More River)
40: On the Night of the Fire
Gaslight
41: Kipps
The Prime Minister
The Feminine Touch
The Voice in the Night
47: The Fugitive
48: An Ideal Husband
51: Tom Brown's School Days
57: Island in the Sun
The Gentle Touch

1449

Frank Yaconelli
1929: Señor Americano
  30: Firebrand Jordan
      Parade of the West
  31: Black Camel
  33: Strawberry Roan
  34: Death Takes a Holiday
  35: The Awakening of Jim
      Burke
      Western Frontier
      Gun Play
  36: Lawless Riders
      Down to the Sea
      The 3 Mesquiteers
      Blazing Justice
      Romance Rides the Range
  37: Wild West Days
      It Could Happen to You
  39: Wild Horse Canyon
      Across the Plains
      Escape to Paradise
  40: The East Side Kids
      Dr. Cyclops
      Pioneer Days
      Wild Horse Range
  41: Forced Landing
      Riding the Sunset Trail
      The Driftin' Kid
      Two in a Taxi
  42: Fiesta
  43: Man of Courage
  46: Slightly Scandalous
      South of Monterey
  47: Beauty and the Bandit
      Riding the California
      Trail
      Wild Horse Mesa
  48: The Dude Goes West
      Madonna of the Desert
  49: Alias the Champ
  50: The Baron of Arizona
      September Affair
  54: Dragon's Gold
  55: The Racers
  56: Serenade

Barton Yarborough (d. 1951)
1941: Let's Go Collegiate
  45: Captain Tugboat Annie
      I Love a Mystery
  46: The Devil's Mask

Red Dragon
The Unknown
Wife Wanted
  47: Kilroy Was Here
  49: Henry the Rainmaker

Dick York (1928-
1955: My Sister Eileen
      3 Steps in the Sun
  57: Operation Mad Ball
  58: Cowboy
      The Last Blitzkrieg
  59: They Came to Cordura
  60: Inherit the Wind

Jeff York (1912-
1945: They Were Expendable
  46: Alias Mr. Twilight
      Little Miss Big
      The Postman Always Rings
      Twice
      Up Goes Maisie
      The Yearling
  47: Fear in the Night
      Blondie's Holiday
  48: Panhandle
      The Paleface
  50: Surrender
      Short Grass
      Kill the Umpire!
      Call of the Klondike
  51: The Lady Says No
  56: The Great Locomotive
      Chase
      Davy Crockett and the
      River Pirates
      Westward Ho, the Wagons!
  57: Johnny Tremaine
      Old Yeller
  63: Savage Sam
  67: Tammy and the Millionaire

Michael York (1941-
1967: The Taming of the Shrew
      Red and Blue
      The Accident
      Confessions of a Loving
      Couple
      Smashing Time
  68: The Strange Affair
      Romeo and Juliet

1450

68: Justine
69: Alfred the Great
The Guru
The Walls Come
Tumbling Down
The Dreamers
The Cook

Susannah York (1942-
1960: Tunes of Glory
There Was a Crooked Man
61: The Greengage Summer
Loss of Innocence
62: Freud (or, The Secret
Passion)
63: Tom Jones
64: The 7th Dawn
Mutiny in Outer Space
65: The Sands of Kalahari
The Doctor and the Devils
66: Kaleidoscope
A Man for All Seasons
68: Sebastian
Lock Up Your Daughters
The Killing of Sister
George
Duffy
69: The Battle of Britain
Oh! What a Lovely War
Country Dance
City Beneath the Sea
Cannon for Cordoba

Edith Yorke (1872-
1929: Fugitives
The Valiant
30: 7 Keys to Baldpate
City Girl
Love Racket

Alan Young (1919-
1946: Margie
48: Chicken Every Sunday
49: Mr. Belvedere Goes to
College
51: Aaron Slick from Punkin
Crick
52: Androcles and the Lion
55: Gentlemen Marry
Brunettes
58: tom thumb

60: The Time Machine
65: Never Too Young

Carleton Young (c1908-
1936: Happy Go Lucky
37: A Man Betrayed
Join the Marines
Get Along, Little Dogies
Navy Blues
Dangerous Holiday
Dick Tracy (ser.)
Young Dynamite
38: The Old Barn Dance
Heroes of the Hills
Cassidy of Bar-20
Gang Bullets
Outlaw Express
39: Convict's Code
Smoky Trail
Port of Hate
El Diablo Rides
40: Pals of the Silver Sage
Gun Code
41: Pride of the Bowery
Billy the Kid's Fighting
Pals
Up in the Air
The Badlands of Dakota
A Missouri Outlaw
Billy the Kid's Roundup
42: Code of the Outlaws
S.O.S. Coast Guard
44: In the Meantime, Darling
Ladies of Washington
Take It or Leave It
45: Abbott & Costello in
Hollywood
Thrill of a Romance
Thunderhead--Son of
Flicka
46: Queen of Burlesque
48: The Kissing Bandit
50: American Guerrilla in the
Philippines
Double Deal
51: Gene Autry and the Mounties
Hard, Fast, and Beautiful
Best of the Bad Men
Fighting Leathernecks
His Kind of Woman
People Will Talk

1451

51: Chain of Circumstance
    The Blue Veil
    The Mob
    The Day the Earth Stood
      Still
    Red Mountain
52: Deadline U.S.A.
    My Six Convicts
    The Brigand
    Battle Zone
    Last of the Comanches
53: Niagara
    The Glory Brigade
    A Blueprint of Murder
    Goldtown Ghost Riders
54: Riot in Cell Block 11
    Bitter Creek
    Arrow in the Dust
    20,000 Leagues Under
      the Sea
55: Battle Cry
    The Racers
    Artists and Models
    The Court-Martial of
      Billy Mitchell
56: The Bottom of the Bottle
    Beyond a Reasonable Doubt
    Julie
    Flight to Hong Kong
    Battle Hymn
58: Cry Terror
    The Last Hurrah
59: The Horse Soldiers
60: The Gallant Hours
    The Music Box Kid
    Sergeant Rutledge
61: The Big Show
    Armored Command

Clara Kimball Young (1891-1960)
1931: Kept Husbands
    Women Go On Forever
    Mother and Son
32: File No. 113
    Probation
    Love Bound
34: I Can't Escape
    Return of Chandu
35: Fighting Youth
    She Married Her Boss
    His Night Out

36: Three on the Trail
    The Last Assignment
    Rogues' Tavern
37: Hills of Old Wyoming
38: The Frontiersman
41: The Roundup
    Mr. Celebrity

Gig Young (1915-
1941: Navy Blues
    Here Comes the Cavalry
      (short)
    Dive Bomber
    They Died with Their
      Boots On
    The Man Who Came to
      Dinner
42: The Gay Sisters
    The Male Animal
    Captains of the Clouds
    One Foot in Heaven
43: Air Force
    Old Acquaintance
45: Tokyo Rose
    Follow that Woman
    Love Letters
    Affairs of Susan
46: Escape Me Never
    They Made Me a Killer
47: Big Town
    7 Were Saved
48: Woman in White
    Main Street Kid
    Pitfall
    Wake of the Red Witch
    The 3 Musketeers
49: Lust for Gold
    Tell it to the Judge
    For Those Who Dare
    Thelma Jordan
    Down Dakota Way
50: Hunt the Man Down
51: Come Fill the Cup
    Slaughter Trail
    Target Unknown
    Only the Valiant
    Too Young to Kiss
52: Holiday for Sinners
    You for Me
    Wait Till the Sun Shines,
      Nellie

53: The Girl Who Had Every-
       thing
    The City that Never
       Sleeps
    Arena
    Torch Song
54: Young at Heart
55: The Desperate Hours
57: Desk Set
58: The Tunnel of Love
    Teacher's Pet
59: Ask Any Girl
    Story on Page One
62: That Touch of Mink
    Kid Galahad
63: 5 Miles to Midnight
    For Love of Money
    A Ticklish Affair
64: Strange Bedfellows
67: The Shuttered Room
68: The Midnight Patient
       (TV pilot)
    Companions in Night-
       mare (TV)
69: They Shoot Horses,
       Don't They?

Loretta Young (1911-
1928: Scarlet Seas   SSE
29: Girl in the Glass
       Cage   PT
    Fast Life
    The Careless Age
    Forward Pass
    Show of Shows
30: The Squall
    The Way of Life
    Man's Estate
    Loose Ankles
    Road to Paradise
    Second Floor Mystery
    Truth about Youth
    The Devil to Pay
    The Man from Blankley's
    Kismet
    Broken Dishes
    Gallagher
31: Right of Way
    The Ruling Voice
    The Honorable Mr. Wong
    Big Business Girl
    I Like Your Nerve!

Working Wives
8 to 5
Platinum Blonde
Beau Ideal
3 Girls Lost
Upper Underworld
Too Young to Marry
32: Three Wise Girls
    Play Girl
    Taxi!
    Weekend Marriage
    Life Begins
    They Call it Sin
    The Hatchet Man
33: Grand Slam
    Heroes for Sale
    She Had to Say Yes!
    Zoo in Budapest
    The Devil's in Love
    The Kid's Last Fight
    The Life of Jimmy Dolan
    Midnight Mary
    A Man's Castle
    Employees' Entrance
    Lady of the Night
34: House of Rothschild
    Born to be Bad
    White Parade
    Caravan
    Bulldog Drummond Strikes
       Back
35: Clive of India
    Call of the Wild
    The Crusades
    Shanghai
36: The Unguarded Hour
    Private Number
    Ramona
    Ladies in Love
37: Love Is News
    Cafe Metropole
    Love under Fire
    Wife, Doctor, and Nurse
    Second Honeymoon
38: 4 Men and a Prayer
    3 Blind Mice
    Suez
    Kentucky
39: Wife, Husband, and Friend
    The Story of Alexander
       Graham Bell
    Eternally Yours

40: The Doctor Takes a Wife   The Invisible Ghost
He Stayed for Breakfast
41: The Lady from Cheyenne   Robert Young (1907-
The Men in Her Life   1931: The Sin of Madelon Claudet
Bedtime Story   Lullaby
42: A Night to Remember   Guilty Generation
43: China   The Black Camel
44: And Now Tomorrow   32: Wet Parade
Ladies Courageous   Unashamed
Home Is the Sailor   Strange Interlude
45: Along Came Jones   The Kid from Spain
46: The Stranger   New Morals for Old
47: The Farmer's Daughter   33: Hell Below
    (OSCAR)   Tugboat Annie
Perfect Marriage   Today We Live
48: The Bishop's Wife   Saturday's Millions
Rachel and the Stranger   Right to Romance
Accused   Men Must Fight
49: Mother Is a Freshman   The House of Connelly
Come to the Stable   Arms and the Girl
50: Key to the City   Frou-Frou
51: Cause for Alarm   34: Carolina
Half an Angel   Whom the Gods Destroy
52: Paula   Death on the Diamond
Because of You   Paris Interlude
53: It Happens Every Thursday   The Band Plays on
                               Lazy River
Polly Ann Young (1908-   Spitfire
1928: Masks of the Devil   S   House of Rothschild
29: The Bellamy Trial   PT   35: West Point of the Air
Tanned Legs   Vagabond Lady
30: Rich People   Calm Yourself
31: One Way Trail   Red Salute
34: The Man from Utah   Remember Last Night?
Stolen Sweets   The Bride Comes Home
35: The Crimson Trail   36: 3 Wise Guys
Sons of Steel   Sworn Enemy
Thunder in the Night   The Longest Night
His Fighting Blood   It's Love Again
Happiness C.O.D.   Secret Agent
36: The Border Patrolman   The Bride Walks Out
Hitchhike to Heaven   Stowaway
39: The Story of Alexander   37: Dangerous Number
    Graham Bell   Married Before Breakfast
The Wolf Call   The Emperor's Candle-
Mystery Plane   sticks
Port of Hate   The Bride Wore Red
40: Turnabout   Navy Blue and Gold
Murder on the Yukon   I Met Him in Paris
The Last Alarm   38: Paradise for Three
41: Road Show   3 Comrades

38:	Toy Wife	Roland Young (1887-1953)	
	The Shining Hour	1929:	Unholy Night
	Josette		Her Private Life
	Rich Man Poor Girl	30:	The Bishop Murder Case
39:	Honolulu		Wise Girls
	Bridal Suite		Madame Satan
	Maisie		New Moon
	Miracles for Sale	31:	The Prodigal
40:	The Mortal Storm		Don't Bet on Women
	Northwest Passage		Annabelle's Affairs
	Dr. Kildare's Crisis		The Guardsman
	Lady be Good		The Pagan Lady
	Florian		He Met a French Girl
	Sporting Blood		Squaw Man
41:	H.M. Pulham, Esq.	32:	One Hour with You
	Western Union		A Woman Commands
	The Trial of Mary Dugan		Wedding Rehearsal
	Married Bachelor		William and Mary
	Highway to Freedom		Lovers Courageous
	Stirling Metal		Lullaby
42:	Joe Smith, American		This Is the Night
	Cairo		Street of Women
	Journey for Margaret		The New Yorker
43:	Slightly Dangerous	33:	Pleasure Cruise
	Claudia		A Lady's Profession
	Sweet Rosie O'Grady		Blind Adventure
44:	The Canterville Ghost		They Just Had to Get
	Secrets in the Dark		Married
45:	The Enchanted Cottage	34:	His Double Life
	Those Endearing Young		Here Is My Heart
	Charms	35:	David Copperfield
46:	Claudia and David		Ruggles of Red Gap
	Lady Luck	36:	The Unguarded Hour
	The Searching Winds		One Rainy Afternoon
47:	Crossfire		Give Me Your Heart
	They Won't Believe Me	37:	The Man Who Worked
48:	Relentless		Miracles
	Sitting Pretty		Gypsy
49:	Adventure in Baltimore		Call it a Day
	That Forsyte Woman		King Solomon's Mines
	Love Is Big Business		Ali Baba Goes to Town
50:	Bride for Sale		Topper
	And Baby Makes Three	38:	Sailing Along
51:	Second Woman		The Young in Heart
	Goodbye My Fancy	39:	Topper Takes a Trip
	On the Loose		Yes, My Darling Daughter
52:	Half-Breed		Here I Am a Stranger
54:	Secret of the Incas		Night of Nights
	Nothing but a Man	40:	He Married His Wife
69:	Marcus Welby, M.D.		Private Affairs
	(TV pilot)		Star Dust

40: Irene
No, No, Nanette
Dulcy
The Philadelphia Story
41: Topper Returns
Flame of New Orleans
Two Faced Woman
42: They All Kissed the
Bride
Tales of Manhattan
The Lady Has Plans
43: Forever and a Day
44: Standing Room Only
45: And Then There Were
None
48: Bond Street
You Gotta Stay Happy
49: The Great Lover
The White Man
50: Let's Dance
51: St. Benny the Dip
53: That Man from Tangier

Tammy Young (d. 1935)
1933: She Done Him Wrong
Tugboat Annie
Gold Diggers of 1933
Heroes for Sale
The Bowery
34: Search for Beauty
Six of a Kind
You're Telling Me
Little Miss Marker
The Old-Fashioned Way
The Lemon Drop Kid
It's a Gift
The Mighty Barnum
35: The Glass Key
Man on the Flying Trapeze
Champagne for Breakfast
Little Big Shot
Wanderer of the Waste-
land

Blanche Yurka (1893-
1940: Queen of the Mob
City for Conquest
Escape
41: Ellery Queen and the
Murder Ring
Ladies for a Night
42: Pacific Rendezvous

43: The Song of Bernadette
A Night to Remember
Tonight We Raid Calais
Hitler's Hangman
44: Cry of the Werewolf
The Bridge of San Luis
Rey
One Body Too Many
45: The Southerner
46: 13 Rue Madeleine
48: The Flame
50: The Furies
52: At Sword's Point
53: Taxi!
58: A Tale of Two Cities
59: Thunder in the Sun

Mai Zetterling (1925-
1946: Frenzy
47: Frieda
48: Bad Lord Byron
49: Quartet (The Facts of
Life seq.)
Portrait from Life
Romantic Age
51: Blackmailed
Hell Is Sold Out
53: Desperate Moment
The Frightened Bride
54: Knock on Wood
55: Dance, Little Lady
A Prize of Gold
57: Abandon Ship! (or, Seven
Waves Away)
Truth about Women
59: Yesterday's Enemy
Jet Storm
Of Love and Lust
60: Operation Mermaid
Faces in the Dark
Piccadilly Third Stop
Offbeat
62: Only Two can Play
The War Game
The Night Is My Future
63: The Main Attraction
The Bay of St. Michel
66: Night Games (writ., dir.)
Loving Couples (writ.,
dir.)
69: The Man Who Finally Died

Efrem Zimbalist, Jr. (1923-
1949: House of Strangers
57: Bombers B-52
A Band of Angels
58: The Deep Six
Violent Road
Girl on the Run
Hell's Highway
Too Much, Too Soon
Home Before Dark
60: The Crowded Sky
61: A Fever in the Blood
By Love Possessed
62: The Chapman Report
65: Harlow (Magna.)
66: The Reward
67: Wait Until Dark

Vera Zorina (1917-
1938: The Goldwyn Follies
39: On Your Toes
40: I Was an Adventuress
41: Louisiana Purchase
42: Star-Spangled Rhythm
44: Follow the Boys
46: Lover Come Back
When Lovers Meet
48: River Lady

George Zucco (1886-1960)
1931: The Dreyfus Case
32: Good Companions
34: Autumn Crocus
36: After the Thin Man
Sinner Take All
37: Parnell
The Firefly
Saratoga
London by Night
Madame X
The Bride Wore Red
Conquest
Rosalie
Souls at Sea
The Man Who Could Work
Miracles
38: Arsene Lupin Returns
Marie Antoinette
Lord Jeff
Fast Company
Vacation from Love

Suez
Charlie Chan in Honolulu
39: Arrest Bulldog Drummond!
The Magnificent Fraud
The Cat and the Canary
Captain Fury
Adventures of Sherlock
Holmes
Here I Am a Stranger
The Hunchback of Notre
Dame
40: New Moon
The Mummy's Hand
Dark Streets of Cairo
Arise, My Love
41: The Monster and the Girl
Topper Returns
International Lady
A Woman's Face
Ellery Queen and the
Murder Ring
42: My Favorite Blonde
Halfway to Shanghai
The Black Swan
Dr. Renault's Secret
The Mad Monster
The Mummy's Tomb
43: Black Raven
Dead Men Walk
Sherlock Holmes in
Washington
Holy Matrimony
Never a Dull Moment
44: One Body Too Many
The Devil's Brood
The 7th Cross
Shadows in the Night
The Mummy's Ghost
Return of the Ape Man
The Voodoo Man
45: Hold that Blonde!
House of Frankenstein
Sudan
Having a Wonderful Crime
Confidential Agent
Fog Island
The Woman in Green
Weekend at the Waldorf
One Exciting Night
46: The Flying Serpent
47: Desire Me

1457